Capital Allowance Transactions and Planning 2016/17

Capital Allowances: Transactions and Planning 2016/17

Nineteenth edition

Martin Wilson MA FCA
and
Steven Bone BSc (Hons) PGDip.BA FRICS ATT

The Capital Allowances Partnership Limited
www.cap-allow.com

Bloomsbury Professional

Bloomsbury Professional Limited, Maxwelton House, 41–43 Boltro Road, Haywards Heath, West Sussex, RH16 1BJ

© Bloomsbury Professional Limited 2016

Bloomsbury Professional is an imprint of Bloomsbury Publishing Plc

A CIP Catalogue record for this book is available from the British Library.

ISBN 978 1 78451 277 4

While every care has been taken to ensure the accuracy of this work, no responsibility for loss or damage occasioned to any person acting or refraining from action as a result of any statement in it can be accepted by the authors, editors or publishers.

Typeset by Compuscript Ltd, Shannon
Printed and bound in Great Britain by CPI Group (UK) Ltd, Croydon, CR0 4YY

Preface

This work is written by authors with more than 40 years of specialist capital allowances experience, gained in both the accountancy and surveying professions. It aims, above all, to save taxpayers money by helping them to legitimately maximise capital allowances and related tax reliefs on a wide range of commercial transactions. Capital allowances are often overlooked, and reading this book can be an easy way of getting ahead of the competition – forewarned is forearmed.

This book is essential to taxpayers (especially property investors and owner-occupiers) and their advisers. Its unique transaction-based structure and special features such as pro forma elections, checklists and comments on pre-contract enquiries make it particularly useful to those advising on property deals.

Important changes have been made to the rules affecting fixtures in property acquisitions. Under these changes, purchasers run a serious risk of failing to qualify for allowances, even though they meet all the existing criteria, simply because they have inadvertently omitted to follow new administrative procedures. Inevitably, a failure to follow these procedures will lead to claims against unwary advisers. Legislation is stated as at 1 August 2016. Unless otherwise stated, references are to the *Capital Allowances Act 2001*. The HMRC material reproduced in the book is Crown copyright.

The views expressed are our own. Although this work aims to be comprehensive and practical, the availability and best use of allowances will depend on the individual circumstances of each transaction. For this reason, the reader is advised to take professional advice before proceeding with a transaction or course of action.

Martin Wilson
Steven Bone
The Capital Allowances Partnership Limited
www.cap-allow.com

Contents

Contents

Contents

Contents

Table of statutes

[all references are to paragraph number or Appendix]

Table of statutory instruments

[all references are to paragraph number or Appendix]

Table of cases

Chapter 1

Practicalities of a claim

GENERAL

1.1   The capital allowances regime has become increasingly complicated. The *Capital Allowances Act 2001* (*CAA 2001*), which was already lengthy when first enacted, has since grown by over a third. In many cases, maximising a claim for capital allowances will require specialist input and a great deal of work, and the question is often asked whether the cost (in both time and money) is justified.

1.2   One answer is that capital allowances are effectively a negative element of the total cost. Failure to exploit allowances fully will therefore effectively increase the post-tax cost of a building, just as surely as if there had been a failure to identify the most competitive construction or fit-out tender. The scope for capital allowances planning extends, of course, far beyond the context of a new building development, as this work demonstrates. On an acquisition, for example, failure to secure the capital allowances can often have the same result as adding 10% to the purchase price.

1.3   With effect from April 2012, so far as fixtures in a second-hand building are concerned, failure to consider capital allowances at the time of purchase can result in a complete and permanent loss of allowances, both for the purchaser and for all future owners, allied to a claw-back or reversal of any allowances previously given to the seller. This could have commercial implications as well as tax ones because it may make the property less attractive to future buyers and could adversely affect the price that a buyer is willing to pay.

1.4   A second consideration is the application of the self-assessment regime to both individual and corporate taxpayers. Responsibility for the correctness of a capital allowances claim falls squarely on the taxpayer, with interest and penalties for claims proved to be incorrect as a result of carelessness or deliberate misstatement, or inadequate record keeping. Following *Langham (Inspector of Taxes) v Veltema* [2004] EWCA Civ 193, the necessity of claims being prepared accurately and expertly is even more apparent if discovery assessments and unexpected tax liabilities are to be avoided. Discovery assessments allow HMRC to reopen tax returns outside the ordinary time limits for doing so (for up to six years for carelessness and 20 years for deliberate actions).

1.5   A prime concern of any taxpayer should be to pay as little tax as possible. This, of course, must be done by legal means. This principle was enunciated by Lord Tomlin in the 1935 case *Duke of Westminster v IRC* (1935) 19 TC 490: 'Every man is entitled if he can to order his affairs so that the tax attaching … is less than it would otherwise be.' This principle has held true through a number of challenges, although with the passage of time some modification has been inevitable, and anti-avoidance schemes generally have been attacked. In some cases, such schemes are now required to be registered with Her Majesty's Revenue & Customs (HMRC) in advance (this does not apply in most capital allowances scenarios). Most recently, legislation has addressed certain uncommercial transactions where capital allowances were used to obtain a tax advantage (see **14.94** *et seq*, **18.53** and **20.56A** *et seq*).

1.6   In general, the taxpayer should seek to claim relief for expenditure in the following order (provided, of course, the facts permit it):

(i)   as land remediation expenditure (relief at 150%) – see **24.1**;

(ii)   as a 'normal' revenue deduction or as expenditure qualifying for the businesses premises renovation allowance or flat conversion allowances (relief at 100%) – see **1.9**, **11.61** and **6.24** *et seq*;

(iii)   as capital expenditure on research and development or as an enterprise zone property (if appropriate) (relief at 100%) – see **19.50** *et seq* and **9.1**;

(iv)   as an item of plant (relieved at between 8% and 100% pa) – see **Chapters 14–16**.

1.7   This is not, however, a hard-and-fast rule and in some cases the order of preference may in part be reversed. The availability of the 100% annual investment allowance for plant (see **14.62** *et seq*) can, depending on the level of expenditure, make plant allowances as attractive as a revenue deduction. Issues relating to choosing between different types of allowance, or disclaiming allowances altogether, are outlined from **21.40** *et seq*.

1.8   Planning is nearly always possible and the amounts involved normally justify at least an initial examination. Where a property is being acquired (or indeed sold), capital allowances must be considered as early as possible in the process, and appropriate contract clauses included. Failure to do so can result in either a loss of tax relief for the buyer, an immediate tax charge for the seller, or both.

Revenue deduction

1.9   The optimal tax relief will normally be obtained if it can be shown that amounts are properly deductible as revenue expenses. Furthermore, a revenue deduction is potentially available for repairs and maintenance works which would not qualify for any capital allowances because the assets in question are not eligible as plant (see **15.7** *et seq*) or machinery (see **15.2** *et seq*). Where capital allowances are available they are generally a poor alternative (with the exception of 150% relief for land remediation expenditure (see **Chapter 24**) and 100% allowances for expenditure on energy-saving or water-conserving plant (see **14.31–14.55**) unless the amount spent is such that it qualifies in full for the annual investment allowance (see **14.62** *et seq*).

1.10   However, whether the expenditure qualifies for a revenue deduction is a question of fact – the taxpayer cannot simply choose to charge expenditure to profit and loss account, in order to secure a tax deduction.

1.11   The nature of expenditure (whether it is revenue or capital) is often assumed to be a question of fact. This is far from true, although admittedly items such as buildings and machinery are usually easier to classify than some of the more esoteric subjects which have been considered by the courts, for example petrol station 'solus' agreements. In connection with the last of these, Lord Upjohn in *Regent Oil Co Ltd v Strick (Inspector of Taxes)* (1965) 43 TC 1 observed:

> 'no part of our law of taxation presents such almost insoluble conundrums as the decision whether a receipt or outgoing is capital or income for tax purposes.'

1.12   A general guide is provided by the rule put forward by Viscount Cave (in *British Insulated & Helsby Cables Ltd v Atherton (Inspector of Taxes)* (1925) 10 TC 155) that expenditure is normally capital if it is made 'not only for once and for all, but with a view to bringing into existence an asset or an advantage for the enduring benefit of the trade'. The distinction between capital and revenue as it applies to tangible assets such as buildings and plant is often largely a question of whether an outlay represents (i) a repair or (ii) an improvement. Generally, the taxpayer will want to claim as much as possible by way of repairs (although, so far as assets which would otherwise qualify for capital allowances are concerned, the availability of the annual investment allowances (see **14.62** *et seq*) can blur the decision). In this way, full tax relief will be given in the year of expenditure, rather than spread over the asset's life. However, as is to be expected, there are legal constraints. Taxpayers should also be aware of special rules regarding repairs to integral features (see **1.37** *et seq*).

3

1.13 One important case gave its name to what is generally known as the *'Law Shipping'* principle. In this case, a ship was purchased in a dilapidated state and subsequently renovated. The courts held that the need for repair was reflected in a low purchase price, and that the subsequent repair costs, to the extent that they were attributable to the period prior to acquisition, were therefore properly to be regarded as capital (*Law Shipping Co Ltd v IRC* (1923) 12 TC 621). Similarly, in *Jackson (Inspector of Taxes) v Laskers Home Furnishers Ltd* (1956) 37 TC 69, a taxpayer leased a premises which had been unused for 18 years and was in a very bad state of repair and unfit for occupation. In return for substantial rent reductions, it incurred expenditure to make it fit for occupation, by dealing with the accumulation of repairs and making small alterations to suit its business, and the expenditure was held to be capital.

1.14 In contrast to *Law Shipping*, another case dealt with a number of cinemas purchased during and immediately after World War II. The cinemas were in need of repair, but were nonetheless capable of use (and were in fact used) before being repaired. When the repairs were eventually carried out, it was held the amounts expended were revenue and not capital (*Odeon Associated Theatres Ltd v Jones (Inspector of Taxes)* (1972) 48 TC 257). This case dealt with similar principles to *Law Shipping*, but was distinguished on three bases. First, the purchase price was not substantially reduced due to the state of repair. Secondly, the cinemas were capable of being used for the purpose of earning profits before the disputed repairs were undertaken. Thirdly, evidence was given that accounting for the repairs as revenue expenditure was perfectly permissible, and indeed standard practice (*Law Shipping* was entirely silent on accounting treatment).

1.15 The conclusion to be drawn from these cases is that, if the expenditure would have been treated as allowable repairs if ownership had not changed, the repairs are normally allowable when expended by the new owner. The points that indicate that, exceptionally, the cost of the work is capital include:

(i)   the asset was not in a fit state for use until the repairs had been carried out or could not continue to be used in the trade without being repaired shortly after acquisition; and

(ii) there is evidence in, for example, the contract for the sale of the asset or in negotiations leading up to the contract or in the surrounding circumstances that the purchase price was substantially less because of the dilapidated state of the asset. Inspectors should not attempt to deny relief where the purchase price merely reflects the reduced value of an asset due to normal wear and tear (eg between normal maintenance cycles).

(HMRC Business Income Manual (hereafter BIM), para 35450)

1.16   The distinction between capital and revenue can be equally indistinct where the expenditure is on an asset already in the ownership of the taxpayer. Any deduction from revenue will be limited to the cost of the repairs actually carried out (as distinct from repairs obviated by the improvement).

1.17   Whether expenditure is capital or revenue is a matter of law, and the accounting treatment is influential, but not conclusive. Generally revenue expenditure is allowed only when it is charged to the profit and loss account (Tax Bulletin 53 (June 2001); BIM, para 42215). Where revenue expenditure is capitalised or 'deferred' (using HMRC's preferred terminology), as, say, part of the cost of a building, it may only attract a tax deduction when it is amortised. Many businesses do not depreciate buildings (eg investment properties), in which case, no deduction is available. Companies must therefore be aware of the problems which can be brought about by accounting policies.

1.18   Special rules apply to repairs to integral features (see **1.37** *et seq*).

Refurbishment

1.19   A fundamental feature of capital expenditure is that some 'enduring benefit' must be created. However, this benefit must be of a certain kind; in particular, a new asset must be brought into existence. The *nature of the asset* is therefore important.

1.20   Where replacements are in point, another important factor is whether the replacement is of an entire asset or merely part of an asset, or whether the original asset has come to the end of its useful working life.

1.21   A replacement may nonetheless be regarded as being on revenue account if it is a *like-for-like replacement* (subject to the application of special rules for integral features – see **1.37** *et seq*). A replacement cannot in strictness be like-for-like if there is an element of *improvement*. However, a replacement which is shown to improve overall operating efficiency, rather than simply doing the same job better, is more likely to be treated as revenue. An element of improvement is often made inevitable simply by the passage of time and associated technological progress. Some leeway is allowed by extending the scope of the term 'like-for-like' to include the *nearest modern equivalent*. Motive for incurring the expenditure is also important.

The nature of the asset

1.22   There is a thin line between revenue and capital items. In general terms, the distinction is not founded upon the quantum of the expenditure, nor upon the size of the assets involved. Rather, the two key principles are:

1.23 *Practicalities of a claim*

(*a*) the durability of any new asset created (see **15.11**); and

(*b*) (in the context of replacements) whether it is the whole or merely a part of an asset which is being replaced.

1.23 There is a wealth of case law on this question. The most commonly quoted case is *British Insulated & Helsby Cables Ltd v Atherton* (*Inspector of Taxes*) (1925) 10 TC 155, which speaks of capital expenditure being made with a view to bringing into existence an asset or an advantage for the enduring benefit of the trade. In *Whitehead* (*Inspector of Taxes*) *v Tubbs* (*Elastics*) *Ltd* [1984] STC 1, it was observed that there was no single test for determining whether expenditure is revenue or capital, but one very important factor was whether, in consequence of the expenditure, an identifiable asset (tangible or intangible) of an enduring nature was acquired or produced. However, Oliver LJ elaborated further, saying that capital expenditure was not evidenced by a simple enduring benefit, but rather by one of a capital nature in the sense that it enabled a company to utilise its capital assets in a way in which it could not have utilised them before. There is a parallel to be drawn here with the case of *Lothian Chemical Co Ltd v Rogers* (*Inspector of Taxes*) (1926) 11 TC 508, where the cost of converting plant for use for a different process was held to be capital.

Entirety

1.24 Alongside this, one needs to consider whether the item concerned is a complete asset, or merely part of an asset. In *Lurcot v Wakely and Wheeler* [1911] 1 KB 905, Buckley LJ said:

> 'Repair is restoration by renewal or replacement of subordinate parts of a whole. Renewal as distinguished from repair is reconstruction of the entirety, meaning not necessarily, but substantially, the whole subject matter under discussion.'

1.25 This 'entirety' concept was highlighted in the two cases of *O'Grady* (*Inspector of Taxes*) *v Bullcroft Main Collieries Ltd* (1932) 17 TC 93 and *Samuel Jones & Co* (*Devondale*) *Ltd v IRC* (1951) 32 TC 513. Both concerned the replacement of chimneys. However, in *Samuel Jones* where the chimney was merely part of a larger building, the expenditure was treated as being in respect of repairs, whilst in *Bullcroft* where the chimney constituted a complete asset in itself, the replacement cost was held to be capital.

1.26 In *Transco plc v Dyall* (*Inspector of Taxes*) [2002] STC (SCD) 199, the 'entirety' was held to be the whole of a gas transmission and distribution network ('from the beach to the meter'). This case outlined some useful pointers to what would constitute capital – see **Appendix 4**.

1.27 HMRC's and the courts' interpretation of what constitutes the 'entirety' can be quite liberal. In *Cairnsmill Caravan Park v HMRC Comrs* [2013] UKFTT 164 (TC), it was held that the entirety was an entire caravan park (with 300 fixed and touring caravan pitches, an office, shop, indoor swimming pool, shower and toilet block, and 14 acres of recreational woodland and open ground). In HMRC's words, the entirety was 'an identifiable asset in its own right'.

1.28 HMRC gives an example of a boiler needing replacing and being moved to a different position. At the same time the kitchen is modernised by stripping out the base units, wall units, sink, fitted cooker and hob and replacing them with units of an equivalent quality but in a different layout to suit the new boiler position. Here HMRC confirms that the entirety is the house, not the fitted kitchen (or put another way, the refurbishment is a repair to a larger entity – the house). In contrast, replacing a whole building (such as a garage or chalet) or stand-alone asset (such as a fridge-freezer) would constitute replacing that entirety (BIM, para 46911).

Like-for-like expenditure

1.29 An asset which is, strictly speaking, a new part will nonetheless not be regarded as a capital item where it is a like-for-like replacement. In theory, the new asset should be identical to the old, but of course some leeway is inevitable. In the case of *Margrett (Inspector of Taxes) v Lowestoft Water & Gas Co* (1935) 19 TC 481, it was ruled inadmissible to apportion the expenditure so as to identify the cost of repairs which would have otherwise been necessary. One key question would be whether the old asset is to be replaced because the new asset can do the job better than the old asset (even when the latter was brand new), or because the old asset is no longer able to perform as it once could, due to obsolescence or deterioration. This was essentially the question proposed (and answered in the taxpayer's favour) in *Rhodesia Railways Ltd v Collector of Income Tax, Bechuanaland Protectorate* [1933] AC 368.

Improvements

1.30 Expenditure on a replacement asset will generally be regarded as capital if that asset is in any way an improvement on the old. However, there is little or no guidance as to what constitutes an improvement. There are two possibilities:

(*a*)   the replacement is in some way intrinsically better than the old asset; or

(*b*)   there is an anticipated future benefit in terms of operating efficiency (of the business as a whole, rather than simply of the machine).

1.31 In the former case, there would be no real basis for claiming that the cost of the replacement was revenue. In the latter case, however, there is considerably more hope. As with like-for-like replacements (above), it is important to look at the reasons behind the incurring of the expenditure. What is the future benefit, and how likely is it? This illustrates an interesting comment made in *Tucker (Inspector of Taxes) v Granada Motorway Services Ltd* [1979] STC 393, where Lord Wilberforce stated that the benefit must 'endure in the way that fixed capital endures; not a benefit that endures in the sense that for a good number of years it relieves you of a revenue payment'.

1.32 In *Moonlight Textiles Ltd v HMRC Comrs* [2010] UKFTT 500 (TC), the taxpayer renovated a curtain showroom, warehouse and workshop with associated offices, etc. The refurbishment involved a complete replacement of the roof, major alterations, redecoration and improvement of the kitchen and other works. The alterations were designed to accommodate a shift in the business to providing a bespoke curtain/blind-making service along with their installation and resulted in a larger refurbished showroom and a reduced warehouse facility. HMRC agreed that the roof repairs and part of the kitchen alterations constituted repairs. Otherwise, there had been a significant improvement of the premises and the work had changed the character of the building as a whole. Therefore, all of the broader expenditure was capital.

1.33 In *Cairnsmill Caravan Park v HMRC Comrs* [2013] UKFTT 164 (TC), it was held that replacing a grassed area for the pitching of caravans with a hardcore area was not an improvement. It was questionable whether the new surface was more durable, because the original grass surface had lasted about 50 years. The new surface cost marginally more to maintain. And the hardcore had less aesthetic appeal than grass, was not suitable as a recreation area for children, nor could caravan awning fixing pins be readily located, which had generated customer complaints.

Nearest modern equivalent

1.34 Replacement parts will generally be allowed as a revenue expense where they are replacing like-for-like. With the passage of time, of course, it is increasingly unlikely that an exactly identical replacement can be found. Hence, HMRC's policy that the 'nearest modern equivalent' is an acceptable substitute. One problem with this is that technology has generally improved over the years, and it is therefore sometimes difficult to say that there has not been an enhancement or improvement. Once again, an important consideration is motive, ie the reason why the expenditure was incurred. If the improvement is merely incidental, and was not instrumental in making the decision to incur the expenditure, it may be discounted. By way of example, HMRC accepts that replacing single-glazed windows with double-glazed ones is allowable as a repair (BIM, para 46904).

1.35   The case of *Conn (Inspector of Taxes) v Robins Bros Ltd* (1966) 43 TC 266 dealt with rather extreme facts, concerning as it did a business trading from 400-year-old premises. Such an extreme instance as replacing an oak floor with a concrete one was held to be a repair, rather than capital, on the grounds that this was the nearest modern equivalent. In defining the 'nearest modern equivalent', one must consider the wider context. It cannot be simply a matter of comparing technical specification or physical properties of the particular asset, one has to look also at, for example, comparative cost or changed operating requirements. A useful (but admittedly very hypothetical) question to ask is whether the purchaser of the old asset would, faced with today's circumstances, purchase the replacement that has been chosen.

1.36   More recently, in *Christopher Wills v HMRC Comrs* [2010] UKFTT 174 (TC), the taxpayer renovated a listed-building outbuilding (attached to a residential rental property). The building was previously used as storage, a games room and additional living space and garage, but had become extremely run down and damp. Indeed, its state of disrepair was so dangerous it risked collapsing. Because the property was listed, the only option was a 'substantial repair scheme'. The works brought the interior more up to date, including adding heating, electric power points and a water supply (but no basins, toilets, kitchen or anything that would allow the space to be anything more than additional living space ancillary to the main house). The taxpayer expensed about 40% of the cost as repairs and capitalised the remainder. The tribunal allowed the taxpayer's claim (that is, held the work was of 'essential repair') and also allowed further structural works not originally treated as repairs.

Integral features

1.37   With effect from 1 April 2008 (corporation tax) and 6 April 2008 (income tax), new rules apply where expenditure is incurred on the *provision or replacement* of an integral feature (see **14.5**). Such assets are allowed by statute to be plant and machinery, qualifying for capital allowances at the rate of 8% per annum, and eligible for the 100% annual investment allowance.

1.38   *Section 33A* defines integral features as:

(*a*)   electrical and lighting systems;

(*b*)   cold water systems;

(*c*)   space or water heating systems, powered systems of ventilation, air cooling or air purification (including floors or ceilings comprised in such a system);

(*d*)   lift, escalators and moving walkways;

(*e*)   external solar shading.

1.39   The new rules apply where expenditure is on the *provision or replacement* of an integral feature. The term 'replacement' is extended by *CAA 2001, s 33B*. Broadly, if expenditure on an integral feature (eg repairs) is more than 50% of the cost of replacing that integral feature, that expenditure will be treated as being in respect of a replacement. In essence, the usual process for determining whether expenditure is capital or revenue is reduced to a mathematical comparison.

1.40   Theoretically, repairs costing 50% of the cost of replacing a heating system could be allowed as repairs, but if that figure were 50.1% they would automatically be treated as capital. It is not possible to circumvent the 50% rule by fragmenting repair expenditure, as the calculation must be based on the cumulative total of expenditure incurred over a rolling 12-month period (*s 33B*).

1.41   Furthermore, in determining whether the repairs have cost more than 50% of the cost of replacing the entire asset, one must consider the cumulative expenditure incurred over a running 12-month period. One cannot avoid expenditure being treated as capital simply by incurring it in several instalments, even if they fall into different accounting periods.

Example

Note: this example is reprinted verbatim (but with current dates) from HMRC Capital Allowances Manual, para 22350

Jonathan designs, makes and sells jewellery. He incurs expenditure on repairing or replacing parts of the central heating system in his large studio/shop. The expenditure he incurs on the system may be summarised as follows:

Date	Repair cost	12 months' cumulative expenditure	Replacement cost	% of original expenditure	50% exceeded?
1 April 2014	£10,000	£10,000	£60,000	16.66%	No
1 Sept 2014	£20,000	£30,000	£65,000	50%	No
1 Dec 2014	£5,000	£35,000 (08–09)	£65,000	58.33%	Yes
1 July 2015	£10,000	£35,000 (1/9/08 to 31/8/09)	£65,000	53.8% (of 1/9/08 cost)	Yes
Totals	£45,000		£65,000	75% or 70%	Yes

The underlying reason for the expenditure is irrelevant – if say the December 2014 repairs in the example were required as a result of vandalism, they would nonetheless be taken into account in determining whether not only the £5,000 repairs, but also the previous £30,000, should be treated as capital. That vandalism has not only cost Jonathan the extra £5,000 on repairs, but also (in the first year at least) 90% of the relief on the £30,000 – if Jonathan is a higher-rate taxpayer, that cost will be £10,800. This calls into question the third stated aim of the changes, namely 'fairness'. It would be fairer to exclude from the calculation any expenditure that is demonstrably not part of an ongoing scheme of replacement, but merely a reaction to circumstances. One would hope for a common-sense approach from Inspectors in such cases.

Whilst many readers will have sympathy with attempts to restrict the possibility of claiming capital expenditure as a repair (though it is not clear whether this was a real or imagined problem), the rather contrived nature of the example given does illustrate how the circumstances 'caught' may be more likely to be found in textbooks or in the exam room, than in real life.

Improvements obviating repairs

1.42   In the 1952 case of *Lawrie v IRC* (1952) 34 TC 20 a new roof was added to a building. Once this work began, it became apparent that the existing roof had been in a poor state of repair. The taxpayer therefore claimed as a repair part of his expenditure on the new roof. This claim was not allowed because the amount claimed was for notional repairs obviated by the alterations, rather than for actual repairs carried out. The concept of 'notional repairs' was also disapproved of in *Moonlight Textiles Ltd v HMRC Comrs* [2010] UKFTT 500 (TC).

DILAPIDATIONS

General

1.43   Dilapidations arise through breach of contract under a lease, where the lease provides that the tenant is responsible for repairs and must, at the end of the lease, deliver the property back to the landlord in the same condition it was in at the beginning. Dilapidations are items of disrepair and works required to repair or reinstate those assets, where the work has not been done during the period of the lease.

1.44   An outgoing tenant's dilapidations expenditure normally falls into one of two categories:

(*a*)   repairs, removals and reinstatements; or

(*b*)   payment to the landlord in lieu of making good the disrepair.

These are discussed below.

Repairs, removals and reinstatements

1.45   Expenditure on repair works (see **1.9**) by an outgoing tenant are deductible for tax purposes if they would have been allowed during the lease, even if they have been deferred until the end of the lease. This is of course providing that no significant improvements are made, which would seem unlikely as a tenant's liability for repair does not generally involve making improvements, or modernising the property (although dilapidations schedules can sometimes include works which have more to do with the landlord's surveyor's aspirations for presenting the premises for re-letting, than with remedying repairs).

1.46   A revenue deduction is not available for any expenditure of a capital nature. This could include the rebuilding of leasehold premises, the reinstatement of any portion of the leased premises that has been demolished, or the removal of any assets installed by the tenant (BIM, para 43255). If the expenditure is capital, it will not qualify for tax relief unless the works qualify for capital allowances instead. Whether any expenditure is capital in such circumstances is doubtful, because it would seem unlikely that an outgoing tenant's dilapidations expenditure would bring into existence an asset or advantage for the enduring benefit of its trade (see **1.12**).

Payment to landlord in lieu of replacement

1.47   Alternatively, on expiry of a lease, the tenant may, instead of making good the dilapidations, agree to pay the landlord a sum by way of composition. This payment is deductible if it relates to repairs that would have been allowable if they had been carried out during the lease and is not conditional on those dilapidations works actually being carried out by the landlord. However, because the composition payment is compensation to the landlord for the tenant not having carried out accrued repairs (which may in fact never be made good), it only becomes deductible for tax purposes when it is accounted for in accordance with generally accepted accounting practice (ie when it is expensed through the tenant's profit and loss account).

1.48   If dilapidations expenditure has been provided for in accordance with generally accepted accounting practice then a tax deduction is available for the provision, providing that it is for allowable repairs and has been estimated with sufficient accuracy (which should normally be possible). It is also worth noting that HMRC recognises absolute accuracy of provisions is impossible, and instructs Inspectors not to substitute a different figure simply because their judgement of the 'right' amount differs from the directors and proprietors of the business. This is of course on the basis that the judgment of the business must have been exercised in a reasonable manner, taking into account the information reasonably available to it and other relevant factors, including its own business expertise (BIM, para 46555).

1.49   To the extent that the composition payment (or provision) relates to capital works then it is disallowable (subject to the concern raised above about whether the tenant receives any enduring benefit from the expenditure anyway). It is possible though that some or all of it may qualify for capital allowances under the contributions provisions of the capital allowances legislation, if the money is spent by the landlord on qualifying expenditure (see **1.119**).

1.50   Where composition payments include revenue and capital elements, it is necessary to apportion them to allow only the estimated costs that qualify for tax relief (BIM, para 43265).

ALTERNATIVE BASES – RENEWALS AND WEAR AND TEAR

1.51   As an alternative to claiming capital allowances on machinery and plant, it was possible by concession to adopt instead what was generally known as the 'renewals basis'. The renewals basis was most often applied to small items such as hotel crockery and linen but could be permitted for larger items. The renewals basis was useful to the taxpayer where the items concerned had a short life, but did not qualify as machinery or plant. This concession was withdrawn for expenditure incurred from 6 April 2013 (income tax) or 1 April 2013 (corporation tax) (BIM, para 46985).

A statutory renewals allowance remained available for the replacement of trade tools (*ITTOIA 2005, s 68* and *CTA 2009, s 68*) but this was abolished from 1 April 2016 (corporation tax) or 6 April 2016 (income tax) by *Finance (No 2) Act 2016 s 71*.

1.52   Where the renewals basis was adopted, no relief (either revenue deduction or capital allowance) was given for the original purchase of an asset, but the cost of any subsequent replacements or renewals were allowed in full as a revenue deduction. The previous availability of this basis as an alternative to formal capital allowances was confirmed by an early case, *Caledonian Rly Co v Banks* (*Surveyor of Taxes*) (1880) 1 TC 487, which was never overturned. Although HMRC stated that the renewals basis related only to plant and machinery, such a conclusion was not clear from the *Caledonian* case itself.

1.53   It was possible for taxpayers to change from the renewals basis to 'normal' capital allowances, provided that where they used more than one item of a class of machinery or plant they changed from the 'renewals' basis to the capital allowances basis for all the items in that class (ESC B1). The commercial written-down value of items transferred was added to the qualifying expenditure for the pool for the period in which the change took place. For this purpose 'commercial written-down value' meant the value arrived at by writing-down the asset from cost at a commercial rate of depreciation having regard for the age of the asset and its expected life.

1.54   It was possible to change *to* a renewals basis, but not in respect of assets which had previously qualified for capital allowances (HMRC Capital Allowances Manual (hereafter CA), para 29220).

Example

Lucas owned a machine on which he had claimed capital allowances. Due to the frequent replacement of the machine, he considered switching to the renewals basis. In practice, the old machine must continue to be dealt with within the capital allowance system. When Lucas replaced the machine, the replacement would have qualified for neither a trading deduction nor capital allowances. However, when the replacement was itself replaced, a full deduction for the cost of the second replacement was given.

1.55   A further alternative, called a wear and tear allowance, used to be available where a person was letting furnished living accommodation. This was withdrawn by *Finance (No 2) Act 2016 s 70* from 1 April 2016 (corporation tax) or 6 April 2016 (income tax). Such landlords could claim a deduction for the wear and tear of plant, equal to 10% of rent, less charges and services that would normally be borne by a tenant but were, in fact, borne by the taxpayer (eg council tax, water and sewerage rates and any other material services costs). This allowance was given to cover plant and machinery chattels (not fixtures) that a tenant or owner-occupier would normally provide in unfurnished accommodation. Examples included moveable furniture and furnishings, televisions, fridges and freezers, carpets, curtains, linen, crockery, cookers, washing machines and dishwashers (ESC B47 and HMRC Property Income Manual (hereafter PIM), para 3200). ESC B47 was withdrawn from 6 April 2013 and replaced by *SI 2011/1037*. The 10% wear and tear allowance was then provided for by *ITTOIA 2005, ss 308A–308C*.

1.56   Following the repeal of the wear and tear allowance, landlords are instead allowed under *Finance (No 2) Act 2016 s 72* to deduct the actual, cost of replacing 'domestic items'. That is, chattels (not fixtures) including furniture, furnishings, household appliances and kitchenware. If the item is not replaced on a like-for-like basis then the deduction is limited to the amount of expenditure that would have been incurred if the asset had remained substantially the same. No relief is available if the property is furnished holiday accommodation or if relief is claimed under the rent-a-room scheme (a tax exemption up to a specified threshold for income arising from letting out furnished accommodation in the taxpayer's home, or bed and breakfast/guest house). The replacement of fixtures is tax-deductible as repairs (see **1.9** *et seq*).

1.57   Note that plant and machinery capital allowances are not generally available for plant let for use in a dwelling-house (see **15.125**).

PROGRESSING A CLAIM

1.58   In the simplest case the negotiation process is compressed into a single letter or a few lines in a computation and, usually, its agreement by the Inspector. In a more complicated case it can be broken down into the following stages:

(*a*)   recording facts and decisions which constitute contemporaneous evidence;

(*b*)   presenting the claim;

(*c*)   settling the claim.

1.59   Sometimes these stages overlap. There is no bar on the inclusion in a claim of innovative ideas, provided the Inspector is supplied with enough information to enable him to make his own judgment. However, retention of credibility is an important factor in the negotiation and settlement of claims.

1.60   In addition, under corporation tax self-assessment (CTSA), a claim may still be challenged by HMRC for a number of years after it is submitted, including, where valuations are used, under HMRC's discovery powers (*Langham* (*Inspector of Taxes*) v *Veltema* [2004] EWCA Civ 193) unless appropriate protective explanatory information is disclosed in the tax return 'white space'. HMRC's practice set out in SP1/06 is that:

'Most taxpayers who state that a valuation has been used, by whom it has been carried out, and that it was carried out by a named independent and suitably qualified valuer if that was the case, on the appropriate basis, will be able, for all practical purposes, to rely on protection from a later discovery assessment, provided those statements are true.'

1.61   Increasingly, standard HMRC practice is for reckless or negligent claims to result not only in unexpected (and unprovided for) tax charges and interest, but also in penalties that can be as much as the tax underpaid. In some circumstances, a penalty can be geared to the amount of tax underpaid, even if that tax has been paid later.

Example

Mr Careless acquires a property and claims capital allowances on the fixtures. Rather than carry out a just apportionment as required by *s 562*, he merely guesses at the amount of the claim and obtains a repayment of tax of £100,000. One year later, the Inspector enquires into the claim, which is agreed in a much lower amount, such that the repayment should only have been £30,000. Mr Careless repays the extra £70,000 with interest. Although there has been no *net* tax loss to the Treasury (as the overpayment has been repaid), HMRC could charge a penalty, potentially up to £70,000 (100% of the tax underpaid).

Recording facts and decisions

1.62   It is important to record the facts and decisions relating to the subject of the claim as they occur or are made. An increasing number of claims now depend for their success upon the ability of the claimant to demonstrate that an asset was acquired for use for a particular purpose. There can be nothing stronger than contemporaneous evidence, especially if the course of events between acquisition of the asset and the making of a claim is not particularly helpful.

1.63   A common example where this is true is partitioning (see **16.52** *et seq*), where a claim is dependent upon the partitions being not only movable but likely to be moved as a commercial necessity in the course of trade due to variations in accommodation requirements. If the circumstances leading to the adoption of the movable system are recorded, and preferably illustrated at the design or planning stage by projections of the likely movements as then perceived, it is so much easier to demonstrate them if subsequently challenged. Likewise, if the claim is to be based on the fact that a complex asset functions as a single item of plant, agreement will be facilitated if the evidence to that effect can be captured and made clear in the design brief or other similar documents. In the event of a formal appeal hearing, this type of information is invaluable.

1.64   Capital allowances claims often revolve around matters of judgment, rather than simply applying hard and fast rules. However, nothing should be included in a claim unless there is a reasonable argument to support it. Under self-assessment, penalties may be imposed for negligent or fraudulent claims.

Presenting the claim

1.65   Generally, a capital allowances claim will be incorporated into the corporation tax or income tax computation of the year in which the expenditure on the asset in question is incurred. It is therefore often the case that capital allowances are only considered when the returns are being prepared. This is not always the best policy. For example, it is possible for a building to be constructed within a period of, say, four months. By the time the year end matters are due to be dealt with, it may be that builders, project managers and so on have been paid and no longer have any involvement with the project (nor any incentive to help maximise allowances). In addition, on very large projects only, there is frequently some merit in opening negotiations with the Inspector on the basis of projected costs, agreeing the principles and then arranging for the revised costings (if necessary) to be prepared while the quantity surveyors, architects, project managers, etc are still on-site. If the claim is negotiated before the final costs are known, the Inspector will expect (and it is good practice to provide) a complete reconciliation of the projected and final figures.

1.66   Early consideration of capital allowances has the advantage of enabling early identification of areas where the additional breakdown of costs is required by the builder, surveyor or architect.

Settling the claim

1.67   A claim is usually settled by agreement, negotiation or withdrawal. Under self-assessment, the Inspector is not obliged to formally agree a claim. If the time limit for the opening of an enquiry expires, a claim will be deemed to be agreed (see **21.6** and **21.16**). If it is agreed, there is nothing more to be said. A reduction of the claim might imply immovable resistance but this is not always so as will be seen later.

1.68   Whilst some Inspectors adopt a pragmatic approach to claims, others do not. Some will also seek guidance from capital allowances specialists within HMRC head office. The approach varies between Inspectors. Taxpayers should remember that they are not bound to accept an Inspector's contentions. The published HMRC Manuals do not have the force of law and have on occasion been shown to misinterpret decided cases. The taxpayer has the option of requesting an HMRC internal review, although many taxpayers feel that such a review is unlikely to be truly objective and impartial. As a last resort, taxpayers (and HMRC) have the right for their claim to be decided by the tribunals.

1.69   Even before the technical arguments have been resolved it is advisable for the claimant to calculate exactly what the claim is worth. This will generally be the allowances expressed in terms of tax saved. This cost (cost A) will need to take into account the speed at which the allowances are likely to be used bearing in mind available profits, etc.

1.70   The next step is to compare this with the likely cost (cost B) of an appeal to the tribunal. This will be an immediate outlay. If an appeal is seriously considered, the likely value of the claim will therefore be reduced to A minus B. However, because no appeal is certain to succeed, the taxpayer must also assess the relative probabilities of success and failure.

1.71   Inspectors sometimes bullishly state that a claim should be reduced to a much lower amount (often calling it the 'correct' figure, which taxpayers should be wary of), and subsequently propose a 'without prejudice' compromise mid-way between the original claim and the Inspector's reduced proposal. In those cases, the taxpayer should consider the strength of its claim – if entitlement has been satisfactorily established, and a proper valuation exercise has been carried out where needed, taxpayers should be wary of hastening to a 'split-the-difference' compromise agreement, without requesting the full details of the information on the basis of which the Inspector's proposal is suggested. Unfortunately it is not unknown for Inspectors' proposals to be somewhat speculative, with no real underlying basis or calculations.

1.72   In some cases, the Inspector is required to involve valuation specialists from the Valuation Office Agency (VOA), for example where a 'just and reasonable apportionment' of purchase consideration is required under *s 562*. However, it remains the responsibility of the Inspector to agree the non-valuation matters such as the taxpayer's entitlement to claim allowances, the eligibility of assets that qualify for capital allowances and the amount of capital allowances with the taxpayer (VOA Manual, para 3.67), although in practice, Inspectors often take guidance from the VOA on such matters. For more difficult or unusual technical issues, Inspectors are also increasingly likely to involve HMRC's head office capital allowances specialists. However, taxpayers should remember that even their word is not law (any more than the opinions of professional advisers).

1.73   The Inspector may ask the VOA for either a 'not negotiated' or a 'negotiated' apportionment.

1.74   Not negotiated apportionments are more often requested in the first instance and are those where the VOA does not contact the taxpayer or carry out an internal inspection of the property. The aim is to decide at high level on the basis of any information provided by the taxpayer (eg its submitted capital allowances claims and correspondence with the Inspector), together with any other knowledge of the property (eg existing VOA records or even public websites), whether the taxpayer's apportionment or valuation may be accepted as falling within the VOA's interpretation of reasonable tolerances. The VOA aims to complete not negotiated apportionments in six weeks.

1.75   Negotiated apportionments are less often asked for in the first instance, but are used for larger or more complicated circumstances, or can follow not negotiated apportionments, if in the VOA's opinion the taxpayer's apportionment falls outside its interpretation of reasonable tolerances. In practice though, in situations where the size and complexity of the claim probably merits a negotiated apportionment, the Inspector may still go through the formality of requesting a not negotiated apportionment in the first instance, before instructing a negotiated one (with the not negotiated apportionment being used as a negotiating tool by HMRC). In negotiated apportionments an internal inspection of the property is often carried out and negotiations take place with the taxpayer or its agent. The VOA aims to complete negotiated apportionments in six months.

1.76   The value of a settlement is sometimes enhanced by the fact that it can be applied for a number of years. This is considered in connection with sampling – see **6.16** *et seq.*

DATE EXPENDITURE INCURRED

General rules

1.77   Capital allowances are first given (subject to other requirements, for example that an industrial building is in use) for the chargeable period in which the capital expenditure has been (or is deemed to have been) incurred. When the rate of an allowance is changed the new rate is effective in respect of capital expenditure incurred on or after a specified date. It is clear, therefore, that the ascertainment of that date is very important. See also **22.21** for rules establishing the date of disposal (which in many cases will be the other side of the same coin!).

1.78   The general rule is that expenditure (other than that which consists of an additional VAT liability – see **22.1** *et seq*) is incurred on the date *on which the obligation to pay it becomes unconditional.* This applies whether or not there is a later date on or before which the whole or any part of that amount is required to be paid (*s 5(1)*, (2)).

1.79   Except in the circumstances explained below, the date on which the expenditure is actually paid is generally irrelevant.

Payment within one month after accounting date

1.80   If the obligation to pay becomes unconditional within one month of the end of a chargeable accounting period as a result of the issue of a certificate or some other event, and the agreement provides that the asset becomes the property of the purchaser or is otherwise under the agreement attributed to him before the end of that period, the obligation to pay is treated as having become unconditional immediately before the end of that period (*s 5(4)*). This subsection recognises the fact that extended contracts (frequently called 'milestone contracts' – see **1.87**) usually provide for monthly payments or other periodical payments based on valuations of work done. If the work done before a year end (and therefore attributable to the purchaser) is not certified (which is generally when the obligation to pay becomes unconditional) until after the year end, this subsection treats the obligation to pay as having become unconditional before that year end. HMRC was asked to comment on the expression 'or is otherwise under the agreement attributed to'. The reply was to the effect that although reference must be made to the contract there are generally clear alternatives – that the asset is either the property of the purchaser or is otherwise attributable to the purchaser. The construction of an asset to the purchaser's own specification would normally satisfy the latter requirement.

1.81   Satisfaction of the test in *s 5(4)* merely fixes the date on which the obligation to pay becomes unconditional. It is still necessary for payment to be required to be paid within a further four months if the provisions of *s 5(5)* (see **1.84**) are not to apply. Furthermore, satisfaction of the condition of attribution does not obviate the requirement that the asset (if machinery or plant) or a relevant interest therein (if an industrial building) must belong to the claimant either during or at the end of the chargeable period.

1.82   For details of HMRC's view on deposits paid shortly before the end of an accounting period, see **14.143** *et seq.*

1.83   *Section 5(4)* cannot be invoked to 'backdate' expenditure to take advantage of the first-year allowances on plant (unless, in effect, the withdrawal of a particular first-year allowance happens to coincide with the end of an actual chargeable period or its basis period).

Payment after four months

1.84   Where an agreement requires any consideration to be paid on (or not later than) a date which is more than four months after the date on which the obligation to pay becomes unconditional, that consideration is treated as incurred on that later date (*s 5(5)*).

1.85   It follows that if an asset is unconditionally purchased with a four-month credit period, allowances will be available for the period in which it is purchased. However, if the credit period is longer than four months, the period in which allowances become available is determined as if the expenditure has been incurred on the last day of the credit period. In either case the actual date of payment is irrelevant. Consequently, if a credit period of three months is allowed, but actual credit of five months is taken, the 'four-months' rule' of *s 5(5)* has no effect.

1.86   For hire-purchase and similar agreements see **18.1**.

Milestone contracts

1.87   In the case of a 'milestone' contract which requires the contract price to be paid in instalments (usually monthly), each instalment will generally be incurred when the surveyor, or more usually the architect or project manager certifies that the work has been performed. The date(s) of payment can usually be ignored because each date will be only a matter of some three or four weeks later than the relevant date of certification and will not, therefore, trigger the application of *s 5(4)*.

1.88   The construction work under such a contract, if it is building or structure, is usually performed on-site, which in most cases will either be owned by the purchaser or be the subject of an interest in land to which he is entitled. Consequently *s 271(3)* (industrial buildings allowance – see **7.33**) will be satisfied. If the contract, as will generally be the case, also includes some expenditure which can be allocated to machinery or plant, HMRC seems generally to accept appropriate apportionment of each instalment without separate examination of the belonging test (see **14.141** *et seq*). Given that in most cases the plant, by virtue of its inclusion in a building, will be a fixture on land in which the purchaser has an interest, the question of ownership will most likely be already satisfied, but for further comment on the question of ownership, see **14.141**.

Reservation of title to goods

1.89   HMRC has stated (CA, para 11800) that, where goods that have been supplied subject to reservation of title have been delivered to the purchaser, then the obligation to pay will have become unconditional for the purposes of *s 5(3)*. However, it also stated that *s 5(4)* will not apply because that subsection applies only when the goods are the property of the purchaser. In these circumstances the goods might be said to have been attributed to the purchaser as envisaged by *s 5(4)*. This will depend on the precise circumstances, the wording of any contracts, and so on.

Retentions

1.90   HMRC's view is that the obligation to pay any part of the purchase price that is the subject of a retention does not become unconditional until the condition which gave rise to the retention is satisfied, for example the end of the defects liability period (CA, para 11800). The same principles will apply where money is paid into an escrow account, pending the satisfaction of any conditions.

Options

1.91   Expenditure on an option to acquire plant may qualify for allowances, but only when the option is exercised, as only then is the ownership requirement (see **14.141**) satisfied. It is worth considering, however, whether the option can be regarded as a contract under which ownership will pass on performance of the contract (see **18.1**).

Anti-avoidance

1.92   Where:

(*a*)   an obligation to pay becomes unconditional on a date earlier than that which accords with normal commercial usage, and

(*b*)   the sole or main benefit which might have been expected to be obtained thereby is that the expenditure would be taken to be incurred in a chargeable period which is earlier than would otherwise have been the case,

the expenditure is taken to have been incurred on the date on or before which it is required to be paid. The date on which the obligation to pay became unconditional is then ignored (*s 5(6)*).

Interaction of other provisions

1.93   Where any other provision of *CAA 2001* would cause any expenditure to be treated as incurred on a date which is later than that which would result from the application of *s 5(3)–(6)*, for example pre-trading expenditure (see **1.101**) that other provision takes precedence (*s 5(7)*).

Date of delivery

1.94   Some Inspectors have contended that until the vendor had fulfilled all obligations imposed upon him (and that included delivery of the asset) the obligation to pay would remain conditional. An alternative legal view is that the question whether a person had incurred capital expenditure has to be looked at from the standpoint of the person who had incurred the expenditure and not that of the vendor. As a matter of general contractual law, if a purchaser and vendor entered into an agreement providing for payment to be made on a particular date, then as soon as that date arrived the purchaser would have incurred the expenditure. If that date were the date of execution of the contract then at that time the purchaser would be under an unconditional obligation to pay the amount due under the contract. If HMRC's view were correct, the words in parenthesis in *s 5(3)* would need to refer to '(whether or not there is *an earlier* or later date …)'.

Revenue practice

1.95   The following Revenue Interpretation was first given in Tax Bulletin 9 (November 1993) and has now largely been incorporated into CA, para 11800, where a number of examples are given.

> 'The normal rule is that expenditure is incurred on the date on which the obligation to pay becomes unconditional.
>
> A person buying goods is legally required to pay for them on delivery unless there is a special agreement as to terms of payment. If the buyer is legally required to pay on delivery the obligation to pay becomes unconditional when the goods are delivered.
>
> If goods are sold subject to reservation of title (a *Romalpa* contract, see CA11700) the obligation to pay becomes unconditional when the goods are delivered. The supplier has then fulfilled his or her part of the contract. This means that the buyer incurs capital expenditure as soon as the goods are delivered.
>
> The date on which the obligation to pay for an asset becomes unconditional and the date on which the purchaser is legally required to pay for that asset may not be the same. For example, the sales agreement may require payment to be made within four weeks of delivery. If so the obligation to pay becomes unconditional on delivery but the purchaser is not legally required to pay until four weeks after delivery.
>
> There is an exception to the general rule. If there is a gap of more than four months between the dates on which the obligation to pay becomes unconditional and the date on which payment is required to be made the

expenditure is not incurred until the date on which payment is required to be made.'

1.96 Not every asset is acquired by a single payment – stage payments or instalments can add a level of complication.

Example

Jones Ltd, a manufacturer of marine engines, has an annual accounting date of 30 September. On 25 May 2010 it signs a contract for the erection of a factory extension for a total cost of £1,500,000. Progress instalments are due to be certified on the 25th of each month with payment due 14 days later. The progress payments were as follows:

Certificate	Amount	Certified	Due
	£		
1	200,000	25.6.10	8.9.10
2	250,000	25.7.10	9.10.10
3	300,000	25.8.10	8.11.10
4	400,000	25.9.10	9.12.10
5	200,000	25.10.10	8.11.10
6 (retention)	175,000	25.6.11	8.10.11

1.97 The dates on which the expenditure has been certified are, in the first instance, the dates on which the expenditure was incurred. On those dates Jones would have an unconditional obligation to pay.

1.98 Payment 5 was not certified until after 30 September 2010, the end of a chargeable period, but it must have referred to work done during that year because the previous certificate was for the period to 25 September 2010. Such work would have been 'under the contract attributable to the person having that obligation [to pay]'. It therefore falls within the scope of *s 5(4)* (see **1.80** above) and the appropriate part of payment 5 can be treated as incurred during the year to 30 September.

1.99 In such circumstances it would be advisable to have the certification of the expenditure apportioned (assuming any additional fee payable would not offset the benefit of advancing the allowances by one year).

1.100 Payment 6 is a retention payment for which the obligation to pay does not become unconditional until the retention period has expired and no construction problems remain outstanding. This part of the expenditure is therefore incurred when certified.

Expenditure prior to commencement of the qualifying activity

1.101 Expenditure on machinery or plant incurred for the purposes of a qualifying activity by a person about to carry it on is treated as incurred on the day on which the activity actually commences (*s 12*).

In determining whether or not any expenditure qualifies for an annual investment allowance (AIA) (see **14.62** *et seq*), the effect of *s 12* on the time when the expenditure is treated as having been incurred is ignored (*s 38A(4)*). What this means is that if expenditure was incurred before April 2008 for a qualifying activity commencing after April 2008, no AIA is available for that expenditure. In contrast, if pre-trading capital expenditure is incurred *after* April 2008 but before that qualifying activity has commenced, this will qualify for an AIA because the expenditure is deemed to be incurred on the first day of trading by *s 12*.

If capital expenditure was incurred before April 2012 or 2014 when the fixed value requirement (see **4.16** *et seq*) or pooling requirement (see **4.27** *et seq*) took effect and was treated by *s 12* as incurred on the first day of trading (ie, after April 2012 or 2014) it would seem logical that the fixed value and pooling requirements should *not* apply to that expenditure. Otherwise, the situation could theoretically arise where a taxpayer bought qualifying assets in say, 2010 before the relevant requirements had even been conceived of, but nevertheless still be caught by them if it did not start trading (eg, secured a tenant) until after April 2012 or 2014.

Similarly, for the purposes of determining whether a first-year allowance is available and the rate applicable, it is necessary to have regard to the actual date on which the expenditure is incurred (*s 50*). Consequently, expenditure incurred (for corporation tax purposes):

(*a*)   before 1 April 2009 in respect of a qualifying activity commenced after 1 April 2009 will not qualify for a first-year allowance;

(*b*)   during the year ended 31 March 2010 in respect of a qualifying activity commenced during that year will qualify (subject to satisfaction of the normal rules);

(*c*)   during the year ended 31 March 2010 in respect of a qualifying activity commenced after that date will qualify (again subject to the normal rules).

1.102   Expenditure incurred prior to incorporation is dealt with in **13.40** *et seq.*

Assets created by the claimant

1.103   This is a subject which, more often than not, is dealt with on a common-sense basis rather than strictly in accordance with the rules. If the materials are purchased specifically for the construction of the asset and do not, therefore, form part of the trader's own trading stock, the expenditure will be incurred on dates ascertained by application, as far as possible, of the general rules.

1.104   If the materials are appropriated from trading stock there will be the usual adjustment to the profit and loss account to recognise the fact that stock has been appropriated other than to trading purposes. Usually such adjustments follow the principle in *Sharkey (Inspector of Taxes) v Wernher* (1955) 36 TC 275 that such an appropriation is deemed to be a sale at market value. However, in Statement of Practice A32 HMRC state that: 'The decision is not considered to apply to … expenditure incurred by a trader on the construction of an asset which is to be used as a fixed asset in the trade.' Capital allowances will be given on the original cost (CA, para 11530) – see **11.89**.

1.105   In all these matters a practical approach is often agreed with the Inspector, if only to arrive at an acceptable basis of dealing with any associated labour costs and overheads charged initially to revenue account.

1.106   For an unincorporated business capital expenditure cannot include any valuation of the owner's time.

CONTRIBUTIONS AND SUBSIDIES

General

1.107   The legislation includes specific provisions to ensure that one person cannot obtain capital allowances on expenditure which is actually borne or 'met' by another (the 'contributor'). However, that other person may obtain capital allowances if the contribution was made for the purposes of his trade or for the purposes of a trade carried on by the tenant of a building in which the contributor has an interest.

Contributions received

1.108 Expenditure is not to be regarded as incurred by any person to the extent that it has been or is to be met directly or indirectly by any other person. Ignored for this purpose are grants made under the provisions of the *Industrial Development Act 1982*, *Pt II*, the *Industry Act 1972*, *Pt I*, or their Northern Ireland equivalents. These equivalents are those specified by *SI 2001/810*, ie:

(*a*) any grant made under the *Industrial Development (Northern Ireland) Order 1982*, *Pt III*, being a grant not exceeding 45% of the expenditure, and made under an agreement entered into before 1 April 2003;

(*b*) any grant made by the Local Enterprise Development Unit out of moneys granted under the *Industrial Development (Northern Ireland) Order 1982*, *art 30*, likewise not exceeding 45% of the expenditure and being a grant made under an agreement entered into prior to 1 April 2003; or

(*c*) where any grant is made at a rate higher than 45% of the expenditure, the first 45% of that grant.

1.109 Also ignored are:

(i) insurance proceeds or other compensation in respect of assets which have been destroyed, demolished or put out of use (the amount, defined by *ss 61* (plant) and *316* (industrial buildings), etc is effectively the net proceeds or compensation (*s 535*); and

(ii) contributions received from a person other than a public body where that person would not be entitled to either capital allowances or a trading deduction in respect of that expenditure (*s 536*). A 'public body' is defined as the Crown or any public or local authority in the United Kingdom (*s 537(3)*).

1.110 In *McKinney (Inspector of Taxes) v Hagans Caravans (Manufacturing) Ltd* [1997] STC 1023, the term 'public authority' (now referred to as a 'public body') was held to include an international fund set up to promote economic and social advance in Northern Ireland. There is no simple test for identifying a public body, but key criteria (not all of which need necessarily be met) include:

(*a*) a constitution which derives from some public source;

(*b*) performance of a public service;

(*c*) public control and accountability;

(*d*) absence of private profit;

(*e*) public funding.

1.111 It is assumed that, for the purposes of establishing whether the contributor is entitled to allowances, that person is within the charge to tax, whether or not that is in fact the case (*s 536(4)*).

1.112 It is understood that where the contribution is made by an exempt pension fund, no account need be taken of that contribution. HMRC regards this treatment as concessionary.

Timing and repayment of grants received

1.113 Little importance is attached to the respective timing of the receipt of a grant and the incurring of the expenditure to which it relates. Expenditure may be incurred before the person becomes entitled to a grant or subsidy or before he has applied for one. However, the grant, once received, should be deducted from the expenditure otherwise qualifying for allowances (CA, para 14100). This follows from the case of *Cyril Lord Carpets Ltd v Schofield* (1966) 42 TC 637 (see **Appendix 4**).

1.114 If a person subsequently repays a grant (whether compulsorily or voluntarily), he might formerly have been able to claim capital allowances on the amount repaid, but only if the circumstances fell within the terms of ESC B49, ie:

(*a*)   the grant was made by the Crown, government or any other public body; or

(*b*)   the repaid grant is taxable in the hands of the person who made the grant as a balancing adjustment or a revenue receipt.

1.115 ESC B49 was withdrawn with effect from 1 April 2013 for corporates and 6 April 2013 for non-corporates. From that date, HMRC believes that no allowance is due where expenditure has initially been met by a grant that is subsequently repaid (CA, para 14300). HMRC's stated reason for withdrawing the concession was as follows:

'It has been decided to withdraw this ESC because:

●   when making the commercial decision to receive a contribution, taxpayers are in a position to take full account of the circumstances in which the contribution might have to be repaid and the business consequences that will follow;

●   any implementing legislation would have to be complex, lengthy, and restrictive (to avoid creating tax planning opportunities) running counter to the Government's ambition to create a simpler tax system.'

1.116 It appears unfair that allowances should be thus arbitrarily denied in respect of qualifying expenditure which, ultimately, has *not* been met by a grant. Setting aside the respective merits of a simple tax system and a fair one, the likely effect may be to discourage potential grant claimants where there is any possibility that the grant may have to be repaid.

1.117 As stated at **1.108** above, *s 532* states that expenditure is not to be regarded as incurred by any person to the extent that it *has been or is to be met* directly or indirectly by any other person. It may be that HMRC interpret this wording to include situations where expenditure is financed in the first instance by a grant, even if that grant is subsequently repaid. An alternative reading would be to say that the question of whether expenditure has, or has not, been 'met' by a grant must be considered at the present time, taking account of all the latest known circumstances. It would seem to be a misuse of language to suggest that expenditure has been 'met' by a grant which has since been repaid. It has always seemed quite clear that the contributions received legislation was intended only to ensure that taxpayers could not claim allowances where they had not incurred expenditure, not to doubly penalise taxpayers for triggering a repayment.

1.118 CA, para 14300 instructs Inspectors that since ESC/B49 has been withdrawn they should 'refuse to give capital allowances in all cases on a grant repaid because there is nothing in the legislation to allow them'. This is arguably untrue, because if expenditure has not been 'met' by a grant, it should be dealt with under general principles. Therefore, if a person has ultimately incurred expenditure on the provision of plant and machinery for the purposes of a qualifying activity, and that plant belongs to him, *s 11* would make allowances available, and it is by no means clear that this can be overruled by HMRC's reading of *s 532*, reflected in CA, para 14300.

Contributions paid

1.119 Subject to certain conditions, capital allowances will be available to a person contributing a capital sum to expenditure incurred on the provision of an asset by another person (*s 537*). This will apply where the contribution is made:

(*a*) for the purposes of a trade or relevant activity (defined in s 536(5)) carried on (or to be carried on) by the contributor (*s 538(1)* (plant) and *s 539(1)* (industrial buildings)); or

(*b*) for the purposes of a trade carried on by a tenant of land in which the contributor has an interest. This allows relief for contributions made, inter alia, by a lessor of a building towards expenditure of his tenants or of anyone else, provided it is for the purposes of his tenant's trade(s) (*s 539(1)(b)(ii)* (industrial buildings)).

1.120   For claims made on or after 29 May 2013, anti-avoidance is introduced to stop gas and electricity distribution companies from claiming tax relief for costs already paid for by business customers. *Section 538* was amended to confirm that plant and machinery allowances are available for contributions to capital expenditure on plant and machinery in the recipient's hands. The contributor's payment is treated as capital expenditure on the provision of plant and machinery for use in its business and it is able to claim capital allowances, instead of the recipient. Also, if the recipient of a contribution has previously pooled expenditure (after 1 January 2013, or before that date but no claim for allowances was made) which would be ineligible to be pooled under this amended legislation, then it must account for a disposal value for the portion of the expenditure not yet written-off.

1.121   These rules do not apply where the person making the contribution and the person receiving it are connected persons (*s 537(2)*) (and see **20.25** *et seq* below).

1.122   If the contribution was made in respect of a trade carried on (or to be carried on) by the contributor, and the trade is transferred, allowances will thereafter be available to the transferee. Where part only of the trade is transferred, an appropriate proportion of the allowances will be transferred (*ss 538(4)–(6) and 542*). If the contribution was made in respect of a trade carried on by a tenant, allowances are given to the person who has the 'contributor's interest' in the land at the end of the relevant chargeable period (*s 539(3)–(5)*).

1.123   A person who makes a contribution towards plant and machinery does not normally have to account for a subsequent disposal of the asset (indeed, he may not even be aware of it). Generally, the contributor will continue to claim allowances regardless of whether the asset is disposed of, or even ceases to exist. Only if the contributor's relevant activity is transferred, does he cease to claim and must account for disposal proceeds (if any).

1.124   A disposal is likely to be a rarity, therefore, where the plant is moveable, or where it is fixed to a building used for the contributor's trade. However, in the case of property investors, any sale of a property will be treated as a transfer of (part of) the relevant activity (ie the property business).

1.125   It appears therefore that where a property investor contributes to fixtures, then later sells that property, he should bring in a disposal value in respect of contribution allowances. This is often overlooked, but can be in the contributor's favour. The contributor could, for example, make an election under *s 198* (see **4.44**) in respect of this disposal value. If this election were for £1, allowances would be retained by the contributor, and a balancing allowance could arise in certain circumstances.

1.126 This possibility is generally overlooked. It is often thought that a *s 198* election does not apply to contribution allowances, because such an election is only possible where a disposal value is brought into account under item 1 of the table in *s 196*, ie where there is a disposal under *s 188*. *Section 188* applies only if a person has been treated as the owner of a fixture under certain named sections. A contributions allowance is given under *s 538*, which is not one of the sections listed in *s 188*. Consequently, a *s 198* election cannot be made in respect of contribution expenditure.

1.127 However, this reasoning is erroneous. *Section 538* does not grant allowances as a right, but merely treats the contributor as if it owned the asset 'for the purposes of Part 2' (ie plant allowances), and that even for contributions allowances, the requirements of *CAA 2001*, *Pt 2*, including the fixtures chapter, must be met. In essence, so the argument runs, *s 538* enables the contributor to benefit from the fixtures rules, but then the claim itself is made under *s 176*, etc. Following this argument to its conclusion, a *s 198* election is possible.

Sums payable in respect of depreciation

1.128 No allowances will be given to a person using machinery or plant for the purposes of a trade, if in a particular chargeable period that person receives sums which:

(*a*) are in respect of, or take account of, the depreciation to the machinery or plant occasioned by its use; and

(*b*) do not fall to be taken into account as income of that person, or in computing the profits or gains of any trade carried on by him (*ss 37* and *209*).

1.129 Where any such subsidies are in respect of part only of any depreciation, the allowances available shall be reduced to such amount as is 'just and reasonable, having regard to the relevant circumstances' (*ss 210(1)* and *212(2)*). What is 'just and reasonable' is a matter for negotiation between the taxpayer and HMRC.

1.130 Expenditure to which these provisions apply is assumed to have been incurred for the purposes of a separate notional trade, and is therefore excluded from the general plant pool. This notional trade is deemed to be permanently discontinued when the asset begins to be used wholly or partly for purposes other than those of the actual trade (*s 211*).

1.131 Where an asset has been used, and allowances have been claimed, in a chargeable period prior to that in which it is first subject to these provisions, then it is deemed at that time to have begun to be used wholly for purposes other than those of the actual trade. Therefore, in accordance with *ss 55* and *61*, a disposal value must be brought into account. Effectively, the relevant asset will be 'depooled' at market value. Taxpayers can unwittingly come within these provisions, for example, where a lessor has incurred expenditure on fixtures, but the lease agreement makes the lessee responsible for maintenance or renewal of these fixtures. It may sometimes be preferable, therefore, for the lessor to retain responsibility for maintenance, with perhaps a compensatory adjustment to the amount of rent payable.

1.132   Assets to which this section applies (where depreciation is subsidised) cannot be treated as 'short-life assets' (see **14.179** *et seq*).

INDUCEMENTS

General

1.133   Often landlords will provide financial incentives or 'inducements' to encourage new tenants to take up leases (eg key tenants to 'anchor' new developments) or existing tenants to renew leases, or to persuade tenants to accept higher rental amounts (which will increase the capital value and scope for borrowing against a property).

1.134   Such inducements can take a number of forms, but there are three main techniques used in practice:

(*a*)   a reduced rent or rent-free period;

(*b*)   a reverse premium;

(*c*)   a contribution to fitting-out works.

1.135   The optimal tax efficiency of these alternatives depends on the particular transaction and tax status of the parties involved and interacts with capital allowances. This is discussed below.

Reduced rent or rent-free period

1.136   The landlord may agree to reduce the rent, or offer a rent-free period (typically to keep the tenant's overheads low whilst it is fitting out the building and so unable to trade from it).

1.137   Where both the landlord and tenant are taxable, offering a reduced rent or rent-free period is a relatively tax neutral option because the landlord will not have to pay tax on the rent it has foregone, but the tenant will be unable to obtain a tax deduction for the rents which would otherwise have been payable.

1.138 However, it may not always be the most cost effective option and, for example, if the landlord is a tax-exempt investor (such as a pension fund), although it will have no tax preference about the incentive method used, it will typically be keen to maximise its income stream and the capital value of the property and so may be reluctant to offer these types of incentives.

Reverse premium

1.139 A reverse premium typically means a cash lump sum payment from a landlord to a tenant.

1.140 Historically reverse premiums could be received tax free by tenants. Now though, because of legislation introduced with effect from 9 March 1999 (for corporation tax *CTA 2009, ss 96–98* ; and for income tax *ITTOIA 2005, ss 99–103*), they are mostly taxable in tenants' hands as trade profits or trading income, with the tax charge following the accounting treatment (ie spread over the duration of the lease, or if shorter the period to the next market rent review date, which under a standard full repairing and insuring lease is normally five or seven years but can be longer). This treatment only applies where reverse premiums are received from a landlord (the 'grantor' of the estate or interest in land), or a nominee of that landlord, or person acting under the directions of, or connected to the landlord (*CTA 2009, s 96(4)*; *ITTOIA 2005, s 99*), so would not apply, for example, if a cash sum was received from an outgoing tenant as an incentive to take on an assignment of its lease. This legislation also does not apply to reduced rents or rent-free periods, as discussed above.

1.141 As an alternative to a reduced rent or rent-free period, the payment of a reverse premium may be attractive, for example, to a trader-developer that sells the property immediately on completion of the development and is able to deduct the lump sum inducement in calculating its profit or loss. As the developer's expenditure is not capital, it would not be able to benefit from any capital allowances.

Contribution to fitting-out works

1.142 Alternatively, the landlord may agree to pay for part of the cost of fitting out the building with fixtures and chattels to equip the building for the particular tenant's needs (ie expenditure which is normally a tenant's responsibility and will not increase the value of the landlord's reversionary interest, because it will be worthless to the landlord when the lease ends). Where this happens the payment is generally subject to the reverse premium rules described above and so is taxable in the tenant's hands. It is irrelevant whether the landlord pays the supplier or contractor directly, or indirectly by reimbursing the tenant.

1.143   There are, however, some exceptions to this, namely where:

(*a*)   The tenant is responsible for completing the fabric of the building (ie the landlord's 'shell') and the landlord reimburses all or part of this cost. This work is an improvement to the landlord's property that increases the value of the reversion and would normally be taken into account in fixing market rent at a rent review.

(*b*)   The landlord meets the tenant's cost, but is reimbursed by, for example, an enhanced rental level to reflect the additional value to the tenant of a building more highly equipped with fixtures and fittings. This means that the tenant has received no taxable benefit. In practice, it is important that this is properly documented to prove the point to HMRC.

(*c*)   The incentive is a contribution towards a tenant's fitting out costs that are eligible for capital allowances. This is because the tenant will effectively already suffer an increased tax liability through its reduced ability to claim capital allowances on qualifying expenditure that it would otherwise have incurred. Conversely, the landlord should be able to claim capital allowances for any contribution to capital allowances qualifying assets (see **1.119** *et seq*).

1.144   The optimum tax treatment depends on the relative tax status of the parties involved (eg whether they are taxable, their effective tax rates and whether they have tax losses they can use), the duration of the lease, the period until the next rent review, and the rates that capital allowances will be available to each party (taking into account any first-year allowances, short-life asset election opportunities, or long-life assets). It should be calculated on a discounted present value cash-flow basis (which may require different discount rates to be used for the landlord and tenant).

1.145   As a general rule of thumb, for two taxable parties entering into a standard institutional lease with a five-year rent review period, and where plant and machinery writing-down allowances are available at the normal 18% and 8% integral features per annum reducing balance bases, it may be more tax efficient for the tenant to forgo capital allowances than to accept a taxable reverse premium. Therefore, a fitting-out contribution agreement should be structured in the following order to be optimally tax-efficient for the tenant (and vice versa for the landlord):

(*a*)   to works required to complete the landlord's shell, which will increase the value of the reversionary interest and do not qualify for capital allowances (not taxable as a reverse premium and do not reduce the tenant's capital allowances claim);

(*b*)   to works required to complete the landlord's shell, which will increase the value of the reversionary interest and do qualify for capital allowances (not taxable as a reverse premium, but will reduce the tenant's capital allowances claim);

(*c*)   to tenant's works, which qualify for capital allowances (not taxable as a reverse premium, but will reduce the tenant's capital allowances claim);

(*d*)   to tenant's works, which do not qualify for capital allowances (taxable as a reverse premium over the period to the next rent review);

(*e*)   as income of the tenant, for example if the landlord's contribution exceeds the cost of the fitting-out works (taxable as a reverse premium over the period to the next rent review or the duration of the lease if shorter).

Chapter 2

Construction of new buildings

INTRODUCTION

2.1   The construction of new premises will for many taxpayers be the most expensive project or type of project ever undertaken, and the availability of capital allowances can often significantly reduce the post-tax cost of a project. Almost invariably, expenditure on a capital project will consist of some elements qualifying for a high rate of allowances, and some elements qualifying for a lower rate, or for no allowances at all. The key to maximising allowances is essentially the proper identification or recognition of the former. There can be no question of artificially inflating the expenditure qualifying for allowances: the availability of allowances must stand or fall on the facts of each individual case. All too often, however, the true facts are not brought out, and a valid claim for allowances is forgone.

2.2   A construction claim must be based on actual costs as far as possible, rather than estimates or valuations, which should only be relied upon where the project-cost documentation is insufficient in detail to identify all expenditure on capital allowances qualifying assets (eg design and build, or direct labour construction procurement methods). Where valuations are necessary, they should be carried out by an appropriately tax-qualified quantity surveyor. It scarcely needs saying that guesswork or 'a finger in the air' does not meet the taxpayer's obligation under self-assessment to file a complete and correct return.

2.3   Taxpayers should also be aware that undue delay can make it difficult to provide sufficient supporting documentation to meet the record-keeping requirements of self-assessment. Once contractors have completed their work (and been paid), it may be difficult to procure further analyses of key expenditure.

2.4   Some of the expenditure will qualify for tax relief only as a deduction in computing a capital gain or loss on a subsequent sale. Other expenditure will qualify for other types of capital allowances, and it is essential that the claim for such allowances is maximised. When considering eligibility for capital allowances, the major areas of expenditure for most taxpayers will be:

(*a*) plant and machinery; and

(*b*) buildings.

2.5   So far as capital allowances for plant and machinery are concerned, the main problem facing the person making a claim is whether or not the particular assets acquired do, in fact, qualify as plant. Once this is accepted, it is generally true that allowances will be given, irrespective of the nature of the particular trade.

2.6   The same was not historically true of expenditure on buildings. With the exception of buildings in enterprise zones (see **Chapter 9**) and hotels (see **8.4** *et seq*), the system of allowances generally discriminated in favour of industrial and agricultural concerns, and against, for example, the financial, retail and service industries (although this discrimination disappeared with the abolition of industrial buildings allowances from April 2011 – see **7.15** *et seq*). The precise rules governing which buildings qualified for allowances and which did not are considered in **Chapter 7**. Depending on the trade carried on, expenditure on a new building could previously qualify for relief at 4% pa, or it could fail to qualify at all. Key considerations were as follows:

(i)   Was the building in an enterprise zone? (See **Chapter 9**.)

(ii)   Was it a qualifying hotel? (See **Chapter 8**.)

(iii) Was the use made of the building such that it will qualify as industrial? (See **Chapter 7**.)

(iv)   To what extent could any of the expenditure be said to be in respect of machinery or plant? (See **Chapters 14–16**.)

LAND AND LANDSCAPING

General

2.7   No capital allowances are available for the costs of acquiring land (*ss 24* (plant)) or, in most cases, for expenditure on work done to the land (*s 22(1)(b)* (plant)), except where for the purpose only of installing plant or machinery (*s 23, List C, Item 22*) (see **2.14**). However, see treatment of land remediation expenditure (**Chapter 24**) and preparatory works below (see **2.11**).

2.8   The cost of landscaping does not generally qualify for allowances. This can appear inequitable, for example, where a new hotel is surrounded by landscaped grounds; the landscaping would undoubtedly be said to perform a function in the hotelier's trade, namely attracting guests by providing pleasant surroundings. Despite this, HMRC argues that the landscaping does not constitute plant but instead is merely part of the premises (see **15.21** *et seq*), relying on the speech of Lord Lowry in *IRC v Scottish & Newcastle Breweries Ltd* (1982) 55 TC 252 (CA, para 31400).

2.9   It may appear confusing that despite being part of the 'premises', HMRC does not regard landscaping as a 'building' or 'structure'. In its Press Release introducing *Sch AA1* to *Capital Allowances Act 1990* (*CAA 1990*) (now *CAA 2001, ss 21–24*) in 1993, it described a structure as 'any substantial man-made asset'. A previous version of HMRC's Capital Allowances Manual (para 22020) expanded upon this to say that the word 'structure' embraced artificial works which might not properly be described as buildings; examples of structures are walls, bridges, dams, roads, culverts and tunnels. The meaning of 'structure' has most often been considered by the courts in a rating context, but the following may provide useful 'leads' in difficult cases:

(*a*)   *IRC v Smyth* [1914] 3 KB 406;

(*b*)   *Cardiff Rating Authority and Cardiff Assessment Committee v Guest Keen Baldwin's Iron & Steel Co Ltd* [1949] 1 KB 385;

(*c*)   *BP Refinery (Kent) Ltd v Walker (Valuation Officer)* [1957] 2 QB 305; and

(*d*)   *Anchor International Ltd v IRC* [2005] STC 411.

2.10   Landscaping in other contexts, for example in the grounds of an office building, is even less likely to qualify for allowances.

Preparatory works

2.11   The cost of work done to land may include expenditure on:

(*a*)   preparing, cutting, tunnelling or levelling land in connection with the construction of a building; or

(*b*)   preparing land as a site for the installation of machinery or plant.

2.12   Expenditure under (*a*) may only qualify if the building is to be used for research and development (see **Chapter 19**), whereas expenditure under (*b*) may qualify for plant allowances, provided the general conditions for plant allowances are met.

2.13   HMRC's view was that expenditure on the drainage or reclamation of land did not qualify for industrial buildings allowances, as it is not expenditure on the construction of a building or structure (CA, para 31400). Although this view related to a form of allowances which has since been abolished, it is indicative of HMRC's approach. Consequently, such costs incurred in connection with the installation of plant are unlikely to qualify for allowances.

2.14 Although works involving the alteration of land do not in the first instance qualify for plant allowances (*s 22(1)(b)*), that does not apply where the alterations are for the sole purpose of installing plant or machinery (*s 23(4)*, *List C, Item 22*). This means that, if work done to land is merely incidental to the installation of plant (eg providing a firm base for heavy plant to rest on), plant allowances should be available.

2.15 However, for plant purposes *s 23, List C, Item 22* does exclude from the *ss 21* and *22* definitions of a 'building' or 'structure' 'the alteration of land for the purpose of only installing plant and machinery'. This permits treating such expenditure as incurred on the 'provision' of the plant or machinery in question (see **14.114** *et seq*). In *Mrs ME McMillin v HMRC Comrs* [2011] UKFTT 65 (TC), the taxpayer sought to claim plant allowances for an earth bund, which it was argued provided thermal insulation to one side of a property and was for the purpose only of installing plant or machinery (ie ground source heat pumps). However, the main purpose was to allow for the disposal of spoil/waste from the building works. So the earthworks were held not to be for the purpose *only* of installing plant.

INCIDENTAL EXPENDITURE – PRELIMINARIES, FEES, ETC

Planning permission

2.16 HMRC's view is that the cost of obtaining planning permission, (or costs associated with a public enquiry) is not expenditure on the construction of an asset. However, if a builder's price for constructing a building includes the cost of obtaining any necessary consents, there is no disallowance of a part of the total cost (CA, para 31400).

Preliminaries

2.17 A conventional contract for the erection or substantial alteration of a building of any size will usually refer to preliminary expenses. Preliminaries is not a precise term, but is generally understood to mean a building contractor's costs of administering a project and providing general plant facilities and site-based services. The nature of the expenditure under this heading can vary considerably but will often include the cost to the contractor of setting up his site organisation and management, for example toilets and canteen for his workers, secure compounds for materials, cabins for visiting surveyors and architects, insurance premiums, etc. The method of allocating these costs to machinery or plant is a frequent cause of disagreement with the Inspector (see **2.22** and **2.28**). At first sight they are building-related but in two respects (and possibly more) significant amounts may refer to machinery or plant:

(*a*)   some of the machinery or plant, common examples being the heating, ventilation and electrical systems and the plumbing and sanitary ware, is installed as part of the actual building process;

(*b*)   the main contractor will often have some responsibility for the offloading, storing and handling of machinery or plant and supervision of its installation.

2.18   The preliminaries relating to such items are claimed on the basis that they are part of the cost of 'providing' the asset, a term which covers transport and installation (ie more than the actual supply).

2.19   Claimants often seek to get round the problem by apportioning preliminary expenses pro rata to the expenditure on plant or machinery or non-allowable items. Sometimes this is accepted but often it is rejected by HMRC, which seeks to impose a restriction.

2.20   Judges of the Upper Tribunal in *JD Wetherspoon plc v HMRC Comrs* [2012] UKUT 42 (TCC) effectively dismissed such a restriction and instead recommended the following approach:

●   Where items claimed as preliminaries may be properly apportioned or attributed to a qualifying or non-qualifying asset (ie they are trade-specific preliminaries that are attributable to particular items of 'measured work'), they are part of the cost of that item of plant.

●   Where overheads or preliminaries relate to the project as a whole (eg site supervision and insurance, etc) they should be pro-rata apportioned globally.

●   For other preliminaries which were not incurred for individual items of measured work, but relate to several categories (eg scaffolding, mobile towers, propping, site hoardings, temporary protection of the works, etc), then a pro-rata apportionment is also appropriate.

2.21   Any pro-rata allocations should be as accurate as possible, but where (as was the case in *JD Wetherspoon*) there are, for example, many preliminaries items, a 'common-sense' global pro-rata apportionment which accords with commercial practice is reasonable in principle and will normally be appropriate. However, it was noted that this might not be legitimate in all cases and HMRC is still entitled to investigate figures on a case-by-case basis to see whether a more specific breakdown is appropriate and proportionate.

2.22   Nevertheless, HMRC appears reluctant to accept the findings of the Upper Tribunal and still routinely rejects pro rata claims in the first instance (although such claims are often agreed after negotiation) and, at the time of writing, its guidance (CA, para 20070) does not reflect this decision. There, it is stated that a pro-rata apportionment is acceptable only for 'small construction projects'. Strangely, much of the text of the relevant guidance has been withheld from the public 'because of exemptions in the Freedom of Information Act 2000', but it is understood that HMRC may regard a 'small construction project' as one costing less than £100,000 in London or £50,000 elsewhere in the UK.

2.23 HMRC may also, with VOA advice, accept a business using a pro-rata approach for all its similar projects. But accepting an agreement for a particular year will not bind HMRC for future years, to which a risk-based approach will be taken.

Fees

2.24 The fees associated with a substantial building project can cover a wide spectrum – lawyers, architects, surveyors, etc. Some of these will qualify as incurred on the provision of machinery or plant in their entirety or in substantial part, eg electrical and mechanical engineers; some will qualify as expenditure on industrial buildings, eg structural engineers; some will not qualify for any allowances, eg lawyers. A considered allocation and/or apportionment is necessary based on the facts.

2.25 HMRC has stated that fees only qualify for capital allowances to the extent that the expenditure is directly related to the acquisition of plant (CA, para 20070). The apportionment to machinery or plant of fees, etc charged on, for example, a building contract therefore needs to be properly planned, with documentation in place to support the claim.

2.26 Where one fee covers both buildings and integral plant, an apportionment is possible, but the onus is on the claimant to prove that a part of the fee does indeed relate to plant. Inspectors are specifically instructed not to accept an apportionment based merely on the cost of plant as a fraction of the total cost (CA, para 20070) although such an apportionment is often accepted in practice and has been supported by the courts (see **2.29–2.30**). Where appropriate, difficulty may be avoided by arranging for fees relating to plant to be separately identified and invoiced.

2.27 Some inspectors have in the past, guided by HMRC VOA, sought to restrict the qualifying element of fees in accordance with the table below (referred to as the 'Newstead' formula). However, this is understood to have originated in a claim where fees were only one of the disputed items, and where both taxpayer and Inspector made concessions.

2.28   The taxpayer should not therefore think that this table represents either statute or official policy, and if encountered in practice, should be aware of its background and status. The artificial restrictions imposed on the final four items have in fact been rejected by the courts (see **2.29–2.30**).

Type of cost	*Percentage qualifying as plant*
Legal	Nil
Surveyors	Nil
Project managers	Nil
Mechanical engineers	Fee × Qualifying plant/total plant
Electrical engineers	Fee × Qualifying plant/total plant
Service engineers	Fee × Qualifying plant/total plan
Lift consultants	Fee × Qualifying plant/total plant
Quantity surveyors	Fee × 30% × Qualifying plant/total project cost (excluding fees)
Architects	Fee × 30% × Qualifying plant/total project cost (excluding fees)
Structural engineers	Fee × 30% × Qualifying plant/total project cost (excluding fees)
Preliminaries	Cost × 50% × Qualifying plant/total project cost (excluding fees)

2.29   In *JD Wetherspoon plc v HMRC Comrs* (2007) SpC 00657; [2009] UKFTT 374 (TC); [2012] UKUT 42 (TCC), it was agreed between HMRC and the taxpayer that structural engineer's fees should be proportionally allocated to those items of expenditure that related to the alterations and amendments to the existing building.

2.30   Furthermore, the Commissioners/tribunal judges effectively dismissed notional restrictions by HMRC and instead recommended a common-sense approach. Where items claimed as fees may be properly apportioned or attributed to a qualifying or non-qualifying asset, they are part of the cost of that item. Where assets relate to several categories of work, or the project as a whole, they may be apportioned on a global pro-rata basis. Any allocation should be as accurate as possible, but a 'common-sense' approach which accords with commercial practice is reasonable in principle and will normally be appropriate. However, it was noted that this might not be legitimate in all cases and HMRC is still entitled to investigate figures on a case-by-case basis to see whether a more specific basis would be appropriate and proportionate.

2.31   Nevertheless, HMRC still routinely rejects pro rata claims (although many claims are nonetheless agreed on this basis) and, at the time of writing, its guidance (CA, para 20070) does not reflect this decision. There, it is stated that a pro-rata apportionment is acceptable only for 'small construction projects'. Strangely, much of the text of the relevant guidance has been withheld from the public 'because of exemptions in the Freedom of Information Act 2000', but it is understood that HMRC may regard a 'small construction project' as one costing less than £100,000 in London or £50,000 elsewhere in the UK.

2.32   HMRC may also, with VOA advice, accept a business using a pro-rata approach for all its similar projects. But accepting an agreement for a particular year will not bind HMRC for future years, to which a risk based approach will be taken.

Example

A new office has been erected at a cost of £2,000,000 exclusive of fees and preliminaries. The Inspector has agreed that this cost can be apportioned to:

	Amount £
Building	1,600,000
Mechanical plant	150,000
Electrical plant	250,000
	2,000,000
Preliminaries	65,000
Fees, etc	
Architect	100,000
Mechanical engineers	50,000
Electrical engineers	60,000

Assuming that the office is of normal design and construction, with no special features, the expenditure qualifying for capital allowances could be derived as follows:

Machinery and plant	Amount £
Mechanical plant	150,000
Electrical plant	250,000
	400,000
Architect	7,500

Mechanical engineers	50,000
Electrical engineers	45,000
Preliminaries	7,500
Total claim for machinery and plant	510,000

The mechanical engineers' fees relate to plant which qualifies in its entirety. The electrical engineers' fees relate to plant which is 71% qualifying (£250,000 out of £350,000). This has been rounded to £45,000, illustrating that the apportionment of fees is not merely a question of applying a formula.

2.33 Although the figures are purely illustrative they demonstrate that the value of a claim can be substantially increased by taking proper account of fees and preliminaries.

2.34 HMRC's view is that fees can only qualify for allowances if the asset to which they relate is actually constructed or provided. If construction is aborted, no allowance is due.

Finance costs

2.35 The cost of financing an acquisition is not capital expenditure (*Ben-Odeco Ltd v Powlson (Inspector of Taxes)* (1978) 52 TC 459). Interest is not converted into capital simply because it is charged to capital in the payer's accounts but this does not mean that a capital price cannot contain an escalating element calculated in part or in whole as if it were interest. If a price adjustment of this sort is part of the contract with the supplier of the plant, as opposed to a financial institution to which interest would normally be paid, there is a better prospect of it qualifying for capital allowances (*Van Arkadie (Inspector of Taxes) v Sterling Coated Materials Ltd* [1983] STC 95).

2.36 It was confirmed in *Barclays Mercantile Business Finance Ltd v Mawson (Inspector of Taxes)* [2002] EWCA Civ 1853 that where expenditure was incurred on the provision of plant or machinery wholly and exclusively for the purposes of the trade, it was immaterial how the trader acquired the funds to incur the expenditure. Whilst the cost of finance will not itself qualify for allowances, the fact that finance has to be obtained by way of loan does not preclude allowances being claimed on the asset itself.

Builder's work in connection

2.37 It is not unknown for builder's work in connection (BWIC) on the installation of plant in a building under construction to be excluded from qualifying expenditure on the ground that *s 25* (see **14.119**) cannot apply because that section refers to alterations to an *existing* building. BWIC on the installation of machinery or plant should be claimable under the general principle that it is part of the cost of 'provision' (*s 11*) (ie a cost of construction or setting up of the machinery or plant into working order), *s 25* being irrelevant.

Preparation of land and other installation costs

2.38   Expenditure on preparing, cutting, tunnelling or levelling of land is not itself eligible for relief. However, see **2.14** in respect of alterations to land which are for the sole purpose of installing plant or machinery, which may qualify for plant allowances (*s 23(4)*, *List C, Item 22*).

Liquidated and ascertained damages

2.39   Liquidated and ascertained damages (LADs) are a contractual mechanism of obtaining reimbursement from a defaulting supplier or contractor, when lateness or failure to perform to specification causes the customer loss, without the need to prove that loss. The loss must be foreseeable at the time the contract was formed and the damages levied at an agreed genuine pre-estimate of the loss, with the level of damages forming the upper limit on the money that can be claimed, even though the actual loss may turn out to be greater or less. The levying of LADs by the customer results in a payment from the contractor to the customer as compensation for its failure to perform.

2.40   For capital allowances purposes LADs should be ignored because they are compensation received to cover the reimbursement of anticipated trading expenses and not a reduction in the cost of the construction works (some or all of which may qualify for capital allowances).

2.41   However, in such circumstances the receipt would normally become taxable by diminishing the admissible trading expenses to which it was intended to relate, by the amount of the LADs received (following *IRC v Granite City Steamship Co Ltd* (1927) 13 TC 1).

2.42   Alternatively, sometimes in practice in situations where LADs could be levied by the customer but technically are not, a negotiated reduction in the contract value is instead agreed between the customer and contractor (ie a discount), which may also take into account a number of other issues. In these circumstances, depending on the particular facts, the discount would become taxable to the extent that it diminished the customer's admissible trading expenses and/or reduced the customer's capital allowances claim to the extent it related to the provision of capital allowances qualifying assets (which for symmetry would not be treated as a taxable receipt in the customer's hands).

TIMING OF THE CLAIM

The traditional claim

2.43   Capital allowances are given in respect of expenditure incurred. This implies therefore that a claim can only be made once the relevant asset has been purchased or built. Certainly the traditional method of making a claim reflects this.

2.44   The practice of many taxpayers is still to consider only capital allowances when the tax computations are being submitted (or when calculating payments on account under CTSA), and to base any claim only on the accounting records of the enterprise concerned. This is all very well where the assets involved are relatively uncontroversial (eg industrial machinery or motor cars), but it is no longer appropriate in more complex cases. The use of evidence other than accounting records is considered at **2.55**. The problems with timing are considered below.

Typical timescale

2.45   The timescale in a typical scenario, for example the construction of a new, medium-sized industrial building with a potentially high plant content, may be as follows. It is assumed the taxpayer's accounts are made up to a date in month 9 of the project, and that it is a large company required to make tax payments on account.

Month

1	The project gets underway; plans are drafted and the expenditure is authorised. Local authority planning procedures are initiated.
3	Plans are finalised.
4	Detailed design briefs are drawn up; contractors are appointed.
4	Corporation tax payment on account under self-assessment.
5	Bill of quantities drawn up; work commences.
6–10	Work progresses; the shell is completed and work begins on fitting out. Payments made on basis of surveyor's valuations.
7	Corporation tax payment on account under self-assessment.
9	Taxpayer's accounts year ends.
10	Corporation tax payment on account under self-assessment.
11–13	Fitting-out progresses to completion.
12	Audit takes place.

13	Corporation tax payment on account under self-assessment.
14	Final payments (subject to retentions) are made.
16	Corporation tax payment on account under self-assessment.
19	Corporation tax payment on account under self-assessment.
21	Taxpayer's accounts year ends. Previous accounts to be filed; also tax returns.
22	Corporation tax payment on account under self-assessment.
24	Audit takes place.
25	Corporation tax payment on account under self-assessment.
28	Corporation tax payment on account under self-assessment.
33	'Enquiry window' ends for claim made for first year of project.

2.46   In the above scenario, it is likely that the capital allowances on the new building will be considered initially around month 15 or 16 when the first year's tax computation is prepared. However, because industrial buildings allowances (other than the initial allowances) are not due until the building is brought into use, it is often the case in such circumstances that many taxpayers and their advisers do not fully consider capital allowances until such time as the building is complete. In the above example, full attention might not be given to capital allowances until month 27. There are numerous reasons for considering capital allowances at a much earlier stage. For example to:

(*a*)   ensure ownership of the asset is in the right hands;

(*b*)   consider whether tax-efficient features can be inserted into planning documentation;

(*c*)   consider the effect of '*Section 106*' agreements under the *Town and Country Planning Act 1990* (see **2.51** *et seq*);

(*d*)   'tweak' the design to improve the tax position;

(*e*)   consider the effect of adoption orders;

(*f*)   form a claim team early on, when all parties are interested (ie inter alia, their fees are outstanding!);

(*g*)   generally increase the time available to think about difficult areas!;

(*h*)   provide greater accuracy when calculating payments on account under CTSA;

(*i*)   ensure any claim is sufficiently well-supported to avoid exposure to interest and penalties under CTSA.

2.47   Note that, although these are advantages in considering capital allowances during construction, they are not essential. Retrospective claims can be made. This is unaffected by the pooling and fixed value requirements introduced by *FA 2012 (CAA 2001, ss 187A* and *187B)* (see **4.27** *et seq*).

Method of ownership

2.48   Certain bodies will have no *direct* interest in capital allowances for the simple reason that they do not pay tax. These include:

(i)   pension funds;

(ii)   charities;

(iii)   local authorities.

2.49   For example, a company pension fund may actually pay for a new building but the company itself will want the allowances. In such cases, it may be possible to arrange the funding in such a way that this is achieved. The pension fund (in this example) could fund the construction before granting a long lease to the company for a premium, allowing the company to receive the allowances under *s 184*.

2.50   In other cases, several persons may be contributing to a 'pot of expenditure'. If this is the case, care must be taken that the right person incurs the 'right' expenditure, ie the taxable person pays for those assets qualifying for allowances. This is also true where contributions are made to a local authority in connection with, for example, agreements under the *Town and Country Planning Act 1990, s 106*.

Planning agreements

2.51   Sometimes when a large development is being planned, the taxpayer will have to fulfil certain conditions specified by the local authority before planning permission will be given. Such agreements are often seen as a burden by the taxpayer; however, that burden can be mitigated.

2.52   At the very least, it may be possible to ensure that money spent is incurred in respect of assets qualifying for tax relief rather than on non-qualifying or unspecified assets. For example, suppose a company constructing a new head office is required by the local authority to contribute £75,000 towards the cost of site access improvements. If nothing is done to identify precisely what assets are the object of the contribution, the transaction may attract no tax relief at all. At best, it may be possible to negotiate an apportionment of the expenditure with the Inspector but the success of this is by no means certain.

2.53 The problem should therefore be dealt with prospectively rather than retrospectively. Once the amount of the contribution has been decided, but before the expenditure has been incurred, the suggestion should be made to the local authority that the contribution should be regarded as being wholly or largely in respect of items of plant (eg traffic lights). The local authority will probably be happy to accept such a proposal and will confirm it in writing. The expenditure may therefore be added to the general pool of expenditure on plant, providing all the other conditions for qualification are satisfied. Of course, it is worth stressing again that the above agreement should be negotiated before any money has been paid!

2.54 Whilst the planning application and planning consent have no statutory impact on the tax treatment, it is often the case that tax-efficient features can be incorporated in the documentation that are of no concern to the planning authorities.

DOCUMENTATION

2.55 The items below suggest what information might be required (and why) in order to maximise a claim for capital allowances in connection with a greenfield or brownfield site development. Such a list can never be exhaustive, and each new case will generate new ideas and new sources of inspiration. Similarly, not all of the following will be relevant in every case:

(*a*) *Copy planning approval documents.* These are likely to mention a number of factors relevant to capital allowances, for example, the reasons behind any special features aimed at preventing contaminating neighbouring sites.

(*b*) *Copy agreements under the Town and Country Planning Act 1990, s 106, etc.* These agreements are a means by which the planning authority can impose an obligation to carry out or bear the cost of works beyond the cost of the building itself. For example, such agreements often compel the taxpayer to carry out and/or pay for improvements to the highway or sewage network or to provide public amenities. These may, in appropriate circumstances, qualify as industrial buildings or as plant.

(*c*) *Details of any arrangements for any payments under (b) above to be attributed to specific aspects of the works.* Reason: a contribution to capital expenditure incurred by others ranks for capital allowances (subject to conditions) only if the expenditure is on an asset which would normally qualify as plant, an industrial building or structure, a mineral extraction asset or an agricultural building. Attribution to specific items qualifying for allowances is preferable to a lump sum contribution towards general improvements.

(*d*)   *Details of moves by an authority towards eventual 'adoption' of any asset.* This will sometimes influence the choice of capital allowance or the negotiating strategy. In particular, adoption can (if properly planned) generate a balancing allowance for IBAs, effectively accelerating allowances.

(*e*)   *Details of the various persons involved in construction – not only the main contractor, but also architects, surveyors, project managers, mechanical and electrical engineers, etc.* Costings will be required on which to base the capital allowances claim but it is extremely unlikely that the requirements will match all of the 'works packages' into which expenditure is conveniently analysed for construction purposes. There will need to be established, generally through the project manager, a line of communication for this to be obtained.

It will be necessary to discuss construction technicalities with the liaising party who may also be a catalyst for the introduction of any novel items into the claim and may be able to assist with the exploration of all possible avenues of claim.

(*f*)   *Design briefs.* These facilitate better understanding of the nature and function of the development and generally provide information on which to base claims.

(*g*)   *Establish a line of communication (generally with the project manager) so that any material changes in the design brief can be 'tax audited'.* The design of a large development invariably changes in detail as the work progresses. It is difficult to be specific on what this might affect.

(*h*)   *Site plans, building plans – whatever is available.* The reasons for these are mainly obvious, but also necessary to establish, for example how many separate buildings exist for IBA and the approach generally.

(*i*)   *Plans and design briefs of any specific item or composite items of plant such as assembly lines which might be supplied/installed by a specialist.* Necessary to maximise opportunities for claims, particularly where a 'plant' claim may be possible on an item which at first sight might appear to be no more than part of a building.

(*j*)   *Plans, design brief, etc of any special aspects of the building, for example a scheme for disposal of effluent.* Again, such detail will assist in identifying where a 'plant' claim may be possible on an item which at first sight might appear to be no more than part of a building.

(*k*)   *Where appropriate, promotional literature.* These may, inter alia, support arguments based on 'ambience' or 'concepts' in, for example, hotel or leisure industries, or in establishing a qualifying use of the building for IBA purposes.

(*l*) *Details of energy-efficient or environmentally beneficial plant qualifying for first-year allowances* (see **14.31–14.53**).

(*m*) *Cost forecast broken down into as many work packages as convenient and showing the likely dates for payment.* This will give an immediate impression of type and magnitude of allowances potentially available, and furthermore, will facilitate agreement of an interim claim for allowances on plant, if as often happens, a development spans a year end.

(*n*) *If development is in phases, the estimated date of completion and commencement of use for each phase.* Necessary for planning claims, and for establishing when IBAs first become due.

(*o*) *Details of the commissioning arrangements.* Commissioning costs are usually mixed. Sometimes they can be claimed as revenue, sometimes as capital. Also the commissioning arrangements can have a bearing on commencement date of allowances.

(*p*) *Accounting treatment.* The accounting treatment can have a bearing on commencement date of allowances, but perhaps more importantly can influence whether an item is regarded as building or plant, and, if the latter, whether it is 'long life' plant or, alternatively, provides scope for a short life asset election.

(*q*) *Details of contamination.* Expenditure on cleaning up contaminated land (remediation) may qualify for tax relief at the rate of 150% (see **Chapter 24**).

(*r*) *Details of interests in the land.* It is important to establish that the person incurring expenditure has a 'relevant interest' for business premises renovation allowances (see **11.82–11.83**) or a qualifying interest for fixtures purposes (see **11.23**). There may be more than one person with an interest in the land, and interests may terminate or be created as the project progresses.

PRIVATE FINANCE INITIATIVE EXPENDITURE

General

2.56   The Private Finance Initiative (PFI) introduces private sector expertise and finance into the design, building and maintenance of public infrastructure projects and the operation of public services. It is sometimes referred to as 'PPP' (Public Private Partnership). Although the latter embraces a wider range of activities, the 'PFI' is the most prolific and successful form of 'PPP' to date, so as far as capital allowances are concerned, although the two terms are essentially interchangeable, 'PFI' is more commonly used.

2.57   PFI projects typically involve the private sector assuming much of the risk, and then designing and constructing PFI property (eg central or local government offices, hospitals, schools, prisons or roads, etc) as well as providing ancillary support services to agreed standards (eg facilities management and maintenance). In return the private sector operator receives an annual service payment (or 'unitary charge'), which may be linked to its performance and the facility's availability and usage criteria. The operator is usually a special purpose vehicle (SPV) set up by a consortium, often comprising a construction company and a service management provider. These contracts are for lengthy periods, typically for 25 to 30 years, and usually for large sums of money with significant debt funding from financial institutions.

2.58   Tax is crucial for private-sector PFI operators because it has a significant impact on the competitiveness of their bids and cash flows, and so affects initial pricing and the financial success of won projects. A tax-efficient proposal will have an advantage over other more tax-inefficient bids and flawed tax structures or assumptions in bid financial models may mean that contracts prove not to be financially viable in practice.

2.59   Probably, the most central tax-related concern in any PFI contract is to find the best means of obtaining tax relief for the substantial cost of building and maintaining the asset. This occurs either through traditional capital allowances for the initial construction cost, with revenue relief for subsequent repairs, or alternatively via 'composite trade' status, which treats the up-front cost as being incurred on revenue account and so being fully tax deductible. It does not matter what type of property is involved, as the same property could be revenue or capital depending on the PFI operator's role and the way the contract is structured.

Capital allowances

2.60   Transaction cash flow models normally assume that the SPV will pay minimal tax and for capital expenditure, maximised capital allowances are crucial to achieve this. In the early years, SPVs usually generate losses, but capital allowances may be available (if not surrendered to investor-shareholders) to be carried forward to provide significant tax shelter for future profits.

2.61   PFI transactions can involve complicated legal structures, asset ownership and funding/expenditure arrangements. So the initial major issues to consider are structuring the transaction to ensure that the desired entity may claim capital allowances in accordance with the capital allowances legislation (particularly for fixtures: see **11.15** *et seq*), making sure that any capital contributions received do not reduce its capital allowances claim (see **1.108**

et seq) and ensuring that there will be no unforeseen claw-backs of allowances at a later date.

2.62 It is then important to ensure that the capital allowances and life cycle repair assumptions used in financial bid models are realistic, as there may be a wide range of possible answers and there is an important balance to be struck between the assumptions being too low (causing the bid to be tax-inefficient and jeopardising its chances of winning), or too high (reducing the subsequent operational performance of a successful bid). Capital allowances available will generally comprise plant and machinery (including potentially long-life assets).

2.63 If the bid is successful and the project proceeds, it is then vital to ensure that any capital allowances claims are accurate, maximised and properly supported to achieve the optimum anticipated tax efficiency in practice and meet the SPV's self-assessment filing obligations. It is also essential during the operation of the assets that tax relief is claimed for any subsequent capital additions and repair and maintenance expenditure in the most efficient way.

2.64 However, claiming capital allowances will still result in a high effective tax rate because the depreciation of the capital allowances non-qualifying expenditure (eg typically the buildings/premises) will not qualify for any tax relief. Therefore, the composite trade approach was developed instead (see **2.65** *et seq* below).

Composite trade

2.65 This more recent development allows the SPV to treat all of its construction expenditure as an allowable trading profit deduction when it is written off to its profit and loss account, or relieved against income receivable by it. This is much more tax-efficient than treating the expenditure as capital and claiming capital allowances and so enables an SPV to reduce its tax burden significantly.

2.66 To qualify for composite trade status the SPV must have a trade of providing design and construction services, as well as ancillary support services and not have a lease in the land, but only a subordinate right of access to provide its services or exploit those rights as a source of rent or other (with the public sector body being the property legal owner and occupier). This type of approach is typically used by PFI bidders from a construction contracting background, who also provide ancillary facilities management services.

2.67 For composite trade status to apply the SPV must demonstrate that the design and construction aspects of the PFI project are performed by it on trading account. This is a question of fact based on the SPV's stated intention, supported by the relevant facts (ie not only what business the taxpayer professes to carry on, but what business it actually carries on). HMRC's instructions confirm that each case will depend on its own particular facts so it is not possible to provide a definitive checklist of all the factors to consider, although the following would normally be relevant (BIM, para 64030):

(*a*)   the stated intention of the operator;

(*b*)   the terms of the PFI agreement; and

(*c*)   what the operator actually does in practice.

2.68   For example, relevant questions to consider would include whether the business is exploiting as a source of rent, an interest or right in or over land (and so is carrying on a property investment business), or whether the PFI property provides a setting for its activities (and so is capital).

2.69   HMRC also recognises that the accounting treatment is of limited assistance in determining the scope of a PFI trade, because if FRS5 applies, ownership of the PFI property might not be reflected in the SPV's balance sheet (ie the asset may be 'off balance sheet'). This is because the criteria which determine whether the property is a fixed asset for accounting purposes are different to those which determine whether it is capital for tax purposes.

2.70   A typical example of a composite trade might be as follows (BIM, para 64050):

> 'A private sector operator enters into a PFI contract with a public sector purchaser (eg a National Health Service (NHS) Trust), to build a hospital and provide non-clinical support services for 25 years. In return the operator receives an annual service payment (the 'unitary charge'). The hospital belongs to the Trust (and not the operator) throughout the period of the contract. The Trust grants only a right of access, or licence, to enable the operator to do no more than go on to the land to provide the construction, support and ancillary support services.
>
> For tax purposes, the operator's trade is the provision of design, construction and support services. The operator is not carrying on a Schedule A investment business since it is not exploiting, as a source of rent or other receipts, the right/licence granted by the purchaser. The operator has not acquired the hospital as a fixed capital asset of its business, or as trading stock.'

2.71   Often in practice the tax benefit of a composite trade approach may be lost to the bidder and its shareholders, because many public authorities insist that it is passed to them by reducing the unitary charge that they must pay. For example, the Department of Health (DoH) recognises that composite trade status will be preferable in most cases and since 4 February 2003 has stipulated for NHS schemes that PFI bidders and NHS Trusts must clear any decision *not* to apply it with the central DoH Private Finance Unit. Furthermore, the DoH instructions *expect* that the full benefit of the tax saving should be passed to NHS Trusts in the form of reduced unitary charges. That being said, even though the PFI bidder will not benefit from the tax efficiency achieved, it should of course help the competitiveness of its bid and improve its chances of success in winning the contract against any less tax-efficient competitors.

Chapter 3

Purchase of a new building

INTRODUCTION

3.1   **Chapter 2** considered the position of a taxpayer incurring expenditure on the construction of a new building, and being involved throughout the construction process. Very often this degree of involvement does not take place; it may be that the taxpayer requires new premises, but has few specific trade-related needs, such that the premises can be of a fairly standard design. In such cases, the taxpayer may simply purchase a suitable property that happens to be on the market. In many respects, the capital allowances issues will be the same as for a building constructed to the taxpayer's own needs, although the fact that the building was constructed without the taxpayer's particular trade in mind may reduce the scope to claim allowances on plant, where it is important that items purporting to be plant do in fact carry on some function related to the trade.

3.2   So far as the building itself is concerned (ie the structure), the most relevant type of allowance was historically that for industrial buildings – for general definition, etc, see **7.47** *et seq.* Industrial buildings allowances were abolished with effect from April 2011, so for most taxpayers, plant allowances (primarily on fixtures) will be the only relevant opportunity for tax savings.

3.3   Note that the requirements of *s 187A* (see **4.16–4.34**), governing allowances on fixtures, do not apply where a new and unused building is purchased from the builder. In practical terms, this means that a purchaser may formulate a claim for allowances on fixtures, then merely claim those allowances in his tax return, rather than having to apply to the First-tier Tribunal for a determination of the qualifying amount. It should be noted that where a property is acquired from the builder or developer (whose expenditure was incurred on revenue account), an election under *s 198* is not possible (see **4.56**). Despite this, ill-advised sellers in such circumstances have been known to demand an election, which can only be invalid.

3.4   The purchase of a second-hand building is dealt with in **Chapter 4**. If the building is in an enterprise zone, see **Chapter 9**, and if research and development allowances may be in point, see **Chapter 19**.

3.5 Note that expenditure on land does not qualify for allowances (*s 24*). If the price paid for a building includes the cost of the site, the latter must be established (by apportionment if necessary) and excluded from the claim (CA, paras 22040, 31305). It is not acceptable merely to deduct the value of the land element from the price paid (*Bostock v Totham* (*Inspector of Taxes*) [1997] STC 764; *Bowerswood House Retirement Home Ltd v HMRC Comrs* [2015] UKFTT 94 (TC)).

PURCHASE OF AN UNUSED BUILDING

3.6 Whether or not expenditure on the structure of a building qualifies for tax relief will depend, generally, on the purpose to which the building is planned to be used. The majority of buildings which qualified historically, ie until April 2011, were those of an industrial nature (see **Chapter 7**). Since then, only buildings used for research and development (see **Chapter 19**) will qualify in their entirety.

3.7 Where a building is not used for research and development, the taxpayer will need to identify and quantify those elements of the building qualifying as plant and machinery for the purposes of allowances.

PLANT

3.8 However a building is purchased, and whatever the nature of the building, it is generally worth considering whether a claim for plant and machinery allowances is possible.

3.9 This is particularly important where no form of buildings allowances is available, which will be the vast majority. Only, for example, where a property is used for research and development will it be unnecessary to identify and separately claim for plant and machinery.

3.10 In such circumstances, to the extent that the purchase price can be allocated to plant, rather than to the fabric of the building, the purchaser will be able to claim allowances. The circumstances of the vendor may need to be taken into consideration, but particularly where the building is acquired from a property developer, he should have no objections. The principles of apportionment of costs are set out at **4.67** *et seq.*

3.11 **Appendix 2** gives a partial checklist of items which have been accepted as plant, whilst the subject of plant within offices and retail premises is dealt with in **Chapters 5** and **6** respectively.

Chapter 4

Purchase of a second-hand building

INTRODUCTION

4.1   The taxpayer incurring expenditure on second-hand assets, whether actual buildings or items of plant included within those buildings, will be able to claim allowances under the same general rules as if he were acquiring the assets brand new. There are, however, certain additional rules to be dealt with, and in many cases the amount qualifying for allowances will be restricted or even eliminated altogether.

4.2   An apportionment of the purchase consideration can often effectively reduce the after-tax cost of a second-hand building by properly identifying all items qualifying for allowances, which might otherwise be ignored in the wider context of a property acquisition.

4.3   Note that expenditure on land does not qualify for allowances. If the price paid for a building includes the cost of the site, the latter must be established (by apportionment if necessary – merely deducting a value for the land element is not acceptable; *Bostock v Totham* (*Inspector of Taxes*) [1997] STC 764; *Bowerswood House Retirement Home Ltd v HMRC Comrs* [2015] UKFTT 94 (TC)) and excluded from the claim (CA, paras 22040, 31305). The legislation currently or historically denying allowances for the acquisition of land is scattered throughout *CAA 2001*, as follows:

- *s 24* – plant and machinery allowances;
- *s 272* – industrial buildings allowances;
- *s 360B* – business premises renovation allowance;
- *s 363* – agricultural buildings allowances;
- *s 393B* – flat conversion allowances;
- *s 440* – research and development allowances.

BUILDINGS

General

4.4   As with newly constructed buildings, the actual structure of a building (the 'bricks and mortar') acquired second-hand only ever qualified for allowances if it fell within one of the prescribed categories, ie:

(*a*)   the building was in an enterprise zone (see **Chapter 9**);

(*b*)   it was a qualifying hotel (see **Chapter 8**);

(*c*)   the use made of the building is such that it would qualify as industrial (see **Chapter 7**); or

(*d*)   the building is used for research and development (see **Chapter 19**).

4.5   All but the last of these categories of allowance was abolished from April 2011. However, whilst no such buildings allowances will be available to a new purchaser, previous claims by the seller (or a predecessor) may restrict or eliminate any scope for the purchaser to claim allowances on plant and machinery (see **4.14**).

4.6   Establishing the capital allowances available when a building is acquired second-hand can be complicated and it is essential that capital allowances due diligence is carried out to review the tax history of the property being acquired and identify any risks and restrictions on the amount that can be claimed. In practice, this is typically dealt with by the solicitor dealing with the transaction. Although a set of British Property Federation endorsed Commercial Property Standard Enquiries exists (form 'CPSE.1' – including capital allowances questions largely written by one of the present authors) and some solicitors have their own in-house pre-contract enquiry questions covering capital allowances, it is an issue that is all too often ignored or forgotten (or the pre-contract enquiry questions are returned blank or with answers that cannot be logically true), which can leave the buyer and his advisers exposed to considerable risk. See **Appendix 9** for discussion of pre-contract enquiries.

4.7   This risk extends also to a solicitor or other agent advising on the purchase contract. In *Hurlingham Estates v Wilde & Partners* [1997] 1 Lloyds Rep 525, a conveyancing solicitor had no intention or expertise to advise on tax, but had no formal engagement letter and the court held the solicitor had a duty to advise on tax, notwithstanding his ignorance on the subject. In *Clarke v Iliffes Booth Bennett (a firm)* [2004] EWHC 1731 (Ch), a case not directly concerned with capital allowances, it was held that a solicitor had a duty to understand a contract to the extent necessary to give proper advice to the client:

> 'If a solicitor who holds himself or herself out as a specialist in corporate matters is involved in the drafting of an agreement for the sale and purchase

of assets, … and the agreement contains tax indemnities, then the solicitor cannot be heard to say that he or she is not under a duty to understand the indemnities and advise as may be necessary in the circumstances, simply because the client is sophisticated and has negotiated the indemnities.'

4.8   By extension, a solicitor should not overlook capital allowances clauses, elections under *s 198*, CPSE.1 replies or, for example, the impact on capital allowances of any apportionment of the price contained in a contract.

4.9   *Finance Act 2012* introduced additional conditions that the purchaser of a property must satisfy before he can claim capital allowances on fixtures. These are the 'fixed value requirement' and the 'pooling requirement' (see **4.16** *et seq* and **4.27** *et seq*). With these new conditions, it is more essential than ever for conveyancing solicitors to be aware of, and deal with, capital allowances issues at the time of the property transaction.

PLANT

4.10   When a building is purchased second-hand, the buyer will be acquiring not only a shell building, but also any plant elements contained therein. This will include not just things that are obviously machinery, but also 'integral features' such as air conditioning or heating, and other plant and machinery fixtures.

4.11   It is possible for the purchaser to claim capital allowances on such plant. To the extent that such items are fixtures, they are treated as belonging to the purchaser of the building (*s 181*) (see **11.30**). This also applies where a purchaser of an interest in land pays a capital sum to discharge the obligations of an equipment lessee to whom the fixtures were previously let (*s 182*).

4.12   Usually, such a claim will be based on a 'just and reasonable' apportionment of the total purchase consideration, in accordance with *s 562* (which operates by default in the absence of a *s 198* joint election – see **4.44** *et seq*). The intention is to apportion the purchase price to reflect the value that each constituent part makes to the value of the whole property (*Salts v Battersby* [1910] 2 KB 155). An apportionment is usually prepared using the VOA's formula approach (see **4.69** *et seq*), which was endorsed by the First-tier Tribunal in *Bowerswood House Retirement Home Ltd v HMRC Comrs* [2015] UKFTT 0094 (TC) (see **Appendix 4**). Any dispute over the apportionment may be resolved by a tax tribunal (*s 563*). In *Wood (t/a A Wood & Co) v Provan (Inspector of Taxes)* (1968) 44 TC 701 (see **Appendix 4**), the Commissioners made an apportionment notwithstanding the fact that a separate price for plant was shown in the purchase contract. However, this decision was made before the 1997 enactment of the provisions for a *s 198* joint election by purchaser and vendor (see **4.44**).

4.13   In some circumstances, the amount will be restricted to whatever amount is properly brought into account as disposal proceeds by the vendor (*s 185*). That said, it must nonetheless be emphasised that the matter is not entirely in the hands of the vendor because it is not the vendor's prerogative to unilaterally choose a disposal value (for example, tax written-down value), and the purchaser is not bound to accept the vendor's apportionment, however unfair that may be.

4.14   Furthermore, in the absence of an election under *s 198* (see **4.44**), the Inspector is not bound by any apportionment agreed between the parties and reflected in the purchase contract (*Fitton v Gilders and Heaton (Inspector of Taxes)* (1955) 36 TC 233; *Tapsell (Mr and Mrs) and Lester (Mr) (trading as Partnership 'The Granleys') v HMRC Comrs* [2011] UKFTT 376 (TC)). The question of whether a contract allocation may be ignored by the purchaser is essentially a matter of contract law. All too often, purchasers and their solicitors agree to an allocation of the purchase price, for example for stamp duty land tax (SDLT) purposes (see **22.30** *et seq*), without any consideration of the impact on capital allowances. Such allocations should be avoided, or it should be made clear they do not apply for the purposes of capital allowances.

4.15   It is worth noting that HMRC cannot deem the *total* proceeds to be an amount other than the actual proceeds, only the apportionment between different assets can be challenged. In order to show that some assets (eg plant) have been overvalued, HMRC must also demonstrate that other assets have been undervalued (CA, para 12100).

Fixtures: 2012 changes – 'the fixed value requirement'

4.16   With effect from April 2012, where the vendor (or an earlier owner since April 2012) has pooled qualifying expenditure on plant or machinery fixtures, *s 187A* makes the availability of capital allowances to a purchaser of fixtures conditional on the value of fixtures being established formally within two years of a transfer (the 'fixed value requirement').

4.17   There is an alternative method of fixing the value that applies only in some (narrowly defined) cases where an intermediate owner or lessee, who was not entitled to claim an allowance (such as a charity or pension fund), had failed to determine a fixtures apportionment with the past owner. It should be appreciated that until April 2014, when the pooling requirement took effect (see **4.27**), the new rules only applied where a relevant prior owner had pooled qualifying expenditure on the fixtures. If expenditure had not been pooled, the rules were initially unaffected.

4.18   *Section 187A(1)* sets out the circumstances in which the new rules apply. They apply if:

4.19 *Purchase of a second-hand building*

- a buyer incurs capital expenditure on acquiring a property containing fixtures from another person (the seller), for the purposes of the buyer's business;

- the seller, or a previous owner, owned the fixtures at a relevant earlier time (see *s 187B(4)*) as a result of incurring expenditure on them for business purposes; and

- the seller, or a previous owner, pooled qualifying expenditure on plant or machinery in respect of the historic expenditure.

4.19 However, the new section does *not* apply if the previous owner was only entitled to relief by virtue of the contributions legislation in *CAA 2001*, *s 538*.

4.20 The key point here is that *s 187A* only applies if the seller, or a previous owner in the *relevant period* (effectively the period since the commencement of these rules in April 2012), had claimed allowances on the fixtures. It is therefore crucial to establish, for example through pre-contract enquiries, whether this is in fact the case. From April 2014, the rules are extended to situations where the seller could have claimed, whether they did so or not (see **4.27**).

4.21 *Section 187A(3)* provides that the new owner's expenditure on fixtures qualifying for allowances is to be treated as nil if the 'fixed value requirement' (see **4.24**) applies but is not satisfied, or the 'disposal value statement requirement' (see **4.22**) applies but is not satisfied.

4.22 So, in all cases to which this section applies, one or other of the 'value' requirements will apply and must be satisfied if the purchaser is to claim allowances. (In practice, the 'fixed value requirement' will apply in the vast majority of cases and the 'disposal value statement requirement' is likely only to apply very infrequently, in circumstances where an election is not permitted and statute imposes disposal proceeds calculated as an apportionment of market value.)

4.23 If either requirement is not met, neither the purchaser nor any future owner of those fixtures will be able to claim allowances. In the first instance, the purchaser's qualifying expenditure is deemed to be nil (see **4.21**). On a subsequent sale, the new owner's claim will be restricted to the seller's disposal value under *s 185* – because the seller's claim cannot exceed nil, his disposal value will also be limited to nil.

4.24 The 'fixed value' requirement applies where the past owner (that is, the current seller) is or has been required to bring the disposal value of the plant or machinery into account, and is met when one of two outcomes occurs. That is, either:

- 'a relevant apportionment of the apportionable sum has been made'; or

- the current owner has obtained certain statements where the property is acquired from someone other than 'the past owner' (the rare exception).

4.25   *Section 187A(7)* explains that a relevant apportionment is made if:

- a tribunal has determined the part of the sale price that constitutes the disposal value of the fixtures, on an application made by one of the affected parties within two years of the purchaser's acquisition; or

- there has been a joint election, under either *s 198* or *s 199*, as appropriate, between the past owner and the purchaser within two years of the acquisition (see **4.44** *et seq*).

4.26   The overwhelming majority of commercial property transactions involving second-hand fixtures should involve a relevant apportionment, so that there will be the requirement for a reference to the tribunal, or for a joint election to be made, within two years of a sale. It must be emphasised that if this requirement is not met, the purchaser will obtain no allowances. However, the seller must still account for disposal proceeds under the underlying legislation (see **11.49** *et seq*, **12.46** *et seq*), possibly giving rise to a tax charge (*s 187B(6)*).

Fixtures: 2014 changes – the 'pooling requirement'

4.27   With effect from April 2014, *s 187A* makes the availability of capital allowances to a purchaser of fixtures further conditional on previous business expenditure on qualifying fixtures being pooled before a subsequent transfer on to that new purchaser (the 'pooling requirement'). This is in addition to the 'fixed value requirement' in **4.16–4.26** above.

4.28   *Section 187A(1)* sets out the circumstances in which the new rules apply. They apply if:

- a buyer incurs capital expenditure on acquiring a property containing fixtures from another person (the seller) for the purposes of his business;

- the seller, or a previous owner, owned the fixtures at a relevant earlier time (see *s 187B(4)*) as a result of incurring expenditure on them for business purposes; and

- the seller, or a previous owner, was entitled to claim plant and machinery allowances (PMAs) in respect of the historic expenditure.

4.29   The key point here is that *s 187A* now applies if the seller, or a previous owner in the relevant period (effectively the period since the commencement of these rules in April 2012), was *entitled* to claim allowances on the fixtures (eg the seller is an owner-occupier or investor subject to UK tax). It is therefore crucial to establish, for example through pre-contract enquiries, whether this is in fact the case. It is worth emphasising that, from April 2014, these rules apply where the seller *could have* claimed; before then, they applied only where the seller had in fact pooled qualifying expenditure.

4.30   The pooling requirement does not apply in circumstances where the seller was not entitled to claim. Generally it will not apply for the following reasons:

- The asset is a chattel (the pooling requirement only applies to fixtures).

- The seller's expenditure was not capital (eg a builder or property dealer).

- The seller was not carrying on a qualifying activity (eg a house-owner selling a home to a business).

- The seller is not within the scope of UK income or corporation tax and capital allowances (eg councils, charities, pension funds).

- The seller's expenditure was not accepted as being in respect of plant and machinery.

4.31   An example of the last-mentioned will be expenditure on cold water systems, general electrical and lighting systems, and external solar shading, where the seller incurred expenditure prior to April 2008. Before that date, such items were not regarded as plant and machinery, but would now qualify as integral features. Such assets are not caught by the fixed value and pooling requirements.

4.32   *Section 187A(3)* provides that the new owner's expenditure on fixtures qualifying for allowances is to be treated as nil if (from April 2014) the 'pooling requirement' (see **4.23**) is not satisfied.

4.33   So, in all cases to which this new section applies, the pooling requirement must be satisfied. Of course, once the expenditure has been pooled, the sale will be one to which one or other of the 'value' requirements will also apply (see **4.16–4.26**).

4.34   The 'pooling requirement' is that the historic expenditure must have been allocated to a pool (see **14.3**) in a chargeable period beginning on or before the day on which the past owner ceased to own the fixture, or the past owner claimed a first-year allowance on the expenditure (or any part of it). Consequently, where this rule applies, a property purchaser will only be able to claim allowances on fixtures if the seller has claimed (or at least pooled the expenditure, whether or not allowances were actually claimed). In practice, pooling requires the expenditure to have been included in a tax return. Where it is essential to demonstrate that this has been done, it would be prudent to refer to the relevant expenditure in the 'white space' for other information on the return.

Restricted claims

4.35   Where the vendor of an interest in land, as defined in *s 175*, has claimed allowances in respect of fixtures attached to that land, he is required to bring into account a disposal value (that is, a negative adjustment to the capital allowances pool in which the expenditure was recorded to reflect the disposal proceeds of that plant). This in turn is restricted to the seller's original cost (*s 62*).

4.36   Where, on or after 24 July 1996, a person incurs expenditure on fixtures, in respect of which a former owner has been entitled to allowances, then the maximum amount on which allowances may be claimed will be equal to the disposal value required to be brought into account by that former owner (together with any incidental expenditure under *s 25* (*s 185*) – see **14.119** *et seq*). Before that date, a purchaser's claim was still restricted to the seller's disposal value, but did not have to consider earlier owners (*CAA 1990, s 59(10)*).

4.37   If the fixtures are acquired from a taxpayer, the qualifying expenditure will, therefore, be limited to the disposal value brought into account by the vendor, which in turn will be restricted to that vendor's original cost (or cost to a person connected with the vendor, if higher – (*s 64*)). If the fixtures are acquired from a non-taxpayer (eg an exempt fund) allowances may still be restricted to the disposal value brought into account, not by the vendor (for whom there will be no disposal value) but by an earlier claimant. This will only apply, however, if that earlier claimant disposed of the fixtures on or after 24 July 1996. If, since that date, there has been no disposal by a taxpayer, the claim by the new purchaser will not be restricted and will be based on a just apportionment of the total expenditure under (*s 562*) (see **4.63** *et seq*). This restriction does not apply where assets have been severed from the building and sold other than as fixtures (*s 185*).

4.38   Two key points emerge, which the prospective purchaser must not overlook:

(*a*)   The capital allowances on fixtures will be of particular value if they have, since 24 July 1996, been continuously owned by a person who was not entitled to allowances (or indeed, a series of such persons).

(*b*)   The quantum of any claim may only be properly established with full knowledge of the history of ownership of the relevant fixtures. The intending claimant should, therefore, require such details from the vendor as part of the acquisition process (see **4.6**). In HMRC's view, the onus is on the purchaser to prove the capital allowances history of the assets acquired, in support of which inspectors refer to *West Somerset Railway Plc v Chivers* (*Inspector of Taxes*) [1995] STC (SCD) 1. However, tax appeals do not impose an absolute obligation on the taxpayer, but rather speak of a 'balance of probabilities' (see **Appendix 4**). From April 2012, the legislation makes explicit that a purchaser must show whether the 'fixed value requirement' (see **4.24**) or 'disposal value statement' (see **4.21**) applies and, if so, that is satisfied (*s 187B(1)*).

Different type of allowances previously claimed

4.39   Where the property acquired includes fixtures which have previously been involved in a claim for IBAs or research and development allowances, the qualifying expenditure is restricted to (in the case of IBAs) the portion of the consideration attributable to the fixtures, on the assumption that the consideration was equal to the residue of expenditure on the relevant interest, or (for research and development) to the portion of the consideration attributed to the fixtures, limited to original cost (*ss 186* and *187*). Where fixtures have previously qualified for agricultural buildings allowances (ABAs), no subsequent purchaser may claim allowances at all (s *9(1)*).

Disposal values: anti-avoidance

4.40   Where, with a view to 'avoidance', a vendor brings into account a disposal value which is less than the notional tax written-down value (TWDV) of the relevant plant, that TWDV is substituted for the actual disposal value. Consequently no balancing allowance will arise. However, this only applies to the vendor – the purchaser's claim will be restricted to the actual (low) consideration. It is assumed for this purpose that all available allowances had been claimed. 'Avoidance' is defined as the obtaining or increase of an allowance or deduction, or the avoidance or reduction of a charge (*s 197*).

4.41   Furthermore, when after 31 March 2008, an asset is sold, and that asset was one allocated to the 'special rate' pool (for integral features, long-life assets, thermal insulation and solar panels), anti-avoidance provisions potentially apply. If the asset is disposed of for less than its TWDV, as part of a scheme or arrangement having the obtaining of a tax advantage as a main purpose, then notional TWDV is substituted for the actual disposal value (*s 104E*). This mirrors *s 197* (see **4.40**); however *s 104E(3)(b)* adds the further proviso that where a long-life asset is concerned, that expenditure had not been prevented from being treated as a long-life asset by the annual *de minimis* (see **14.165–14.167**). Given that *s 104E* only applies where an asset has been added to the special rate pool (including, inter alia, long-life assets), it is not evident in what circumstances *s 104E(3)(b)* operates.

4.42   In *HMRC Comrs v Lloyds TSB Equipment Leasing (No 1) Ltd* [2014] EWCA Civ 1062, it was held that a transaction could serve a genuine commercial purpose but still have a main purpose of obtaining capital allowances and, therefore, fall foul of relevant anti-avoidance legislation (see **Appendix 4**).

4.43   The disposal value may be below TWDV for genuine commercial reasons, rather than for reasons of tax avoidance, in which case it may not be challenged by HMRC (*s 197*).

Apportionment of consideration: joint election

4.44   In either of the above situations, the parties to a sale may elect to fix the amount to be allocated to fixtures (*s 198* or *s 199* for leases). The amount so allocated may not exceed the original cost of those fixtures. Obviously, if the total sale price is less than the original cost of the fixtures, then the amount apportioned cannot exceed that. The irrevocable election must be made jointly within two years after the date of the relevant transaction, and must include:

(*a*)   the names and Unique Taxpayer References (UTR) of both parties (from April 2012 where a party does not have a UTR the election should say so (*FA 2012, Sch 10, para 4; CAA 2001, s 201(3)(f)*));

(*b*)   sufficient information to identify both the relevant land (to which the fixtures are attached) and the machinery or plant;

(*c*)   details of the interest acquired; and

(*d*)   the amount fixed by the election.

4.45   If an application has been made to the Tax Chamber of the First-tier Tribunal in time, but has not been determined or has been withdrawn, and the parties to sale reach agreement, an election may be accepted even though the normal time limit has passed (*s 201(1A)*).

4.46   See pro forma election, **Appendix 5**.

4.47   A formal election is the only way to guarantee an agreed apportionment at the outset (subject to it not being rejected by HMRC for technical reasons, such as not being submitted in time or deficient drafting: see **4.55** *et seq*) – it is not sufficient that an apportionment is included in the purchase contract, as such an apportionment is not binding on HMRC (*Fitton v Gilders and Heaton* (*Inspector of Taxes*) (1955) 36 TC 233; *Tapsell (Mr and Mrs) and Lester (Mr)* (*trading as Partnership 'The Granleys'*) *v HMRC Comrs* [2011] UKFTT 376 (TC)).

4.48   In most practical situations, it will *not* be to the purchaser's advantage to enter into an election, rather than rely on the default 'just apportionment' provisions of *s 562*. Professional advice should be sought whenever a *s 198* election is proposed by the vendor.

4.49   HMRC accepts a single election covering all the fixtures in a single property (but not multiple properties) – HMRC Tax Bulletin 35 (June 1998) and CA, para 26850. In practice, where an amount has been agreed between vendor and purchaser covering several properties, HMRC will accept an apportionment between the properties on a reasonable basis, such as book value or floor area.

4.50   On the subject of HMRC accepting an election covering all the fixtures in a property, it is worth looking closer at what the Revenue Manual actually says. CA, para 26850 states:

'The fixtures rules work on an asset-by-asset basis. In practice, you may accept a degree of amalgamation of assets where this will not distort the tax computation. Provided that there are no specific factors which could give rise to distortion, you may accept an election covering all the fixtures in a particular property but not for a portfolio of properties.'

4.51   It is unclear what is meant by the term 'distortion'. It is arguable that distortion of 'the tax computation' does take place where the amount allocated to fixtures by an election under *s 198* is clearly insufficient, in that it bears no relation to the amount which has actually been paid for those fixtures, for example where an election for £1 covers assets clearly worth millions.

4.52   Distortion may also be relevant where the plant acquired consists of both integral features and other plant, and the election fails to allocate separate amounts to each.

4.53   It must be of the greatest importance to realise that an election under *s 198* can only cover plant on which the vendor has claimed allowances. The purchaser may still be able to claim allowances on an 'unrestricted' basis on other items of plant which were not identified as such by the vendor, and are in consequence not covered by the election. It should also be remembered that an election under *s 198* relates only to fixtures, and not to movable plant (that is, chattels).

4.54   A Real Estate Investment Trust (REIT), as permitted from 1 January 2007 by *Finance Act 2006*, cannot make a *s 198* election on joining or leaving the REIT regime, or on transfer of property across the 'ring fence' to its non tax-exempt activities, but is otherwise able to elect when a property is acquired or disposed of by the company.

Common errors in s 198 elections

4.55   In practice, many elections appear to be technically invalid, for a variety of reasons.

Vendor did not claim

4.56   It is explicitly stated that the *s 198* legislation applies 'if the disposal value of a fixture is required to be brought into account', which can only be the case if the vendor has claimed allowances on the fixtures concerned (*s 64*). Some *s 198* elections purport to be made in cases where the vendor has not claimed allowances (for example, where the seller is a developer holding the property as trading stock, and therefore clearly not eligible for capital allowances).

Missing information

4.57   *Section 201* sets out certain information which a *s 198* election *must* contain, including:

(*a*)   the amount fixed by the election;

(*b*)   the name of each party to the election;

(*c*)   information sufficient to identify the plant or machinery;

(*d*)   information sufficient to identify the relevant land;

(*e*)   particulars of the interest being acquired (and the date of the transaction); and

(*f*)   the UTR of each party to the election (from April 2012, where a party does not have a UTR the election should say so (*FA 2012, Sch 10, para 4*; *CAA 2001 s 201(3)(f)*)).

4.58   Oddly, nothing in the legislation requires the election to be signed. It simply must be a joint election, so any evidence of agreement should suffice, such as being a contractual obligation within a sale and purchase agreement for a property.

4.59   Some of this information is often omitted, with the result that the election may be arguably invalid. For example, an inspector would seem to be within his rights if he rejected an election which failed to give the tax reference numbers of each party. With the introduction of the 'fixed value requirement' (see **4.16**) and the 'pooling requirement (see **4.27**) it is increasingly likely that HMRC will reject invalid elections, as to do so may mean that allowances are entirely clawed back from sellers, but denied to purchasers. Already, it is far more common for elections to be rejected, and taxpayers would be unwise to rely on poorly worded elections, just because they have been accepted in the past. The drafting of elections presents a major risk to professional advisers, and capital allowances specialists should be involved.

Identifying the fixtures

4.60   The requirement presenting the greatest practical difficulty appears to be the obligation for 'information sufficient to identify the plant or machinery'. In a great many cases, the lack of detail could arguably invalidate the whole election. The following are the problems most commonly seen.

4.61   First, many elections refer simply to 'all the fixtures at the property', 'all fixed plant and machinery', or equivalent wording. This either purports that a perfect capital allowances claim has been made, covering every conceivable qualifying item (which is improbable), or there must be serious doubt (apparently shared by HMRC) whether this is sufficient to identify the plant or machinery which is purportedly subject to the election.

4.62   Secondly, some elections merely refer to a standard list of fixtures which may be typically found in a building (normally with no values against any of the descriptions), but which may or may not be present in the actual property which is the subject of the election. Again, this is insufficient to identify the plant or machinery which is purportedly subject to the election. For example, some elections have listed a lift among the items of plant, when no lift actually existed.

4.63   Thirdly, some elections in effect combine the two points above by referring to 'all the fixtures at the property, including but not limited to' the assets shown on an attached standard list. It is difficult to see how such terminology can be consistent with the legislation.

4.64   Fourthly, some elections refer to an inventory of fixtures and fittings, which typically includes both fixtures and chattels. *Section 198* can only relate to fixtures. Therefore, if an election purports to relate to fixtures and chattels (with no separate amounts allocated), the entire election would appear to be invalid. This is because the legislation states that the amount fixed by an election must be quantified at the time the election is made. Where the amount allocated to the fixtures (rather than the chattels) is not clear, the amount cannot be said to be fixed.

4.65   Fifthly, when elections refer to 'all fixtures at a property', they often do so without considering whether or not the fixtures concerned have been subject to a claim. Frequently, allowances will only have been claimed on some of the fixtures, in which case, the election is invalid, as to the extent that it relates to assets which have not been subject to a claim, no disposal value is required to be brought into account.

4.66   Sixthly, the election sometimes claims to cover assets that appear to be ineligible (broadly, assets which are not accepted as plant), in which case it is clearly invalid. If an election purports to relate to both eligible assets and ineligible assets (with no separate amounts allocated), the entire election would again appear to be invalid, as the amount fixed by the election (for qualifying assets) has not been quantified at the time the election is made.

Quantifying expenditure on plant

4.67   If the qualifying expenditure is to be calculated on a full apportionment basis, there will be a good deal of work necessary to maximise the claim. The process of establishing the amount qualifying for plant will consist broadly of the following steps:

(*a*)   Land valuation –

(i)   No allowances are due in respect of the purchase of land (*s 24*). The first task, therefore, is to establish the market value of the land (the so-called 'bare site value'). Any land valuation must be referred by the Inspector to the District Valuer (CA, para 12300).

(ii)   The District Valuer will also advise the Inspector, if requested, on the question of apportioning building expenditure between qualifying and non-qualifying (see **1.72** *et seq*).

(*b*)   Building and plant valuation –

(i)   Having determined the value of the land, the taxpayer then needs to split the balance of the purchase consideration between buildings and plant.

(ii)   It is usual to estimate those relative values at the date of the purchase. Bear in mind that the purpose of this exercise is merely to establish the relative proportions of buildings and plant so that those percentages may then be applied to the purchase consideration.

(iii)   It is essential to compare like with like. The easiest route to take is to value plant and building as at the purchase time (which is also consistent with the market value for land being used). Both elements should, therefore, be valued according to their replacement value at the time of purchase. It is commonly thought that the plant (but not the building) should be depreciated to reflect its actual age and condition. This is, however, neither logical nor correct. Any depreciation is, in effect, reflected in the purchase price, which is then reflected in the apportioned values of the elements of the property. However, when a building is near the end of its life the purchase price may reflect substantial redevelopment value. In such circumstances the building's obsolescence may not be fully reflected in the purchase price and it may sometimes then be necessary to adjust the replacement costs to allow for obsolescence

(iv) When inspecting a property for the purpose of identifying plant, the taxpayer and his advisers must be aware of the respective interests, ie who has paid for what. For instance, it may be that the freeholder now selling his interest was responsible only for the shell building, and that all fitting out was funded by tenants. In this case, the allowances on fittings will remain with the tenants.

(v) For transactions on or after 1 April 2008, it is also necessary to attribute separate values to 'integral features' (see **14.5** *et seq*) and other plant.

Apportionment formulae

4.68 The method of apportioning costs to determine qualifying expenditure is not prescribed by statute. It is, therefore, a matter for negotiation between the taxpayer, his advisers and HMRC. In accordance with the decision in *Salts v Battersby* [1910] 2 KB 155, the underlying aim of any method of apportionment should be to apportion the purchase price in proportion to the values of the constituent parts that go to make up the property. Simply deducting a value for the land is not sufficient (*Bostock v Totham (Inspector of Taxes)* [1997] STC 764). In *Bowerswood House Retirement Home Ltd v HMRC Comrs* [2015] UKFTT 94 (TC) the tribunal accepted that the VOA's preferred apportionment formula (see **4.69**) had been used extensively over many years in the context, and the tribunal was satisfied that it gave a just and reasonable result.

4.69 Set out below are just two of the possibilities when quantifying, say, the plant content of an office building. The VOA has expressed a preference for the following formula, which is almost always used in practice (VOA Manual, para 3.31):

$$Q = P \times (A/(B + C))$$

Where Q = qualifying expenditure

A = the replacement cost of the qualifying assets

B = the replacement cost of the building (including plant content)

C = the land value (ie bare site value)

P = purchase consideration

4.70 As mentioned above, the VOA formula is not mandatory. A less commonly used alternative (using the same notation) is:

$$Q = (P - C) \times (A/B)$$

4.71 Although the two formulae above are not mandatory, in practice, the VOA will almost always insist on the first formula and is normally extremely reluctant to accept different apportionment methods, unless there are very strong grounds for doing so. One area where the VOA does sometimes seek to depart from use of the formulae is where fixtures and chattels are acquired together. In such instances, it is not uncommon for the VOA to argue that because the chattels are not fixed to, and part of, the land/building they should not be valued with it, but should instead be valued separately (for example, based on their written-down values in the financial accounts, or individual second-hand market values). Nonetheless, the chattels must still form part of the overall apportionment under *s 562*.

4.72 The apportionment formula can have a significant impact on the value of a claim.

Example

Snowden Ltd acquired an office building for £40 million in such circumstances that any expenditure qualifying for allowances was to be determined by a just apportionment under *s 562*. Its accountants later obtain estimates of the market/replacement values of the various components as follows:

Land	£5 million (C)
Building	£50 million (B)
Plant therein	£20 million (A)

The two formulae give the following qualifying expenditure.

VOA formula:

Qualifying expenditure = £40 million × 20/(50 + 5) = 14.5 million

Alternative formula:

Qualifying expenditure = (40 − 5) × 20/50 = 14 million

In this example, therefore, a mathematical detail can cost (at current tax rates) £140,000 in additional tax. With different figures, however, the result could be reversed, with the alternative formula giving the better result.

4.73 The VOA Manuals include a number of helpful instructions affecting the method of apportionment. They confirm (para 3.31) that plant ('A' in the formula) does not need to be written down due to its age, as age and obsolescence will be reflected in the purchase price. An exception is that if the purchase price is based 'largely or wholly' on the value of the land then the obsolete nature of the building will not be reflected in that price and it may be necessary to adjust the replacement costs for obsolescence (para 3.35).

4.74   The bare site ('C') should be taken as the open market value of the actual site at the date of purchase valued on the assumption that:

(i)   any reclamation works which have been carried out on the site which permanently enhance the value of the land should be included (eg removing underground obstructions or treating contamination);

(ii)   the valuation reflects the circumstances existing at the valuation date; and

(iii)   the interest valued will be the interest actually acquired (eg if a long leasehold, taking account of ground rent).

Presumably, where appropriate the assumptions will also still include the following factors listed in a previous version of the manual:

(iv)   the site is cleared of all building and external works;

(v)   access and services are available up to the boundary; and

(vi)   planning permission is available for the existing type of development (para 3.33).

4.75   The replacement costs used in the formula ('A' and 'B') should be taken as the estimated cost of replacing the building if work had commenced at the appropriate time as to have the building available for occupation at the date of purchase. It should include: (i) site works, but not any reclamation works which permanently enhance the value of the bare land; (ii) the cost of external works; (iii) professional fees; and (iv) finance charges (para 3.66). The last-mentioned is often ignored in practice, as finance charges do not generally qualify for capital allowances, following *Ben-Odeco Ltd v Powlson (Inspector of Taxes)* (1978) 52 TC 459. If, due to the use of modern materials and building techniques, the cost of erecting a modern substitute would be less than the cost of an identical replacement building, the cost of the modern substitute should be used (para 3.66). Informally, however, the VOA has sought to disapply this rule where the property is listed, or where the old-fashioned materials were prestigious, even at the original time of construction. No deduction should be made for any regional development grants that may be available (para 3.66).

Practical considerations

4.76   Where a claim for allowances is to be restricted, the requirements of the vendor and of the purchaser may be in direct opposition (but not where the vendor has not made a claim, as is often the case).

Example

A Ltd purchased an office building on 1 July 1994 for £750,000. The following year it spent £200,000 on the addition of an air-conditioning system and claimed capital allowances.

In 2004, A Ltd agreed to sell the building to B Ltd for a total consideration of £2 million. The one matter outstanding was the amount to be apportioned to the air-conditioning. B Ltd would want as high an amount as possible allocated to the plant to maximise its capital allowances claim. A Ltd, however, wants to bring into its pool a low disposal value if indeed it has to introduce one at all.

4.77   In other cases, it may be that the position of, say, the vendor is slightly different. If, in our example, A Ltd had been steadily making losses then its own capital allowances position is of little concern. There may, in fact, be scope for A Ltd to permit a very high allocation to plant in exchange for a slightly larger selling price.

4.78   The optimum allocation is thus not always achieved, and should not be taken for granted by either party. If the vendor and the purchaser can reach agreement, the inclusion of an allocation of expenditure in the documentation, though not binding on HMRC, should avoid any later dispute between the parties themselves. Inclusion of the agreed allocation in an election under *s 198* (see **4.44**) will be binding on HMRC.

4.79   If the vendor wishes to continue to claim capital allowances, this can be achieved by including in the sale contract (or a *s 198* election) the lowest sustainable valuation of the plant. As plant is generally pooled for capital allowances purposes, the effect is that allowances will continue to accrue to the vendor almost indefinitely.

4.80   Of course, it must always be borne in mind that tax matters should not be allowed to overrule commercial considerations. However, as a minimum, potential claimants should consult a specialist in order to gauge the potential quantum of allowances – only then can they assess whether the capital allowances are worth pursuing.

4.81   Ignoring capital allowances altogether is not an option where the 'fixed value requirement' (see **4.16**) and the 'pooling requirement (see **4.27**) apply. In such cases, ignoring capital allowances issues completely will generally result in the worst possible result for both buyers and sellers.

4.82   Both parties should beware of ignoring capital allowances simply for an easy life; such a move may cost more in terms of both time and money in the long run. At an early stage, a 'desk top review' should be undertaken in order to establish entitlement and to be sure that the likely savings from capital allowances exceed the cost of putting the claim together. The purchaser should make standard enquiries of the vendor, using the form CPSE.1 or equivalent, and insist on proper answers. If necessary, specialist capital allowances advice should be sought.

4.83   If necessary, appropriate clauses should be included in the purchase contract (the present authors have drafted a number of those included in online databases commonly referred to by those drafting contracts). The reasons for taking such action at this stage are threefold:

(i)   The vendor will be put on notice that he has certain obligations to fulfil and information to provide.

(ii)   If appropriate, the relevant clauses may be 'traded' against others onerous to the purchaser.

(iii)   If such thoughts are only raised when the contract is on the verge of completion, such technical details may be sacrificed in order to 'clinch the deal'.

4.84   The vendor may, of course, have requirements of his own regarding capital allowances. He may, for example, be seeking a relatively low apportionment of the consideration to plant so as to mitigate any claw-back. The final agreement is a matter for negotiation. A vendor may often argue for a *s 198* election for an amount equal to tax written-down value on the grounds of 'fairness'. Such fairness is, however, an illusion where (as is generally the case) a property is sold at a profit. Consider the following example:

Example

Albert buys a building for £1 million and claims allowances on fixtures of £250,000. After three years (when the fixtures are written down to £128,000; for simplicity assuming 20% writing down allowances) he sells the building to Bertram for £1.2 million. In the absence of a *s 198* election, the amount apportioned to fixtures could reasonably be expected to be around £300,000, but as Albert made a claim, the amount would be restricted to the original cost of £250,000. A *s 198* election for £128,000 would allow Albert to keep allowances (intended, do not forget, to compensate for a fall in value) of £122,000 relating to assets on which he has in fact made a gain.

DOCUMENTATION

4.85   Using the typical scenario of the purchase of a second-hand office building, inclusive of an unquantified plant content, this section considers what documentation should be put in place.

4.86   The requirements of the purchaser and the vendor are often mirror images of the same problem. For clarity, the requirements below have been considered from the point of view of the purchaser. Not all the items mentioned will be appropriate in every case. It is often better, however, to begin with many demands, which can if appropriate be 'traded' in the course of the purchase negotiations.

- Ideally, a full inventory should be taken of all potential plant included within the building and being sold.

- The purchaser should seek to obtain confirmation from the vendor that the value attributed to each item is less than the 'ceiling' imposed by *s 185* (see **4.37** *et seq*). In most cases this will be the original acquisition cost to the vendor, but may be further restricted by the disposal value used on previous transfers. The purchaser may wish to seek a warranty from the vendor that this has been considered.

- The vendor should also state which of the items listed on the inventory have been accepted as plant by HMRC, and whether any have been treated as long-life assets (see **14.153**). Whether the assets continue to be treated as plant will depend on the purchaser's use of them.

- In the context of the fixtures legislation, the qualifying expenditure of the purchaser may be restricted by the disposal value brought into account by the vendor (see **4.35** *et seq*). The purchaser should seek, therefore, to at least be kept informed of the vendor's negotiations with HMRC in respect of the relevant plant. If the figures are material, the purchaser may even wish to review the correspondence in draft.

- The purchaser should seek to incorporate in the purchase documentation a statement that the vendor will make available all relevant information to the purchaser, and will provide him with all reasonable assistance for the preparation of his capital allowances claim.

- The parties may also wish to incorporate in the contract a statement that an election under *s 198* will be entered into, at the request of either party (see **4.44** *et seq*). However, although it theoretically avoids the need to prepare an apportionment, entering into a *s 198* election is generally inadvisable for a purchaser, because the amount is likely be much less than the *s 562* apportionment that would otherwise apply by default.

- In some cases, the purchaser may try to obtain an indemnity from the vendor regarding the right to capital allowances. That is to say, a failure to obtain allowances would result in the purchaser being reimbursed by the vendor. This is commonly the situation where a landlord constructs a building to his tenants' requirements and the rent payable varies with the success or otherwise of the landlord's capital allowances claim.

4.87 *Purchase of a second-hand building*

4.87   Where an industrial building is being purchased, the following will also be relevant:

- Evidence of the date on which the building was first brought into use, and/or on which additional expenditure on the building was incurred. For expenditure incurred after 5 November 1962, allowances were given over a period of 25 years; prior to that date, over a period of 50 years (see **4.7**).

- Confirmation of the amount on which the vendor has successfully been claiming allowances and details of the residue of expenditure (that is, TWDV) after the sale (see **4.40** *et seq*). This will impact on the purchaser's qualifying expenditure in that in most cases his claim will be based on the lower of the amount he pays, and the amount paid by the vendor.

- Details of use of the building by lessees or licensees and confirmation that the lease agreements oblige the tenants to use the building only for purposes qualifying for industrial buildings allowances.

4.88   Where contaminated land is acquired, including where, for example, asbestos is present, the purchaser should retain all environmental reports. Note, however, that if the purchase price is reduced because of the contamination, land remediation relief (see **Chapter 24**) may be denied. This is generally no more than a hypothetical risk.

Chapter 5

Offices – special features

GENERAL

5.1   For expenditure on the structural elements of offices, as opposed to the plant and machinery contained within them, if they are used for research and development, see **Chapter 19**. For expenditure that meets the requirements of the legislation governing business premises renovation allowances, see **11.61**.

5.2   Offices did not generally qualify for industrial buildings allowances (IBAs), although there were exceptions, notably IBAs where the office, rather than merely being the seat of administration, was closely linked to a manufacturing or other qualifying process. An office formerly could, in appropriate circumstances, qualify for IBAs in an enterprise zone (see **Chapter 9**).

5.3   Although IBAs were abolished with effect from April 2011, a present-day purchaser of a property could potentially have his claim for plant allowances restricted if the building had previously qualified for IBAs (*s 186*). Consequently, in borderline cases, it will be helpful to know the former legislation, so as to rule out this possibility.

5.4   The most important case was *IRC v Lambhill Ironworks Ltd* (1950) 31 TC 393 (see **Appendix 4**). In that case it was stated:

'An office must be something which clearly has not got anything of an industrial character or is not directly ancillary to the industrial operations conducted or carried on in the rest of the works.'

5.5   In the *Lambhill* case, IBAs were given in respect of a drawing office used by a structural engineering company. The drawing office was clearly very closely related to the 'industrial' activities carried on by the taxpayer, rather than being, for example, used for management or administration purposes.

5.6   A similar line of reasoning was followed in the Irish case of *O'Conaill v Waterford Glass Ltd* (1982) TL(I) 122 (see **Appendix 4**). Here, a computer building was deemed to be an industrial building, because it, and the computer it housed, existed solely or primarily to perform a function related to industrial activities carried on in other buildings on the same site. A similar English case, *Abbott Laboratories Ltd v Carmody (Inspector of Taxes)* (1968) 44 TC 569, is discussed at **7.118** in the context of what constitutes a separate building.

5.7   A later consideration of the term 'office' was in *Girobank Plc v Clarke (Inspector of Taxes)* [1998] STC 182. An office was here defined as 'the place where the central management emanates and where the manager and his staff do their work' (following a Canadian case, *Carter v The Standard Ltd* (1915) 30 DLR 492).

5.8   Examples of offices which did *not* qualify for industrial buildings allowances are accommodation for:

(*a*)   directors and senior executives;

(*b*)   planning and administration;

(*c*)   personnel;

(*d*)   wages staff;

(*e*)   works manager and staff dealing with costing and despatch; and

(*f*)   purchasing, sales and marketing departments (CA, para 32312).

5.9   As the vast majority of offices will not qualify for any form of buildings allowances, it is essential to identify items qualifying as plant or machinery.

PLANT

5.10   A modern office building will generally contain numerous assets which may qualify as plant. A more complete list of items potentially qualifying is given in **Appendix 2**, but the principal items in an office environment *may* include (those in italics are now regarded as integral features – see **14.5** *et seq*):

- *air conditioning including ducting and vents*;

- *air purification systems*;

- blinds and curtains;

- *boilers*;

- burglar alarms;

- *bus bars* (that is, metal conductors inside trunking which distribute heavy duty electrical current);

- close circuit television;

- cameras;

- canteen fittings and equipment;

- car park illumination and barrier equipment;

- carpets and other loose floor coverings, such as mats;

- computers and associated specialised flooring and ceilings;

- communications equipment;

- conduit for security alarm systems;

- *cold water systems for drinking and air conditioning*;

- *cold water systems acquired on or after 1 April 2008* (see **14.5**);

- counters and fittings;

- data installations;

- *document lifts*;

- electrically operated doors – electrical and mechanical components;

- *electrical systems designed to suit a particular trade* (see **5.13**);

- *electrical systems, including lighting acquired on or after 1 April 2008* (see **14.5**);

- *emergency lighting*;

- fans and heaters;

- fire alarms;

- fire protection equipment (eg extinguishers and hoses), systems (eg alarms) and sprinklers;

- furniture and furnishings, such as loose furniture, fitted desks, notice boards, racking, cupboards and shelving, soft furnishings, etc;

- gas fire extinguishing systems (eg halon);

- *gas heating*;

- *generators*;

- hand dryers;

- *heating installations, fittings, pipes and radiators*;

- *hot water services and related plumbing*;

- intercom installations;

- kitchen equipment;

- *lighting systems acquired on or after 1 April 2008* (see **14.5**);

- lightning protection systems;

- machinery, such as lever handles and door closers;

- moveable partitions (where a commercial necessity) (see **16.52** *et seq*);

- *passenger lifts*;

- paging systems;

- sanitary appliances and fittings;

- signage (eg directional or fire action);

- smoke detectors and heat detectors;

- solar panels (see **15.67**);

- *solar shading*;

- sprinkler systems;

- *suspended ceilings forming an integral part of an air conditioning system* (ie so-called 'plenum' ceilings—see **16.51**);

- *switchboards (electrical, not telephone)*;

- tea and coffee dispensers and vending machines;

- telecommunications systems;

- addition of thermal insulation (see **15.69** *et seq*);

- *ventilation systems*;

- wet and dry risers (fire fighting equipment); and

- window cleaning cradles (including tracks and anchorages).

5.11   Not all of these will qualify as plant in every situation, and the general principles of what constitutes plant (see **Chapter 15**) must be borne in mind. The specific issues concerning some of the more common items are dealt with in **Chapter 16**.

Electrical systems

5.12   Electrical systems (including lighting) have, since April 2008, been treated as integral features, qualifying for allowances under *s 33A* (see **14.5** *et seq*). Before April 2008, such systems did not generally qualify as plant, but could do so in certain circumstances.

5.13   For expenditure incurred before 1 April 2008 (since when electrical systems qualify as integral features), it would often be possible to demonstrate that the electrical system was such that it would qualify as a single entity eligible for plant allowances, within the guidelines set out in CA, para 21180, ie:

(i) the electrical system is designed and built as a whole, and is a fully integrated entity;

(ii) it is designed and adapted to meet the requirements of the trade, rather than being a general purpose or standard system designed to meet the needs of a range of occupants;

(iii) the end-user items of the installation function as apparatus in the trader's business; and

(iv) the electrical system is essential for the functioning of the business (CA, para 21180).

5.14 A system qualifying under these old rules would continue to attract allowances at the main pool rate (currently 18%). For expenditure incurred on or after 1 April 2008, such a system would qualify as plant under *s 33A*, albeit at the 10% or 8% 'special rate' of writing down allowance applicable to integral features (see **14.5** *et seq*).

5.15 If an electrical installation did not satisfy the above conditions, inspectors were instructed to adopt a piecemeal approach (*Cole Bros Ltd v Phillips (Inspector of Taxes)* (1982) 55 TC 188). They would accept that the following items were plant:

(*a*) the main switchboard, transformer and associated switchgear provided that a substantial part of the electrical installation – both the equipment and the ancillary wiring – qualifies as plant;

(*b*) a standby generator and the emergency lighting and power circuits it services;

(*c*) lighting in sales areas if it is specifically designed to encourage the sale of goods on display;

(*d*) wiring, control panels and other equipment installed specifically to supply equipment that is plant or machinery;

(*e*) lighting which within (*c*) qualified even if there was no other lighting. The public areas in businesses such as banks and building societies were regarded as sales areas.

Chapter 6

Retail property – special features

GENERAL

6.1   Retail shops will not generally qualify for any form of buildings allowances, such as IBAs (*s 277(1)*). Industrial buildings allowances were abolished with effect from April 2011. However, any claim (eg for plant allowances) by a later purchaser of a property may be restricted if IBAs had been claimed by a previous owner (*s 186*), and for that reason, the relevant rules on IBAs are set out below.

6.2   A retail shop includes any premises of a similar character where retail trade or business (including repair work) is carried on (*s 277(1)(b)*). Inspectors were instructed to regard the public areas in businesses such as banks and building societies as sales areas. These presumably were, therefore, tantamount to a retail shop (CA, para 21180).The question of whether a particular building is to be regarded as a retail shop has been considered regularly by the courts, though not often for capital allowances purposes. In general terms, a 'retail shop' is characterised not by the design of the building, but by the nature of the trade which is carried on there. Consequently, a redundant church used as a workshop may qualify for allowances, whereas shop premises used as an office will not.

6.3   In broad terms, a retail shop has been said to consist of a place where facilities are offered and to which the general public can resort for the satisfaction of their wants and needs (*Turpin v Assessment Committee for Middlesbrough Assessment Area* [1931] AC 446). HMRC has confirmed that trade customers are not the public, and so a building which serves only trade customers is not a retail shop (CA, para 32311). Similarly, the premises from which a mail order business is operated are in use for a retail trade but they are not a retail shop because the public does not have access to them.

6.4   A retail shop can encompass much more besides the traditional image of a glass-fronted high street store. The reference in *s 277(1)(b)* to 'repair work' would extend the definition to include garages; however, vehicle repair premises are covered by a long-standing agreement with HMRC (see **7.105** *et seq*).

6.5   Following an early case, *Finn v Kerslake* [1931] AC 446, a commonly used example of what does or does not constitute a retail shop (or ancillary premises) is a bakery. A bakery would certainly have qualified for IBAs under *s 274*, that is, it was used for the purposes of a trade consisting of the manufacture of goods or materials or the subjection of goods or materials to a process. This would have remained so even if it primarily supplied retail outlets owned by the same concern. Making something is not ancillary to selling it. For example, a bakehouse that produced bread was not in use for purposes ancillary to the shop where the bread was sold because making the bread was not ancillary to selling it (CA, para 32313). However, if the bakery formed part of a shop (as is now prevalent in large supermarkets), or if it supplied only one shop, it was likely that the bakery would be considered to be in use for purposes ancillary to the purposes of a retail shop. It is understood that HMRC would take this approach if at least 90% of the bakery's output is sold in the shop.

6.6   The principles emerging from this example may be applied to other types of business or activity.

6.7   A retail shop is often easily identifiable. A more difficult issue is often whether a building is *ancillary to the purposes of a retail shop* – expenditure on such a building was also prohibited from qualifying for IBAs by *s 277(1)*. To a great extent, it is a matter of degree whether a building was used for such purposes. To return to our bakery example, where a bakery supplied:

(*a*)   an attached retail shop;

(*b*)   other retail shops owned by the bakery; and

(*c*)   retail shops owned by others;

it would have been necessary to take into account factors such as the proportion of output going to the attached shop, the mix of wholesale and retail sales, and so on.

6.8   Delivery men are treated as retail outlets if a retail shop exists, but otherwise they are not. Retail sales do not, of themselves, constitute a retail shop, and by extension, if no retail shop exists, there can be no purposes ancillary to it.

6.9   The question of whether a building was used for a purpose ancillary to the purposes of a retail shop was one of the matters discussed in *Kilmarnock Equitable Co-operative Society Ltd v IRC* (1966) 42 TC 675 and in *Sarsfield (Inspector of Taxes) v Dixons Group Plc* [1998] STC 938. In the latter case, it was stated:

> 'A building is used for a purpose which is ancillary to the purposes of a retail shop if its user is confined to furthering the purposes of the retail shop, ie subservient and subordinate to retail selling.'

6.10 In the case of *Dixons Group*, a transport undertaking carried on by one group member consisted of receiving, storing and delivering goods to be sold in retail shops operated by other companies in the group. The transport undertaking was of a substantial size in terms of investment, number of employees and turnover, and made a taxable profit. Despite this, it was held to remain 'subservient and subordinate, and therefore ancillary' to the purposes of the retail shops.

6.11 In practical terms, the availability of allowances is likely to revolve around the degree to which the 'qualifying' activity can be shown to be independent of other 'excluded' activities with which it interacts.

6.12 Following the decision in the *Kilmarnock* case, HMRC has confirmed that a building can only be ancillary to one purpose. This means that if a building is used for two purposes it is not in use for purposes ancillary to either. For example, a wholesale distribution warehouse that supplies goods in broadly equal measure to retail shops owned by a connected person and to arm's-length customers is not in use for purposes ancillary to either (CA, para 32313).

6.13 Further examples of buildings that are used for purposes ancillary to the purposes of a retail shop are:

- a printing works used solely for the printing requirements of a multiple shop concern;

- a garage for the delivery vans of a multiple shop concern;

- a workshop used by the maintenance staff of a retail shop for the repair and maintenance of the shop fittings;

- a hotel laundry that serves a group of hotels (though if the hotels are qualifying hotels, allowances will be due on the laundry as well as on the hotels (CA, para 32313)).

PLANT

6.14 It remains true, however, that the vast majority of retail premises will not qualify for any form of buildings allowances, and as a result it is essential to identify items qualifying as plant or machinery. Listed below are the main items one would expect to find in a retail shop which, in appropriate circumstances, *may* qualify as plant for the purposes of capital allowances (those in italics will now be regarded as integral features – see **14.4** *et seq*):

- False ceilings –
    - allowed only where the false ceiling is an integral part of an air-conditioning system (eg a so-called 'plenum' ceiling forming one side of a duct – see **16.51**);
    - surface mounted lighting track.

- Decorative screeds –
    - only if informative, eg giving directions or advertising services.
- Floor finishes –
    - carpet and reusable carpet tiles;
    - coverings/finishes serving a particular function, eg non-slip, heavy duty.
- Internal partitions –
    - moveable, where the movement of the partitions is a commercial necessity, not merely commercial convenience (see **16.52** *et seq*). (Note: the reasons why the movable partitioning is needed for the trade should be formulated in advance.)
- Doors –
    - mechanical or electrical components (eg for revolving or sliding doors);
    - internal doors forming 'airlock' to preserve internal temperature, regulate flow of customers;
    - automatic doors: electrical and mechanical parts, pressure pads.
- Security –
    - automatic door closers and similar fittings. Mesh link and roller shutters where required in addition to ordinary doors for the purposes of the trade;
    - kiosk/gondola shutters;
    - security shutters in addition to ordinary doors, where they form an active part of a security alarm system;
    - burglar bars, if part of alarm system;
    - security mirrors, eg two-way or convex type.
- Windows –
    - hygiaphones acting as security windows (a hygiaphone is a glass screen through which staff can speak to the public);
    - security windows around cash desks, etc.
- Walls and ceiling finishes –
    - allowable only where it can be demonstrated that they perform some function specific to the trade.

6.14   *Retail property – special features*

- Fire safety expenditure –

    – fire-fighting apparatus, eg sprinklers, hydrants, reservoirs, extinguishers;

    – semi-structural items, eg fire shutters, fire and smoke curtains.

- Plumbing –

    – cold water piping serving toilets, etc;

    – *cold water system acquired after 31 March 2008* (see **14.5**);

    – hot water piping from source of heat to appliance;

    – *hot water system acquired after 31 March 2008* (see **14.5**);

    – tiling and splash backs (in *JD Wethersoon Plc v HMRC Comrs* [2012] UKUT 42 (TCC) it was held that small areas of splashback wall tiling and plastering around sinks, lavatory basins or other equipment were building alterations incidental to the installation of plant or machinery qualifying under what is now *CAA 2001, s 25* – see **14.119** *et seq*).

- Vehicle access, etc –

    – dock levellers, platforms;

    – speed restrictors ('sleeping policemen');

    – car park lighting;

    – automatic barriers (eg card-controlled);

    – signs;

    – security cameras;

    – bollards;

    – trolley parks (metalwork only);

    – floodlighting;

    – skips (including cost of levelling prepared land).

- Outbuildings –

    – fuel stores, fuel tanks.

- Protective structures –

    – brick, concrete, metal or wooden structures built around plant for the protection of the plant itself or of employees/members of the public, eg around liquefied petroleum gas (LPG) stores.

- Cost of alterations to buildings –

    – alterations to an existing building incidental to the installation of plant and machinery, eg metal framework for space heaters, strengthening floors for the installation of racking, alterations to the building so that plant can be installed (*s 25* – see **14.119** *et seq*).

- Miscellaneous –

    – *external solar shading*;

    – security cages.

- Heating systems, etc –

    – items of machinery, eg air handling plant, boilers, radiators, space heaters;

    – builder's work in connection with the above;

    – services of gas, electricity and water to the plant which are exclusive to that item of plant (eg water piping back to the point where the pipe serving only a particular item of plant branches off from the distribution system);

    – *space or water heating systems generally, acquired after 31 March 2008* (see **14.5**).

- Sanitary –

    – toilets;

    – toilet accommodation (eg cubicles);

    – sinks/washbasins;

    – urinals;

    – hand dryers;

    – towel and soap holders;

    – mirrors;

    – showers;

    – additional fittings for the disabled;

    – drinking fountains;

    – macerators, etc;

    – supply or waste pipes solely serving the above;

    – hot water piping;

    – potable water system.

6.14 *Retail property – special features*

- Fire protection –
  - smoke detectors;
  - heat detectors;
  - fire and smoke alarms;
  - sprinklers;
  - break glass call points;
  - emergency lighting;
  - fixtures to emergency exits (eg panic latches);
  - fire corridors;
  - electricity/water supplies to alarms, etc;
  - roof lights forming part of smoke control system;
  - smoke extraction systems.
- Electrical –
  - electrical system serving particular items of plant (eg electronic point of sale (EPOS) equipment/heating);
  - telemecanique or similar trunking system;
  - *electrical system generally, acquired after 31 March 2008* (see **14.5**);
  - display lighting;
  - high bay lighting system;
  - *lighting system generally, acquired after 31 March 2008* (see **14.5**);
  - sockets and cabling used exclusively by items of plant, eg computers, EPOS equipment;
  - temperature and light level sensors;
  - distribution boards;
  - generators;
  - switchgear;
  - security cameras;
  - videoscan equipment;
  - video recording equipment.

- Fixtures and fittings –
    - external signs;
    - aisle/product signs;
    - display units;
    - shelving;
    - display lighting and lighting track;
    - entrance barriers;
    - lockers (eg for staff);
    - gondolas;
    - litter bins;
    - bicycle holders.
- Communications, etc –
    - paging system/intercom;
    - piped music/PA system.
- Shop fronts –
    - external signs;
    - lettering (removable);
    - window display – floors and backs.
- Lifts and escalators –
    - *lifts and escalators generally acquired after 31 March 2008* (see **14.5**);
    - lift cars;
    - lift machinery and indicators;
    - escalators;
    - electrical supply.

6.15   The HMRC guidelines previously allowed that an entire electrical system could be regarded as plant if certain conditions were met (CA, para 21180 – see **5.13**). These guidelines were first formulated following a claim successfully made by a supermarket chain. With effect from 1 April 2008, electrical systems generally will qualify for plant allowances (*s 33A*), albeit at the 8% rate of writing down allowance applicable to integral features.

SAMPLING

6.16 Where a taxpayer incurs expenditure of a recurring nature, it may be possible to agree the capital allowances treatment on the basis of a sample, thus obviating the need to analyse all the expenditure involved. This is most commonly met in the case of multiple property owners, notably (but not exclusively) retailers.

6.17 If the claim is based on a review of, say, repetitive minor refurbishment of public houses or shops, it might be possible to agree that a percentage of that expenditure will be deemed to qualify for allowances for a number of years thereby avoiding time-consuming yearly detailed analysis. Situations of this nature can sometimes be useful trade-offs when negotiations founder upon technical problems.

6.18 From 20 October 2003, HMRC changed its approach to sampling of this kind, and issued new instructions to Inspectors (CA, para 20075). These are self-explanatory and are as follows:

'Where a taxpayer incurs significant expenditure in a chargeable period on a number of properties that contain fixtures that qualify for PMA [plant and machinery allowances], it may be possible to arrive at the amount of qualifying expenditure for those fixtures by means of sampling. For example, sampling may be appropriate where a company acquires a number of similar sized retail units and fits them out in their "corporate style" to create a standard type of shop.

Sampling is acceptable in principle, both as a method for preparing PMA claims and in checking them.

It is not possible to provide hard and fast rules on the method of sampling to be adopted as the facts and circumstances of each case will be different. However, if sampling is appropriate, statistically acceptable sampling methodologies must be adopted.

You should discuss with the taxpayer the size of the sample, and the expenditure included in the sample, which will depend on identifying the relevant population. These discussions should take place before a PMA claim is prepared or checked using a sampling method. Appropriate cases may be agreed without reference elsewhere but the Revenue's Analysis and Research team may be able to advise on sample sizes and techniques, where necessary.

You should not agree, in advance, claims for future years based on an earlier year's sample. However, you may decide to examine claims by means of enquiries to identify variances in accounting systems and spending patterns from those previously examined. If there is little variance it may well be that no further enquiry would be necessary into that claim.

Similarly, you cannot automatically roll forward an earlier sampling methodology to similar projects in later years. However, you should be able to judge the extent of sampling required in the later years in the light of work done on the earlier project. The relevance of earlier sampling work to later expenditure may be affected by changes in the underlying statutory provisions and related case law.

If the bulk of expenditure has been incurred before the end of the chargeable period then sampling discussions can begin between you and the taxpayer then. However, you must not agree the extent of sampling before the beginning of a chargeable period.

The above guidance applies only to fixtures. It does not apply to chattels.'

6.19 However, on 17 August 2012, HMRC expressed concern that many businesses had submitted sampling proposals that were not statistically acceptable, largely because the sample size was too small, and there was published revised guidance for consultation. At the time of writing, this is not known to have been officially adopted, but is reproduced below:

'Where a business undertakes large programmes of work on their properties on a regular basis and the nature of the work is very similar, HMRC will, in certain circumstances, accept claims for plant and machinery allowances for expenditure incurred on qualifying fixtures, based on a detailed breakdown of expenditure in a sample of those properties. The "qualifying proportion" of expenditure in the sample may then be applied to the other properties. For example, sampling may be appropriate where a company acquires a number of similar sized retail units and fits them out in their "corporate style" to create a standard type of shop.

Sampling is acceptable in principle in appropriate cases, both as a method for preparing PMA claims and of checking them.

When is it appropriate to use sampling?

Sampling should be considered where:

- the overall size of the population (the total number of properties or units) allows for a reasonable sample size to be drawn from it (HMRC does not consider any sample size that is less than 15 to be reasonable)

- there would be a considerable and demonstrable burden involved for the business in analysing the expenditure for the whole population

- the nature of the works undertaken is reasonably similar across the whole population, or appropriate stratified sampling will be undertaken (see below under the heading "Categories")

Methodology

When estimating something using a sample drawn from a population, a confidence interval can be used as a measurement of how good, or how accurate the estimate (often an average) is. A confidence interval gives a likely range in which the "true" value will lie. It is always given together with the confidence level, which is the likelihood that the "true value" will lie within this range. The confidence level is often expressed as a percentage.

If the gross capital expenditure for a claim does not exceed £25 million

HMRC require that the capital allowances qualifying proportions derived from a sample are within a 95 per cent confidence interval of plus or minus (+/–) 5 per cent of the gross expenditure. In other words, if the estimated qualifying proportion of gross expenditure is 40 per cent, we would expect that the true value would lie within a range of 35 per cent to 45 per cent of the gross expenditure.

If the gross capital expenditure for a claim is more than £25 million

HMRC require that the capital allowances qualifying proportions derived from a sample are within a 95 per cent confidence interval of +/– 5 per cent of **the qualifying proportion**.

For example:

- if the estimated qualifying proportion of gross expenditure is 40 per cent, the range would be from 38 per cent to 42 per cent (5% of 40% is 2%, so the range would be +/– 2% of the estimated qualifying proportion of 40%)

- if the estimated qualifying proportion of gross expenditure is 60 per cent, the range would be from 57 per cent to 63 per cent (5% of 60% is 3%, so the range would be +/– 3% of the estimated qualifying proportion of 60%)

Categories

In many cases there may be considerable diversity across the population. For example, retail units may be categorised as "superstores" or "high street stores" and the work carried out might be new build, extensions or re-fits. There could be substantial variation in the proportion of qualifying expenditure across the different categories.

Additionally, standard programmes of work on outlets can vary significantly with regard to the proportion of qualifying expenditure depending on the location of the property. For example, where some of the outlets are located in mainline train terminals or airports the work requirements may be far more stringent than for those in other locations.

HMRC will not consider sampling unless the nature of the work undertaken is shown to be reasonably similar across units, because otherwise it will be almost impossible to achieve the accuracy required.

In cases where there are different categories of work it may be possible to reduce the variation in qualifying expenditure by drawing separate sub-samples from each category. This is sometimes referred to as stratified sampling or stratification.

Similarly, if there are one or two projects within a total population that are markedly different, it will probably be necessary to exclude these from the sampling exercise and submit individual claims.

Sample size

A minimum sample size of 15 units is required for each identifiable category (stratum).

If the number of units being analysed is 15 or fewer then all the data should be analysed and sampling is not permitted.

It is important to note that this is a minimum figure and that in most cases a larger sample will be necessary to meet HMRC's accuracy requirements stated above.

Sampling method

HMRC require random sampling, where every unit in the population has a chance of being selected. We will need to see evidence that the sample has been chosen randomly. "Representative" sampling is not permitted.

Information to be provided

Ideally, the sampling exercise should be discussed with the business before a PMA claim is submitted. This is to ensure an adequate sample is drawn to avoid the need for further sampling at a later stage. The business should set out the population information (number of units, level of expenditure), the method for selecting the sample and the method for estimating the qualifying proportion. The business should also undertake calculations to demonstrate that the proposed sample size is likely to meet accuracy requirements.

When the claim is submitted the following information must be supplied:

1.   A high level summary of the number of units in the population and the gross capital expenditure for both the population and the sample.

2.   A list of all the units by gross capital expenditure split by category.

3.   Details of the method used to select the sample - this needs to be demonstrably random.

4. Estimates of the total "qualifying proportion" and total qualifying expenditure for the population (or each category where appropriate) and how they were calculated from the sample results.

5. Evidence that the estimate of the "qualifying proportion" meets HMRC's accuracy requirements. (This requires calculating a confidence interval for the sample.) This is a crucial component of the claim.

Other issues

The Finance Act 2008 introduced a new classification of "integral features" of a building or structure, expenditure on the provision or replacement of which qualifies for writing-down allowances at the special rate. Guidance on "integral features" can be found at CA22300. For qualifying expenditure incurred from April 2008 it will be necessary for businesses to calculate separate percentages for expenditure on:

- "Integral features" and, where appropriate, any other fixtures, such as "long-life assets" (see CA23720), that qualify for writing-down allowances at the special rate

- Other fixtures that qualify for writing down allowances at the main rate

Businesses do not have an automatic right to use sampling. HMRC reserves the right to examine all the records where appropriate. You should therefore ensure that businesses are aware that they must retain all the underlying records relating to the whole population.

You should not agree, in advance, claims for future years based on an earlier year's sample. However, you may decide to examine claims to identify variances in accounting systems, spending patterns and the nature of work carried out from those previously examined. If there is little variance it may well be that no further enquiry would be necessary into that claim.

Similarly, you cannot automatically roll forward an earlier sampling methodology to similar projects in later years. However, you should be able to judge the extent of sampling required in the later years in the light of work done on the earlier project.

The relevance of earlier sampling work to later expenditure may be affected by changes in the underlying statutory provisions and related case law.

If the bulk of expenditure has been incurred before the end of the chargeable period then sampling discussions can begin between you and the taxpayer then. However, you must not agree the extent of sampling before the beginning of a chargeable period.

Sampling is not an appropriate way to arrive at the qualifying expenditure for PMA on property acquisitions. The part of the capital expenditure incurred on the property that relates to fixtures is found by apportioning the capital sum between the fixtures and the rest of the land (subject to the limit of original cost or a previous owner's disposal value). The apportionment is made under s 562 *CAA 2001, s 562* (CA12300) except where the purchaser and vendor decide to make a joint election under *CAA 2001, s 198* (CA26800) to fix the amount to be apportioned to the fixtures.

It will be necessary to look at each acquisition individually to establish whether an election under *s 198* has been made (from April 2012 an election under *s 198* will be used to fix the price of fixtures in most property transactions). Additionally, where there has been a previous PMA claim in relation to the fixtures acquired the qualifying expenditure of the purchaser is limited to the historic cost of the fixture (CA26400). Again, each property will need to be looked at individually to establish the maximum amount that may be claimed.

The above guidance applies only to fixtures. It does not apply to chattels.

Appropriate cases may be agreed without reference to HMRC's Knowledge, Analysis and Intelligence (KAI) team, but KAI may be able to advise on sample sizes and techniques, where necessary.'

6.20   The key points are that any sample must be 'statistically valid', and that agreements cannot be *automatically* rolled forward to subsequent years. Regarding statistical validity, Inspectors have an element of discretion over the sampling techniques to use. However, on major exercises, HMRC normally requires samples to be large enough to ensure that there is a 95% likelihood that the capital allowances qualifying percentage estimated from the sample is within plus or minus 5% of the true answer if every expenditure project had been analysed in detail. For smaller exercises, inspectors generally exercise a good deal of discretion.

6.21   Alternatively, for multiple property portfolios pro forma approaches are commonly used. These seek to create and use a standard pro forma to accurately capture and classify expenditure for capital allowances purposes.

6.22   Theoretically, pro forma approaches are a good idea because they are meant to ensure that *all* expenditure incurred is reviewed and analysed for capital allowances purposes (which should result in the most accurate answer). Furthermore, they should also result in a streamlined and efficient claim preparation process.

6.23   In practice, experience has shown that for many taxpayers these objectives are not met and in fact very often the opposite result occurs. This is because pro forma approaches are subject (notoriously) to the following major weaknesses:

(*a*)   No two buildings or construction projects are the same, so it can be impractical to design a standard pro forma to suit all circumstances.

(*b*)   Claims generated by pro forma are only as good as the data captured on them – an inadequate or incorrectly compiled pro forma will invariably lead to an incorrect claim.

   They can give the dangerous illusion that all expenditure is being analysed accurately, whereas in practice that is far from true. For example, forms may be completed using budget or contract costs (rather than out-turn costs) and not be properly reconciled to the expenditure recorded in the accounts. Or some forms might not be completed at all (so the tax relief is lost) and other forms may be completed inaccurately and inconsistently (resulting in under and overclaims), especially if they are completed by a number of building contractors or surveyors with little understanding of, or training in tax.

(*c*)   A pro forma may not be technically up to date, as legislation, case law and best practice develop over time. For example, any pro forma not updated to reflect integral features (see **14.5**) will almost certainly undervalue a claim.

(*d*)   Even if a pro forma works reasonably well to capture and classify expenditure incurred, very often that information will not flow through into the tax return as it was intended to.

FLAT CONVERSION ALLOWANCES

6.24   For expenditure incurred between May 2001 and April 2013, a 100% first-year allowance, called a 'flat conversion allowance', was available where parts of business premises were converted into flats (*s 393A*). The relief was given as a letting expense of the business and was most commonly met where flats were sited above shops. This was one of a number of provisions aimed at urban regeneration. Other measures included a reduced rate of VAT, and enhanced relief for cleaning up contaminated land (**Chapter 24**).

6.25   Flat conversion allowances were withdrawn for expenditure incurred on or after 1 April 2013 (corporation tax) or 6 April 2013 (income tax) and the entitlement to claim writing-down allowances on any outstanding residue of qualifying expenditure ceased with effect from the same dates (*FA 2012, s 225 and Sch 38, para 36 et seq*).

6.26   Capital allowances, including a 100% first-year allowance, were available for expenditure on converting or renovating certain flats above business premises, incurred on or after 11 May 2001. The relevant part of the premises must have been vacant, or only used for storage, throughout the period of one year ending immediately before the commencement of the conversion or renovation (*s 393B(2)*). Somewhat perversely, the legislation could encourage a taxpayer whose premises had been vacant for a few months, and who was considering work of this kind, to postpone the works until such time as the property had been vacant for a full year, so as to ensure the 100% allowance may be claimed.

6.27   Flat conversion allowances were not available for expenditure on or in connection with the acquisition of land, the extension of a qualifying building (except where to provide a means of access to or from a qualifying flat), the development of land next to a qualifying building, or the provision of furnishings or chattels (*s 393B(3)*).

6.28   Where qualifying expenditure was incurred, a first-year allowance of 100% was given. If all or part of this was disclaimed, writing-down allowances of 25% per annum were available on a straight-line basis.

6.29   Expenditure which qualified was the renovation or conversion of a 'qualifying building' into a 'qualifying flat' (see **6.25**). A 'qualifying building' was one which:

(*a*)   was built before 1 January 1980 (even if extended after that date, as long as any extension was completed before 1 January 2001);

(*b*)   where all or most of the ground floor of the qualifying building (not necessarily all of the buildings on the footprint of the site) was authorised for business use (ie within planning classes: A1 (shops), A2 (financial and professional services), A3 (food and drink), B1 (business, eg offices, laboratories and light industry) or D1 (non-residential institutions such as clinics, libraries, nurseries, and places of worship, etc);

(*c*)   when it was built the upper floors (not more than four storeys, excluding the attic unless it has been used as a dwelling) were originally intended to be used as dwellings (*s 393C*); and

(*d*)   was previously vacant, or used for storage, for a year or more (see **6.26**).

6.30   Condition (*b*) had to be satisfied *after* the works were complete. The relief was not available, for example, where retail premises were converted to residential in their entirety.

6.31   A flat is a dwelling which is a separate set of premises, forms part of a building and is divided horizontally from another part of the building (*s 393A(3)*). For these purposes, a dwelling is a building (or part of one) that is occupied, or intended to be occupied, as a separate dwelling (*s 393A(4)*). There are detailed rules as to what constitutes a 'qualifying flat' (*s 393D*). It must:

(*a*)   be in a qualifying building (see **6.29**);

(*b*)   be suitable for, and held for the purposes of, short-term letting as a dwelling (ie a lease not exceeding five years);

(*c*)   have its own entrance separate to the business part of the premises (ie not be accessed through the business ground floor); and

(*d*)   have four rooms or less (excluding bathrooms, kitchens, small closets and hallways that each do not exceed 5m² in area).

6.32   It must *not*:

● be a high-value flat (or part of a scheme involving high-value flats); and

● be let to a person connected with the person incurring the expenditure (eg a family member – see **20.25** *et seq*).

6.33   Whether or not a flat is a high-value flat is determined by reference to the following table of notional rents included in *s 393E(5)*:

No of rooms in flat	*Greater London*	*Elsewhere*
1 or 2	£350 per week	£150 per week
3	£425 per week	£225 per week
4	£480 per week	£300 per week

6.34   Balancing adjustments (allowances or charges) may arise on disposal (ie the flat is sold, or a long lease is granted, or it is demolished, or ceases to meet the qualifying conditions above). However, no balancing adjustment is made if the disposal, etc occurs more than seven years after the time when the flat was first suitable for letting as a dwelling.

6.35   A balancing allowance is denied where the proceeds of the balancing event are less than they would have been as the result of a tax avoidance scheme (*s 570A*). The provisions of *s 570A* apply for flat conversion allowances as they did for IBAs (see **12.28**).

Chapter 7

Industrial property – special features

INTRODUCTION

7.1   Expenditure on most types of building will not qualify for allowances. The main exception to this rule has historically been where the building concerned was an industrial one.

7.2   Legislation included in *Finance Act 2008* implemented the gradual phasing-out of industrial buildings allowances by April 2011. The way that this was achieved is considered fully in **7.15** *et seq*. From April 2011, however, definitions of qualifying buildings and qualifying expenditure are relevant primarily where a property is purchased second-hand and the purchaser needs to establish whether his claim for allowances on fixtures is restricted by *s 186* as a result of a previous owner having claimed industrial buildings allowances (see **4.39**).

7.3   The provisions relating to industrial buildings allowances are included, despite their abolition, as:

(i)   advisers will still be dealing with earlier years; and

(ii)   claims by new purchasers or lessees of industrial buildings will be affected by the tax history of the building.

7.4   The question of whether or not a building qualified was not governed by whether it had a broadly industrial character, but whether the use to which it was put was one of the qualifying activities specified by the legislation.

7.5   A separate system of allowances applied to agricultural buildings (see **Chapter 10**). In many ways, agricultural buildings allowances were similar to IBAs and were given in respect of expenditure on farmhouses, cottages, fences and other works. In appropriate circumstances, taxpayers could find that a claim for either type of allowance (but not both) could have been possible.

QUALIFYING EXPENDITURE

General

7.6   Industrial buildings allowances were generally given where a person incurred capital expenditure on an industrial building or structure, as defined in the legislation. The definition is considered below under **7.47** *et seq* (*s 271*).

7.7   Allowances could also be given for certain revenue expenditure incurred on trading account by a property developer or trader (see **7.37** *et seq*). This was a rare exception to the rule that capital allowances are available only for capital expenditure.

The site

7.8   No allowances were due in respect of expenditure on the acquisition of any land, or of rights in or over land (*s 272(1)*). Where land was acquired and a new building constructed, the separate cost elements were usually easy to identify. However, on a subsequent sale and purchase, any consideration would be for both the building and the site upon which it stands. In this case, the consideration would need to be justly apportioned, so as to isolate that part that qualified for allowances (*s 356(1)*).

7.9   Expenditure incurred on preparing the land so as to render it suitable for supporting a building would qualify as part of the cost of the building, eligible for allowances. Allowances would also be due on the cost of preparing, cutting, tunnelling or levelling land for the purposes of preparing the land as a site for the installation of machinery or plant where no allowance could otherwise be made (*s 273*). Of course, it would normally be preferable if such expenditure could be claimed to be incurred on the provision of the machinery or plant (see **14.110** *et seq*), thus qualifying for a higher rate of allowances.

Building alterations and repairs

7.10   Where a trader incurs capital expenditure on alterations to an existing building incidental to the installation of machinery or plant, that expenditure itself qualifies for allowances as if it were part of the machinery or plant (see **14.119**) (*s 25*). Other alterations to a qualifying building and repairs which are not allowed as trading deductions did qualify for IBAs (*s 272(2)*). In general terms, allowances were given on an improvement to a building as if the improvement were a separate building.

Demolition costs

7.11   Where a building was to be demolished, and a balancing adjustment arose in accordance with *s 314* if the person incurring the costs of demolition owned a relevant interest, the net cost of demolition was added to the residue of expenditure incurred on construction of the property (*s 340*).

7.12   Where no balancing adjustment could arise (eg if the demolished building was a non-qualifying one), the demolition cost might form part of the cost of preparing the site for a replacement building, if any.

Roads on industrial estates

7.13   Expenditure in respect of a road on an industrial estate was treated as qualifying for allowances if the estate consisted wholly or mainly of buildings that were treated as industrial buildings within the definition of *s 271* (which included 'qualifying trades' defined by *s 274* (*s 284(1)*). If a road was included in the lease of a building, it would qualify for IBAs only if that building so qualified (CA, para 32340). This applied equally to private roads on a trading estate in an enterprise zone, where the buildings were commercial buildings within the extended meaning of 'industrial' (*s 284(2)*) and also applied to roads on hotel property (see **8.32**).

7.14   HMRC's view is that if a road was taken over by a local authority, it did not qualify for IBAs because the person incurring the expenditure did not have a relevant interest (see **7.35** *et seq*). This could be overcome by proper timing of construction, use and adoption.

ALLOWANCES AVAILABLE

New buildings

7.15   Allowances are no longer available.

7.16   Prior to 1 April (corporation tax) or 6 April 2008 (income tax), a writing-down allowance (WDA) of 4% of qualifying expenditure was made where certain conditions (see **7.33**) were fulfilled (*s 310(1)*). Where the accounting period was less or more than a year, the WDA was proportionately decreased or increased (*s 310(2)*).

7.17   This 4% allowance was reduced by one-quarter in each of the four years to April 2011 (on a straight-line basis). So a business claiming 4% pa, saw this reduce to 3% from April 2008, 2% from April 2009, 1% from April

2010 and 0% from April 2011. If the property was acquired second-hand with say ten years of its 25 year IBA life left to run, such that the initial claim was 10% pa (see **7.27** *et seq*), this reduced to 7.5%, then 5%, 2.5% then nil.

7.18   These changes applied from 1 April each year for corporation tax, and 6 April for income tax. Where an accounting period overlapped these dates, the respective rates were time-apportioned. For example, a company with a September 2009 year-end was entitled to IBAs at the rate of 2.5% (6/12 × 3% plus 6/12 × 2%).

7.19   All this meant that after April 2011, any unrelieved balance of expenditure was simply written off, and would not attract tax relief, resulting in substantially increased future tax bills for affected businesses.

Example

Gordon spent £5 million on constructing a factory in 2006, expecting that the whole of this expenditure would attract tax relief via IBAs over the next 25 years. At his marginal tax rate of 40%, this would be worth £2 million over time. Instead, he began claiming allowances at the expected 4% pa, but then saw this gradually reduce to 1% for 2010/11, before allowances ceased altogether.

In April 2011, the residue of expenditure (that is the unrelieved part of the original cost) was £4.3 million, which was written off without relief. So in future years, Gordon will pay total additional tax of £1.72 million.

7.20   A key effect of the abolition of IBAs is that it is vital to maximise plant and machinery allowances, as this is the only way that many taxpayers may obtain any tax relief for expenditure on property.

7.21   It may also be beneficial to review recent years' IBA claims and where possible, re-classify expenditure from IBA treatment to plant and machinery. This is likely to be unproblematic for open tax returns (eg those still within the statutory window to amend a capital allowances claims). However, it is otherwise only possible if the property is sold, and then the claim must be based on an apportionment of the vendor's residue of expenditure (ie the tax written down value amount not written off yet).

7.22   HMRC's view (Revenue & Customs Brief 12/09) is that once a business has exercised its choice to claim one type of capital allowance rather than another, that choice may not be revisited and effectively reversed in respect of expenditure incurred in a closed year, under the old 'error or mistake' provisions (see **21.23** *et seq*). Therefore it was not permissible to submit 'error or mistake' claims to substitute claims for plant and machinery capital allowances in respect of expenditure on certain building fixtures for part of previous IBA (or ABA) claims on expenditure on the building as a whole. With effect from 1 April 2010, an error or mistake claim is no longer permitted in respect of capital allowances (see **21.23**).

7.23   If any industrial buildings writing down allowances were disclaimed in prior years it may be worth reversing these, where possible.

7.24   Also marketed were some artificial arrangements to accelerate IBAs to ensure they are claimed in full before abolition (eg using numerous group companies with different year ends and repeated intra-group sales of properties). However, these were ineffective, except in the rarest of circumstances, because of a variety of tax technical and commercial reasons. The WDAs were deducted from the cost (or in later years, the brought forward 'residue' or tax written-down value) to give a residue carried forward (*s 334*). This residue (and by extension, the previous allowances deducted) was historically important, for example when a property was sold to a second potential claimant (see **7.27** *et seq*), though with effect from 21 March 2007, the rules for claiming allowances on second-hand property were changed.

7.25   Where at any time, the relevant interest (see **7.35** *et seq*) in the building was held by the Crown or a person who is not within the charge to tax, the residue was nonetheless reduced by the allowances that would have accrued if the owner had been a taxpayer paying income tax (*s 339*).

7.26   Allowances could be disclaimed in a particular year (see **21.38**).

Second-hand buildings

7.27   Allowances are no longer available.

7.28   Before the abolition of IBAs in April 2011, the purchaser of a second-hand industrial building could claim allowances. However, the calculation of those allowances changed with effect from 21 March 2007.

Purchase on or after 21 March 2007

7.29   Where an industrial building was sold on or after 21 March 2007, the purchaser effectively 'inherited' the vendor's claim (*FA 2007, s 36*). The purchaser's claim was based on the vendor's tax written-down value (and the sale of an existing industrial building did not, as hitherto, give rise to a balancing charge or allowance – see **12.9** *et seq* and the example below).

. Purchase prior to 21 March 2007

7.30 Where an industrial building was acquired second-hand before 21 March 2007, the WDA was ascertained by taking the residue of qualifying expenditure at the date of acquisition and writing it off on a straight-line basis over the period beginning with the sale and ending with the 25th anniversary of when the building was first used (*s 311*). As with 'first-hand' buildings, allowances could be disclaimed in a particular year, thereby effectively extending the tax life of the building (see **21.38**). Where the accounting period was less or more than a year, the WDA was proportionately decreased or increased (*s 310(2)*).

7.31 The residue of expenditure (commonly called the tax written-down value) was generally the original cost, written down by net allowances given, including any balancing allowance or charge on the sale itself – see **12.9** *et seq* for details of calculation. Where, prior to 21 March 2007, a building was sold for more than original cost within 25 years of first use, all allowances given would be clawed back, such that the residue of expenditure was the same as original cost. A second-hand purchaser could never claim allowances on an amount higher than this. Where a property was acquired from a non-taxpayer, any calculation of the residue nonetheless had to be made as if the building had been owned by a taxpayer since the date of its first use (*s 339*).

Example

X Ltd built a factory at a cost of £1 million, and after claiming IBAs for 20 years, sold the factory to Y Ltd for £2 million. The residue of expenditure (tax written-down value) at that time was £200,000, ie cost of £1 million less allowances given of £800,000.

If the sale took place prior to 21 March 2007, X Ltd would have suffered a balancing charge of £800,000 (all the allowances previously given would be 'clawed back'). Y Ltd would have been able to claim IBAs based on £1 million (original cost) and allowances would have been given over five years (the unexpired potion of the 25-year 'tax life' of the factory), ie £200,000 pa.

If the sale took place on or after 21 March 2007, X Ltd would not suffer any clawback of allowances. Y Ltd would have been able to claim IBAs based only on the residue of expenditure (£200,000), at an annual rate 'inherited from X Ltd, ie £40,000 pa.

Furthermore, IBAs were abolished from April 2011, so Y Ltd's claim would be reduced to nil from that time.

7.32 Where the expenditure was incurred before 6 November 1962, the duration of the writing-down period was 50 years, rather than 25, and WDAs were at a rate of 2% pa (*Sch 3, para 66*). The purchaser of a second-hand building needed not assume, therefore, that no allowances were available merely because the building was more than 25 years old.

CONDITIONS FOR ALLOWANCES

7.33 Before April 2011, WDAs could have been claimed where three conditions were fulfilled:

(*a*)   qualifying expenditure has been incurred on a building;

(*b*)   the claimant was, at the end of a chargeable period, entitled to the 'relevant interest' (see **7.35** *et seq*) in relation to that expenditure; and

(*c*)   the building or structure was at that time an industrial building (*ss 271(3)* and *309*).

Time conditions must be met

7.34 It is worth emphasising that the conditions only needed to be met at the end of the chargeable period. Even if a building only qualified for IBAs on the last day of an accounting period, that sufficed for full allowances to be given. In extreme cases, a difference of one day in bringing a building into use (see **7.48** *et seq*) could have resulted in either an acceleration or a delay of allowances by a whole year.

RELEVANT INTEREST

7.35 A claim for IBAs in respect of any expenditure could be made only by the holder of the 'relevant interest' relating to that expenditure. When the relevant interest changed hands so did the entitlement to relief. However, it should not be thought that all transactions in a property resulted in a change to the relevant interest or its ownership. In particular, the grant of a lease out of the relevant interest did not generally cause allowances to cease, providing the building continued to be in qualifying use (but see **12.34** *et seq* regarding the realisation of a capital value).

7.36 When a person incurred expenditure on a building, his relevant interest was in essence whatever 'interest' he had in that building, at the time that the expenditure was incurred (*s 286(1)*); that is, the interest relevant to the capital allowance – there being no need to 'invent' some notional interest in the building apart from the land on which it is built (*Bostock v Totham (Inspector of Taxes)* [1997] STC 764). In the absence of a list of permissible 'interests' in land, as is specified for plant fixtures (see **11.23**), the term 'interest' was understood to take its normal legal meaning (of real estate proprietary 'interests', ie those *in rem* directed against property and capable of binding a third party purchaser, rather than those directed against a specific person). So a relevant interest could, therefore, take a variety of forms. In most circumstances the relevant interest was a recognised legal estate such as a freehold or leasehold. However, it was also possible for other 'interests' to qualify. These might include contractual rights such as licences (ie the concept of 'interested in' rather than 'interest in'). This is because although a licence is just a permission that makes it lawful to do what would otherwise be a trespass and does not in itself create an 'interest' in land (*Ashburn Anstalt v W J Arnold & Co* [1989] Ch 1), a licence to occupy would normally be legally protectable and licences may also be coupled with recognised 'interests' in land. A tenancy at will would qualify because it is a form of lease (CA, para 33040). Likewise, an equitable interest or an agreement to obtain the freehold or a lease could be the relevant interest (CA, para 33040) and it is understood that HMRC accepted a wayleave could be a relevant interest. Where the same person held more than one interest in a property, and one was reversionary upon the others, that would be the relevant interest (*s 286(3)*).

Example

Timms Ltd bought a freehold plot of land in 2005 and in the same year constructed a factory thereon. The following year, Timms granted a long lease to a pension fund in return for a significant premium. The pension fund then granted a shorter lease back to Timms.

In 2007, Timms added an extension to the factory. The relevant interest for this extension was the freehold, which was reversionary on all others (both that held by Timms and that held by the pension fund).

IBAs FOR PROPERTY DEVELOPERS AND TRADERS

Background

7.37   In certain cases, property traders could claim WDAs on industrial buildings (CA, paras 33040 and 34510). It was often assumed that no IBAs could be claimed for properties on trading account, as there was a common belief that the expenditure incurred by the claimant must be capital.

7.38   *Section 309* set out the requirements for claiming WDAs:

(*a*)   'qualifying expenditure' must have been incurred;

(*b*)   the would-be claimant had the relevant interest; and

(*c*)   at the end of the chargeable period, the building was an industrial building (ie in qualifying use, not more than 25 years old, etc).

7.39   For property traders and developers, the key requirement was the first. Qualifying expenditure is defined by *s 294* as capital expenditure incurred on the construction of a building. *Sections 295* and *296* extended allowances where a capital sum is paid to a developer. Previously, it was assumed that the present claimant must have himself incurred qualifying expenditure, so if his expenditure was not capital, no allowances would be due.

7.40   However, the precise wording of the legislation merely states the requirement that 'qualifying expenditure has been incurred on a building', ie at some time, not necessarily by the current owner. Therefore, provided someone has previously incurred capital expenditure or paid a capital sum (at any time), that condition is met.

7.41   This relates to WDAs. Consequently, a property trader or developer could identify any qualifying industrial building held on trading account, and claim industrial buildings WDAs. These at least accelerated tax relief (some or all of which could have been clawed back if the property was sold for more than the residue of expenditure, see **7.27** *et seq*) and could have been a permanent saving.

7.42   If a trader could claim WDAs, there would seem to be no reason why he should not also have been subject to the rules on balancing adjustments. Under *s 314*, a balancing adjustment was made if:

(*a*)   qualifying expenditure was incurred on a building; and

(*b*)   a balancing event occurred while the building was an industrial building or after it had ceased to be an industrial building.

7.43   Condition (*a*) is the same as for WDAs, so the availability of balancing allowances (and charges) would seem to have been confirmed. Condition (*b*) is interesting because, whereas WDAs were only given if the building remained in qualifying use, a balancing allowance could arise even if the property was vacant (provided it was still within its 'tax life').

Example

Payne, a trader, bought a factory, 20 years old, and allowed the tenant to operate it for one year before demolishing it to build houses. Payne could get WDAs for the first year, then a balancing allowance. However, he would already get a trading deduction for the cost of the factory, so a balancing allowance was only of any value if it was given in addition to the trading deduction.

7.44   The normal rule for preventing double deductions or allowances is in *s 4(2)*:

> '*Capital expenditure* and *capital sums* do not include … any expenditure or sum that may be deducted in calculating the profits or gains of a trade … or property business.'

7.45   However, as shown above, *ss 309* and *314* made no mention of capital expenditure or capital sums – that is precisely why this opportunity arose.

7.46   Therefore, it was seemingly possible for a trader to obtain a double deduction.

THE MEANING OF 'INDUSTRIAL'

General

7.47   There was no requirement that an industrial building or structure should rise above ground level; therefore, roads, car parks and yards could be eligible for allowances. The type of assets which could qualify could often in practice be deduced from *ss 21* and *22*, which define buildings and structures for the purpose of denying plant allowances.

7.48   An 'industrial building or structure' was defined by *ss 271(1)(b)*, *274* and *275* as a building or structure being in use for the purposes of one of a number of trades or activities (see *Tables A* and *B* of *s 274* below). In a sense it is therefore incorrect to speak of a 'qualifying building' as it is in fact the use to which a building was put that was either qualifying or not. It is possible to conceive of two buildings identical in construction, one of which was used as a warehouse and qualified for allowances, whilst the other was used as a retail shop (perhaps a carpet or furniture store) and attracted no allowances.

'Table A
Trades which are "Qualifying Trades"

1.   *Manufacturing* A trade consisting of manufacturing goods or materials.

2.   *Processing* A trade consisting of subjecting goods or materials to a process. This includes (subject to *s 276(3)*) maintaining or repairing goods or materials (see **7.53**).

3. *Storage* A trade consisting of storing goods or materials –

    (*a*) which are to be used in the manufacture of other goods or materials,

    (*b*) which are to be subjected, in the course of a trade, to a process,

    (*c*) which, having been manufactured or produced or subjected, in the course of a trade, to a process, have not yet been delivered to any purchaser, or

    (*d*) on their arrival in the United Kingdom from a place outside the United Kingdom.

4. *Agricultural contracting* A trade consisting of –

    (*a*) ploughing or cultivating land occupied by another,

    (*b*) carrying out any other agricultural operation on land occupied by another, or

    (*c*) threshing another's crops.

For this purpose "crops" includes vegetable produce.

5. *Working foreign plantations* A trade consisting of working land outside the United Kingdom used for –

    (*a*) growing and harvesting crops,

    (*b*) husbandry, or

    (*c*) forestry.

For this purpose "crops" includes vegetable produce and "harvesting crops" includes the collection of vegetable produce (however effected).

6. *Fishing* A trade consisting of catching or taking fish or shellfish.

7. *Mineral extraction* A trade consisting of working a source of mineral deposits.

"Mineral deposits" includes any natural deposits capable of being lifted or extracted from the earth, and for this purpose geothermal energy is to be treated as a natural deposit.

"Source of mineral deposits" includes a mine, an oil well and a source of geothermal energy.

Table B
Undertakings which are "Qualifying Trades" if carried on by way of trade

1. *Electricity* An undertaking for the generation, transformation, conversion, transmission or distribution of electrical energy.

2. *Water* An undertaking for the supply of water for public consumption.

3. *Hydraulic power* An undertaking for the supply of hydraulic power.

4. *Sewerage* An undertaking for the provision of sewerage services within the meaning of the *Water Industry Act 1991*.

5. *Transport* A transport undertaking.

6. *Highway undertakings* A highway undertaking, that is, so much of any undertaking relating to the design, building, financing and operation of roads as is carried on –

   (*a*) for the purposes of, or

   (*b*) in connection with,

the exploitation of highway concessions.

7. *Tunnels* A tunnel undertaking.

8. *Bridges* A bridge undertaking.

9. *Inland navigation* An inland navigation undertaking.

10. *Docks* A dock undertaking.

    A dock includes –

    (*a*) any harbour, and

    (*b*) any wharf, pier, jetty or other works in or at which vessels can ship or unship merchandise or passengers,

other than a pier or jetty primarily used for recreation.'

7.49   The precise activity carried on in the individual building should not be looked at in isolation. Rather, one had to consider the taxpayer's trade and overall activity in respect of which the building is used (*Blunson v West Midlands Gas Board* (1951) 33 TC 315).

7.50   In the context of deciding whether a building was used or unused, 'use' meant use for any purpose and not just for a purpose qualifying for IBAs. 'Use', however, did not include occupation by a tenant for fitting out by that tenant prior to the commencement of actual production or other use.

The fitting-out process was regarded by HMRC as merely the completion of construction (CA, para 33520).

PART OF A TRADE

7.51 It is worth observing that allowances could still be available where only part of a trade qualified. *Section 276(2)* reads:

'If a building is in use for a partly qualifying trade, allowances are only available if that building is in use for the qualifying part of the trade.'

7.52 The qualifying activity did not have to be the major part of the trade carried on. In *Kilmarnock Equitable Co-operative Society Ltd v IRC* (1966) 42 TC 675, it was held that it was necessary only to distinguish 'a definitely identifiable part of their individual operations ... a quite separate activity'. In *Girobank Plc v Clarke (Inspector of Taxes)* [1998] STC 182, the High Court held that the sorting of documents by a bank was sufficiently identifiable to be regarded as a part of a trade, however the claim failed on other grounds.

7.53 The relative size of each separate part of the trade or undertaking ought to have been irrelevant. However, it was held in *Bestway (Holdings) Ltd v Luff (Inspector of Taxes)* [1998] STC 357 that in order to be regarded as a part of a trade for this purpose, the activities in question had to be a 'significant, separate and identifiable part of the trade'. This was confirmed by Tax Bulletin 40 (April 1999) and affirmed in the House of Lords in *Maco Door & Window Hardware (UK) Ltd v Revenue and Customs Comrs* [2008] UKHL 54, which confirmed that the relevant part of the trade or undertaking must in itself be an activity in the nature of trade (ie a commercial trading activity carried out in its own right directed towards making a profit) (see **7.57**).

7.54 In *Farnell Electronic Components Ltd v HMRC Comrs* [2011] UKFTT 597 (TC), it was confirmed that to determine what a trade consists in, it is necessary to consider the composite whole of the activities involved, rather than any one or more constituent activities, however important or essential.

7.55 The question of part of a trade qualifying is considered further in the context of storage at **7.77** *et seq.*

OTHER QUALIFYING UNDERTAKINGS

7.56 Tables A and B extended IBAs to a number of activities which qualified for allowances if carried on by way of trade. Some of these activities are highly specialised, and are not considered in detail here. These were:

(*a*) water, sewerage, electricity and hydraulic power undertakings;

(*b*)   tunnel, bridge and highway and inland navigation undertakings;

(*c*)   mineral extraction;

(*d*)   catching or taking of fish or shellfish; and

(*e*)   agricultural contracting and the working of foreign plantations.

7.57   The activities most commonly met in practice will be transport and dock undertakings.

Transport undertakings

7.58   Falling under this heading was any undertaking providing commercial transport, whether of passengers or of goods. This would therefore have included a haulage company, a bus company or an airline. Also included were private rail companies and taxi firms. However, a trade which consisted of hiring out 'self-drive' vehicles would not qualify.

7.59   The provision of transport as part of wider trade could also qualify – see *Buckingham (Inspector of Taxes) v Securitas Properties Ltd* (1979) 53 TC 292, where allowances were given in respect of the vehicle service bay of a security service company.

7.60   In practice, allowances were given in respect of such premises as waiting rooms, garages or freight sheds, but not in respect of general administrative buildings or retail outlets. The question of whether a transport undertaking was ancillary to the purposes of a retail shop was considered in *Buckingham (Inspector of Taxes) v Securitas Properties Ltd* [1998] STC 938 – see **6.8**.

7.61   It was important to bear in mind the rule that where the cost of non-qualifying parts of a building was not more than one quarter of the total (the so-called 'de minimis' rule), the whole could be regarded as qualifying for allowances (*s 283(2)*) (see **7.114** *et seq*). For example, retail units at an airport terminal could well represent only a small part of the total expenditure and therefore be allowed.

Dock undertakings and inland navigation

7.62   A 'dock' included any harbour, wharf, pier or jetty or other works in or at which vessels can ship or unship merchandise or passengers (*s 274, Table B, item 10*). Excluded, however, were any piers or jetties used primarily for recreation. However, as the exclusion only extended to piers and jetties, there was sometimes scope for negotiation. Examples of expenditure qualifying under this heading included:

(*a*)   walls and floors of docks, basins, locks and gates thereto;

(*b*)   piers, breakwaters, jetties and mooring facilities, whether fixed or floating;

(*c*)   roads and other hard surfaces; and

(*d*)   buildings and structures within the dock area, together with others elsewhere specifically used for the purposes of the dock undertaking.

MANUFACTURING AND PROCESSING

General

7.63   Manufacturing and processing share many common features, and the two activities are considered together in the following paragraphs.

Manufacture

7.64   The meaning of 'manufacture' was not considered by the courts in the context of IBAs. Decided cases from other areas of the law suggested, however, that the term could be construed widely, and that manufacture did not necessarily mean the creation of an end product from raw materials. The construction of a product from component parts (or a step in such production) would be regarded as manufacture (*Prestcold (Central) Ltd v Minister of Labour* [1969] 1 All ER 69).

Goods or materials

7.65   In most cases, 'goods or materials' will be recognised for what they are. In three cases, certain items were excluded from the definition:

(i)   In *Bourne (Inspector of Taxes) v Norwich Crematorium Ltd* (1967) 44 TC 164 it was held that human remains were not 'goods or materials' and that cremation was not, therefore, the subjection of goods or materials to a process.

(ii)   Similarly, in *Buckingham (Inspector of Taxes) v Securitas (Properties) Ltd* (1979) 53 TC 292 it was held that coins and bank notes were not 'goods or materials'.

(iii)   More recently, the Court of Appeal, reversing the decision of the High Court, held that information-bearing documents were not 'goods or materials' in *Girobank Plc v Clarke* [1998] STC 182.

7.66   The interpretation of the word 'goods' in the *Securitas* case as only meaning 'merchandise or wares' was supported by Nourse LJ in *Girobank*, who derived comfort both from the commercial context of *s 274* and also from Parliament's choice of the words 'goods or materials' rather than 'goods or chattels'. Nourse LJ also thought, at least so far as the items dealt with by Girobank were concerned, that if they were not goods, then they could not be materials. However, no further explanation was given. Clearly, whether or not items qualify will depend on the context. Coins and bank notes (whether British or foreign) would be 'goods or materials' for the purpose of a trade consisting of their manufacture.

7.67   Increasingly, data is stored, transferred and analysed in electronic form, without ever being printed in hard copy. Although the point has not been tested by the courts, it is extremely unlikely that such data would have been regarded as 'goods or materials'.

7.68   In *Next Distribution Ltd, Next Group Plc and The Paige Group Ltd v HMRC Comrs* [2012] UKFTT 405 (TC), fashion and homeware 'goods' were held to be the individual items, rather than bulk deliveries of large numbers of the same item.

Subjection to a process

7.69   In *Kilmarnock Equitable Cooperative Society Ltd v IRC* (1966) 42 TC 675, it was said that the subjection of goods or materials to a process may be something other than manufacture, and still qualify for allowances. The Lord President said:

> 'An industrial building may connote something other than a place where goods or materials are manufactured: it may include … a place where goods or materials are subjected to a process which falls short of the manufacturing of a new article.'

7.70   In this particular case, the screening and bagging of coal was held to qualify as such a process. To put this in a wider context, a building used for the sorting of goods, breaking bulk, packing and so on could therefore have qualified for IBAs.

7.71   A process ought certainly not have been thought of as something restricted to heavy industry. Examples of other processes qualifying for relief included:

(*a*)   cleaning and bagging of coal;

(*b*)   breeding rodents for experimental purposes;

(*c*)   developing and printing photographs;

(*d*)   cutting steel tubes to customers' requirements;

(*e*)   cutting and binding carpets to customers' requirements;

(*f*)   sorting of rags, scrap metal, etc;

(*g*)   preparation of pre-packed cooked meals;

(*h*)   cleaning, sorting and pre-packing fruit and vegetables;

(*i*)   ripening fruit (after picking, not while still growing);

(*j*)   egg packing;

(*k*)   tea or coffee blending;

(*l*)   wine bottling;

(*m*)   whisky blending;

(*n*)   car servicing (unless part of a retail shop – see **7.105**);

(*o*)   fitting tyres and exhausts (unless part of a retail shop – see **7.105**);

(*p*)   packaging and breaking bulk, assuming uniformity of treatment;

(*q*)   shrink wrapping; and

(*r*)   seed cleaning.

7.72   This list is indicative of the type and range of activities that did qualify; there were many others.

7.73   In *Bestway (Holdings) Ltd v Luff (Inspector of Taxes)* [1998] STC 357, the term 'process' was not extended to activities which were merely preliminary to sale, and which in isolation were 'limited, mundane and of no substantial significance'. In contrast, *obiter dicta* in *Buckingham (Inspector of Taxes) v Securitas Properties Ltd* (1979) 53 TC 292 suggested that the cleaning of antique coins in preparation for sale would be regarded as a process. There are conflicting authorities on the necessity for a process to change the goods in some way. On balance, the absence of any physical change did not prevent an activity from being a 'process'. This may have enabled IBAs to be claimed, for example, on buildings used for quality control.

7.74   In *Bestway*, Lightman J said that since the word 'process' was used in the legislation in conjunction with the words 'manufacture' and 'production', a uniform treatment or system of treatment of some real significance was postulated.

7.75   In *Next Distribution Ltd, Next Group Plc and The Paige Group Ltd v HMRC Comrs* [2012] UKFTT 405 (TC), the work done was essentially ancillary (ie, unloading, checking, holding, labelling, transporting and dispatch) and overall nothing was physically done to most of the goods: 'we do not consider that attaching an address label (whether physical or electronic) is sufficient'. Because the individual fashion and homeware goods remained unchanged, they were not subjected to a process.

Repairing

7.76 The reference to the subjection of goods or materials to a process included the maintaining or repairing of goods or materials (*s 274, Table A, item 2*). However, where those goods or materials were used in the repairer's trade, one had to examine whether that trade itself qualified for IBAs. The expression 'used in a trade' probably connoted that the assets were held as fixed assets, rather than trading stock.

STORAGE OF GOODS OR MATERIALS

General

7.77 Four particular types of storage qualified under *s 274, Table A, item 3*. These were:

(*a*)   the storage of goods or materials which are to be used in the manufacture of other goods or materials;

(*b*)   the storage of goods or materials which are to be subjected, in the course of a trade, to any process;

(*c*)   the storage of goods or materials which, having been manufactured or produced or subjected, in the course of trade, to any process, have not yet been delivered to any purchaser; and

(*d*)   the storage of goods or materials on their arrival in the United Kingdom from a place outside the United Kingdom.

7.78 In each case, to qualify for allowances, the storage activity had to constitute a trade. For many years, HMRC held the view that qualifying storage could not be merely an incidental part of another trade (eg wholesaling or retailing). Either storage had to constitute the only trade (ie the storage of goods on behalf of the owners of the goods for a fee), or it should be a separable part of the trade (capable perhaps of being contracted out on a commercial basis). In the 1951 case *Dale (Inspector of Taxes) v Johnson Bros* (1951) 32 TC 487, which the claimant lost because it held the goods as purchaser, Sheil J stated: 'it will not do that the trade is storage plus something else or something else plus storage. It must simply be a keeping or custody.'

7.79   This view appeared to be in contradiction of *s 276* (see **7.51** *et seq*). In *Bestway (Holdings) Ltd v Luff (Inspector of Taxes)* [1998] STC 357, it was held that storage in this context referred to a form of warehousing, and not merely the storage that any wholesaler wants for his goods. The court rejected the taxpayer's claim that storage should be taken to mean 'keeping in reserve for future use or disposal'. Lightman J found that the key factor was the purpose for which the goods are stored – storage must be an end in itself, and not merely incidental to some other purpose, such as sale. This was confirmed by Tax Bulletin 40 (April 1999) and led HMRC to believe that a wholesaler could never claim IBAs (although a warehouse or store might qualify under another heading, for example because it was used for the purposes of a manufacturing trade, even if the storage was not an end in itself).

7.80   The *Bestway* decision was initially contradicted by the Special Commissioners' decision in *Maco Door & Window Hardware (UK) Ltd v Revenue and Customs Comrs* [2005] SWTI 1996, where it was held that expenditure incurred to build a wholesale warehouse used to store window and door hardware qualified for IBAs. This was because the Commissioners found as a fact that the building was used for storage and part of the taxpayer's trade consisted in storage. In the Special Commissioner's view *Bestway* did not automatically prevent any wholesaler from claiming IBAs and, because the taxpayer had to hold stock in excess of its immediate needs, the building was used for storage. Furthermore, a company's trade may include different activities (ie be a 'composite' trade) and because it was necessary that it had to store products, storage was a separate part of the company's trade (*s 276*).

7.81   This view was subsequently upheld by the Court of Appeal [2007] All ER (D) 183 (June) (reversing the decision of the High Court [2006] EWHC 1832 (Ch)), but overturned by the House of Lords in *Maco Door and Window Hardware (UK) Ltd v Revenue and Customs Comrs* [2008] UKHL 54. It was held that that although as a matter of ordinary language the goods were clearly 'stored', the expenditure did not qualify for IBAs, because to qualify any storage must itself be an activity in the nature of trade (ie a commercial trading activity carried out in its own right and directed towards making a profit) that is 'significant, separate and identifiable'. In this context physical separation was of no consequence; commercial separation was the key, and Maco's storage was simply carried out to support its wholesale trading operation and not as a trading activity in itself.

7.82   In *Saxone, Lilley & Skinner (Holdings) Ltd v IRC* (1967) 44 TC 122, it was considered appropriate to look at the use to which the building was put, rather than at the general trade carried on by the claimant. The most important case on this subject, however, is *Crusabridge Investments Ltd v Casings International Ltd* (1979) 54 TC 246, where it was held that the claimant need not carry on a trade of storage nor even a trade qualifying under another heading, provided that some part of the trade consisted of a qualifying storage activity, and the building in question was used for that part of the trade. The same case confirmed that, if a claim is in respect of storage of goods which are to be subjected to any process, the storage and the processing need not be carried on by the same person.

Example

Askham operated as a manufacturer and wholesaler of electrical goods. He occupied two warehouses. Warehouse A was used for the storage of electrical components which were to be used in the manufacture, by Askham, of televisions and radios. Warehouse B was used to store compact disc players, which Askham did not have the technology to manufacture himself. The machines were therefore held in Warehouse B only until sold to customers.

Warehouse A qualified as an industrial building by virtue of its use to store goods or materials (ie components) to be used in the manufacture of other goods or materials (ie electrical products). Warehouse B, on the other hand, did not qualify. It was used for the storage of finished goods, but these goods had been delivered to a purchaser, ie Askham. The fact that the whole trade was not a qualifying one did not preclude allowances for Warehouse A. In contrast, Warehouse B did not attract allowances because it was not itself used for the qualifying part of the trade.

Askham would have been well advised to reconsider his warehousing policy. He might have found it feasible to store both his manufactured and bought-in goods indiscriminately throughout both warehouses. He might then have been able to take advantage of the decision in *Saxone, Lilley & Skinner*, also discussed at **7.125** and **Appendix 4**.

Imported goods storage

7.83   In order to have qualified, it was originally the case that a warehouse for imported goods need not necessarily have been in the immediate vicinity of a port or airport (or indeed the Channel Tunnel). The acid test was whether the goods were being stored for the first time in the United Kingdom, and were still in transit and had not, therefore, reached their final destination. This was put forward in *Copol Clothing Co Ltd v Hindmarch (Inspector of Taxes)* (1983) 57 TC 575, and confirmed by HMRC Instructions.

7.84   *Finance Act 1995* added the requirement that storage had to be on the goods' arrival 'in any part of the United Kingdom from a place outside' the UK. This requirement was deemed always to have effect. In *Next Distribution Ltd, Next Group Plc and The Paige Group Ltd v HMRC Comrs* [2012] UKFTT

405 (TC), it was concluded that 'arrival' connoted the act or instance of reaching a place (in this instance, the UK). This had to be given a pragmatic meaning in the context of each case and did not solely mean when goods came into territorial waters or UK airspace. Goods arrived by ship and were then transported by road or rail to storage facilities about 200 miles away. This was held not to be storage on arrival in the UK.

7.85   Note that the place of storage needed not to be a warehouse in the conventional sense – the 'goods' may have arrived by pipeline and been stored in tanks.

Delivery

7.86   It can be seen that the concept of delivery could have been important in deciding whether certain stores and warehouses qualified for allowances. Delivery may have been something less than actual physical delivery. One important factor was the passing of title and it may have been that delivery merely implied the 'making available' to a purchaser of the goods or materials. In *Dale (Inspector of Taxes) v Johnson Bros* (1951) 32 TC 487, goods were delivered to a selling agent and title passed. It was held that the agent did fall within the term 'any purchaser' in *s 274, Table A, item 3(c)*, and IBAs were therefore not available.

STAFF WELFARE FACILITIES

7.87   The term 'industrial building or structure' included any building or structure provided by the person carrying on a qualifying trade or undertaking for the welfare of workers employed in that trade or undertaking and in use for that purpose (*s 275*). Note, however, that a landlord could not claim relief for expenditure in respect of his tenants or their employees. Examples of qualifying buildings included:

(*a*)   canteens;

(*b*)   crèches or day nurseries;

(*c*)   garages;

(*d*)   sports facilities (eg a hard tennis court or indoor sports hall);

(*e*)   hostels (CA, para 32320);

(*f*)   rest rooms;

(*g*)   car parks;

(*h*)   social clubs; and

(*i*)   medical facilities.

7.88   Where the person providing the welfare facilities was carrying on a trade which qualified in part for IBAs, then only the welfare facilities used wholly or partly by employees in that part of the trade would have qualified for allowances (CA, para 32320).

7.89   So, if a business with a manufacturing operation and a retail shop provided separate canteens for the employees in each, only the one used by the factory workers would attract allowances. It would have been best in such circumstances to allow all employees to visit either canteen. Provided there were no separate areas set aside for either factory or shop workers, the canteens should have qualified in full, by virtue of *Saxone, Lilley & Skinner (Holdings) Ltd v IRC* (1967) 44 TC 122 (see **7.125**).

7.90   A building which was sometimes used by outsiders (ie non-employees) would nonetheless qualify for allowances if it was provided for the welfare of workers (CA, para 32320). HMRC suggested that a shop provided by an employer for his workers could not attract IBAs, because *s 277* denied allowances to retail shops (CA, para 32320). However, the long-standing definition of a shop is 'a place where facilities are offered and to which the general public can resort for the satisfaction of their wants and needs' (*Turpin v Assessment Committee for Middlesbrough Assessment Area* [1931] AC 446). A shop which is open only to employees of a particular business could not be said to be open to the general public. HMRC also claimed that office staff and management were not 'workers' and that welfare facilities provided for them could not therefore qualify (CA, para 32320). However, this point did not seem to be taken in practice.

Sports pavilions

7.91   Allowances were given where a building was occupied by a person carrying on a trade and used as a sports pavilion for the welfare of employees (*ss 271(1)* and *280*). At first sight, sports pavilions appeared to be another example of welfare facilities (see **7.87** *et seq*) but the important difference was that sports pavilions attracted allowances regardless of the nature of the trade, unlike welfare facilities where the trade had to be one qualifying for IBAs. However, the allowance was not extended to those carrying on a profession or vocation.

7.92   The important factor was not the original design or intended purpose of the building but the use to which it is put. HMRC's view was that a 'sports pavilion' should:

(*a*)   be by a playing field, pitch or track; and

(*b*)   exist primarily for the convenience of the players (rather than the spectators) for changing, bathing, waiting for their turn to compete, etc.

7.93 Social clubs, therefore, would not normally have qualified as sports pavilions. However, if the club was close to, say, a tennis court or bowling green and provided any of the facilities referred to in (*b*) above, a claim might have been possible in respect of expenditure apportioned to the qualifying parts. Alternatively, social clubs may have been staff welfare facilities (see **7.87**).

7.94 Note that it was at least doubtful whether the term 'sports pavilion' included buildings where the sport actually took place, for example squash courts or pool or snooker rooms. HMRC did not generally draw a distinction.

7.95 Normally, occupation by the trader was a prerequisite for claiming IBAs. However, it was understood that where a trader contributed towards a sports pavilion owned by another person, allowances were given. Where the 'other person' was a public or local authority, the allowance was given to the trader where use by the trader, his staff, etc was reasonably commensurate with the level of the contribution.

NON-QUALIFYING BUILDINGS

General

7.96 A number of types of building were excluded from qualifying for industrial buildings allowances (*s 277*). These included buildings and structures in use as, or as part of, any of the following:

(*a*)   a dwelling-house;

(*b*)   a retail shop;

(*c*)   a showroom;

(*d*)   a hotel (subject to special rules for 'qualifying hotels' – see **8.4**);

(*e*)   an office.

7.97 A building was also ineligible for allowances if it was used for any purpose ancillary to the purposes of a dwelling-house, retail shop, showroom, hotel or office.

7.98 HMRC confirmed that, based upon the Kilmarnock decision, a building could only be ancillary to one purpose. This meant that if a building was used for two purposes it was not in use for purposes ancillary to either. For example, a wholesale distribution warehouse that supplied goods to retail shops owned by a connected person and to arm's-length customers was not in use for purposes ancillary to either (CA, para 32313).

7.99 This is examined further, in connection with retail shops at **6.13**.

Dwelling-houses

7.100   As stated above, expenditure on dwelling-houses did not qualify for IBAs. This remained true when the dwelling-house was situated in an enterprise zone, in contrast to expenditure on hotels, offices, etc.

7.101   'Dwelling-house' was not defined for IBA purposes. In the case of *Riley v Read* (1879) 1 TC 217, the meaning of 'to dwell' was described, albeit in another context, as 'to live in a house; that is, to live there day and night; to sleep there during the night, and to occupy it for the purposes of life during the day'.

7.102   For many years, HMRC stated that a dwelling-house was a building, or part of a building, which was a person's home. It included a person's second or holiday home, but did not include accommodation used for holiday letting or as a university hall of residence, hospital, nursing home or prison. Nor was a block of flats a dwelling-house, although the individual flats may have been (CA, para 11520). Consequently, allowances could have been available for plant in communal areas, and for lifts, air conditioning equipment, and so on.

7.103   In relation to capital expenditure incurred on or after 22 October 2010, HMRC's published view changed, such that the distinctive characteristic of a dwelling-house was its ability to afford to those who use it all the facilities required for day-to-day private domestic existence (*Gravesham Borough Council v Secretary of State for the Environment* (1982) 47 P&CR 142) (see also **15.125** *et seq*).

Retail shops

7.104   A retail shop included any premises of a similar character where retail trade or business (including repair work) was carried on (*s 277(1)*). The question of whether a particular building was to be regarded as a retail shop (or as ancillary to a retail shop) is considered in **6.1** *et seq.*

7.105   The reference above to 'repair work' would extend the definition to include garages. A vehicle repair workshop was considered to fall within *s 274, Table A, item 1* or 2, but was normally excluded from an allowance by *s 277(1)*, as being in use as, or for purposes ancillary to, a retail shop. However, in an agreement with the Motor Trade Association, HMRC indicated that it would accept a workshop as an industrial building where:

(*a*)   it was completely separated from the rest of the motor dealer's premises;

(*b*)   it did not include the reception area for motor cars; and

(*c*)   access to it by the public was discouraged (CA, para 32221).

7.106 Subsequent HMRC Guidance (CA, para 32221) substituted the word 'prohibited' for 'discouraged', thereby misrepresenting the actual agreement.

7.107 Allowances would not be refused because the workshop was not physically separated from showrooms, offices, etc. Unless the whole building was occupied for a non-qualifying purpose, for example showrooms, allowances may have been given where the workshop occupied a distinguishable part of the building which was not used to any substantial extent for purposes other than vehicle repair.

7.108 Where the workshop was used partly but not mainly for a non-qualifying purpose, for example the storage of parts or accessories sold in the retail part of the business or partly but not mainly for a purpose ancillary to the purposes of a retail shop (eg the preliminary inspection and preparation of cars for sale in the showroom) a proportionate part of the allowance may have been given. Where, however, a non-qualifying use was less than one-quarter of the total use, no restriction was made (*s 283(2)*) (see **7.114** *et seq*).

Showrooms

7.109 Showrooms were generally excluded from being regarded as industrial buildings, irrespective of whether they were used for retail or wholesale purposes. There appeared to be no authority as to what constituted a showroom, and dictionary definitions were not always helpful. In *Bestway (Holdings) Ltd v Luff (Inspector of Taxes)* [1997] STC (SCD) 87, the Commissioners stated: 'In the last resort the decision as to what is and what is not a showroom must be one of impression.' The same might also apply for other types of premises where legal authority is lacking, for example, a mill or office. In many cases, such as in the motor trade, it is impossible to distinguish between a showroom and a retail shop.

7.110 Whether or not a room was a 'showroom' was a matter of degree. The display of a manufacturer's wares in a reception area did not change the nature of that room into a showroom.

7.111 In many cases, the problem was avoided because expenditure on the 'showroom' part of such a building was not more than 25% of the total, and therefore fell to be allowed by virtue of *s 283(2)* (see **7.114** *et seq*).

Hotels

7.112 Hotels in general were outside the definition of an industrial building, but expenditure incurred on a 'qualifying hotel' after 11 April 1978 did qualify for relief under *s 271(1)(b)(ii)* (see **8.4**).

Offices

7.113 Offices did not generally qualify for IBAs, although there were exceptions, notably where the office, rather than merely being the seat of administration, was closely linked to a manufacturing or other qualifying process. A drawing office or sorting office would often qualify for IBAs in this way. Of course, it was open to debate whether either was really an 'office' in the first place. A more complete consideration of this question is set out in **5.1** *et seq.*

De minimis exception

7.114 Where part of a building qualified for IBAs and part did not, allowances were given on the whole cost of the building providing the expenditure incurred in respect of the non-qualifying part was not more than 25% of the total expenditure on the building (the so-called 'de minimis' rule) (*s 283(2)*). Before 16 March 1983, the appropriate percentage was 10%.

7.115 It was important to remember that cost was the deciding factor: some claimants fell into the trap of looking instead at floor space. A calculation based on floor space may have sometimes been an acceptable substitute for one based on cost, but it should not have been assumed that the two calculations would always give the same result due, for example, to office and other areas being fitted out to different specifications. Where expenditure on the non-qualifying part of a building exceeded 25% of the total, allowances were given only on the expenditure incurred in respect of the qualifying part (*ss 283(2) and 571(1)*).

Example

Bailey, who carried on a manufacturing trade, constructed two new buildings in the year ended 31 December 2006. Details were as follows:

	Building A	*Building B*
Total cost (£m)	5.0	8.0
Office cost (£m)	1.0	2.5
Total area (sq ft)	15,000	20,000
Office area (sq ft)	5,000	5,000

Allowances given were based on expenditure of:

(*a*) building A: £5 million (non-qualifying expenditure was not more than 25% of the total);

(*b*) building B: £5.5 million (non-office part only).

Separate building or extension?

7.116   In general terms, it was possible to obtain allowances on, say, an office by adding it on to an existing (qualifying) building, rather than constructing a new, separate building just a few feet away. This depended, however, on the expenditure on the office not being more than 25% of the total cost of the shop and the existing building. This would usually only be the case if the existing building was itself relatively large or not very old. Even a small extension was, at recent prices, likely to cost in excess of 25% of the total, if the original building was constructed many years ago.

7.117   There was no real definition of what constituted a separate building either in statute or case law. The question of what was a 'unified structure' was considered in *Lancashire Electric Power Co v Wilkinson* (1947) 28 TC 427.

7.118   The most regularly quoted case was *Abbott Laboratories Ltd v Carmody (Inspector of Taxes)* (1968) 44 TC 569. Here the taxpayer had constructed four buildings on a 53-acre site, which were treated as a single unit for the purposes of rates and, up to 1962/63, for Schedule A (property) income tax. One block, used solely for administration and not in itself qualifying for IBAs, was connected to another block by a covered passage. In view of this, the company claimed that the two blocks should be treated as one building for IBA purposes. This contention was not accepted by the courts, which ruled that no allowances could therefore be given for expenditure on the administration block by taking advantage of the *de minimis* rule. It was held that on the particular facts of the case, the administration block was not sufficiently physically integrated with the other structural units. This did not necessarily apply in every case.

7.119   Other cases, however, conflicted with this decision. In an Irish case, *O'Conaill v Waterford Glass Ltd* (1982) TL(I) 122 expenditure on a separate building housing a computer was held to qualify for allowances, as the computer installation existed to serve the other parts of an industrial complex. Under the Irish equivalent of the *de minimis* rule, the whole complex was treated as one building.

7.120   Following the *Abbott Laboratories* case, it was often assumed that buildings connected by covered walkways were always regarded as separate buildings. This was not necessarily so. The precise circumstances of the case had to be looked at. In *Cadbury Bros Ltd v Sinclair (Inspector of Taxes)* (1933) 18 TC 157, it was held that a block containing dining facilities and changing rooms, connected by bridges and walkways to a factory, was rightly treated as a single part of an entire complex. However, the reader should be aware that this case considerably pre-dated the introduction of IBAs as we knew them. Key features for a successful claim on this basis may have included:

(*a*)   a common power supply, water supply or heating system;

(*b*)   the fact that one part could not be demolished without seriously damaging the other parts; and

(*c*)   the impossibility (legally or practically) of selling one part without the others.

7.121   It should be noted that even if a number of buildings were accepted as forming single composite premises, the view of HMRC was that each building must individually satisfy the 25% *de minimis* rule (see **7.114** *et seq*) in order to qualify for allowances (CA, para 32750). A block used wholly for administration would fail to attract IBAs, even if its size and cost were minimal compared to the whole site. In such circumstances, allowances might be obtained by moving some qualifying activities to the administration block, with some administrative functions moved to 'qualifying' buildings (provided that did not infringe the *de minimis* rule).

Successive extensions

7.122   When extensions or alterations caused the non-qualifying expenditure on a building to exceed 25% of the total for the first time, no adjustment was required to be made in respect of allowances given in earlier periods. A new *de minimis* calculation had to be made following each incurral of expenditure.

Example

Smith Ltd, which made up its accounts to 31 December each year, operated from a single building, which it built and extended as follows:

	Factory £	*Office* £	*Total* £
Construction			
1 April 1995	80,000	20,000	100,000
Extension			
30 June 1998	–	10,000	10,000
	80,000	30,000	110,000
Extension			
4 July 2004	25,000	5,000	30,000
	105,000	35,000	140,000

The effect was:

Accounting periods	Non-qualifying percentage	
1995–1997	20%	The whole of the expenditure qualified for IBAs
1998–2003	27%	Only the expenditure on the factory qualified
From 2004	25%	The whole of the expenditure qualified as the non-industrial part was 'not more than' one-quarter of the whole

Impact of mixed claims

7.123   Due to the generally higher rate of allowance available, it was normally advisable to claim as much expenditure as possible as plant, rather than as an industrial building. However, if the plant claim was particularly successful, there may have been an adverse impact on the *de minimis* calculation.

Example

Barnes incurred expenditure of £100,000 on an industrial building, of which £24,000 related to an office. IBAs were available on the whole of the expenditure, as the non-qualifying part was less than 25%. Allowances were therefore at a rate of up to £4,000 pa (assuming 4% WDAs before IBAs were phased out).

It then occurred to Barnes that expenditure totalling £8,000 (treated as industrial) could validly have been said to be in respect of items of plant, and he notified HMRC of this. However, the net cost of the building was now £92,000, and the non-qualifying part now exceeded 25%. The expenditure, therefore, had to be apportioned, and although overall allowances were higher in early years, £24,000 of the expenditure would never be relieved at all.

Duality of purpose

7.124   It was possible, of course, for a building as a whole to be in use for a number of purposes, one (or more) of which qualified for IBAs, whilst the others did not.

7.125   Following the case of *Saxone, Lilley & Skinner (Holdings) Ltd v IRC* (1967) 44 TC 122, it was established that in such circumstances, allowances were available on the whole building provided the extent of the qualifying use was not negligible. To paraphrase Lord Reid in that case, the legislation referred only to 'use for the purposes of a trade' – it did not say 'wholly or mainly in use for the purposes of a trade'. Qualifying use was regarded by HMRC as being negligible if it was less than 10% of the total use (CA, para 32315). This only applied where the part of a building used for a non-qualifying purpose was not separately identifiable. Thus, in the *Saxone, Lilley & Skinner* case, a warehouse was used to store shoes, one-third of which came within *s 274, Table A, item 3(c)*: the storage of goods or materials 'which, having been manufactured or produced ... have not yet been delivered to any purchaser'. The remaining two-thirds of the shoes stored had been bought from third parties and were being stored prior to delivery to retail shops. The predominant use of the warehouse, therefore, did not qualify for allowances. However, because 'qualifying' goods were stored throughout the whole building, the whole building was in use for a qualifying purpose. Any taxpayer who occupied a building for purposes which did not all qualify for allowances would need to ensure, if he could, that the qualifying and non-qualifying areas were not physically segregated.

Example

Wells carried on a trade falling into two parts. Buildings used for activity A would qualify for IBAs; those used for activity B would not. Wells incurred expenditure on two buildings used as follows:

	Building 1	*Building 2*
Cost	£4m	£4m
Percentage qualifying use	30%	40%

Building 1 contained a separate area dedicated to the non-qualifying use, unlike building 2 where both activities were carried out alongside each other. Allowances would have been given as follows.

Building 1 clearly divided into two parts – one qualified, the other did not. In such circumstances, it was necessary to apportion the expenditure incurred between the two parts. If the apportioned cost of the non-qualifying part exceeded 25%, no allowances in respect of it were given (see **7.116** *et seq* regarding the *de minimis* rule under *s 283(2)*). Let us assume (for the purposes of this example only) that the expenditure incurred in respect of the non-qualifying part of the building was in proportion to the intended use (ie 30%). Allowances would then only have been given for the remaining 70%, ie £2.8 million.

Building 2 did not have any parts used only for non-qualifying purposes. Instead, the whole building could have been said to be used for a qualifying purpose, albeit alongside a non-qualifying purpose. As a result, allowances would be given on the whole of the expenditure, ie £4 million.

7.126 It should be noted that, as a result of these rules, the greater allowances would have been given in respect of the building with the greater non-qualifying use. Such possibilities should have been considered when planning a building to be used for more than one purpose. In the example above, we referred to the qualifying percentage. This was normally thought of in terms of, say, floor space, but could equally have been calculated on a time or usage basis.

Practical steps to strengthen the claim for allowances

7.127 Where businesses operated at least partly from industrial premises which supplied retail shops, certain steps were advisable to strengthen the claim for allowances:

(*a*) Physical separation. If possible, the 'industrial' and the 'retail' activities should have been carried on from different premises, with no physical link between them. If the cost of the retail premises was less than 25% of the cost of the retail and industrial premises combined, it would be better to group the two in a single building (see **7.116** *et seq*). As was stated in the agreement with the Motor Trade Association referred to at **7.105**, the public should not have had access to any building or part of a building deemed to be industrial.

(*b*) Legal separation. It would have been of some assistance to the claimant if the 'industrial' and the 'retail' operations were carried out by separate legal entities, for example two different companies, albeit in the same group.

7.128 It must be stressed, however, that such steps in themselves did not guarantee the granting of allowances. In addition, such reorganisations of buildings or companies involved issues (and costs) beyond the scope of this book. Capital allowances should never be considered in isolation.

NON-INDUSTRIAL USE

General

7.129 A building would only have qualified for IBAs in an accounting period if it was in use for one of the prescribed purposes at the end of that accounting period (*s 309(1)(c)*). For a building which would generally be considered an industrial building, there were three circumstances when the building would not have been in qualifying use:

(*a*) where a building had been completed, but was yet to be used for any purpose;

(*b*) where a building was, at the end of an accounting period, in use for a non-qualifying purpose; or

(*c*) where a building was in temporary disuse.

7.130 Each of these sets of circumstances had a different impact on the capital allowances computation.

Buildings yet to be used for any purpose

7.131 The 25-year life of an industrial building only began to elapse (and WDAs were only available) when the building was brought into use. Note that for agricultural buildings, this was not the case (see **10.20**). Thus, if the construction and fitting out of an industrial building took more than one year, allowances (other than initial allowances) could not be claimed in the first year. This was a disadvantage for most taxpayers, however in most cases the delay was only a temporary one. This provision was necessary to ensure that allowances were not given to taxpayers who had no real intention of using the building for a qualifying purpose.

7.132 A positive aspect, however, was that there is no requirement to account for 'notional' WDAs, as there was in the case of buildings in use for other than a qualifying purpose (see **7.133**).

Building used for a non-qualifying purpose

7.133 If a building was, at the end of an accounting period, in use for a purpose which did not attract IBAs, then it was necessary to deduct from the written-down value notional WDAs (*s 336*). These notional allowances reduced the residue of expenditure that may be carried forward, and hence reduced the total allowances that may be claimed in future. However, the notional allowances themselves could not be treated in such a way as to give relief from tax.

Example

East Ltd began to construct a building in its year ended 31 December 1996. The building was completed by September 1997, but was only brought into use as a warehouse (qualifying for IBAs) in March 1998. Expenditure on the building was as follows:

	Amount
	£'000
Year ended 31 December 1996	500
Year ended 31 December 1997	1,500

From June 2002 to September 2003, East used the building as a retail shop, before reverting to its original use. Allowances were available as follows:

Year ended 31 December 1996	
Expenditure	500
Allowances (nil as not yet brought into use)	–
Carried forward	500
Year ended 31 December 1997	
Brought forward	500
Expenditure	1,500
	2,000
Allowances (nil, as still not brought into use)	–
	2,000
Year ended 31 December 1998	
Brought forward	2,000
Allowances (4% – now in use for the first time)	(80)
Carried forward	1,920
Year ended 31 December 1999–2001	
Brought forward	1,920
Allowances (3 × 4% of £2 million)	(240)
Carried forward	1,680
Year ended 31 December 2002	
Brought forward	1,680
Allowances (Note: this allowance was notional only and could not be offset against profits)	(80)
	1,600
Year ended 31 December 2003	
Brought forward	1,600
Allowance	(80)
	1,520

7.134   It is worth pointing out that 'real' allowances were available to reduce profits, despite the fact that for most of the year the building was not in use for a qualifying purpose. The use of a building at the end of the relevant period was the only criterion which decided the availability of allowances. The existence of a period of non-qualifying use would, however, affect the calculation of a balancing allowance or charge (see **12.21** *et seq*). If a building was first used for a non-qualifying purpose before subsequently being brought into use for a qualifying purpose, the qualifying expenditure must have been reduced by notional allowances in respect of that earlier period of non-qualifying use.

Building let partly to a non-qualifying licensee

7.135   Where a building or structure was used by more than one licensee of the same person, it would not be regarded as 'industrial' for the purposes of allowances unless each of the licensees used the building (or that part of it to which the licence relates) for a qualifying trade (*s 278*). This would appear in the first instance to deny allowances for expenditure on a building where even one licensee used it for a non-qualifying purpose. However, the precise treatment depended on the circumstances (CA, para 32350). Either there would be completely mixed use of the building, with no part of it used exclusively for non-qualifying trades, or each licensee would use an identifiable part of the building. If the former applied, *s 278* would deny any relief. In some ways, this was *Saxone, Lilley & Skinner* (see **7.125**) in reverse. If the latter applied, it was necessary to look at the separate identifiable parts of the building. Allowances would be given in respect of (apportioned) expenditure on those parts of the building used for a qualifying trade. If the non-qualifying parts were not more than 25% of the whole, allowances were given on the whole of the expenditure by virtue of *s 283(2)*.

Temporary disuse

7.136   An industrial building did not cease to be regarded as such simply by reason of temporary disuse (ie not being used for any purpose whatsoever) (*s 285*). During a period of temporary disuse, therefore, WDAs continued to be given as normal. Note, however, that this was only the case where the period of disuse was preceded by a period of qualifying use.

7.137   Temporary disuse differed from non-qualifying use in that, where the disuse was only temporary, the allowances given were not merely notional, and could be set against profits in the normal way.

7.138 If, during a period of temporary disuse, there occurred any of the events set out in *s 315* then a balancing charge or allowance would be made in the normal manner. A balancing charge was to be taxed under the *Income Tax (Trading and Other Income) Act 2005* (*ITTOIA 2005*), *Pt 2* (income tax) or as property business profits (corporation tax).

Chapter 8

Hotels – special features

INTRODUCTION

8.1   As a rule, hotels offer a much greater scope for capital allowances claims than most other types of building. This is due largely to four reasons:

(*a*) Hotels are often rich in plant of a type integral to the building. This is discussed in more detail in **Chapter 16**, but typical examples will be:

    (i) lifts;

    (ii) air-conditioning;

    (iii) heating;

    (iv) sanitary equipment;

    (v) signs;

    (vi) fire detection equipment.

    For expenditure incurred on or after 1 or 6 April 2008, items falling within (i), (ii) and (iii) will be treated as integral features (see **14.5** *et seq*).

(*b*) Hotels will often include other assets which are not generally found in other buildings, and which will be regarded as plant in their own right, without applying any special principles. For example:

    (i) swimming pools;

    (ii) gymnasium equipment;

    (iii) laundry equipment.

(*c*) Hotels can claim plant allowances on a whole variety of assets aimed at creating an ambience (eg works of art, bric-a-brac). Such a claim would not be possible in, for example, an office (see **8.2**).

(*d*) Hotels of a certain type *used to* qualify for IBAs (though this relief was abolished from April 2011) (see **8.4**). Although IBAs no longer exist, a purchaser of a hotel may find that his claim for plant allowances will be restricted by IBAs claimed (*s 186* – see **4.39**). The former IBA rules are therefore outlined from **8.4** below, as it will be helpful for a purchaser to understand whether the hotel may previously have qualified for IBAs.

AMBIENCE

8.2 Nothing in the statute expressly permits assets to be regarded as plant for capital allowances purposes simply because they contribute to creating a certain ambience or atmosphere. Rather, the eligibility of such assets is an extension of general principles, as set out in the case of *IRC v Scottish & Newcastle Breweries Ltd* (1982) 55 TC 252, where the taxpayer, carrying on the trade of a hotelier, incurred significant expenditure on lighting and decor (such as murals and sculptures) in its licensed premises. These items were successfully claimed as plant. The Special Commissioners found that the company's trade was not just the provision of food and accommodation, but also the creation of atmosphere or ambience, conducive to attracting custom. The importance of attracting custom had already been shown to be relevant for plant allowances purposes in the case of a swimming pool in *Cooke (Inspector of Taxes) v Beach Station Caravans Ltd* [1974] STC 402, which was found to perform the active function of attracting visitors to a caravan park. The Special Commissioners' view in *Scottish & Newcastle Breweries* was ultimately upheld in the House of Lords. In consequence of this decision, decorative items in hotels, restaurants and 'similar trades' (*s 23, List 3*) (eg public houses) may qualify as plant. The same items would not, of course, be plant if purchased by anyone carrying on a trade of which the provision of hospitality (and therefore, ambience) was not a fundamental part. This was effectively stressed by Lord Wilberforce in the *Scottish & Newcastle* case:

> 'In the end each case must be resolved, in my opinion, by considering carefully the nature of the particular trade being carried on, and the relation of the expenditure to the promotion of the trade.'

8.3 Anyone acquiring or refurbishing a hotel should, therefore, consider to what extent individual assets contribute (whether actively or passively) to the ambience or atmosphere, whether that is one of luxury, homeliness or liveliness.

INDUSTRIAL BUILDINGS ALLOWANCES

8.4 With effect from 12 April 1978, expenditure on a *qualifying hotel* qualified on the same basis (with slight modification) as an industrial building (*s 271(1)(b)(ii)*). However, in common with other IBAs, allowances for hotels were abolished from April 2011 (see **7.15** *et seq*).

8.5 Although IBAs no longer exist, a purchaser of a hotel may find that his claim for plant allowances will be restricted by IBAs claimed (*s 186* – see **4.39**). The former IBA rules are therefore outlined below, as it will be helpful for a purchaser to understand whether the hotel may previously have qualified for IBAs.

8.6   A qualifying hotel was a hotel which complied with the following requirements:

(*a*)   The accommodation was in a building of a permanent nature (which was likely to exclude some caravan sites, etc, although see **8.33**). It was irrelevant that the hotel might consist of more than one building as long as all of the buildings were used for the same trade and were (broadly) at the same location, enabling them to be regarded by the guests as all part of the one hotel.

(*b*)   It was open for at least four months during April to October (see below).

(*c*)   During that time –

(i)   it had at least ten letting bedrooms;

(ii)   the sleeping accommodation offered at the hotel consisted wholly or mainly of letting bedrooms (see below); and

(iii)   the services provided (see below) for guests normally included the provision of breakfast and an evening meal, the making of beds and the cleaning of rooms (*s 279*).

The season

8.7   The 'season' was the period from April to October, inclusive, which excluded a hotel open only for winter seasons (or, remembering that IBAs were also given to buildings sited overseas, to hotels open in the summer months of the southern hemisphere). Such a hotel could have qualified for allowances if it remained open in the season, but operated on a reduced basis (eg no entertainment, pool or hairdresser). The value of the allowances had to be measured against the additional costs of staff, heating, etc. HMRC stated that, in practice, 120 days was regarded as equivalent to four months (Consultative Committee of Accountancy Bodies TR 308; CA, para 32401). It should be noted that out of season there were no restrictions on the use of the accommodation.

Letting bedrooms

8.8   A 'letting bedroom' was a private bedroom available for letting to the public generally and not normally in the same occupation for more than one month (*s 279(9)*). A hotel with a large residential guest list could, therefore, have difficulty with this rule. 'Public' meant just that and excluded clubs, hostels and similar premises open only to members or specified groups of people. As accommodation in a qualifying hotel had to consist wholly or mainly of letting bedrooms, a large establishment which otherwise would not qualify could not do so merely by setting aside ten or more bedrooms for use by the general public. The possibility of 'hiving off' the hotel function had therefore to be considered in appropriate cases.

Provision of services

8.9   HMRC stated that the mere availability of services did not satisfy the test in *s 279(1)(c)(iii)*: there had to be reasonable use (CCAB TR 308). However, in CA, para 32401, of which the following is an extract, they adopted a revised interpretation of the meals requirement:

> 'HMRC regard the "meals test" as satisfied where the offering of breakfast and dinner is a normal event in the hotel's carrying on of its business. HMRC do not regard it as satisfied where the service of meals is exceptional, for example, if either breakfast or an evening meal is available only on request.'

Expenditure incurred before 12 April 1978

8.10   Expenditure incurred before 12 April 1978 could never have qualified for hotel allowances. *Sections 295(3)* and *296(4)* (which referred to expenditure being deemed to have been incurred on a date later than that on which it was actually incurred) did not apply, when ascertaining entitlement to allowances, to deem expenditure on hotels to have been incurred after 11 April 1978 if, in fact, it was incurred on or before that date (*Sch 3, para 58*).

Conversion costs

8.11   The cost of converting an existing building into a hotel could have qualified in the same manner as construction expenditure. This applied equally where a non-qualifying hotel was converted into a qualifying one, for example by beginning to open during the 'season'.

8.12   Furthermore, where a hotel was extended so that for the first time it had ten or more bedrooms, allowances were available on earlier expenditure, provided it was incurred after 11 April 1978. In such circumstances, the qualifying expenditure was written-down by allowances representing the previous period of non-qualifying use.

Meaning of 'hotel'

8.13   There was no statutory definition of a hotel for the purpose of capital allowances, so it was necessary to have regard to what is commonly regarded as such. Usually the answer lay in the consideration of a 'bundle' of facts. It is clear that a hotel is something more than a collection of rooms which are let without any other type of service whatsoever. Many roadside restaurants have a separate residential block in which a furnished room can be booked without the right (or the requirement) to enjoy any services other than basic accommodation. Such arrangements would not generally have amounted to the provision of hotel services, but allowances have, in practice, been granted.

8.14   A hotel is normally evidenced by the provision of hospitality which in turn is normally evidenced by the availability, at no extra charge, of room service in the form of bed-making and other 'creature comforts' and the availability of facilities such as 'public' rooms and lounges available to all residents. The decision in the *Scottish & Newcastle* case (see **8.2** above) indicated that a hotel normally provided a degree of ambience in its decor. HMRC accepted that an establishment was a hotel if it met the requirements of the *Hotel Proprietors Act 1956, s 1(3)* (CA, para 32402), that is, it was:

> 'held out by the proprietor as offering food and drink and, if so required, sleeping accommodation, without special contract, to any traveller presenting himself who appears able and willing to pay a reasonable sum for the services and facilities provided and who is in a fit state to be received.'

8.15   Many hotels are now part of a complex providing a wide range of conference and/or recreational activities. It was often difficult to decide whether the hotel was part of the latter or the latter was part of the hotel. If possible, it was best to ensure that the hotel operated as the 'umbrella' organisation managing in some way the provision of the leisure facilities with special terms for its residents.

Creation of a leasehold

8.16   An election under *s 290*, transferring allowances to a lessee, may have been made in respect of a hotel (see **11.7** *et seq*).

Staff welfare

8.17   Buildings provided for the welfare of workers could have been included in a claim irrespective of whether they were on the same site or separate buildings (*s 279(7)*). HMRC confirmed that this provision covered hostels which employees occupied but was not intended to give relief for flats and houses provided for the individual employees.

8.18   Where the running of a hotel was carried on by an individual, either alone or in partnership, any living accommodation normally occupied by him or his family when the hotel was open during the season was excluded (*s 279(8)*). Where accommodation was excluded by this provision there was no restriction of allowances provided the 25% *de minimis* rule (see **7.114** *et seq*) was satisfied (CCAB TR 308).

Actual use

8.19   A qualifying hotel must have been in use for the purposes of a trade carried on by the claimant or a lessee throughout a period of 12 months. Such a period would normally be the 12 months ending with the last day of a chargeable period or its basis period (*s 279(3)*) but if the hotel was first used on a date after the beginning of that period, the period throughout which such use must extend would be the 12 months beginning on that date (*s 279(4)*). If during the period of 12 months just mentioned, a hotel had fewer than ten letting bedrooms until a date which was too late for it to qualify by reference to those 12 months, it may have instead qualified by reference to the 12 months beginning on that *date* (*s 279(5)*).

Example

The Restawhile Hotel Ltd commenced to trade on 1 January 2006. Its accounting date was 31 December. The hotel complied with the definition of a qualifying hotel in all respects except that prior to 30 June 2008 it had only eight letting bedrooms. The status of the hotel was as follows:

(*a*)   Accounting periods to 31 December 2006 and 2007 – non-qualifying for both years.

(*b*)   Accounting period to 31 December 2008 – qualifying hotel by virtue of *s 279(5)* because it had complied with the definition in *s 279(1)* for 12 months beginning on 30 June 2008 (even though only part of that period had elapsed by 31 December).

(*c*)   Accounting period to 31 December 2009 – qualifying hotel by virtue of *s 279(3)* because it had complied with the definition for the whole of its accounting period.

If the hotel had ceased to qualify in March 2006, it would not have met the requirements of *s 279(5)* for a full 12 months of qualifying use. No allowances would, therefore, have been available.

Allowances and charges

8.20   The WDA was 4%, as for industrial buildings (or a different percentage if acquired second-hand – see **7.27** *et seq* for calculation) (*s 310*). It continued during any period of temporary disuse until two years after the end of the

141

chargeable period or basis period in which the temporary disuse commenced (*s 317(4)*). The WDA then ceased.

8.21   This 4% allowance was reduced by one-quarter in each of the four years to April 2011 (on a straight-line basis). So a business initially claiming 4% pa saw this reduce to 3% from April 2008, 2% from April 2009, 1% from April 2010 and 0% from April 2011. If the property was acquired second-hand with say ten years of its 25-year IBA life left to run, such that the initial claim was 10% pa (see **7.27** *et seq*), this reduced to 7.5%, then 5%, 2.5% then nil.

8.22   These changes applied from 1 April each year for corporation tax, and 6 April for income tax. Where an accounting period overlapped these dates, the respective rates were time-apportioned. For example, a company with a September 2008 year end was entitled to IBAs at the rate of 3.5% (6/12 × 4% plus 6/12 × 3%).

8.23   All this meant that after April 2011, any unrelieved balance of expenditure would simply be written off, and would not attract tax relief.

8.24   A key effect of the abolition of IBAs is that it is vital to maximise plant and machinery allowances, as this is the only way that many hoteliers will obtain any tax relief for their expenditure on property.

8.25   It may also be beneficial to review recent years' IBA claims and, where possible, re-classify expenditure from IBA treatment to plant and machinery. This is likely to be unproblematic for open tax returns (eg those still within the statutory window to amend a capital allowances claims). However, it is otherwise only possible if the property is sold, and then the claim must be based on an apportionment of the vendor's residue of expenditure (ie the tax written-down value amount not written off yet).

8.26   HMRC's view (*Revenue & Customs Brief 12/09*) is that once a business has exercised its choice to claim one type of capital allowance rather than another, that choice may not be revisited and effectively reversed in respect of expenditure incurred in a closed year, under the old 'error or mistake' provisions (see **21.23** *et seq*). Therefore it is was not permissible to submit 'error or mistake' claims to substitute claims for plant and machinery capital allowances in respect of expenditure on certain building fixtures for part of previous IBA claims on expenditure on the building as a whole.

8.27   If any industrial buildings WDAs were disclaimed in prior years, it may be worth reversing these where possible.

8.28   Also marketed were some artificial arrangements to accelerate IBAs to ensure they are claimed in full before abolition (eg using numerous group companies with different year ends and repeated intra-group sales of properties). However, these were ineffective, except in the rarest of circumstances, because of a variety of tax technical and commercial reasons.

8.29 A balancing adjustment arose on the occurrence of any of the events specified for industrial buildings in *s 315* (see **12.9**), provided the transaction took place before 21 March 2007. It was irrelevant whether, at that time, the building was a qualifying hotel. If the event was the sale of the relevant interest (see **7.35** *et seq*) the WDA was re-computed as for an industrial building (see **7.30–7.32**). If none of the events specified in *s 315* occurred and a period of two years elapsed during which the building was not a qualifying hotel, the relevant interest therein was deemed to have been sold at the end of that period at its market value and a balancing allowance or charge calculated accordingly (*s 317(2)*). The deemed sale could occur up to (almost) five years after the building ceased to be a qualifying hotel given that the temporary disuse provisions operated for the first (almost) three years.

8.30 This 'two-year rule' did not apply to hotels in enterprise zones (*s 317(5)*).

8.31 However, for transactions on or after 21 March 2007, the purchaser effectively 'inherited' the vendor's claim at tax written-down value, and there was no calculation of balancing allowances or charges (*FA 2007, s 36*).

Roads on hotel property

8.32 Industrial buildings allowances were sometimes available for roads on hotel property (eg hotels in large grounds with private access roads). As discussed in **7.13** *et seq*, expenditure in respect of a road was treated as qualifying for IBAs if the estate consisted wholly or mainly of buildings that were treated as industrial buildings (*s 284(1)*). Industrial buildings were defined in *s 271(2)*, as including buildings or structures within *s 271(1)(b)*, which included a qualifying hotel. So a qualifying hotel was an industrial building and if an estate consisted wholly or mainly of hotels, IBAs may be available for expenditure on roads.

Holiday camps and caravan parks

8.33 HMRC accepted that a holiday camp might qualify for IBAs (CA, para 32402). This was because it was understood to accept that prefabricated chalets provided accommodation of a permanent nature, as did mobile homes provided with mains water, electricity and other permanent features such as concrete steps and a garden fence. However, it was important to ensure that the holiday camp or caravan park met all the conditions to be a qualifying hotel (see **8.4**), including having at least ten chalets or mobile homes of a permanent nature, being open during the season, and offering breakfast and an evening meal in the normal course of business (although this did not, of course, have to be taken up by visitors). If these conditions were met, then all expenditure on buildings and structures on the site should have qualified, including accommodation, entertainment and administration facilities (and if the site consisted wholly or mainly of qualifying accommodation, even roads – see **8.32**).

Chapter 9

Enterprise zones

INTRODUCTION

9.1   There were previously a small number of specially designated areas where, in addition to other privileges, an initial allowance of 100% was available for new buildings. This was a type of industrial buildings allowance (IBA). The designation of enterprise zones was generally reserved for what were considered areas of special need (see **Appendix 3**).

9.2   The most recently designated IBA enterprise zone expired in October 2006. This, combined with the abolition of IBA enterprise zone allowances in 2011 (**see 9.3**), means that they will be rarely met with in practice.

9.3   IBA enterprise zone allowances were withdrawn from 1 April 2011 (corporation tax) and 6 April 2011 (income tax). Where a business's chargeable period spans the relevant date, the amount of writing-down allowance was time apportioned (*FA 2008, s 83*), and where a business disposed of a building within seven years of first use, it would potentially be liable for a balancing charge. This reduction from the former period of 25 years applied for chargeable periods beginning on or after 1 April 2011 (corporation tax) or 6 April 2011 (income tax) (*FA 2008, Sch 27, paras 31* and *32*).

9.4   However, in Budget 2011 the government announced the creation of new so-called enterprise zones in disadvantaged areas. These give business rates discounts, simplified planning approaches and superfast broadband. A limited number of these areas, mainly where there is a strong focus on manufacturing, have been designated as enhanced capital allowances enterprise zones where investment in plant and machinery will benefit from 100% capital allowances (**see 9.45** *et seq*).

State aid rules stipulate that enhanced capital allowances (ECAs) in enterprise zones cannot be offered alongside other forms of regional aid such as selective finance assistance, business rates discounts, etc. ECAs will therefore only be attractive for large, capital-intensive projects where the benefits from ECAs would outweigh other forms of available support.

9.5   The comments below (**9.8–9.44**) refer to the previous (abolished) system where IBAs were available.

9.6   This will still be relevant where, for example, a taxpayer buys a property in a former enterprise zone, and considers making a capital allowances claim on the existing fixtures. If they had previously been included in a claim for enterprise zone allowances, no plant claim will be possible.

9.7   The new system of 100% allowances for expenditure on plant is considered from **9.45**.

ALLOWANCES FORMERLY AVAILABLE (IBA SYSTEM)

9.8   A building in an enterprise zone would, provided the appropriate conditions were met, attract a 100% initial allowance (*s 306*) against qualifying enterprise zone expenditure (*ss 298–300*). No allowances were available, however, for the cost of the land itself. If the building was never completed, and construction was permanently abandoned, the initial allowance was withdrawn (*s 307*). If, on the other hand, construction work was halted temporarily, for example during a recession in trade, the allowance would not be withdrawn.

9.9   A taxpayer could choose to limit his claim to a specified amount, or indeed not claim the allowance at all (see **21.38** *et seq*) (*s 306(2)*). Where less than the whole initial allowance was claimed, the balance of expenditure was available as a WDA of 25% pa on a straight-line basis (*s 310(1)(a)*). Such WDAs only commenced when the building was brought into use. Use was not a prerequisite for the initial allowance to be given.

9.10   Writing-down allowances could be disclaimed in any particular year (*s 309(2)*), in which case they were available in later years, still at the rate of 25%.

9.11   Despite the accelerated rate of allowances compared to buildings elsewhere, buildings in enterprise zones nonetheless had a 25-year tax life and a clawback of allowances was possible if the building was sold within that time. See **Chapter 12** for the treatment of the sale of property. It should also be noted that a subsequent purchaser (within the 25 years) would be entitled to allowances, on the same basis as with any other 'industrial' building (see **7.30–7.32**).

9.12   Because enterprise zone property was often seen primarily as an investment-based tax shelter, it was perhaps more likely than was normally the case that a person claiming allowances would be incurring expenditure on a building that he did not intend to occupy for his own trade. If the intention was to let the building to tenants, the allowances were given as an expense of that rental business (*s 353*). In order to make enterprise zone allowances available to smaller investors, the concept of an enterprise zone property unit trust (EZPUT) was created. If investment was made via such a vehicle, it nonetheless remained the individual investors who were entitled to the allowances (CA, para 39700).

Time limit on expenditure

9.13   To qualify for the special allowances, expenditure had to be incurred:

(*a*)   within ten years of the enterprise zone first being designated as such; or

(*b*)   under a contract entered into within the ten-year period, provided the expenditure was actually incurred not more than 20 years after such designation (*s 298*).

9.14   In cases falling within (*b*) above, Inspectors were instructed to consider the validity of the contract and whether the building ultimately constructed was that which was originally contracted for. If changes had been made, HMRC would be concerned to see that they were indeed merely variations of the original contract, rather than constituting an entirely new contract (CA, para 37150). These rules were in any case subject to the abolition of IBAs generally.

Extent of enterprise zones

9.15   Enterprise zones generally covered only a relatively small area, for example individual industrial estates. The initial allowance did not extend to the rest of the town or area. Details of recent enterprise zones are given in **Appendix 3**.

9.16   It must be stressed that the boundaries of enterprise zones were not flexible – it was possible to miss out on the initial allowance simply by building on one side of the road rather than the other, and if a building straddled the boundary, then the expenditure had to be apportioned into qualifying and non-qualifying parts (CA, para 37390). The *de minimis* rule (see **7.114** *et seq*) was not relevant.

9.17   A building already situated in what was subsequently designated as an enterprise zone would not qualify for the initial allowance because qualifying expenditure could only be incurred during the ten-year life of the zone. Additions to such a building carried out during the life of the zone could also fail to attract the initial allowance because the extent of the enterprise zone may well have been designated in such a way as to exclude existing buildings.

The onus was on the would-be claimant to make sure his building fell within the zone.

QUALIFYING BUILDINGS

General

9.18   Enterprise zone allowances were a form of IBAs, and given in respect of buildings and structures that would otherwise have qualified for IBAs under *s 274* (see **7.47** *et seq*). However, the range of buildings qualifying in an enterprise zone extended beyond this. *Section 271(1)(b)(iv)* extended allowances to commercial buildings and structures.

Commercial buildings

9.19   A commercial building was defined by *s 281* as a building which was used for the purpose of a trade, profession or vocation or, whether or not for such a purpose, as an office or offices.

9.20   Unusually, an office could qualify despite not being used for a trade. Expenditure on a building which was occupied by, for example, a charity would therefore qualify for allowances.

9.21   One type of building that would seldom, if ever, qualify for enterprise zone allowances was a 'dwelling-house', that is to say, houses, flats and other properties used for residential purposes (see **7.100** *et seq*). The one exception to this was where the dwelling-house was classified as industrial by being part of a larger qualifying building and represented not more than 25% of the total cost thereof (see **7.114** *et seq*) (*s 283(2)*). This provision often removed the need, for example, to calculate and disallow that part of the expenditure relating to a caretaker's lodging.

Hotels

9.22   To qualify for 'normal' IBAs, a hotel had to fulfil certain conditions, for example having a minimum number of letting bedrooms (*s 279*) – see **8.4** *et seq*. However, smaller hotels or establishments operating in a slightly different way (eg motels) could qualify for allowances in enterprise zones. This is because they could nonetheless qualify under the heading of commercial buildings.

9.23   It was important however not to fall into the trap of assuming that all types of building providing lodging could be brought under the broad umbrella of hotels. HMRC had, for example, resisted claims for allowances on time-share apartments on the grounds that they constituted a dwelling-house (see **7.100** *et seq*).

Change of use

9.24 The person incurring the expenditure did not have to occupy the building himself, but could grant a lease or licence without suffering any withdrawal of allowances (*s 305*), unless he realised a *capital value* (*s 328*) (see **12.34** *et seq*).

9.25 Any change of use of a building which had previously qualified for enterprise zone allowances would be ignored with the one exception of commencement of use as a dwelling-house.

9.26 If a building had begun to be used as a dwelling-house, WDAs, if any, would be suspended but there would be no balancing adjustment. This effectively meant that where the 100% initial allowance had been claimed, any change of use to that of a dwelling-house was without any immediate effect for capital allowances purposes. This rule was in any case not invoked if the dwelling represents no more than 25% of the whole building.

PLANT

9.27 One area of interest was the treatment of plant which became an integral part of an enterprise building, and could arguably qualify either for plant allowances or buildings allowances. The normal priorities of the investor were reversed, of course, by the existence of the 100% initial allowance for expenditure on buildings. Outside enterprise zones, the priority was normally to have as much of the total expenditure as possible classified as non-'integral features' or non-'long-life' plant, in order to obtain the WDAs of 20% pa, as opposed to 10% for those assets or 4% on industrial buildings (and nothing at all on commercial buildings). Where an initial enterprise zone allowance was available, the incentive was to classify all debatable expenditure as building. Fortunately, there ought to be no major disputes on this point, because although *s 7* excludes the possibility of claiming more than one type of allowance on the same expenditure, it does not specify any order of precedence. Consequently, where a taxpayer was entitled to the 100% initial allowance, he could choose to treat as qualifying expenditure any amounts spent on the provision of machinery or plant which was an integral part of the building.

9.28 The question arose of whether plant was actually attached to a building. Consider, for example, storage racking in an enterprise zone property.

If the racking was free-standing and would be removed upon vacation of the building, it would not qualify for the 100% allowance. If, however, the racking was fixed to the building and would remain in the building through a succession of tenants, the enterprise zone allowances should have been available.

9.29   Expenditure on the thermal insulation of a building in an enterprise zone would be treated as expenditure on the building. *Section 28*, which would normally treat such expenditure as being on the provision of machinery or plant, did not apply.

PURCHASE OF A COMPLETED BUILDING

9.30   In most enterprise developments, it was not the case that the individual or company looking to claim allowances would itself be incurring expenditure on the construction of a building. It was more likely that it would be purchasing a completed building from a developer. The 'history' of an enterprise zone development was likely to be similar to the following scenario:

(*a*)   The freehold interest in the site was owned by an enterprise zone authority.

(*b*)   The authority entered into a building agreement with a developer.

(*c*)   Under the terms of such an agreement, the developer was obliged to construct a building, and in return, was entitled to call for the transfer of an interest in the land upon completion of the development.

(*d*)   The interest transferred may have been the interest held by the authority or a long lease granted out of it, and the developer may have had the right to have that interest granted to a named third party, rather than to itself.

(*e*)   The developer would incur these costs on trading account, and would not itself be eligible for capital allowances.

(*f*)   At that stage, if not before, the developer would seek investors to whom he could sell the building in order to make his profit.

(*g*)   In order to make the investment more attractive, the developer could also be prepared to give some form of rental guarantee.

The importance and meaning of use

9.31   The treatment of an acquisition depended on whether or not the building had been 'used', and whether the purchase took place within two years of first use. In the context of deciding whether a building was unused, 'use' meant use for any purpose and not just for a purpose qualifying for IBAs. 'Use', however, did not include occupation by a tenant for fitting out by that tenant prior to the commencement of actual production or other use. The fitting-out process was regarded by HMRC as merely the completion of construction (CA, para 33520).

Purchase of an unused building before expiry of the zone

9.32   The most straightforward situation would be where an investor purchased an unused building directly from a developer before the expiry of the enterprise zone. In such circumstances, *s 296(2)* required the construction expenditure actually incurred (by the developer) to be ignored, and instead the investor was deemed to have incurred expenditure on construction on the date on which the purchase price became payable.

9.33   Where the building was purchased directly from a developer, the amount paid by the investor would be the amount qualifying for allowances. Where, however, the building was purchased not from the developer, but from an intermediary, the expenditure qualifying for allowances would be the lower of the amount paid by the investor, and the amount paid to the developer on the sale of his interest (*s 296(3)*). The effect of this was to give allowances based on original cost plus developer's profit, but not on the profit of any intermediary.

9.34   Where the vendor of the building was not a developer, but, for example, a trader who intended the building for his own use but had changed his mind, then that vendor's profit was excluded from expenditure qualifying for allowances. The new investor would only be able to claim allowances on the lower of the amount he paid for the interest, and the actual expenditure incurred in the original construction of the building (*s 295(2)*). A building purchased directly from a developer could therefore be worth more in terms of allowances than an identical building purchased from someone else because qualifying expenditure in respect of the former would be augmented by the developer's profit. The purchaser would therefore need to be certain that the vendor is a genuine developer. This fact could not just be assumed, and a warranty of this fact may well have been required.

9.35   Where only part of a building had been brought into use, there are two possibilities:

(*a*)   the whole building would be regarded as having been brought into use; or

(*b*)   only the relevant part of the building would be regarded as having been used, in consequence of which any expenditure will be apportioned between the 'used' part and the 'unused' part, and each part of the expenditure dealt with separately.

9.36 The question of which was the correct treatment would depend on the circumstances. The former treatment was likely to be appropriate where, for example, the person constructing the building was the sole user but chose not to occupy the whole. Where, however, a building was divided into distinct units and only some of those units were let, it could be possible to adopt the alternative treatment.

Purchase of unused building after expiry of zone

9.37 Where an enterprise zone building was sold before being brought into use (but after the expiry of the zone), then the actual expenditure was in the first instance ignored for the purposes of calculating allowances and instead the purchaser was entitled to allowances based on a deemed amount of expenditure. This deemed amount was the lesser of the price paid by him or the actual expenditure on construction (*s 295*). Furthermore, where construction operations continued after the expiry of the zone, the deemed amount qualifying for allowances was restricted to reflect the proportion of work undertaken before that expiry (*s 302*).

Example

Lovell incurred expenditure on the construction of an office building in an enterprise zone which was first designated as such on 24 April 1984. The expenditure was analysed as follows:

	Amount	
	£	
Land	200,000	20 December 1993
Building	500,000	20 December 1993
Extension	100,000	15 May 1994

The 100% initial allowance was claimed but, before use commenced, the building was sold to Marian and Terry on 4 July 1994 for £650,000, of which £200,000 related to the land. The effect of the sale on allowances was as follows:

(*a*) Lovell: the 100% allowance given was claimed back.

(*b*) Marian and Terry: the expenditure qualifying for allowances was –

Qualifying expenditure × The part of the construction expenditure/Total expenditure on construction

that is, 450,000 × 500,000/600,000 = £375,000

Marian and Terry were able to claim an initial allowance of £375,000 in the chargeable period in which they purchased the building. Where the building was sold more than once before being brought into use, the provisions of *s 302* only had effect as regards the last of those sales. In all cases the rules contained in this section were subject to *s 298*, that is, that expenditure must have been incurred within 20 years of the enterprise zone first being designated as such.

Purchase within two years of first use

9.38   For expenditure incurred on or after 16 December 1991, the 100% initial allowance was also available to the purchaser of a *used* building, provided that the building was first used not more than two years before the purchase (*s 303*).

9.39   As with the purchase of an unused building after the expiry of the zone, the amount of expenditure qualifying for initial allowances was calculated by reference to that proportion of the construction work undertaken during the ten-year life of the zone. The provisions of *s 303* applied only to the first sale of the relevant interest after the building had been brought into use, and operated regardless of whether the interest was sold before the building was first used (*s 303(1)(d)*).

9.40   It should be noted that if the sale of the relevant interest took place more than two years after the building was first used, the purchaser would be entitled to neither the initial allowance nor the enhanced 25% WDA. Instead, the WDA was calculated so as to write off the residue of expenditure over the balance of the building's 25-year life.

9.41   Clearly, any potential purchaser of a used building needed to know exactly when that building was brought into use, and might well have required a warranty to be given in this regard by the vendor (see **9.44**). On the other hand, the vendor himself may have been holding out the availability of enterprise zone allowances as an inducement to potential purchasers, and so he too would have needed to establish the date of first use.

9.42   One inherent problem was that 'use' was not satisfactorily defined. HMRC indicated that it did not regard a building as having come into use simply because it was occupied by a tenant who was fitting it out (see **9.30**).

9.43   It was announced at the time of Budget 2008 that where a business disposed of an enterprise zone building within seven years of first use, it would potentially be liable for a balancing charge.

WARRANTIES

9.44　The purchaser of an enterprise zone building would need to seek certain warranties from the vendor, in order to establish that the allowances available would be as expected. These warranties included the following:

- Confirmation that the whole site was in an enterprise zone, so that expenditure would not need to be apportioned into a qualifying and non-qualifying part.

- Confirmation that the whole of the developer's expenditure was incurred prior to the expiry of the zone, again to prevent any need for apportionment of expenditure into qualifying and non-qualifying elements.

- Confirmation that the vendor was a genuine property developer and had been accepted by HMRC as such, or alternatively details of the circumstances of acquisition by the vendor.

- Confirmation that the building had not been brought into use, or that it had been used for less than two years (in which case precise dates should have been given).

- Agreement by the vendor to provide the purchaser with all information necessary for the submission of a claim for allowances.

- Details of any other interests in the property.

NEW ENTERPRISE ZONES (2011 SYSTEM)

9.45　A new enterprise zones scheme was announced in 2011. Although the main benefits for businesses in the new zones were simplified planning and business rates discounts, the government also introduced 'enhanced' (that is, accelerated) capital allowances for expenditure on plant and machinery (in other words, first-year capital allowances (FYAs)). In contrast to the 'old' enterprise zones, however, no allowances are available for expenditure on buildings.

9.46　The government made 100% FYAs available from 1 April 2012 in various designated assisted areas within specific enterprise zones. It should be noted that it is *not* the case that 100% plant allowances are available in *every* enterprise zone. First-year capital allowances are available only for expenditure within designated assisted areas, which are not identical with the enterprise zones themselves. These assisted areas were designated by statutory instrument *SI 2014/3183*.

9.47   ECA areas were designated by *SI 2014/*3183 and *2015/*2047. A list of zones and designated assisted areas is published by the government:

- Zones in England are found at http://enterprisezones.communities.gov. uk/enterprise-zone-finder.

- Zones in Scotland are listed at http://www.gov.scot/Topics/Economy/ EconomicStrategy/Enterprise-Areas/Incentives/Capital-Allowances.

- Zones in Wales are set out at http://business.wales.gov.uk/enterprisezones.

- At the time of writing, there were no enterprise zones in Northern Ireland, although a pilot site was planned for a site adjacent to the University of Ulster Coleraine campus. In the 2016 Budget it was announced that the Northern Ireland Executive had set the boundaries for the zone and the first investors were expected on site later in 2016.

Useful further discussion is provided by House of Commons Library Briefing Paper 5942 by Matthew Ward (http://researchbriefings.files.parliament.uk/ documents/SN05942/SN05942.pdf).

9.48   To qualify, the expenditure must be incurred in the period after the area is designated as an assisted area, and initially had to be incurred before 1 April 2017 (*s 45K*). However, with effect from 17 July 2014 this was extended to 1 April 2020 by *Finance Act 2014 s 64(5)*. The fact there was a specific end date meant that the relief was less attractive in areas which were designated later than others. As a result, *Finance (No 2) Act 2016 s 68* changed the rules so that FYAs are available for expenditure incurred in the period of eight years from the date when the area was (or is treated as) designated.

9.49   The relief is restricted to UK resident companies liable to corporation tax in respect of a trade or a mining, transport or similar undertaking, and the expenditure must be on new and unused plant. There are sundry exceptions to eligible companies based on European state aid rules. Thus, for example, agricultural firms do not qualify, and nor do vehicles or transport equipment acquired by transport undertakings.

9.50   The plant must be acquired for use primarily in a designated assisted area, and anti-avoidance rules exist to ensure this requirement is not abused. Amongst other things, there is scope for a claw-back of allowances where the plant begins to be used primarily *outside* of the designated assisted area within five years. Also, the expenditure must be incurred to expand a business or start a new type of business not previously carried on by the company (*ss 45K, 45N*).

9.51   Qualifying expenditure is capped at £125 million per investor (*s 212U*).

Chapter 10

Agricultural property – special features

INTRODUCTION

10.1 Capital allowances were historically available for expenditure on *agricultural* buildings and other works (including, for example, fences and walls).

10.2 Agricultural buildings allowances (ABAs) were abolished from April 2011.

10.3 The provisions relating to ABAs are included, despite their abolition, as advisers will still be dealing with earlier years.

10.4 In addition, an understanding of the previous system will be relevant where, for example, a taxpayer buys a property that had previously qualified for ABAs, and considers making a capital allowances claim on the existing fixtures. If those fixtures had previously been included in a claim for ABAs, no plant claim will be possible (*s 9*). It is therefore essential to a buyer, in relevant cases, to satisfy himself that ABAs cannot have been an issue, or to identify and exclude from his claim such fixtures.

10.5 Agricultural buildings allowances were in many ways similar to IBAs, but not identical to them.

QUALIFYING EXPENDITURE

General

10.6 ABAs were given where a person incurred capital expenditure on an agricultural building, or fences or other works, as defined in the legislation and the expenditure was incurred by a person having the freehold or leasehold interest in land in the United Kingdom wholly or mainly for the purposes of husbandry on that land (*s 361*). The meaning of land is defined by the *Interpretation Act 1978*, *Sch 1* to include buildings, and see the definitions of 'husbandry' (at **10.31** *et seq*) and 'agricultural building' (at **10.35** *et seq*).

The site

10.7   No allowances were due in respect of expenditure on the acquisition of any land, or of rights in or over land (*s 363*).

Buildings alterations and repairs

10.8   Where a trader incurs capital expenditure on alterations to an existing building incidental to the installation of machinery or plant, that expenditure itself qualifies for plant and machinery allowances as if it were part of the machinery or plant (see **14.119** *et seq*) (*s 25*). Other alterations and improvements or reconstruction of a qualifying building, as well as repairs which are not allowed as trading deductions, qualified for ABAs, as did an appropriate allocation of professional fees, such as architects', which were a necessary part of the cost of the works (CA, para 40200).

Demolition costs

10.9   ABAs were available for demolition costs where the demolition was preliminary to replacing a building, unless the building demolished was an industrial building and the cost of demolition had been added to the residue of expenditure for IBA purposes (see **7.11**) (CA, para 40200).

ALLOWANCES AVAILABLE

New buildings

10.10   With effect from April 2011, allowances are no longer available.

10.11   Prior to 1 April (corporation tax) or 6 April 2008 (income tax) a WDA of 4% of qualifying expenditure was made over 25 years, when certain conditions (see **10.20**) were fulfilled (*s 373(1)*). Where the accounting period was less or more than a year, the WDA was proportionally decreased or increased (*s 373(2)*).

10.12   This 4% allowance was reduced by one-quarter in each of the four years to April 2011 (on a straight-line basis). So a business initially claiming 4% pa, saw this reduce to 3% from April 2008, 2% from April 2009, 1% from April 2010 and 0% from April 2011. If the property was acquired second-hand with say ten years of its 25-year ABA life left to run, such that the initial claim was 10% pa (see **7.27** *et seq*), this reduced to 7.5%, then 5%, 2.5% then nil.

10.13 These changes applied from 1 April each year for corporation tax, and 6 April for income tax. Where an accounting period overlapped these dates, the respective rates were time-apportioned. For example, a company with a September 2008 year end was entitled to ABAs at the rate of 3.5% (6/12 × 4% plus 6/12 × 3%).

10.14 All this meant that after April 2011, any unrelieved balance of expenditure was simply written off, and would not attract tax relief resulting in substantially increased future tax bills for affected businesses.

Example

Gordon spent £500,000 on constructing a farm building in 2006, expecting that the whole of this expenditure would attract tax relief via ABAs over the next 25 years. At his marginal tax rate of 40%, this would be worth £200,000 over time. Instead, he began claiming allowances at the expected 4% pa, but then saw this gradually reduced to 1% for 2010/11, before allowances ceased altogether.

In April 2011, the residue of expenditure (that is the unrelieved part of the original cost) was £430,000, which was then written off without relief. So in future years, Gordon will pay total additional tax of £172,000.

A key effect of the abolition of ABAs is that it has become vital to maximise plant and machinery allowances, as this is the only way that many farmers may obtain any tax relief for expenditure on property.

It may also be beneficial to review recent years' ABA claims and where possible, re-classify expenditure from ABA treatment to plant and machinery. This is likely to be unproblematic for open tax returns (eg those still within the statutory window to amend a capital allowances claims). However, it is otherwise only possible if the property is sold, and then the claim must be based on an apportionment of the vendor's residue of expenditure (ie the tax written-down value amount not written off yet).

HMRC's view (*Revenue & Customs Brief 12/09*) was that once a business has exercised its choice to claim one type of capital allowance rather than another, that choice may not be revisited and effectively reversed in respect of expenditure incurred in a closed year, under the 'error or mistake' provisions (see **21.23** *et seq*). Therefore it was not permissible to submit 'error or mistake' claims to substitute claims for plant and machinery capital allowances in respect of expenditure on certain building fixtures for part of previous ABA claims on expenditure on the property as a whole.

Also, if any agricultural buildings WDAs were disclaimed in prior years, it may have been worth reversing these where possible.

10.15   Allowances may have been disclaimed in a particular year (see **21.38** *et seq*). Where allowances were disclaimed and there was no subsequent sale of the property, unlike IBAs (see **21.3**) the tax life of the building could not be extended, meaning that the expenditure would never be fully written off. This was because ABAs could only be claimed during the expenditure's 25-year tax life ('writing-down period') (*s 372(1)(c)* and (2)).

Second-hand buildings

10.16   Until the abolition of ABAs in 2011, where an agricultural building was sold unused, the person who constructed the building could not claim ABAs, but the buyer could. The buyer's expenditure was based on the lower of the construction cost incurred by the seller and the price paid by the buyer to acquire the building. Where only part of the related agricultural land was sold, then it was necessary to apportion on a just and reasonable basis the expenditure between the part of the land sold and the part retained (eg where a farm road was built that crossed land retained as well as land sold). If a building was sold more than once before it was used, ABAs could only be claimed in relation to the last sale (*s 370*).

10.17   Where an agricultural building was acquired second-hand, the rules operated differently to those that applied for IBAs before 21 March 2007 (see **7.27–7.32**). Where a used agricultural building was sold the seller was prevented from claiming any future WDAs (*s 375(3)*) and the buyer was able to claim the remaining unrelieved WDAs going forward at the same rate, as if it had stepped into the seller's shoes (*s 375(4)*) (with the WDA being proportionally decreased or increased if the accounting period was less or more than a year). If, because of the vendor and purchaser having different chargeable period ends, these rules meant that the total WDAs available for the full 25-year ABA writing down period would be less than the original expenditure, then the new owner could claim the balance as an additional amount in the final chargeable period of the 25-year ABA tax life (*s 379*). If the new owner acquired the relevant interest in only part of the related agricultural land, then he became entitled to only the part of the previous owner's ABAs that related to that part of the land, which was treated as if it were a separate allowance (*s 375(5)*).

Example

Jack had an accounting year end of 30 June and owned the freehold of a farm. Between August and October 2001 he built a barn on his land for £200,000. On 1 September 2003 he sold his farm to Dick whose year end was 31 December.

The construction of the barn took place in Jack's income tax year of assessment 2001/02 and the 25-year writing down period for ABAs began on 6 April 2001.

The sale happened two months into Jack's accounting year ending 30 June 2004, but with only four months remaining before the end of Dick's year ending 31 December 2003.

The ABA WDAs that may have been claimed by Jack and Dick were as follows

2001/02	Jack	£200,000 × 4%	=	£8,000
2002/03	Jack	£200,000 × 4%	=	£8,000
2003/04	Jack	£200,000 × 4% × 2/12ths	=	£1,333
2003/04	Dick	£200,000 × 4% × 4/12ths	=	£2,666
2004/05	Dick	£200,000 × 4%	=	£8,000

Dick then continued to claim £8,000 for each subsequent year (reduced by one-quarter in each of the four years to April 2011, whereupon ABAs were abolished).

10.18　In contrast to the position that existed for IBAs prior to 21 March 2007, there could be no ABA balancing adjustment unless an election was made within two years of the period end in which the sale took place, to treat the sale (or demolition/destruction) as a balancing event (*ss 381* and *382*). Where such an election was made, like the former position for IBAs, the buyer's WDA was ascertained by taking the 'residue of qualifying expenditure' (*ss 376* and *386*) and writing it off on a straight-line basis over the period beginning with the sale and ending with the 25th anniversary *of the first day of the period* in which the construction expenditure was incurred (*s 373(2)*). Anti-avoidance measures existed to prevent such elections being made where it appeared that the sole or main benefit that might be expected to accrue to the parties from the acquisition was a tax advantage (ie obtaining an allowance or a greater allowance) (*s 382(2)*).

10.19　See pro forma election, **Appendix 5**.

CONDITIONS FOR ALLOWANCES

10.20　WDAs may have been claimed where three conditions were fulfilled:

(*a*)　qualifying expenditure was incurred;

(*b*)　the claimant was, at any time during that chargeable period, entitled to the relevant interest in relation to that expenditure; and

(*c*)　that time fell within the writing-down period (25 years beginning with the first day of the chargeable period in which the expenditure was incurred) (*s 372(1)*).

First use

10.21   No allowances were available if the *first* use of the building was not for the purposes of husbandry (see **10.31** *et seq*). If, however, the first use was for husbandry then ABAs continued until the end of the expenditure's 25-year ABA tax life irrespective of what the building was used for in later years. This was unlike the IBA rules in relation to non-industrial use (see **7.129**). If ABA WDAs had been given before the building had been brought into use, they had to be withdrawn if the first use was not for the purposes of husbandry, or the person who claimed sold the relevant interest (see **10.23** *et seq*) before the building was brought into use (*s 374*).

Time conditions must be met

10.22   It is worth emphasising that unlike IBAs, which only became available if the building was in use at the end of that accounting period (see **7.129**), ABAs (like plant and machinery allowances) could be claimed as soon as the expenditure was incurred, irrespective of whether the building was complete or had yet been brought into use.

RELEVANT INTEREST

10.23   A claim for ABAs in respect of any expenditure could only be made by the holder of the 'relevant interest' relating to that expenditure. The meaning of 'relevant interest' differed though from that used for IBA purposes (see **7.35**).

10.24   When a person incurred expenditure on an agricultural building, his relevant interest was whatever interest he had in the 'related agricultural land' at the time that the expenditure was incurred. The related agricultural land was the land that was being used for agricultural purposes (see **10.31** *et seq*) (*s 361(1)(b)* and *(2)(b)*).

10.25   The relevant interest could only be a freehold or leasehold interest in land in the United Kingdom. This meant that land outside the United Kingdom could never be agricultural land for ABA purposes (*s 364(1)*) though it was of course possible for expenditure on non-UK land to qualify for IBAs under the definition of 'working foreign plantations' (see **7.48**) (*s 274(1)*). The ABA definition of relevant interest also focused narrowly on freehold and leasehold interests, which were defined in *s 393* to include agreements to acquire freeholds or leases, but for leases, excluded mortgages. This narrow focus meant that other legal interests such as licences, grazing or commons rights, rent of grass, etc could not be relevant interests for ABAs (CA, para 41000).

10.26 Where a person held more than one legal interest (eg the freehold and a lease in the same land) then the relevant interest was the one that was reversionary on the others (in this example, the freehold) (*s 364(3)*).

10.27 If a person was entitled to different relevant interests in different parts of the related agricultural land, the expenditure had to be apportioned between those parts on a just and reasonable basis and that person was treated as if he had incurred the expenditure apportioned to each part separately (*s 371*).

10.28 If a subordinate interest was created out of the relevant interest (eg a new lease was granted), the relevant interest was not affected and continued to be the relevant interest (*s 365*).

10.29 Where an interest in land was conveyed or assigned by way of security, but remained subject to a right of redemption (ie the right to have the security discharged on performance of the agreement), the person with that interest was deemed to hold it instead of the creditor (*s 366*).

10.30 Where a lease ceased to exist because it was surrendered, or the person owning it acquired the interest which was reversionary on it (ie immediately superior to it), then the interest into which the extinguished lease merged became the new relevant interest, unless a new lease of all or part of the related agricultural land was granted to take effect when the former lease ceased to exist (*s 367*).

MEANING OF 'HUSBANDRY'

10.31 ABAs were available for expenditure on land used for the purposes of husbandry. Husbandry was not defined in the legislation, although statute did specify that it included 'any method of intensive rearing of livestock or fish on a commercial basis for the production of food for human consumption' as well as 'the cultivation of short rotation coppice' (ie trees planted at high density where stems were harvested at intervals of less than ten years) (*s 362*).

10.32 Otherwise the meaning of husbandry was decided by an extensive body of court cases. The key definition accepted by HMRC, based on the statement made by Lord Clyde in *Lean v IRC* (1926) 10 TC 341, was that land is occupied for the purposes of husbandry if the trade carried on by the person occupying the land depended to a *material extent* on the fruits (natural or commercial) of that land (CA, para 40100). The reference to material extent was included because Lord Clyde recognised that many farms depend to a large extent upon imported foodstuffs which are not, and could not, be produced on those farms.

10.33   Court cases have held husbandry to include: growing medicinal herbs for distillation and treatment (*IRC v William Ransom & Son Ltd* (1918) 12 TC 21); sheep grazing (*Keir v Gillespie (Surveyor of Taxes)* (1920) 7 TC 473); simple poultry rearing and keeping (*Lean v IRC* – see **10.32**); battery farming of hens (*Peter Reid v CIR* (1947) 28 TC 451); and rearing stud cockerels and hatching pedigree chicks (some later sold and some used to supply future breeding stock) (*Long v Belfield Poultry Products Ltd* (1987) 21 TC 221). It is also understood that HMRC would normally accept that market gardening, as defined by *CTA 2009, s 1317*, was in use for the purposes of husbandry, as was land used to grow 'normal crops' with fuel production as the objective (eg oil-seed rape, beet, cereals and miscanthus).

10.34   The courts have held the following not to be husbandry: breeding silver foxes (to sell their pelts) and production of eggs for their consumption (*IRC v Melross* (1935) 19 TC 607); 'custom hatching' of eggs for customers (*Long v Belfield Poultry Products Ltd* – see **10.33**); purchase of eggs and sale of the chicks (*Thornber Bros Ltd v Macinnes* (1987) 21 TC 221).

MEANING OF 'AGRICULTURAL BUILDING'

10.35   An agricultural building was defined in *s 361* as a building (such as a farmhouse, farm building or cottage) or fence or other works. So dwellings could therefore qualify for ABAs. The asset also did not have to be physically located on the agricultural land in question.

10.36   A 'farmhouse' was the farmer's dwelling that the farm was run from. Following the decision in *Lindsay v IRC* (1953) 34 TC 289 this was based on the duties of the occupant, rather than who the occupant was (eg if the farm owner delegated the running of the farm to a manager, then it was the manager's house which was the farmhouse and not the owner's).

10.37   If the farm was run from more than one house, then it may have had more than one farmhouse (eg if it was owned by brothers who ran it in partnership, both of their houses would be farmhouses) (CA, para 40100). It was held in *Arnander (executors of McKenna, deceased) v Revenue and Customs Comrs* [2006] STC (SCD) 800 (the so-called '*McKenna*' case) that a building was only a farmhouse if it was occupied by an individual who farmed on a day-to-day basis, rather than the person in overall control of the agricultural business conducted on the land. Furthermore, if the premises were extravagantly large, or on a more elaborate or expensive scale than the agricultural purpose for which they were used, then they should be treated as having been converted into something grander (ie they may be a primarily rich man's residence, rather than a farmhouse).

10.38 Where the expenditure was on a farmhouse, ABAs were only available for up to one third of the expenditure incurred constructing it, and the full one third would only be given if the accommodation and amenities of the farmhouse were proportionate to the nature and extent of the farm. This was because the farmhouse was also residential accommodation. If the farmhouse was larger or more luxurious than the average farmhouse that a farm of that size and type would normally be expected to have, then ABAs would only be available on a reasonable proportion (never exceeding one third of the cost). If more than one third of a farmhouse was used for farm business, the cost qualifying for ABAs still could not exceed one third (*s 369(3)* and (*4*)) (CA, para 40200).

10.39 A 'farm building' was a structure like a barn, a cowshed, a chicken shack, a milking parlour or a stable (CA, para 40100).

10.40 The legislation did not define the meaning of 'cottage', so it took its ordinary meaning. HMRC accepted that this was a small dwelling-house, although there was no clear boundary where Inspectors would draw the line between cottages and buildings that were so large and costly that they could not reasonably be regarded as cottages. HMRC also accepted that cottages occupied by retired farm workers and buildings used to provide welfare facilities for farm employees were agricultural buildings (CA, para 40100).

10.41 'Other works' were not defined by the legislation, but HMRC would accept that they had a wider definition than 'buildings or structures' that qualified for IBAs (see **7.47** *et seq*). They included: drainage and sewage works; water and electricity supply installations; walls; planting shelter belts of trees; silos; farm roads; reclamation of former agricultural land; and removal of trees or hedges that were dead, diseased or obstructed agricultural operations (CA, para 40100).

10.42 Where stone or gravel from a quarry or gravel pit on an agricultural estate was used in the construction of an agricultural building, ABAs were available on a proportion of the working costs of the quarry or pit that were reasonably attributable to the stone or gravel used in the construction of the building (unless those costs were already allowable as a property business profits deduction for corporation tax or *ITTOIA 2005, Pt 3* for income tax) (CA, para 40200).

10.43 A final difference between ABAs and IBAs was that whereas IBAs were not available for expenditure in use as, or part of, or ancillary to, a retail shop (see **7.104**), the same exclusion did not exist for ABAs, so they were available for buildings used as retail shops, providing that they sold farm-produced produce. ABAs were not available to the extent that bought-in produce was sold (CA, para 40100). Where this occurred it was necessary to apportion the expenditure on a just and reasonable basis between the part used for the purposes of husbandry, which would qualify for ABAs (ie selling produce produced by the farm) and the part used for other purposes, which would not (ie selling bought-in produce) (*s 369(5)*). For example, this apportionment may have reasonably been based on the proportions of turnover of each type of produce.

Chapter 11

Property investors – specific issues

INTRODUCTION

11.1 For most types of capital allowance, it is not a requirement that the assets should be used, or the premises occupied, by the person incurring the expenditure. The effect of this is that allowances are available, in appropriate circumstances, to property investors, as well as to owner-occupiers.

11.2 An exception to this rule is the case of research and development allowances (see **Chapter 19**), where there is a specific requirement that the expenditure is related to the trade of the person incurring the expenditure. Where a property investor (for example, a group property company holding properties occupied and used by its trading associates) incurs expenditure on an asset to be used for research and development by its tenant, that requirement is not met.

BUILDINGS

11.3 Allowances on buildings, rather than on plant within those buildings, are no longer generally available, with the exception of business premises renovation allowances (see **11.61** *et seq*) and research and development allowances (see **Chapter 19**). Historically, buildings held by a property investor, if they are to qualify for allowances, had to meet the same conditions as those held by owner-occupiers. In essence, this means allowances were generally only available for:

(*a*)   industrial buildings – abolished from April 2011 (see **Chapter 7**);

(*b*)   qualifying hotels – abolished from April 2011 (see **Chapter 8**); and

(*c*)   commercial buildings in enterprise zones – abolished from April 2011 (see **Chapter 9**).

11.4 The provisions relating to industrial buildings allowances are included, despite their abolition, as:

(i)   advisers will still be dealing with earlier years, and

(ii)   claims by new purchasers or lessees of industrial buildings will be affected by the tax history of the building.

11.5   The broad requirement was merely that the building was in use for a qualifying purpose at the end of a chargeable period, whether by the owner or by a tenant, licensee, etc. The landlord, therefore, needed to ascertain, when considering a potential tenant, whether that tenant's trade would enable the building to qualify for allowances. All else being equal, it was advantageous to select a tenant who was carrying on a qualifying trade, rather than one who was not.

11.6   Similarly, it is worth stressing that in order to qualify for a full year's allowances, the property only needed to be in qualifying use on the last day of that year. The landlord should be mindful, however, that a building needed to actually be *in use* (see **7.48** *et seq*). It was not sufficient that a tenant had moved into the building and was fitting it out for his own needs, or had signed a lease but not yet moved in.

Transferring allowances to lessee

11.7   Where a long lease was granted out of the relevant interest in an industrial building, the allowances generally remained with the holder of the relevant interest. The lessor and lessee could elect jointly to transfer the right to allowances to the lessee, where the new lease was for a period exceeding 50 years (*s 290(1)*). The long lease was then regarded as the relevant interest, and any capital sum paid by the lessee in consideration of the grant of the lease was regarded as consideration for purchase of that relevant interest (*s 290(2)*). The capital sum had to be apportioned between land and buildings, so that the former could be excluded from the claim for allowances (CA, para 12300).

11.8   See pro forma election, **Appendix 5**.

11.9   The election needed to be made within two years after the date on which the lease took effect (*s 291(4)*). Inspectors were formerly instructed to refuse a late election unless, within the two years, there had been a clear indication of an intention to elect, or all parties concerned had submitted computations on the basis that such an election had been or would be made. This concession now appears to have been removed, making a formal election essential (CA, para 33100). An election was not possible where:

(*a*)   the lessor and the lessee were connected (*s 291(1)*) (see **20.25–20.30**); or

(*b*)   it appeared that the sole or main benefit which may be expected to accrue to the lessor from the grant of the lease and the making of an election was the obtaining of a balancing allowance (*s 291(2)*) (see **12.9** *et seq*).

11.10 Condition (*a*) above did not prevent an election being made where the lessor was a body discharging statutory functions and the lessee a company of which it has control (*s 291(1)*).

11.11 No such election was possible where construction was yet to commence (*s 290(1)(a)*).

PLANT

General

11.12 Expenditure on plant will qualify for allowances if it is incurred for the purposes of a qualifying activity (see **14.104**). This includes ordinary UK and overseas property businesses (ie property letting) (*s 15(1)(b)* and (*d*)).

11.13 Relief on fire safety expenditure has historically been given by ESC B16. However, the legislation to which this Concession refers (*s 29*) was abolished with effect from 1 April 2008 (corporation tax) and 6 April 2008 (income tax), so logically the Concession ceased to apply after those dates. The eligibility of expenditure on fire safety expenditure now depends therefore on general principles (see **Chapter 15**).

11.14 Expenditure incurred by a property investor on fixtures in a let building does not generally qualify for first-year allowances (see **14.20** *et seq*). Expenditure may qualify for the AIA (see **14.62** *et seq*).

Fixtures

Historical position – an anomaly

11.15 Prior to 11 July 1984, where a person (normally a lessee) incurred expenditure on an item of machinery or plant (eg a lift or heating system) which formed part of a building he did not own, no allowances were strictly available. This anomaly, brought to public attention by *Stokes* (*Inspector of Taxes*) *v Costain Property Investments Ltd* (1984) 57 TC 688 (see **Appendix 4**), resulted from the application of general property law and its interaction with specific capital allowances legislation. In brief, such fixtures, being inseparable from the building and installed under a development agreement, became in law the property of the owner of the building (that is, generally the freeholder). Capital allowances were not, therefore, available to the person incurring the expenditure because the building, and hence the fixtures, did not belong to him as required by *s 11(4)(a)*. Nor could the landlord claim allowances, for although he owned the building, and hence, under general land law principles, owned the fixtures, he had not incurred the expenditure. Concern regarding this perceived injustice eventually led to the specific rules on fixtures which now make up *CAA 2001, Pt 2, Ch 14*.

11.16 *Finance Act 2001* removed the requirement for the person incurring expenditure to have an interest in land, where that person is an energy services provider (*FA 2001, s 66, Sch 18* – see **18.71** *et seq*).

The nature of fixtures

11.17 A fixture is defined by *s 173(1)* as:

(*a*) 'plant or machinery that is so installed or otherwise fixed in or to a building or other description of land as to become, in law, part of that building or other land'; and

(*b*) 'includes any boiler or water-filled radiator installed in a building as part of a space or water heating system'.

11.18 This is most commonly applied to lifts, heating systems, air conditioning, telephone systems and wiring, etc, although the net can be stretched wider. Where any question arises as to whether any machinery or plant has become, in law, part of a building or other land and that question is material with respect to the liability to tax (for whatever period) of two or more persons, that question is determined, for the purposes of the tax of all those persons, by the Special Commissioners (*s 204(1)–(3)*).

11.19 The case *of J C Decaux (UK) Ltd v Francis (Inspector of Taxes)* [1996] STC (SCD) 281 considered the distinction between chattels and fixtures. Key factors were held to be the method and degree of annexation to the land (broadly, *how* it is fixed) and, most importantly, the object and purpose of that annexation (broadly, *why* it is fixed). This approach is reflected in HMRC guidance (CA, para 26025). In *Decaux*, the essential question was whether the items (automated public conveniences, bus shelters, etc) were fixed for the better enjoyment of the items themselves, or whether they were installed as an amenity or feature of the land to which the public had recourse.

11.20 The question of what constitutes a fixture is more usually a question of land law, rather than revenue law, and full consideration of this subject is, therefore, beyond the scope of this work. However, a useful summary of the relevant law (since 1872) is to be found in *TSB Bank Plc v Botham* (1996) 73 P & CR D1, CA, *Holland v Hodgson* (1872) LR 7 CP 328 and *Berkley v Poulett* (1976) 241 Estates Gazette 911, CA. The method and degree of annexation has historically had the greatest significance and suggests that property is *prima facie* a fixture if it is physically fixed or substantially connected to the land. If the asset cannot be removed without causing serious damage to some part of the land or building to which it is attached, then it is likely to be a fixture. However, more recently, the courts have given greater prominence to the object and purpose of annexation. This considers whether the asset's attachment to the land is meant to be a permanent and lasting improvement of the land or building (in which case it is a fixture), or whether it was fixed on a temporary basis and merely so the asset may be used and better enjoyed as a chattel (in which case it is not a fixture).

11.21   Following the *Decaux* case above, *FA 1997, Sch 16* directed that where affixation to the land is merely incidental, allowances are available on leased fixtures irrespective of whether the lessee is carrying on a trade. For this to apply, the following conditions must be met (*s 179*):

(*a*)   The plant is fixed to land (and not to a building).

(*b*)   The equipment lessee has an interest in that land (see **11.23**) at the time he takes possession of the plant.

(*c*)   The plant may be severed from the land (and will belong to the lessor) at the end of the lease.

(*d*)   The plant is of a type which may be re-used following such severance.

(*e*)   The lease is accounted for as an operating lease (ie, one that does *not* transfer substantially all of the risks and rewards of ownership to the lessee; *not* a finance lease).

11.22   In *Melluish (Inspector of Taxes) v Barclays Mercantile Insurance Finance (No 3) Ltd* [1995] STC 964, it was held, following the non-tax case *Hobson v Gorringe* [1897] 1 Ch 182, that the intention of the parties as to the ownership of fixtures was only material so far as such intention could be presumed from the degree and object of the affixation. The contractual terms between the parties could not affect the question of whether, in law, a chattel had become a fixture and, therefore, belonged to the owner of the land.

11.23   Various provisions require the person incurring expenditure to have an 'interest in land'. This is defined as (*s 175*):

(*a*)   the fee simple estate or an agreement to acquire such estate (generally the freehold);

(*b*)   a lease or (except in the context of leasing plant and machinery) an agreement to acquire a lease (defined in *s 174*);

(*c*)   Scottish equivalents of the above;

(*d*)   an easement or servitude or an agreement to acquire such an interest; or (*e*) a licence to occupy land provided it is an 'exclusive' licence (that is, giving permission to enter and remain on land to exert control over that land) (CA, para 26100).

11.24 HMRC has confirmed that where a tenant is permitted to occupy land without a formal lease or licence, that nonetheless qualifies as an interest in land for this purpose.

11.25 The reference in (*b*) to leasing machinery or plant must relate to plant leased as a trade, separate from any building to which it is fixed. It cannot apply to fixtures in a let property, as to do so would be for *s 175* to contradict itself.

Expenditure on 'new' fixtures

11.26 *Section 176* applies where the holder of an *existing* interest in the relevant land (see the *Decaux* case below – **11.27**) incurs expenditure on 'new' fixtures (eg installed during a construction project). The 'relevant land' in relation to a fixture means the building or other description of land of which the fixture becomes part, or, in the case of a boiler or water-filled radiator, the building in which it is installed (*s 173*). Such fixtures are treated as belonging to the person incurring the expenditure. Where two or more persons with an interest in the relevant property incur expenditure on the same fixture, the fixture is treated as belonging under *s 176* only to the person with the lowest interest (although the other person may be able to claim under the contributions rules – see **1.119** *et seq*). If both persons have the same level of interest, then they will both be able to claim under *s 176* for the part of the expenditure they incur (CA, para 26150).

Example

John owns a freehold office and Adrian is his leasehold tenant. Adrian installs an air conditioning unit and John agrees to pay half of its cost. Adrian is the only person entitled to claim plant and machinery allowances for the expenditure under the fixtures rules of *s 176* because he has the lowest interest. However, John may claim plant and machinery allowances for his expenditure under the contributions rules of *s 538* (and Adrian is prevented from claiming for that expenditure, because he has not incurred it, by *s 532*).

11.27 In the case of *Decaux* [1996] STC (SCD) 281, it was confirmed that the interest must be in place when the expenditure is incurred; it is not sufficient that it comes into being upon, and as a result of, the incurring of the expenditure. However, a formal agreement to create such an interest may itself enable allowances to be under (*a*) or (*b*) in **11.23**.

Expenditure on fixtures incurred by equipment lessor

11.28 **Chapter 18** deals with the situation where machinery or plant which becomes a fixture is not owned by the tenant of the building, but rather is leased to him by a third party (ie not the owner of the building or indeed anyone with an interest in the building).

Acquisition of existing interest in land – 'second-hand' fixtures

11.29 The person who first installs fixtures in a building is catered for by *s 176* (see **11.26** *et seq*).

11.30 Where a building is sold second-hand for an amount which includes a capital sum in respect of existing fixtures, those fixtures are treated as belonging to the purchaser, unless another person has a 'prior right' in relation to the fixture, in which case the fixture is treated as belonging to that other person instead. Another person has a prior right if immediately before the sale he is treated as the fixture owner by (*s 181*):

(*a*) having incurred expenditure on the provision of the fixture (but not by virtue of the contributions rules – see **1.119** *et seq*);

(*b*) being entitled to an allowance (ie having allocated the expenditure to a pool (see **14.3**)) (as defined by *s 202*) in respect of that expenditure; and

(*c*) making or having made a claim for allowances (as defined by *s 202*) in respect of that expenditure.

11.31 The most commonly encountered example is a tenant that has installed plant into its leased premises.

11.32 This treatment also applies where a purchaser of an interest in land pays a capital sum to discharge the obligations of an equipment lessee to whom the fixtures were previously let (*s 182*). However, allowances are denied if another person has an interest in the same land, was treated as owning the fixtures prior to the sale, is entitled to an allowance in respect of those fixtures, and has made such a claim (*s 182(2)*).

11.33 The amount qualifying for allowances may be restricted by reference to original cost (*s 185*). The practical implications of this are considered in **4.35** *et seq*.

11.34 In addition, where second-hand fixtures are acquired after April 2012, the purchaser may, depending on the tax history of those fixtures and the terms of the acquisition, only be able to claim allowances by applying to the Tax Chamber of the First-tier Tribunal (see **4.16–4.34**).

Creation of a new interest in land – 'second-hand' fixtures

Lessor entitled to allowances

11.35 *Section 181* (above) covers the situation where an existing interest in a building changes hands. *Section 183* deals with the creation of a new lease where the incoming lessee pays a capital sum for existing fixtures. In such circumstances, the lessor and lessee may elect jointly for the fixtures to be treated as belonging to the lessee provided that the lessor would have been entitled to allowances on the fixtures in the chargeable period (or its basis period) in which the lease was granted. A lessor who cannot fulfil this condition through not being within the charge to tax (eg a pension fund) will be regarded as being within the charge to tax for this purpose (*s 183(1)(b)*). The election must be made within two years of the lease taking effect. No election may be made if the parties are connected (*s 183(1)(d)*). Note that it is the lessor's position and not that of the lessee which is important here. An election under *s 199* may be used in conjunction with one under *s 183* to fix the amount allocated to fixtures in this way.

11.36 See pro forma election, **Appendix 5**.

Lessor not entitled to allowances

11.37 Where the lessor was not entitled to allowances (other than simply through not being within the charge to tax), the fixtures are treated as belonging to the lessee, who will then be entitled to capital allowances, but only if (at the time the lease is granted) no person has previously been entitled to allowances (*s 184*).

11.38 This would apply, for example, where the lessor was a property developer.

11.39 Allowances will be denied where another interest in the land exists, and the person with that interest was treated as owning the fixtures prior to the sale, has made a claim, and remains entitled to claim allowances on those fixtures – a 'prior right' (*s 184(2)*).

11.40 In *West Somerset Railway Plc v Chivers (Inspector of Taxes)* [1995] STC (SCD) 1, the onus of proving that no person had previously been entitled to allowances was held to fall on the claimant. In that case the taxpayer paid a capital sum to acquire a 99-year lease of a railway line and claimed plant and machinery allowances on the railway fixtures. However, the

Special Commissioner held that the company failed to prove that no person had previously been entitled to claim capital allowances for the fixtures (albeit acknowledged to be an almost impossible task) and on the *balance of probabilities* (ie is it more likely than not) it was likely that a prior freehold owner had become entitled to allowances. Therefore, no allowances were available to the purchaser of the long lease. This is also relevant where *s 185* is in point (see **4.36**).

11.41   The key point is to look at the *balance of probabilities* – this case should not be interpreted as imposing a burden of absolute proof on the taxpayer in every case. In many cases, particularly where a freehold is being acquired, the balance of probabilities is that the purchaser will be entitled to allowances.

11.42   A Plc is a property developer. During 2001 it incurred expenditure of £2 million in erecting an office building including £50,000 in respect of air conditioning. In 2004 the building was leased at a premium to B. Of the total premium £75,000 was allocated to the air conditioning.

11.43   B will obtain capital allowances on the £75,000 as A Plc was not entitled to allowances (its own expenditure was on trading account and not capital), and the fixtures have not been used for the purpose of A Plc's trade.

11.44   Where the property acquired includes fixtures which have previously been involved in a claim for IBAs or research and development allowances, the qualifying expenditure is also restricted (*ss 186* and *187*) – see **4.39**.

Deemed disposal of fixtures

11.45   A person claiming capital allowances on fixtures is required to bring a disposal value into account on the occurrence of a sale or any of the similar events listed in *s 61*. In addition, a fixture is treated as ceasing to belong to a person when that person ceases to have the qualifying interest in the building to which the plant is fixed (*s 188(2)*).

11.46   In certain circumstances, the qualifying interest is deemed to continue even though it has actually ceased. It is assumed in each of the following cases that the interest has continued in the form of the new interest. The relevant circumstances are as follows:

(*a*)   The qualifying interest ceases to exist because it is merged into another interest acquired by the same person (*s 189(2)*).

(*b*)   The qualifying interest is a lease and, on its termination, a new lease of the relevant land (with or without other land) is granted to the lessee (*s 189(3)*).

(c)   The qualifying interest is a licence and, on its termination, a new licence to occupy the relevant land (with or without other land) is granted to the licensee (*s 189(4)*).

(d)   The qualifying interest is a lease and after expiry of the lease, the lessee remains in possession of the relevant land with the consent of the lessor but without a new lease being granted to him (*s 189(5)*).

11.47   When, on the termination of a lease (or of a licence) a fixture is treated as ceasing to belong to the lessee (or licensee) then it is treated as beginning to belong to the lessor (*s 193*).

11.48   If a 'fixture' ceases to be a fixture by virtue of being permanently severed from the relevant land, it is treated as ceasing to belong to the person to whom the 'fixtures' legislation deems it to belong. This is not the case where the severed fixture does actually continue to belong to that person (*s 191*).

Disposal value of fixtures

Continuation of qualifying interest

11.49   If the qualifying interest is sold and the fixture is not permanently severed from the land, the vendor's disposal value is taken to be the amount treated as expenditure incurred by the purchaser. This will, in most cases, be the actual proceeds. If the amount is less than the open market value, then that value is substituted for the actual proceeds unless the purchaser's expenditure on the fixture will qualify for capital allowances as plant or for scientific research allowances (*s 196*). *However*, the disposal value cannot exceed the capital expenditure originally incurred on the provision of the machinery or plant (*s 62*).

Expiry of qualifying interest

11.50   If the fixture ceases to belong to the former owner because of the expiry of the qualifying interest, then, except insofar as the former owner receives any capital sum, the disposal value will be nil. Any actual proceeds or compensation received will, of course, be taken into account (*s 196, Table, item 4*).

Example

Rhubarb Ltd is the lessee of an office building and during the tenancy it installs a small lift for distributing internal post. The total cost of the lift and installation is £20,000. The following year, Rhubarb Ltd goes into receivership and the residue of the lease is assigned to Custard Ltd for £30,000 of which £10,000 is agreed to refer to the fixture. After a further two years, Custard Ltd is liquidated and the residue of the lease is abandoned.

The lift ('the fixture') is deemed to belong to Rhubarb Ltd and normal capital allowances are available. On the assignment of the lease by the receiver, Rhubarb Ltd has to bring into account a disposal value. This is the agreed consideration of £10,000, even if it is below market value, because Custard Ltd is entitled to allowances. Custard Ltd is entitled to normal capital allowances on expenditure of £10,000. When the company ceases to trade a disposal value has to be brought into account by virtue of *s 61, Table, item 6.* This value would in practice be nil.

Immediately after the abandonment of the lease, the fixture is deemed to belong to the lessor. No capital allowances are available, however, because it has not itself incurred any capital expenditure.

Restriction of qualifying expenditure

11.51   Where, on or after 24 July 1996, a person incurs expenditure on fixtures, in respect of which a former owner has pooled qualifying expenditure, then the maximum amount on which allowances may be claimed will be equal to the disposal value required to be brought into account by that former owner, together with any incidental expenditure incurred by the new owner under *s 25* (*s 185*). The disposal value is taken to be the amount treated as expenditure incurred by the purchaser, which will, in most cases, be the actual proceeds (see **11.49**).

Landlord's energy saving allowance

11.52   Since 6 April 2004, tax relief is available under *ITTOIA 2005, s 312* for non-corporate landlords who incur capital expenditure installing energy-saving insulation to residential property. For expenditure incurred on or after 8 July 2008, this was extended to corporate landlords (*CTA 2009, s 251* and *SI 2008/1520*).

11.53   It was announced at Budget 2015 that the landlord's energy saving allowance will no longer be available after 31 March 2015 for corporate landlords or after 5 April 2015 for non-corporate landlords.

11.54   The landlord's energy saving allowance provides a tax deduction in computing rental income until 5 April 2015 of up to a maximum of £1,500 for the installation of:

- cavity wall insulation and loft insulation from 6 April 2004 (*Energy-Saving Items* (*Deductions for Expenditure etc*) *Regulations 2004, SI 2004/2664*);

- solid wall insulation from 7 April 2005 (*Energy-Saving Items Regulations 2005, SI 2005/1114*);

- hot water system insulation and draught proofing from 6 April 2006 (*Energy-Saving Items* (*Deductions for Expenditure etc*) *Regulations 2006, SI 2006/912*); and

- floor insulation from 6 April 2007 (*Energy-Saving Items Regulations 2007, SI 2007/831*).

11.55   For expenditure incurred up to and including 5 April 2007, the £1,500 deduction was available per 'building', but for expenditure incurred on or after 6 April 2007 it is available per 'property' so that the maximum £1,500 is deductible for each flat in a block of flats (*FA 2007, s 18*).

11.56   No deduction is available if the energy-saving item is installed during the course of construction (that is to say, the relief is only intended for the retro-fitting of insulation), or if the person incurring the expenditure does not have an interest in the property or is in the course of acquiring an interest in the property (*ITTOIA 2005, s 313(2)*). However, confusion arises where a person currently does not have an interest, but is trying to obtain one. A literal reading of the legislation suggests that the person would not qualify because he is in the course of acquiring an interest in the property. However this would be illogical because:

(i)   that person would not qualify anyway (because he already does not have an interest in the property, so the extra wording is unnecessary); and

(ii)   if a person with a qualifying interest (eg a tenant) was looking to improve his interest (eg was acquiring the freehold), then he would no longer qualify.

11.57   Therefore, the logical conclusion is that the legislation is poorly drafted and the allowance was intended to be made available to a person with an interest, or who was looking to acquire an interest or a further interest.

11.58   Furthermore, no deduction is available if the property is furnished holiday accommodation or let under the rent-a-room scheme.

11.59   For new property investment businesses the deduction is available for expenditure incurred in the six months before the business commenced, providing that it was not incurred before 6 April 2004 (*ITTOIA 2005, s 313(5), Sch 2, para 73*).

11.60   Where only part of the expenditure would qualify for the relief, but the remainder would not, then the tax deduction is calculated using a just and reasonable apportionment (*ITTOIA 2005, s 312(4)*).

Business premises renovation allowance

11.61   *Finance Act 2005* announced a new 100% allowance for expenditure on the renovation of business premises, whether owned or let, with the intention that those premises are brought back into business use. After a long delay whilst waiting for EU approval, it was finally announced that the allowance would be available from 11 April 2007 (*SI 2007/945*), and would operate for at least five years (*s 360B*). It was announced on 23 March 2011 that the scheme would be extended for another five years, ending on 10 April 2017 (*SI 2012/868*). The premises must have been vacant for a year or more and be situated in a designated disadvantaged area (*FA 2005, s 92, Sch 6*).

11.62   Somewhat perversely, the legislation may encourage a taxpayer whose premises have been vacant for a few months, and who is considering work of this kind, to postpone the works until such time as the property has been vacant for a full year, so as to ensure the 100% allowance may be claimed.

11.63   The allowances are only available to the person incurring the expenditure, not to a subsequent purchaser, and may be 'clawed back' if there is a sale or other balancing event within five years (seven years for expenditure incurred before 1 April 2014 for corporation tax purposes or 6 April 2014 for income tax purposes) (*s 360I*).

11.64   Three basic conditions must be met in order for expenditure to qualify for the business premises renovation allowance (BPRA). These are (*s 360A*):

(i)   it must be qualifying expenditure;

(ii)   it must be on a qualifying building; and

(iii)   the person incurring the expenditure must have a relevant interest (see **11.56**) in the building.

Qualifying expenditure

11.65   Qualifying expenditure is capital expenditure incurred in connection with:

(i)   the conversion of a qualifying building (see **11.77**) into qualifying premises (see **11.80**);

(ii) the renovation of a qualifying building that is or will be qualifying premises; or

(iii) repairs to a qualifying building, incidental to the above conversion or renovation.

(*s 360B(1), (2A)*)

11.66 With effect for expenditure incurred from 1 April 2014 for corporation tax purposes or 6 April 2014 for income tax purposes, this is known as Condition A, and a further Condition B is introduced.

11.67 Condition B is that the expenditure is incurred on:

(*a*) building works,

(*b*) architectural or design services,

(*c*) surveying or engineering services,

(*d*) planning applications, or

(*e*) statutory fees or statutory permissions.

(*s 360B(2B)*)

11.68 Other expenditure not listed in Condition B may still qualify for relief, but only to the extent that that expenditure (in total) does not exceed 5% of the qualifying expenditure incurred on the matters mentioned in (*a*) to (*c*) above, ie building works, architectural or design services, and surveying or engineering services. Project management costs may therefore qualify under this provision.

11.69 However, the following expenditure will not qualify (*s 360B(3)*):

(i) the demolition of existing buildings;

(ii) the extension of a qualifying building, except where to provide access to or from qualifying business premises;

(iii) the development of land adjoining or adjacent to a qualifying building;

(iv) the provision of plant and machinery (other than certain fixtures); or

(v) the acquisition of land or rights in or over land.

11.70 With effect for expenditure incurred from 1 April 2014 for corporation tax purposes or 6 April 2014 for income tax purposes, the definition of 'fixtures', expenditure on which may qualify for relief, is further curtailed. In such cases, the fixtures concerned must be listed in *s 360B(3A)*.

11.71   That subsection includes:

(*a*)   integral features within the meaning of *s 33A*;

(*b*)   automatic control systems for opening and closing doors, windows and vents;

(*c*)   window cleaning installations;

(*d*)   fitted cupboards and blinds;

(*e*)   protective installations such as lightning protection, sprinkler and other equipment for containing or fighting fires, fire alarm systems and fire escapes;

(*f*)   building management systems;

(*g*)   cabling in connection with telephone, audio-visual data installations and computer networking facilities, which are incidental to the occupation of the building;

(*h*)   sanitary appliances, and bathroom fittings which are hand driers, counters, partitions, mirrors or shower facilities;

(*i*)   kitchen and catering facilities for producing and storing food and drink for the occupants of the building;

(*j*)   signs;

(*k*)   public address systems; and

(*l*)   intruder alarm systems.

(*s 360B(3A)*)

11.72   Expenditure is excluded to the extent that it exceeds the market value amount for the works, services or other matters to which it relates. The 'market value amount' means the amount of expenditure which it would have been normal and reasonable to incur on the works, services or other matters in the market conditions prevailing when the expenditure was incurred, assuming the transaction as a result of which the expenditure was incurred was between persons dealing with each other at arm's length in the open market (*s 360B(3B)*, (*3C*)).

11.73   Allowances are not available for property previously used or to be used for the following trade sectors: fishery, shipbuilding, the coal industry, synthetic fibres, the primary production of certain agricultural products, and the manufacture and marketing of products which imitate or substitute for milk or milk products.

11.74 Furthermore, expenditure only qualifies for relief if the works to which it relates are completed before the end of the period of 36 months beginning with the date when the expenditure was incurred.

11.75 To the extent that it relates to works that are not completed or provided before the end of that period, the expenditure is to be treated for the purposes of BPRA as never having been incurred (unless and until the works are actually completed).

11.76 If a person who has made a tax return becomes aware that anything in it has become incorrect because of the operation of this provision, that person must give notice to an officer of Revenue and Customs specifying how the return needs to be amended. The notice must be given within three months beginning with the day on which the person first became aware that anything in the return had become incorrect because of the operation of this provision (*s 360BA*).

Example

Biggs incurs £100,000 on work potentially qualifying for BPRA on 15 April 2014. However, only 90% of the works are carried out by the third anniversary of incurring the expenditure, ie 15 April 2017. Consequently, £10,000 of the BPRA is withdrawn, and the 2014/15 tax return amended. Biggs will be able to claim the final £10,000 when the works are actually completed.

Qualifying buildings

11.77 The whole or a part of a building or structure may qualify, provided all of the following conditions are met (*s 360C*):

(i)   It must be situated in a designated disadvantaged area (see **11.79**), *on the date on which the work begins.*

(ii) It must have been unused for at least 12 months before the date on which the work begins.

(iii) It must have last been used for the purposes of a trade, vocation or profession, or as an office (for any purpose).

(iv) It must not have last been used as a dwelling, or as part of a dwelling.

11.78 It should be emphasised that if the building was last used as an office, it need *not* have been used for a trade, vocation or profession. This potentially extends the relief, therefore, to premises last used by governmental bodies or charities (but only if they were used as offices).

Designated disadvantaged areas

11.79   Although the Treasury may designate additional areas, the initial list of qualifying areas is the same as for the purposes of stamp duty land tax (SDLT) disadvantaged areas relief (*FA 2006, Sch 6*). There are approximately 2,000 such designated disadvantaged areas across the UK designated by the *Assisted Areas Order 2007* (*SI 2007/107*). An online postcode database is available at www.ukassistedareasmap.com/ieindex.html. Where a property lies across the boundary of a designated area, a just and reasonable apportionment may be made, to determine what proportion of expenditure qualifies for relief (*s 360C(6)*). It should be noted that the assisted areas are not necessarily the same as those which used to be treated as such for SDLT reliefs, or for the 100% plant allowances available in newly-designated enterprise zones (see **9.45** *et seq*).

Qualifying business premises

11.80   Qualifying business premises consist of a qualifying building which is used (or is available and suitable for letting for use) for the purposes of a trade, vocation or profession, or as an office (for any purpose), and which is not a dwelling or part of one (*s 360D*).

11.81   Essentially, then, the relief aims to encourage the restoration to qualifying use of premises which last had a qualifying use, but have then been unused for 12 months.

Relevant interest

11.82   The rules for determining the relevant interest generally mirror those for flat conversion allowances and for IBAs. Generally, the relevant interest will be the interest held by the person incurring the expenditure, at the time the expenditure was incurred (*s 360F*), or acquired by him as a result of the work being done (*s 360G*).

11.83   Where that person has more than one interest, the reversionary or superior interest will be the relevant one. As with IBAs, the interest does not cease to be the relevant interest just because a new interest (eg a lease) is created out of it. If the relevant interest merges with a superior interest (eg if a lessee acquires the freehold) that superior interest becomes the relevant one. No WDA is given, however, if the owner of the relevant interest has granted a long lease (ie exceeding 50 years) for a capital sum (*s 360I(1)*).

Allowances given

11.84   The relief is given as an expense of the claimant's property investment business, or trade, profession or vocation. The allowance given is equal to 100% of the expenditure incurred, in the year that the expenditure is incurred. The taxpayer may choose to take a lesser amount, in which case the balance is relieved by way of WDAs at the rate of 25% pa (*s 360G*). WDAs are only given where the taxpayer still has the relevant interest at the year-end.

Balancing events

11.85   A balancing adjustment will be made if a balancing event takes place within five years (seven years for expenditure incurred before 1 April 2014 for corporation tax purposes or 6 April 2014 for income tax purposes) of the date on which the premises were first used (or available for use) as qualifying business premises (that is, after the renovation, etc). A balancing adjustment can be a charge or an allowance, and is calculated by comparing the disposal proceeds (eg the sale price) with the 'residue of qualifying expenditure' (ie the tax written-down value not yet written off, which, if the 100% allowance has been taken, will be nil, resulting in a 'claw-back', so taxpayers may wish to postpone major changes of use, or the sale of property until seven years have passed) (*s 360P*).

11.86   The proceeds to be taken into account are as follows:

Balancing event	Proceeds
Sale of relevant interest	Net sale proceeds
Grant of a long lease for a capital sum	The capital sum received, or if higher, the commercial premium that would have been paid
End of lease if a connected person has a superior interest	Market value
Death of person who incurred qualifying expenditure	Residue of qualifying expenditure immediately before death
Demolition or destruction	Net amount received for the remains of the building, plus any insurance money or capital sums received by way of compensation
Qualifying building ceases to be qualifying business premises	Market value

Grants

11.87   No allowance is given in respect of expenditure which is met by grants received (*s 360L*).

Appropriations to or from trading stock

11.88   It may be that a taxpayer has both a trade and a property rental activity. For example, a company may hold some properties as trading stock for sale, and others as investment properties to generate rental income. As circumstances or intentions change, properties may be transferred from trading stock to fixed assets, or vice-versa.

11.89   Where an asset is transferred from trading stock, there is a deemed sale at market value (*ITTOIA 2005, s 172B* (income tax), *CTA 2009, s 157* (corporation tax)). However, for capital allowances purposes, the qualifying expenditure is the original cost (CA, para 11530). *CAA 2001, s 13* (use for qualifying activity of plant or machinery provided for other purposes) would not apply because the 'actual expenditure' was not capital expenditure.

11.90   Where an asset is transferred from fixed assets to trading stock, there is a deemed sale at market value, and if capital allowances have been claimed, a disposal value must be brought into account (limited under normal principles to original cost) (*ITTOIA 2005, s 172C* (income tax), *CTA 2009, s 158* (corporation tax)).

Chapter 12

Sale of property

INTRODUCTION

General

12.1   The primary tax implication on the sale of fixed assets is often the realisation of a capital gain or loss. The interaction of capital allowances with capital gains tax is dealt with in **Chapter 22**.

12.2   It is worth emphasising that, contrary to common misconception, claiming capital allowances does *not* reduce the capital gains base cost, thereby increasing any subsequent gain (although this can occur if land remediation relief has been claimed – see **24.35** *et seq*). However, where the property being sold has in the past qualified for capital allowances, there may as a completely separate issue, be a claw-back of the allowances previously given (a balancing charge), or, dependent on the circumstances, a reduction in future allowances or an additional immediate balancing allowance (see **12.49**). Where fixtures are concerned, the risk of a balancing charge may be mitigated by making an election under *s 198* (see **4.44** *et seq*).

12.3   It is also worth emphasising that the vendor's obligation to account for a disposal value (in turn potentially leading to a claw-back of allowances) is unaffected by whether or not the purchaser intends to claim allowances going forward. In particular, if the purchaser fails to meet the 'fixed value requirement' (*s 187A*) (see **4.24**), the seller nonetheless is required to account for a disposal value based on a just apportionment under *s 562* (see **4.12** and **4.68** *et seq*).

12.4   From the vendor's point of view, it is essential to plan to minimise any claw-back of allowances – doing nothing will inevitably lead to a loss of allowances, and possibly an immediate tax charge. Many property owners seek to avoid a claw-back or reduction of allowances on sale by entering into an election under *s 198* (see **4.44**) for a minimal amount. Since the introduction of the fixed value requirement (see **4.16**) it seems that more *s 198* elections are being rejected. Depending on timing, it may be that a seller who relied on a flawed election (see **4.55** *et seq*) finds it is rejected, such that a claw-back (and hence an additional tax charge) arises, based on a market value apportionment of the total sale price.

Ascertainment of proceeds

12.5 The proceeds of a sale will in many cases be obvious. Any part of the sale price which ultimately proves to be irrecoverable, however, is disregarded. If the vendor disposes of his right to receive any part of the proceeds, those proceeds are not taken into account, but any consideration received for disposing of his rights will be. If consideration for the sale consists of shares in the purchasing company, the proceeds will be the value of the shares issued (CA, para 11540).

12.6 Where a site (with a building on it) is sold for redevelopment, it may be arguable that the building is worthless, and the whole of the proceeds relate to the site (see **4.68** *et seq*). This could be good for vendors, but bad for a purchaser wishing to claim allowances. This will depend on the facts of each individual case.

Buildings

12.7 Historically, so far as buildings themselves were concerned (ie the 'bricks and mortar', rather than the plant within a building), the only capital allowances implication of a disposal was where the building had been an 'industrial building'. Industrial buildings allowances were abolished from April 2011, so the following comments relate to earlier accounting periods, with which agents may still be dealing.

12.8 So far as buildings are concerned, a similar adjustment may arise when a building that has qualified for research and development allowances is disposed of (see **19.59**). A taxpayer may also suffer a claw-back if flat conversion allowances or business premises renovation allowances have been claimed and a sale occurs within five years after the time when the flat was first suitable for letting as a dwelling (see **6.34**) or the date that the premises were first used as qualifying business premises (see **11.85**).

Balancing adjustments

12.9 Industrial buildings allowances are abolished from April 2011. Before their abolition, and with effect from 21 March 2007, balancing adjustments on industrial or agricultural buildings no longer arose (*FA 2007, s 36*). The following paragraphs therefore relate to events on or prior to that date.

12.10 Prior to 21 March 2007, when an industrial building was sold, then depending on the level of proceeds, compared to its tax written-down value (or 'residue of expenditure'), there might be either a further 'balancing allowance' to write the cost down to zero, or a claw-back of allowances already given (a 'balancing charge'). It should be noted that where the building concerned qualified for *agricultural*, rather than *industrial*, buildings allowances, a balancing adjustment was only ever made following a joint election by vendor and purchaser – otherwise WDAs were given, apportioned on a time basis in the year ownership changes (see **10.18**).

12.11 In addition to an outright sale, a balancing allowance or charge also arose when one of the following events occurred in respect of the *relevant interest* (*s 315*) (see **7.35** *et seq*):

(*a*)   that interest, being an interest dependent on a foreign concession, came to an end on the coming to an end of that concession;

(*b*)   that interest, being a leasehold interest, came to an end otherwise than on the person entitled thereto acquiring the interest which was reversionary thereon;

(*c*)   the building or structure was demolished or destroyed (see **12.17** *et seq*) or, without being demolished or destroyed, ceased altogether to be used;

(*d*)   any capital value was realised under *s 328* (see **12.34** *et seq*); or

(*e*)   an additional VAT rebate (see **22.7** *et seq*) in respect of any of the capital expenditure was made under *s 350* to the person entitled to the relevant interest.

12.12 This is subject to the proviso that no balancing adjustment (either allowance or charge) was made where the relevant event occurred more than 25 years after the date of the original expenditure (50 years for expenditure incurred before 6 November 1962) (*s 314(4)*).

12.13 This rule also applied to buildings in enterprise zones. Thus it is the case that, although expenditure on such buildings was generally written-off over a maximum of four years (there was a 25% WDA as an alternative to the 100% initial allowance), the building was still deemed to have a 25-year tax life and a claw-back of allowances was possible if the building was sold within that time. However, enterprise zone allowances too were abolished in April 2011 (see **Chapter 9**).

12.14 The proceeds which had to be brought into account were set out in *s 316* – they generally consisted of the net sale proceeds, insurance, salvage or compensation moneys. Where these were less than the residue of expenditure, a balancing allowance was made equal to the shortfall (*s 318(2), (3)*). If the amount of those moneys or proceeds exceeded the residue of expenditure, a balancing charge was made equal to the excess (*s 318(4)*, *(5)*). A balancing charge, however, could not exceed the total allowances given. For this purpose, only 'real' allowances were taken into account – a 'notional' allowance (see **7.133**) could never give rise to or increase a balancing charge (*s 320*).

12.15   Note that, in contrast to allowances on plant, the discontinuance of a trade (without an actual sale, etc) was not a balancing event requiring a disposal value to be brought into account for IBA purposes.

Example

Church Ltd (making up accounts to 31 December each year) incurred expenditure of £200,000 in constructing a factory which was first brought into use on 1 April 1984. WDAs were given at the rate of 4%, ie £8,000 pa. On 1 April 2005, the building was sold to Chapel Ltd for £100,000. The residue was calculated thus:

	£
Cost	200,000
Allowances	
(20 × £8,000)	(160,000)
	40,000
Proceeds	(100,000)
Balancing charge	60,000

The *residue of expenditure* before sale (£40,000) was increased by the amount of the balancing charge. The *residue of expenditure* at the time of sale was therefore £100,000. Chapel Ltd was entitled to WDAs of:

$$\frac{\text{Residue at the time of sale}}{\text{Years from sale to end of 25 years}} = \frac{100}{5} = £20,000 \text{ pa}$$

The WDA for any period could not exceed the residue of qualifying expenditure. The sum of all WDAs (together with any initial allowance) could not therefore exceed the amount of the original qualifying expenditure (*s 312*).

Use and disuse

12.16   Temporary disuse (see **7.136** *et seq*) was treated as industrial use, and did not, therefore, give rise to a balancing adjustment (*s 285*). HMRC considered that a building had 'ceased altogether to be used' where (inter alia) (CA, para 35050):

(*a*)   it had become derelict;

(*b*)   it had become unfit for further use;

(*c*)   it was to be demolished because it is in the path of new roads;

(*d*)   it was in a site which is to be redeveloped.

Demolition

12.17   HMRC gave guidance on the meaning of 'demolition', and on related issues, in a letter to the London Docklands Development Corporation on 23 May 1996. They requested that the letter be made available to all parties concerned with buildings damaged by the terrorist bombing on the Isle of Dogs, the majority of which had qualified for IBAs under *s 305* (enterprise zones). Although written in that specific context, the content of the letter is of more general application.

12.18   The letter stated that, for the purposes of *s 315*, a building would not be treated as demolished or destroyed to the extent that the cost of reinstating it was treated for tax purposes as an allowable deduction as expenditure on repairs. Whether work amounted to a repair or to an improvement is a question of fact or degree. One needed to consider whether the building as a whole had been materially improved or altered. HMRC accepted that where the original steel frame of the building remained standing and was re-used, expenditure would remain allowable as a deduction. Further, where the steel frame or other part of the structure required straightening or realigning, this too would amount to a repair rather than an improvement or alteration.

12.19   For more general guidance on the meaning of 'demolition', see the non-tax case of *Drake v Foottit* (1881) 7 QBD 201.

12.20   HMRC acknowledged that where a building was demolished shortly *after* a sale, it may well be that the building was worthless, and the entire proceeds related to the land alone.

Buildings which have not only been 'industrial'

12.21   Special rules applied where a building or structure had to some extent been used other than as an industrial building or structure, or for research and development (*s 319*). In such circumstances, any balancing allowance or charge was adjusted by reference to (*s 323*):

(*a*)   'the relevant period of ownership', which was the period beginning with the date the building was first used for any purpose, and ending with the date of the event giving rise to the balancing allowance or charge (note: if in that period the building has been sold, the relevant period began only on the day following the most recent sale) (*s 321*);

(*b*)   'the starting expenditure', which was the capital expenditure incurred on construction of the building or structure, unless the person receiving or suffering the balancing allowance or charge was not the person who incurred that expenditure (eg a subsequent purchaser), in which case the 'capital expenditure' was the residue of expenditure at the beginning of the relevant period (*s 322*); and

(*c*)   'the adjusted net cost', which was the difference between the capital expenditure and the amount of any proceeds, reduced by applying the fraction (I/R) where –

I = parts of relevant period for which building was used as an industrial building; and

R = total relevant period (in days).

12.22   Where the sale proceeds were more than the starting expenditure, a balancing charge was made equal to the net allowances made (*s 319(4), (5)*). Where the sale proceeds, etc were less than the starting expenditure then, if the adjusted net cost of the building or structure:

(*a*)   exceeded the allowances given, a balancing allowance was made of an amount equal to the excess; or

(*b*)   was less than the allowances given, a balancing charge was made of an amount equal to the shortfall (*s 319(3)*).

12.23   A balancing charge or allowance was not made where a building was sold between connected persons, and treated by *s 569* (see **20.5** *et seq*) as having been sold for a sum equal to the residue of expenditure immediately prior to the sale (*s 569(5)*).

Example

Potts Ltd (accounting date 31 December) incurred expenditure of £130,000 on the construction of a factory which was first brought into use on 1 April 1994. Apart from being used for non-industrial purposes for 15 months from

1 July 1998, it was used as a factory up until 30 April 2004, when it was sold for £125,000. The impact on capital allowances was as follows:

	£
Cost	130,000
Writing-down allowances	(20,800)
1994–1997 (4 × 4% × £130,000)	109,200
Notional allowances (see **7.133**)	
1998 (4% × £130,000)	(5,200)
	104,000
Writing-down allowances	
1999–2003 (5 × 4% × £130,000)	(26,000)
	78,000
Balancing charge	42,420
2004 – see below	
Residue after sale	120,420
Capital expenditure	130,000
Net sales proceeds	(125,000)
Net cost	5,000

Relevant period (1 April 1994–30 April 2004) = 121 months

Period of qualifying use = 106 months

	£
Adjusted net cost 5,000 × 106	
$\dfrac{(5,000 \times 106)}{121}$	4,380
Allowances given (not notional) (20,800 + 26,000)	46,800
Balancing charge	42,420

Anti-avoidance: restriction of balancing allowance

12.24   Where the relevant interest in an industrial building was sold to a connected person, *s 568* required open market value to be substituted for the actual proceeds received (if any). In the absence of anti-avoidance legislation, this would be open to abuse, in that if the market value could be artificially depressed, the value of any balancing allowance would be proportionately increased. For example, one way of depressing the market value would be to grant a lease in the building to a connected person on such terms that the value of the landlord's relevant interest decreased. If this interest was then transferred to another connected person, a balancing allowance would be triggered. *Section 325* countered such schemes where:

(*a*)   the relevant interest in a building or structure was sold subject to a subordinate interest (*s 325(1)–(3)*);

(*b*)   a balancing allowance would (but for these rules) be made; and

(*c*)   any of the three persons involved were connected, or it appeared that the sole or main benefit arising (from the sale or from the grant of the subordinate interest) would be the obtaining of an allowance.

12.25   In such circumstances, the net proceeds to the vendor:

(i)   were increased by the amount of any premium receivable by him for the grant of the subordinate interest; and

(ii)   where no rent, or no commercial rent, is payable in respect of the subordinate interest, were taken to be what the proceeds would have been if a commercial rent had been payable and the relevant interest had been sold in the open market (increased by the amount in (i) above) (*s 325(4)*).

12.26   The net proceeds were not increased, however, beyond such amount as eliminated the entire balancing allowance – this provision could not create a balancing charge (*s 325(5)*).

12.27   Despite the provisions of *s 325* (see **12.24** *et seq*), some taxpayers still sought to generate balancing allowances on related party transactions using tax avoidance schemes, which sought to artificially reduce the market value of an asset by making it subject to, for example, a mortgage or restrictive covenant. The asset would then be transferred between connected persons such that the low market value would generate a balancing allowance.

12.28   With effect for balancing events occurring on or after 27 November 2002 (unless they were in pursuance of a contract entered into earlier), *s 570A* denied a balancing allowance where:

•   a claim was made for industrial buildings allowances;

•   a balancing event (eg a sale) occurred which gave rise to a balancing allowance; and

● the proceeds of that balancing event were lower than they would otherwise be, as the result of a tax avoidance scheme.

12.29   It appears that even if a genuine balancing allowance would have arisen on the sale of the property, the use of a tax avoidance scheme would rule out entitlement to that allowance. This form of tax avoidance could therefore leave the taxpayer in a worse position than he would have been if applying the rules normally. HMRC's Explanatory Note suggests that only the 'artificial' part of the balancing allowance will be denied, but that view is not borne out by the legislation as drafted.

12.30   So far as the purchaser or transferee is concerned, any claim was based on the reduced amount of proceeds (ie as if the tax avoidance scheme had worked) (*s 570A(4)*).

LEASES

12.31   The relevant interest did not cease to be so by reason of the creation of a lease to which that interest was subject (*s 288*). The grant of a lease did not generally, therefore, give rise to a balancing adjustment. See, however, **12.34** *et seq* on realisation of a capital value where a subordinate interest was created in an enterprise zone property.

12.32   In *Woods v R M Mallen* (*Engineering*) *Ltd* (1969) 45 TC 619, the holder of a 99-year lease had constructed an industrial building. After a number of years, he granted a sub-lease for the remainder of the term of his own interest, less three days. It was held by the courts that he had not disposed of the relevant interest. The sub-lease was not the same interest as that held by the person granting that sub-lease. The effect was therefore that the holder of the head-lease was able to continue to claim allowances, rather than suffer a balancing adjustment. For many years, the tax avoidance possibilities of this fact were exploited to the full, particularly by investors in enterprise zones.

Example

Denton acquired a freehold industrial unit in an enterprise zone for £2 million in 2000. At the same time, and for the same price, his twin brother acquired the unit next door. Five years later, Denton sold his unit for £2.5 million.

His brother granted a 199-year lease of his unit, again for a premium of £2.5 million. Their capital allowances claims are as follows:

	Denton	Twin
	£	£
2000		
Additions	2,000,000	2,000,000
Allowances	(2,000,000)	(2,000,000)
2005		
B/fwd	Nil	
Proceeds	(2,000,000)	Nil
(restricted to cost)	2,000,000	
Balancing charge		
Carried forward		Nil

Long leases – joint election to transfer allowances

12.33   As described above, where a long lease was granted out of the relevant interest in an industrial building, the allowances generally remained with the holder of the relevant interest. However, the lessor and lessee could elect jointly (provided they were not connected) to transfer allowances to the lessee on the grant of a lease, for more than 50 years (*s 290*). This is more fully explored in **11.7** *et seq.*

Realisation of capital value

12.34   As shown above, it was possible for many years to avoid a balancing charge by granting a lease of a building, rather than selling it outright. This was open to abuse, particularly where the building concerned was in an enterprise zone. Typically, an enterprise zone investor would have received 100% tax relief in year one. In the absence of anti-avoidance legislation, he could dispose of a lesser interest in the property (normally the grant of a long lease) and thus recoup all or most of his original investment, without suffering a claw-back of relief. In some cases, the subsequent creation of the lesser interest was envisaged as part of a scheme to attract the initial investment. These were known as 'guaranteed exit schemes'.

12.35   Rules to prohibit such abuse were in *s 328*, which has effect for expenditure incurred under a contract entered into on or after 13 January 1994.

When the legislation was first proposed, it was intended to apply wherever a capital value was realised in respect of a current or former industrial building. This intention was modified, however, before the legislation came into force. Instead, except where a guaranteed exit scheme is concerned, the 'capital value' rules only applied:

(*a*)   where a capital value was realised within, broadly, the first seven years of a building's life (*s 330*); and

(*b*)   where the building concerned was in an enterprise zone (*CAA 2001, s 327*).

12.36   Where this applied, the capital value realised was brought into account, and gave rise to a balancing charge or claw-back of allowances (*s 328(1)*), but these provisions could not give rise to a balancing allowance (*s 328(2)*).

12.37   A capital value is realised when, in respect of a building in an enterprise zone, on which industrial buildings allowances have been given, there is paid an amount of capital value which is attributable to an interest in land (the 'subordinate interest') to which the *relevant interest* is or will be subject (*s 328(5)*). For example, where a lease is granted out of a freehold for a premium, the freehold is the relevant interest, which will thereafter be subject to the lease. The lease is an interest in land to which the premium is attributable. Capital value equal to that premium must therefore be brought into account. This applies only if the payment (in this case, the premium) is made not more than seven years after the agreement relating to the capital expenditure was entered into. This might be open to abuse. For example, it might be that a taxpayer could enter into a contract for capital expenditure, but the contract would only become unconditional after three years. Thus, of the seven-year period covered by the capital value rules, three would expire before the expenditure was irrevocably committed. Therefore, where the agreement for capital expenditure is conditional, the seven-year period runs from the time when it becomes unconditional (*s 330(1)(b)*).

12.38   Capital value is deemed to be attributable to the subordinate interest if it is paid (*s 329(1)*):

(i)   in consideration of the grant of that interest;

(ii)   in lieu of any rent payable by the person having the subordinate interest (eg a leaseholder) or in consideration of the assignment of such rent; or

(iii)   in consideration of the surrender of the subordinate interest, or the variation or waiver of any terms on which it was granted.

12.39   Capital value means any capital sum, monetary or otherwise. It excludes any amounts which are treated as rent or profits by virtue of *CTA*

2009, s 217 (s 331(1)). *CTA 2009 s 217* deals with cases where a short lease (ie one for a term not exceeding 50 years) is granted at a premium, and part of the premium is treated as an income receipt, rather than capital.

12.40 Where no premium is given, or the premium is less than would be the case if the transaction were at arm's length, then the latter 'arm's-length' premium will be brought into account, rather than the actual premium paid. This only applies where no commercial rent is payable. Therefore genuine transactions on normal commercial terms should not be 'caught' by this provision (*s 329(2)*).

12.41 The capital value rules also apply where any of the following events occur (*s 329(4)*) and ((*5*)):

(*a*) any rent payable is assigned;

(*b*) the subordinate interest is surrendered; or

(*c*) there is a variation or waiver of any of the terms on which the subordinate interest was granted, and where any consideration given is less than would be the case if the transaction were at arm's length.

Capital value – guaranteed exit arrangements

12.42 As referred to above, the capital value rules normally only apply in the first seven years after the expenditure is incurred. This limitation is removed where:

(*a*) the person acquiring the relevant interest did so in accordance with arrangements which provided for the subsequent sale of that interest or the realisation of a capital value; and

(*b*) such a sale or other relevant event is required by the acquisition arrangements, or is made more likely by virtue of such arrangements (*s 330(3), (4)*).

12.43 In such cases, a balancing charge may arise under the capital value rules at any time in the first 25 years after the expenditure is incurred. The 'capital value' rules will not apply where an election is made under *s 290* (see **12.33**), thus transferring allowances to, for example, the lessee. Where, within the seven years following the incurring of expenditure, an agreement giving rise to the realisation of a capital value becomes unconditional, then even if the capital value is actually not realised until after the expiry of those seven years, it will be treated as being realised within that period.

Capital value – effect on grantee

12.44   The capital value rules require a disposal value to be brought into account by the person granting the lease etc, but they do not deem any qualifying expenditure to be incurred by the grantee. This is less favourable, of course, than if the relevant interest were actually sold, in which case the purchaser would be entitled to allowances.

Termination of leases

12.45   The table below summarises the treatment when a lease comes to an end.

Lease ends; no new lease granted; lessee remains in possession	Lease is treated as continuing as long as the lessee is in possession (*s 359(2)*)
Lease contains option for grant of new lease; new lease is granted	New lease is treated as continuation of old lease (*s 359(3)*)
Lessor pays any sum to lessee; sum is in respect of leased building	Lease treated as surrendered in consideration of the payment (*s 359(4)*)
Lease granted to new lessee; new lessee pays a sum to old lessee	Leases treated as same lease, assigned to new lessee in consideration of payment (*s 359(5)*)

PLANT

Balancing allowances and charges

12.46   When plant is disposed of (called a 'disposal event' by *s 60*), a disposal value (*s 61* and *s 196*) (also called a 'disposal receipt' (*s 60*) or 'disposal proceeds') may have to be accounted for, giving rise to a balancing allowance or charge (a so-called 'claw-back'). The precise treatment, especially whether a balancing charge arises, will depend on whether the original expenditure on the plant was pooled.

12.47   No disposal value need be accounted for, if the plant in question had not been the subject of a capital allowances claim (*s 64*). This was specifically highlighted by HMRC as a change in law, upon the enactment of *CAA 2001*.

12.48   This latter rule does not apply where the plant was previously acquired from a connected person who did have to bring in disposal proceeds (*s 64(2), (3)*). It is not therefore possible to 'trap' allowances in a group by transferring plant intra-group for a nominal value, with the transferee then failing to make a claim.

Pooled assets

12.49 These rules apply on the disposal of assets which have been included in the general pool or the 'special rate pool'. If, in a chargeable period, the total disposal proceeds exceed the qualifying expenditure (ie the brought forward written-down value plus additions in the period), there will be a balancing charge equal to the excess (*s 56(6)*). Such an occurrence is relatively rare, but it is far more common than the occurrence of a balancing allowance. A balancing allowance on plant (other than depooled plant such as short-life assets) will generally only arise where the trade is permanently discontinued (or is deemed to be permanently discontinued).

12.50 Note that even the disposal of all the assets in the pool does not generate a balancing allowance, so long as the trade continues.

Depooled assets

12.51 Balancing allowances or charges will arise on the disposal (or deemed disposal) of individual assets not included in a pool, for example 'short-life' assets or 'old', expensive motor cars. These are discussed in **14.179** *et seq* and **17.12** *et seq*.

12.52 The amount brought in as a disposal value will in most cases be the net proceeds to the person disposing of the asset, including any compensation or insurance proceeds (*s 61*). Market value is substituted for actual proceeds where the plant is sold at below market value, unless:

(*a*) the buyer will be entitled to capital allowances on the expenditure; or

(*b*) there is a charge to tax under *Income Tax (Earnings and Pensions) Act 2003 (ITEPA 2003)* (for example where the asset is given to an employee) (*s 61, Table, item 2*).

12.53 The disposal value cannot exceed the capital expenditure originally incurred on provision of the machinery or plant (*s 62*).

12.54 Where the plant was acquired from a connected person, the limitation is to the highest capital expenditure incurred by any of the connected parties (*s 62(2), (3)*).

Fixtures

12.55   Special rules apply where fixtures are disposed of with a building. These are fully considered in **Chapter 11.** However, it is worth stating here that the deemed disposal value of fixtures depends primarily on the price achieved for the property as a whole. In particular, in determining the value attributed to fixtures, no account is to be taken of their condition or obsolescence (see **4.73**). Consequently, sellers should not assume that the sale of very old fixtures will be free of any potential tax charge.

Anti-avoidance

12.56   Where the sale of property includes assets which were allocated to the special rate pool (see **14.3**), anti-avoidance provisions potentially apply. If the asset is disposed of for less than its tax written-down value, as part of a scheme or arrangement having the obtaining of a tax advantage as a main purpose, then notional tax written-down value is substituted for the actual disposal value (*FA 2008, Sch 26*).

Chapter 13

Acquisition of a business

ACQUISITION OF SHARES

13.1　Where the acquisition of a business is effected by purchasing the shares in the company carrying on that business, there are no implications for capital allowances. Allowances continue to be due to the company as if the share transfer had not taken place. If the company's accounting date is changed in order to match that of its new parent, then to the extent that that results in an accounting period of more or less than 12 months, WDAs will be restricted or increased accordingly.

13.2　Note, however, that anti-avoidance legislation applies where a company is acquired in order that a tax advantage may be obtained using that company's capital allowances (*ss 212A–212S*). This is dealt with at **20.31–20.52**.

Due diligence

13.3　During the course of sale negotiations the buyer will normally carry out tax due diligence to identify any historic tax liabilities within the target company. In asset-rich businesses this can focus on capital allowances claims, which are typically one of the largest aspects of the tax return. Buyers should therefore ensure that any capital allowances risks and liabilities are identified and that they are adequately protected from them (as well as identifying any unforeseen opportunities that might exist, for example the scope to remedy historic under claims of capital allowances and benefit from the improvement in post-transaction periods). Similarly, sellers should seek to ensure that capital allowances claims are accurate and optimised, and that robust supporting records are available so that the company obtains a clean bill of capital allowances health.

13.4　If the due diligence process identifies any areas of potential concern, there are typically two main forms of protection available to buyers. The first is tax warranties, whose principal purpose is to elicit information on tax matters. These assist the buyer in assessing any future tax liabilities that may be suffered and operate as contractual terms, with breach of contract claims possible by the buyer if any warranties given turn out to be false (eg misleading pre-contract enquiry statements about capital allowances claims or their agreement status). Secondly, a tax deed or indemnity can be agreed, which is a covenant by the seller to pay the buyer an amount in respect of particular tax liabilities of the target company. The tax deed will also usually allocate and deal with tax administration matters in respect of pre-completion tax periods (eg allocating responsibility for preparing and agreeing capital allowances claims, which will of course also affect the buyer post-completion because of carried-forward pool balances) (see also **4.67** *et seq*).

13.5   In certain circumstances, a change in ownership combined with a major change in the nature of the trade can result in the prohibition of losses being carried forward. This equally applies to losses representing surplus capital allowances and to other losses (*Corporation Tax Act 2010 (CTA 2010), ss 673-674*).

ACQUISITION OF A TRADE

General

13.6   Where there is a succession to a trade or other business, the treatment of assets qualifying for capital allowances will depend on whether those assets are machinery and plant, or other assets.

Plant and machinery

13.7   Where there is a change in the ownership of a trade, the trade is generally treated as discontinued by reason of *CTA 2009, s 41(2)* (companies) or *ITTOIA 2005, s 882, Sch 1, para 94* (other persons, where no person is engaged in the trade both before and after the change). In such circumstances, any property which, without being sold, was in use for the trade immediately before and immediately after the change, is treated as if it was sold (at market value) to the person taking over the trade (*s 265*). The twin effects of this are that the former owner of the trade must bring in a disposal value (ie market value), and the successor is entitled to writing-down allowances, but not an annual investment allowance or first-year allowances, on the same amount (see **13.14**). The assets may be treated as integral features in the hands of the transferee. It was held in *Parmar (t/a Ace Knitwear) v Woods (Inspector of Taxes)* [2002] EWHC 1085 (Ch), [2002] STC 846 that the absence of actual consideration for plant did not mean that plant had not been transferred, if that was in fact the case.

13.8   The legislation is explicit that the requirement for the property to be in use *is* met where it is merely provided and available for use (*s 265(3)*). These provisions apply to all qualifying activities (see **14.108** *et seq*) other than an employment or office (*s 265(5)*).

13.9   An occurrence which commonly takes place in connection with a succession to a trade, although it need not, is that a person begins to use for trading purposes an asset which he already owns. Where a person brings into use for a trade an asset which he had purchased himself other than for use in a trade (or which is received by way of gift), the amount to be brought into account as qualifying expenditure is the open market value of that asset, restricted to original cost if the asset is brought into trading use on or after 21 March 2000 (*ss 13* and *14*).

Connected persons

13.10   Where the parties involved in the succession are connected an election may be made (within two years of the succession), the principal effect of which is that the plant in use at the time is deemed to be transferred at tax written-down value (ie at such a price which does not give rise to a balancing allowance or charge) (*ss 266* and *267*). In addition to being connected (as defined by *CAA 2001, ss 575* and *575A* as amended by *ITA 2007, Sch 1, para 411*) the two parties must fulfil two conditions:

(*a*)   each of them must be within the charge to tax in the United Kingdom; and

(*b*)   the successor must not be a dual resident company within *CTA 2010, s 109* (*s 266(1)*).

13.11   For the purposes of corporation tax only, for successions occurring on or after 5 December 2005, no election under *s 266* is possible where the business concerned is one of leasing plant or machinery (*s 267A*).

So far as plant and machinery fixtures (see **11.17** *et seq*) are concerned it may be more advantageous not to make a *s 266* election and instead enter into a joint election under *CAA 2001 s 198* (see **4.44** *et seq*) for a low value, such as £1 or £2, because this may generate a balancing allowance.

13.12   See pro forma election, **Appendix 5**.

Integral features

13.13   Anti-avoidance provisions may apply where the transfer of trade is between connected persons, and involves the transfer of integral features (assets listed in **14.5**). These provisions apply to prevent expenditure on existing assets which *did not* previously qualify for allowances (eg non-qualifying elements of cold water systems) being transferred to a connected person such that a claim would become possible under the new rules on the whole of the original expenditure (*FA 2008, Sch 26, para 15*). In essence, the new owner may only claim allowances on such assets if the vendor had previously claimed allowances.

13.14 However, where an asset *did* previously qualify for plant allowances at the full rate of writing-down allowance, but would now fall to be treated as an integral feature, members of a *group* may elect to transfer the asset (known as a 'pre-commencement integral feature') such that: (i) no balancing adjustment need be made by the transferor (ie the asset is transferred at tax written-down value); and (ii) the expenditure may be allocated to the main pool (not the special rate pool) by the transferee (*FA 2008, Sch 26, para 15*). See pro forma election in **Appendix 5**.

13.15 However, this election applies only to members of a group, not to connected persons generally. So a trade may be transferred within a group without assets beginning to be treated as integral features, but where a trade is transferred between other connected persons, there is no such scope.

Succession to a qualifying activity by inheritance

13.16 Where a person succeeds to a qualifying activity either as a beneficiary under a will or on the intestacy of a deceased person, he may elect that any plant passing to him with the activity is treated as transferred at the lower of:

(*a*)   the open market value;

(*b*)   unrelieved capital expenditure (ie the tax written-down value of the pool) (*s 268*).

13.17 If no election is made, then the succession is treated as a deemed sale at market value (*s 265*). However, if the inheritance is from a connected person (see **20.25**), then the anti-avoidance rule in *s 214* applies so that the deemed sale is limited by *s 218* (see **20.9**) to the lower of market value and the prior owner's disposal value (or if they did not claim capital allowances, to their original capital expenditure).

13.18 Where the successor later sells or otherwise disposes of the machinery and plant, the disposal value brought into account will be limited to the capital expenditure incurred by the deceased (*s 268(6)*).

Assets other than plant

13.19 Similar provisions apply to all expenditure qualifying for allowances except machinery and plant (considered above), research and development and dwelling-houses let on assured tenancies.

13.20 Where under *ITTOIA 2005, s 882, Sch 1, para 94* or *CTA 2009, s 41(2)* (see **13.7**), the transferred activity is treated as ceasing, and any property which, without being sold, was in use for the trade immediately before and immediately after the change, that property is treated as if it was sold (at market value) to the person taking over the activity (*s 559*). Again, the twin effects of this are that the former owner of the trade must bring in a disposal value (ie market value), and the successor is entitled to WDAs, but not initial allowances, on the same amount. Relevant activities include a trade, property business, profession or vocation, but not an employment or office (*s 559(5)*).

13.21 In contrast to the treatment of plant (see above), the legislation does not make clear whether the requirement that the property must be in use is satisfied by merely being provided and available for use. (In connection with this, see the case of *Schapira v Kirby* (1970) 46 TC 320.)

Election by connected persons

13.22 Where the parties involved in the succession are connected an election may be made under *s 569* (within two years of the succession), the principal effect of which is that the assets are deemed to be transferred at tax written-down value, thereby avoiding a balancing allowance or charge (see **20.5** *et seq*).

13.23 See pro forma election, **Appendix 5**.

COMPANY RECONSTRUCTIONS WITHOUT A CHANGE OF OWNERSHIP

General

13.24 Special rules apply (*CTA 2010, s 941*) where one company ceases to carry on a trade (or part of a trade) and another company begins to carry on that trade, and:

(*a*) the trade (or a 75% interest in it) belongs to the same persons at some time in the two years following the transfer as it did at some time in the year preceding the transfer (*CTA 2010, s 941*); and

(*b*) within the three-year period referred to above, the trade is not carried on otherwise than by a company which is within the charge to tax in respect of it (*CTA 2010, s 943*).

13.25 *Section 948* refers only to a trade, and not to other 'qualifying activities' under *s 15*. Consequently, for example, a property business may not be governed by these special rules.

13.26   The provision does not apply if the successor company is a dual resident investing company, ie, a company that is both UK resident and also subject to non-UK tax because it derives its status as a company from non-UK law, its place of management is in that overseas territory, or it is for some other reason treated under that law as resident in that territory for tax purposes (*CTA 2010, s 948*).

13.27   Where these conditions are met, then for the purposes of capital allowances and losses, the trade is not treated as permanently discontinued and then recommenced, as would otherwise be required by *CTA 2009, s 41(2)* (see **13.7**). Instead, *CTA 2010, s 948* operates so as to treat the successor as effectively standing in the shoes of the former owner for the purposes of capital allowances. No balancing allowances or charges are calculated in connection with the transfer, and WDAs available to the successor will be identical to those which would have been available to the former owner, had he continued to carry on the trade. In effect, therefore, the machinery and plant is transferred at tax written-down value.

13.28   Where only part of a trade is transferred, the expenditure transferred, and hence the allowances, shall be determined on the basis of just and reasonable apportionments (*CTA 2010, s 952*).

13.29   When dealing with company reconstructions, it is important not simply to assume that *CTA 2001, s 948* will apply. If the '75% rule' (see **13.24**) is not met, it may be possible to obtain the same result for plant by making an election under *s 266* (see **13.10** *et seq*). Such election, of course, is optional, unlike the mandatory provisions of *CTA 2010, s 948*.

13.30   What purports to be a transfer of a trade may not always be so, notably where the trade consists solely of providing services to the transferee. For example, if the trade is one of leasing plant to the transferee, the trade will simply disappear – the transferee company cannot lease plant to itself! However, advantage may normally be taken of *s 61* to transfer the plant at a value convenient for tax purposes.

Anti-avoidance

13.31   *Finance Act 2008* introduced new legislation (*CTA 2010, ss 954-957*) to prevent a perceived abuse where a trade was sold to an unconnected buyer in order to generate a balancing allowance. Where the creation of a balancing allowance is the main purpose, or one of the main purposes, of a transaction, no balancing allowance arises. Instead, s 948 is deemed to apply (see **13.27**), such that there is no balancing allowance, and the buyer merely steps into the shoes of the seller.

Transfer of trade during an accounting period

13.32　The transfer of a trade can often be made most smoothly on the accounting date of one (if not both) of the companies involved. For commercial reasons, this is not always possible. In such circumstances, HMRC's view is that allowances should be apportioned between the two companies. This is set out in ICAEW Technical Release TR 500:

> **'Transfer Of Trade Part Way Through Accounting Period: Entitlement To Capital Allowances March 1983**
>
> The transfer of a trade may take place during the currency of the accounting period of the companies concerned. In those circumstances, the Inland Revenue take the view that [*ICTA 1988, s 343(2)*] should normally be applied as follows:
>
> (*a*)　writing-down allowances are calculated on the "pool" of qualifying expenditure held by the transferee at the end of its accounting period, and those allowances are apportioned on a time basis for the period in which each company carried on the trade;
>
> (*b*)　first-year allowances are given to the company which actually incurred the expenditure, no apportionment being necessary;
>
> (*c*)　any balancing adjustments (whether charges or allowances) are made on the company carrying on a trade in the relevant time, without any apportionment.'

13.33　This treatment applies not only to assets already in the pool at the date of transfer, but also to new assets subsequently acquired (in the same chargeable period) by the transferee. In effect, part of the allowances apportioned to the transferor will relate to these new assets, even though the transferor never actually owned them. If the transferee wishes to avoid this, he may do so by bringing the accounting period to an end immediately after the transfer.

Change of trade, or conversion of an investment company to a trading company, or vice versa

13.34　When an investment company is converted into a trading company, or vice versa, or where a person discontinues one trade and commences another one, any machinery or plant owned by that person is deemed to have been disposed of and reacquired at market value (*ss 13 and 61(2), Table, item 7*). In practice, this requirement is often overlooked and WDAs continue to be claimed as if the conversion had not taken place. In certain circumstances, it may be to the company's advantage to insist on the correct treatment, for example where to do so would give rise to a balancing allowance.

13.35 If capital allowances have previously been added to trading losses or excess management expenses carried forward as the case may be, they will be lost. In such circumstances, it may be appropriate to disclaim allowances for 'open' years of assessment.

Incorporation

13.36 In the majority of cases, the rules and practicalities of capital allowances are of equal application to companies and to unincorporated businesses. However, it would be a mistake to think that because of this, incorporation of a business can automatically take place with no impact on the capital allowances position.

13.37 The basic rule is that on incorporation of a business, assets are deemed to be sold and reacquired at their open market value (*s 265*). A person wishing to incorporate his business therefore runs the risk of crystallising a balancing charge where the market value of plant is higher than its tax written-down value. The reverse situation is relatively rare, as is the scope, therefore, for claiming a balancing allowance. Note that no first-year allowances are available to the incorporated business (*s 265(4)*), nor can the incorporated business claim allowances on an amount greater than the disposal value brought in by the unincorporated business, or (if the latter never claimed) to the original capital expenditure incurred by the unincorporated business. Furthermore, assets treated as 'normal' plant by the unincorporated business may fall to be treated as 'integral features' after incorporation.

Example

Mr Smith has a trade which he incorporates after some years. He bought fixtures for £400,000 and claimed capital allowances of £37,000. At the date of incorporation, when they have a tax written-down value of £30,000, they are valued at £1,400,000.

The incorporation is treated as a sale at market value, ie £1.4 million. However, the qualifying expenditure is limited by *s 218* to £400,000 original cost to the 'seller'. This will also be the amount brought into the account by the unincorporated business, as its disposal value cannot exceed the original cost of the plant transferred (*s 62*). The overall effect is that in the year of incorporation, the new company can claim WDAs of £100,000 (restricted if its first period of account is less than one year), whilst the old business suffers a balancing charge of £370,000.

13.38 A potential balancing charge on plant may be avoided by making an election under *s 266* (see **13.10**), the broad effect of which is to transfer the plant at tax written-down value. For certain other assets, an election for 'tax written-down value' under *s 569* (see **13.22**) may be made where that value is less than open market value, and so can be used to avert a balancing charge arising on incorporation.

13.39 Where an individual incorporates his business but retains ownership of a building which is nonetheless used by the new company for its trade, HMRC has stated that *s 559* 'does not appear to permit' allowances to remain with the individual (CCAB Memorandum to the Inland Revenue, December 1982 and reply). In practice this point is rarely taken.

Expenditure prior to incorporation

13.40 When the incorporation of a company is delayed it is not uncommon to find 'pre-incorporation expenditure'. Such expenditure is outside the scope of *s 12* (pre-trading expenditure – see **1.101**) because it could not have been incurred by the company as a person about to carry on the trade or other qualifying activity due to the simple fact that the company was then not in existence. It might be possible to show that the person who did incur the expenditure commenced to use the asset for trading purposes and that the trade was subsequently transferred to the company. *Section 266* might then offer a route for the claiming of allowances. Alternatively, the individual could simply invoice the company following incorporation. Obviously, the assets concerned must be excluded from those acquired on incorporation.

13.41 If the asset is acquired by the company without the original purchaser having used it for the purposes of a trade, and therefore without having been required to bring a disposal value into account, the expenditure on which the company may claim allowances will be the smallest of:

(*a*)   the open market value;

(*b*)   the capital expenditure incurred by the seller; and

(*c*)   the capital expenditure incurred by any person who is connected with the seller (*s 218(3)*).

13.42 If the seller did not acquire the asset on capital account, such that conditions (*b*) and (*c*) are inapplicable, the restriction will simply be to open market value.

Chapter 14

Plant: system of allowances

INTRODUCTION – THE TREATMENT OF PLANT IN THIS WORK

14.1   For most businesses carrying on a 'qualifying activity' (see **14.108**), machinery and plant will form the majority of any claim for capital allowances. The capital allowances implications of plant are part of almost any transaction involving capital assets, and relevant planning ideas, etc are discussed in the chapter dealing with that transaction. For example, where a retail shop is acquired second-hand, the key chapter will be **Chapter 6**. **Chapters 14** to **16** deal with certain matters which affect plant, regardless of the context. These are as follows:

(*a*)   **Chapter 14 –**

    (i)   the manner in which allowances are given;

    (ii)   types of allowances, and conditions which must be met;

    (iii) special treatment for long-life assets;

    (iv) special treatment for short-life assets.

(*b*)   **Chapter 15 –**

    (i)   the meaning of the term 'plant';

    (ii)   the development of case law;

    (iii) the impact of statute.

(*c*)   **Chapter 16 –**

    (i)   the treatment of items of plant commonly found in buildings.

14.2   In addition, **Appendix 2** lists various assets which have, in appropriate circumstances, been accepted as qualifying as plant.

MANNER OF GIVING ALLOWANCES

Pooling of expenditure

14.3   Since 1971, expenditure on machinery and plant has (with some exceptions) been 'pooled' for capital allowance purposes. This means that all qualifying expenditure with similar characteristics for tax purposes is accumulated in one total (ie recorded in a ledger for tax purposes), from which the allowances are deducted. The resultant balance is known as the 'main pool' (*s 54*). However, expenditure on various types of assets is excluded from the main pool and accumulated separately in either a 'single asset pool' or a 'class pool'(*s 54*). These assets are:

Single Asset Pools

(*a*)   expensive cars (see **17.12** *et seq*);

(*b*)   assets used only partly for the purposes of the trade (see **14.128** *et seq*);

(*c*)   assets attracting a partial depreciation subsidy (see **1.129** *et seq*);

(*d*)   assets qualifying for contribution allowances (see **1.119** *et seq*);

(*e*)   short-life assets (see **14.179** *et seq*);

(*f*)   ships.

Class Pools

(*a*)   'special rate pool' for integral features (see **14.5** *et seq*), thermal insulation, solar panels, certain cars, and long-life assets (see **14.153** *et seq*);

(*b*)   'old' expenditure on plant used for overseas leasing (see **18.15**).

14.4   It is generally assumed that the pooling must be reflected on a tax return. However, whilst the corporation tax return (CT600) includes a box for showing expenditure incurred, there is no equivalent on income tax returns. Arguably, the return should disclose in the 'white space' box that expenditure has been incurred, even where no allowances are claimed.

Integral features

14.5   With effect from 1 April 2008 (corporation tax) or 6 April 2008 (income tax), there is a separate special rate pool for 'integral features' (and other expenditure - see **14.162**), for which a WDA of 8% pa is given. The integral features included in this new pool are:

- electrical systems (including lighting systems);

- cold water systems;

- space or water heating systems (ie heating and hot water), powered systems of ventilation, air cooling or air purification (ie mechanical ventilation and air conditioning), and any floor or ceiling comprised in such a system;

- lifts, escalators and moving walkways; and

- external solar shading (ie *brise soleil*).

(*s 33A*)

14.6 Active façades (ie external cladding systems equipped with technologies, such as two glazing layers separated by a ventilated air cavity, that improve thermal performance) were included in the draft legislation included with Budget 2008 Notice BN07, but omitted from the final legislation, as in HMRC's published view they are already included as part of air conditioning systems.

14.7 The legislation does not define a 'system' so the term takes its ordinary meaning (ie broadly an assembly of interconnected parts that forms a more complex whole). However, HMRC has published guidance clarifying its understanding of what is meant by this. In HMRC's view:

- an electrical system is a system for taking electrical power (including lighting) from the point of entry to the building or structure, or generation within the building or structure, and distributing it through the building or structure, as required. The system may range from the very simplest to the most complex. It does *not* include systems intended for other purposes, which may include wiring and other electrical components (eg communication, telecommunication and surveillance systems, fire alarm systems or burglar alarm systems etc;

- a cold water system is a system for taking water from the point of entry to the building or structure and distributing it through the building or structure as required, which again may range from the very simplest to the most complex;

(CA, para 22330)

- a powered system of ventilation would include, for example, a radon sump with extractor fan.

(CIRD, para 61425)

14.8 However, it is highly questionable whether a stand-alone asset such as an extractor fan would fall within the definition of a 'system'.

14.9   Where an asset is sold, and that asset was one allocated to the special rate pool, anti-avoidance provisions potentially apply. If the asset is disposed of for less than its tax written-down value as part of a scheme or arrangement having the obtaining of a tax advantage as a main purpose, then notional tax written-down value is substituted for the actual disposal value (*s 104E*).

14.10   Anti-avoidance provisions also apply to prevent expenditure on existing assets which did not previously qualify for allowances (eg non-qualifying elements of cold water systems) being transferred to a connected person such that a claim would be possible on the whole of the original expenditure (*FA 2008, Sch 26, para 15*).

14.11   However, members of a group may elect to transfer a 'pre-commencement integral feature' such that: (i) no balancing adjustment need be made by the transferor; and (ii) the expenditure may be allocated to the main pool (not the special rate pool) by the transferee (*FA 2008, Sch 26, paras 16, 17*). See pro forma election, **Appendix 5**.

14.12   There are special rules relating to the repair or replacement of integral features, which can sometimes overturn the 'normal' rules on repairs (see **1.37** *et seq*).

ALLOWANCES

14.13   Relief is given by a combination of:

(i)   first-year allowances (see **14.14** *et seq*),

(ii)   the annual investment allowance from 1 April 2008 (corporation tax) or 6 April 2008 (income tax) (see **14.62** *et seq*),

(iii)   WDAs at 8% for integral features, long-life assets, adding thermal insulation to buildings, and solar panels, and 18% for other expenditure (see **14.99** *et seq*), and

(iv)   balancing allowances or charges (see **12.46** *et seq*).

First-year allowances

14.14   First-year allowances have at various times been introduced for different types of expenditure, and for different classes of taxpayer. Most of these are now withdrawn.

Current first year allowances

(*a*) Expenditure on energy-saving plant and machinery on or after 1 April 2001, an allowance of 100% is available (*s 45A*) (see **14.31** *et seq*). This allowance was extended to assets used for leasing with effect for expenditure incurred on or after 17 April 2002 (*s 46(5)*). With effect from 1 April 2006, the allowance for leased assets is restricted to those cases where the assets concerned are 'background plant or machinery' as defined by *s 70R* (see **18.50**).

(*b*) Expenditure on electric cars and cars with low CO^2 emissions, on or after 17 April 2002 but before 1 April 2018 (*s 45D*) at a rate of 100% (see **17.39**).

(*c*) Expenditure on gas refuelling stations on or after 17 April 2002 but before 1 April 2018 (*s 45E*), at a rate of 100%. With effect from 1 April 2006, the allowance was withdrawn for leased assets (*Finance Act 2006 (FA 2006), Sch 9, para 11*). From 1 April 2008 the relief was extended to refuelling equipment for biogas, which is defined as 'gas produced by the anaerobic conversion of organic matter and used for propelling vehicles' (*FA 2008, s 75*).

(*d*) Expenditure incurred on or after 17 April 2002 in a ring-fence trade (oil extraction) (*s 45F*), at a rate of 100% (24% for long-life assets – see **14.153** *et seq*).

(*e*) Expenditure incurred on or after 1 April 2003, an allowance of 100% is available for environmentally beneficial (ie water-conserving) plant (*s 45H*) (see **14.44** *et seq*). This allowance was extended to assets used for leasing with effect for expenditure incurred on or after 1 April 2003 (*s 46(5)*). With effect from 1 April 2006, the allowance for such assets which are leased is restricted to those cases where the assets concerned are 'background plant or machinery' as defined by *s 70R* (see **18.50**).

(*f*) Expenditure incurred in the period 1 April 2010 to 31 March 2018 (corporation tax) or 6 April 2010 to 5 April 2018 (income tax) on zero-emission goods vehicles (*s 45DA*). A 100% first-year allowance is available. A goods vehicle is one which is designed primarily for the conveyance of goods, and 'zero-emission' means that the vehicle cannot in any circumstances emit carbon dioxide (CO_2) while being driven. This allowance was due to be withdrawn on 31 March 2015 for income tax purposes and 5 April 2015 for corporation tax purposes, but was extended by *FA 2015, s 45* (see **17.37–17.38**).

(*g*) Expenditure incurred by a company in the period 1 April 2012 to 31 March 2020 on plant and machinery for use primarily in a designated assisted area (*s 45K*). This is considered at **9.45** *et seq*.

14.15   *Plant: system of allowances*

Former first year allowances

(*h*)   Expenditure incurred (other than on motor cars) in the 12 months ended 31 October 1993, or for any additional liability arising in respect of such expenditure (*Sch 3, para 47*) – a first-year allowance of 40% was available.

(*i*)   Expenditure incurred (other than on certain excluded assets – see **14.20**) by a small or medium-sized enterprise (see **14.17**), in the 12 months ended 1 July 1998 (*Sch 3, para 48*) – a first-year allowance of 50% (12% for long-life assets – see **14.153** *et seq*) was available.

(*j*)   Expenditure incurred (other than on certain excluded assets – see **14.20**) by a small or medium-sized enterprise (see **14.17**), on or after 2 July 1998 (*ss 39* and *44*) – a first-year allowance of 40% is available (see also (*j*) below). In contrast to (*b*) above, no first-year allowance is due in respect of long-life assets. From 1 April 2008 (corporation tax) or 6 April 2008 (income tax), this was repealed and in part replaced by a new annual investment allowance available to all businesses (see **14.62** *et seq*).

(*k*)   Expenditure incurred by a small enterprise (see **14.17**) on information and communications technology (ICT) in the period from 1 April 2000 to 31 March 2004 (*s 45*) – a first-year allowance of 100% was available (see **14.24**). This is repealed by *Finance Act 2008* (*FA 2008*), *s 73*.

(*l*)   Expenditure incurred in the 12 months beginning 1 April 2004 (6 April 2004 for income tax) or in the 24 months beginning 1 April 2006 (6 April 2006 for income tax) *for small enterprises only*, at a rate of 50% (*s 52(3)*). Note: the allowance was *not* available for expenditure incurred between 1 April 2005 and 31 March 2006 (5 April for income tax purposes). From 1 April 2008 (corporation tax) or 6 April 2008 (income tax), this was repealed and in part replaced by an annual investment allowance available to all businesses (see **14.62** *et seq*).

(*m*)   Expenditure incurred in the period 12 May 1998 to 11 May 2002 by small companies or businesses acquiring plant for use in Northern Ireland, an allowance of 100% was available (*s 40*) (see **14.28**). This was repealed by *FA 2008, s 73*.

(*n*)   Expenditure incurred in the 12 months beginning 1 April 2009 (corporation tax) or 6 April 2009 (income tax), at a rate of 40% (*FA 2009, s 24*). Note: this applied to businesses of any size, but not (inter alia) where the plant is leased, so it is not available to landlords, unless the relevant plant is 'background plant' (see **18.50**) which is not also an integral feature (see **14.5**).

14.15   The meaning of 'incurred' for this purpose is, as for other transactions, set out in *s 5* (see **1.78**). *Section 12*, which deems pre-trading expenditure to have been incurred on the first day of trading, is specifically disapplied (*Sch 3, paras 47(2)* and *48(2)*).

14.16   No first-year allowance is given where the provision of the asset is connected with a change in the nature or conduct of a trade or other qualifying activity carried on by a person other than the person incurring the expenditure, and the obtaining of a first-year allowance would be the main benefit (or one of the main benefits) arising from the change (*s 46(2)*). Certain other assets are excluded from qualifying for some or all types of first-year allowances (see **14.20** *et seq*).

The meaning of 'small' and 'medium-sized'

14.17   The availability of some former first-year allowances depended on the business being small or medium-sized. A company or business was regarded as small or medium-sized for a particular year if (having assumed that an unincorporated business was in fact a company) it qualified as small or medium sized in accordance with *Companies Act 2006, ss 382* and *465* or *Companies (Northern Ireland) Order 1986, art 255*. These provisions required a company to meet two or more of the following requirements in that year or the previous year:

	Turnover	*Balance sheet total*	*Number of employees*
Small company	Not more than £5.6 million	Not more than £2.8 million	Not more than 50
Small group	Not more than £5.6 million net (or £6.7 million gross)	Not more than £2.8 million net (or £3.36 million gross)	Not more than 50
Medium-sized company	Not more than £22.8 million	Not more than £11.4 million	Not more than 250
Medium-sized group	Not more than £22.8 million net (or £27.36 million gross)	Not more than £11.4 million net (or £13.68 million gross)	Not more than 250

14.18   Note: in the context above 'net' is understood to mean based on consolidated accounts and 'gross' is without adjusting for intra-group items. The balance sheet total means the aggregate of amounts shown as assets in the balance sheet (before deducting both current and long-term liabilities). A trust, or a partnership of which a company is a member, is not within the definition of 'business', which means that it cannot claim first-year allowances (CA, para 23170).

14.19 These limits apply for accounting periods ending on or after 30 January 2004. Before that date, the limits were as follows (*CA 1985, s 247(3)*):

	Small	Small or medium-sized
Turnover not more than	£2.8 million	£11.2 million
Assets not more than	£1.4 million	£5.6 million
Number of employees not more than	50	250

Excluded assets

14.20 First-year allowances are not available for expenditure on:

(*a*)   motor cars, except for electric cars and cars with low CO^2 emissions (see **Chapter 17**), sea-going ships or railway assets (*s 46*);

(*b*)   machinery or plant for leasing (see **Chapter 18**) – see also below (*s 46*);

(*c*)   long-life assets (see **14.153**) (*s 44(2)*);

(*d*)   deemed expenditure under *s 13A* on assets previously leased under a long funding lease (see **18.43**) (*s 46(2)*); or

(*e*)   integral features (see **14.5**) (*FA 2009, s 24(2)(c)*) – only relevant for first-year allowances in 2009/10.

14.21 *Finance Act 2013 s 69* removes the general exclusions to first-year allowances for expenditure incurred on railway assets and ships with effect from 1 April 2013.

14.22 The Treasury notes accompanying this legislation when first published make it clear that the leasing ((b) above) exemption extends to expenditure incurred by property investors on fixtures attached to a building which is let. Therefore, a landlord cannot generally claim first-year allowances in respect of plant and machinery fixtures. This is now incorporated in HMRC instructions (CA, para 23110). However, an exception to this rule is where the plant is 'background plant' (see **18.50**) and is not an integral feature (see **14.4**). This may include, for example, built-in furniture, alarms, signage, PA or music systems, telephone and data systems, and movable partitions. However, this exemption only applies to the first-year allowances available between April 2009 and April 2010 (item (*n*) in **14.14**), not to the earlier forms of first-year allowance.

14.23 So far as the various types of energy-efficient (see **14.31**) and environmentally beneficial (see **14.44**) plant are concerned, the leasing exclusion applies as follows:

Energy-efficient plant (*s 45A*)	FYAs available from 1 April 2001
	Extended to leased assets from 17 April 2002
	Withdrawn for leased assets from 1 April 2006, unless the assets concerned are 'background plant or machinery' as defined by *s 70R* (see **18.50**) (*FA 2006, Sch 9, para 11*)
Cars with low CO_2 emissions (*s 45D*)	FYAs available from 17 April 2002
	FYAs available until 31 March 2018 (*FA 2013, s 67*)
	FYAs always available on leased assets
Gas refuelling stations (*s 45E*)	FYAs available from 17 April 2002
	FYAs available on leased assets from that date until 31 March 2006 (*FA 2006, Sch 9, para 11*)
	FYAs available until 31 March 2018 (*FA 2013, s 68*)
Environmentally beneficial plant (*s 45H*)	FYAs available from 1 April 2001
	Extended to leased assets from 1 April 2003
	Withdrawn for leased assets from 1 April 2006, unless the assets concerned are 'background plant or machinery' as defined by *s 70R* (see **18.50**) (*FA 2006, Sch 9, para 11*)

14.24 In addition, software did not qualify for the 100% ICT allowance (see **14.14**(*k*), **14.27**) if it was acquired with a view to granting to another person a right to use or otherwise deal with the software in question (*s 45(4)*). This applied to expenditure incurred on or after 26 March 2003 (*FA 2003, s 166(4)*, which was repealed by *FA 2008, s 76*).

14.25 Any form of hire is regarded as leasing for the purposes of *s 46*, whether or not a formal lease is in place. The HMRC manual (CA, paras 23110 and 23115) accepts that there is a distinction between: (i) the hiring of an asset; and (ii) the provision of services which require the use of an asset. The long-standing test, which was not particularly helpful in the concept of fixtures, was whether the overall supervision and control of the asset rested with the owner of the asset, or the person who had 'hired' it.

14.26 HMRC's view was adapted following the decision in a non-tax case, *Baldwins Industrial Services Plc v Barr Ltd* [2003] BLR 176. A company hired a crane with an operator to another company to help in a construction project.

The courts held that the relevant contract was a construction contract, and was not simply the letting of plant on hire. HMRC regard this case as establishing the principle that 'the supply of plant or machinery with an operator, by a business, is the provision of a service and not mere hire'. The labour element was held to be crucial.

14.27 In *MGF (Trench Construction Systems) Ltd v HMRC Comrs* [2012] UKFTT 739 (TC), the taxpayer was successful in claiming first-year allowances for plant and machinery supplied without labour, but with a package of services including design, assembly and transport. Accordingly, such a supply is not excluded from being 'first-year qualifying expenditure' by *s 46(2)*. (See CA, para 23115, updating Revenue Interpretation RI 262, issued in August 2003.)

Northern Ireland

14.28 For small companies or businesses acquiring plant for use in Northern Ireland, a first-year allowance of 100% was available on expenditure incurred in the period 12 May 1998 to 11 May 2002 (*s 40*). Excluded assets are as above (**14.20** *et seq*), with the addition of aircraft and hovercraft (*s 41(1)*). Allowances were also not available for goods vehicles used by freight hauliers, nor for plant used in the agriculture or fisheries sector (*s 41(1)* and *(2)*). The first-year allowance will be clawed back where the relevant plant is used outside Northern Ireland within two years of the date the expenditure was incurred (five years if the expenditure exceeded £3.5 million) (*s 43*).

International groups

14.29 The position of a company which is part of an international group depends on whether the expenditure was incurred on or after 12 May 1998. The initial position, which applies to expenditure incurred before that date, was outlined by the Financial Secretary to the Treasury in a Finance Bill debate:

'When a small or medium-sized company is a subsidiary of an overseas parent, it will be considered in isolation because it would not be worth imposing on business the compliance costs involved in establishing the position of an overseas group for the sake of a one year tax relief.'

14.30 This does not directly address the position where there are a number of UK subsidiaries, all owned directly by an overseas parent, but on a straightforward reading of the Financial Secretary's words, there is no need to aggregate the various UK companies. In their press releases of 12 May and 24 June 1998, HMRC announced a change. From 12 May 1998 for 100% allowances in Northern Ireland (see **14.28**), and from 2 July 1998 for other first-year allowances (see **14.14**), the international group must itself satisfy the 'small or medium-size' test.

Energy-saving plant and machinery

14.31   *FA 2001* introduced a 100% first-year allowance (called an 'enhanced capital allowance') on energy-saving plant or machinery (*s 45A*; *FA 2001, s 65*). The introduction of this allowance was part of a wider package of measures aimed at helping businesses reduce their energy consumption, and so help the United Kingdom reduce emissions of greenhouse gases.

14.32   The rules on energy-saving plant or machinery are slotted into the existing legislation on first-year allowances. Consequently, issues such as the manner of giving allowances, and the scope to disclaim all or part of the allowance, are identical to the existing provisions governing first-year allowances. Note, however, that first-year allowances on energy-saving plant or machinery are *not* restricted to small or medium-sized enterprises.

14.33   The expenditure must be on plant which is new (ie not second-hand) (*s 45A(1)*), and must be incurred on or after 1 April 2001.

14.34   Certain categories of asset are excluded from first-year allowances. These include:

- cars, ships and railway assets; and

- assets used for leasing, where the expenditure was incurred prior to 17 April 2002 (*s 46(2)*; *FA 2002, s 62*).

14.35   In addition, no 100% FYA is available for expenditure on plant where that plant is in receipt of a tariff under either the Feed-in Tariff (FiT) or Renewable Heat Incentive (RHI) schemes as set out in the Energy Act 2008 or, in Northern Ireland, the Energy Act 2011(*s 45AA*).

14.36   In order to qualify, plant must be of a description specified by Treasury order, or must meet the energy-saving criteria specified by Treasury order for plant of that description. The Treasury may also require that a certificate of energy efficiency is in force, issued by the Secretary of State (Department of Energy and Climate Change) or devolved equivalents in Scotland, Wales and Northern Ireland. If such a certificate is later revoked, it is treated as never having been issued.

14.37   If only some components of an item of plant qualify for first-year allowances under this heading, the amount qualifying is limited to the amount specified by Treasury order – this overrides the 'just' apportionment which would otherwise apply.

14.38 *Plant: system of allowances*

14.38 Amendments to the types of qualifying technologies were set out in Statutory Instruments:

- *SI 2002/1818* (from 5 August 2002);

- *SI 2004/2093* (from 26 August 2004);

- *SI 2005/2424* (from 22 September 2005);

- *SI 2006/2233* (from 7 September 2006);

- *SI 2007/2165* (from 16 August 2007);

- *SI 2008/1916* (from 11 August 2008);

- *SI 2009/1863* (from 4 August 2009);

- *SI 2010/2286* (from 8 October 2010);

- *SI 2011/2221* (from 1 October 2011);

- *SI 2012/1832* (from 2 August 2012);

- *SI 2012/2602* (from 7 November 2012);

- *SI 2013/1763* (from 7 August 2013);

- *SI 2014/1868* (from 7 August 2014), and

- *SI 2015/1508* (from 4 August 2015).

14.39 The classes of energy-efficient assets are specified on the government's Energy Technology List (see *https://etl.decc.gov.uk/etl/site.html*). They include:

- air-to-air energy recovery;

- automatic monitoring and targeting equipment;

- boiler equipment;

- combined heat and power (CHP);

- compact heat exchangers;

- compressed air equipment;

- heat pumps for space heating;

- heating, ventilating and air conditioning (HVAC) equipment;

- high speed hand air dryers;

- lighting;

- motors and drives;

- pipework insulation;

- radiant and warm air heaters;

- refrigeration equipment;

- solar thermal systems and collectors;

- thermal screens; and

- uninterruptible power supplies (UPS).

14.40 Within these groups there are many sub-technologies, such as single speed motors and biomass boilers. For some of the technology categories, the Energy Technology List lists the specific products eligible for enhanced capital allowances. These are known as 'listed' products. Eligible products in the four other technologies (component based automatic monitoring and targeting; combined heat and power; lighting and pipework insulation) do not appear on the list but qualify based on meeting specified performance criteria. These are known as 'unlisted' products.

14.41 It was announced in Budget 2014 that the Energy Technology List would be updated by Treasury Order, to include two new sub-technologies: active chilled beams, and desiccant air dryers with energy-saving controls. The criteria for 12 current technologies would be revised.

14.42 Support for solar thermal screens (included on the list since 2001) and electronic drain traps (on the list since 2003) was withdrawn from 7 September 2006 because the market penetration of that technology grew substantially during the period of inclusion on the list. From April 2012 (or April 2014 for CHP installations) ECAs are not available for machinery or plant which generates electricity or heat (or produces biogas or biofuels) that attract payments under the Government's Feed-in Tariff (FiT) or Renewable Heat Incentive (RHI) schemes (*s 45AA*).

14.43 Many taxpayers do not realise how difficult it is to claim the first-year allowance. For a CHP system, for example, the taxpayer must complete a lengthy self-assessment process, analysing in detail and measuring accurately the degree of energy efficiency. This can only be done by a specialist electrical engineer. He will then be issued with a certificate of energy efficiency, which he must in turn use to obtain another certificate from the Secretary of State, entitling him to claim the first-year allowance on his tax return.

Environmentally beneficial plant and machinery

14.44 *FA 2003* introduced a second 100% first-year allowance (called an 'enhanced capital allowance') for expenditure on environmentally beneficial (ie water-conserving and quality-improving) plant and machinery incurred on or after 1 April 2003. This is available to both large and small businesses (*s 45H*; *FA 2003, s 167*).

14.45   The plant acquired must be of a description specified by Treasury order, and meet the environmental criteria set out by Treasury order. In essence, 'environmentally beneficial' plant will have been designed to remedy or prevent damage to the physical environment or natural resources (*s 45H(3)*).

14.46   In some cases, allowances are due only if a 'certificate of environmental benefit' is in force, confirming that particular plant (or plant constructed to a particular design) meets the relevant environmental criteria (*s 45I*).

14.47   The plant acquired must be new and not second-hand (*s 45H(1)*), and must not be a long-life asset (ie having an estimated useful economic life of greater than 25 years) (*s 46(2)*) (see **14.153** *et seq*). In addition, it must not fall within the general exclusions of *s 46*, which include cars, ships and railway assets.

14.48   Until 31 March 2006, allowances for environmentally beneficial plant and machinery were always available for leased assets. However, from 1 April 2006 allowances are only available where leased plant is provided under an excluded lease of background plant and machinery (see **18.50**).

14.49   Allowances are available for environmentally friendly components of larger plant, even if the plant as a whole would not qualify. The amounts qualifying are those specified by the relevant Treasury order, and not a just apportionment of the whole cost (*s 45J*).

14.50   If a certificate of environmental benefit is revoked, it is regarded as never having been issued, and tax returns must be amended accordingly. A taxpayer who becomes aware that amendment is needed has three months in which to notify HMRC.

14.51   Amendments to the types of qualifying technologies were set out in Statutory Instruments:

- *SI 2004/2094* (from 26 August 2004);
- *SI 2005/2423* (from 22 September 2005);
- *SI 2006/2235* (from 7 September 2006);
- *SI 2007/2166* (from 16 August 2007);
- *SI 2008/1917* (from 11 August 2008);
- *SI 2009/1864* (from 4 August 2009);
- *SI 2010/2483* (from 8 November 2010);

- *SI 2011/2220* (from 1 October 2011);

- *SI 2012/1838* (from 2 August 2012);

- *SI 2013/1762* (from 7 August 2013);

- *SI 2014/1869* (from 7 August 2014), and

- *SI 2015/1509* (from 4 August 2015).

14.52   The classes of water-conserving assets are specified on the government's Water Technology List (see *www.wtl.defra.gov.uk*). They include:

- cleaning in place equipment;

- efficient showers;

- efficient taps;

- efficient toilets (including urinals);

- efficient washing machines;

- flow controllers;

- greywater recovery and reuse equipment;

- leakage detection equipment;

- meters and monitoring equipment;

- rainwater harvesting equipment;

- small scale slurry and sludge dewatering equipment;

- vehicle wash water reclaim units;

- water efficient industrial cleaning equipment; and

- water management systems for mechanical seals.

14.53   It was announced in Budget 2014 that the scheme would be amended to clarify the qualifying criteria for a number of technologies and to incorporate changes in technical standards. The primary amendment would be to the criteria for efficient washing machines, to enable a slighter wider range of businesses to benefit from the scheme.

Practical difficulties – energy-efficient and environmentally beneficial plant

14.54   There are a number of practical difficulties to be aware of when claiming enhanced capital allowances. First, the expenditure must be on plant and machinery (*s 45A(2)* and *s 45H(2)*). This means that expenditure on some assets included on the technology lists might not always qualify for *any* capital allowances, let alone enhanced capital allowances because it is not plant or machinery. Before April 2008 and the introduction of 'integral features' (see **14.5**), this would have included very common assets such as general lighting in some circumstances (see **16.32** *et seq*). Secondly, as mentioned in **14.31** *et seq* above, the assets must be unused and not second hand (*s 45A(1)* and *s 45H(1)*) and long-life assets are excluded (*s 46(2)*) (see **14.153** *et seq*).

14.55   Finally, in practice the process of identifying qualifying assets and their costs and claiming the tax relief can be cumbersome and includes several steps, ie:

(*a*)   The up-front services of a consultant mechanical and electrical services engineer, and/or specialist mechanical and electrical subcontractor, may be helpful to check the design brief against the energy and water technology lists and specify appropriate products. These are mostly specified by manufacturer and model (ie so-called 'listed' assets), but for some assets (ie so-called 'non-listed' assets) must meet defined performance criteria (eg lighting or pipework insulation).

(*b*)   Appropriate records should be retained to prove to HMRC that assets qualifying for enhanced capital allowances were installed and how much they cost (including where the qualifying products are components of larger systems, ensuring that the amount claimed does not exceed the maximum specified by government).

(*c*)   The records must be provided to the person preparing the tax computation and return to allow the tax relief to be claimed (making sure that the expenditure is on plant and machinery that is not a long-life asset).

First-year tax credits

14.56   From 1 April 2008 it is possible for companies (and only companies) to surrender the element of any trading losses attributable to claiming enhanced capital allowances in return for a cash payment from government (new *CAA 2001, Sch A1* introduced by *FA 2008, Sch 25*). Broadly, a company which has a 'surrenderable loss' (*CAA 2001, Sch A1, para 1(2)*) may claim a first-year tax credit equal to 19% of that loss. The amount of the loss surrendered is the lower of: (i) the amount of the first-year tax allowance; or (ii) the actual loss (*CAA 2001, Sch A1, para 1(3)*).

14.57   The availability of first-year tax credits was due to end on 31 March 2013, but has been extended for a further five years to 31 March 2018 (*CAA 2001, Sch A1, para 3(1)(b)*).

Examples

If a first year allowance of £40,000 is deducted in computing a loss of £30,000, the tax credit payable will be £5,700 (ie 19% of £30,000).

However, if a first-year allowance of £50,000 is deducted in computing a loss of £60,000, the tax credit payable is £9,500 (ie 19% of £50,000).

14.58   The repayment is subject to an upper limit, which is the greater of: (i) the total amount of the company's PAYE and NIC liabilities for payment periods ending in the chargeable period; or (ii) £250,000. The company may restrict its claim for the first-year tax credit to only part of the total amount claimable (*FA 2008, Sch A1, para 2(3)*).

14.59   The tax credit will usually be paid to the company, although HM Revenue & Customs does not have to make a repayment where the company has outstanding PAYE or NIC liabilities. Or the tax credit may be used to discharge any outstanding corporation tax liability (*FA 2008, Sch 25, Part 2*). The repayment does not count as income of the company for any purpose (*FA 2008, Sch 25, para 23*).

14.60   There is also a 'claw-back' period, defined as ending four years after the end of the chargeable period for which the first-year tax credit was paid. This applies where a first-year tax credit is claimed in respect of an asset and that asset is then sold before the end of the claw-back period. Then the tax credit must be repaid to HM Revenue and the relevant loss reinstated (*FA 2008, Sch 25, Part 3*).

14.61   Anti-avoidance applies to prevent tax credits where arrangements have been entered into which have the claiming of a tax credit as a main purpose (*FA 2008, Sch 25, para 28*).

Annual investment allowance

Introduction

14.62   From 1 April 2008 (corporation tax) or 6 April (income tax), *FA 2008, s 71* and *Sch 24* introduced a new 'annual investment allowance' (AIA).

14.63   The AIA is available to most businesses, regardless of their size or legal form, including sole traders, companies, partnerships (including LLPs) of which all the members are individuals, registered friendly societies and certain corporate bodies that are not companies, but are within the charge to corporation tax. However, it does not include trusts or mixed partnerships (ie, those of which a company is a member) (*Hoardweel Farm Partnership v HMRC Comrs* [2012] UKFTT 402 (TC); *Drilling Global Consultant LLP v HMRC Comrs* [2014] UKFTT 888 (TC); CA, para 23082).

14.64 The AIA is available to landlords, as there is no exclusion from the allowance of expenditure on assets used for leasing, including fixtures in a let building.

14.65 The AIA has, since its introduction, been something of a political football. The qualifying amount has been reduced to as low as £25,000, on the grounds that the availability of a larger allowance would distort business decisions, but then the same government has increased the allowance first to £250,000 and then to £500,000.

14.66 The allowance reduced again from 1 January 2016 to £200,000 (described by the Chancellor as an increase!).

Amount qualifying for AIA

14.67 The AIA provides for a 100% capital allowance for a set amount of expenditure on qualifying plant and machinery each year.

14.68 The amounts qualifying in income tax cases are:

- £50,000 from 6 April 2008 to 5 April 2010;
- £100,000 from 6 April 2010 to 5 April 2012;
- £25,000 from 6 April 2012;
- £250,000 from 1 January 2013;
- £500,000 from 6 April 2014;
- £200,000 from 1 January 2016.

14.69 For corporation tax, rather than income tax, the relevant dates are:

- £50,000 from 1 April 2008 to 31 March 2010;
- £100,000 from 1 April 2010 to 31 March 2012;
- £25,000 from 1 April 2012;
- £250,000 from 1 January 2013;
- £500,000 from 1 April 2014;
- £200,000 from 1 January 2016.

14.70 The person incurring the expenditure must own the plant as a result of incurring the expenditure (*CAA 2001, s 51A*).

14.71 The value of the AIA each year is therefore limited to between £25,000 and £500,000 (according to when the expenditure is incurred) multiplied by the taxpayer's marginal rate of tax. It is also merely an acceleration of the relief that would otherwise be available via 'normal' capital allowances. In general terms, the AIA is perceived to be more valuable to smaller businesses than to larger ones, as a greater proportion of their overall expenditure is relieved in the year it is incurred.

Use of AIA

14.72 The AIA can be offset against virtually all plant and machinery (excluding cars, as defined by s 81 and s 468D), including fixtures, 'integral features' (see **14.5**) and long-life assets (see **14.153**).

14.73 As well as the exclusion relating to cars, the AIA will *not* be available for expenditure incurred:

● in the period in which the capital allowances qualifying activity is permanently discontinued (*David Alexander Keyl v HMRC Comrs* [2014] UKFTT 493 (TC)); or

● for certain expenditure incurred in connection with ring fence trades (oil extraction); or

● where the provision of the plant is connected with a change in the nature or conduct of the trade carried on by a person other than the person incurring the expenditure, and the obtaining of an AIA is a main benefit from the making of the change, or.

● in circumstances where the succession rules of *s 265* apply (see **Chapter 13**).

14.74 Furthermore, no AIA is available where the expenditure is *deemed* rather than actual (typically, where plant was first acquired for a non-trading purpose, and only later used for the trade or other qualifying activity), or where the plant or machinery concerned was previously used for long funding leasing, or was a gift (*s 38B*).

Groups of companies, and related business carrying on similar activities

14.75 Stand-alone companies each receive a single annual allowance (*s 51B*).

14.76   Groups of companies (*s 51C*), companies under common control (*ss 51D–51F*), or related companies (*s 51G*), will receive a single allowance, which they can allocate between themselves in any way they wish. So, if a group consists of two companies, one of them may use the whole of the £50,000 or £100,000 AIA – a sensible measure which obviates the need to artificially split expenditure between group companies in order to maximise the tax relief.

14.77   The same approach applies where two or more similar 'qualifying activities' (defined by *s 15* for the purposes of capital allowances) are carried on under common control (*ss 51H–51J*). Whether commonly controlled businesses are engaged in a similar qualifying activity is determined by reference to the well-established international classification system 'NACE' (Nomenclature Générale des Activités Économiques dans les Communautés Européennes), which divides industries into 17 main classifications (information on these classifications is available on the website of the Office of National Statistics and will be included in the relevant HMRC guidance).

14.78   These rules aim to prevent the fragmentation of a business to form 'related' businesses and to prevent duplication of the AIA where qualifying activities are under common control. They should apply to only a small minority of businesses, as most taxpayers do not control a multiplicity of related businesses. However, it appears to be the case that where one business is owned by an individual, and another by that individual and a connected person (eg a spouse) in equal shares or with the connected person having a greater share, then the businesses are not under common control, so two AIAs are available.

Allocation of AIA

14.79   As the AIA may be allocated between different types of expenditure in any way the taxpayer wishes, it should generally be allocated to expenditure which would otherwise qualify for the lowest rates of relief (eg in the first instance to 'integral features' or long-life assets, normally qualifying for 10% writing down allowances).

Example

A taxpayer with an accounting period of 12 months to 31 March 2015 is able to use the full AIA limit of £500,000. He incurs the following expenditure:

- £250,000 on integral features qualifying for 8% writing-down allowances;

- £75,000 on environmentally beneficial (ie water-conserving) plant qualifying for enhanced capital allowances (ie a 100% first-year allowance); and

- £375,000 on other plant and machinery additions to the main/general pool qualifying for 18% writing-down allowances.

The taxpayer should allocate his £100,000 AIA firstly to the £250,000 8% integral features, then the remaining £250,000 to the 18% main pool plant, thus preserving the 100% enhanced capital allowance on environmentally beneficial plant and leaving £125,000 of general pool plant qualifying at 18%.

Effectively, the taxpayer has converted the 8% allowance on the integral features into a 100% allowance and done the same for the 18% allowance that would have otherwise been available for two-thirds of the general pool plant.

This freedom to allocate the AIA operates as a proxy for a *de minimis* provision, meaning some businesses may be able to dispense with a 8% 'special rate' pool if the amounts of integral features do not exceed the AIA limit.

The AIA may only be claimed in the chargeable period in which the expenditure is actually incurred (*s 51A(2)*), so may not be deferred to a later period (although it can be used to augment a loss carried forward). However, like most other allowances, all or part of the AIA may be disclaimed (*s 51A(7)*), such that a larger pool of expenditure is carried forward, qualifying at either 18% or 8% per annum, although this will rarely be appropriate.

Prevention of double allowances

14.80   The same expenditure may qualify only once for tax relief. If for example, expenditure could qualify for the AIA or the enhanced capital allowances first year allowance for energy-saving, or environmentally beneficial plant, the taxpayer must decide which to claim (*s 52A*).

Accounting periods overlapping 1 or 6 April 2008

14.81   Where a business has a chargeable period which is more or less than a year, the maximum AIA is proportionally increased or reduced. Similarly, the AIA is time-apportioned where the chargeable period overlaps 1 April 2008 (corporation tax) or 6 April 2008 (income tax). This is calculated by reference to the precise number of days falling before and after the relevant date (not forgetting that 2008 was a leap year!).

Example

A company with a 30 September 2008 year end will be entitled to an AIA for the chargeable period of £25,000 (ie 183/366 × £50,000).

Accounting periods overlapping 1 or 6 April 2010

14.82 Similarly, the AIA is time-apportioned where the chargeable period overlaps 1 April 2010 (corporation tax) or 6 April 2010 (income tax). This is calculated by reference to the precise number of days falling before and after the relevant date.

14.83 However, so far as concerns expenditure actually incurred before the relevant date, the maximum is calculated as if the increase in AIA had not taken place. In most cases (ignoring short accounting periods), this will mean that the AIA for expenditure incurred before the relevant date will be restricted to £50,000 (*FA 2010, s 5(5)*).

Example

A company with a calendar year chargeable period from 1 October 2009 to 30 September 2010 would calculate its maximum AIA entitlement based on:

(*a*)   the proportion of a year from 1 October 2009 to 31 March 2010, that is, 6/12 × £50,000 = £25,000; and

(*b*)   the proportion of a year from 1 April 2010 to 30 September 2010, that is 6/12 × £100,000 = £50,000.

The company's maximum AIA for this transitional chargeable period would therefore be the total of (a) + (b) = £25,000 + £50,000 = £75,000.

However, the restriction in *FA 2010 s 5(5)* would then apply to expenditure incurred on or before 31 March 2010 – if £60,000 was incurred before that date, and £10,000 thereafter, the maximum AIA would be £60,000 (rather than the full £75,000 calculated above), namely:

(*a*)   £50,000 for the 'early' expenditure; plus

(*b*)   £10,000 for the later expenditure.

It is not possible to claim the full £75,000 AIA because of the restriction imposed by *FA 2010 s 5(5)* and the fact that there is insufficient expenditure post-31 March. If the expenditure incurred *after* the relevant date had been £30,000 rather than £10,000, the AIA would be the full permitted £75,000, effectively:

(*a*)   £50,000 for the 'early' expenditure; plus

(*b*)   £25,000 (the balance up to the £25,000 maximum) for the later expenditure.

This calculation merely establishes the maximum AIA – there is no requirement to calculate separate 'pre' and 'post' AIAs and allocate each to the relevant expenditure. It is not possible to claim the new maximum of £100,000 just because one has incurred expenditure of more than £100,000 after the relevant date.

Accounting periods overlapping 1 or 6 April 2012

14.84 Similarly, the AIA is time-apportioned where the chargeable period overlaps 1 April 2012 (corporation tax) or 6 April 2012 (income tax). This is calculated by reference to the precise number of days falling before and after the relevant date (not forgetting that 2012 is a leap year!) (*FA 2011, s 11(6)*).

14.85 However, so far as concerns expenditure actually incurred *after* the relevant date, the maximum is restricted to the time-apportioned amount of the AIA relating to the part of the chargeable period falling after the change (*FA 2011, s 11(7)*).

Example

A company with a calendar year chargeable period from 1 January 2012 to 31 December 2012 would calculate its maximum AIA entitlement based on:

(a)   the proportion of a year from 1 January 2012 to 31 March 2012, that is, 91/366 × £100,000 = £24,863; and

(b)   the proportion of a year from 1 April 2012 to 31 December 2012, that is 275/366 × £25,000 = £18,784.

The company's maximum AIA for this transitional chargeable period would therefore be the total of (a) + (b) = £24,863 + £18,784 = £43,647.

However, the restriction in *s 11(7)* would then apply to expenditure incurred after 31 March 2012 – if £10,000 was incurred before that date, and £30,000 thereafter, the maximum AIA would be £28,784:

(a)   £18,784 for the 'later' expenditure (limited as above); plus

(b)   £10,000 for the 'early' expenditure.

It is not possible to claim the full £43,647 AIA because of the restriction imposed by *s 11(7)* and the fact that there is insufficient expenditure pre-31 March 2012. If the expenditure incurred *after* the relevant date had been £10,000 rather than £30,000, and the expenditure *before* that date had been £300,000 rather than £10,000, the AIA would be the full permitted £43,647, effectively:

(a)   £10,000 for the 'later' expenditure; plus

(*b*) £33,647 (the balance up to the £43,647 maximum) for the 'earlier' expenditure.

This calculation merely establishes the maximum AIA - there is no requirement to calculate separate 'pre' and 'post' AIAs and allocate each to the relevant expenditure. Consequently the apparent anomaly in the above example, where an 'early' AIA of £33,647 is calculated, even though only £30,000 was incurred in the 'early' period, is perfectly possible.

Accounting periods overlapping 1 January 2013

14.86 The AIA is time-apportioned where the chargeable period overlaps 1 January 2013 (*FA 2013, s 7, Sch 1*).

14.87 The most complex situation is where a chargeable period straddles both the relevant date in April 2012 and 1 January 2013. In such cases, the maximum AIA is determined firstly by an overall time-apportionment calculation, and secondly by restricting the actual expenditure that may qualify for the AIA in each part of the chargeable period.

Example

A company makes up its accounts to 31 January each year. The year to 31 January 2013 may be split into three periods:

1. Period X runs from 1 February 2012 to 1 April 2012; the maximum time-apportioned AIA is $2/12 \times £100,000 = £16,667 +$

2. Period Y runs from 1April 2012 to 1 January 2013; the maximum time-apportioned AIA is $9/12 \times £25,000 = £18,750 +$

3. Period Z runs from 1 January 2013 to 31 January 2013; the maximum time-apportioned AIA is $1/12 \times £250,000 = £20,833$

Total = £56,250

However, there is a further restriction, made by looking at each component period in isolation.

Restriction for period X

This is limited to the maximum which would have been due if the 1 January 2013 change had not happened, that is:

2 months × £100,000 = £16,667 +

10 months × £25,000 = £20,833

Therefore, up to £37,500 incurred before 1 April 2012 may be sheltered by AIA

Restriction for period Y

The restriction is given by the formula A – B, where:

('A') = Total AIA for periods Y + Z if 1 January 2013 change had not happened

('B') = Actual AIA claimed for period X ('C'), minus maximum time-apportioned AIA for period X (*as if it had been a stand-alone period*) ('D')

In our example,

('A') = 10/12 × £25,000 = £20,833

('C') Actual expenditure in period X (say, £20,000)

('D') Maximum time-apportioned AIA for period X (as above) = £16,667

So, ('B') = ('C') – ('D') = £20,000 minus £16,667 (as above) = £3,333

Therefore, ('A') – ('B') = £20,833 – £3,333 = £17,500. The maximum AIA for period Y is £19,500.

Restriction for period Z

This is calculated by adding together the maximum AIA for periods Y and Z (*as if they were stand-alone periods*):

Period Y = 9/12 × £25,000 = £18,750

Period Z = 1/12 × £250,000 = £20,833

Therefore, the maximum AIA for period Z is £39,583.

Total 'restriction' for periods X + Y + Z

The individual component period restrictions are £37,500, £19,500 and £39,583. These total £96,583, but the AIA given cannot exceed the maximum £56,250 permitted for entire period, as calculated earlier in this example.

In effect, the maximum for period Z becomes £56,250 less the £20,000 actual claim in periods X and Y, ie £36,250

Accounting periods overlapping 1 or 6 April 2014

14.88 The AIA is time-apportioned where the chargeable period overlaps 1 or 6 April January 2014 (*FA 2014, s 10*).

14.89 Again, the maximum AIA is determined firstly by an overall time-apportionment calculation, and secondly by restricting the actual expenditure that may qualify for the AIA in each part of the chargeable period.

Where a business has a chargeable period of 12 months that spans the operative date of the increase on 1 April 2014, the maximum allowance for that business's transitional chargeable period comprises two parts:

(a) its AIA entitlement, based on the £250,000 annual cap for the portion of the period falling before 1 April 2014; and

(b) its AIA entitlement, based on the £500,000 cap for the portion of the period falling on or after 1 April 2014.

Example

A company with a 12 month chargeable period from 1 January 2014 to 31 December 2014 would calculate its maximum AIA entitlement based on:

(a) the proportion of the period from 1 January 2014 to 31 March 2014, that is, $3/12 \times £250,000 = £62,500$; and

(b) the proportion of the period from 1 April 2014 to 31 December 2014, that is, $9/12 \times £500,000 = £375,000$.

The company's maximum AIA for this transitional chargeable period would therefore be the total of $(a) + (b) = £62,500 + £375,000 = £437,500$, although in relation to (a) (the part period falling before 1 (or 6) April 2014, no more than a maximum of £250,000 of the company's actual expenditure in that particular part period would be covered by its transitional AIA entitlement (the maximum claimable before the increase to £500,000).

Accounting periods overlapping 1 January 2016

14.90 Where a business has a chargeable period that spans the date of end of the temporary increase on 31 December 2015, the maximum allowance for that business's transitional chargeable period comprises two parts:

(a) the AIA entitlement, based on the temporary £500,000 annual cap for the portion of the period falling before 1 January 2016; and

(b) the AIA entitlement, based on the £200,000 cap for the portion of the period falling on or after 1 January 2016.

Example

A company with a 12 month chargeable period from 1 April 2015 to 31 March 2016 would calculate its maximum AIA entitlement based on:

(a)   the proportion of the period from 1 April 2015 to 31 December 2015, that is, 9/12 × £500,000 = £375,000; and

(b)   the proportion of the period from 1 January 2016 to 31 March 2016, that is 3/12 × £200,000 = £50,000.

The company's maximum AIA for this transitional chargeable period would therefore be the total of (a) + (b) = £375,000 + £50,000 = £425,000, although in relation to (b) (the part period falling on or after 1 January 2016) no more than £50,000 of the company's actual expenditure in that part period would be covered by its transitional AIA entitlement.

Similar businesses with different year ends

14.91   On occasion, the AIA may be required to be shared between related businesses, ie those under common control. Where more than two businesses with different chargeable periods share an AIA, the maximum AIA that a business can claim is reduced (but not below nil) by any amounts allocated to another business or businesses with the same or later (ending) chargeable period(s).

Example (from HM Treasury Explanatory Notes)

If four companies in a company group with different chargeable periods ending in the financial year 2012–2013 were required to share a single AIA their individual maximum amounts might look like this:

Company	CP ending on	Maximum time-apportioned AIA
		£
A	30 April 2012	93,750
B	31 December 2012	43,750
C	31 March 2013	25,000
D	31 March 2013	25,000

The rule *in subsection (9)* provides that the absolute maximum AIA that the companies can share is £93,750. However, *subsection (11)* provides that companies C & D cannot each claim £25,000 AIA and if between them companies C & D did claim amounts totalling £25,000 then companies A & B's maximum claim would be reduced by £25,000. Similarly if company B did claim the reduced maximum of £18,750 following claim(s) by companies C & D, then company A could only claim the reduced balance of £50,100.

Subsection (3) restricts HM Treasury's power to amend the amount of the maximum AIA by way of secondary legislation to a power to increase the maximum amount (*FA 2011, s 11(3)*).

Subsequent disposal

14.92 Where an AIA is claimed in respect of an asset, and that asset is sold, disposal proceeds must be brought into account. The mechanism for this is that on acquisition, the initial expenditure is allocated to whichever pool is appropriate, then the 'available qualifying expenditure' (*s 57*) in that pool is reduced by the same amount. There is no immediate effect on the pool, but the mechanism is then in place which will require the taxpayer to bring in a disposal value on the sale, etc of the asset (*s 58(4A)*).

Anti-avoidance

14.93 Anti-avoidance also exists to prevent the artificial use of unused annual investment allowances. These deny a taxpayer an AIA where there is an arrangement entered into wholly or mainly to enable that person to obtain an AIA to which the person would not otherwise be entitled (*s 218A*).

14.94 In addition, *Finance Act 2010* introduced a new *ITA 2007, s 127A*, denying loss relief against general income where a property loss is attributable to the Annual Investment Allowance and arises in connection with 'relevant tax avoidance arrangements'.

14.95 The restriction applies (*s 127A(1)*) where:

- a person makes a loss in a UK property business or overseas property business;

- the loss has a capital allowances connection (defined by *ITA 2007, s 123(2)*), and

- the loss arises in consequence of, or in connection with, relevant tax avoidance arrangements.

14.96 *Section 127A(2)* makes it clear that, if this section applies, no property loss may be relieved against general income to the extent that the loss is attributable to the annual investment allowance (assuming that the loss relates to the AIA before any other deductions or allowances).

14.97 'Relevant tax avoidance arrangements' are those which have as their main purpose, or one of their main purposes, to make use of an annual investment allowance to reduce a tax liability by means of property loss relief against general income. Genuine commercial arrangements should not, therefore, be affected.

14.98   These rules apply for arrangement entered into on or after 24 March 2010, unless an unconditional obligation existed before that date.

Writing-down allowances

14.99   Before 1 April 2008 (corporation tax) and 6 April 2008 (income tax) WDAs were generally given at a rate of 25% pa of the balance of qualifying expenditure in the pool. However, from those dates until 31 March 2012 (corporation tax) and 5 April 2012 (income tax), this reduced to 20% pa. From 1 April 2012 and 6 April 2012, the rate was again reduced to 18% pa (*FA 2012, s 10(2)*).

14.100   The balance of qualifying expenditure upon which WDAs are given consists of the balance brought forward from the previous chargeable period, plus any new expenditure incurred in the year (together referred to as 'available qualifying expenditure' or 'AQE') (*s 57*), less the total disposal receipts (TDR) brought into account (see **12.49** *et seq*) (*s 56(1)*). WDAs and first-year allowances are not given in the same accounting period.

14.101   In calculating the rate of WDA available, the date the expenditure is incurred is irrelevant. In the accounting period which overlaps 31 March 2008 (corporation tax) or 5 April 2008 (income tax), a 'hybrid' rate of allowances is used on the basis of time apportionment. For example, a company with a September 2008 year-end was entitled to allowances at the rate of approximately 22.5% (183/366 × 25% plus 183/366 × 20%). Where the hybrid rate would be a figure with more than two decimal places, it was rounded up to the nearest second decimal place (*FA 2008, s 80(10)*).

14.102   Identical principles apply where an accounting period overlaps 31 March 2012 (corporation tax) or 5 April 2012 (income tax).

14.103   The rate of 25%, 20% or 18% is proportionately increased or reduced if the chargeable period is less or more than one year, or *if the qualifying activity has been carried on for part only of the chargeable period.* The words in italics apply for corporation tax purposes from 6 April 1995. One impact of the change is where a company begins a second or subsequent trade part of the way through an accounting period. From 6 April 1995, WDAs for expenditure on plant used in that new trade will be restricted; prior to that date, they were not (*s 56(3)* and (*4*)).

14.104   WDAs are given where the following conditions are met:

(*a*)   a person carrying on a *qualifying activity* (see **14.108**) has incurred capital expenditure (see **1.12** *et seq*, **15.11** *et seq*) on the *provision* (see **14.114** *et seq*) of machinery or plant *wholly or partly* (see **14.128** *et seq*) for the *purposes of the qualifying activity* (see **14.135** *et seq*); and

(*b*)   in consequence of his incurring that expenditure, the machinery or plant *belongs* or has belonged (see **14.141** *et seq*) to him (*s 11*).

14.105 For the most recent consideration of whether expenditure had been 'incurred', see *ABC Ltd v M (Inspector of Taxes)* [2002] STC (SCD) 78 (see **Appendix 4**).

14.106 It was confirmed in *Barclays Mercantile Business Finance Ltd v Mawson* [2002] EWCA Civ 1853, [2003] STC 66; affd [2004] UKHL 51, [2005] STC 1 and in *Barclays Mercantile Industrial Finance Ltd v Melluish (Inspector of Taxes)* [1990] STC 314, that provided the expenditure was incurred on the provision of machinery or plant wholly and exclusively for the purposes of the trade, it was irrelevant whether or not the trader's objective was or included the obtaining of capital allowances, and the *Ramsay* principle (ie that the scheme should be looked at as a whole to disregard any steps that have no business purpose, apart from avoiding tax) could not apply (*WT Ramsay Ltd v IRC*; *Eilbeck (Inspector of Taxes) v Rawling* [1981] STC 174). The extent to which expenditure was incurred was also considered in *Commissioners for HM Revenue & Customs v Tower MCashback LLP 1* [2011] UKSC 19.

Small pools

14.107 With effect from 1 April 2008 (corporation tax) or 6 April 2008 (income tax), where the written-down value of a plant and machinery pool is no more than £1,000, businesses may claim a WDA equal to the entire value of the pool (*CAA 2001, s 56A*). This applies to the main 18% pool and to the 'special rate' 8% pool, but not to single asset pools (see **14.3**).

Qualifying activity

14.108 *Section 11* is the main rule that determines entitlement to claim capital allowances in respect of machinery or plant. One of the conditions precedent is that the claimant must be carrying on a qualifying activity (*s 15*). This includes the following (provided the profits or gains, if any, are subject to tax):

(*a*)   a trade;

(*b*)   an ordinary property business (ie UK property investment);

(*c*)   a furnished holiday lettings business (see below);

(*d*)   an overseas property business (ie non-UK property investment);

(*e*)   a profession or vocation;

(*f*) a concern listed in *Income Tax (Trading and Other Income) Act 2005* (*ITTOIA 2005*), *s 12(4)* or *Corporation Tax Act 2009* (*s 39(4)* (mines, transport undertakings, etc);

(*g*) the management of an investment company;

(*h*) special leasing of plant or machinery (ie let otherwise than in the course of a qualifying activity); and

(*i*) an employment or office (provided the expenditure is *necessarily* incurred) (*s 36*).

14.109 It was observed *per curiam* in *Barclays Mercantile Industrial Finance Ltd v Melluish (Inspector of Taxes)* [1990] STC 314 that it may be that if it could be shown that a company which was a member of a group entered into a transaction apparently in the course of its trading operations but in fact at the direction of the parent company and without exercising any discretion in the matter, the Special Commissioners would be justified in finding that it was not part of the trading activities.

14.110 With effect for chargeable periods ending on or after 21 March 2000, any reference to a qualifying activity in relation to allowances on plant relates only to that part of the activity which is taxable in the United Kingdom.

14.111 This does not apply to the legislation dealing with overseas leasing, oil profit sharing contracts, sale and leaseback transactions or successions to a trade, as that legislation includes references to a trade which is not intended to be restricted to a trade taxable in the United Kingdom (*s 15(1)*).

Furnished holiday letting

14.112 A furnished holiday lettings business is effectively treated as a trade by the UK tax system, rather than as a UK or overseas property business. This has an effect on, for example, loss relief (see **22.35**). Furthermore, the dwelling-house restriction (see **15.125**) does not apply to a furnished holiday let which is so treated (the HMRC Manuals confirm that accommodation genuinely let for profit, rather than being primarily a holiday home, is not in any case a dwelling-house – CA, para 11520).

14.113 In order to be treated as a trade, rather than a property business, a furnished holiday let must meet certain criteria:

● It must be within the UK (England, Wales, Scotland and Northern Ireland, but not the Isle of Man or Channel Islands) or the European Economic Area (EEA) (comprising the member states of the EU plus Iceland, Liechtenstein and Norway). UK-based furnished holiday lettings are treated as one business and EEA lettings are treated as an entirely separate business;

- The letting must be carried out commercially with a view to a profit (business plans and accounts may be required in support);

- It must have furniture for normal occupation and the occupants must be entitled to use it, and

- It must be available for letting for 210 days, with no more than 31 days of letting to the same person (and such periods of longer term occupation must not exceed 155 days in the tax year), and it must be actually occupied by the public as furnished holiday accommodation for at least 105 days. For accounting periods ending before 1 April 2012 (corporation tax) or 6 April 2012 (income tax), these criteria were respectively 140 days and 70 days (*ITTOIA 2005, s 325* and *CTA 2009, s 267*).

If there is more than one furnished holiday lettings property, but one or more of them is not occupied for at least 105 days, an 'averaging election' may be made. This averages the occupancy rates of all the furnished holiday properties in that UK or EEA furnished holiday lettings business (*ITTOIA 2005, s 326* and *CTA 2009, s 268*).

A 'period of grace' election may also be made if there was a genuine intention to let a property which was occupied for at least 105 days in the previous year (*ITTOIA 2005, s 326A* and *CTA 2009, s 268A*). Such an election can be made for two consecutive tax years, but if the property is not occupied for at least 105 days in the third year then it ceases to qualify as a furnished holiday let.

14.113A   Plant and machinery allowances are available for furnished holiday lettings businesses in the UK (*s 15(1)(c)*) and European Economic Area (EEA) (*s 15(1)(da)*). The allowances are given as an expense of that particular furnished holiday lettings business (*s 249* for the UK and *s 250A* for the EEA).

Where a furnished holiday let property no longer meets the relevant conditions (see **14.113**) that business may be treated as ceasing and capital allowances will not be available. A balancing charge will crystallise, based on the market value of the qualifying assets (for chattels, *s 61(1)(e)(f)*, *s 61(2)* Item 7 and for fixtures, *s 196* Item 12), but no sale proceeds will be received to pay the tax with. However, this outcome rests upon the failure to meet the conditions being regarded as a permanent cessation of the furnished holiday lettings business. If that business is continuing (eg, there are other FHL properties, or the intention that the conditions may be met in future years), it is arguable that there has been no permanent discontinuance. HMRC appear to allow for a wider concession:

> 'Strictly, if a property qualifies in one year but does not do so in the next, the disposal value of plant and machinery should be brought into account. If income from a property temporarily ceases to qualify solely because not all the tests are satisfied for that year, capital allowances may be continued. But

if a property is let on a long-term basis, or sold, or otherwise seems unlikely to qualify in the foreseeable future, disposal value should be brought into account.' (PIM4120)

Provision

14.114 'Provision must cover something more than the actual supply' (*IRC v Barclay, Curle & Co Ltd* (1969) 45 TC 221). It is worth highlighting that what qualifies for allowances is not merely expenditure *on* machinery or plant, but expenditure *on the provision of* machinery or plant (*s 11*). By implication, and in practice, this may therefore go beyond the actual purchase price of the asset to include any expenditure on acquiring title, bringing the asset to the location in which it is to be used and setting it up in working order. This was considered in *Ben-Odeco Ltd v Powlson* (*Inspector of Taxes*) (1978) 52 TC 459 (see **Appendix 4**). Common examples would include:

(*a*)   irrecoverable VAT;

(*b*)   VAT adjustments under the capital goods scheme (see **22.7** *et seq*);

(*c*)   import duties;

(*d*)   engineers and legal fees;

(*e*)   commissions;

(*f*)   delivery costs; and

(*g*)   installation costs.

14.115   Commissioning expenses paid to the supplier of the asset normally qualify as part of the qualifying capital expenditure without any difficulty. The treatment of other costs, normally of a revenue nature, incurred by the purchaser (eg labour and fuel) is sometimes complicated by the adoption of special accounting treatment to avoid distortion of profits. Any such additional expenses charged to revenue will generally be allowed as such in the computations of an established trade or if the requirements of *s 12* (relief for pre-trading expenditure) are satisfied. The relief of capitalised expenditure is likely to be by way of capital allowances but a revenue deduction can sometimes be negotiated.

14.116   The cost of removal and re-erection of plant qualifies for allowances (CA, para 21190), but the taxpayer should consider first whether it qualifies as a trading deduction. For example, HMRC accepts that when a trader moves to new premises, the expense of removing equipment should be allowed in *all* cases, where the cost falls on the trader and is not effectively reimbursed (BIM, para 46701).

14.117   A payment by a company to enable it to retain its title to an item of plant has been held to be part of the cost of provision of that plant (*Bolton (Inspector of Taxes) v International Drilling Co Ltd* [1983] STC 70).

14.118   Fees and financing costs are dealt with in **2.24–2.36**, and hire purchase in **18.1**.

Building alterations

14.119   The cost of building alterations connected with the installation of machinery or plant will also qualify for allowances, provided certain conditions are met. Such expenditure must be incurred by a trader on alterations to an *existing* building incidental to the installation of machinery or plant for the purposes of that trade (*s 25*). In this context, 'incidental' means 'in connection with' and not 'small, minor or insignificant'. The following statement by Lord Reid in the House of Lords in *Barclay, Curle* is also helpful:

> 'Incidental is a wider meaning than necessary. In my view, expenditure necessary for the installation of the plant is already covered by ITA 1952, *s 279* [ie a predecessor to *CAA 2001, s 11*]. But it may be that the exigencies of the trade require that when new machinery or plant is installed in existing buildings, more shall be done than mere installation in order that the new machinery or plant may serve its proper purpose. Where that is the case this section [ie *CAA 2001, s 25*] enables the cost of the additional alterations to be included.'

14.120   So long as the trader is occupying the building for his trade, it is irrelevant who owns the building. It is similarly irrelevant whether the plant itself is leased by the trader or owned outright.

14.121   *Section 25* overrides *ss 21* and *22* (assets treated as buildings or structures) (see **15.97** *et seq*), but does not apply to expenditure by a lessor for the purposes of a lessee's trade.

14.122   In HMRC's view, *s 25* is interpreted narrowly to cover only the direct costs of installing plant that 'can properly be considered to be part of the cost of providing the plant' and where there is a 'direct link' between the incurring of the expenditure and the installation of the plant it is incidental to. Therefore, it considers that *s 25* does not apply to additions to a building, but only to alterations to a building (CA, para 21190). However, this narrow view is difficult to reconcile with Lord Reid's statement above (see **14.37**) and at odds with HMRC's more inclusive approach to allow expenditure on installing lift shafts into existing buildings, as well as *Disability Discrimination Act* expenditure (see **16.76**(*b*)).

14.123 In *Wimpy International Ltd v Warland* (*Inspector of Taxes*) [1989] STC 273 when building a restaurant rooftop air cooling and extraction plant room it was held that the expense of sinking the floor into the concrete of the ceiling below was incidental to the installation of the plant, but building a brick housing was not.

14.124 In *B&E Security Systems Ltd v Commissioners for HM Revenue & Customs* [2010] UKFTT 146 (TC), an entire control room to contain surveillance monitoring equipment was held to be incidental to monitoring equipment. The works included strengthening walls, floors and ceilings; providing a raised access computer floor for extensive cabling; fireproof security doors and an interlock; providing independent amenities including washroom facilities and a kitchen; and independent power supplies including backup batteries and a generator.

14.125 In *JD Wetherspoon plc v HMRC* [2012] UKUT 42 (TCC), the Upper Tribunal concluded that the purpose of *s 25* was that if plant is installed in an existing building it is possible that something will not fit, which will lead to alterations having to be made to the existing building. Therefore, *s 25* is intended to level the playing field between new and existing buildings by affording taxpayers relief for expenditure on existing buildings which would not be needed if the same plant was installed in new buildings or in the open air.

14.126 They considered a number of assets and the following decision was reached in relation to public house fit outs:

Asset	*Decision*
Wipe clean kitchen tiling	Not incidental to kitchen plant (ie, cookers and other equipment) because the tiles did not have sufficient 'nexus' to that plant (however, splash backs to sinks and the immediate surrounds of lavatory basins were incidental to that plant)
Waterproof floor coatings and non-slip/wipe clean floors generally	Not incidental to toilet sanitary ware or other equipment (however, PVC sheeting in disabled toilets qualified because it had the special function of assisting wheelchair traction)
Plastering and painting generally	Not incidental to toilet sanitary ware or other equipment
Doors and frames in general areas of the toilets (outside cubicles)	Not incidental to toilet sanitary ware

Brickwork and blockwork lavatory partitions	Not incidental to toilet sanitary ware
Panelled lavatory partitions including doors/cubicles and back panelling to conceal cisterns and pipes	Incidental to toilet sanitary ware, which could not be used without partitions or cubicles (but the Tribunal indicated that it would have found these ineligible if HMRC had appealed on this point)
Strengthened upper floors to take load of kitchen equipment	Incidental to kitchen equipment
Pattresses (ie mountings) to support equipment	Incidental to equipment
Drainage system	Incidental to toilet, kitchen and cellar beer distribution plant
Toilet and kitchen lighting builders work	Incidental to toilet and kitchen lighting (on kitchen lighting the Upper Tribunal indicated that it was not sure that it would necessarily have reached the same conclusion as the First-tier Tribunal, but the point was not appealed by HMRC)

14.127   If the conditions for allowances under *s 25* are not met, allowances may still be available under general principles, as expenditure on the provision of plant (see **14.114** and **14.119**). See also the treatment of installation costs, site preparation and BWIC in **2.37–2.38**.

Example

Brown buys a printing machine which has to be fixed to an abnormally strong floor, so he puts down an extra six inches of concrete on the floor of his existing building. This qualifies for allowances by virtue of *s 25*. If the problem had been anticipated by incorporation of the extra thickness of flooring into the building at the time of construction the expenditure on that extra thickness would not have qualified as expenditure on machinery or plant.

Wholly or partly

14.128   In order to qualify for allowances, expenditure must be incurred 'wholly or partly' for the purposes of the qualifying activity (*s 11*). However, the effect of the expenditure must be distinguished from the object of the expenditure at the time it was incurred. If there is an unavoidable or incidental effect or benefit of a non-qualifying nature the expenditure may nevertheless be treated as incurred with the sole object of being wholly for the purposes of the trade. *CAA 2001* uses the phrase 'wholly or partly' instead of 'wholly and exclusively' used in *CAA 1990* because that was considered to be potentially misleading. It was considered that taxpayers might conclude they were not entitled to plant and machinery allowances if they used an asset partly for other purposes, yet *CAA 1990, s 79* already made explicit provision for allowances for plant or machinery used partly for a qualifying activity and partly for other purposes.

14.129 Where a person carrying on a qualifying activity incurs capital expenditure on the provision of machinery or plant partly for the purposes of that activity and partly for other (eg, private) purposes, the expenditure is included in a single asset pool, ie dealt with outside the main pool, etc (*s 206*). The allowance (or charge) is restricted to an amount which is just and reasonable for the proportion of business use (*s 207*). HMRC accepts that expenditure incurred by an employer in providing an asset for a director's or employee's private use as part of a remuneration package (giving rise to a taxable benefit under *s 205* ITEPA 2003), is incurred wholly and exclusively for the purposes of the business' qualifying activity. However, if there is a 'blatant incongruity' between the asset provided for the director or employee and the commercial requirements of the business, Inspectors may seek to use *G H Chambers (Northiam Farms) Ltd v Watmough*, 36 TC 711 to restrict the capital allowances on the grounds of personal choice (CA, para 27100).

14.130 Where there is a reduction in trading use on or after 21 March 2000, and the market value of the asset at that time exceeds the tax written-down value by at least £1 million, the notional trade is treated as ceasing, with a requirement to bring in disposal proceeds equal to market value. The effect is to claw back allowances, to the extent that they exceed the real fall in the value of the asset. The separate pool recommences the following year, based on that same market value (*s 208*).

14.131 Where machinery or plant is used for the purposes of an office or employment, there is an additional requirement that the plant must be *necessarily* provided (*s 36*). 'Necessarily' implies that the duties must objectively require the use of machinery and plant, and the employee or office holder must be obliged to incur the expense of providing it.

> 'The test is not whether the employer imposes the expense but whether the duties do, in the sense that irrespective of what the employer may prescribe, the duties cannot be performed without incurring the particular outlay' (*Brown v Bullock (Inspector of Taxes)* (1961) 40 TC 1 at 10, per Donovan LJ).

14.132 For example, a claim by a vicar in respect of a projector to illustrate his sermon failed because the Commissioners found as a fact that another vicar could perform religious ministry without the equipment and that the taxpayer would have been able to do his job without the equipment (*White* (*Inspector of Taxes*) *v Higginbottom* [1983] STC 143). The fact that the job could have been done better with the projector seems to have been irrelevant.

14.133   It seems that HMRC interprets the 'necessarily' test in respect of offices and employments as being in place of, rather than in addition to, the 'wholly or partly' test applied to other qualifying activities. This is not of great practical importance for the following reasons:

(*a*)   the 'necessarily' test is normally more difficult to satisfy than the wholly or partly test; and

(*b*)   the 'necessary adaptation' of *s 207* (use partly for a qualifying activity and partly for other purposes) requires that a just and reasonable apportionment shall be made when the machinery or plant is used partly in the performance of the duties and partly for other purposes.

14.134   The 'necessarily' test is specifically excluded in respect of expenditure on the provision of a motor vehicle incurred partly for the purposes of an office or employment and partly for other purposes (*s 80(2)*) (see **Chapter 17**).

Purposes of the qualifying activity

14.135   Expenditure will almost certainly have been incurred for the purposes of the qualifying activity if the asset is being used in the earning of the profits of the activity and is not being used for any other purpose. The phrase 'for the purposes of a trade' is discussed in some depth in *Usher's Wiltshire Brewery Ltd v Bruce* (*Surveyor of Taxes*) (1914) 6 TC 399 and the principles may be extended to other qualifying activities.

14.136   In *Union Cold Storage Co Ltd v Jones* (*Inspector of Taxes*) (1923) 8 TC 725, Pollock MR said at 737:

'in following Usher's case you must look at what is the direct concern and direct purpose for which the money is laid out, and I do not think that you can go to the remoter or indirect results for which it may be possibly useful to lay out money.'

14.137   Problems may sometimes be encountered when a company in a group allows use of its plant by other group members. In *Union Cold Storage Co Ltd*, a company which allowed its plant to be used by an associated company was refused capital allowances. Rowlatt J said at 736:

'I think "used for the purposes of the trade of the appellant company" means that the appellant company are making profits by using and causing wear and tear of the machinery.'

14.138 Machinery and plant used by an employee for private purposes is generally treated as in use for the purposes of the employer's trade because such use will usually be part of the employee's remuneration package and therefore constitutes use of the plant 'in making profits by using and causing wear and tear of the machinery'. However, when the employee is a controlling shareholder he is able to exercise more personal choice, the effect of which upon a claim for capital allowances in respect of a motor car was considered in *G H Chambers (Northiam Farms) Ltd v Watmough (Inspector of Taxes)* (1956) 36 TC 711. In that case there was ample evidence to show that (in the words of Vaisey J at 717):

'the car would not have been bought by anyone who in considering the question of its purchase was directing his mind, solely and exclusively, to the necessities of the trader or of the trade as such.'

14.139 The car had therefore been purchased partly for purposes other than those of the trade, ie personal choice, which was sufficient to invoke the provisions of what is now *s 206* (see **14.129** *et seq*). However, in *Kempster v McKenzie* (1952) 33 TC 193 (in the context of a sole trader, not an employee), the opposite conclusion was reached. Clearly, each case will be decided on its facts. HMRC may seek to restrict allowances where there is a 'blatant incongruity' between the asset provided and the commercial needs of the business (CA, para 27100).

14.140 Use of machinery or plant for providing business entertainment is treated as use otherwise than for the purposes of the trade (*CTA 2009, s 1298*). If such use is only partial, restricted allowances might still be available. In contrast, expenditure on security assets (see **15.91** *et seq*) is always treated as incurred for the purposes of the trade, provided the conditions of *s 33(1)*, *(2)* are satisfied (*s 33(3)* and *(4)*).

Ownership

14.141 WDAs on machinery or plant are given where a person incurs expenditure as a result of which that person owns the machinery or plant (the so-called 'belonging' test) (*s 11(4)(b)*). The phrase 'as a result of which' has only once been given any prominence by the courts, in *Bolton (Inspector of Taxes) v International Drilling Co Ltd* [1983] STC 70. A drilling rig belonged to the company, but was subject to an option to purchase held by a third party. The company paid £500,000 for cancellation of the option. It was held that, although the rig belonged to the company before the incurring of the £500,000, it would have ceased to do so had this amount not been paid, and therefore (after the date of the option) the rig did belong to the company in consequence of incurring the expenditure of £500,000.

14.142 The term 'owns' is not defined by statute and one must therefore look to its ordinary meaning. Whether or not a person owns an item of plant is dependent on the relevant facts of each case. In *Melluish v BMI (No 3) Ltd* [1995] STC 964, the ownership requirement was held to be satisfied where the claimant was able to show that it was, in law or in equity, the absolute owner of the equipment (ie the beneficial owner). In most instances, 'ownership' is not a problem because either the asset is purchased outright or it is deemed to belong to a person by specific provision of the legislation, for example, assets acquired under a hire-purchase agreement (*s 67*). Under general property law, fixtures attached to a building become part of it, and in effect belong to the freeholder of the land on which the building stands. The case of *Stokes (Inspector of Taxes) v Costain Property Investments Ltd* (1989) 57 TC 688 highlighted the anomaly that a lessee could not therefore claim capital allowances, even if the fixtures had been added at his own expense, because the fixtures did not belong to him. *CAA 2001, Pt 2, Ch 14* generally rectifies this situation, allowing the lessee to claim allowances (see **11.17** *et seq*).

Deposits

14.143 A common problem is where a taxpayer pays a deposit for an item of machinery or plant in one accounting period, but the plant is not actually completed or delivered until the following accounting period. In most cases, the purchase contract (or the supplier's standard terms of sale) will state that title shall not pass until all amounts have been paid.

14.144 In such circumstances it may be that, although the taxpayer has incurred capital expenditure under an unconditional obligation, he is initially precluded from claiming capital allowances because the plant does not yet belong to him. In many cases, relief is obtained via *s 67* (see **18.1**), which refers to expenditure incurred by a person who 'shall or may' become the owner of the machinery or plant. If an agreement can be brought within the scope of that section, a deposit will almost certainly qualify for relief when made. HMRC has confirmed that in such circumstances, allowances are available even if the asset is never ultimately owned.

14.145 Alternatively, one must rely on the facts, and influence them if one can. For example, if the deposit paid is substantial, the supplier may agree to transfer title at an earlier time than would normally be the case.

14.146 In some cases, *constructive ownership* has been accepted by HMRC, such as where a machine is being constructed to the customer's specification, and is so specialised that it would be of little or no use to anyone else. In these circumstances, failure to proceed with the contract would result in legal action effectively forcing performance of the contract.

14.147 This may be contrasted with, for example, an aborted contract for construction of an aircraft, in which case the partially constructed aircraft could be readily adapted for supply to another customer. The question of abortive expenditure on machinery or plant is dealt with at **14.151** *et seq* below.

14.148 Another factor which may influence the Inspector is the state of completion of the machinery and whether it is merely awaiting delivery at the taxpayer's year end.

Reservation of title to goods

14.149 HMRC has stated that where goods which have been supplied subject to reservation of title have been delivered to the purchaser then the obligation to pay will have become unconditional for the purposes of *s 5(1)* (CA, paras 11700 and 11800). However, it also stated that *s 5(4)* will not apply because that subsection applies only when the goods are the property of the purchaser. In these circumstances it may be arguable that the goods could be attributed to the purchaser as envisaged by *s 5(4)(d)*.

Milestone contracts

14.150 The construction work under such a contract, if it is a building or structure, is usually performed on-site which in most cases will either be owned by the purchaser or be the subject of an interest in land to which he is entitled. Consequently, *s 271(3)* (industrial buildings allowance – see **7.30**) will be satisfied. If the contract also includes some expenditure which can be allocated to machinery or plant, as will generally be the case, HMRC seems generally to accept appropriate apportionment of each instalment without separate examination of the ownership test (see **14.104** *et seq*). Given that in most cases the plant, by virtue of its inclusion in a building, will be a fixture on land in which the purchaser has an interest, the question of ownership is likely to be already satisfied.

Abortive expenditure

14.151 HMRC has confirmed that allowances will be available where expenditure has been incurred towards the manufacture of plant, but the supplier goes into liquidation before completion (CCAB statement 1972). This would only be the case, however, if the semi-constructed plant did in law *belong* to the taxpayer. Otherwise, the position of the prospective purchaser is less secure. Tax Bulletin 2 (February 1992), contained the following comment on abortive capital expenditure on machinery or plant:

'The side note to *s 60 CAA 1990* [the predecessor of *CAA 2001, s 67*] identifies its application to transactions of hire purchase. [Note: the heading to *s 67* no longer refers to hire-purchase; however the remainder of this Bulletin remains valid.] However, in certain circumstances this legislation may also apply to abortive capital expenditure incurred on machinery or plant.

A trader may incur capital expenditure on machinery or plant which is never actually owned – perhaps because the buyer withdraws from the supply contract or because the supplier defaults, or for some other reason. In such cases the trader will not qualify for writing down allowance on the expenditure incurred under [*s 11*] because it will not be possible to satisfy the "belonging" condition in [*s 11(4)(b)*].

[*Section 67*] deals, however, with a trader who incurs capital expenditure on the provision of machinery or plant for the purposes of the trade "under a contract providing that he shall or may become the owner of the machinery or plant on the performance of the contract". If such a contract exists, [*s 67(2)*] treats machinery or plant as belonging to the trader.

In many cases abortive expenditure (eg a deposit paid on machinery which is never actually supplied) may well be incurred under a contract which provides that the taxpayer "shall or may become the owner". If so, that expenditure will qualify for writing down allowance by virtue of [*s 67(2)*].

[*Section 67(4)*] will bring the disposal value of the machinery or plant into account at the time when the taxpayer ceases to be entitled to the benefit of the contract without becoming the owner of the machinery or plant. The disposal value will be calculated by reference to the rules in [*s 61*].'

14.152   The provisions of *s 67* are outlined further in **Chapter 18**.

LONG-LIFE ASSETS

14.153   With regard to expenditure on machinery or plant incurred on or after 26 November 1996 (*FA 1997, Sch 14*), certain assets are deemed to be 'long-life assets'. These originally qualified for a reduced rate of WDAs at 6% pa rather than the 25% pa as was generally the case (*s 102*). However, with effect from 1 April 2008 (corporation tax) and 6 April 2008 (income tax), the rate of WDAs increased to 10% pa to match the rate for integral features (see **14.5**). The rate reduced to 8% pa from 1 April 2012 and 6 April 2012 (*FA 2012, s 10(3)*).

14.154   For long-life assets existing before the rate change, a 'hybrid' rate of WDA applies on the basis of time-apportionment (where this would be a figure to more than two decimal places it is rounded up to the nearest second decimal place). For expenditure incurred shortly after the change, the full 10% rate applied for the chargeable period in which the expenditure was incurred, even if it was a transitional period. Where the cost of an asset straddles the relevant date, the expenditure before and after the date is treated as being upon separate tranches of expenditure (ie in effect, separate assets).

Example

Longevity 25 Ltd has a 30 June 2008 period end and had a long-life asset pool before April 2008 of £200,000. It then incurred a further £125,000 on long-life assets in May 2008. For the £200,000 pre-existing assets it will be entitled to writing down allowances for the period ended 30 June 2009 at the rate of approximately 7% (ie 275/366 × 6% plus 91/366 × 10%). Plus for the £125,000 incurred after the rate change it will be entitled to the full 10%.

Expenditure on long-life assets potentially qualified for first-year allowances of 12% if it was incurred in the period 2 July 1996 to 1 July 1997, but attracts no first-year allowances if incurred after that date (*s 44(2)*). Expenditure incurred on or after 17 April 2002 in a ring-fence trade (oil extraction) may qualify for a first-year allowance of 24% (*FA 2002, s 63*).

The concept of long-life assets was originally interpreted as an attack on recently privatised utilities; however, the legislation has proved to be of much wider application. It is unwise to ignore the risk of long-life asset treatment applying, when submitting and negotiating a claim. Otherwise, it is possible to put considerable time and effort into proving that an item should be regarded as plant, rather than as part of a building, only to then be forced into accepting that the lower rate of allowances applies.

Definition

14.155 A long-life asset is an item of plant or machinery which, *when new*, is estimated to have a useful economic life of at least 25 years (*s 91(1)*). In contrast to short-life assets (see **14.179** *et seq*), the question of whether or not an asset has a 'long life' is not determined simply by looking at the period of ownership of the person incurring the expenditure. Rather, that person must estimate (*at the time it is first brought into use*) the full life of the asset over a number of owners, until such time as it ceases to be used as a fixed asset of *any* business (*s 91(3)(b)*). Clearly, there will often be difficulties in making such an estimate. For example, many assets, whilst they might be regarded as obsolete or superseded by new technology well within 25 years, could nonetheless continue to be used much longer by a less demanding purchaser.

14.156 The definition of 'useful economic life' for this purpose also conflicts with that in FRS 15 which, again, considers only the period of ownership of the present owner. Also in contrast to FRS 15, there is no possibility of revising the estimate once it has been made. Unexpected obsolescence does not, therefore, affect the level of WDAs, which, if once given at 8% pa, will always be given at the long-life asset rate. It is possible, therefore, that a purchaser can find himself bound by long-life asset treatment agreed by a prior owner. Where the assets concerned are fixtures, it may be possible to mitigate the exposure by use of elections under *s 198*, such that the purchase consideration is allocated primarily to non-long-life assets. Conversely, once allowances have been given at 18% pa, the conventional rate will continue to apply, both for the original owner and for subsequent purchasers, regardless of whether the asset proves to have a longer life than was first estimated. This is implicit in *s 91*, which states that the question of whether an asset is 'long-life' is to be determined when it is new and is not to be varied subsequently.

14.157 The fact that this treatment is not dealt with explicitly by the legislation has led to some Inspectors seeking to revisit the treatment, and recategorise assets as long-life assets, on the basis that full facts were not disclosed in the first instance. Full disclosure is generally advised, but if a taxpayer genuinely believes that an asset does not have a long-life (as defined), then it can hardly be recommended that he should set out to plant doubts in the Inspector's mind. However, the expenditure on the relevant asset should be capable of being identified from the tax computation (rather than just being 'hidden' in a total plant additions figure for the year) and an appropriate form of wording should be provided in the tax return 'white space'. That way, the Inspector should not be able to claim later that he was unaware of the potential issue.

14.158 The HMRC Manual (CA, para 23750) confirms that once an asset has been treated as long-life, it cannot later be changed, even if sold to a new owner. The Manual also instructs Inspectors not to revisit 'normal life' assets if dealing with a purchase. It would have been inequitable for Inspectors to be able to revisit the decision where there is continuing ownership if: (a) the owner could not do the same; and (b) the owner is disadvantaged compared to a new purchaser.

14.159 Key evidence as to asset life will be provided by the depreciation policy applied to relevant assets. Assets depreciated over more than 25 years risk being regarded as long-life assets. It has been common practice for many businesses to include certain items of plant (eg heating systems) within the 'buildings' category in their accounts and depreciate them accordingly. In future, qualifying plant should instead be separately identified and depreciated over a shorter period. Tax savings may thereby be achieved, but only at the expense of accounting profit.

14.160 Following the introduction of the long-life asset legislation, it is understood that Inspectors were instructed to identify and investigate changes in depreciation policy. Other factors indicating estimated lives of assets might include manufacturers' or suppliers' literature, past experience (where the taxpayer has owned the same type of asset previously) and published data (eg RICS Building Cost Information Service *Component Life Expectancy* data and the *Building Services Component Life Manual* (Blackwell Science)).

Pooling

14.161   Until 31 March 2008 (corporation tax) and 5 April 2008 (income tax), all long-life assets were included in a single, separate pool for the purpose of calculating capital allowances (*s 101*). This separate pool was discontinued only when the actual trade ceased: disposal of all long-life assets did not in itself, therefore, cause a balancing allowance or charge to arise (*s 65(1)*).

14.162   With effect from 1 April 2008 (corporation tax) and 6 April 2008 (income tax) *FA 2008* introduced a 'special rate' pool to include new expenditure on long-life assets and 'old' expenditure on long-life assets not previously allocated to a pool, as well as new expenditure on thermal insulation of buildings under *s 28* and new expenditure on integral features under *s 33A* (see **14.5**).

Also treated as special rate are expenditure incurred:

- on or after 1 April 2009 (corporation tax) and 6 April 2009 (income tax) on the provision of a car that is not a main rate car (see **17.43**);

- on or after 1 April 2010 on the provision of cushion gas (within the meaning given by *s 70J* - that is, gas that functions or is intended to function as plant in a particular gas storage facility); and

- on or after 1 April 2012 (corporation tax) and 6 April 2012 (income tax) on solar panels.

(*s 104A*)

14.163   Old long-life asset expenditure that was allocated to a pool was to be carried forward as special rate expenditure and qualified for WDAs at 10% (*FA 2008, s 80*). From April 2012 this reduced to 8% (*FA 2012, s 10(3)*).

Exemptions

14.164   There are, broadly speaking, three types of exemption from the rules dealing with long-life assets – one relates to the amount of the expenditure, the second to certain types of asset, and the third to fixtures in particular types of buildings.

De minimis limit

14.165 The rules will not apply where the taxpayer's expenditure on potential long-life assets does not exceed £100,000 in a chargeable period of 12 months (*ss 97* and *99*). This limit is varied pro rata where the chargeable period is of more or less than 12 months (*s 99(3)*). Where the taxpayer is a company having associated companies, the £100,000 limit is divided by the number of associates (including, of course, the taxpayer itself) (*s 99(4)*).

14.166 The *de minimis* limit does not apply in the case of:

- shares in plant or machinery;

- contributions; and

- plant used for leasing (*s 98(4)*).

14.167 Each chargeable period is viewed in isolation, with no question of 'averaging' over a period of years. This means that a taxpayer who generally incurs no expenditure on long-life assets will still be subject to the restriction on allowances if, in one particular year, his relevant expenditure exceeds £100,000. Consequently, so far as is commercially possible, it is advisable for a taxpayer to 'stagger' such expenditure over two or more years, so as to fall below the *de minimis* level in each year.

Exempted assets

14.168 Long-life asset legislation does not apply to expenditure on:

(*a*) cars (including those which are hired out, and are generally not regarded as motor cars for capital allowances purposes by virtue of *s 81, 82, 96* or *268A*);

(*b*) seagoing ships (other than those primarily used for sport or recreation, or in connection with offshore mineral workings) (*s 94*);

(*c*) railway assets (where the expenditure was incurred before 1 January 2011) (*s 95*).

Fixtures in exempted buildings

14.169 The long-life asset rules do not apply to expenditure on fixtures in a building used *wholly or mainly* as (*s 93*):

(*a*) a dwelling-house (see **15.125** *et seq*);

(*b*) a retail shop or showroom;

(*c*)   a hotel; or

(*d*)   an office.

14.170 Fixtures in a building used for purposes ancillary (see **7.98**) to the above are also exempted (*s 93(1)*). HMRC has confirmed (CA, para 23730) that the 'wholly or mainly' rule in *s 93(1)* will be satisfied if at least 75% of the building is used for one of the exempted purposes. It is largely the case, therefore, that fixtures will only be long-life assets where they are attached to buildings which would (if new expenditure were incurred on them) qualify as industrial buildings under *s 274* (see **7.47**). There are exceptions – many leisure facilities, for example, are unlikely to qualify for IBAs and yet are not exempted from the rules on long-life assets. Some relief may be had if buildings can be brought within the 'retail shop' exemption, which is extended to include 'any premises of a similar character where retail trade or business, including repair work, is carried on' (*s 93(1)(b)*, *(2)*). This includes pubs and bars, banks, restaurants and cafés but excludes hotels, cinemas and theatres (Tax Bulletin 30 (August 1997), now superseded).

Anti-avoidance – disposal value

14.171 If a long-life asset is disposed of, and the amount brought into account as the actual disposal value is less than the notional written-down value of the asset, then the actual disposal value is ignored for capital allowance purposes and a deemed disposal value equal to the notional written-down value is substituted. This only applies where the disposal is part of a scheme of arrangement which had avoidance as its main subject, or as one of its main objects (*s 104*). If a low disposal value is commercially tenable, this rule will not apply.

HMRC practice

14.172 HMRC will apply the following procedure to determine whether expenditure has been incurred on a long-life asset.

14.173 The first step is to determine whether the expenditure is on one asset, more than one asset or only part of an asset. The 'long-life' test is to be applied to the item of plant which is regarded as an entity for tax purposes. The case of *Brown (Inspector of Taxes) v Burnley Football and Athletic Co Ltd* [1980] STC 424 is helpful in this respect. Case law dealing with repairs and replacements (eg *O'Grady (Inspector of Taxes) v Markham Main Colliery Ltd* (1932) 17 TC 93 and *Samuel Jones & Co (Devondale) Ltd v IRC* (1951) 32 TC 513) will also be relevant – see **1.24** *et seq*. Where an asset consists of various component parts, some of which have lives longer, and some shorter, than

25 years, HMRC's approach is understood to be to treat the asset either wholly as a long-life asset, or wholly as a 'normal' asset – there is no provision for treating different components differently (CA, para 23720). This is regardless of provisions in FRS 15 for 'component accounting'. In the absence of other guidance, it must be assumed that if more than 50% of the asset has a life in excess of 25 years, the asset as a whole will be treated as a long-life asset. Conversely, if more than 50% of the asset has a life expectancy of under 25 years, none of the asset will be treated as a long-life asset.

14.174   Step two, having established whether there is a single asset or not, is to determine the life of any such asset. It is understood that fixtures will not be regarded as long-life assets simply because they are attached to a building which is itself likely to have a long life. It is the anticipated lifespan of the fixtures themselves which will determine the treatment. Many fixtures (eg light fittings) will not have a long life, as defined. Exceptions to this, however, may be quasi-structural items such as air-conditioning ducts, water or gas pipes, and some parts of electrical systems. Evidence such as design specifications or manufacturers' literature may also be relevant.

14.175   HMRC's approach to long-life assets is confirmed in CA 23790. Although that paragraph deals specifically with printing equipment, a number of the points made are of more general application.

14.176   CA 23790 emphasises that each asset must be dealt with on its own facts. It is possible that two identical assets could have different expected economic lives because of the predicted use of the asset in the particular trade in which it is employed.

14.177   Where there is no established second-hand market for a particular category of asset, HMRC will generally follow the depreciation policy for the asset used in the accounts, provided this is reasonable. Where, however, there is an active second-hand market other factors are relevant. These include how long the particular business typically keeps that type of asset before it is replaced, whether the business has a history of selling assets into the second-hand market or scrapping them, and whether there are rapid technological or market changes in the sector.

14.178   HMRC has entered into a number of agreements covering the application of the long-life asset legislation across the following industries:

- airlines (jet aircraft capable of a configuration of 60 or more seats and used primarily for the carriage of passengers or freight for profit);
- greenhouses;
- water supply; and
- printing.

SHORT-LIFE ASSETS

Introduction

14.179 Short-life assets are not assets with short lives; rather, they are assets which are only expected to be actively used in a trade for a short time, after which they will be sold or scrapped. It would be more accurate, therefore, to describe them as 'short ownership assets'. This is a fundamental difference to 'long-life' assets. In certain circumstances, electing to treat assets as short-life assets can accelerate tax relief, but this should not be taken for granted.

The problem

14.180 The concept of a short-life asset was introduced in 1986 with the intention of solving a specific problem resulting from the pooling system normally applying to machinery and plant. Unless the trade ceases, balancing allowances or charges will not generally occur, and therefore an individual item of plant can continue to attract WDAs at an ever-decreasing rate long after the item has been sold or scrapped. This can be grossly unfair when dealing, for example, with a computer which after three or four years can be so obsolete as to be of no further use in the business.

The solution

14.181 HMRC therefore announced in a press release of 15 January 1986 a new system designed to be 'of particular assistance to businesses whose machinery and plant has a short working life because of heavy use or rapid obsolescence'. It is not sufficient for the active useful life of the asset to be 'short'. The assets must actually be sold, scrapped or otherwise destroyed for the advantages of the special treatment to be felt. Thus it is that prudent retention of assets taken out of active use (eg to be used as back-up in an emergency) is not encouraged.

Details of the special treatment

14.182 It is possible to elect that named assets are dealt with outside the pool system: the legislation achieves this by deeming that each asset for which an election is made is included in a single asset pool (*s 86(1)*). As such, each asset (or group of assets – see **14.190**) will be dealt with separately for capital allowances purposes, and will qualify for the normal 18% WDA available on plant. If the asset is sold or scrapped before the eighth anniversary (or, as was appropriate, the fourth anniversary – see following paragraph) of the end of the chargeable period in which it was acquired, this is regarded as the 'final chargeable period', and the disposal proceeds (if any) will be used to calculate a balancing allowance or charge (*s 65(2)*). If, however, the asset has not been sold or scrapped by that date, the balance of qualifying expenditure will be transferred into the general plant pool and will continue to attract allowances in the normal way (*s 86(2)*).

14.183   The current cut-off point, for expenditure incurred on or after 1 April 2011 (corporation tax) or 6 April 2011 (income tax), is eight years from the end of the chargeable period in which the asset is acquired (*FA 2011*, s *12*). Previously it was four years.

Making an election

14.184   For a company, an election for the above treatment to apply must be made to the Inspector in writing not more than two years after the end of the chargeable period in which the expenditure was incurred. For individuals, etc operating under the system of self-assessment (including non-resident corporate investors), the deadline for notification will be 12 months after the 31 January following the year of assessment in which the period of account ends (*s 85(2)*). Such an election is irrevocable (*s 85(4)*), and must identify the assets involved, the amount of capital expenditure and the date it was incurred (*s 85(1)*). If parts of the expenditure are incurred at different times, the two-year deadline for making the election is triggered by the date on which the first part is incurred (*s 85(3)(b)*).

14.185   See pro forma election, **Appendix 5**.

Ineligible assets

14.186   Certain assets are not eligible for treatment as short-life assets. These are (*s 84*):

(*a*)   ships;

(*b*)   cars (as defined by *s 81* or *s 268A*), other than cars hired to disabled persons (*s 268D*) (see **Chapter 17**);

(*c*)   machinery or plant used for 'special leasing', ie let otherwise than in the course of a qualifying activity (see **18.64** *et seq*);

(*d*)   machinery or plant used only partly for the purposes of a qualifying activity (see **14.128** *et seq*);

(*e*)   machinery or plant which is subject to a partial depreciation subsidy (see **1.129** *et seq*);

(*f*)   machinery or plant received by way of gift or originally provided for another purpose (see **13.9**);

(*g*)   leased machinery or plant on which expenditure is incurred after 26 July 1989, except –

(i)   machinery or plant used for short-term leasing and governed by *ss 122–125*, and

(ii)   vehicles provided wholly or mainly for persons receiving certain disability allowances, listed in *s 82*;

(*h*)   long-life assets (see **14.153**);

(*i*)   integral features (*s 33A*) (see **14.5**), and other expenditure qualifying for the 'special rate' of allowances (but not cars let to disabled persons);

(*j*)   machinery or plant leased to two or more persons jointly in circumstances where *s 116* precludes the making of a first-year allowance;

(*k*)   machinery or plant leased outside the United Kingdom which only qualifies for a 10% WDA in accordance with *s 109* (see **18.16**);

(*l*)   deemed expenditure under *s 13A* on machinery or plant previously used for leasing under a long funding lease provided for another purpose (see **18.43**).

Connected persons

14.187   Transfers of short-life assets between connected persons are given special treatment. If a trader disposes of a short-life asset to a connected person (defined by *CAA 2001, s 575* and *s 575A* as amended by *ITA 2007, Sch 1, para 411* – see **20.25** *et seq*) before the end of the eighth anniversary of the period in which the asset was acquired, that asset will be treated as being a short-life asset in the books of the transferee. The relevant 'eighth anniversary' will be determined by the date that the transferor incurred the original expenditure (*s 89(5)*).

14.188   Furthermore, both parties may elect (within two years) for the transfer to be deemed to have been at tax written-down value, so that no balancing adjustment arises on the transfer (*s 89(2)* and (*6*)). In the absence of such an election, the normal rules for transfers between connected persons apply (see **20.25** *et seq*).

14.189   Where an asset is sold for less than market value, and the transferee will be claiming capital allowances on his expenditure, the normal rule is that actual proceeds should be substituted for market value. This rule does not apply for short-life assets. Unless an election under *s 89(6)* is made or there is a charge to tax under *Income Tax (Earnings and Pensions) Act 2003 (ITEPA*

2003), market value will be included as the disposal value in the books of the transferor (*s 88*).

Groups of assets

14.190   In certain cases where it may be appropriate to make a short-life asset election, there may be real practical difficulties in doing so. Most commonly, it may be that separate identification of the assets is impossible or impractical in the circumstances of the case. It would be completely unrealistic, for example, to expect the taxpayer with a stock of several thousand returnable containers to be able to keep track of each one. Details of HMRC's approach to such cases are given in Statement of Practice SP 1/86, set out below. Similar guidance appears in the HMRC Manual, CA, para 23640.

'Capital Allowances: Machinery And Plant: Short Life Assets (15 January 1986)

1. Several representative bodies have raised with the Revenue some practical questions arising out of the new rules for capital allowances on certain short life machinery and plant which come into effect on 1 April 1986. The new rules enable allowances on machinery and plant for which an election is made to be dealt with outside the main capital allowance pool.

2. In discussions between these bodies and the Revenue several areas were identified where businesses and their accountants might find guidance helpful. This note sets out, in broad terms, how they can be dealt with in ways which will be acceptable to local inspectors. In general, inspectors will want to be satisfied that the accounting and other records are adequate to support short life asset elections and computations and that the new legislation is not being abused.

3. These guidelines are not, however, a substitute for the statutory rules. Their aim is to complement the legislation so that the new arrangements are introduced and continue to operate as efficiently as possible for businesses themselves, their professional advisers and the Revenue. The intention is to review the guidelines when the arrangements have settled in and, if necessary, revise them in the light of experience.

Election for Short Life Asset Treatment

4. The rules for making elections are set out in *FA 1985, s 57(2)* [*CAA 2001, s 85*]. They enable all the machinery and plant acquired in a chargeable period (or its basis period) for which short life asset treatment is wanted, to be included in one.

Election signed by the taxpayer for that period.

5.   In general, inspectors will want to ensure that elections and any supporting material, such as a schedule attached to the election or cross references to schedules or analyses supplied with the accounts, provide sufficient information to minimise the possibility of any difference of view at a later date (for example, on a disposal) about what was and what was not covered by an election for any chargeable period etc and that the assets are not in one of the clauses excluded by *FA 1985, Sch 15 [CAA 2001, s 84]*.

6.   In particular, however, where separate identification of the short life assets acquired in a chargeable period etc is either impossible or possible but impracticable (for example, similar small or relatively inexpensive assets held in very large numbers perhaps in several locations) then the information on the election about the assets, required by *FA 1985, s 57(2)(b) [CAA 2001, s 85]*, may be provided by reference to batches of acquisitions. Where large numbers of similar short life assets are acquired throughout a chargeable period etc it will be acceptable if the costs of those assets for the period are aggregated and shown on the election in one sum.

Capital Allowance Computations

7.   The Revenue accept that it may not be practicable for individual capital allowance computations to be maintained for each and every short life asset especially where the assets are held in very large numbers.

8.   Where, therefore, the inspector is satisfied that the actual life in the business of a distinct class of assets having broadly similar average lives before they are sold or scrapped is likely to be less than five years (that is, the year of acquisition plus the four following years) computations in the form set out in Example 1 below will be acceptable. On this basis a balancing allowance will normally become available for the last year of the agreed life of the assets.

9.   Where disposal proceeds can be attributed to assets acquired in a particular year they should be brought into the appropriate column(s) of the computation relating to those assets for the year(s) in which the proceeds are received. If attribution in this way is not possible, disposal proceeds may be credited on a FIFO basis; that is all receipts from disposals in any chargeable period etc are to be regarded as related to the earliest period for which a short life asset pool on the lines of these arrangements is in existence.

10. This form of computation is intended primarily for short life assets costing similar amounts which cannot be identified individually. It is possible however that similar arrangements may be helpful where short life assets which have a separate identity are acquired in large numbers such that the business does not in fact keep track of them individually and it would not be reasonable to expect it to do so. Where this is the case, computations based on the above principles and along the lines of Example 2 below will normally be acceptable to inspectors.

11. Given the wide variety of potential short life assets and the widely varying circumstances of individual businesses, other forms of computation may also be acceptable.

Submission of election and computations to inspectors

12. It is suggested that either on the first occasion when an election is made or when any abridged or simplified computations are submitted to inspectors for the first time, an explanation of the way in which the computations will be or have been put together is provided together with a description of the underlying records on which they are based. Inspectors will want to be satisfied that, together, the elections and the computations provide the correct statutory result and that if, for any reason, questions are asked about individual items (for example, on a disposal several years after acquisition), sufficient information will be available to the business or to its accountants to enable complete and satisfactory answers to be given.'

Example 1

This example uses the previous four-year cut-off point.

Assets held in large numbers with a very short life where individual identification is impossible (eg returnable containers, linen, tools).

The taxpayer satisfies the inspector that the average actual life (note: not useful life) of tools used in his trade is three years, it is therefore reasonable to presume that those items acquired in year 1 are all disposed of in year 4. He elects for short-life asset treatment. Accounts are made up to March each year.

Year of acquisition	*2006*	*2007*	*2008*	*2009*	*Total allowances each year*
Cost of tools	1,000	1,200	800	1,000	

2006 WDA	250			250
	750			
2007 WDA	188	300		488
	562	900		
2008 WDA	140	225	200	565
	422	675	600	
2009				
Presumed scrapped Disposal value	Nil			
Balancing allowance	422			
WDA		135	120	200	877
Qualifying expenditure carried forward		540	480	800	

Where scrap or sale proceeds are not in practice taxed as trading receipts and can be identified but not related to particular acquisitions, they should be regarded as disposal value of the earliest period for which a short-life asset pool is in existence. For example, if proceeds from the sale of all tools scrapped in 1999 were 50, the balancing allowance in the example would be 372.

Example 2

Assets held in large numbers where individual identification is possible but impracticable in the circumstances of the case.

The taxpayer uses in his trade large numbers of relatively small items such as scientific or technical instruments, calculators, or amusement machines and elects for short-life asset treatment. His accounting records enable him to identify for each kind the number and cost of acquisition, and both the number and sale proceeds of disposals and the number on hand at the end of the short-life asset period related to those acquisitions. Accounts are made up to March each year.

Technical instruments	*Number*	*Cost*	*Disposal value*
Acquisition in 2005	100	10,000	
Sold in 2007	20	500	
Sold in 2008	40	400	
On hand 2009	40		

Computation		*Cost*	*Total allowance*
2005 expenditure on 100		10,000	
Instruments			
WDA		2,500	2,500
		7,500	
2006 WDA		1,875	1,875
		5,625	
2007 disposals: 20 instruments			
Expenditure unallowed			
5,625 × 20/100 =	1,125	1,125	
Disposal value	500	4,500	
Balancing allowance	625		
			1,750
WDA		1,125	
80 instruments		3,375	
2008 disposals: 40 instruments			
Expenditure unallowed			
3,375 × 40/80 =	1,688	1,688	
		1,687	
Disposal value	400		
Balancing allowance	1,288		
			1,710
WDA		422	
40 instruments		1,265	
2009 WDA		253	253
Expenditure unallowed (40 instruments)		1,012	
2010 transfer to main pool		1,012	

It is presumed in this example that all the items cost the same amount; where similar items cost different but broadly similar amounts, this method of computation may still be used.

Disadvantages of short-life asset election

14.191 As mentioned above, the election is irrevocable. It will be beneficial in most cases, but some thought must be given to likely future events before electing. The most important factor is often the expected disposal value, as the following example illustrates.

Example

Walker has a general pool of expenditure with a tax written-down value of £10,000. In his year ended March 2008, he acquired a new computer for £12,000 and elected to treat it as a short-life asset. In 2010 he sold the computer for £10,000. His allowances were as follows:

		General pool	*S/L asset*	*Total allowances*
2008	B/fwd	10,000		
	Additions		12,000	
	WDA	(2,500)	(3,000)	5,500
2009	B/fwd	7,500	9,000	
	WDA	(1,500)	(1,800)	3,300
2010	B/fwd	6,000	7,200	
	Proceeds		(10,000)	
	Balancing charge		2,800	(2,800)
	WDA	(1,200)		1,200
	C/fwd	4,800	0	7,200

265

14.191 *Plant: system of allowances*

If Walker had not made the election, his allowances would have been as follows:

		General pool	Total allowances
2006	B/fwd	10,000	
	Additions	12,000	
	WDA	22,000	
		(5,500)	5,500
2007	B/fwd	16,500	
	WDA	(4,125)	4,125
2008	B/fwd	12,375	
	Proceeds	(10,000)	
	WDA	2,375	
		(594)	594
		1,781	10,219

Walker would therefore have received almost £2,500 more allowances if the election had not been made. This is because the balancing charge would have been absorbed by the pool. The converse can apply where there is a balancing allowance on the short-life asset and a large general pool.

Chapter 15

Plant: the meaning of the term

INTRODUCTION

15.1   One major problem, or opportunity, arising in connection with capital allowances on plant is that the term 'plant and machinery' is not defined by statute. In a capital gains tax case (dealing with whether a painting was a 'wasting asset', which would be the case if it was plant or machinery) LJ Rimer said in the Court of Appeal: 'I would regard it as tolerably obvious that "plant and machinery" is a composite phrase and that the Yarmouth v. France test [see 15.6] applies to all of it' *(Executors of Lord Howard of Henderskelfe (deceased) v HMRC Comrs* [2014] EWCA Civ 278). However, in a capital allowances context that assertion flies in the face of a substantial body of statute, case law and practice, and would appear to be questionable to say the least. For example, *s 11(4)* (see **14.108** *et seq*) refers to expenditure on the provision of plant or machinery (making clear that they are different things). Also 'machinery' is expressly identified as the first item in *s 23*, List C (separately from various items of plant which follow it) (see **15.109**).

15.2   'Machinery' is generally more easily identifiable than plant, but experience has shown it can often be forgotten in practice, with HMRC and taxpayers instead focusing initially on whether expenditure is on 'plant'.

15.3   Machinery is not defined in statute or case law and so takes its ordinary meaning, which is typically a device or assembly of interconnected fixed and movable parts, which transmits force to do useful work and often (but not always) has a power supply. HMRC accepts that the term 'machinery' includes machines and the working parts of machines, which usually have moving parts. It also accepts that assets like motor vehicles and lathes are machines, as are computers and similar electronic devices, and other less obvious assets such as door handles with moving parts (CA, para 21010).

15.4   For expenditure incurred on or after 30 November 1993, the scope of the term 'plant and machinery' is further limited by *ss 21* and *22* (see **15.102** *et seq*). Nevertheless, apart from integral features (see **14.5**) and a small number of other types of expenditure specifically treated as plant by statute, the eligibility of individual assets will be decided either by established practice or by decided cases.

15.5   As First-tier Tribunal Judge Radford concluded in *The Executors of Lord Howard of Henderskelfe v HMRC Comrs* [2011] UKFTT 493 (TC):

> 'machinery is easily recognised and has an intrinsic character and quality that identifies it. However, "plant" has no such innate quality: it is merely an asset that is put to a particular use in a particular context and acquires its colour from the context in which it is used.'

CASE LAW

General

15.6   Full details of relevant cases (in date order) are given in **Appendix 4**. The following sections concentrate on the most important cases and illustrate the general principles that have developed over more than a century.

15.7   The earliest case of relevance was in 1860. Like many cases dealing with plant, *Blake v Shaw* (1860) 8 WR 410 was heard long before the introduction of capital allowances as they are now known. Over the years, the definition of plant has been important for the purposes of such areas as employer's liability and compensation for war damage. The conclusions, however, remain of relevance for the purposes of capital allowances. In *Blake v Shaw*, plant was said to commonly include: 'all the matters permanently used for the purposes of the trade as distinguished from the fluctuating stock'. This distinction was taken further in the case of *Yarmouth v France* (1887) 19 QBD 647 where the question arose as to whether a horse was plant. In a judgment which has come to be regarded as the most fundamental definition of plant, Lindley LJ said:

> 'There is no definition of plant in the Act but, in its ordinary sense, it includes whatever apparatus is used by a businessman for carrying on his business – not his stock-in-trade which he buys or makes for sale; but all his goods and chattels, fixed or moveable, dead or alive, which he keeps for permanent employment in his business.'

15.8   Important points to extract from this are that plant is *apparatus*:

(*a*)   used for carrying on a business; and

(*b*)   kept for permanent employment (ie an element of durability is required).

15.9   This definition has generally withstood the test of time but, of course, after more than a century, it has been qualified by subsequent decisions. Various major themes and sub-themes have emerged over the years. These include:

(i)   durability of the asset (see **15.11**);

(ii)   the 'functional' test (see **15.14**);

(iii)   the 'premises' test (see **15.21**);

(iv)   the 'business use' test (see **15.50**); and

(v)   the 'completeness' test (see **15.66**).

15.10   To a greater or lesser extent these overlap and in fact stem from a relatively small number of cases. They are sufficiently important, however, to examine the development of each.

Durability of the asset

15.11   This is essentially the most fundamental of tax questions, ie the distinction between revenue and capital expenditure (see **1.9** *et seq*). An important case specifically on this subject is *Hinton (Inspector of Taxes) v Maden and Ireland Ltd* (1959) 38 TC 391, where the subject of the claim was expenditure on knives and lasts used by a footwear manufacturer. By a three to two majority it was held in the House of Lords that the lasts and knives were plant; this was in spite of the fact that they were numerous, small and cheap. The vital factor was the durability of the assets which in this case was between one and five years. Lord Jenkins said:

> 'The reference to "permanent employment" (in *Yarmouth v France*) in the business demands some degree of durability ... The intention no doubt is to keep and use [the knives] for so long as they are serviceable and I cannot regard the circumstance that they wear out in [a] relatively short period as investing them with so transitory a character as to take them out of the category of plant to which they would otherwise belong.'

15.12   The alternative would presumably have been to allow the cost of the knives and lasts on a renewal basis like the cost of replacement tyres for a lorry or crockery for a hotel. This argument was put forward by Lord Denning but was not adopted by the majority. (See **1.51** *et seq* regarding the renewals basis.)

15.13   HMRC will generally regard an asset as sufficiently durable if it has a normal working life of more than two years (CA, para 21100). However, each case must be considered on its merits. With effect from April 2008 special rules apply with respect to repairs to integral features (see **1.37**).

The functional test

15.14   No distinction is generally drawn between machinery and plant. The man in the street, if asked to describe machinery, would generally accredit it with moving parts (see **15.3**). To describe plant is more complicated. In order to qualify as plant for capital allowance purposes, there is no strict requirement that the asset should have moving parts in the nature of machinery. Indeed, it may appear to be quite passive in nature. Examples of such 'passive plant' may include, for example, radiators, moveable partition or the bric-a-brac popular in hotels and public houses.

15.15   The term 'passive plant' is, however, something of a misnomer; the plant can invariably be shown to perform a function as business apparatus of some kind. In the examples given, the spray booth will enable the spraying of vehicles to be carried out without either polluting the surrounding areas or endangering employees or members of the public. The bric-a-brac helps to create a relaxing and pleasant atmosphere necessary for the attraction of customers. However, the more obvious the function, the more readily an asset will be accepted as plant. The term 'passive plant' was discussed in *Cooke (Inspector of Taxes) v Beach Station Caravans Ltd* [1974] STC 402.

15.16   A starting point for considering the importance of the 'functional test' is the 1969 case of *IRC v Barclay, Curle & Co Ltd* (1969) 45 TC 221. The taxpayers constructed a dry dock. This involved not only items such as pumps and valves that were clearly machinery, but also the excavation of 200,000 tons of earth and the lining of the hole with concrete. It was held that the whole of the expenditure was incurred on the provision of plant. The dry dock was more than just a hole in the ground – it performed the active function of lifting and lowering ships and could be drained to facilitate repairs. Lord Reid said:

> 'The only reason that a structure should also be plant … is that it fulfils the function of plant in the trader's operations … I do not say that every structure which fulfils the function of plant must be regarded as plant, but I think that one would have to find some good reason for excluding such a structure.'

15.17   He also pointed out that the cost of providing plant could perfectly well exceed the cost of the plant itself, and that an asset was not excluded from being plant merely by virtue of size.

15.18   Another dockside case was heard in 1974 – *Schofield (Inspector of Taxes) v R&H Hall Ltd* (1974) 49 TC 538. In this case the taxpayer erected a silo for the purpose of holding grain in a position where it could conveniently be discharged for delivery to purchasers; tankers could pass below the silo and the grain could be loaded by the operation of gravity. Before the construction of the silo, the grain had been bagged by hand, carried ashore and loaded by hand onto customers' lorries. The silo effectively carried out these functions plus the cooling, turning over and fumigation of the grain. Simple storage alone was but 'a trifling part' of the silo's function. Of course, with the progress of technology, designs may change. A modern silo might, for example, be more horizontal than vertical, with delivery effected by means other than gravity. This should not alter the fact that the whole installation qualifies as an item of plant. Dry docks and silos are relatively rare, but there are in practice a number of other types of structure which have been regarded as composite items of plant, although none of these has reached the courts.

15.19   By way of illustration, an interesting case was heard by the Australian courts (*Wangaratta Woollen Mills Ltd v Federal Comr of Taxation* (1969) 119 CLR 1 (Aust HC)), which has been quoted, with approval, in the House of Lords. A dye house, although a building, was held to be almost entirely an item in the nature of plant; certain unusual features meant that the dye house itself played an essential part in the dyeing process. These features included a complex ventilation system and drains to remove volatile liquids. It is, however, debatable whether the decision would have been the same, had *ss 21–23* then been in force (see **15.102** *et seq*).

15.20   It is important to stress, of course, that allowances for plant are by no means restricted to businesses where an industrial process is carried on. Another useful case to consider is therefore *Leeds Permanent Building Society v Procter (Inspector of Taxes)* [1982] STC 821. Here, decorative screens used for window displays were held to be plant, on the grounds that by providing security, privacy and publicity they played a part in the commercial activities of the society.

The premises test

15.21   The 'premises' test is often wrongly confused with the concept of 'setting', such that the two are often regarded as indistinguishable. The idea of 'setting' is in fact part of the 'functional test' (see **15.14**).

15.22   This test was developed further in the case of *Wimpy International Ltd v Warland (Inspector of Taxes)* [1989] STC 273, where the word 'premises' was substituted for 'setting'. Fox LJ commented:

'There is a well established distinction in general terms, between the premises in which the business is carried on and the plant with which the business is carried on. The premises are not plant.'

15.23   He also approved the comment of Lord Lowry in *IRC v Scottish and Newcastle Breweries Ltd* (1982) 55 TC 252 case that 'something which becomes part of the premises, instead of merely embellishing them, is not plant'.

15.24   The question of whether or not something becomes part of the premises is largely a matter of fact. Hoffmann J in the *Wimpy* case (High Court) proposed four considerations:

(i)   whether the item appears visually to retain a separate identity;

(ii)   the degree of permanence with which it has been attached to the building;

(iii) whether the building or structure would be incomplete without it;

(iv)   the extent to which it was intended to be permanent.

15.25   It is worth setting out his statement in full (our italics):

'The question seems to me to be whether it would be *more appropriate to describe the item as having become part of the premises than as having retained a separate identity.* This is a question of fact and degree, to which some of the relevant considerations will be:

1.   whether the item appears visually to retain a separate identity,

2.   the degree of permanence with which it has been attached,

3.   the incompleteness of the structure without it, and

4.   the extent to which it was intended to be permanent or whether it was likely to be replaced within a relatively short period.

[Counsel for the company] submitted that if this was the proper test, *those considerations constituted a series of separate hurdles which had to be overcome ... I do not agree.*'

15.26   It is clear from this that Hoffmann J did *not* intend to set out four tests, all of which needed to be satisfied in order for an asset to be treated as plant (as has commonly been stated). Rather, his intention was to reaffirm the single test laid down by previous court decisions, namely 'whether it would be *more appropriate* to describe the item as having become part of the premises than as having retained a separate identity'. The four specific points mentioned are merely *some* of the *considerations* which may help to decide.

15.27   Considerations 1 and 3 are self-explanatory. Regarding his second consideration, it is not the case that an asset will fail to qualify for wear and tear allowances because it is in some way 'attached', either to a building or to the land. *Yarmouth v France* refers to plant being 'goods and chattels, *fixed* or moveable' and no-one since has sought to suggest that plant cannot be fixed. Indeed, Chapter 14 of *CAA 2001* deals expressly with allowances on fixtures.

15.28   Equally, attachment to the land, rather than to a building or structure, does not preclude the claiming of plant allowances. Buckley LJ in *Benson v*

The Yard Arm Club (Court of Appeal) observed that in determining whether an item was plant, 'it is no matter that it consists of some structure attached to the soil'.

15.29 Hoffmann J's fourth point is in essence concerned with the expected life of the assets claimed as plant (the issue considered by *Hinton (Inspector of Taxes) v Maden and Ireland Ltd* (1959) 38 TC 391 (see **15.11**)). It has never been considered that an asset fails to be regarded as plant simply because it has a relatively lengthy period of use. Case law has always been clear on the point. *Yarmouth v France* spoke of plant including:

'whatever apparatus is used by a businessman for carrying on his business … which he keeps for *permanent* employment in his business.'

15.30 By way of illustration, the dock in *Barclay, Curle* was held to be plant despite the fact that it was agreed it might last for 80 to 100 years.

15.31 Hoffmann J expressly mentioned 'whether it (the alleged plant) was likely to be replaced within a relatively short period'. His intention was presumably simply to suggest that a relatively short period of use would indicate that an asset has prima facie *not* become part of the premises; in the context of existing case law (referred to with approval by Hoffmann J), it cannot have been intended that assets not 'replaced within a relatively short period' were therefore premises. It is, of course, unclear what is meant by 'a *relatively* short period'. It cannot mean short by comparison with the life of the larger asset to which the plant is attached, in this case the land, which will endure infinitely longer than the structures.

15.32 The *Wimpy* case was subject to appeal, and consequently the comments of Hoffmann J were subject to review by a higher court.

15.33 The Court of Appeal unanimously endorsed the reasoning of Hoffmann J, in particular his assertion that the key question was be whether it would be more appropriate to describe the item as having become part of the premises than as having retained a separate identity. Lord Justices Lloyd and Glidewell both acknowledged (as Hoffmann J had done) that the phrase 'something which becomes part of the premises' was borrowed from Lord Lowry in *Scottish & Newcastle*. Lloyd LJ observed (and in so doing affirmed the continuing applicability of *Yarmouth v France*):

'Of course, in one sense, everything on the premises, especially if it is fixed, may be said to form part of the premises. But obviously that is not what Lord Lowry had in mind. It would have been inconsistent with Lord Lindley's test in *Yarmouth v France* that plant includes all goods and chattels, fixed or movable.'

15.34 Glidewell LJ, after commenting that the decision in *Scottish & Newcastle* was binding on the *Wimpy* case, went on to say (our italics):

'when Lord Lowry referred to "something which becomes part of the premises", he cannot have meant simply something which is affixed to the premises. He must have been expressing in other words the point made by Oliver L.J. in *Cole Brothers v Phillips* about something which "performs *simply and solely* the function of housing the business".'

15.35 This echoes the comments of Brightman J in *Dixon v Fitch's Garage* [1975]:

'there is a clear thread running through the recent cases … that a structure is not plant if its *only* purpose is to provide shelter and if it plays *no* part in what may be termed "the commercial process"'.

15.36 To sum up, an asset only fails the premises test (ie it fails to qualify as plant) if its *only* function is to act as premises.

15.37 Nevertheless, in *JD Wetherspoon plc v Comrs for HM Revenue and Customs* SpC 00657 (2008); UKFTT 374 (TC) [2009]; UKUT 42 (TCC) [2012], the Commissioners sought to apply to decorative timber wall panelling the four 'considerations' set out in *Wimpy*, but seemingly drew conclusions incompatible with the facts. Despite noting that three of the four 'considerations' pointed to the panelling not being premises (and the meaning of the fourth being unclear), they concluded that 'some of the considerations … point one way and some the other'. It appeared that they then sought to add an additional test of their own devising, namely whether the panels were 'an unexceptional component which would not be an unusual feature of premises of [this] type'.

15.38 In other words, if it is not unusual to find a particular asset in a particular type of property, then (in the Commissioners' view) that asset must be part of the premises, and consequently not plant. This apparent test appeared to be inherently flawed; in practical terms, when applied to many common assets, it gave results which were unequivocally wrong. A lift, for example, would not be plant or machinery using this test, but is expressly allowed by *s 33A* (and even before the enactment of *s 33A* was never challenged). Or one would normally expect to find a fitted bar in a pub but no-one would seriously suggest this to mean it could not be plant.

15.39 Wetherspoon appealed and contended that this represented a new and wholly illegitimate legal test. However, surprisingly the Upper Tribunal concluded that the Commissioners were not seeking to lay down some principle of general application (ie a new test) but simply explaining their reasoning. This was that it was that the panelling was ordinary (ie 'unexceptional') panelling which simply turned an un-panelled room into a panelled room. By way of contrast, they referred to *Wimpy*, where the Special Commissioners allowed as plant (which was not appealed) some purportedly 'exceptional' wall panelling finished in bronze or silver mirrors, or infills of melamine, hessian or a textured sandstone effect.

15.40 The decision in the *Wetherspoon* case is at odds with principles laid down by higher courts, which appear to have been overlooked by the Tribunal. As discussed above, Lord Justice Oliver commented in the leading Court of Appeal judgment in *Cole Bros* (subsequently endorsed by the House of Lords and referred to with approval by the House of Lords in *Scottish & Newcastle* and the Court of Appeal in *Wimpy*) that the 'premises' is something that 'simply and solely' houses the business. Therefore, given that the parties had already agreed that the panelling created ambience, following binding precedent the Tribunal should have had no option but to conclude that it was plant.

15.41 *Wimpy* (Court of Appeal) therefore remains the prime source for guidance on the question of plant and premises, and any attempt by an inspector to rely on *Wetherspoon* (Upper Tribunal) should be treated with caution.

15.42 The dividing line between plant and setting is at times a very indistinct one. In *Jarrold (Inspector of Taxes) v John Good & Sons Ltd* (1962) 40 TC 681, movable partitions were the subject of dispute. Pennycuick J said: 'the setting in which a business is carried on, and the apparatus used for carrying on a business, are not always necessarily mutually exclusive' and Ormerod LJ said 'the dividing line between what is "plant" and what is not is a narrow one, and the facts of this particular case come near to that dividing line'. The finding was determined by the requirements of the particular trade. In fact, the same asset may be plant in one business and not in another. This is considered further in **15.50** *et seq.*

15.43 One thing which is certain is that an asset is not precluded from being plant simply because of its great bulk or high cost. Lord Reid in *Barclay, Curle* (see **15.16**) said: 'one would have to find some good reason for the exclusion of [such] a structure [from the definition of plant]. And I do not think that mere size is sufficient'. Similarly, Blackburne J in *Bradley (Inspector of Taxes) v London Electricity plc* [1996] STC 1054 stated that simply because something was a substantial fixed structure, with a roof and inner and outer walls and floors, and has in it what is accepted to be plant used for the purposes of the business, does not mean that it must be regarded as premises rather than plant. Entire buildings and structures have been regarded as plant (see **Chapter 16**). The question of whether structures can be plant has also been considered in a number of cases. The dry dock in *Barclay, Curle* was followed into the plant category by another 'hole in the ground' – the swimming pool in *Cooke (Inspector of Taxes) v Beach Station Caravans Ltd* [1974] STC 402. In this case, swimming pools together with their attendant machinery for purifying and heating the water were considered as a single unit. It was found that the pools performed the active function of attracting visitors to the caravan park.

15.44   Not all buildings or structures can be categorised as plant. In the following cases such treatment was rejected, although sometimes the taxpayer appears to have been unfortunate. In *Dixon (Inspector of Taxes) v Fitch's Garage Ltd* [1975] STC 480 the item not allowed as plant was a canopy over a filling station. It was held to be part of the setting, providing light and shelter for customers. A similar shelter used for advertising purposes was held to be plant in the Irish case *O'Culachain v McMullan Bros* [1991] 1 IR 363 and it may be that if *Fitch's Garage* came to court today, the decision could be reversed. Certainly the decision has been doubted twice in the House of Lords, by Lord Hailsham in *Cole Bros Ltd v Phillips (Inspector of Taxes)* [1982] STC 307 and by Lord Cameron in *Scottish and Newcastle Breweries*. Another case, *Thomas v Reynolds* [1987] STC 135, concerning an inflatable tennis court cover, might have had a better chance of success for the taxpayer if more pertinent facts had been established before the Commissioners.

15.45   On other occasions the court's refusal of plant status is difficult to argue with. In the case of *St John's School v Ward (Inspector of Taxes)* (1974) 49 TC 524 the supposed items of 'plant' were a gymnasium and a laboratory. Both were prefabricated buildings, bolted together on site and with mains electricity connected. A key factor in deciding that the buildings were part of the setting rather than plant was that neither had any function to perform other than sheltering the persons who used them.

15.46   The reasoning was similar in *Brown (Inspector of Taxes) v Burnley Football and Athletic Co Ltd* [1980] STC 424, where it was held that a football stand was the place 'from where' spectators watched the match rather than them watching the match 'by means of the stand. However, it is of interest that in the Irish case of *O'Grady v Roscommon Race Committee* [1992] IR 425, an improved racecourse stand was held to be part of the means to attract patrons and was therefore plant like the swimming pool in *Cooke v Beach Station Caravans Ltd.*

15.47   In *Benson (Inspector of Taxes) v Yard Arm Club Ltd* (1979) 53 TC 67, an old ferry boat and barge converted for use as a floating restaurant were held not to be plant. The vessels were the structure in which the business was carried on, rather than apparatus used to carry on the business. If the vessels had not been moored, but had been used for, say, dinner cruises on the river, the decision might have been different.

15.48   In *Bradley (Inspector of Taxes) v London Electricity plc* [1996] STC 1054, Blackburne J thought the key question was to ask what plant-like function the structure as an entity performed in the taxpayer's trading activity:

'The fact that features of the structure were carefully designed to accommodate the equipment within does not convert what is otherwise plainly the premises in which the activity is conducted into the plant or apparatus with which that activity is conducted.'

15.49 In *Shove (Inspector of Taxes) v Lingfield Park 1991 Ltd* [2004] STC 805, an artificial 'all-weather' racetrack was held to fail the 'premises test', and consequently plant allowances were denied. Similarly, in *Family Golf Centres Ltd v Thorne (Inspector of Taxes)* [1998] STC (SCD) 106, it was held that putting greens on a golf course were premises, rather than plant, because they were part of the place where the company's trade was carried on. They were not a mere adjunct, for they were part of the essence of the taxpayer company's trade.

The business use test

15.50 Reference has been made to *Jarrold v John Good & Sons Ltd (1962) 40 TC 681* (see **15.42**), and to the fact that identical assets may be regarded as plant in one business and not in another. In fact, this was already an old idea having been suggested by, amongst others, Uthwatt J in *J Lyons & Co Ltd v A-G* [1944] 1 All ER 477 when he speculated that certain lighting might qualify as plant if it were connected with the particular needs of the trade carried on.

15.51 In the *Jarrold* case, the items in question were movable partitions. It was successfully argued that these partitions performed a particular function in the taxpayer's business, namely that they enabled different departments to be segregated from each other, regardless of whether individual departments expanded or contracted.

15.52 The importance of the nature of the particular trade came to greatest prominence with the concept of ambience. This idea was put forward in *IRC v Scottish and Newcastle Breweries Ltd* [1982] STC 296, where the taxpayer, carrying on the trade of a hotelier, incurred significant expenditure on lighting and decor in its licensed premises. These items were successfully claimed as plant. The Special Commissioners found that the company's trade was not just the provision of food and accommodation, but also the creation of atmosphere or ambience. This view was ultimately upheld in the House of Lords.

15.53 In consequence of this decision, items of bric-a-brac in hotels, restaurants and public houses will qualify as plant. The same items would not be plant if purchased by anyone carrying on a trade of which the provision of hospitality (and therefore ambience) was not a fundamental part (indeed *s 23* prevents this – see **15.110**).

15.54 The comments of Lord Wilberforce in the *Scottish and Newcastle Breweries* case serve as a fitting conclusion:

'In the end each case must be resolved, in my opinion, by considering carefully the nature of the particular trade being carried on, and the relation of the expenditure to the promotion of the trade.'

15.55 In HMRC's view the business use test is 'basically the same as the functional test' (CA 21140).

The concept of 'setting'

15.56 The concept of 'setting' is often wrongly confused with the 'premises' test, such that the two are often regarded as indistinguishable. The idea of 'setting' is in fact more properly regarded as part of the 'functional' or 'business use' tests.

15.57 Plant was first formally contrasted with 'setting' in a 1944 case concerned, not with taxes, but with the *War Damage Act 1943: Lyons v A-G.* Uthwatt J asked:

'Are the lamps and fitments properly to be regarded as part of the setting in which the business is carried on, or as part of the apparatus used for carrying on a business?'

15.58 In this particular case, it was found that the majority of the lighting in a Lyons cafe was not plant (further consideration of the eligibility of lighting for allowances is given at **16.32** *et seq*). Consequently, inspectors considering the concept of 'setting' often rely on the *Lyons* case. There are, however, particular reasons why this case should be treated with caution.

15.59 The case dealt with whether compensation was due under the *War Damage Act 1943* for lamps damaged by enemy action. The Act provided for compensation in respect of damage to land, *extended to include both buildings and plant.*

15.60 The comments of Uthwatt J (in the *Lyons* case) on 'setting' have often been confused with the premises test. The comments of Hoffmann J in *Wimpy International Ltd v Warland [1989]* make it clear that Uthwatt J thought he had identified a category of asset which was *neither the premises nor used for carrying on the business.* It is the second part of this definition that is important. Uthwatt J asked:

'Are the lamps and fitments properly to be regarded as part of the setting in which the business is carried on *or* as part of the apparatus used for carrying on the business?'

15.61   The key question he was asking was whether the assets were 'used for carrying on the business' – it followed from his narrow (and subsequently revised) interpretation of this phrase, taken of course from *Yarmouth v France*, that the light fittings in the case were not regarded as plant. In Uthwatt J's view, the light fittings in the restaurant were not *directly* concerned with the provision of food and drink, and therefore must be part of something which Uthwatt J christened the 'setting'. In his own words, Uthwatt J thought that, if something formed part of the 'setting', it could not be used for carrying on the business, and was therefore not plant under *Yarmouth v France.*

15.62   This narrow view of what is meant by 'carrying on the business' has now been discounted, notably in *Scottish & Newcastle.*

15.63   Furthermore, in *Wimpy* (Court of Appeal), Fox LJ observed:

'The case *[J Lyons & Co Ltd]* is *only* of any note for present purposes because of the distinction drawn by Uthwatt J between "plant" and "setting".'

15.64   Following *Scottish & Newcastle*, it is clear that Uthwatt J misunderstood the distinction between plant and setting, believing there could be no overlap. More explicitly, in *Jarrold v John Good*, Pennycuick J comments directly on the *Lyons'* decision:

'I do not want to appear to doubt in any way the correctness of that decision on the facts of that case, but it seems to me that the setting in which a business is carried on, and the apparatus used for carrying on a business, are not always necessarily mutually exclusive.'

15.65   Given that this distinction drawn by Uthwatt J was the only reason the *Lyons* case was of note, and given that that distinction has later been rejected by a higher court, *Lyons* is of limited relevance.

The completeness test

15.66   Another test that is sometimes mentioned is the 'completeness' test (CA, para 21150). This involves considering whether the building would be complete for carrying on the qualifying activity that is to be carried on within it without the item of expenditure that is being considered as plant (ie if the asset would be needed to complete the building, then it is not plant). This question should probably not be elevated to the status of a separate test in its own right, because although it was considered in *Cole Bros* (see **16.26**), it is merely the third of the four premises considerations later expounded by Hoffmann J in *Wimpy* (see **15.24**).

STATUTE – ELIGIBLE EXPENDITURE

General

15.67 Various types of expenditure, some of which would otherwise not obviously qualify as plant, are expressly stated to qualify. These include:

(i)   thermal insulation (*s 28*) – see **15.69** *et seq*;

(ii)   computer software (*s 71*) – see **15.73** *et seq*;

(iii)   films, etc (*Sch 2, para 82*);

(iv)   fire safety (*s 29*) – withdrawn for expenditure incurred since 1 April 2008 (corporation tax) or 6 April 2008 (income tax) – see **15.81** *et seq*;

(v)   safety at sports grounds (*ss 30–32*) – withdrawn for expenditure incurred since 1 April 2013 (corporation tax) or 6 April 2013 (income tax) – see **15.88**;

(vi)   personal security assets (*s 33*) – see **15.91**;

(vii)   integral features (*s 33A*) – see **14.5**;

(viii) solar panels (*s 104A(1)*).

15.68 The expenditure covered by these sections has in each case been perceived as being worthy of relief for non-tax reasons. In addition, building alterations connected with the installation of machinery or plant are treated as plant by virtue of *s 25* (see **14.119** *et seq*).

Expenditure on thermal insulation

15.69 Thermal insulation will be treated as plant if it is added to an existing building occupied for the purposes of a qualifying activity (*s 28*). Prior to 1 April 2008 (corporation tax) or 6 April 2008 (income tax), this treatment was granted in respect of industrial buildings only. If the insulation was added during the course of construction of a new industrial building, it would qualify only for industrial business allowances (IBAs). See also **11.52** *et seq* for details of the landlord's energy saving allowance for installing thermal insulation into existing residential property.

15.70 The legislation also provides that on a disposal of the asset a disposal value of nil has to be brought into account, so as to ensure that relief is only given to the person installing the insulation (*s 63(5)*). Assets likely to qualify for allowances will include:

●   roof lining;

●   double glazing;

- draught exclusion;

- cavity wall insulation.

(*CA, para 22220*)

15.71   Where expenditure is incurred on assets which serve more than one purpose (eg, double glazing which retains heat and excludes noise), allowances will nonetheless be available provided that insulation against loss of heat is *one of the reasons* why it is incurred. It does not have to be the main reason (CA, para 22220).

15.72   It should be noted that the provisions cover only prevention of the loss of heat, and not the prevention of the loss of cold, for example to assist in the creation of a low ambient temperature. Where the latter is relevant, however, it may well be that the insulation qualifies as plant under general principles. *Sections 21* and *22*, for example, envisage that cold stores, cold rooms, and air cooling equipment may be eligible as plant (see **15.102** *et seq*). With effect from April 2008, *s 33A* confirms beyond doubt that air cooling equipment is indeed eligible as plant (see **14.5**).

Computer software

15.73   Expenditure on computer software may be treated as plant in accordance with *s 71* (though for expenditure on or after 1 April 2002, companies, but not individuals, must elect for the treatment to apply – see **25.22**).

15.74   A helpful definition of 'computer software' was given by a government Minister in the following response to questions on *Finance (No 2) Bill 1992, cl 55* (which later became *CAA 1990, s 67A* and *CAA 2001, s 71*) during Standing Committee: '… the legislation should apply to a wide range of products, including not only computer operating programmes, but databases, CD encoded reference books and similar innovations in future, including mailing lists, which could, under some circumstances, be bought in the form of computer software'. HMRC instructions now confirm Inspectors should treat computer programs of any type and data of any kind as computer software (ranging from operating systems like Windows to games like Solitaire), even where there is no physical asset because the software has been transferred by electronic means (eg transmitted over the Internet) (CA, para 23410).

15.75   Prior to the enactment of *s 71*, some doubt existed as to the availability of capital allowances in respect of expenditure on computer software, though many such claims were agreed. The perceived problem was that software was not generally purchased outright. Instead, it was (and still is) common for a payment to be made for the right to use software under licence. Under such an arrangement, it could not be said that the software was owned by the user of the software, as is required by *s 11(4)(b)*.

15.76   Allowances under *s 71* are extended to capital sums paid for computer software licences and software distributed by electronic means. Such software is treated as machinery or plant, and as satisfying the belonging requirement. HMRC has confirmed that allowances are only available to the grantee. Thus, if A incurs the expenditure, but requires the licence to be granted to B, no allowances will be available.

15.77   It is of course generally better to claim the cost of software as a revenue expense, thus obtaining full tax relief in the year in which it is incurred. Whether or not this is possible will depend upon the facts. When software is acquired at the same time as hardware, HMRC will seek to treat it as capital. However, this is not a firm rule. The borderline between capital and revenue is as uncertain for 'deemed' plant such as software as it is for 'true' plant.

15.78   In most cases, an election to treat software as a short-life asset under *s 83* will not confer any benefit. This is because under those rules, the benefit of the election is only felt where the asset is disposed of within the prescribed period (see **14.182** *et seq*). It is not sufficient that the software has been taken out of use. The question arises, of course, as to whether software can physically be disposed of – unlike hardware it is not a tangible asset and so the question is not easily answered. It appears the following would qualify as a disposal:

- where software is acquired under a fixed-term licensing agreement, expiry of that term;

- where dedicated software can only be used with certain items of hardware, disposal of that hardware;

- in other cases, deletion of software from hard disks and destruction of any other media.

15.79   Where, under the provisions outlined above, computer software (or the right to use such software) is treated as machinery or plant, then if a right is granted to another person to use that software, a disposal value must be brought into account. This is the case whenever a capital sum is received for the grant of such a right, regardless of whether the right granted is in respect of the whole or part only of the software.

Example

Kingston, a trader, makes up his accounts to 31 March annually. On 1 April 2007, the value of his general plant pool was £30,000. He subsequently had the following transactions:

- 30 April 2007 – purchased computer for £5,000, together with associated software for £2,000.

- 10 June 2007 – purchased for £3,000 from a young inventor the exclusive right to a specialist software package for investment analysis which he used in his trade. He also employed the young inventor.

- 30 November 2007 – granted a licence to Bowley to use the specialist package for £1,500. Bowley did not intend to use the software for trading purposes.

- 6 June 2008 – granted a similar licence to Potter for £2,000. Potter also did not intend to use the software for trading purposes.

- 10 June 2008 – granted a similar licence back to the original inventor of the software. No consideration was given.

Allowances are as follows:

Year ended 31 March 2008

		£	£
Plant pool b/fwd		30,000	
Additions:	Computer	5,000	
	Software	2,000	
	Software	3,000	
			10,000
			40,000
Disposals:	Licence 30.11.07		(1,500)
			38,500
Writing-down allowance @ 25%		(9,625)	
			28,875

Year ended 31 March 2009

		£	£
Plant pool b/fwd		28,875	
Disposals:	Licence 6.6.08		(2,000)
	Licence 10.6.08		(nil)(Note)
			26,875
Writing-down allowance @ 20%			(5,373)
			21,502

Note: It is assumed that the licence granted on 10 June will give rise to a tax charge on the inventor, who is employed by Kingston. Market value is therefore not brought into account. See **12.52** *et seq.*

15.80   HMRC is understood to accept that allowances are due where a person incurs capital expenditure on writing software programs for his own use, even if these are never stored in a tangible form (eg disk).

Fire safety

15.81   Since 1 April 2008 (corporation tax) or 6 April 2008 (income tax), there have been no special rules enabling fire safety expenditure to qualify for capital allowances. Eligibility will now depend on whether an asset is, or is not, plant under general principles. For example, a smoke detector would be plant whereas a reinforced ceiling and walls creating a fire 'haven' would generally not. For discussion on fire doors see **16.62**.

15.82   Until 1 April 2008 (corporation tax) or 6 April 2008 (income tax), when the relief was abolished, *s 29* gave relief for traders incurring expenditure in taking steps to comply with a notice issued under the *Fire Precautions Act 1971, s 5(4)* (which was repealed on 1 October 2006 and replaced by the *Regulatory Reform (Fire Safety) Order 2005*), where the notice was issued on an application for a fire certificate in respect of premises used for the purposes of the trade and where relief would not otherwise be available (*s 29*). Relief was also available, although no formal notice was issued, where a trader incurred expenditure in taking, in respect of any premises used by him for the purposes of the trade:

(*a*)   steps specified, in a letter or other document sent or given to him by or on behalf of the fire authority or an application for a fire certificate under the *Fire Precautions Act 1971* in respect of those premises, as steps that would have to be taken in order to satisfy the authority as mentioned in *s 5(4)* of that Act, being steps which might have been, but were not, specified in a notice under that subsection; or

(*b*)   steps which, in consequence of the making of an order under *s 10* of that Act prohibiting or restricting the use of the premises, had to be taken to enable the premises to be used without contravention of the order (*s 29(4)*).

15.83   Under *s 538*, relief was given to lessors who make contributions towards their tenants' or licensees' fire safety expenditure, provided the expenditure satisfies the conditions of *s 29* or Northern Ireland equivalents. In practice, relief was also allowed where the lessor incurs the expenditure himself, if similar expenditure by the tenant or licensee would have qualified for relief (ESC B16).

15.84   As with expenditure on thermal insulation, a disposal value of nil is deemed to be brought into account in the period in which the asset(s) represented by the expenditure is disposed of (*s 63(5)*), thereby ensuring that relief is only given to the person incurring the initial expenditure.

15.85   The *Fire Precautions Act 1971* did not apply in Northern Ireland. However, ESC B16 granted relief under Northern Ireland equivalents, on the same basis as in Great Britain.

15.86   There were, however, two other problem areas:

(i)   Buildings covered by the relevant parts of the *Fire Precautions Act 1971* include:

   (*a*)   factories;

   (*b*)   offices;

   (*c*)   shops;

   (*d*)   railways;

   (*e*)   boarding houses; and

   (*f*)   hotels.

   Other premises, for example hospitals and nursing homes, are not included. HMRC is believed to have denied relief for fire safety expenditure in such cases.

(ii)   As stated above, relief is strictly given only where expenditure is incurred as a result of fire authority instructions. Where a new building is being constructed, the architect will incorporate fire safety features from the first draft in accordance with the planning requirements, before there is any need for them to be specified by a fire authority. Expenditure on these safety features would not strictly qualify for relief under *s 29* but may constitute plant for other reasons.

15.87   The potential claimant should be aware that the wording of *s 29* is strictly adhered to. For example, HMRC instructions state that 'expenditure on a fire door can qualify under *s 29* but *only* if its installation is required by law' (ie, in taking steps to comply with a notice issued under the *Fire Precautions Act 1971*). Otherwise fire doors will generally *not* qualify as plant because 'doors' are included within the *s 21* definition of 'buildings', which cannot be plant (see **15.104**). Although fire doors *might* be included within the *s 23* item 10 exemption for 'other equipment for extinguishing or containing fires' (see **15.110**) they must still qualify as plant under basic case law principles (see **15.6** *et seq*) and were specifically held *not* to qualify as plant in a fast food restaurant context in the High Court in *Wimpy International Ltd v Warland (Inspector of Taxes)* (1989) 61 TC 51 where Hoffmann J said 'these were rejected [by the Special Commissioners] by the application of the business use test, although ... I think they would probably have failed the premises test as well. The finding was not seriously challenged'.

Safety at sports grounds

15.88   Plant and machinery allowances for safety at sports grounds expenditure will be withdrawn for expenditure incurred on or after 1 April 2013 (corporation tax) or 6 April 2013 (income tax) (*FA 2012, s 225* and *Sch 38, para 33*).

15.89   The rules under this heading are similar to those affecting that used to apply in respect of fire safety, as set out above. Expenditure will be treated as plant, if incurred to comply with the terms and conditions of a safety certificate issued under the *Safety of Sports Grounds Act 1975* or certified by a local authority as falling within those requirements if such a certificate had been applied for (*s 30*). Not all sports grounds are regulated by this Act. However, safety expenditure on other (non-designated) sports grounds may qualify for similar relief if it is incurred to comply with safety certificate requirements of a local authority (*ss 31* and *32*).

15.90   If the assets are disposed of, the disposal value to be brought into account is nil, so that allowances can only be given to the person originally incurring the expenditure (*s 65(4)*).

Security assets

15.91   *Section 33* gives plant allowances for expenditure by individuals or partnerships (and not companies) on the provision of a 'security asset' where relief could not otherwise be given. A 'security asset' is one which is used to meet a 'special threat' to an individual's personal physical security, arising wholly or mainly by virtue of his trade, profession or vocation (*s 33(2)*). It was held in *Brockhouse v HMRC Comrs* [2011] UKFTT 380 that 'special' means 'exceptional in quality or degree, unusual, out of the ordinary' (Shorter English Dictionary; *Lord Hanson v Mansworth* (2004) SpC 410). If the expenditure is incurred partly for security and partly for other reasons, the amount qualifying under this section will be based on an appropriate proportion of the whole (*s 33(5)*). Incidental use of a security asset for other purposes (eg staff welfare) does not preclude the allowance being given (*s 33(3)* and ICAEW Technical Release TR 759). Similarly, allowances are still available where the benefit of increased security is felt not only by the trader, but also by members of his family or household (*s 33(4)*).

15.92 A HMRC Press Release of 13 April 1989 first detailed the types of assets intended to be covered, now set out in CA, para 22270. These include:

(*a*) alarm systems;

(*b*) bullet-resistant windows in houses;

(*c*) floodlighting and similar facilities;

(*d*) reinforced doors and window; and

(*e*) perimeter walls and fences.

15.93 Certain assets are excluded from being security assets:

(i) cars;

(ii) ships;

(iii) aircraft; and

(iv) dwellings and grounds appurtenant to a dwelling (*s 33(6)*).

15.94 In considering whether an asset qualifies for relief, it is immaterial whether or not it becomes affixed to land (whether constituting a dwelling or otherwise) (*s 33(6)(b)*). It should be noted, however, that this allowance is only available to individuals carrying on a 'relevant qualifying activity', ie: a trade; an ordinary property business; a furnished holiday lettings business; an overseas property business; or a profession or vocation (*s 33(1)*). Expenditure by a company for the benefit of an employee will not qualify for an allowance.

Demolition costs

15.95 Where any machinery or plant *in use for the purposes of a qualifying activity* is demolished, then:

(*a*) if that machinery or plant is replaced by the person carrying on that qualifying activity, the net cost of demolition is treated as expenditure incurred on the provision of the new machinery or plant; and

(*b*) if the machinery or plant is not replaced by the person carrying on that qualifying activity, the net cost of demolition is treated as qualifying expenditure in the chargeable period in which the demolition takes place (*s 26*).

15.96 Exceptions to (b) above are encountered in the context of the offshore oil industry, which is beyond the scope of this book (*s 163*).

STATUTE – INELIGIBLE EXPENDITURE

Background

15.97   As a result of case law, the dividing line between plant and buildings has shifted over the years in favour of the taxpayer, as a result of the courts or the Special Commissioners/Tax Tribunal Judges being convinced of the 'correctness' of taxpayers' claims, in the sense that they fell within the definition laid down by the premises, functional and business use tests (see **15.14** *et seq*). One result of this was that certain items were eligible for the accelerated allowances available for plant, despite having a life which was just as long as the building in which they were incorporated. In respect of accounting periods ending on or after 26 November 1996, this anomaly was addressed by the introduction of a lower rate of allowance for plant which is a long-life asset (see **14.153** *et seq*). Furthermore, with effect from April 2008 the lower rate of allowances was extended to integral features (see **14.5**).

15.98   An earlier attempt to address the issue, at least in connection with plant which is incorporated into a building, reached the statute book in what are now *ss 21–23*. These consist largely of tables (reproduced below) which firstly list items in a building or structure which are not generally plant, then set out the circumstances in which such items may nonetheless qualify (ie they might be plant if they satisfy the plant tests (see **15.14** *et seq*)). These rules apply to expenditure incurred on or after 30 November 1993, or in pursuance of a contract entered into before that date. (*Finance Act 1994 (FA 1994), s 117.*)

15.99   These provisions were not intended to change the treatment of assets which had been accepted as plant by the courts (Statement by the Financial Secretary to the Treasury, *Hansard*, Standing Committee A, 10 March 1994, col 602). However, this did not extend to cases where the Special Commissioners had decided in the taxpayers' favour (prior to publication of the Special Commissioners' decisions), and HMRC had chosen not to appeal, or where the treatment of certain assets had been the subject of a long-standing agreement between taxpayer and HMRC.

15.100   However, it must be remembered that these rules were intended only to clarify and strengthen existing case law.

15.101   The second claim made for the new rules was that they would 'help clarify the boundary between buildings, structures and land on the one hand and plant on the other'. Such a 'reclarification of boundaries' was always a Herculean task, attempting as it does to clarify a term that, as we have seen, has long defied definition by many learned judges. Modern commercial buildings have a variety of hi-tech features built into their very fabric. For example, a computer centre may incorporate a so-called 'Faraday cage' to prevent corruption of data. In the light of such technological advances, the clarification of the boundary between buildings and plant would have taxed the most competent draughtsman. One may perhaps see the 1996 rules on long-life assets and the 2008 rules on integral features as recognition that *ss 21–23*, as originally enacted, were less than fully successful in this attempted clarification.

Details of ss 21–23

15.102   Buildings, structures and interests in land are all dealt with separately.

Buildings

15.103   For expenditure incurred on or after 30 November 1993, expenditure on the provision of machinery or plant does not include any expenditure on the provision of a building (*s 21(1)*). The term 'building' is not defined so takes its ordinary meaning and includes any asset in the building which is incorporated into the building or is normally so incorporated, and in particular any asset in or in connection with the building which appears in List A. (*s 21(3)*). HMRC regards 'in connection with' as merely indicating physical connection (Revenue reply to ICAEW representations on the *Finance Bill 1994*).

15.104   In addition to these general exclusions, the question of whether or not an asset is an item of plant is initially determined by List A of *s 21* (reproduced below). This is subject to List C in *s 23* (see **15.110**).

'List A
Assets Treated as Buildings

1.   Walls, floors, ceilings, doors, gates, shutters, windows and stairs.

2.   Mains services, and systems, for water, electricity and gas.

3.   Waste disposal systems.

4.   Sewerage and drainage systems.

5.   Shafts or other structures in which lifts, hoists, escalators and moving walkways are installed.

6.   Fire safety systems.'

Structures, assets and works

15.105 For expenditure incurred on or after 30 November 1993, expenditure on the provision of machinery or plant does not include any expenditure on:

(*a*)   the provision of any structure or asset in List B; or

(*b*)   any works involving the alteration of land (*s 22(1)*).

15.106 A structure means a fixed structure of any kind, other than a building (*s 22(3)*). The Revenue Press Release accompanying the draft legislation declared that 'a structure is any substantial man-made asset'. The meaning of this is not entirely clear, as no doubt some structures are less 'substantial' than many machines and items of plant (see also **2.9**).

15.107 As with buildings, the legislation gives a list of structures excluded from being plant. This is set out below. This is subject to List C in *s 23* (see **15.110**):

'List B
Excluded Structures and Other Assets

1.   A tunnel, bridge, viaduct, aqueduct, embankment or cutting.

2.   A way, hard standing (such as a pavement), road, railway, tramway, a park for vehicles or containers, or an airstrip or runway.

3.   An inland navigation, including a canal or basin or a navigable river.

4.   A dam, reservoir or barrage, including any sluices, gates, generators and other equipment associated with the dam, reservoir or barrage.

5.   A dock, harbour, wharf, pier, marina or jetty or any other structure in or at which vessels may be kept, or merchandise or passengers may be shipped or unshipped. HMRC has confirmed that a floating pontoon is plant even if it is attached to a pile or other fixed structure, whereas a 'fixed' pontoon is not plant (CA, para 21215)

6.   A dike, sea wall, weir or drainage ditch.

7.   Any structure not within items 1 to 6 other than –

  (*a*)   a structure (but not a building) within Chapter 2 of Part 3 (meaning of 'industrial building'),

  (*b*)   a structure in use for the purposes of an undertaking for the extraction, production, processing or distribution of gas, and

  (*c*)   a structure in use for the purposes of a trade which consists in the provision of telecommunication, television or radio services.'

Land

15.108 Expenditure on the provision of machinery or plant on or after 30 November 1993 does not include expenditure on the acquisition of any interest in land. Items which are attached to land such that, under general land law, they become part of it, are not covered by this provision (*s 24*).

General exemptions

15.109 The rules in *ss 21* and *23* do not affect:

(*a*)   thermal insulation (*s 28*) (see **15.69** *et seq*);

(*b*)   computer software (*s 71*) (see **15.73** *et seq*);

(*c*)   films etc (*Sch 2, para 82*);

(*d*)   fire safety expenditure (*s 29*) (see **15.81** *et seq*);

(*e*)   safety equipment at sports grounds (*ss 30–32*) (see **15.88**);

(*f*)   security assets (*s 33*) (see **15.91** *et seq*);

(*g*)   integral features (*s 33A*) (see **14.5**).

Specific exemptions

15.110 Lists A and B (see **15.104** and **15.107**) are subject to List C (*s 23*). This does not mean that assets included in List C are automatically plant, but merely that they are not precluded from being plant by *ss 21* and *22* (Lists A and B). These assets will only attract plant allowances if they meet the usual criteria, including the functional, premises and business use tests (see **15.119** and **15.14** *et seq*) (the words in square brackets and italics below are deleted by *FA 2008, s 70* with effect from 1 April 2008 (corporation tax) and 6 April 2008 (income tax)):

'List C
Expenditure Unaffected by Sections 21 and 22

1.   Machinery (including devices for providing motive power) not within any other item in this list.

2.   [*Electrical systems (including lighting systems) and cold water*] gas and sewerage systems provided mainly –

  (*a*)   to meet the particular requirements of the qualifying activity, or

  (*b*)   to serve particular plant or machinery used for the purposes of the qualifying activity.

3.   [Space or water heating systems; powered systems of ventilation, air cooling or air purification; and any floor or ceiling comprised in such systems.]

4.   Manufacturing or processing equipment; storage equipment (including cold rooms); display equipment; and counters, checkouts and similar equipment.

5.   Cookers, washing machines, dishwashers, refrigerators and similar equipment; washbasins, sinks, baths, showers, sanitary ware and similar equipment; and furniture and furnishings.

6.   [Lifts,] hoists[, escalators and moving walkways].

7.   Sound insulation provided mainly to meet the particular requirements of the qualifying activity.

8.   Computer, telecommunication and surveillance systems (including their wiring or other links).

9.   Refrigeration or cooling equipment.

10.   Fire alarm systems; sprinkler and other equipment for extinguishing or containing fires.

11.   Burglar alarm systems.

12.   Strong rooms in bank or building society premises; safes.

13.   Partition walls, where movable and intended to be moved in the course of the qualifying activity.

14.   Decorative assets provided for the enjoyment of the public in hotel, restaurant or similar trades.

15.   Advertising hoardings; signs, displays and similar assets.

16.   Swimming pools (including diving boards, slides and structures on which such boards or slides are mounted).

17.   Any glasshouse constructed so that the required environment (namely, air, heat, light, irrigation and temperature) for the growing of plants is provided automatically by means of devices forming an integral part of its structure.

18.   Cold stores.

19.   Caravans provided mainly for holiday lettings.

20.   Buildings provided for testing aircraft engines run within the buildings.

21.   Moveable buildings intended to be moved in the course of the qualifying activity.

22. The alteration of land for the purpose only of installing plant or machinery.

23. The provision of dry docks.

24. The provision of any jetty or similar structure provided mainly to carry plant or machinery.

25. The provision of pipelines or underground ducts or tunnels with a primary purpose of carrying utility conduits.

26. The provision of towers to support floodlights.

27. The provision of –

    (*a*) any reservoir incorporated into a water treatment works, or

    (*b*) any service reservoir of treated water for supply within any housing estate or other particular locality.

28. The provision of –

    (*a*) silos provided for temporary storage, or

    (*b*) storage tanks.

29. The provision of slurry pits or silage clamps.

30. The provision of fish tanks or fish ponds.

31. The provision of rails, sleepers and ballast for a railway or tramway.

32. The provision of structures and other assets for providing the setting for any ride at an amusement park or exhibition.

33. The provision of fixed zoo cages.'

(Note: Zoos are defined in the *Zoo Licensing Act 1981*.)

15.111 Items 1–16 of List C above (ie only up to and including swimming pools) do not include any asset whose principal purpose is to enclose the interior of a building or to provide an interior wall, floor or ceiling which is intended to remain permanently in place (*s 23(4)*). Such assets are therefore 'buildings' that cannot qualify as plant. In *Bowerswood House Retirement Home Ltd v Commissioners for HM Revenue and Customs* [2015] UKFTT 0094 (TC), a company was unsuccessful in claiming plant and machinery allowances for a conservatory-type covering over a swimming pool (see **Appendix 4**).

15.112 HMRC has also confirmed that the reference to 'water heating systems' includes the whole of the system, and not just heating apparatus (Revenue reply to ICAEW representations on the *Finance Bill 1994*).

15.113 *Item 17* of *List C* above refers to glasshouses. HMRC guidance (CA, para 22090) confirms that, in its view, most glasshouses are not plant or machinery because they are buildings or structures (see **16.68** *et seq*). However, Inspectors are instructed to accept that a glasshouse and its attendant machinery are inter-dependent and form a single entity which functions as plant if the following conditions are met:

1   The structure and its equipment were designed to operate as one unit to operate as a single entity.

2   It operates extensive computer controlled equipment, without which the structure cannot operate to achieve the optimum artificial growing environment for the particular crops involved.

3   The equipment was permanently installed during the construction of the greenhouse.

4   The equipment includes computer systems which control boiler and piped heating systems, temperature and humidity controls, automatic ventilation equipment and automatic thermal screens or shade screens.

15.114 Depending on the crops grown, the equipment may include: equipment for carbon dioxide enrichment of the glasshouse atmosphere (eg cucumbers or tomatoes), hydroponic culture (eg capiscums or tomatoes), mobile benching or transport tables (eg pot plants) or lighting to control day length or to supplement natural light (eg pot and cut chrysanthemums and plant propagators).

15.115 A qualifying glasshouse is likely to be used for year-round growing of high-value crops.

15.116 Polytunnels are usually metal-framed semi-circular tunnels covered in polythene that are used predominantly by the farming and horticulture industry. In a VAT case *Argents Nurseries Ltd v HMRC Comrs* [2007], polytunnels were held to be plant because they functioned as part of the production process. However, HMRC capital allowances guidance instructs inspectors that, if a polytunnel is used to provide shelter for livestock, machinery or stores, it is not plant because its primary, if not only, use is the provision of shelter and it will therefore comprise the premises (see **15.21** *et seq*) in which the qualifying activity is carried on. Furthermore, if a polytunnel is a fixed structure, it is ruled out from being plant by *s 22*. Nevertheless, HMRC does acknowledge that neither 'fixed' nor 'fixed structure' is defined by *CAA 2001* and there is a spectrum of potential definitions.

15.117 Otherwise (ie, where a polytunnel is not a 'fixed structure', depending on the precise definition that is appropriate), HMRC accepts that, for the growing of plants, it can do more than just provide shelter from the elements (eg, increase air and soil temperature and humidity, extend the growing season and protect plants from insects). But it is necessary to look at the facts, including exactly how the polytunnel is to be used. For example, where strawberries and raspberries are grown in the ground, the same ground can only be continuously used for between four and seven years, after which the polytunnels and crops must be moved. In such circumstances, HMRC will accept that the polytunnels are plant. However, if strawberry crops are grown in raised beds, the crops will not need to be moved and it is more likely that the polytunnels will be fixed structures that cannot be plant. Other crops must be looked at on their merits. For example, HMRC considers that blackberries, gooseberries and black/ redcurrants can remain in the same ground for ten years or more, so it is 'far more likely' that the polytunnel will be a fixed structure.

15.117A   Caravans occupying residential sites are not eligible as plant. The only exception to this is that HMRC will accept as plant a caravan provided by a farmer to house a farm employee (even if it occupies a fixed site and is used solely for residential purposes) – this remarkable concession does not apply in other, non-farming, circumstances.

A caravan *is* accepted by HMRC as plant if it does not occupy a fixed site and is regularly moved as part of normal trade usage (even if it is only moved between summer and winter quarters).

HMRC guidance also accepts a caravan is plant, irrespective of whether it is moved, if it is provided mainly for holiday lettings on a holiday caravan site (that is, licensed as such by the local authority, but not including holiday camps, leisure parks, hotels or conference centres). For this purpose a caravan is anything treated as a caravan by the Caravan Sites and Control of Development Act 1960 or the Caravans Act (Northern Ireland) 1963. It includes units delivered in two sections and then joined together, as well as moveable wooden lodges. It does not include non-moveable structures (even if they are otherwise identical to moveable ones).

In the 1950s an agreement was reached with the National Caravan Council, which applies to businesses that hire out caravans or provide caravan sites. Taxpayers can still ask for this to be applied (accepting both the allowances and disallowances agreed). Under the agreement the following assets are eligible for plant and machinery allowances:

● Water supplies (including mains and apparatus used to convey water to or around sites, and hot water);

● Electricity supplies (including cables, wiring, diesel generating equipment and general electrical apparatus);

● Sanitary fittings, baths and wash basins (which are nowadays routinely treated as plant - see 16.17).

No allowances are given for:

- Roads;

- Proposed sites for individual caravans;

- Buildings erected as sanitary blocks (although plant and machinery within the buildings, such as sanitary fittings, would qualify);

- Sewage and drainage pipes installed as part of public health requirements.

(CA, para 22100)

15.118   For an example of the scope *of Item 22*, see *Anchor International Ltd v IRC* [2005] STC 411 (**Appendix 4**), dealing with the base for an artificial sports pitch.

The interaction of *s 23* with existing case law, in particular the 'premises test'

15.119   HMRC's published view is that assets in *s 23* are not automatically regarded as plant, but rather must meet the usual tests set out by case law. Some inspectors of taxes have thus sought to refuse a claim for plant allowances for assets listed in *s 23*.

15.120   However, it was the clear intention of the legislators that the assets listed in *s 23* should be treated as plant and machinery (provided, of course, that they are used in a relevant business activity). HMRC replied to the Institute of Taxation representations at the time the legislation (or rather, its predecessor, *CAA 1990, Sch AA1*) was proposed, as follows:

> 'The intention behind the legislation is therefore to strengthen the current boundary (between plant and buildings or structures) and to ensure that no further erosion takes place ... *The broad aim is to provide exclusions for assets currently regarded as plant as a result of court decisions, so as to leave the present position unchanged.*

> The specific amendments which ministers have introduced ... are intended to ensure that this is so.'

15.121   A similar statement was made by the Financial Secretary to the Treasury the following day. The 'specific amendments' included the items towards the end of what is now List C in *s 23*. These were added to the *Finance Bill* as it passed through Parliament. It is clear therefore, for example, that existing practice was to treat fixed modular structures as plant, and that treatment was intended to continue.

15.122 It would be illogical to have specifically exempted some assets from the operation of the new rule (which was, after all, stated by the Revenue to be a tightening of the existing tests) if those assets were not plant anyway. Consequently, most of the items listed in *s 23* are, despite the Revenue's contentions that the case law tests must still be met, quite clearly plant.

15.123 This is not unexpected – *s 23* was stated, both by the Inland Revenue and by the Financial Secretary to the Treasury, to reflect and maintain existing case law and practice. At the time this legislation was first proposed, case law principles were well established. So, assets which were exempted by *s 23* were in fact assets which had previously qualified as plant in line with case law principles.

15.124 It should therefore be no surprise to discover that, when the case law principles are applied to any item in *s 23*, those principles direct that the item be regarded as plant. In a sense, it is superfluous to consider that *s 23* assets must nonetheless pass the case law tests, because they are in many cases the very assets that established the case law tests in the first place.

Plant in dwelling-houses

15.125 Expenditure on plant does not qualify for allowances if the plant is to be used in a dwelling-house, in connection with a qualifying activity which is either a property business or special leasing as defined by *s 19* (see **18.64**) (*s 35(2)*). A dwelling-house (see also **7.101** *et seq*) used to be defined by the HMRC Manual as a building, or part of a building, which is a person's home. This extended to a second or holiday home.

15.126 However, in relation to capital expenditure incurred on or after 22 October 2010, HMRC's preferred definition changed, such that in its view the distinctive characteristic of a dwelling-house became its ability to afford to those who use it all the facilities required for day-to-day private domestic existence [*Gravesham Borough Council v Secretary of State for the Environment* (1982) 47 P&CR 142] (Revenue & Customs Brief 45/10) (CA, para 11520).

15.127 The restriction does not apply where plant is used in a dwelling-house in connection with a qualifying activity which is *not* a property business or special leasing, including a trade. Where a trader's premises include accommodation (eg staff accommodation at a pub or hotel), there is no requirement to restrict allowances.

15.128 A block of flats is not a dwelling-house although the individual flats within the block may be. Consequently, allowances may be available for plant in communal areas, and for lifts, air-conditioning equipment, fire alarms and so on. HMRC guidance suggests that where a complex asset, such as a fire alarm, serves a block of flats as a whole, there is no requirement to disallow expenditure on those parts of the system (eg smoke detectors) which are within individual flats (CA, para 23060). In practice, HMRC will not seek to apportion expenditure where the non-qualifying part (ie, the expenditure relating to assets within the individual flats) is less than 25% of the whole.

15.129   University halls of residence, accommodation used for holiday letting, hospitals, nursing homes and prisons are not dwelling houses (CA, para 23060). However, the nature of student accommodation has evolved in recent years, so HMRC guidance was updated to reflect this. In contrast to old-style halls or colleges, many student residences are now indistinguishable from ordinary blocks of flats, other than the nature of the inhabitants.

15.130   Before 22 October 2010 it was HMRC's view (see Revenue & Customs Brief 66/08) that within the flats only the 'communal' areas (eg living rooms and kitchens) were *not* dwelling-houses. Outside the flats other areas of the building to which tenants do not have access were also not dwelling-houses. However, all other areas are dwelling-houses. In effect, each student's own private room or rooms would be regarded as a dwelling-house, so plant therein will not qualify for allowances.

15.131   From 22 October 2010, HMRC's preferred definition of a dwelling-house changed such that the distinctive characteristic of a dwelling-house became its ability to afford to those who use it all the facilities required for day-to-day private domestic existence (see **15.125**). In effect, this meant that the entire student flat (including all heating, cooking and washing facilities) fell within the demise of the dwelling. The same principle applies to other residential properties such as houses in multiple occupation (so-called HMOs; defined by the *Housing Act 2004*, broadly, as properties occupied by more than one household and more than one person).

Chapter 16

Plant: treatment of common items in buildings

PLANT IN BUILDINGS

16.1   It is true to say that historically, many of the areas of dispute regarding plant were common to the majority of buildings, whether newly built or purchased second hand. These included:

(*a*)   mains services generally (see **16.4** *et seq*);

(*b*)   hot and cold water and drainage systems (see **16.8** *et seq*);

(*c*)   sanitary installations (see **16.17** *et seq*);

(*d*)   gas installations (see **16.19** *et seq*);

(*e*)   electrical systems (see **16.22** *et seq*);

(*f*)   substations (see **16.28** *et seq*);

(*g*)   lighting (see **16.32** *et seq*);

(*h*)   lightning protection (see **16.40** *et seq*);

(*i*)   lift installations (see **16.42** *et seq*);

(*j*)   suspended ceilings (see **16.47** *et seq*);

(*k*)   partition walls (see **16.52** *et seq*);

(*l*)   doors (eg, roller shutters) (see **16.58** *et seq*); and

(*m*)   mezzanine floors (see **16.64**).

16.2   The treatment of items (*b*), (*e*), (*g*) and (*i*) has been greatly clarified with regard to expenditure incurred on or after 1 April 2008 (corporation tax) or 6 April 2008 (income tax), where these assets will in many cases be regarded as 'integral features' qualifying for the (now) 8% rate of plant allowances (see **14.5**).

16.3   What follows is a brief discussion of the historical treatment of such items. This treatment will still be relevant to taxpayers and their advisers, due to the time lag in preparing claims and submitting tax returns. As ever, the merits of an individual claim will depend on the precise facts of the case, and the application of the general principles described in **Chapter 15**.

Mains services generally

16.4   With effect from 1 April 2008 (corporation tax) or 6 April 2008 (income tax), electrical, lighting, cold water and heating *systems* are treated as 'integral features' qualifying for the (now) 8% rate of plant allowances (see **14.5**). The following analysis will still be relevant in respect of historical expenditure or retrospective claims, or where the mains services fall outside the demise of the relevant system (given that in HMRC's view the system starts from the point of entry to, or generation within, the building or structure).

16.5   When considering the question of machinery or plant in buildings, the first port of call has historically been what are now *ss 21–23*, which, with effect from 30 November 1993, sought to codify existing case law and practice (see **15.102** *et seq*). *Section 21* rules that the term 'building' includes 'mains services, and systems, of water, electricity and gas'. Such items could not, therefore, be regarded as plant, unless they were provided:

(*a*)   to meet the particular requirements of the trade; or

(*b*)   to serve particular machinery or plant used for the purposes of the trade.

16.6   The question had been raised by the accountancy bodies many years earlier, and an answer given by Sir William Pile, Chairman of the Board of Inland Revenue. This answer (released by the Institute of Chartered Accountants in England and Wales (ICAEW) as Technical Release TR 256) still provides an invaluable insight into this area, and may in some ways be seen as a commentary (albeit well in advance) on the relevant parts of *ss 21–23*.

16.7   The specific clarification sought by the CCAB (Consultative Committee of Accountancy Bodies) was with regard to the eligibility for capital allowances of expenditure on the installation of 'main services' in new hotels. This followed the case of *St John's School v Ward* (*Inspector of Taxes*) (1974) 49 TC 524. HMRC's reply is set out below:

> 'You have asked about the treatment of expenditure on the installation of the "main services" in new hotels. You said that hitherto the Revenue had regarded such expenditure as expenditure on plant and machinery which, therefore, qualified for capital allowances, but that recently, in the light of a court case about school buildings, Inspectors of Taxes had begun to challenge this view and to suggest that no relief was due as such expenditure should be regarded as part of the cost of the building.

There has, in fact, been no recent change in Revenue practice in this area. What has happened is that the recent case to which you refer – *St John's School v Ward* – has focused fresh attention on the distinction which has always had to be drawn for the purposes of capital allowances between expenditure on plant and machinery and expenditure on buildings. As a result, Inspectors of Taxes have no doubt recently been looking more critically at borderline expenditure. But there has been no change in our view of what falls on either side of the dividing line, and there is, of course, no question of any "attack" on the hotel industry. It is our job to apply the law as we understand it, and the treatment of hotels and restaurants is in this respect no different from that of any other business.

It may be helpful if I summarise our practice in this area, which is based on the views expressed by the courts over the years. Expenditure on the provision of main services to buildings such as electrical wiring, cold water piping, and gas piping is regarded as part of the cost of the building, and therefore, as not qualifying for capital allowances. We do, however, regard as eligible for capital allowances expenditure on *apparatus* to provide electric light or power, hot water, central heating, ventilation or air conditioning, and expenditure on alarm and sprinkler systems. Relief is also given on the cost of all hot water pipes, and on the cost of baths, washbasins, etc although the *St John's School* case suggests that the courts might regard such expenditure as part of the cost of the building. We do not, however, propose any change of practice in this respect. Finally, to complete the picture, and since you mentioned modernisation, I should say that expenditure on alterations to *existing* buildings which is incidental to the installation of plant or machinery qualifies for relief under a separate provision [*s 25*].'

Hot and cold water and drainage systems

16.8　For expenditure incurred on or after 1 April 2008 (corporation tax) or 6 April 2008 (income tax), cold water systems, and space or water heating systems are treated as 'integral features' qualifying for plant allowances (see **14.5**). However, whilst a cold water system is an integral feature, a sewerage or drainage system (discussed below) is not, so still needs to be considered under normal principles.

16.9　*Section 21* regards as part of a building both a mains water system and a sewerage or drainage system and, in *Bridge House (Reigate Hill) Ltd v Hinder (Inspector of Taxes)* (1971) 47 TC 182, a restaurant's below-ground extension connecting its drains to the public sewer was held not to be plant because it presented 'no special feature' (although Salmon LJ said 'I do not wish, however, to be understood as deciding that sewers carrying trade effluent from a factory or even from a large hotel could in no circumstances be called plant'). However, in *JD Wetherspoon plc v HMRC SpC 657*; UKFTT 374 (TC) [2009]; UKUT (TCC) [2012], during a pub fit out the whole drainage system had to be amended because the existing drainage system was nowhere near adequate, including adding additional below ground outlet points, and was held to qualify as plant because it was a 'trade specific sewerage system'. Cold water and sewerage systems may still be regarded as plant though if they are provided mainly to meet the particular requirements of the trade, or to serve particular machinery or plant used for the purposes of the trade. As discussed below, hot water installations are not generally considered to be a contentious item of plant.

16.10   Very often, analyses of building expenditure include one amount only in respect of plumbing, to cover both hot and cold water systems (and sometimes also waste water drainage). The claimant should go further, and attempt to break down further this amount into a hot water element and a cold water element (and waste water disposal element). The tax treatment of each can be different.

Hot water installations

16.11   With effect from 1 April 2008 (corporation tax) or 6 April 2008 (income tax), water heating systems are treated as 'integral features' qualifying for the 8% rate of plant allowances (see **14.5**).

16.12   Items included within a hot water installation were accepted as plant by HMRC in the case of *Lupton (Inspector of Taxes) v Cadogan Gardens Developments Ltd* (1971) 47 TC 1. Water heaters were also inferred to be plant in the case of *Jarrold (Inspector of Taxes) v John Good & Sons Ltd* (see **16.52** *et seq*). In addition, apparatus to provide hot water, along with all hot water pipes, was allowed as plant in Sir William Pile's letter reported in *Accountant* magazine in August 1977, and subsequently forming part of Technical Release TR 256 of the ICAEW (see **16.6**). HMRC has confirmed that the reference to a 'hot water system' includes the whole of such a system, and not just the heating apparatus.

Cold water installations

16.13   With effect from 1 April 2008 (corporation tax) or 6 April 2008 (income tax), cold water systems are treated as 'integral features' qualifying for the now 8% rate of plant allowances (see **14.5**).

16.14   In general terms, before the introduction of the 'integral features' legislation (see **14.5**) cold water installations were not usually regarded as plant. To all intents and purposes, the question of their eligibility for allowances has only once been specifically considered by the courts. A cold water installation is generally seen from the outset of a project as an asset which is part of the actual structure of the building, rather than an item of plant.

16.15   The one significant occasion of cold water systems being considered by the courts was in *Wimpy International Ltd v Warland* (*Inspector of Taxes*) (1989) 61 TC 51, referred to above at **15.22**. On that occasion, the items in dispute were cold water tanks and piping installed solely due to the requirements of Wimpy's catering trade (because their 'capacity greatly exceeds that for other commercial premises' and 'were required solely because Wimpy wanted to conduct a catering trade on the premises').

16.16   Due to this particular fact, the tanks and piping were allowed as plant. In the words of the published decision: 'Insofar as the installations they serve are plant they too are plant. But if they form part of a general water supply such as any occupier would need they are not.' The need for special cold water installations is by no means restricted to the restaurant trade. Such a system may be necessary, for example, where there is a requirement for machinery to be constantly cooled or where water is consumed in processing or manufacturing. Water tanks were also regarded as plant in *Cattermole* (*Inspector of Taxes*) *v Reigate Corpn* (1941) 24 TC 359, though capital allowances were not the matter of dispute in that case. However, in most other circumstances before the introduction of the integral features legislation, the nature of the properties and the trades carried on there did not suggest that there was any significant scope for claiming allowances in respect of general cold water installations. A claim was more likely to succeed where the installation consisted of a separate potable water supply, or where it consisted of pipes, etc dedicated to serving accepted items of plant (eg a hot pressings machine).

Sanitary installations

16.17   Items included within a sanitary installation are normally accepted as plant by HMRC. An early case dealing with this was *Lupton* (*Inspector of Taxes*) *v Cadogan Gardens Developments Ltd* (1971) 47 TC 1, where baths, lavatories and cisterns, washbasins, and showers and fittings were held to qualify.

16.18   Published HMRC guidance instructs Inspectors of Taxes to accept that baths, wash basins and toilet suites are plant (CA, para 21200).

Gas installations

16.19 These are usually treated in their entirety as items of plant or machinery. Not all buildings are supplied with gas, which normally only serves qualifying machinery and plant (such as boilers, etc). So it would seem logical that in the majority of cases any gas installations are provided either to meet the particular requirements of the trade, or to serve particular machinery or plant used for the purposes of the trade and therefore should qualify for capital allowances (see **16.4**).

16.20 In contrast to electrical systems, the eligibility of gas installations has not been specifically considered by the courts. HMRC's practice is again set out in Sir William Pile's letter incorporated within the ICAEW Technical Release TR 256 (see **16.6** *et seq*). That letter states that 'the provision of mains services to buildings such as … gas piping is regarded as part of the cost of the building'. However, the same letter then goes on to say that capital allowances are given for expenditure on 'apparatus to provide … hot water [and] central heating'.

16.21 With effect from 1 April 2008 (corporation tax) or 6 April 2008 (income tax) heating and hot water systems are treated as 'integral features' qualifying for the now 8% rate of plant allowances and, depending on the facts, it may well be the case that any gas installations are part of those systems.

Electrical systems

16.22 Prior to the introduction of the 'integral features' legislation (see **14.5**), the electrical system of a building was in the first instance precluded from being regarded as plant by *s 21*. A system could, nonetheless, have been regarded as plant if it was provided mainly for one of two purposes:

(*a*) to meet the particular requirements of the trade; or

(*b*) to serve particular machinery or plant used for the purposes of the trade (*s 23*).

16.23 In a standard electrical system, some items would qualify and some would not. However, it was sometimes possible to claim allowances on the whole of the system, provided certain conditions were met (CA, para 21180). These were:

(i) It was specifically designed and built as a whole, and was a fully integrated entity.

(ii)   It was designed and adapted to meet the particular requirements of the trade.

(iii)   The end user items of the system functioned as apparatus in the trader's business.

(iv)   It was essential for the functioning of the business.

16.24   By way of illustration, these rules were first formulated in respect of a claim for the entire electrical system of a supermarket. The electrical installation in that case was regarded as one gigantic complex system, the function of which was apparatus to enable the supermarket to sell its merchandise. It went far beyond merely providing the essential housing of the business.

16.25   For the application of these rules to lighting, see **16.32** *et seq*.

16.26   If a system did not meet these criteria, a piecemeal approach was adopted in deciding which elements were plant and which are not (CA, para 21180). *Cole Bros Ltd v Phillips (Inspector of Taxes)* [1982] STC 307 was the authority for determining which electrical assets could qualify as plant on a piecemeal basis. In that case, which considered the electrical installations in a department store, the entire electrical system was held not to be a single item of plant and the following piecemeal treatment was decided:

Asset description	*Function*	*Plant/Not plant*
Substation containing equipment belonging to electricity board	Accepted high voltage power onto site and directed it to switchgear owned by Cole Bros	Not discussed
Main switchgear owned by Cole Bros outside substation (associated to transformers – see below)	Directed high voltage power from substation to transformers	Entirely plant (with associated transformers – see below)
Transformers (× 3) owned by Cole Bros	Converted high voltage power to standard single phase and three phase voltages suitable to use in buildings	Entirely plant. There was no basis for apportioning the cost of the transformers between plant and non-plant assets

Asset description	Function	Plant/Not plant
Main switchboard owned by Cole Bros	Directed low voltage power from transformers around the whole building	Entirely plant because '… a very substantial part of the total electrical installation had … been agreed or found to be "plant" … it does seem to me to be very difficult to argue either that the wiring which is agreed or found to be plant can be segregated from its attendant control switches or that the size and nature of this switchboard was not dictated by the necessity to incorporate into it those control switches'. There was no basis for apportioning the cost of the transformers between plant and non-plant assets
Conduits, cables and cubicles containing switches, fuses and contractors in riser cupboards	Directed and carried power to each of the building's three floors and controlled the power for each floor	Plant where serving machinery or plant (see below). Otherwise not plant (but parts of the general equipment of the building forming the 'reticulation system')
Cables to equipment (including, heating ventilating and air conditioning, fire alarm, clocks, TV workshop, cash registers, lifts and escalators, burglar alarm, etc.)	Directed and carried power to equipment	Plant
Local wires from cubicles serving shop floor, in trunking	Directed power throughout shop floor, including light fittings and electrical sockets	Not plant (parts of the general equipment of the building forming the 'reticulation system')

Asset description	Function	Plant/Not plant
Emergency lighting		Plant
Standby generator		Plant
'Special' lighting (eight tube, square fluorescent lights, suspended from ceiling)		Not plant (had no special significance to the trade)
'Normal' lighting		Not plant
Window panel lighting, sockets and controls, and external sign wiring		Plant (attracted customers)
Kitchen equipment sockets and wiring		Plant

16.27   With effect from 1 April 2008 (corporation tax) or 6 April 2008 (income tax), electrical and lighting systems are treated as 'integral features' qualifying for the now 8% rate of plant allowances (see **14.5**).

Ductwork

16.27 A The installation of underground cables (eg, electricity, telecommunications or television) usually includes costs of excavation and ductwork to house the cables. Where those ducts are installed as a direct incident of installing qualifying cables, the costs of the associated excavation and ductwork are treated as part of the 'provision of' (see **14.114**) the cables – regardless of whether the excavation, ducts and cabling have been treated as separate components in the accounts and depreciated at different rates. If the cabling is not itself a long-life asset (see **14.153** *et seq*), then the long-life asset rules will not apply to the ducting (CA, para 21200).

Expenditure on ducting within a building or structure follows the tax treatment of the system that the ducting supports. For example, expenditure on ducting for a building's electrical system is treated in exactly the same way as that electrical system (ie, recorded in the special rate pool). Where ducting supports two or more systems the expenditure should be apportioned between them on a just and reasonable basis (CA, para 22230).

Electrical substations

16.28　An electrical substation would normally generally fall outside the definition of an electrical system for integral features purposes. Expenditure under this heading is likely to fall into two broad categories:

(*a*)　expenditure on transformers, and

(*b*)　expenditure on switch gear.

16.29　Both transformers and switch gear were considered in the *Cole Bros* case (see **16.26**). The Special Commissioners had found that the transformers were plant, but that the switch gear was not. When the case went to court, HMRC did not dispute the decision regarding transformers, however, there is some confusion regarding the treatment of switch gear. It is believed that the switch gear ancillary to the transformer was allowed as part of the cost of the transformer itself. It is likely that switch gear will qualify in full if the items it serves have been substantially allowed as plant.

16.30　Much depends on the precise nature of each relevant electrical system, and the way in which it operates. However, in most cases, it is unlikely that the cost of housings will qualify for allowances.

16.31　In order to substantiate any claim, the claimant will need precise details both of the substations and of the electrical systems which they serve. It may be that such information can only be provided by the relevant electrical engineers.

Lighting

16.32　With effect from 1 April 2008 (corporation tax) or 6 April 2008 (income tax), lighting systems are treated as 'integral features' qualifying for the now 8% rate of plant allowances (see **14.5**).

16.33　Prior to the introduction of the 'integral features' legislation, lighting was not generally allowed as plant. Although exceptions to this rule were reported, these were relatively rare, and normally turned on the particular circumstances of the case. For example, lighting was allowed as plant where it could be properly said to perform a function in the trade of a restaurateur. This, however, was often tied in with the question of 'ambience', necessary to attract custom. This particular argument was, therefore, unlikely to be of relevance to most claimants. Another very common example of qualifying lighting was that used for display purposes in shops. The key factor to consider was whether the lighting could be regarded as something more than part of the premises in which the trade is carried on. The leading case on this subject was for many years not a tax case at all, but rather one dealing with compensation under the *War Damage Act 1943*. This was *J Lyons & Co Ltd v A-G* [1944] 1 All ER 477, although it was acknowledged in *Wimpy International* that the *Lyons* case was dealing with 'setting' (rather than 'premises') in a very special sense (see **15.56**). This reasoning was confirmed more recently in the *Cole Bros* case (see **16.26**), where general lighting was one of the elements claimed as plant in respect of a department store at Brent Cross.

16.34   *Section 23* recognised that lighting systems may on occasion qualify as plant, where provided mainly to meet the particular requirements of the trade, or to serve particular machinery or plant used for the purposes of the trade. Building specifications would often refer to 'special light fittings' or some such term. In order to be successfully claimed, such fittings really must have performed a special function, for example:

(*a*)   providing ambience in a trade dealing with members of the public;

(*b*)   providing daylight lamps for examining fabrics, etc;

(*c*)   display lighting in shops.

16.35   Lighting was not sufficiently 'special', for example, if it was intended solely to provide an attractive feature or focal point in the reception area of an office.

16.36   The HMRC document 'ECA – 100% Enhanced Capital Allowances for Energy-Saving Investments' illustrates how the rules were to be applied in practice. This is set out below.

'Lighting systems – when entire systems are plant

A complete lighting system may be treated as plant, and so can qualify for capital allowances, if the system is provided mainly to meet the particular requirements of the trade carried on in the building in which the system is installed. This means that general lighting installed in a building is not plant unless it is required to meet the particular demands of the trade carried on in the building. This approach is sometimes referred to as the "completeness test". It is applied to an asset in a building by considering whether the building would be complete for the purpose of carrying on the particular business activity for which the building is used if that asset had not been installed.

For lighting, the distinction is between a lighting system added to a building that is otherwise complete for its intended use by the particular occupier and lighting that is needed to make the building complete. In the first case the lighting system will function as plant but in the second it will not. This will be a question of fact, to be considered in the light of the particular facts and circumstances of the case.

A lighting system can still be plant even if the building would be incomplete if the lighting system was removed, provided that the lighting system is specially adapted for the particular requirements of the business to be carried on in the building.

A lighting system in a building is a single entity of plant where the following conditions are satisfied:

- it is specifically designed and built as a whole, that is it is a fully integrated entity, and

- it is designed and adapted to meet the particular requirements of the occupier's business, and

- the particular lighting system is essential for the functioning of the business.

Examples

These examples are aimed at helping to define what lighting means for capital allowances purposes generally.

(*a*)   A new supermarket is built containing a lighting system that has been designed to help display the goods throughout the shop to their best advantage. The whole system may be plant, even though there is no other lighting in the building.

(*b*)   A trader commissions a new office for its business, and specifies anti-glare lighting throughout so that staff can use their computers effectively. The lighting system may be plant.

(*c*)   A trader purchases an office into which the business expands. The building has an existing lighting system. The lighting system is not plant. It was not installed to meet the particular requirements of the trader's business.

Parts of lighting systems

Parts of a lighting system may qualify for capital allowances even if the whole system does not. The same general criterion applies – are the parts of a system installed to meet the particular requirements of the person's business?

Examples

These examples are aimed at helping to define what lighting means for capital allowances purposes generally.

(*a*)   lighting in display cabinets, or in those parts of a building used as sales areas, if the lighting is specifically designed to encourage the sale of goods on display. This can include the public areas in businesses such as banks and building societies.

(*b*)   lighting installed specifically to supply light to particular items of plant or machinery can qualify, for example, lighting designed for use with computer equipment.

(*c*)   lighting specifically installed to provide ambience in a hotel or restaurant may qualify.

Lighting to illuminate sports pitches may qualify, but not the general lighting in changing rooms and areas available to the general public.'

16.37   The comments on lighting did not necessarily apply to emergency lighting and floodlighting. Emergency lighting was claimed as plant in the *Cole Bros* case referred to above (see **16.26**). The claim was not disputed by HMRC. It seems clear that, perhaps unusually for lighting, emergency lighting would qualify for allowances as an item of plant. In HMRC's view emergency lighting is now normally part of a lighting system qualifying as an integral feature.

Floodlighting

16.38   In general terms, there can only be two reasons for the installation of floodlighting:

(*a*)   to draw attention to a property at night, to advertise its pleasant aspect and its occupiers' trades; and

(*b*)   for security purposes.

16.39   In either case, it is likely that the lighting performs a function in the trade of the building's owners or tenants. Furthermore, *s 23* specifically provides that expenditure on the provision of towers to support floodlights may qualify for plant allowances.

Lightning protection

16.40   Systems of lightning protection may qualify as plant for capital allowances purposes. The risk of lightning striking is not so great that every building must be protected, so they are only installed where the likelihood of lightning striking is greater than normal (eg to prevent structural damage to high or isolated buildings), or where the use of the building means that the consequences would be particularly damaging for its contents and occupants (ie to protect valuable and sensitive electrical and computer equipment, or 'life critical' equipment, eg in hospitals). Therefore, lightning protection is unlikely to be prevented from qualifying as plant by the 'premises' test (see **15.21** *et seq*) or 'completeness' test (see **15.66**) because it is not installed into most buildings as a matter of course. Instead, it is usually installed by specialist electrical contractors to protect sensitive electrical and computer equipment necessary for the occupant's trade. However, the treatment does vary and some Inspectors maintain that where the building is of a type or size normally equipped with such protection, it could be said to be a part of the building or 'setting', rather than part of the cost of the 'provision' of plant used for the purposes of a trade.

16.41   Where the existence of lightning protection is not only normal but is also essential because of the trade carried on, it may be that the lightning protection qualifies as plant in accordance with the 'business use' test. Examples may include the explosives store of a fireworks manufacturer or the premises of an electronics manufacturer.

Lift installations

16.42   On or after 1 April 2008 (corporation tax) or 6 April 2008 (income tax), lifts are treated as 'integral features' qualifying for the now 8% rate of plant allowances (see **14.5**).

16.43   Historically, lift cars and their attendant machinery (including wiring) were items of plant, not disputed by HMRC, although it may sometimes be contended that they were long-life assets attracting relief at a reduced rate (see **14.153** *et seq*). They were allowed as plant in the following cases:

(a)   *Macsaga Investment Co Ltd v Lupton (Inspector of Taxes)* (1967) 44 TC 659;

(b)   *Lupton (Inspector of Taxes) v Cadogan Gardens Developments Ltd* (1971) 47 TC 1;

(c)   *Benson (Inspector of Taxes) v Yard Arm Club Ltd* (1979) 53 TC 67.

16.44   In the *Macsaga* case, Pennycuick J stated, 'I would say at the outset that it is, I think, perfectly clear that … lifts … are machinery or plant in any ordinary use of those words'. This was not questioned in the other cases referred to above, and has now been formally confirmed by HMRC (CA, para 21190).

16.45   The treatment of lift shafts will depend on when the expenditure was incurred. If this was after 30 November 1993, then lift shafts are specifically prohibited from being regarded as plant by *s 21*, which, inter alia, denies machinery and plant capital allowances to expenditure on 'Shafts or other structures in which lifts, hoists, escalators and moving walkways are installed' (List A). For expenditure on or before 30 November 1993, the treatment depends on the facts. A lift shaft was specifically allowed as plant in the case of *Schofield (Inspector of Taxes) v R& H Hall Ltd* (1974) 49 TC 538, although it has to be said that the circumstances in this case were somewhat unusual, as the whole of the structure that the lift served (a grain silo) also qualified as plant.

16.46 Where a lift is added to an existing building, for instance one added to an external wall, it is clear that the building is complete without the lift or its shaft. The shaft should qualify under *s 25* (as an alteration to an existing building incidental to the installation of machinery or plant) (see **14.119** *et seq*). Where the lift forms an integral part of the structural entity of the building from the start, it will be regarded as part of the structure, rather than as machinery or plant (CA, para 21190). In most cases the treatment of lift pits will follow the treatment of shafts.

Suspended ceilings

16.47 Suspended or false ceilings do not usually qualify as plant, and are regarded as part of a building by *s 21*. However, it is possible for them to so qualify in certain, very restricted circumstances. The leading case on this subject is *Hampton (Inspector of Taxes) v Fortes Autogrill Ltd* [1980] STC 80. In this case a company operating a number of restaurants claimed capital allowances in respect of false ceilings in areas used by the public. The basis of this claim was that:

(*a*) The ceilings served to clad or hide services such as piping and wiring.

(*b*) The ceilings acted as support for items such as loudspeakers and ventilation grilles.

16.48 The claimant further contended that the ceilings were, therefore, part and parcel of the equipment which they supported and covered. Fox J said:

'It is clear that in determining whether something is plant the test to be applied is a functional test; that is to say, does that thing perform a function in the actual carrying out of the trade?'

16.49 Fox J found no suggestion that the ceilings were strictly necessary for the functioning of any apparatus.

16.50 This view was generally endorsed in the later case of *Wimpy International Ltd v Warland (Inspector of Taxes)* [1989] STC 273. However, in this case there was one suspended ceiling which did qualify as plant. The reasons for this were connected with the idea of providing a particular atmosphere or 'ambience' for customers, which is a concept normally peculiar to the hotel and restaurant trades. This argument is unlikely to be of relevance to most potential claimants.

16.51 The other instance in which a suspended ceiling would qualify as an item of plant is where it forms an integral part of another item of plant. This is most likely to be appropriate in the case of a plenum ceiling which effectively acts as, or as part of, a return air duct forming part of an air-conditioning system. However, it must be the case that the air flows directly through the void created by the ceiling: it is not sufficient for the air to flow through pipes or ducts hidden by the ceiling. In buildings that have already been constructed, this will be a matter of fact. *Section 23* reflects this possibility, permitting plant allowances for any ceiling comprised in a system of ventilation, air cooling or purification. Such plenum ceilings are now treated as integral features (see **14.5**).

Partition walls

16.52 Walls have never been widely regarded as items of plant, and are regarded as part of a building by *s 21*, particularly where the wall's principal purpose is to enclose the interior of a building or is intended to remain permanently in place (*s 23(4)*). However, *s 23* still allows treatment as plant, in appropriate circumstances, of 'Partition walls, where moveable and intended to be moved in the course of the qualifying activity'. This reflects the earlier case of *Jarrold*. For partitions to qualify as plant they must fulfil two criteria:

(*a*)   they must be truly demountable or movable; and

(*b*)   they must be intended or likely to be moved as a commercial necessity in pursuance of trade.

Are partitions moveable?

16.53 Very often, an initial claim for allowances will include what claimants or their advisers have identified as 'demountable or moveable partitions'. It has to be said that, perhaps in a majority of cases, the claim that the partitions involved are demountable is not sustainable once challenged by HMRC. 'Demountable' may have different meanings for construction technique and for revenue law. Very often, terms such as 'demountable partitions' are attached to any internal wall that is not made of bricks and mortar. In strict terms, of course, any wall may be dismantled: it is a question of the degree of difficulty of so doing. The acid test is whether the partition or wall can be taken down and reassembled elsewhere with relatively little effort (eg without employing a builder), and without necessitating wholesale structural alterations or repairs. If this is not possible, then it is more likely that the partitions will be regarded as part of the structure or setting where the trade is carried on, rather than as items of plant used for carrying on the trade.

16.54 In the case of *John Good & Sons Ltd*, the partitions were required to be movable so as to accommodate fluctuations in the size of various internal departments. In order for the partitions to qualify as plant, it was not enough that they should be demountable or movable; it was also necessary that they actually had been moved or were intended to be moved as a *'commercial necessity'* (rather than merely a commercial convenience). As a matter of fact, the partitions owned by John Good had virtually not been moved at all.

16.55 It is understood that a small number of proprietary brands of partitions have been accepted by the Inspectors as being demountable. Where such partitions are installed, however, they still have to meet the second requirement, that they are *intended to be moved as a commercial necessity* in the course of a trade.

Are partitions intended to be moved?

16.56 This is in many ways the more difficult criterion to meet. It is often a simple matter to identify partitions that are physically demountable, for example where they are fixed merely by screws at floor and ceiling, and most modern proprietary partitions are capable of being moved in this way. The question, therefore, is whether the partitions meet the second criterion to qualify as plant, namely whether it is envisaged that the partitions will be moved as a commercial *necessity* in the course of a trade (rather than merely a commercial *convenience*).

16.57 If a claim is being submitted subsequent to the installation, and in the period since the partitions were installed, they have actually been moved, the claim should generally succeed with little difficulty. If, on the other hand, a claim is being prepared or planned alongside the construction or development of a property it will not be possible to rely on historical fact to support the claim. In these circumstances, it is important to ensure the appropriate evidence is available and it may be necessary to commission special reports solely for capital allowance purposes. In the case of demountable partitions, it may be appropriate to document formally the need for individual departments to be physically expanded or contracted, perhaps linked to budgets and forecasts based on different scenarios regarding sales or stockholding requirements. The important factor is that the partitions are intended to be moved – it is not necessary for any movement to actually take place (the partitions owned by John Good had virtually not been moved at all).

Doors – roller shutters and fire doors

Roller shutters

16.58 It is a common misconception that capital allowances for plant can be claimed on all roller shutters, especially those operated by electricity. It is often argued that, whilst a door is a prerequisite for any building, the need for roller shutters is a factor arising from the particular trade being carried on. In HMRC's view this is not a valid argument, as the real test is one of what is normally provided in a building of that type, not just in a building generally. For example, it would be senseless to construct a warehouse which did not have large doorways suitable for the loading and unloading of goods. In practical terms, roller shutters or sliding doors are the only way of filling in or securing such a doorway, and might properly be regarded as nothing more than part of the structure or premises. This is certainly the approach taken by *s 21*.

16.59   That being said though, arguably a roller shutter door is simply a machine in its 'entirety' and should qualify for plant and machinery allowances (although *s 21* treats doors and shutters as 'buildings', *s 23, List C* treats 'machinery' as unaffected by *s 21*). This is because roller shutters are normally bought from, and installed by, specialist suppliers as single assets that comprise an assembly of interconnected moving parts that transmit force to do useful work (see **15.3**). It seems rather inequitable that this kind of machine should be treated differently to most other machines by requiring the cost of the opening mechanism to be segregated and claimed (ie the pulley or motor), whereas the remainder of the machine is treated as not qualifying for capital allowances (see also **16.61**).

16.60   There are instances where a plant claim is even stronger. For example, where the requirements of the trade decree the complete exclusion of dust, insects, etc a claim would be justified where roller shutters were added in addition to existing doors to form a sort of 'air lock'.

16.61   HMRC has conceded to the ICAEW that any mechanism, electrical or mechanical, for opening doors is allowable as plant.

Fire doors

16.62   HMRC instructions state that 'expenditure on a fire door can qualify under *s 29* [which only applied until 1 April 2008 (corporation tax) or 6 April 2008 (income tax) (see **15.81** *et seq*)] but only if its installation is required by law' (CA 22230) – in other words, in very restricted circumstances when taking steps to comply with a notice issued under the *Fire Precautions Act 1971*.

16.63   Otherwise, fire doors will generally *not* qualify as plant because 'doors' are included within the *s 21* definition of 'buildings', which cannot be plant (see **15.104**). Although, in some circumstances, fire doors *might* be included within the *s 23, item 10* exemption for 'other equipment for extinguishing or containing fires' (see **15.110**), they must still qualify as plant under basic case law principles (see **15.6** *et seq*) and were specifically held *not* to qualify as plant in a fast food restaurant context in the High Court in *Wimpy International Ltd v Warland (Inspector of Taxes)* (1989) 61 TC 51 where Hoffmann J said 'these were rejected [by the Special Commissioners] by the application of the business use test, although ... I think they would probably have failed the premises test as well. The finding was not seriously challenged'.

Mezzanine floors

16.64   A common misconception is that mezzanine floors always qualify as plant. That is because a form of mezzanine was held to qualify in *Hunt (Inspector of Taxes) v Henry Quick Ltd*; *King (Inspector of Taxes) v Bridisco Ltd* [1992] STC 633 (see **Appendix 4**). However, those mezzanines comprised a free-standing horizontal steel grid on steel pillars, covered by chipboard panels (described as 'no more than a strengthened form of meccano'), which were removable but bolted and anchored to avoid them being dislodged and toppling. They were not part of the 'premises' (see **15.21** *et seq*), in effect, because of their impermanent nature. They qualified as plant because they were storage racking (ie business apparatus). This contrasts markedly with more typical 'mezzanine floors' which are generally constructed from structural steel or concrete and intended to remain permanently in place. Mezzanines such as these fall foul of the prohibitions for 'buildings' and 'structures' now provided for by *ss 21* and *22* (see **15.103–15.107**) (which were not on the statute book at the time of *Hunt v Henry Quick* and *King v Bridisco*) as well as undoubtedly comprising the 'premises'.

SPECIALISED STRUCTURES TREATED AS PLANT

General

16.65   Prior to the implementation of what are now *ss 21–23*, which have effect from 30 November 1993, the boundary between buildings or structures and plant had become increasingly blurred. As business operations became more complex it was increasingly possible to argue that what, at first sight, might have appeared to be a building or a structure, or a major part of one, was in fact functioning, actively or passively, as an item of plant.

16.66   In 1989 the 'premises test' (see **15.21** *et seq*) was clarified in the *Wimpy* case in which Hoffmann J acknowledged (at 170) that:

'even a building or a structure ... could be plant if it was more appropriate to describe it as apparatus for carrying on the business or employed in the business than as premises or place in or upon which the business was conducted.'

16.67   In the light of *ss 21* and *22*, however, it is certain that any claim that a building or structure is an item of plant will be more strongly resisted.

16.68   HMRC announced (Tax Bulletin 5 (November 1992) p 46 (superseded by CA, para 22090)) the following policy relating to claims in respect of 'single entities'. It is included here because, although it deals with glasshouses, the principles set out are of much wider application.

> 'In the past couple of years, there has been a great deal of publicity suggesting that all glasshouses are plant and thus qualify for [plant] allowances [...]. This is not the case. We consider the majority of glasshouse structures to be the premises or setting in which a grower's trade is carried on and on that basis they qualify for agricultural buildings allowance.
>
> However, we do accept that, in some cases, a glasshouse unit and its attendant machinery are interdependent, forming a single entity which will function as apparatus within a grower's business and as such will be plant.
>
> These units will be of extremely sophisticated design, including extensive computer controlled equipment, without which the structure cannot operate to achieve the optimum artificial growing environment for the particular crops involved. The equipment will have been permanently installed during construction of the glasshouse and will normally include a computer system which monitors and controls boiler and piped heating systems, temperature and humidity controls, automatic ventilation equipment and automatic thermal or shade screens.'

16.69   In *Gray (Inspector of Taxes) v Seymour's Garden Centre (Horticulture) (a firm)* [1995] STC 706, a plant claim in respect of a glasshouse failed on the grounds that '[the glasshouse concerned] falls well on the premises side of the line wherever it may be drawn'. It was clear that the glasshouse lacked the 'extremely sophisticated design' etc on which the position of qualifying glasshouses is founded. See also **15.113**.

16.70   The door for such claims was not closed completely, however, despite the requirements of *ss 21* and *22* (see **15.102** *et seq*), and the decision in *Attwood (Inspector of Taxes) v Anduff Car Wash Ltd* [1996] STC 110 that so-called 'single units' must still satisfy the premises test.

16.71   Blackburne J in *Bradley (Inspector of Taxes) v London Electricity Plc* [1996] STC 1054 stated that just because something was a substantial fixed structure, with a roof and inner and outer walls and floors, and has in it what is accepted to be plant used for the purposes of the business, does not mean that it must be regarded as premises rather than plant.

16.72   HMRC admits, in the case of cold stores, that whilst some stores will consist of a building housing an insulated 'box' (in which case only the box will qualify as plant), others may be incapable of independent existence as a building, in which case the entire store may qualify for plant allowances (CA, para 22120). Cold stores were accepted as plant in *Union Cold Store Co Ltd v Simpson/Elleker* (1939) 22 TC 547 and the New Zealand case *CIR v Waitaki International Ltd* [1990] 3 NZLR 27.

Structures protecting plant

16.73 A claim for plant allowances in respect of a housing for an item of plant is made more difficult by *ss 21* and *22* (see **15.102** *et seq*), but may still be possible, if it can be shown that the housing is an integral part of the plant installation. Despite new legislation, the underlying principles have changed little since they were set out in a Revenue Press Release of March 1953, in the context of allowances for the iron and steel manufacturing industry:

'Where an installation of machinery or plant is protected or sheltered by a structure which is an integral part of the installation in the sense –

(i)   that the structure with its supports could not be adapted to any other use, and

(ii)   that the machinery or plant could not be removed without demolishing the structure,

the structure may be treated for Income Tax purposes as plant eligible for the same rate of wear and tear as the protected or sheltered installation.'

Example

Smith constructs a new automated storage facility, controlled entirely by computers. As a result, the goods can be accepted, identified, stored, sorted by date or type, made up into delivery batches and ejected in customer batches and in order of lorry routes, all under the control of a computer. The method of construction is that the foundation slab is cast first, the frame of the storage racks follows with the roof and cladding being added last. The latter are fastened to and supported solely by the racking. In such circumstances, it is likely that the cost of any purely structural elements would be minimal, with the result that the whole, or substantially the whole, would qualify as plant.

16.74 It must be emphasised that each case will be decided on its facts, and the structural items claimed to be plant must be a genuinely integral and essential part of the plant which they house and protect, rather than being a structure first and foremost. A claim (ultimately unsuccessful) was in respect of an underground electrical substation in the *Bradley* case. Following an extensive review of relevant cases, Blackburne J thought the key question was to ask what plant-like function the structure as an entity performed in the taxpayer's trading activity:

'The fact that features of the structure were carefully designed to accommodate the equipment within does not convert what is otherwise plainly the premises in which the activity is conducted into the plant or apparatus with which that activity is conducted.'

DISABILITY DISCRIMINATION ACT EXPENDITURE

General

16.75   From 1 October 2004 the *Disability Discrimination Act 1995* requires building occupiers who provide goods, facilities and services to members of the public to take reasonable steps to remove physical barriers to access. What is reasonable will depend on the type of services being provided and the size and resources of the service provider and could include, for example, simple measures such as installing access ramps and using contrasting colours, better lighting and clearer signs, through to installing automatic opening doors and lifts. There is no specific legislation that treats *Disability Discrimination Act* expenditure as qualifying for tax relief, so it is necessary to determine whether it qualifies for capital allowances or a revenue deduction in the normal way. HMRC has published guidance on its approach to *Disability Discrimination Act* expenditure ('Disability Discrimination Act – new access requirements – tax guidance'), which is summarised below.

Plant and machinery

16.76   HMRC will accept a range of *Disability Discrimination Act* compliant additions to qualify for plant and machinery allowances, for example:

(*a*)   moveable ramps;

(*b*)   new sanitary ware (eg toilets and basins), including where installed into existing buildings, the costs of altering the premises 'incidental' to the installation of the sanitary ware, with Inspectors taking a 'broad view regarding normal installation costs' (see **14.119**);

(*c*)   permanent signs;

(*d*)   new handrails to help customers with mobility impairments;

(*e*)   special anti-glare lighting, or lighting installed in sales areas or their equivalent (where specifically required for the purposes of that trade) (now integral features);

(*f*)   some door handles (see **15.3**);

(*g*)   evacuation chairs; and

(*h*)   lifts (now integral features) and hoists, including where installed into existing buildings, the 'incidental' costs of installing the lift shaft.

16.77   Where expenditure is incurred on or after 1 April 2008 (corporation tax) or 6 April 2008 (income tax), some of these assets, such as (*e*) and (*h*), may be regarded as 'integral features' qualifying for writing down allowances at the 'special rate' of 8% (see **14.5**). It seems unlikely that when including lifts in the definition of 'features integral to a building', it was the Government's intention to halve the rate of allowances on disabled persons' lifts. Nonetheless, they do appear in the first instance to be 'caught'. However, dictionary definitions of lifts generally refer to cars running within a shaft, and it may be that many stair or wheelchair lifts, which are essentially merely moving seats or platforms covering short distances, not within a shaft, do not fall within such a definition. Consequently, such apparatus should still qualify for writing down allowances at the rate of 18%.

Revenue

16.78   Similarly, HMRC will also accept that a range of minor *Disability Discrimination Act* compliant adjustments to existing buildings will qualify for revenue relief (see **1.9** *et seq*). Examples given include:

(*a*)   changing doors on cubicles from opening inwards to outwards;

(*b*)   fixing warning transparencies on glass doors;

(*c*)   using coloured paints or fluorescent strips to make things easier to see (eg painting walls, floors or doors, step edges or passages in contrasting colours);

(*d*)   replacing handrails with special handrails;

(*e*)   repairs to floors to level out uneven surfacing caused by wear and tear over time;

(*f*)   redefining parking areas by repainting parking bays to provide wider, designed disabled parking bays, and car park resurfacing (providing there is no element of improvement);

(*g*)   replacing cracked or uneven paving slabs and cutting back protruding or overhanging objects, grass or other vegetation; and

(*h*)   replacing doors that are no longer fit for use (exceptionally).

Chapter 17

Vehicle fleet

INTRODUCTION

17.1   The treatment of company vehicles will depend on whether they are cars or other vehicles and, if they are cars, whether they were acquired before or after 6 April 2009 (for income tax) and 1 April 2009 (for corporation tax). Before that date, the key point was whether they cost in excess of £12,000. After that date, the emphasis changes, and allowances instead depend on carbon dioxide (CO_2) emission levels.

17.2   This chapter begins by discussing the system in place up to April 2009, although some matters, including definitions, are common to both old and new systems. The new rules are outlined from **17.39** onwards.

17.3   The legislation begins by defining a car as 'any mechanically propelled road vehicle'. There are, however, a number of exclusions, the first being those vehicles which are of a construction primarily suited for the conveyance of goods (*s 81*). Lorries and vans are, therefore, generally excluded from the special treatment accorded to cars. Some vehicles can be designed either for goods or for passengers, and the tax treatment will depend on the precise construction of the relevant vehicle.

17.4   HMRC has confirmed that a car that is capable of being used as a private vehicle is to be treated as a car for plant and machinery allowances purposes, no matter how the taxpayer actually uses it (*Roberts v Granada TV Rental Ltd* (1970) 46 TC 295, CA, para, 23510). In *Morris v Revenue and Customs Comrs* [2006] EWHC 1560 (Ch), [2006] SWTI 585, it was held that a motor home was a car ('any mechanically propelled road vehicle'), even though, in the unusual circumstances of the case, it was used primarily as an office.

17.5   Exclusions from the scope of the term 'motor car' are considered at **17.28** *et seq*.

17.6   Under the old system, if the relevant vehicles are not cars costing more than £12,000, they are dealt with in the same manner as most other items of plant, ie as part of the general pool (see **14.3** *et seq*).

CARS – EXPENDITURE BEFORE APRIL 2009

17.7   The treatment of a particular car depends on its original cost as separate rules govern cars costing in excess of £12,000. Cars were historically excluded from the general pool of qualifying expenditure (see **14.3** *et seq*). This changed for cars costing up to £12,000 from April 2000 (see **17.9**).

17.8   The long-life assets rules (see **14.153**) do not apply to expenditure on cars (including those which are hired out, and are generally not regarded as cars for capital allowances purposes by virtue of *ss 74(2), 82*). Expenditure on cars does not qualify for the 100% annual investment allowance (see **14.62**).

INEXPENSIVE CARS – EXPENDITURE BEFORE APRIL 2009

17.9   The term 'inexpensive cars' does not appear in the statute, but is here used to indicate those cars with a cost to the present taxpayer of £12,000 or less (£8,000 for expenditure prior to 1 April 1992). From 1 June 1980, all new expenditure on such vehicles was deemed to be incurred for the purposes of a notional trade separate from the actual trade carried on. Allowances given were, nonetheless, treated as arising in the course of the actual trade. The effect of this was that all such expenditure was put into a separate pool (often colloquially called the 'car pool') and allowances could be used in the same way as those from the general pool.

17.10   The requirement for separate pooling is abolished for chargeable periods ending on or after 1 April 2000 for corporation tax, or 6 April 2000 for income tax. The taxpayer may formally elect to delay the effect of the abolition by one year.

17.11   The closing written-down value (WDV) of the separate pool for the last chargeable period before abolition is to be added to the opening WDV of the general pool in the following chargeable period (*FA 2000, s 74*).

EXPENSIVE CARS – EXPENDITURE BEFORE APRIL 2009

17.12   Cars costing in excess of £12,000 are not included in the 'car pool'. Instead, each such car is kept in its own single asset pool (*CAA 2001, s 74*). It follows from this that, unlike disposals from the general or car pools, a balancing adjustment will arise where the individual 'expensive' car is disposed of.

17.13   *Section 74* refers to capital expenditure exceeding £12,000. Therefore, a car costing £12,000 exactly will be included in the car pool. 'Cost' is stated to be cost when new, inclusive of factory-fitted extras. In practice, a car acquired second hand for under £12,000 will not be treated as 'expensive', even if its cost when new was over that limit.

17.14   Additions made to a car after it has been brought into use, being additions not contracted for or paid for by the time of the acquisition of the car, do not form part of the cost of the car and will be added to the general pool.

17.15   Expensive cars qualify for a WDA but this is restricted to £3,000 pa (*s 75*), proportionally adjusted where the accounting period is more or less than a full year.

17.16   Because of the fact that balancing adjustments are made on the disposal of an expensive car, it may be worth paying slightly more to ensure that a new car is deemed to be 'expensive'. In general terms, it will be advantageous to do this where it is anticipated that the car will be sold after a relatively short time for a low value.

Example

X Ltd has a brought forward car pool of £20,000. In 2005 it intends to purchase a new car. Two models are considered, one costing £11,500 and the other £12,500. It is expected that each car will be sold in 2008 for one-quarter of its original cost. The capital allowances position will be as follows:

	Option 1 pool	*Option 2 pool*	*Expensive car*	*Total allowances under option 2*
Pool b/fwd	20,000	20,000		
Additions	11,500		12,500	
	31,500	20,000	12,500	
2005 WDAs	(7,875)	(5,000)	(3,000)	
	23,625	15,000	9,500	
2006 WDAs	(5,906)	(3,750)	(2,375)	6,125
	17,719	11,250	7,125	
2007 WDAs	(4,430)	(2,812)	(1,781)	4,593
	13,289	8,438	5,344	
2008 proceeds	(2,875)		(3,125)	
	10,414			
WDA/bal allowance	(2,604)	(2,109)	(2,109)	4,328
C/fwd	7,810	6,329	Nil	

17.17 Total allowances given over the four years will be £20,815 if the cheaper car is purchased, £23,046 for the more expensive one. This is because the 'balancing allowance' for the cheaper car remains in the pool and is effectively allowed over an infinite number of years. This principle is normally clouded by the numerous other movements in the pool.

17.18 However it is a fact that in these circumstances, the dearer car has turned out to be the cheaper of the two in terms of relief for capital expenditure. This may be tax planning for the sake of it, in the case of a business with only two or three cars, because the potential gain is in any case dependent upon the ratio of purchase price to sale price. In the case of a large fleet user, it is a point which might be exploited.

Further restrictions on allowances

17.19 The WDA is proportionally reduced in the following circumstances:

(*a*) where the chargeable period is less than one year (*s 75(2)*);

(*b*) where the person carrying on the trade receives a subsidy towards the qualifying expenditure (*s 532*);

(*c*) if the car is used partly for purposes other than the purposes of the actual trade (*s 77*);

(*d*) if the person carrying on the trade is paid an amount in respect of wear and tear (*s 78*);

(*e*) where a person contributes towards an expensive car, the allowances he may claim will be restricted to such proportion of £3,000 as his contribution bears to the total expenditure; and

(*f*) HMRC may also seek to restrict allowances where it appears that the purchase of an expensive car was determined partly by personal choice and only partly by the needs of the trade.

Leasing expensive cars

Leases commencing before April 2009

17.20 The £3,000 limit on the annual WDA for expensive cars is only a deferment of relief. This is in contrast to the treatment of lease rental payments on cars costing more than £12,000. In the latter case, there is a permanent disallowance calculated annually in accordance with the following formula set out in *CTA 2009, s 56*:

$$\frac{\text{Rental payments in year 3 (cost less £12,000)}}{2}$$

17.21   Where an 'expensive car' is sold in connection with a 'relevant transaction' for anti-avoidance purposes (*s 213*) (see **18.80**, **20.11**) the disposal value brought into account is the lower of market value and original cost (*s 79*).

17.22   This disallowance does not apply if the car is either an electric car or one with low CO_2 emissions (*CTA 2009 s 58*), provided the expenditure is incurred on or after 17 April 2002 on a car first registered on or after that date. The period of hire must begin on or before 31 March 2008.

Leases commencing on or after 1 or 6 April 2009

17.23   With general effect from 6 April 2009 (for income tax) and 1 April 2009 (for corporation tax), the calculation outlined above is replaced by a simple disallowance of 15% of the hire cost, where the car in question has CO_2 emissions of more than 160g per kilometre (*FA 2009, Sch 11, para 36*).

17.24   Leases that commenced before April 2009 will continue to be subject to the old rules for the duration of the lease (*para 65*).

17.25   In certain circumstances, the taxpayer may elect for the new system not to apply.

17.26   This is where a hire contract was entered into before 8 December 2008, but the hire period did not begin until after 1 or 6 April 2009 (but before 1 or 6 April 2010).

17.27   If the election is made, the old rules will continue to apply (*para 67*).

VEHICLES EXCLUDED FROM SPECIAL TREATMENT

17.28   Many vehicles continue to be dealt with within the general pool, including:

(*a*)   cars costing £12,000 or less (with effect for chargeable periods ending after 5 April 2000 or one year later if an election is made) – see **17.9**;

(*b*)   vehicles constructed in such a way that they are primarily suited for the conveyance of goods or burden of any description (*s 81(a)*);

(*c*)   vehicles of a type not commonly used as a private vehicle and unsuitable to be so used (eg driving school cars fitted with dual controls, in *Bourne v Auto School of Motoring* (1964) 42 TC 217) (*s 81(b)*);

(*d*)   'qualifying hire cars' (*s 74(2)(a)*). These are defined as vehicles provided wholly for hire to, or for the carriage of, members of the public in the ordinary course of trade, provided the following conditions are met (*s 82*):

(i) the vehicle must normally be on hire to (or used for the carriage of) the same person for less than 30 *consecutive* days, and for less than 90 days in any period of 12 months (*s 82(2)*), or

(ii) the vehicle is provided for hire to a person who will himself use it so as to comply with the above conditions (*s 82(3)*).

The restrictive provisions given above relating to the hire of vehicles do not apply where the vehicles are made available wholly or mainly for the use of persons in receipt of mobility allowance or supplement (*s 82(4)*);

(*e*) cars with low CO_2 emissions, and electric cars (see **17.39** *et seq*); and

(*f*) double cab pick-ups with a payload of one tonne or more (payload is a vehicle's maximum gross weight less its empty kerbside weight) (CA, para 23510). More detail is given in the HMRC Employment Income Manual (EIM), para 23150.

17.29 Mini-vans licensed as goods vehicles and used as such were held to be of a type not commonly used as private vehicles and unsuitable to be so used (*Roberts* case). However, the opposite conclusion was reached in respect of the mini-van of a radio dealer (*Tapper (Inspector of Taxes) v Eyre* (1967) 43 TC 720) and an electrical contractor's van which was not adapted in any way for business use (*Laing v IRC* (1967) 44 TC 681).

MOTOR CYCLES

17.30 Motor cycles are specifically included in the definition of a car for capital allowances purposes where the expenditure was incurred before 1 or 6 April 2009. Expenditure incurred on a motor cycle after these dates is not treated as being on the provision of a car. A motor cycle is defined (in the Road Traffic Act of 1988) as a mechanically propelled vehicle, other than an invalid carriage, with less than four wheels. The unladen weight must not be more than 410 kilograms (CA, para 23510).

17.31 Quadricycles (quadbikes) do not meet the definition of a 'motorcycle'. If they are road vehicles within the definition above then they will be treated as cars for capital allowances purposes (CA, para 23510).

CAR REGISTRATION PLATES

17.32 A registration plate is not plant unless it is attached to a vehicle. In particular, personalised or 'cherished' number plates are not accepted by HMRC as plant, but merely as evidence of certain intangible rights, not qualifying for allowances (CA, para 21250). Arguably, amortisation of the cost will qualify for relief under *CTA 2009, s 729* – see **Chapter 25**. If a car is acquired for a price which reflects the fact that a cherished plate is already fitted, it is, in practice, unlikely that allowances will be denied on the part of the expenditure attributable to the plate.

ELECTRIC CARS, AND CARS WITH LOW CARBON DIOXIDE EMISSIONS

17.33   Electric cars, and cars with low CO_2 emissions are exempt from the single asset pool requirement, and qualify for 100% first-year allowances (*FA 2002, s 59*). The provisions apply to taxis, but not to motorcycles.

17.34   This is provided the expenditure on such cars is incurred in the period from 17 April 2002 to 31 March 2013, the car is unused, not second-hand, and is first registered on or after 17 April 2002, and the asset is not precluded from qualifying for first-year allowances by *s 46* (see **14.20**). The availability of first year allowances for expenditure on cars with low CO_2 emissions was due to expire on 31 March 2008. This was extended by five years, to 31 March 2013, by *FA 2008, s 74*.

17.35   A qualifying car is one which has a UK approval certificate, or an EC certificate of conformity, showing that the CO_2 emissions do not exceed 110g/km. The qualifying emission level, above which a car cannot be regarded as a low CO_2 car, was reduced to 110g/km from 120g/km with effect from 1 April 2008 (*FA 2008, s 74*). However, cars under existing leasing contracts are unaffected by this reduction.

ZERO-EMISSION GOODS VEHICLES

17.36   A 100% first-year allowance has been available since April 2010 for expenditure on zero-emission goods vehicles (*s 45DA*). A goods vehicle is one which is designed primarily for the conveyance of goods, and 'zero-emission' means that the vehicle cannot in any circumstances emit CO_2 while being driven.

17.37   This allowance was due to be withdrawn on 31 March 2015 for income tax purposes and 5 April 2015 for corporation tax purposes. However, *FA 2013, s 45* postpones the withdrawal until 31 March 2018 for corporation tax purposes and 5 April 2018 for income tax purposes.

17.38 Furthermore, *FA 2013, s 45* provides that the allowance is not available at all if state aid is received towards the expenditure, where the expenditure was incurred after 31 March 2015 (corporation tax) or 5 April 2015 (income tax). Previously, the receipt of state aid meant that 100% allowances were not available only to the extent that state aid was received.

Example

ABC Limited incurred expenditure of £100,000 on a zero-emission goods vehicle and receives state aid amounting to £40,000. Until April 2015, it could still claim the 100% allowance on the balance of £60,000. With effect from April 2015, ABC could claim no 100% allowance (but could instead claim ordinary writing-down allowances).

In effect a claimant must choose either the timing benefit of the 100% allowance or the absolute benefit of state aid. In these circumstances, it seems unlikely that a taxpayer would choose to claim the allowance.

NEW SYSTEM – EXPENDITURE ON OR AFTER 1 OR 6 APRIL 2009

17.39 With general effect from 6 April 2009 (for income tax) and 1 April 2009 (for corporation tax), capital allowances for new expenditure cars will be based on CO_2 emissions (*FA 2009, Sch 11, para 26*).

17.40 Electrically propelled cars, and those with very low CO_2 emissions (defined as equal to or less than 110g per kilometre) continue to qualify for a 100% first year allowance (*CAA 2001, s 45D*). *Finance Act 2013, s 68* reduces the threshold to 95g/km and extends this treatment for a further two years beyond the expiry date of 31 March 2013. It also aligns the treatment of cars with other assets provided for leasing by excluding expenditure on cars provided for leasing from qualifying for FYAs.

Following the changes made by this measure, cars will qualify for allowances as follows:

- expenditure on electric cars or cars with very low CO_2 emissions (up to 95g/km driven from 1 April 2013 – previously 110g/km) qualify for 100 per cent FYAs;

- expenditure on 'main rate cars' (those with CO_2 emissions over the 95g/km threshold for FYA but no more than 130g/km - previously 160g/km) will be allocated to the main rate pool and qualify for 18 per cent writing down allowances;

- expenditure on cars with CO_2 emissions exceeding 130 g/km (previously 160g/km) will be allocated to the special rate pool and qualify for eight per cent writing down allowances.

17.41 For expenditure incurred in the five years beginning on 1 April (corporates) or 6 April (non-corporates) 2010, 100% first-year allowances are extended to goods vehicles, which cannot in any circumstances emit CO_2 by being driven (so-called 'zero-emission' goods vehicles).

17.42 Cars with CO_2 emissions of between 110g and 160g per kilometre will continue to qualify at the 'main rate' of writing down allowance, currently 18% per annum. This rate will also apply to all cars first registered before 1 March 2001 (*FA 2009, Sch 11, para 8*). These thresholds were changed from April 2013 to between 95g/km and 130g/km (*FA 2013, s 68*).

17.43 Expenditure on other cars, that is, those with CO_2 emissions in excess of 160g/km (130g/km from April 2013), will be allocated to the special rate pool (alongside, for example, long-life assets and integral features), qualifying at a rate of 8% per annum (*FA 2009, Sch 11, para 7*).

'Old' expenditure – cars already owned at 1 or 6 April 2009

17.44 Expenditure incurred before April 2009 was subject to the old rules for a further five years, that is, until April 2014 (*FA 2009, Sch 11, para 29*).

17.45 Any balance of expenditure not yet written off at that date was transferred to the main pool at the start of the first chargeable period to commence on or after 1 or 6 April 2014 (*FA 2009, Sch 11, para 31*).

Consequential amendments

17.46 Amendments are made to relevant sections of the Capital Allowances Act to ensure the continuing application of certain rules, including:

- *CAA 2001, s 46*, which prevents cars qualifying for the first year allowances (*FA 2009, Sch 11, para 3*);

- *CAA 2001, s 81*, which prevents cars qualifying for the annual investment allowance (*FA 2009, Sch 11, para 2*);

- *CAA 2001, s 84*, which prevents cars from being treated as short-life assets (*FA 2009, Sch 11, para 6*).

Anti-avoidance

17.47   *FA 2009, Sch 11, para 9* inserts new *CAA 2001, s 104F*, which prevents the artificial creation of balancing allowances in groups where one company carries on the business of providing cars for other companies in the group. This applies only to 'special rate cars'.

Chapter 18

Leasing and hire-purchase

MACHINERY AND PLANT ON HIRE-PURCHASE

General

18.1   In the absence of specific legislation, a person acquiring plant under a hire-purchase (HP) agreement would not immediately be able to fulfil the 'ownership' requirement of *s 11(4)(b)* (see **14.141** *et seq*), because title will not generally pass until all instalments have been paid. However, special rules apply where a trader incurs capital expenditure on plant *under a contract* providing that he *shall or may* become the owner of that plant *on the performance of that contract*. The scope of these special rules goes beyond HP alone, but it is in connection with HP that they are most commonly met. Where expenditure could be subject both to the fixtures rules in *ss 172–204* and the 'hire-purchase' provisions of (*s 67*), it is the former which apply, such that the HP provisions are irrelevant for fixtures (*s 69*) (see **11.15** *et seq*).

18.2   HMRC's view is that expenditure is *incurred under a contract* if and only if the contract is legally binding, and the contract commits the taxpayer to incur that expenditure (CA, para 23310). In such cases, the legislation deems two effects:

(*a*)   the 'belonging' requirement is treated as satisfied at any time when the trader is *entitled to the benefit of the contract (s 67(2))*; and

(*b*)   all capital expenditure to be incurred under the contract after the plant has been brought into use is treated as having been incurred at that time (ie, when the plant is brought into use) (*s 67(3)*).

18.3   The provisions of (b) do not apply where the machinery or plant is to be let under a finance lease, ie one which transfers substantially all the risks and rewards of asset ownership to the lessee and where generally accepted accounting principles treat the lessor as providing finance (*s 229(3)(a)*). This means that, in such circumstances, expenditure on an asset will only qualify for allowances when it is incurred, and not when (as would otherwise be the case) the asset is brought into use.

18.4   It must be noted that *s 67* applies to a contract only if it provides that the intended purchaser 'shall or may become the owner ... on the performance of the contract'. If the contract provides for ownership to pass before all the payments have been made (as in some ship construction contracts) *s 67* does not apply because in those circumstances the ownership does not pass 'on the performance of the contract'.

18.5   The second effect (*s 67(3)*) deals only with expenditure incurred after the plant has been brought into use. Any expenditure incurred in advance of that time is dealt with under the normal rules for determining the date it is incurred (see **1.62** *et seq*). This was confirmed by the Revenue in May 1996 (ICAEW Technical Release 580). Payments made under a hire purchase agreement should be split between revenue payments to hire the asset (which are tax-deductible in the lessee's hands) and capital payments to purchase the asset (which are not tax-deductible but may qualify for capital allowances) (BIM, para 45350).

18.6   Where a person to whom any plant is treated as belonging by virtue of *s 67(2)* ceases to be entitled to the benefit of the contract (without in fact becoming the owner) the following rules apply:

(i)   the plant is treated as ceasing to belong to him at the time when that entitlement ceases;

(ii)   if the plant has already been brought into use, the disposal value cannot exceed the total capital expenditure which he would have incurred if he had wholly performed the contract; and

(iii)   subject to that limitation, the disposal value consists of so much of the capital expenditure as he has not in fact incurred, and any compensation, damages or insurance moneys (*ss 67(4)* and *68*).

Example

Cartons Ltd buys a carton printing machine on a hire-purchase contract. The total price, inclusive of finance charges of £9,600, is £91,200 and is payable in 24 instalments of £3,800 on the first day of each month beginning 1 June 2012. The machine was delivered on 1 June 2012 but was not brought into use until 1 October 2012. The company's accounting date is 31 August. The finance charges of £9,600 will be allowable over the period of the agreement.

The expenditure qualifying for capital allowances will be £91,200 – £9,600 = £81,600 ie £3,400 per month. The qualifying expenditure will be as follows:

		£
Year ended 31 August 2012		
Instalments due June, July and August 2012 – (*s 5(5)* applies)	£3,400 × 3 =	10,200
Year ended 31 August 2013		
Instalment due September 2012 – (*s 5(5)* applies)		3,400
Instalments due October 2012 to May 2014 – (*s 67(3)* applies)	£3,400 × 20 =	68,000
		81,600

LEASING MACHINERY OR PLANT

Introduction

18.7   The treatment of leased plant and machinery may depend on whether the lease was finalised before or after 1 April 2006. *Finance Act 2006* introduced a new regime which generally has effect for leases which are:

(*a*)   either finalised on or after 1 April 2006 and commence on or after that date; or

(*b*)   finalised and commencing before 1 April 2006, but with the plant or machinery first being brought into use after that date.

18.8   Transitional 'grandfathering' rules apply where there was an agreement to lease in place before 21 July 2005 and the following conditions were met:

(*a*)   the plant was under construction before 1 April 2006;

(*b*)   the lease was finalised before 1 April 2007;

(*c*)   the lease is to begin before 1 April 2007.

18.9   The most significant feature of the new regime is that, provided certain conditions are met, capital allowances will be available to the lessee, rather than (as was previously the case) the lessor. However, there are far-reaching exceptions to the new regime, notably that it will not apply to most fixtures.

18.10   The new rules are considered in detail at **18.29** *et seq*.

18.11   With effect from 9 December 2009, one should consider the anti-avoidance legislation in *s 64A* and *ss 228MA* to *228MC* (see **18.81**).

Pre-April 2006 expenditure and exceptions to the FA 2006 rules

18.12 It is a general requirement for claiming capital allowances on plant that the plant must be owned by the person incurring the expenditure (see **14.137**) (*s 11(4)(b)*). Where plant is merely leased, this requirement will not be met by the lessee. This applies whether the agreement takes the form of an operating lease or a finance lease. In each case, the lessee will obtain tax relief other than by using capital allowances, by means of rental payments, finance charges or depreciation calculated in accordance with SSAP 21.

18.13 The entitlement to allowances therefore remains with the lessor. This no longer applies for many leases finalised on or after 1 April 2006 (though there are important exceptions) – see **18.29**. When negotiating leasing agreements, it is important that the intending lessee and lessor are both aware of the allowances available to each or either of them, so that they may understand the economics of the transaction. Plant allowances are available under *s 15* for a number of qualifying activities – these include trades, ordinary property businesses, etc which could be relevant to leasing, and also a category called 'special leasing' (see **18.64** *et seq*).

18.14 The pre-*FA 2006* rules continue to apply to short leases (see **18.46**), and leases of background machinery or plant and plant leased with land (see **18.50–18.51**). In such cases, expenditure may qualify for the annual investment allowance (see **14.62** *et seq*).

Leasing as a trade or as part of another 'qualifying activity' and overseas leasing

18.15 Expenditure on plant and machinery does not fail to attract capital allowances simply because the plant is leased out, rather than used for some other type of trade. However, there are a number of restrictions. Assets used for leasing do not generally qualify for first-year allowances although an exception is where the asset is energy-efficient or environmentally beneficial, and a claim is made under *s 45A, 45D, 45E* or *45H* (see **14.31–14.53** and **17.39**) (*s 46(2)* and *(5)*).

18.16 Prior to April 2006, writing-down allowances were given at a reduced rate of 10% (*s 109*) where, at any time in the 'designated period' (broadly, the ten years following first use by the lessor) (*s 106*), the asset was leased to a person who:

(*a*) was not resident in the United Kingdom; and

(*b*) did not use the asset for the purposes of earning profits subject to UK tax (*s 105*).

18.17   For leases finalised on or after 1 April 2006, the reduced rate of allowances was withdrawn (*FA 2006, Sch 9, para 13*). From that date, assets used for overseas leasing qualify for allowances at the 'usual' rate.

18.18   Allowances on leased assets can be denied altogether if the lease to a non-resident falls within the following list (*s 110*):

'**List**
Leases in Relation to which Allowances are Prohibited

1. The lease is expressed to be for a period of more than 13 years.

2. The lease, or a separate agreement, provides for –

   (*a*)   extending or renewing the lease, or

   (*b*)   the grant of a new lease,

   making it possible for the plant or machinery to be leased for a period of more than 13 years.

3. There is a period of more than one year between the dates on which any two consecutive payments become due under the lease.

4. Any payments are due under the lease or a collateral agreement other than periodical payments.

5. If payments due under the lease or a collateral agreement are expressed as monthly amounts due over a period, any payment due for that period is not the same as any of the others.

   But, for this purpose, ignore variations made under the terms of the lease which are attributable to changes in –

   (*a*)   the rate of corporation tax or income tax,

   (*b*)   the rate of capital allowances,

   (*c*)   any rate of interest where the changes are linked to changes in the rate of interest applicable to inter-bank loans, or

   (*d*)   the premiums charged for insurance of any description by a person who is not connected with the lessor or the lessee.

6. The lessor or a person connected with the lessor will, or may in certain circumstances, become entitled at any time to receive from the lessee or any other person a payment, other than a payment of insurance money, which is –

   (*a*)   of an amount determined before the expiry of the lease, and

   (*b*)   referable to a value of the plant or machinery at or after the expiry of the lease.

For this purpose, it does not matter whether the payment relates to a disposal of the plant or machinery.'

18.19 There are exemptions for 'protected leasing' (*s 110(2)*) – broadly, short-term leasing or certain leasing of ships, aircraft and transport containers (*s 105(5)*).

18.20 Where the lessee is resident in a European Community country that gives the lessee tax depreciation that is broadly equivalent to capital allowances HMRC will apply *s 109* to restrict the rate of WDAs to 10%, but will not apply *s 110*. Where that country does not give the lessee a broadly equivalent relief, HMRC will accept that the lessor is entitled to the conventional 25% rate of WDAs (HMRC Brief 40/07 issued on 24 May 2007).

Finance lessors – restriction of allowances in first year

18.21 For most claimants, allowances will be given in full in the year the expenditure is incurred, even if the expenditure was incurred on the final day of the year. However, it was historically common practice for finance lessors to set up a group of perhaps four or even 12 companies with staggered year ends so that new assets could be purchased by the company closest to its year end. In this way, the group could minimise the delay between incurring the expenditure and obtaining the allowance.

18.22 With effect for accounting periods ending on or after 2 July 1997, where expenditure is incurred on assets to be used for leasing under a finance lease, ie one which transfers substantially all the risks and rewards of asset ownership to the lessee and where GAAP treats the lessor as providing finance, the allowances in the first year will effectively be time-apportioned. Thus if relevant expenditure is incurred mid-way through a 12-month accounting period, allowances in the first year will be at the rate of half of 20% (*s 220*). This restriction does not apply where the expenditure was incurred before 2 July 1997, or is incurred within 12 months of that date in pursuance of an earlier contract (*F(No 2)A 1997, s 44(5)*).

Lessor's expenditure – fixtures

18.23 Where machinery or plant which becomes a fixture is owned neither by the owner of the building nor by a tenant, but rather is leased to the tenant by a third party (ie an equipment lessor) a problem arises. This is that allowances are not available to the property owner or the tenant (because they have not incurred capital expenditure), nor are they available to the equipment lessor (because he has no interest in the building, and hence under general land law, the fixtures do not belong to him). Where the lessee is using the fixtures for the purposes of a qualifying activity, the problem may be alleviated by an election under *s 177* whereby the fixture may be treated as belonging to the equipment lessor. Such an election must be made jointly by the lessor and lessee, in writing, within two years of the end of the chargeable period in which the expenditure is incurred. The owner of the building, if different, is not a party to the election.

18.24   See pro forma election, **Appendix 5**.

18.25   The election is not possible where the equipment lessor and the lessee are connected as set out *in ss 575–575A* (see **20.25** *et seq*) (*s 177(1)(b)*), nor where the plant is leased for use in a dwelling-house (*s 178(c)*). In connection with this latter point, HMRC accepts that plant is not leased for use in a dwelling-house if it is installed in a block of flats, and serves the whole of the block (eg a central heating system) (CA, para 23060). The HMRC Manual also formerly said that to the extent that such plant serves individual flats, it will not qualify for allowances, unless such use is less than 25% of the total use (CA, para 2708). This rule is relaxed for expenditure on boilers, heat exchangers, radiators or heating controls installed in residential property where such plant is leased under the Affordable Warmth Programme (*ss 177(1)(a)(iii)* and *180*).To qualify under the affordable warmth programme, expenditure must be incurred on or after 28 July 2000 and before 1 January 2008 (*s 180, Sch 3, para 33*).

18.26   Allowances are available only if the lessee is carrying on a qualifying activity (see **14.108**). By definition, this must be within the charge to tax (*s 15(1)*). If the lessee is yet to commence a qualifying activity, then the plant is only deemed to belong to the lessor once the activity has commenced (*s 177(3)*). The HMRC Manual formerly said that if the building has mixed use (trading and non-trading premises), the expenditure on plant common to the whole building must be apportioned (CA, para 2726).

18.27   Following the *Decaux* case (see **11.19** *et seq*), where affixation to the land is merely incidental, allowances are available on leased fixtures irrespective of whether the lessee is carrying on a trade. For this to apply, the following conditions must be met (*ss 177(1)(a)(ii)* and *179*):

(*a*)   the plant is fixed to land (and not to a building);

(*b*)   the equipment lessee has an interest in that land at the time he takes possession of the plant;

(*c*)   the plant may be severed from the land (and will belong to the lessor) at the end of the lease;

(*d*)   the plant is of a type which may be reused following such severance;

(*e*)   the lease is accounted for as an operating lease.

18.28   These events may take place in any practical order.

Post-March 2006 expenditure – long funding leases

Introduction

18.29   *FA 2006, Sch 9* puts forward a new regime for dealing with leased plant and machinery, together with provisions aimed at curtailing the avoidance of tax by artificial transactions involving the sale of leasing companies and similar measures.

18.30   The most significant feature of the new regime is that, provided certain conditions are met, capital allowances will be available to the lessee, rather than the lessor. This is the case where expenditure is incurred on an asset let under a long funding lease (see **18.43–18.49**).

18.31   The rationale for the change was a perceived anomaly in the previous tax rules, namely that loan finance and leasing finance were treated differently even though they had the same commercial effect – that one business used an asset though another business had funded its purchase. It was perceived that this difference in treatment, and in particular the availability of capital allowances, meant that in some cases, commercial decisions may have been unduly affected by the tax relief available.

18.32   Provided certain conditions are met, *FA 2006* moves the entitlement to capital allowances from the lessor to the lessee, for leases that are essentially financing transactions. The broad effect is to tax lease finance in the same way as loan finance, eliminating the potentially distorting impact of the previous tax treatment. There is no change in treatment where the previous difference in treatment was minimal.

18.33   In such cases, expenditure may qualify for the annual investment allowance (see **14.62** *et seq*).

Entitlement and quantification of expenditure

18.34   Expenditure by a lessor does not qualify for capital allowances where it is incurred on an asset to be leased under a long funding lease (*s 34A*). Instead, it is deemed that a person leasing plant or machinery under a long funding lease (ie the lessee) is treated as owning that plant or machinery, and having incurred capital expenditure at the start of that lease (*s 70A*).

18.35 Where the lease is a long funding *operating* lease, the deemed capital expenditure under *s 70A is* the market value of the plant at the commencement of the lease or (if later) the date the asset is brought into use (*s 70B*). However, note the anti-avoidance provisions of *s 70DA(5A)* which have effect from 25 February 2015 (*FA 2015, s 46, Sch 10*) – see **18.53** *et seq.*

18.36 Where the lease is a long funding *finance* lease, the deemed capital expenditure under *s 70A* is the present value of the minimum lease payment, plus any unrelievable pre-commencement rentals. If it appears that one of the purposes of the transaction is to obtain capital allowances on an amount greater than the market value of the plant, the qualifying amount is limited to that market value (*s 70C*). With effect from 9 March 2011 *s 70C* is amended to counter avoidance involving arrangements that guarantee the value of the leased asset at the end of the lease but which also enable the amount guaranteed to be taken into account a second time when paid (*ss 70C(4A)–(4C)*).

18.37 Where, under a long funding lease, additional capital expenditure is incurred by the lessor and reflected in the lease payments, the lessee is permitted to be treated as incurring such expenditure (*s 70D*). With effect from 9 March 2011 *s 70D* is amended to counter avoidance involving arrangements that guarantee the value of the leased asset at the end of the lease but which also enable the amount guaranteed to be taken into account a second time when paid (*s 70D(1A)–(1B)*).

18.38 When an asset ceases to be used for long funding leasing and is transferred into qualifying use (use in a trade, etc) allowances will henceforth be available, on an amount equal to the termination amount under *s 70YG* (*s 13A*). Deemed expenditure of this kind does not qualify for first-year allowances (*s 46(2)*) (see **14.20**), nor is it eligible for short-life asset treatment (*s 84(1)(aa)*) (see **14.186**).

Disposal events

18.39 When a long funding lease comes to an end, a disposal value must be brought into account. This is part of the mechanism to ensure that a lessee obtains allowances for an amount equal to his lease rentals, neither more nor less.

18.40 Where the lease is a long funding *operating* lease, the disposal value is in effect equal to the deemed capital expenditure less refunds of rentals and reductions under *CTA 2010, s 379; ITTOIA 2005, s 148I*.

18.41 Where the lease is a long funding *finance* lease, the disposal value is equal to the amounts receivable on termination, plus the present value of the minimum lease payment (at the time of disposal), less any amounts payable to the lessor (*s 70E*). With effect from 9 March 2011, *s 70E* is amended to counter avoidance involving arrangements that guarantee the value of the leased asset at the end of the lease but which also enable the amount guaranteed to be taken into account a second time when paid.

18.42 *Finance Act 2012, s 46* made further changes to *s 70E* for disposal events for long funding leases occurring on or after 21 March 2012. This measure countered arrangements where lessees under long funding leases sought to avoid including amounts received connected to the lease, which are not otherwise brought into account for tax purposes. The definition of a 'rebate' in *s 70E(2A)* is now extended to include any other lease-related payment.

Definitions

Long funding lease

18.43   A long funding lease is:

- not a short lease (*s 70I*);

- not an excluded lease of *background plant or machinery* (*s 70R*);

- not excluded because the plant is leased with land and is of a low percentage value (*s 70U*).

18.44   Treatment of the relevant assets as long funding lease assets is required in a tax return. Once a lessee has treated a lease as a long funding lease, that treatment must be followed in future. It is not possible to change the treatment using an error or mistake claim (*s 70H*).

18.45   A lessee does not have to come within the new regime if he does not want to, but can instead claim a deduction for lease rentals in the usual way (*s 70G*).

Short lease

18.46   The treatment of 'short leases' is untouched by the *FA 2006* rules. In the first instance, it is defined as a lease of five years or less. A lease with a term of between five and seven years may also be a 'short lease', provided certain conditions are met. These conditions are:

- the lease must be accounted for under GAAP as a finance lease;

- the implied residual value of the plant is not more than 5% of the market value at the commencement;

- rentals do not fluctuate unduly (*s 70I*).

Funding lease

18.47 A 'funding lease' is a lease of *plant and machinery* which passes one or more of three tests. These are set out in *ss 70N–70P*, but are broadly:

- the lease must be treated as a finance lease under GAAP;

- the present value of the minimum lease payments must equal at least 80% of the fair value of the plant;

- the term of the lease must be for more than 65% of the useful economic life of the asset.

18.48 Excluded are leases to which *s 67* applies, including hire purchase contracts (*s 70J*).

18.49 An asset cannot be treated as being under a long funding lease (with allowances thereby available to the lessee) if the lessor is entitled to claim – there can be no double claim (*s 70Q*).

Background plant or machinery

18.50 A lease of 'background plant or machinery' cannot be treated as a long funding lease. This relates to plant which is leased with a building to which it is fixed, which is of a description that might reasonably be expected to be installed in a building, and whose sole or main purpose is to add to the functionality of the building. More detail is provided in *SI 2007/303* and HMRC guidance is reproduced below. There is scope for detail to be added by Treasury Order (which may be retrospective) (*s 70R*).

'BLM 21330 – Defining long funding leases: funding leases that are not long funding leases: short leases: excluded leases: examples of background plant or machinery

The first list, in article 2 of SI2007/303, provides examples of the kinds of plant or machinery that should be treated as being background plant or machinery for a building. These are:

a.   heating and air conditioning installations,

b.   ceilings which are part of an air conditioning system,

c.   hot water installations,

d.   electrical installations that provide power to a building, such as high and low voltage switchgear, all sub-mains distribution systems and standby generators,

e.   mechanisms, including automatic control systems, for opening and closing doors, windows and vents,

f.   escalators and passenger lifts,

g.   window cleaning installations,

h.   fittings such as fitted cupboards, blinds, curtains and associated mechanical equipment,

i.   demountable partitions,

j.   protective installations such as lightning protection, sprinkler and other equipment for containing or fighting fires, fire alarm systems and fire escapes, and

k.   building management systems.

Note that the list is not exhaustive – it just provides examples – and that it refers to 'kinds' of plant or machinery. The definitions should therefore not be interpreted too narrowly but equally if the plant or machinery in question is to be background plant or machinery it should of a similar kind to one of those listed at items (a) to (k) above or otherwise meet the criteria in the primary legislation.

If it is argued that plant or machinery meets the definition in the primary legislation, but is not obviously one of the kinds listed, please contact CTIS (CT&BIT) for advice before agreeing that plant or machinery is background plant or machinery. The principle reason for this request is to ensure consistency and, where appropriate, to enable this guidance to be updated to include examples of background plant or machinery that are not explicitly included in the list above.'

'BLM 21335 – Defining long funding leases: funding leases that are not long funding leases: short leases: excluded leases: plant or machinery treated as background plant or machinery

The second list, in article 3 of SI2007/303, is an exhaustive list of plant or machinery that is not, or may not be, background plant or machinery on the basis of the definition in CAA01/S70R, but which is treated as if it were background plant or machinery. Plant or machinery which is to be treated as background plant or machinery is

a.   lighting installations including all fixed light fittings and emergency lighting systems,

b.   telephone, audio-visual and data installations incidental to the occupation of the building,

c.   computer networking facilities incidental to the occupation of the building,

d.   sanitary appliances and other bathroom fittings including hand driers, counters, partitions, mirrors, shower and locker facilities,

e.   kitchen and catering facilities for producing and storing food and drink for the occupants of the building,

f.   fixed seating,

g.   signs,

h.   public address systems, and

i.   intruder alarm systems and other security equipment including surveillance equipment.

Note that not all assets on this list are necessarily plant or machinery in the first place. For example, some types of lighting are plant or machinery, others are not. But where they are plant or machinery this list serves to treat them as background plant or machinery.'

'BLM 21340 – Defining long funding leases: funding leases that are not long funding leases: short leases: excluded leases: plant or machinery that is not to be treated as background plant or machinery

The third list, in article 4 of SI2007/303, describes types of plant or machinery that are deemed not to be background plant or machinery even if they would otherwise be treated as background plant or machinery. These are plant or machinery which is used for any of the purposes of

1.   storing, moving or displaying goods to be sold in the course of a trade, whether wholesale or retail,

2.   manufacturing goods or materials,

3.   subjecting goods or materials to a process,

4.   storing goods or materials–

   1   which are to be used in the manufacture of other goods or materials,

   2   which are to be subjected, in the course of a trade, to a process,

   3   which, having been manufactured or produced or subjected in the course of a trade to a process, have not yet been delivered to any purchaser, or

   4   on their arrival in the United Kingdom from a place outside the United Kingdom.

These definitions are based on concepts used for the purposes of Industrial Buildings Allowances. The relevant guidance at [paragraph] CA 30000 onwards should be followed.'

Plant leased with land

18.51 Where plant (other than background plant – see **18.50**) is leased with land, it is excluded from the effect of the new rules, provided the value of the plant does not exceed:

- 10% of the value of the background plant and machinery; and

- 5% of the value of the land and buildings (*s 70U*).

Fixtures

18.52 The normal fixtures rules are disapplied where plant is subject to the long funding lease rules (but is not 'background plant' which is automatically excluded – see **18.50**).

Anti-avoidance

18.53 Where plant is leased into, and then out of, the UK in order to obtain capital allowances, no allowances are due. The provision does not apply to normal commercial arrangements, for example where an aircraft leasing company enters into a long funding lease as part of its arrangements for the acquisition of an aircraft from the manufacturer (*s 70V*).

18.54 Further anti-avoidance measures were introduced with effect from 25 February 2015, potentially affecting transactions where a person transfers plant to another person but the plant is still available, after the transfer, to be used by the transferor or a person connected with him under the terms of a leaseback under a long funding lease.

18.55 In such circumstances, HMRC perceived there was scope for abuse of the system, which potentially permitted allowances following a sale and leaseback where the seller had not incurred qualifying capital or revenue expenditure.

18.56 Before 25 February 2015, where an asset was sold or transferred, and leased back under a long funding lease, the new owner's qualifying expenditure was limited to the seller's disposal value or (if the seller was not required to bring in a disposal value, generally because its original expenditure was non-qualifying) the lowest of:

- the market value of the asset;

- capital expenditure incurred by the seller; or

- capital expenditure incurred by a person connected with the seller (*s 218*).

18.57   Therefore, if the seller had incurred its expenditure on revenue account (or possibly as non-business expenditure of any kind), the buyer would have been able to make a claim based on market value. From 25 February 2015, for relevant long funding leases, if the seller is not required to bring in a disposal value, and did not incur its expenditure on either capital or revenue account, then the buyer's claim is nil (*s 70DA(5A)*; *FA 2015, s 46, Sch 10*).

Transfers of leased assets

18.58   Where an asset has previously qualified for allowances, but begins to be used for long funding leasing, a disposal value is required to be brought in, thereby taking the asset outside the lessor's capital allowances regime at that point (*s 61*).

18.59   Where a leased asset is transferred from one *lessor* to another, the legislation applies to allow the taxation of the old and new lessors to proceed independently whilst preserving the classification of the lease as a long funding lease or otherwise (*s 70W*).

18.60   Where a leased asset is transferred from one *lessee* to another, this section applies to allow the taxation of the old and new lessees to proceed independently whilst preserving the classification of the lease as a long funding lease or otherwise (*s 70X*).

Sale and leaseback

18.61   Where an asset leased under an existing long funding lease is subject to a sale (by the lessor) and leaseback, the new head lease is treated as a long funding lease, so the new head lessor cannot claim allowances (*s 70Y*).

Variation of lease terms

18.62   When a lease is extended, or where the accounting treatment changes, the old lease is deemed to come to an end, and a new one deemed to begin. Where a non-long funding lease is extended, this can mean that it becomes a long funding lease from that point (*ss 70YA, 70YB* and *70YC*).

Lessor's election

18.63   There is provision for a lessor to elect that all new leases entered into by it shall be treated as long funding leases (if they would not otherwise be so). This does not apply to leases of cars, or of assets which cost more than £10 million (*FA 2006, Sch 8, para 16*, and *SI 2007/304*).

SPECIAL LEASING

Lessor's expenditure

18.64   One of the qualifying activities (*s 15*) for plant allowances is 'special leasing', which is defined as hiring out plant or machinery other than in the course of any other qualifying activity (*s 19(1)*). Each such hiring out is treated as a separate qualifying activity (*s 19(4)*).

18.65   An example of 'special leasing' is the letting of 'investment assets' by a life assurance business (*s 545*).

18.66   Because each non-trade leasing is deemed to be a separate trade beginning on the commencement of the lease, capital allowances in the first year may need to be time-apportioned, because the qualifying activity will not have been carried on for a full year (*s 56(4)* – see **14.108** *et seq*).

18.67   The term 'lease' includes an agreement for a lease where the term to be covered by the lease has begun, and any tenancy, but does not include a mortgage, and 'lessee' and 'lessor' are construed accordingly (*s 70(6)*).

18.68   An asset used for special leasing cannot be a short-life asset (see **14.179**) (*s 84, Table, item 2*). Some assets within the scope of *s 19* attract a WDA of only 10%. They are machinery or plant which is leased (under a lease finalised before 1 April 2006 – see **18.16**) to a person who is not resident in the United Kingdom and who does not use the asset for the purposes of a trade carried on in the United Kingdom or for earning profits chargeable to tax under *CTA 2009, s 1313(2)* (exploration or exploitation activities etc). Certain leasings of ships, aircraft or transport containers and certain short-term leasings of other assets are exempt from this restriction of WDAs (*s 109*).

Lessee's expenditure

Non-fixtures/chattels

18.69   It may be that a lessee is required to incur capital expenditure on plant under the terms of the lease. If that plant does not become a fixture, it is treated as belonging to him as long as it is used for the purposes of his qualifying activity (*s 70(1)* and (2)). On determination of the lease, no disposal value need be brought in by the lessee (*s 70(3)*). On a subsequent sale, etc *s 61* has effect as if the capital expenditure had been incurred by the lessor and not by the lessee (*s 70(4)*). Consequently, a disposal value may be brought into account by the lessor, even though he had not incurred any capital expenditure. This assumes, of course, that the machinery or plant is not removed by the lessee when the lease ends.

Fixtures

18.70 Allowances may be available where the lessee of a building incurs expenditure on plant which becomes a fixture (see **11.15** *et seq*).

ENERGY SERVICES PROVIDERS

18.71 On occasions, an 'energy services provider' may install and operate plant and machinery in a building in which he does not have a legal interest. In such circumstances, the normal requirement for an interest in land is removed (*FA 2001, s 66* and *Sch 18*). The plant may not be formally leased, in which case an election under *s 177* (see **18.23**) is not possible.

18.72 This provision is part of a wider package of measures aimed at helping businesses reduce their energy consumption, and so help the United Kingdom reduce emissions of greenhouse gases.

18.73 An energy services provider is essentially a person providing services under an energy services agreement, as defined by *FA 2001; CAA 2001, s 175A(1)*.

18.74 The plant is effectively deemed to belong to the energy services provider, provided a joint election is made by the energy services provider and the 'client'.

18.75 This election is not possible where the client would not be entitled to an allowance if he incurred the expenditure himself. Typically, this will apply where the client is not within the charge to tax. An exception to this is where the plant is of an energy-saving nature, as specified by Treasury order.

18.76 Where a subsequent purchaser of the property pays a capital sum to discharge obligations under the energy services agreement, the plant is treated as ceasing to belong to the energy services provider, and the capital sum is treated as expenditure qualifying for allowances.

SALE AND LEASEBACK OF PLANT

18.77 Sale and leaseback arrangements were unsuccessfully challenged by HMRC in *Barclays Mercantile Business Finance Ltd v Mawson* (*Inspector of Taxes*) [2002] EWCA Civ 1853, [2003] STC 66; affd [2004] UKHL 51, [2005] STC 1 and *BMBF* (*No 24*) *Ltd v IRC* [2002] EWHC 2466 (Ch), [2002] STC 1450. In essence, a finance lessor may obtain allowances, even though the availability of those allowances is a fundamental reason for the acquisition of the plant.

18.78 Special rules apply where plant is sold, but continues to be used in the vendor's trade or that of a connected person (ie in sale and leaseback transactions) (*s 216*). The primary effect is the same as where vendor and purchaser are connected, namely that the qualifying expenditure of the purchaser is restricted to the disposal value brought into account by the vendor (*s 218(2)*). Where no disposal value falls to be brought into account (eg because the vendor is a non-taxpayer) the purchaser's qualifying expenditure is the smallest of:

(*a*)   the open market value of the machinery and plant;

(*b*)   the capital expenditure incurred by the seller on the provision of the machinery or plant; and

(*c*)   any expenditure on the provision of the machinery or plant incurred by any person connected (see **20.25** *et seq*) with the seller (*s 218(3)*).

18.79   If the seller did not incur capital expenditure, condition (*b*) is ignored – it is *not* the case that the capital expenditure is deemed to be nil, such that no allowances were available.

18.80   *Section 216* also applies, with necessary adaptation, where a person enters into a contract under which, on the performance thereof, he will or may become the owner of machinery or plant belonging to another person, or is the assignee of such a contract (*s 213*).

18.81   Where plant which is used for non-trading activities is sold and leased back under a finance lease, *ss 221–226* impose, generally with effect from 2 July 1997, two further restrictions on the finance lessor. First, no allowances will be given to the lessor if the terms of the lease or of related transactions are such that he has substantially divested himself of any risk that the lessee will not comply with his obligations. Guarantees from persons connected with the lessee are ignored (*s 225*). Secondly, even if the finance lessor has not divested himself of risk, his qualifying expenditure will be limited to the 'notional written-down value' of the plant, if no disposal value is required to be brought into account by the vendor (or market value, if lower) (*s 224(2)* and (*3*).) These rules do not apply where expenditure is incurred before 2 July 1998 in pursuance of an earlier contract (*F(No 2)A 1997, s 46(3)*).

18.82   The requirement to restrict the lessor's qualifying expenditure to open market value under *s 222* or notional tax written-down value under *s 224* (see **18.81**) is relaxed where certain conditions are met and the buyer and seller make a joint election. This election must be in writing, not more than two years after the date of the sale. Such an election will deem the disposal value, and hence the lessor's qualifying expenditure, to be the cost to the lessor or the cost to the lessee, whichever is the lower (*s 228*).

18.83   The conditions are (*s 227*):

- The seller incurred capital expenditure on the asset (rather than treating it as trading stock).

- The asset was new when acquired by the seller. 'New' means unused and not second-hand.

- The asset was not acquired from a connected person, or as part of a transaction whose main benefit was to obtain an allowance.

- The sale is within four months of the asset first being used for any purpose by any person.

- The seller has not claimed allowances on the asset or included it in a pool of qualifying expenditure.

Acquisition of a lease portfolio

18.84   Where assets are acquired together with rental agreements, it is likely that expenditure qualifying for allowances will be challenged by HMRC if it exceeds the original cost of the assets concerned (CA, para 12200).

Anti-avoidance: leasing of plant & machinery

18.85   Anti-avoidance rules apply from 9 December 2009. They address arrangements where:

- a company is created that is taxed on very little income from the leasing of an asset (eg where the right to the majority of the income is sold when the company is offshore), but which is potentially able to claim capital allowances on the full cost of the asset, creating tax losses where there is a commercial profit; or

- where a lessor that has claimed capital allowances in the initial loss-making phase of a lease of plant or machinery avoids tax on the income that arises once the lease moves into its tax-profitable phase by leaving the charge to tax. The intended effect is to turn a tax-timing advantage into a permanent loss of tax on a transaction that is commercially profitable.

18.86   New *CAA 2001, ss 228MA* to *228MC*, are inserted to ensure that in relevant circumstances, the amount qualifying for capital allowances is limited to the present value of the amounts expected to be received as lease rentals or other income (other than disposal receipts brought in for capital allowances purposes) plus the present value of any residual lease ('V').

18.87 The rules will operate at the time the capital expenditure is incurred and so require a lessor to consider what is likely to happen in the future. However, subsequent events, such as default by the lessee (which is in any case unlikely to be an 'arrangement'), which result in the future amount of taxable income being less than the capital expenditure, will not affect the amount on which the lessor may claim capital allowances.

18.88 The rules will not affect normal commercial leases, merely those where arrangements exist which result in 'V' being lower than the capital expenditure which qualify for allowances if such arrangements did not exist.

18.89 In addition, new *CAA 2001, s 64A* is inserted to deal with arrangements reducing the disposal value of a leased asset, in so far as that reduction is attributable to rentals payable under the lease. It requires the disposal value to be calculated as if those arrangements did not exist.

Example (from HMRC Technical Note of 9 December 2009)

'A finance lessor is entitled to receive rentals with a remaining present value of £100 million. No residual value accrues to the lessor. It sells 90 per cent to a third party bank for £90 million, guarantees the income, and immediately leaves the UK. [Leaving the UK triggers a disposal event for capital allowances purposes].

The value of a finance leased asset is generally accepted as being based on the value of the lease rental stream (plus any residual value accruing to the lessor) and so, ignoring the sale of the rentals means that the disposal value of the leased asset will be £100 million rather than £10 million.'

ANTI-AVOIDANCE – SALE OF LESSOR COMPANIES

18.90 *Finance Act 2006, Sch 10* introduced new rules applying to companies carrying on a business of leasing plant and machinery. In particular, the rules address situations where there is a change of ownership of the company or a change in the arrangements for sharing partnership profits.

18.91 They aim to remedy what was seen as an unacceptable permanent deferral of tax. Previously, it had been possible for a leasing company to generate losses in the early years, due to the availability of capital allowances, which could be group relieved. Later in the term of the lease, there would be less relief through capital allowances, and the company would become profitable. Before that happened, though, the company could be sold to a loss-making group, so that the leasing profits were themselves covered by losses surrendered by its new owners.

18.92   The anti-avoidance provisions have effect for changes in ownership, etc which occur on or after 5 December 2005.

18.93   On a change in ownership, etc, the company is treated as receiving an amount of income and the accounting period ends. On the following day, the company is treated as incurring an expense and a new accounting period begins. The deemed income and expense are of the same amount.

18.94   The deemed income cancels out any prior relief for the losses, while the deemed expense ensures that relief is available for future leasing profits. Any loss arising from the deemed expense may not be carried back.

18.95   For the purposes of these provisions, a company is carrying on a business of leasing if:

● half of the plant owned by the company is subject to a qualifying lease; or

● half of the company's income in the last 12 months is derived from qualifying leased plant or machinery.

18.96   'Background plant' (*s 70R*) (see **18.50**) is excluded, so property companies are unlikely to be caught.

18.97   The provisions are extended to include situations where a leasing business is carried on in partnership, and transactions take place which, while they do not constitute a change in ownership of the company, would nonetheless have the same effect, ie a permanent deferral of tax.

18.98   *Finance Act 2012, s 24* further extends the provisions where a lessor company becomes subject to the tonnage tax rules so that its profits cease to be calculated by reference to the normal corporation tax rules. The move into tonnage tax can be achieved in a number of ways without triggering the effect of the sales of lessors provisions and the change in the method of computing profits for tax purposes means that the deferred profits will not brought into charge to tax.

18.99   The changes made by *FA 2006, s 24* ensure that the effect of the sales of lessors provisions is triggered when a company enters the tonnage tax regime so that tax can be collected on the deferred profits of the company.

18.100 Further changes made by this section refocus these restrictions so that any loss from an accounting period after a change of ownership cannot be carried back against the profits of the company that are derived from the income amount. This restriction prevents groups from arranging their affairs so that losses are available in the lessor company after the change of ownership which can be used to cancel the effect of the income amount.

Chapter 19

Research and development, patents and know-how

INTRODUCTION

19.1   This chapter deals with allowances due for expenditure on:

(*a*)   research and development (see **19.5**);

(*b*)   patents (see **19.104**); and

(*c*)   know-how (see **19.119**).

19.2   Each of the three, perhaps, represents a different stage in the acquisition and exploitation of knowledge. However, the capital allowances treatment differs greatly between the pure intangibles, patents and know-how, where the allowances are similar to those on plant, and research and development, where a 100% initial allowance is available, and comparisons with enterprise zone allowances are inevitably drawn.

19.3   There are similarities between allowances on research and intangibles, and the more commonly encountered allowances on plant and buildings. However, the allowances are not identical, and the taxpayer should not assume that the treatment of an item or event will be the same as for the allowances with which he is more familiar.

19.4   With effect from 1 April 2002, most expenditure on intellectual property (including patents and know-how) incurred by a company, attracts relief under *CTA 2009, Pts 8* and *9* – see **Chapter 25**.

RESEARCH AND DEVELOPMENT

General

19.5   Capital expenditure in connection with research and development (R&D) is one of the few remaining instances where a 100% first-year allowance is still available. However, there is still an incentive to classify expenditure as revenue rather than capital, as revenue expenditure may qualify for relief at much more than 100% (see **19.7** *et seq*). R&D allowances are by no means as rare as might be imagined, and many taxpayers have realised, belatedly, that a potential claim has been overlooked.

19.6 For accounting periods ending on or after 1 April 2000, the legislation was amended to substitute the term 'research and development' for 'scientific research', wherever it occurs. This was intended to be a change of nomenclature only, with no impact on the allowances available.

Revenue R&D relief

19.7 Revenue expenditure on research and development activities (see **19.63** *et seq*) by *companies* (*CTA 2009, s 1039*) may qualify for tax relief at an enhanced rate. An outline of R&D tax deductions and credits is given below, but R&D advice for revenue expenditure is a specialist area, and reference should be made to Bloomsbury Professional's *Research and Development Tax Reliefs* by Maria Kitt.

19.8 Relief is available to small or medium-sized enterprises (SMEs) (see **19.24** *et seq*) at:

- 150% for expenditure incurred between 1 April 2000 and 31 July 2008 (*FA 2000, Sch 20*);

- 175% for expenditure incurred between 1 August 2008 and 31 March 2011 (*CTA 2009, s 1044*);

- 200% for expenditure incurred between 1 April 2011 and 31 March 2012 (*FA 2011, s 43*);

- 225% for expenditure incurred between 1 April 2012 and 31 March 2015 (*FA 2012, s 20* and *Sch 3, para 2*); or

- 230% thereafter (*FA 2015, s 27*);

- 130% (previously 125%) under the large companies scheme rules (*CTA 2009, ss 1063* and *1073*) when –

  - R&D is contracted to the SME by a large company (see **19.33**) or a person not carrying on a qualifying trade and the R&D is undertaken 'in-house' by the SME (ie by itself) (*CTA 2009, s 1066*), or is contracted out by the SME to a 'qualifying body' (eg a charity, higher education institution, etc, as defined by *CTA 2009, s 1142*), an individual, or a firm where each member is an individual, which carries out the R&D and is paid for it by the SME (*CTA 2009, s 1067*),

• the expenditure is subsidised by someone else (see **19.34**) and undertaken 'in-house' by the SME or contracted out by the SME to a 'qualifying body' as above. It is subsidised as defined by *CTA 2009, s 1138* if the SME has received a subsidy or grant in respect of it, or the expenditure has been met (directly or indirectly) by another person, or any notified state aid has been received, or

• the expenditure exceeds the relevant cap of €7.5 million for the project (see **19.29** and **19.31**).

To replace the large companies scheme (including SMEs claiming under it) FA 2012 introduced new CTA 2009, Pt 3, Ch 6A. This provides for an 'above the line' tax credit called the 'R&D expenditure credit'. See 19.19.

Example

A Ltd pays a SME, B Ltd, £100,000 to carry out some R&D. In undertaking the R&D, B Ltd spends £70,000 on R&D qualifying expenditure (staffing costs etc, see **19.35**). B Ltd is able to claim a tax deduction of £91,000 (ie £70,000 × 130%).

19.9   Relief is available to large companies at 125% for expenditure incurred between 1 April 2002 and 31 March 2008 (*FA 2002, Sch 12, para 20*) or 130% on or after 1 April 2008 (*CTA 2009, s 1074*).

19.10   To replace the large companies scheme *FA 2012* introduced new *CTA 2009, Pt 3, Ch 6A*. This provides for an 'above the line' tax credit called the 'R&D expenditure credit' (see **19.20**).

Revenue small or medium-sized enterprises R&D tax credit

19.11   Alternatively, loss-making SMEs can surrender their loss and claim an immediately payable tax credit from HMRC (*CTA 2009, s 1054 et seq*; Corporate Intangibles Research and Development Manual – hereafter CIRD, para 80520).

19.12   Before 1 August 2008, the tax credit was 16% of the surrendered loss (ie up to £240 for every £1,000 of R&D expenditure; calculated as £1,000 × 150% × 16%).

19.13   From 1 August 2008 to 31 March 2011, this was limited to a maximum of 14% of the surrendered loss (ie up to £245 for every £1,000 of R&D expenditure; calculated as £1,000 × 175% × 14%) (*CTA 2009, s 1058*).

19.14   From 1 April 2011 to 31 March 2012, this was limited to a maximum of 12.5% of the surrendered loss (ie up to £250 for every £1,000 of R&D expenditure; calculated as £1,000 × 200% × 12.5%) (*FA 2011, s 43*).

19.15   From 1 April 2012 to 31 March 2014, this is limited to a maximum of 11% of the surrendered loss (ie up to £247.50 for every £1,000 of R&D expenditure; calculated as £1,000 × 225% × 11%) (*FA 2012, s 20* and *Sch 3, para 2*).

19.16   From 1 April 2014, this is limited to a maximum of 14.5% of the surrendered loss (ie up to £326.25 for every £1,000 of R&D expenditure; calculated as £1,000 × 225% × 14.5%) (*Finance Act 2014, s 31*).

19.17   The repayment used to be capped at a maximum of the company's Pay As You Earn (PAYE) and National Insurance payments for its own employees in the period and could not be made if:

(*a*)   the company had outstanding corporation tax liabilities;

(*b*)   there was an enquiry open into the company's tax return for the chargeable period for which the R&D tax credit was claimed; or

(*c*)   the company had outstanding PAYE or class 1 national insurance liabilities for payment periods ending in the chargeable period (*CTA 2009, ss 1058* and *1059*).

19.18   The PAYE and national insurance cap is abolished for accounting periods ending on or after 1 April 2012 (*FA 2012, s 20* and *Sch 3, paras 15* and *39*).

19.19   The repayment must be claimed (or amended or withdrawn) within one year of the self-assessment filing date for the accounting period (*FA 1998, Sch 18, para 83E(1)*).

19.20   For expenditure incurred after 1 April 2013, an 'above the line tax credit', called the 'R&D expenditure credit', is available to companies who claim under the large company scheme (including SMEs claiming under those rules because they carry out work sub-contracted to them or receive subsidies). This allows claimants not paying tax to obtain a fully payable tax credit, at 10% of the qualifying R&D expenditure in the period, subject to a cap related to the PAYE and NIC liabilities of the qualifying staffing costs (*CTA 2009, s 104M*). The rate increases to 11% for expenditure from 1 April 2015 (*FA 2015, s 27*). Initially, this scheme is optional, but from 1 April 2016 it will become mandatory.

Small or medium-sized enterprise's pre-trading expenditure

19.21 If a SME incurs qualifying R&D expenditure in a pre-trading accounting period then it can elect to deem an amount equal to 230% of its qualifying expenditure as a trading loss for that period (so that *CTA 2009, s 61* does not apply to treat the expenditure as incurred on the day that trading begins) (*CTA 2009, s 1045*).

19.22 Previously, the rates were 225% for expenditure incurred between 1 April 2012 and 31 March 2015, 200% for expenditure incurred between 1 April 2011 and 31 March 2012, 175% for expenditure incurred between 1 August 2008 and 31 March 2011, or 150% for expenditure incurred before 1 August 2008.

19.23 This deemed loss can be:

(*a*) set off against other profits for the period or the previous year;

(*b*) surrendered as group relief or for a payable tax credit (see **19.11** *et seq*); or

(*c*) carried forward as a loss of the future trade under *CTA 2010, s 45* (*CTA 2009, ss 1045* and *1048*).

Definition of small or medium-sized enterprises for R&D purposes

19.24 For accounting periods ending on or after 1 August 2008, the SME scheme thresholds were doubled to include companies with less than 500 employees and either an annual turnover not exceeding €100 million or an annual balance sheet total not exceeding €86 million (*CTA 2009, s 1119*).

19.25 Prior to this, a SME was defined for R&D tax relief purposes as a micro, small or medium-sized enterprise by EC recommendation *2003/361/EC* of 6 May 2003 (imported into UK law by *SI 2004/3267*) (*CTA 2009, ss 1119* and *1120*). This set out two tests: a quantitative test and an independence test.

19.26 A company was a SME if it had less than 250 employees *and either* an annual turnover not exceeding €50 million or an annual balance sheet total not exceeding €43 million (including adding figures of other legal entities they were associated with) and satisfied the independence test that less than 25% of its capital or voting rights were held directly or indirectly, individually or jointly, by enterprises that were not SMEs.

19.27 From 1 December 2008 HMRC changed its interpretation of how a company's size alters after an acquisition, merger or linking. Previously a company that was an SME during an accounting period was treated as one for the entire period. However, going forward it would be viewed as large for the entire period when the change occurs (CIRD, para 92000).

19.28   With effect for accounting periods ending on or after 31 December 2005, *SI 2005/3376* corrected a mistake in the legislation by amending the *FA 2000, Sch 20, para 2(1)(b)* SME definition to prevent the possibility that a company may fall outside the definition of a SME earlier than intended once it exceeds the relevant employee or financial tests. Furthermore, *SI 2005/3376* amended the large companies R&D legislation (*FA 2002, Sch 12, para 2(1)(b)*) to align the definitions in the SME and large companies schemes, to prevent a company simultaneously being both a SME under the SMEs scheme and a non-SME under the large companies scheme.

Conditions for claiming R&D relief

19.29   The R&D tax relief is available provided that the taxpayer:

Generally

(a)   Is a company (*CTA 2009, s 1039*).

(b)   Carries on a trade in the period and incurs expenditure that is allowable as a deduction in a tax return (ie, is revenue in character) (*CTA 2009, ss 1044(5), 1055, 1063(4), 1068(4)* and *1074(6)*).

Or in the case of SMEs only, incurs expenditure that would have been allowable as a deduction if it had been trading by the time the expenditure was incurred (upon making an election) (*CTA 2009, ss 1044(4), 1045(4), 1055(1), 1063(4), 1068(4)* and *1074(4)*).

For accounting periods beginning up to and including 31 December 2004, R&D relief was only available for development costs that were deferred as an intangible asset under SSAP 13, when that expenditure was amortised through the profit and loss account. For periods beginning from 1 January 2005 companies may claim R&D relief for expenditure incurred in the year, even if the expenditure has been treated as an intangible fixed asset (*FA 2004, s 53*), except where they are performing a long-term contract (because work in progress is not an intangible fixed asset).

(c)   Claims the relief in a tax return (*CTA 2009, ss 1044(6), 1054(2), 1063(5), 1068(4)* and *1074(5)*; *FA 1998, Sch 18, para 83B*).

For accounting periods ending on or after 1 April 2006, the time limit is two years from the end of the accounting period to which the claim relates (*FA 2006, Sch 3*). For periods before this, the time limit was six years (ie the normal self-assessment time limit specified in *FA 1998, Sch 18, para 55*).

(*d*) For expenditure incurred before 1 April 2012, incurs expenditure on R&D of £10,000 per annum (see **19.30**) (*CTA 2009, ss 1044(3), 1050, 1063(3), 1064, 1068(3), 1069, 1074(3)* and *1075*). For expenditure incurred on or after 1 April 2012, this threshold is abolished (*FA 2012, s 20* and *Sch 3, paras 3–8*).

(*e*) Incurs expenditure on one of the various categories of qualifying expenditure (see **19.35**) (*CTA 2009, ss 1052(2), 1066(3), 1124, 1126* and *1132* or *1068(5), 1074(7)* and *1076–1078*).

SMEs only

(*f*) Is a SME (see **19.24**) (*CTA 2009, ss 1039(3), 1043(1), 1044(2), 1045(2), 1063(2)* and *1068(2)*).

(*g*) Was not sub-contracted to carry out the R&D by another person (*CTA 2009, ss 1052(5)* and *1053(4)*). This is because the general principle is that the SME rules are intended to incentivise the company that bears the cost of the R&D project, whereas the large company regime rewards the company actually carrying out the R&D.

Although for 'qualifying chapter 3 expenditure' (ie contracted to it by a large company or person not carrying on a chargeable trade) it may still be possible for the SME to claim under the large company scheme (see **19.33**) (*CTA 2009, s 1063*).

(*h*) Incurs expenditure on 'relevant R&D' (ie that is related to the company's trade, or one to be carried on by it) (*CTA 2009, ss 1044(5), 1051, 1052(3)* and *1053(2)*).

This does not apply where qualifying chapter 3 and 4 expenditure is relevant (ie where the SME is claiming relief at the lower rate available to large companies).

(*i*) Must be a 'going concern'. With effect from 1 August 2008 (*SI 2008/1929*), SMEs in financial difficulty (ie those that are not a going concern) cannot claim the repayable tax credit, or SME or large companies R&D tax relief.

A company is a going concern if its latest published accounts were prepared on a going concern basis and nothing in the accounts suggests that that status depends on it receiving R&D relief. Where a company is in administration or liquidation, it is not a going concern (*FA 2012, s 20* and *Sch 3, paras 9–14*).

Where a company in financial difficulty has claimed a tax credit it is treated as if it had never made the claim, although if the relief applied, or credit was fully or partly paid before the company ceased to be a going concern then the company may keep the benefit (*CTA 2009, ss 1046* and *1057*). Although this does not apply where qualifying chapter 3 and 4 expenditure is relevant (ie where the SME is claiming relief at the lower rate available to large companies).

(*j*)   For expenditure incurred in accounting periods ending before 9 December 2009 (after which this requirement is abolished by *F(No 3)A 2010, s 13*), has the intellectual property (IP) rights resulting from the R&D vesting in it, ie the SME owns the IP (*CTA 2009, ss 1052(4)* and *1053(3)*).

Although this does not apply where qualifying chapter 3 and 4 expenditure is relevant (ie where the SME is claiming relief at the lower rate available to large companies).

In practice, HMRC will accept that this condition is generally met, as long as the claimant company has a real and material interest in any IP that has arisen, or the IP is to be placed in the public domain. However, where there is an agreement recording that all intellectual property created belongs to another party, then the test will be failed (CIRD, para 81550). Where joint ownership is relevant, HMRC's view is that this should provide an equal undivided share, so that either party is entitled to exploit the IP without the consent of the other.

(*k*)   The maximum R&D aid (ie the tax benefit, not the expenditure qualifying for relief) received per project does not exceed €7.5 million, including both tax credits and tax relief (*CTA 2009, ss 1044(9)* and *1113 et seq*) see **19.31**.

Although this does not apply where qualifying chapter 3 and 4 expenditure is relevant (ie where the SME is claiming relief at the lower rate available to large companies).

(*l*)   Has not received any subsidy, either directly or indirectly, or received any notified State Aid for the R&D project (eg certain government funded grants, because the SME scheme is classified by the EU as state aid) (*CTA 2009, ss 1052(6), 1053(5)* and *1138*).

If any notified State Aid is received then the SME loses all ability to make any claim under the SME scheme. If a grant or subsidy is received that is not notified State Aid then the expenditure is subsidised only to the extent that the expenditure does not exceed the subsidy, so only the expenditure net of the subsidy will qualify for R&D relief. However, for expenditure incurred in accounting periods beginning on or after 9 April 2003 expenditure may qualify partly under the SME scheme and partly under the large company scheme (any balance of expenditure not eligible under the SME scheme) (CIRD, para 81650).

(*m*) To qualify for the enhanced tax deduction, incurs –

- 'qualifying chapter 2 expenditure' (ie in-house direct, or contracted out R&D);

- 'qualifying chapter 3 expenditure' (ie contracted to it by a large company or person not carrying on a chargeable trade); or

- 'qualifying chapter 4 expenditure' (ie subsidised in-house direct, or contracted out R&D) (*CTA 2009, ss 1044(5)* and *1051; 1063(4)* and *1065; 1068(5), 1070–1073* and *1138*).

(*n*) To qualify for the repayable tax credit, has a 'chapter 2 surrenderable loss' (ie unrelieved trading loss) (*CTA 2009, ss 1054(1), 1055* and *1056*).

Large companies only

(*o*) Is a large company (ie not a SME – see **19.24**) (*CTA 2009, ss 1074(2)* and *1119–1122*).

(*p*) To qualify for the enhanced tax deduction (the repayable tax credit not being available to large companies), incurs 'qualifying chapter 5 expenditure' (ie in-house direct or contracted out R&D, or contributions to independent research) (*CTA 2009, ss 1074(7)* and *1076–1079*).

If the R&D work has been sub-contracted to the company by a third party it may only claim if it was sub-contracted to it by other large companies or persons otherwise than in the course of carrying on a chargeable trade (*CTA 2009, s 1078(5)*). Where a large company's expenditure is partly or wholly 'refunded', then an additional uplift equal to 30% of the refund is treated as income in the accounting period in which the refund is received (*CTA 2009, s 1083*).

De minimis

19.30   For accounting periods ending before 1 April 2012, a company may only claim the relief where its R&D expenditure exceeds £10,000 (previously £25,000) per annum. For large companies the reduction in threshold from £25,000 to £10,000 had effect for accounting periods ending on or after 9 April 2003 (*FA 2002, Sch 12, para 1*) and for SMEs it applied for accounting periods ending on or after 27 September 2003 (*FA 2000, Sch 20, para 1*). The de minimis is now abolished for all companies.

Maximum for SMEs

19.31   With effect from 1 August 2008, the maximum R&D aid (ie the tax benefit, not the expenditure qualifying for relief) per project under the SME scheme may not exceed €7.5 million, including both tax credits and tax relief (*CTA 2009, ss 1044(9)* and *1113 et seq*).

19.32 Any additional R&D expenditure above this amount may qualify under the less generous (ie, 130% relief) large companies scheme, if the expenditure is incurred by the SME on R&D contracted to it by a large company, or person otherwise than in the course of a trade or profession etc (*CTA 2009, s 1065*).

R&D sub-contracted to SMEs

19.33 A SME can obtain the 'large company' R&D tax relief where it is acting as sub-contractor to a large company (*CTA 2009, s 1063*). This relief is extended to cases where the expenditure is subsidised, and would not therefore qualify for the SME R&D tax relief (*CTA 2009, s 1068*).

Subsidised expenditure incurred by a large company

19.34 Under generally accepted accounting practice, subsidised expenditure is recognised in full and the subsidy is recognised as a receipt. Therefore, because there is no provision in the large company scheme that denies R&D relief for expenditure that is subsidised (unlike the SME rules, see **19.29**(*i*)), a claimant under the large company scheme (including SMEs making such a claim, see **19.7** and **19.33**) may claim R&D relief for the gross amount of any subsidised expenditure (ie without deducting any subsidy received) (CIRD, para 89000).

Categories of qualifying expenditure

19.35 Relief is available for a variety of categories of qualifying expenditure including:

(*a*) Staffing costs *directly and actively* engaged in R&D, ie earnings consisting of money such as salaries, some expenses, class 1 national insurance contributions and pension payments (as well as benefits in kind incurred in accounting periods ending on or after 6 April 2003 and before 1 April 2004; CIRD, para 83250) (*CTA 2009, ss 1123–1124*) (see **19.36**).

(*b*) Consumable stores, including materials or equipment used up in the R&D activity (until 31 March 2004) (*FA 2000, Sch 20, para 6; FA 2002, Sch 12, para 17(c)*). There is no general accountancy definition of consumable stores so the definition follows the wording of the statute, ie the subject matter must be consumable *and* stored by the company, eg 'fuel, ink or paper actually used' (*BE Studios Ltd v Smith & Williamson Ltd* [2005] EWHC 1506 (Ch), [2006] 2 All ER 811).

(*c*)   'Consumable or transformable materials', including water fuel and power (from 1 April 2004) (*CTA 2009, ss 1125–1126*). Consumable or transformable materials has a wider definition than consumable stores because it includes consumable or transformable items that need not be stored (see **19.23**). For expenditure incurred from 1 April 2015, the cost of materials incorporated into products sold on no longer qualifies (an apportionment is required where not all of the material is sold or transferred – so if some material is kept for additional trials or discarded as waste it will still qualify) (*CTA 2009, ss 1126A–1126B*). For expenditure on prototypes see **19.65** and **19.83**.

(*d*)   Computer software *directly* employed in R&D (from 1 April 2004) (*CTA 2009, ss 1125–1126*).

(*e*)   'Externally provided workers' *directly and actively* engaged in the R&D, ie those provided by an agency or other intermediary (from 9 April 2003 for large companies and 27 September 2003 for SMEs) (*CTA 2009, ss 1127–1132*) (see **19.41** *et seq*).

(*f*)   Contributions to independent research (large companies only – see **19.49**) (*CTA 2009, ss 1079* and *1142*).

(*g*)   Sub-contracted activities (see **19.46** *et seq*) (*CTA 2009, ss 1078* and *1133–1136*).

(*h*)   Relevant payments to the subjects of a clinical trial (*CTA 2009, s 1140*).

Employee and management costs

19.36   For expenditure incurred on or after 9 April 2003 (large companies) and 27 September 2003 (SMEs), employee costs qualify for relief in proportion to the time spent on R&D (*CTA 2009, s 1124(4)*). Best practice is that individuals concerned should complete detailed timesheets. Taxpayers should be reasonable because HMRC's view is that no matter how dedicated or efficient the employee is, it is inevitable that they will have some administration or other down-time so it is unrealistic to treat 100% of that person's time as being spent on R&D.

19.37   Previously, no relief was available if an employee spent less than 20% of his time on research and development, but the whole cost qualified for relief if the percentage was greater than 80%.

19.38   Secretarial, administrative or managerial services in support of activities carried on by others do not qualify at all because they are not 'directly and actively engaged' in R&D (*CTA 2009, 1124(5); BE Studios*). *Support* activities which *do* directly contribute to achieving R&D include:

(*a*)   creating or adapting necessary software, materials or equipment;

(*b*)   scientific or technological planning activities; and

(*c*)   scientific or technological design, testing and analysis [DTI guidelines (hereafter DTI), para 27 (see **19.72** *et seq*)].

19.39   Recruitment fees do not qualify (*BE Studios*). In *Gripple Limited v HM Revenue and Customs Comrs* [2010] EWHC 1609 (Ch), payments made by Gripple to an associated company (Loadhog) for a mutual director's services were held not to be 'staffing costs' because they were not 'emoluments' (as required formerly by *FA 2000, Sch 20, para 5*) paid by Gripple, to that director (see also **19.45**).

Consumable or transformable materials/software

19.40   Where consumable or transformable materials are partly employed directly in R&D an appropriate apportionment of the expenditure should be made (eg HMRC will accept that a broad brush apportionment of heating or lighting based on floor area or staff numbers may be suitable, where there is no particular high power consumption based on the nature of the R&D). Inspectors are instructed to take a pragmatic approach and if the taxpayer offers a reasonable apportionment HMRC does not envisage detailed enquiries being desirable to establish a slightly more accurate alternative (CIRD, para 82300). Partly employed software may be apportioned on a similar basis (CIRD, para 82500).

Externally provided workers

19.41   For externally provided workers, the amount qualifying depends in the first instance on whether the research company and the intermediary (the 'staff controller') are connected. For expenditure incurred before 1 April 2012, the narrower term 'staff provider' was used.

19.42   For expenditure incurred on or after 1 April 2012, the legislation was amended to remove a restriction that there had to be only three contractual parties in the arrangements.

19.43   If the research company and the intermediary are not connected, and if no election is made under *CTA 2009, s 1130* (see **19.44**), then 65% of the cost incurred by the company will qualify for relief.

19.44 If the parties are connected, the qualifying amount will be the lower of the cost to the research company and the cost to the staff provider. This may be greater than the 65% available for unconnected persons, who would therefore be at a disadvantage. Consequently, an unconnected research company and staff provider may jointly elect to be treated under the connected person rules (see the pro forma at **Appendix 5**) (*CTA 2009, s 1130*). The election is irrevocable and must be made within two years of the end of the research company's accounting period in which the staff provision contract is entered into.

19.45 The externally provided workers relief is not available for recruitment fees, which as 'qualifying indirect activities' (see **19.74**) do not fall within the relevant category of qualifying expenditure (*BE Studios*) (see **19.29**(*e*) and **19.35**). In *Gripple Limited v HM Revenue and Customs Comrs* [2010] EWHC 1609 (Ch), payments made by Gripple to an associated company (Loadhog) for a mutual director's services were held not to be qualifying expenditure on 'externally provided workers' because that individual's position as a director of Gripple meant he could not qualify as an 'externally provided worker' (see also **19.39**).

R&D sub-contracted to others

19.46 For SMEs the rules about R&D sub-contracted to others (*CTA 2009, s 1053*) are similar to those described above for externally provided workers. A SME's qualifying sub-contracted expenditure can include payments to another person (which need not be R&D when viewed in isolation), but if the parties are unconnected it is limited to a maximum of 65% of the payment made to the sub-contractor (*CTA 2009, s 1136*).

19.47 For connected parties the qualifying amount will be the lower of the payment that it makes to the sub-contractor and the relevant expenditure incurred by the sub-contractor.

19.48 An unconnected research company and sub-contractor may jointly elect to be treated under the connected person rules of *CTA 2009, s 1134* within two years of the end of the research company's accounting period in which the sub-contract is entered into (*CTA 2009, s 1135*). See pro forma election in **Appendix 5**.

19.49 Large companies may only claim for expenditure on R&D that they carry out themselves unless it is sub-contracted to certain qualifying bodies, individuals or partnerships of individuals (ie contributions to independent research 'qualifying bodies' including charities or universities) (*CTA 2009, ss 1076* and *1078–1079*). However, where a large company receives a payment refunding some or all of any sub-contracted R&D then an additional uplift equal to 25% of the refund is treated as income in the accounting period in which the refund is received (*CTA 2009, s 1083*).

Capital expenditure

19.50   Where the expenditure is of a capital nature, it will not be allowed as a deduction from trading profits. There is no alternative to the 100% allowance, for example by way of writing-down allowances (WDAs) (*CAA 2001, s 441(1)*). If the tax relief is not immediately required it is possible to disclaim the relief (*s 441(3)*) but there would seem little point in doing so as the relief would be lost, so it would normally be advisable to claim and carry forward any loss in the usual way. The deduction is given for the chargeable period in which the expenditure was incurred or, if it was incurred before the commencement of the trade, it is given for the chargeable period beginning with that commencement (*s 441(2)*).

19.51   The 100% allowance is available where a person carrying on a trade incurs capital expenditure on R&D related to that trade and undertaken either directly by him or on his behalf (*s 439*). Relief is equally available where the trade begins following the R&D (*s 441*). It is important to note, however, that allowances are only available to a trader, and not to a person carrying on a profession or vocation. Research is related to the trade if:

(*a*)   it may lead to or facilitate an extension of that trade or class of trades; or

(*b*)   it is research of a medical nature having particular relevance to workers employed in that trade or class of trades.

19.52   If an asset is acquired for a different purpose, and only subsequently begins to be used for R&D, no R&D allowances are due.

Groups

19.53   Often, research will be carried out by one company for the sole benefit of others in the same group and will constitute that company's sole activity. There is some doubt that the 100% deduction would be given for expenditure incurred by the research company itself, because that company may not have a trade and any expenditure cannot therefore comply with *s 439*. In practice the 100% deduction will be available, provided any receipts from other group members for carrying out the research are included within trading profits. Any payments made by the group members will qualify for the deduction under normal principles as the research need only be undertaken by the trader himself or 'on his behalf'. The words in *s 439(1)* – 'directly undertaken by him or on his behalf' – were considered in the case of *Gaspet Ltd v Elliss (Inspector of Taxes)* [1987] STC 362. A claim failed because the link between the person incurring the expenditure and the work undertaken was not sufficiently close. The mere provision of finance was not enough.

Property companies

19.54 For a variety of commercial reasons, a group property company is often used to hold all the various properties occupied and used by the trading members of a group. Where such a company incurs expenditure on an asset to be used for research, no R&D allowances will be due. *Section 439* requires the existence of a trade – a property business is not sufficient for this purpose.

Exclusions from allowances

19.55 No R&D allowance is available in respect of expenditure on an interest in land, except where all or part of the expenditure may be apportioned to the acquisition of a building or other structure already constructed on the land, or to plant and machinery forming part of such a building (*s 440*).

19.56 As with industrial buildings, (see **7.100** *et seq*) no allowance is available for expenditure incurred on a dwelling, unless:

(*a*)   the dwelling forms part of a building otherwise used for R&D, and

(*b*)   the expenditure justly apportioned to the dwelling is not more than 25% of the total expenditure on the building (*s 438(3)*).

19.57 If expenditure is incurred which is only partly attributable to R&D, a just apportionment of the total expenditure may be made (*s 439(4)*). This would be of relevance, for example, where a new building was to be used partly for research and partly for manufacture.

19.58 References to expenditure incurred on R&D do not include any expenditure incurred in the acquisition of rights in, or arising out of, research (*s 438(2)*). Such rights would include patents etc. Capital allowances may be available (though at a lower rate) for expenditure on patents or know-how (see **19.104** and **19.119**). In this, the legislation appears to recognise that in order for, say, patents to be an issue, the scientific research must have already reached the stage where a marketable product can be identified. Expenditure at this stage carries a lower commercial risk and is therefore less likely to require the 'encouragement' of a 100% deduction.

Disposal

19.59 In a similar way to industrial buildings, a balancing adjustment may arise when an asset qualifying for R&D allowances is disposed of. There is no provision for balancing allowances. Where part of the initial allowance has been disclaimed, and proceeds are less than the 'residue of expenditure' or 'unclaimed allowance' (*s 441(3)*), a loss has arisen, but no balancing allowance is possible. A balancing charge is calculated in accordance with *s 442*, in much the same way as for industrial buildings. In effect, it will be equal to the excess of disposal proceeds over the tax written-down value of the asset, restricted, of course, to the allowances actually given. Where an asset is destroyed, rather than sold, insurance proceeds or costs of demolition must be taken into account (*s 443*).

Avoiding the balancing charge

19.60   Particularly in the early years of an asset's life, a balancing charge may be much more damaging when the asset sold was one qualifying for R&D allowances rather than for, say, industrial buildings allowances. This is because more allowances will have been given, and can therefore be clawed back.

19.61   In some cases, it may be possible to avoid a balancing charge by not selling the whole interest in the asset, but by granting some minor interest, for example a long lease. This idea is discussed further in connection with industrial buildings (see **12.31** *et seq*). The capital value rules applying in enterprise zones (see **12.34** *et seq*) do not apply to R&D, and it is therefore still possible to avoid a balancing charge in this way.

Change of use

19.62   No balancing adjustment is made where an asset which has qualified for allowances subsequently ceases to be used for a qualifying purpose. Thus, for example, if a building constructed to house research facilities is turned over to commercial production after, say, one year, there is no clawback of the 100% allowance given (CA, para 60600). The taxpayer may therefore be able to maximise his allowances by proper planning of the use to which a new building will be put. If a manufacturer with existing premises constructs a new building to carry out R&D, the new building will qualify for R&D allowances. If, on the other hand, he plans to move his manufacturing operations into the new building and use the old one for research, no R&D allowances will be due.

Definition of research and development

19.63   The question of what constitutes scientific research (now called 'research and development' – see **19.5** and **19.72** *et seq*) was dealt with in the House of Commons (by written answer) on 6 July 1994. The text was as follows:

'*CAA 1990 s 139(1)* defines scientific research as covering any activities in the fields of natural or applied science for the extension of knowledge.

Whether any particular activities fall within this definition will depend on the facts of the case. However, in general terms, activities constitute scientific research if they involve the application of new scientific principles in an existing area of research or the application of existing principles in a new area of research. The essential test is innovation.

Scientific research is generally regarded as including the development of a piece of fundamental research up to the production stage. Expenditure on construction of prototypes, pilot plant and so on qualifies for scientific research allowances if the prototypes are used to test the result of the basic research or the possibility of applying the results of the basic research to manufacture.'

19.64   Although the term 'research and development' is now used, and the definition in *Capital Allowances Act 1990 (CAA 1990), s 139(1)* has not been replicated in *CAA 2001*, the above statement is indicative of the underlying principles.

19.65   As stated above, expenditure on prototypes constructed to test the results of the basic research will qualify for capital allowances (or an enhanced tax deduction under the 'consumable and transformable items' heading), but no relief is due if the prototypes concerned are constructed solely to explore commercial possibilities. For example, research into the possibility of environment-friendly aerosols would qualify as research. Once such a device was commercially viable, and was being produced and marketed, any further expenditure incurred would be towards the development of a product. This would be a normal trading activity not qualifying for any special relief (but potentially qualifying for industrial buildings allowances as the manufacture of goods or materials (*s 274, Table A, item 1*)). See also **19.83**.

19.66   For both capital and revenue expenditure research and development is now defined as being those activities which are treated as such under generally accepted accounting principles (*CAA 2001, s 437(2); CTA 2009, s 1041; CTA 2010, s 1138*).

Accountancy definition of research and development

19.67   Research and development is defined under UK generally accepted accounting principles (GAAP) by SSAP 13, or Part 6 of FRSSE, and internationally by IAS 38.

19.68   SSAP 13 distinguishes R&D activity from non-R&D through the presence or absence of an appreciate element of 'innovation' and is based on the definition developed by the Organisation for Economic Co-operation and Development (OECD), commonly referred to as the 'Frascati' definition. This defines R&D as comprising 'creative work undertaken on a systematic basis in order to increase the stock of knowledge ... and the use of this stock of knowledge to devise new applications'.

19.69   The SSAP 13 definition divides 'research' into two types. These are:

- pure research (experimental or theoretical work undertaken primarily to acquire new scientific or technical knowledge for its own sake, rather than directed towards any specific aim or application); and

- applied research (original or critical investigation undertaken to gain a new scientific or technical knowledge directed toward a specific aim or objective).

19.70   'Development' is the use of scientific or technical knowledge whereby new or substantially improved materials, devices, products or services are produced, new processes or systems are installed prior to the commencement of commercial production or applications, or substantial improvements are made to those already installed.

19.71   SSAP 13 gives companies the choice to capitalise developmental expenditure within intangible fixed assets or charge it to the profit and loss account. However, under international accounting standards, when certain conditions are met, companies will be obliged in accordance with IAS 38 to defer developmental expenditure by carrying it on the balance sheet.

BIS definition of research and development

19.72   Importantly, the SSAP 13 definition is subordinated to extensive Department for Business, Innovation and Skills (BIS) (formerly the Department of Trade and Industry) (DTI) guidelines, issued on 5 March 2004 (replacing previous guidelines issued on 28 July 2000).

19.73   These guidelines are given legal force by *SI 2004/712* and form, for all practical tax purposes, the basis of defining R&D activities (and indeed Inspectors are instructed to start from the DTI (or, now, the BIS) guidelines; CIRD, para 81300). This means that it is not necessary for R&D expenditure to have been accounted for under SSAP 13, Part 6 of FRSSE, or IAS 38 for it to be eligible for R&D tax relief. Conversely, some expenditure may not be tax-qualifying R&D, even if it has been treated as such in the accounts, because for accountancy purposes a wider range of expenditure can be included as R&D than is the case under the R&D tax relief legislation.

19.74 It is also worth noting that the definition of R&D under the tax relief legislation is subtly narrower than the definition used for R&D capital allowances, because 'qualifying indirect activities' are R&D (DTI, paras 5 and 31) and so will qualify for R&D capital allowances, but not R&D tax relief (ie activities which do not *directly* contribute to the R&D, but are related to it, for example, information services, maintenance, security etc).

19.75 The DTI guidelines have a statutory start date of 1 April 2004, although in practice the DTI and HMRC regard them as clarification of the historic position and having always had effect, unless the taxpayer takes a different view to the equivalence to the two sets of guidelines and prefers to use the 2000 guidelines for periods before the 2004 guidelines were introduced (CIRD, para 81300).

19.76 The 2004 guidelines define R&D as taking place when '*a project* seeks to achieve an *advance* in *science* or *technology*' (DTI, para 3), with 'the activities that directly contribute to achieving this advance in science or technology through the *resolution of scientific or technological uncertainty*' being R&D (DTI, para 4).

19.77 *Crucially*, it is not simply enough that the work is in some general sense 'innovative' or 'at the cutting-edge' (as is often thought to be the case), but that it *must also* be in an area of uncertainty and seek to lead to a scientific or technological advance, as defined by the DTI guidelines (see **19.72** and **19.78** *et seq*) (*BE Studios*). This, for example, does not include work in the arts, humanities and social sciences (DTI, para 15). Furthermore, cosmetic or aesthetic qualities are not themselves science or technology, so work to improve the cosmetic or aesthetic appeal of a process, material, device, product or service would not itself be R&D unless it required the resolution of scientific or technological uncertainty and a scientific or technological advance to achieve it (DTI, para 42).

Definition of 'project'

19.78 A '*project*' (see **19.76**) consists of a number of activities conducted to a method or plans in order to achieve an advance in science or technology' and should encompass 'all the activities that collectively serve to resolve the scientific or technological uncertainty associated with achieving the advance, so it could include a number of different sub-projects' (DTI, para 19). Importantly, this means that HMRC will expect there to be some evidence of a 'systematic project', which should leave its trace in the records available, rather than the 'R&D' being simply an ad hoc or unexpected discovery (CIRD, para 80550). Inspectors are also told to look at the largest project in deciding whether expenditure on any sub-project, or part of it, qualifies as directly contributing to it (CIRD, para 81300).

Definition of 'advance'

19.79 An *'advance'* (see **19.76**) means an increase in overall knowledge or capability in a field of science or technology (see below), not just a company's own state of knowledge or capability alone. It can include the adaptation of knowledge or capability from another field of science or technology to make the advance (where the advance was not readily deducible by a competent professional working in the field) (DTI, para 6). An advance can also still occur even if several companies working at the cutting-edge are doing similar work independently, or the work has been done elsewhere, but the details of how are still a trade secret or not readily available (DTI, para 21). It can also occur if the advance is not achieved or fully realised (DTI, para 10).

Definition of 'science' and 'technology'

19.80 *'Science'* is defined as 'systematic study of the nature and behaviour of the physical and material universe' (DTI, para 15) and *'technology'* is defined as 'the practical application of scientific principles and knowledge (DTI, para 17), where "scientific" is based on the definition above' (see **19.76**).

Definition of 'scientific or technological uncertainty'

19.81 *'Scientific or technological uncertainty'* (see **19.76**) exists 'when knowledge of whether something is scientifically possible or technically feasible, or how to achieve it in practice is not readily available or deducible by a competent professional working in the field'. This includes turning something that has already been established as scientifically feasible into a cost-effective, reliable and reproducible process, material, device, product or service (DTI, para 13) and 'system uncertainty' (ie resulting from the complexity of a system rather than uncertainty about how its individual components behave) (DTI, paras 29–30).

Examples of R&D

19.82 So R&D takes place where a project seeks to:

(*a*) extend overall knowledge or capability in a field of science or technology (ie the knowledge or capability that is publicly available, or is readily deducible from the publicly available knowledge or capability, by a competent professional working in the field); or

(*b*) create a process, material, device, product or service which incorporates or represents an increase in overall knowledge or capability in a field of science or technology; or

(c)   make an appreciable improvement to an existing process, material, device, product or service through scientific or technological changes (ie changing or adapting the scientific or technological characteristics of something to the point where it is 'better' than the original and more than a minor or routine upgrading, and representing something that would generally be acknowledged as a genuine and non-trivial improvement by a competent professional working in the field); or

(d)   use science or technology to duplicate the effect of an existing process, material, device, product or service in a new or appreciably improved way (eg a product that has exactly the same performance characteristics as existing models, but is built in a fundamentally different manner).

(DTI, para 9)

19.83   A distinction must be drawn between R&D and commercial pre-production, which is *not* R&D. R&D work starts when work to resolve a scientific or technological uncertainty starts (DTI, para 33). And it ends when:

(a)   that uncertainty is resolved; or

(b)   work to resolve the uncertainty ceases; or

(c)   knowledge is codified in a form usable by a competent professional working in the field; or

(d)   when a prototype with all the functional characteristics of the final process, material, device, product or service is achieved - the design, construction and testing of prototypes (eg under the 'consumable items' category, see **19.35**) or the operation of pilot plants while testing their operations is normally R&D, but modifications following the test findings are not).

(DTI, paras 33–34.)

19.84   HMRC's view was that expenditure on prototypes is disallowable if those prototypes are subsequently sold on to customers rather than being scrapped (ie so-called 'pre-production prototypes'). Furthermore, any expenditure on goods produced from a production run, whether a pilot or otherwise (eg so-called 'early production runs') which are finished products are not eligible for R&D relief. See also **19.65**.

19.85   However, draft guidance has been published relaxing this. If the main point of the activity is experimentation, then there are circumstances where HMRC will now accept the activity as forming part of the R&D process. These are when there is real, quantifiable and significant scientific or technological uncertainty which the activity seeks to resolve, and the activity is necessary to carry out or test the R&D. Where production trials are necessary in such circumstances, the whole or part of the expenditure may be on R&D.

19.86 'First-in-class' normally refers to high-value items of a similar design and specification where it is not commercially feasible to construct the item purely for R&D purposes and which are intended from the outset to be fully functional and saleable products, built to final specifications and intended for sale to a customer. They may involve a significant element of innovation and R&D sub-projects. HMRC will now accept that R&D projects included within the larger commercial project will qualify if the company can demonstrate the qualifying activities.

19.87 HMRC may publish guidance on industries where there are particular difficulties in determining whether projects are R&D. Guidance is currently published on two fields: pharmaceuticals (CIRD, para 81920) and software (CIRD, para 81960).

19.88 The Special Commissioners have held that research into the dramatic construction of films, albeit in a manner that was analytical and in the common sense of the word 'scientific', nonetheless did not qualify as scientific research (*Salt v Golding* [1996] STC (SCD) 269).

HMRC's approach

19.89 The availability of generous tax deductions for revenue expenditure and 100% capital allowances is likely to mean that any claim for tax relief, will be closely scrutinised and HMRC has six R&D units around the country, with designated R&D specialist Inspectors who will deal with all R&D tax relief claims apart from those dealt with by the large business service.

19.90 HMRC has set up a voluntary advance assurance pilot to help small companies to make their first R&D relief claim. It was announced during the Autumn statement 2014 that from 2015 voluntary assurances lasting three years would be introduced for small businesses (including companies claiming SME relief, and smaller businesses claiming under the large company scheme and the R&D expenditure credit scheme) making their first claim for R&D tax relief. In effect, this is a guarantee from HMRC that it will accept R&D claims for three consecutive years.

This procedure is only available to new claimants (including those which have yet to start trading) which have fewer than 50 employees and annual turnover not exceeding £2 million. If another group company has previously claimed R&D relief, then advance assurance is not available.

19.91 HMRC has also issued a practice note setting out how its R&D units will handle claims (CIRD, para 80525). This makes it clear that HMRC will be sympathetic and supportive when dealing with queries from companies or when making enquiries into their claims. However, in return companies will be expected to be open and clear about their R&D activities, and helpful and cooperative if HMRC has any queries concerning their claims.

19.92   HMRC undertakes to issue 95% of payable tax credit claims within 28 days of the specialist unit receiving the claim, or to open any enquiry within 30 days of receiving the claim (although if a tax credit payment has been made, HMRC reserves the right to open an enquiry within the normal statutory time limit, which in most circumstances, is within two years from the accounting period end). During the Autumn statement 2014 it was announced that from 2016 the time taken to process a claim would be reduced.

19.93   A specialist R&D Inspector will normally visit the company's premises to request information and discuss the R&D claim with its management and technical experts. The Inspectors will also not hold themselves out to be scientific or technological experts, but will ask questions and rely on the company's own experts to show that they are competent professionals in the relevant field and have correctly understood the definition of R&D used for tax purposes (see **19.72** *et seq*).

19.94   Inspectors are instructed to take the size of the company and nature of its trade into account and will normally carry out a risk assessment process, focusing on factors, such as whether there is an analysis of how the relief has been arrived at (and whether it is technically correct, or includes arithmetical or typographical errors), the solvency of the company (which may make it difficult to recover money paid out or owed as a result of incorrect claims) and the accounting treatment of the expenditure (CIRD, para 80530). Companies are also encouraged to contact their Inspector in advance if they have any doubts about how the scheme operates, or to discuss how the Inspector will approach the claim and whether the provision of additional information will be helpful in reassuring the Inspector that an enquiry will not be necessary (CIRD, para 80520).

19.95   Inspectors are also told to adopt an open-minded approach about whether activities are R&D and to gather all the facts and listen to the company's representations before making a decision, with the Inspector's aim being to test the information provided against the DTI guidelines and their own instructions. Inspectors are instructed normally to ask the taxpayer to explain in plain, jargon-free language, answers to the following questions:

(*a*)   What was the R&D project, and if relevant what was the larger commercial project?

(*b*)   What were the particular scientific or technological uncertainties involved in the project?

(*c*)   How were the particular uncertainties overcome?

(*d*)   What methods were used to overcome the uncertainties?

(*e*)   Were the methods of overcoming the problems scientific or technological advances, and if so what were those advances?

(*f*)   In what way does the project go beyond what was the current state of knowledge?

(*g*)   Why was the knowledge or capability that they were seeking not readily deducible by a competent professional working in the field?

(*h*)   When were the particular uncertainties overcome?

19.96   Although Inspectors are instructed to be flexible in considering what records will be of assistance to them (CIRD, para 80550) and reminded that reference to underlying records should not be an automatic feature of an enquiry (CIRD, para 80570), nor always be formally documented, HMRC would commonly expect to see contemporaneous project planning documentation (CIRD, para 80560) that may cover:

(*a*)   the aim of the R&D project;

(*b*)   a link between the outcome of the R&D project and its effect on the commercial prospects of the company;

(*c*)   a review of the current state of knowledge;

(*d*)   the difficulties foreseen for the project;

(*e*)   a structure for the project (setting out the activities, who will undertake them, and what the stages are that need to be achieved to get the desired result);

(*f*)   notes on the particular expertise of the R&D personnel involved;

(*g*)   notes on how the uncertainties or other challenges were overcome (or not);

(*h*)   information about any major changes to the aims, or new uncertainties that have been uncovered;

(*i*)   details of any patent applications filed, or how any resultant, identified intellectual property is to be protected;

(*j*)   internal progress reports.

19.97   Where the company has obtained funding for the project, HMRC would also typically look to review funding applications or other relevant documentation, as well as publicity material to provide useful background information (although it accepts that this is likely to focus on the final product and its degree of innovation and customer appeal, rather than concentrating on its scientific or technological uncertainties).

19.98 HMRC's view is also that where the background material shows that the final period is deliverable in a 'short timescale' this may be indicative that there was not the required element of scientific or technological uncertainty needing to be resolved (although no clear boundary exists for a 'short timescale').

19.99 The Inspector may also want to visit the site to see the research and speak to the scientific personnel involved at first hand.

Practicalities

19.100 With this in mind, a well-constructed claim may stress, inter alia, the following features:

(*a*)   the objectives, and in particular the innovative nature of the research, the scientific or technological uncertainties being resolved and the advance being sought;

(*b*)   whether DTI or other grants are received for research and innovation;

(*c*)   the anticipated period of time before research results in a marketable product;

(*d*)   the fact that research is carried out by specific members of staff, who are not involved in production generally;

(*e*)   whether the research is carried out by science graduates;

(*f*)   specific identification of the need to 'take out the thinking side' – ie to remove research staff from the production environment;

(*g*)   specific examples of desired aims and results;

(*h*)   whether production testing will be kept separate, either in an existing building, or in a separate building;

(*i*)   the fact that prototypes are constructed, not to explore commercial viability, but rather to test the results of basic research, or to investigate the possibility of manufacture;

(*j*)   past history of successful innovation and research.

19.101 Even where expenditure does validly qualify for R&D tax relief or allowances, the claim may fail if the true nature of the research is not adequately identified. The steps to be taken vary from the simple (eg not inadvertently describing genuine research as 'product development' on plans and in board minutes) to the more complex. As with any claim for tax relief it is important to establish adequate evidence. In the case of research, it is essential that competent professionals from the particular scientific or technological field are involved in preparing the claim (ideally, the key staff members who carried out the R&D). Furthermore, it may be appropriate to commission one or more independent reports on the nature and purpose of the research by experts in the field. Such scientists will be in the best position to understand the nature of the research – yet another example of the principle that capital allowances claims are not purely the domain of accountants, surveyors and lawyers.

19.102   In *BE Studios* the company specialised in the design, production and sale of computer software for games and other commercial uses, with the aim of producing a better form of software rather than any appreciable element of innovation. It claimed substantial R&D tax credits, which were paid in full by HMRC. However, the High Court held that the payments were made in error and the claims should have been dismissed.

19.103   Evans-Lombe J held that the legislation intended a two-stage process where it was firstly necessary to identify the R&D activities and then establish the qualifying expenditure incurred on them. However, the company had not kept any systematic record of what work its staff were engaged in from day to day and the person who prepared the claim was not a software technical specialist and failed to consult the company's technical personnel. So the company was unable to show that its activities met the necessary criteria (ie what technological advances were being sought and what uncertainties had to be overcome). Instead it focused on the new products' features and benefits and based its claim on the supposition that because it was producing 'innovative' or 'cutting edge' software that permitted uses not at that time achieved by any competitor, then *all* of its work (that was not involved in administration, sales or marketing) must be R&D. This approach was entirely rejected.

PATENTS

General

19.104   The treatment of expenditure on patents will depend on whether the expenditure is incurred by the 'inventor', or whether an existing patent is being purchased from the inventor or a subsequent owner. In addition, expenditure incurred on or after 1 April 2002 *by a company* qualifies for relief under *FA 2002, Sch 29*, rather than by way of capital allowances (see **Chapter 25**). The remainder of this chapter deals with the allowances available before 1 April 2002, and which are still available to individuals.

19.105   The distinction between capital and revenue is as relevant to expenditure on patents as to expenditure on other assets, and the taxpayer should not seek to build up a capital allowances claim where a revenue deduction would be more appropriate. Important cases in this respect are *British Salmson*

Aero Engines Ltd v IRC (1938) 22 TC 29 and *Desoutter Bros Ltd v JE Hanger & Co Ltd* [1936] 1 All ER 535.

19.106   Expenditure, whether capital or revenue, related to the assets which are subject to the patent, rather than to the patent itself, is dealt with in accordance with normal principles, for example, by giving capital allowances in respect of any expenditure on machinery or plant. Allowances can be claimed when the expenditure on the patents has been incurred by a person who:

(*a*)   uses or intends to use the rights for the purposes of a trade which is within the charge to tax ('qualifying trade expenditure') (*ss 467–469*); or

(*b*)   is otherwise liable to income tax or corporation tax on any income from the rights ('qualifying non-trade expenditure').

New patents

19.107   Any fees or expenses incurred in creating or registering one's own patent are treated as a revenue deduction, in accordance with *CTA 2009, s 89*, if the patent is for the purposes of the trade. Otherwise, such costs are allowed by virtue of *CTA 2009, s 924*.

19.108   The cost of renewing or extending the term of a patent are allowed as a trading deduction, as is the cost of an unsuccessful application to register a patent (CA, para 75300).

Existing patents

19.109   For all expenditure incurred on or after 1 April 1986 on acquiring an existing patent, an allowance is given of 25% pa on a reducing balance basis (*s 472(1)*). Prior to that date, allowances were given over a maximum period of 17 years. This unusual writing-down period reflected the life of the patents which between 1949 and 1977 was for an initial period of 16 years with provision for extension (*Sch 3, para 95*).

Rights purchased from a connected person

19.110   In the case of rights purchased from a connected person the expenditure qualifying for allowances is restricted to the relevant amount, namely:

(*a*)   where a disposal value falls to be brought into account, that disposal value;

(*b*)   where no disposal value falls to be brought into account, any capital sum received by the seller and chargeable to tax under *CTA 2009, s 913*;

(*c*)   in any other case, the smallest of:

   (i)   the price which the rights would have fetched in the open market;

   (ii)   any capital expenditure incurred by the seller on acquiring the rights;

   (iii) any capital expenditure incurred by any person connected with the seller (*s 481*).

Definition of patent rights

19.111   Allowances are given for capital expenditure incurred on the purchase of 'patent rights'. 'Patent rights' are defined as 'the right to do or authorise the doing of anything which would, but for that right, be an infringement of that patent' (*s 464(2)*). Any reference to a purchase or sale of patent rights includes a reference to an acquisition or grant of a licence in respect of a patent (*s 466*). Expenditure also qualifies where it is incurred in obtaining a right to acquire, in the future, patent rights in respect of an invention for which the patent has not yet been granted (*s 465*).

19.112   Expenditure on patent rights incurred prior to the commencement of a trade is treated as incurred on the first day of trading, unless the rights have been resold before that day (*s 468(3)*). In such circumstances it appears there is no provision for allowances, and if the rights were sold at a profit, tax could be charged under *CTA 2009 ss 752 and 979* (formerly *ICTA 1988 s 18 Schedule D Case VI*; ie, miscellaneous profits) (corporates) and *ITTOIA 2005, Pt 2* (non-corporates).

Allowances due

19.113   In most respects, allowances for patents mirror those available for plant. All 'new' expenditure is pooled and an annual allowance is given equal to 25% of the written-down value of the pool (ie on a reducing balance basis). This is proportionately reduced if the chargeable period is less than a full year or if the trade has been carried on for only part of the chargeable period (*s 472(2), (3)*).

Disposals

19.114   A disposal value must be 'brought into account' (ie deducted from the pool) whenever patent rights are sold, in whole or in part, or when a licence is granted in respect of such rights (*s 476(2)*). If the disposal proceeds are less than the amount of the pool, the WDA will be given on the net amount. If, on the other hand, the disposal proceeds exceed the value of the pool but not the original cost, there will be a balancing charge equal to the excess (*s 472(5)*, *(6)*). A balancing allowance will be given if the trade is discontinued, or the last of the patent rights included in the pool expire and are not revived (*s 471(6)*). The taxpayer more familiar with plant allowances should note this second event, where the treatment differs from that of plant, where no balancing allowance is given, even if the last plant in a pool has been disposed of.

Example

On 31 March 2005, Monty incurred £30,000 on the purchase of patents rights for use in his trade. The rights had a life of five years. Trade commenced on 30 June. Allowances are given as follows:

		£
Year ended 31.12.2005	Expenditure	30,000
	WDA: 25% 3 6/12	(3,750)
		26,250
Year ended 31.12.2006	WDA: 25%	(6,563)
		19,687
Year ended 31.12.2007	WDA: 25%	(4,922)
		14,765
Year ended 31.12.2008	WDA: 'hybrid' 21.25%	(3,138)
		11,627
Year ended 31.12.2009	WDA: 20%	(2,325)
		9,302
Year ended 31.12.2010	Balancing allowance	(9,302)
		0

Had Monty sold the rights on 30 June 2008 for £15,000, he would have suffered a balancing charge of £235 (£15,000 – £14,765). The disposal value brought into account will be restricted to original cost.

19.115   Where the disposal proceeds exceed not only the written-down value of the pool but also the original cost, the excess over cost is taxable under *CTA 2009* (formerly *ICTA 1988 s 18* Schedule D Case VI) (corporates) and *ITTOIA 2005, Part 2* (non-corporates), in equal parts in each of the next six years, beginning with the year in which the proceeds are received (*CTA 2009, s 913*). The taxpayer may elect within two years for the whole of the excess to be taxed in the year in which the proceeds are received (*CTA 2009, s 913*). Where the election is not made and tax is charged over a period of six years, it is possible that one of a number of events may take place. These include:

(*a*) the death of an individual taxpayer;

(*b*) the winding-up of a taxpayer company; or

(*c*) a change in the members of a partnership.

19.116 When one of these events occurs, there are two consequences prescribed by *CTA 2009, s 918*:

(i) no amount will be charged to tax for any chargeable period subsequent to that in which the event occurs; and

(ii) the amount charged to tax in that period will be increased by any amounts which would otherwise be charged to tax in subsequent periods.

Sale in exchange for shares

19.117 Under ESC B17 (now obsolete), where an inventor sells the patent rights in his invention to a company under his control for less than market value, the assessment on the inventor is limited to actual proceeds, providing the company undertakes to only claim allowances on that amount.

19.118 Where the rights are sold in exchange for shares in that company, HMRC is believed to have accepted that the vendor's tax liability should be computed on the basis that the value of the consideration was the nominal value of the shares, again provided the company undertook to restrict its capital allowances claim by reference to the same figure.

KNOW-HOW

General

19.119 The capital allowances described in this section apply generally to individuals and others chargeable to income tax, and to companies only for expenditure incurred before 1 April 2002. From that date, expenditure incurred by a company qualifies for relief under *FA 2002, Sch 29* (see **Chapter 25**) rather than by means of capital allowances.

19.120 'Know-how' is, almost by definition (see **19.122**), secret knowledge or information. It cannot, therefore, be subject to the same public disclosure, and hence protection, as patents. However, the capital allowances treatment of know-how is, with one important exception, identical to the treatment of patents. All expenditure on know-how is pooled (but pooled separately from other types of asset such as plant or patents). Allowances are given at the rate of 25% pa on a reducing balance basis (*s 458*). Allowances are not given in respect of expenditure incurred on acquiring know-how if the parties to the transaction are connected (*s 455(2), (3)*).

Disposals

19.121 The significant difference between patents and know-how is that when know-how is sold, all disposal proceeds are deducted from the pool. There is no restriction to original cost as with patents where any excess over cost is taxed under *CTA 2009* (formerly *ICTA 1988 s 18* Schedule D Case VI) (corporates) or *ITTOIA 2005, Pt 2* (non-corporates). In the case of know-how, therefore, any excess of proceeds over written-down value will give rise to a balancing charge, taxable in most instances under *CTA 2009 s 35* (formerly *ICTA 1988 s 18* Schedule D Case I; ie, profits from trades) (corporates) (*ss 458(5)* and *462(2)*) or *ITTOIA 2005, Pt 2* (non-corporates).

Definition of know-how

19.122 'Know-how' is defined by *s 452* as:

'any industrial information and techniques likely to assist in –

(*a*)   manufacturing or processing goods or materials;

(*b*)   working a source of mineral deposits (including searching for, discovery or testing mineral deposits or obtaining access to them); or

(*c*)   carrying out any agricultural, forestry or fishing operations.'

19.123 Excluded, therefore, is know-how connected with other fields, for example marketing or financial services.

19.124 This area was the subject of a Revenue Press Release of August 1993 which stated:

'We are sometimes asked whether capital allowances are available for capital expenditure incurred on the acquisition of commercial know-how.

In our view there are no capital allowances available for such expenditure because of the statutory definition of know-how.

[*Section 452*] permits capital allowances to be given on capital expenditure incurred on the acquisition of know-how. "Know-how" is defined at [*s 452(2)*] as "… any industrial information and techniques likely to assist in manufacturing or processing goods or materials …"

The terms of this definition accordingly restrict allowances to capital expenditure incurred in acquiring information relevant only to industrial or technical processes. Information relevant to commercial processes is not included.

Our view is that know-how which does not assist directly in the manufacturing and processing operations is commercial know-how. Examples include information about marketing, packaging or distributing a manufactured product. Such information does not assist directly in the manufacture of that product. Rather it is concerned with selling the product once it has been manufactured.

As such it is not in our view within the definition of know-how in [*s 542(2)*] and so cannot qualify for allowances under [*s 540*].'

Computer software

19.125 Where know-how is held or transmitted by means of computer software (see **15.73** *et seq*), capital expenditure could be eligible for allowances under either heading. The taxpayer will be able to choose which claim is made, which could be important with regard, for example, to a short life asset election, which is not possible where know-how is concerned. Note that, after 1 April 2002, a company wishing to claim capital allowances on computer software has to elect to disapply (*FA 2002, Sch 29*) (see **25.22**).

Acquisition of know-how with a trade

19.126 Where know-how is purchased along with the trade (or part of the trade) to which it relates, any part of the consideration attributed to the know-how is not treated as qualifying for allowances, but rather as a payment for goodwill and therefore not qualifying for tax relief at all (other than on a subsequent sale on which a chargeable gain or loss arises). The person disposing of the know-how is also treated as receiving a sum in respect of goodwill (*CTA 2009, s 178(2)* for corporates and *ITTOIA 2005, ss 193–194* and *ss 583–585* for non-corporates). This treatment does not apply in two circumstances:

(*a*) to the purchaser if the trade was previously carried on wholly outside the United Kingdom; or

(*b*) to either the seller or the purchaser if an election is made jointly by the purchaser and the vendor within two years of the sale (*CTA 2009, s 178(5)*; *CAA 2001, s 454(1)(c)* for corporates and *ITTOIA 2005, ss 193–194* for non-corporates).

19.127 See pro forma election, **Appendix 5**.

19.128 Neither of the above exceptions will apply where the purchaser and vendor are connected or are under common control (*s 455(2)*).

19.129 Where a trade is acquired, the purchaser should investigate whether any part of the consideration may properly be apportioned to know-how, rather than merely to goodwill. Even if the know-how is not of a type qualifying for allowances as such (ie industrial information and techniques), it may be arguable that it qualifies as plant. In *Munby v Furlong* [1977] STC 232, the definition of plant was said to encompass 'the intellectual storehouse which any professional man has in the course of carrying on his profession'.

Restrictive covenants

19.130 Where, in connection with any disposal of know-how, a person gives an undertaking (whether absolute or qualified, and whether legally valid or not) to restrict his or another's activities in any way, any consideration received in respect of the undertaking is treated as consideration for the disposal of know-how (*CTA 2009, s 176(3)* for corporates; *ITTOIA 2005, s 583(1)*). However, this is only true as far as the vendor is concerned and does not apply to the purchaser (CCAB memorandum on the *Finance Bill 1968*). Any such expenditure will not, therefore, qualify for know-how allowances. Furthermore, such a payment is open to be regarded as not made wholly and exclusively for the purposes of the trade and may therefore be denied tax relief under general principles by virtue of *CTA 2009, s 54* – see *Associated Portland Cement Manufacturers Ltd v Kerr* (1945) 27 TC 103. From a tax point of view, such payments should be avoided, although it is recognised that they can be a commercial necessity.

Chapter 20

Transactions within groups and between connected persons

TRANSFER OF ASSETS

Assets other than machinery and plant, know-how and patents

20.1 A general anti-avoidance measure applies (subject to the exceptions referred to below), where either:

(*a*) the buyer is a body of persons over whom the seller has control, or the seller is a body of persons over whom the buyer has control, or both the buyer and the seller are bodies of persons and some other person has control over both of them, or the buyer and the seller are connected (see below) with each other (ie 'the control test') (*s 567(2)*); or

(*b*) it appears with respect to the sale, or with respect to transactions of which the sale is one, that the sole or main benefit which might be expected to accrue to the parties or any of them was the obtaining of an allowance or deduction, the obtaining of a greater allowance or deduction or the avoidance or reduction of a charge (ie 'the tax advantage test') (*s 567(4)*).

20.2 In these circumstances the sale is deemed to have taken place for a consideration equal to the open market value, even if one of the parties to the transaction is resident outside the United Kingdom. The term 'body of persons' includes a partnership (*s 567(3)*).

20.3 The transaction, nevertheless, remains a sale. Consequently, where the transaction took place before 21 March 2007, then for industrial buildings allowance purposes the writing-down allowance had to be re-computed by reference to the number of years remaining out of a period of 25 (or 50) years (see **7.30–7.32**).

20.4 Where one of the parties to the transaction is a pension scheme, the potential risks go beyond the application of the specific capital allowances anti-avoidance legislation. Where tax avoidance is, or could be said to be, involved, it has been suggested that the Audit and Pension Schemes Service could regard this as inconsistent with approval. This might apply in quite routine scenarios, such as a sale and leaseback of property between a company (which could claim capital allowances) and a pension scheme (which could not).

Election by connected persons

20.5   Where the sale is one between connected persons, but no tax advantage as described above is sought, the parties to the sale may elect, within two years of the date of the sale (not within two years of the year end), that the tax written-down value (eg for industrial buildings, the residue of expenditure immediately before the sale), if it is lower, be substituted for the market value (*s 569*). The effect is to transfer any balancing charge, which otherwise would have fallen on the seller, to the buyer and this will manifest itself in the form of reduced allowances and perhaps, ultimately, a balancing charge.

20.6   See pro forma election, **Appendix 5**.

20.7   An election cannot be made:

(*a*)   if the circumstances of the sale (including those of the parties to it) are such that, although falling within the scope of the *CAA 2001*, allowances or charges falling to be made will be incapable of being so made (eg because one of the parties is outside the scope of UK tax) (*s 570(2)(a)*);

(*b*)   if the buyer is a dual resident investing company (*s 570(2)(b)*); or

(*c*)   in the case of a qualifying dwelling-house, unless both the seller and the buyer at the time of the sale are or at any earlier time were approved bodies, as defined in the *Housing Act 1980, s 56(4)* (*s 570(4)*).

Plant or machinery

20.8   *Sections 567–570* do not apply to plant or machinery. Instead, where one of the conditions below applies, no first-year allowance can be made and the purchaser's qualifying expenditure (including any additional VAT) is limited to the disposal value brought into account by the seller (*s 218*). The conditions are:

(*a*)   the purchaser and the seller are connected with each other (see **20.25** *et seq*);

(*b*)   the plant or machinery continues to be used for the purposes of a qualifying activity carried on by the seller or a person connected to the seller (*s 216*) (see **18.77–18.83**); or (*c*) it appears with respect to the sale, or with respect to transactions of which the sale is one, that the sole or main benefit which, but for this section, might have been expected to accrue to the parties or any of them was the obtaining of a tax advantage (*s 215*) (see **20.53**).

20.9 Where no disposal value falls to be brought into account (eg because the vendor is not within the scope of UK taxation) the purchaser's qualifying expenditure is the smallest of:

(i) the market value of the plant and machinery;

(ii) the capital expenditure incurred by the seller on the provision of the machinery or plant; and

(iii) any expenditure on the provision of the plant and machinery incurred by any person connected (see **20.25** *et seq*) with the seller (*s 218(3)*).

20.10 The restriction under *s 218* does not apply where the seller is a manufacturer or supplier, and the plant (which must be unused) is sold in the ordinary course of the seller's business (*s 230*). With effect from 12 August 2011, this exemption applies only providing the sale was not effected for the purpose of obtaining a tax advantage (*FA 2012, s 41*).

20.11 *Section 218* also applies, with necessary adaptation, where a person enters into a contract under which, on the performance thereof, he will or may become the owner of machinery or plant belonging to another person, or is the assignee of such a contract (*s 213*).

20.12 Nothing in *s 218* applies to a short-life asset. Where short-life assets are transferred between connected persons, special rules apply (see **14.187** *et seq*).

20.13 Further anti-avoidance measures were introduced with effect from 25 February 2015, potentially affecting transactions where a person transfers plant to another person but the plant is still available, after the transfer, to be used by the transferor or a person connected with him under the terms of a leaseback under a long funding lease (see **18.43** *et seq*).

20.14 In such circumstances, HMRC perceived there was scope for abuse of the system, which potentially permitted allowances following a sale and leaseback where the seller had not incurred qualifying capital or revenue expenditure.

20.15 Before 25 February 2015, where an asset was sold or transferred, and leased back under a long funding lease, the new owner's qualifying expenditure was limited to the seller's disposal value or (if the seller was not required to bring in a disposal value, generally because its original expenditure was non-qualifying) the lowest of:

- the market value of the asset;

- capital expenditure incurred by the seller; or

- capital expenditure incurred by a person connected with the seller (*s 218*).

20.16   Therefore, if the seller had incurred its expenditure on revenue account (or possibly as non-business expenditure of any kind), the buyer would have been able to make a claim based on market value. From 25 February 2015, for relevant long funding leases, if the seller is not required to bring in a disposal value, and did not incur its expenditure on either capital or revenue account, then the buyer's claim is nil (*s 70 DA (5A)*; *FA 2015, s 46, Sch 10*).

20.17   Where plant which is used for non-trading activities is sold and leased back under a finance lease, *s 222* imposes, generally with effect from 2 July 1997, two further restrictions on the finance lessor (see **18.81**).

20.18   Where one of the parties to the transaction is a pension scheme, the potential risks go beyond the application of the specific capital allowances anti-avoidance legislation. Where tax avoidance is, or could be said to be, involved, it has been suggested that the Audit and Pension Schemes Service could regard this as inconsistent with approval. This might apply in quite routine scenarios, such as a sale and leaseback of property between a company (which could claim capital allowances) and a pension scheme (which could not).

Integral features

20.19   Anti-avoidance provisions may apply where integral features (see **14.5**) are transferred between connected persons. These provisions apply to prevent expenditure on existing assets which *did not* previously qualify for allowances (eg non-qualifying elements of cold water systems) being transferred to a connected person such that a claim would become possible under the new rules on the whole of the original expenditure (*FA 2008, Sch 26, para 15*). In essence, the new owner may only claim allowances on such assets if the vendor had previously claimed allowances.

20.20   However, where an asset *did* previously qualify for plant allowances at the full rate of writing-down allowance, but would now fall to be treated as an integral feature, members of a group may elect to transfer the asset (known as a 'pre-commencement integral feature') such that (i) no balancing adjustment need be made by the transferor (ie the asset is transferred at tax written-down value) and (ii) the expenditure may be allocated to the main pool (not the special rate pool) by the transferee (*FA 2008, Sch 26, para 15*). See pro forma election in **Appendix 5**.

Know-how

20.21 *Sections 567–570* do not apply to sales of know-how. There is, therefore, no requirement to substitute market value for actual consideration. This is a question of practicality, as the market value of know-how, which by its very nature is kept secret and not revealed to any market, would be difficult to establish.

20.22 Note too that for expenditure by companies on or after 1 April 2002, *CTA 2009, Pt 8* applies—see **Chapter 25.**

Patents

20.23 *Sections 567–570* do not apply to sales of patents. Instead, the legislation provides that, in such circumstances, the purchaser's qualifying expenditure is fixed as:

(*a*) where a disposal value falls to be brought into account, that disposal value;

(*b*) where no disposal value falls to be brought into account, any capital sum received by the seller and chargeable to tax under *CTA 2009, s 912*;

(*c*) in any other case, the smallest of –

(i) the price which the rights would have fetched in the open market;

(ii) any capital expenditure incurred by the seller on acquiring the rights; and

(iii) any capital expenditure incurred by any person connected with the seller (*s 481*).

20.24 Also note that for expenditure by companies on or after 1 April 2002, *CTA 2009, Pt 8* applies—see **Chapter 25.**

DEFINITION OF CONNECTED PERSONS

Individuals

20.25 An individual is connected with a person if that person is the individual's spouse or civil partner, or is a relative, or the spouse or civil partner of a relative of the individual or of the individual's spouse or civil partner. 'Relative' means brother, sister, ancestor or lineal descendant. 'Lineal descendant' includes any descendant of the spouse by a previous marriage though not a later marriage (*CAA 2001, ss 575* and *575A* as amended by *ITA 2007, Sch 1, para 411*).

Example

'Person' is connected with all of the individuals in the following chart:

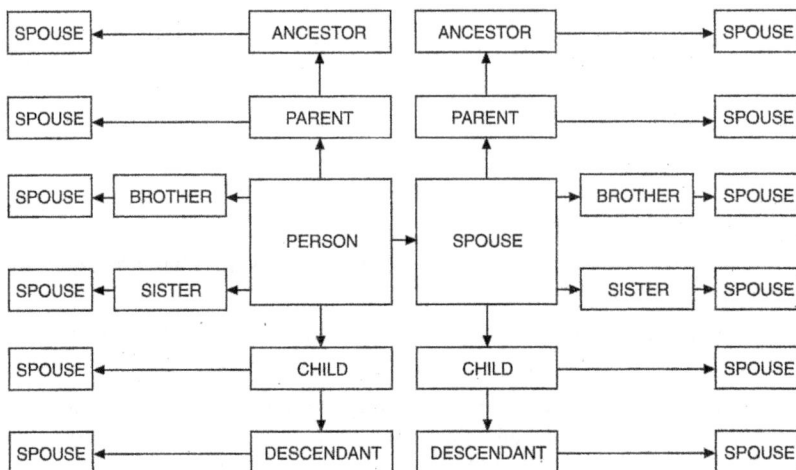

SPOUSE	←	ANCESTOR	ANCESTOR	→	SPOUSE
SPOUSE	←	PARENT	PARENT	→	SPOUSE
SPOUSE ← BROTHER	←			→	BROTHER → SPOUSE
		PERSON →	SPOUSE		
SPOUSE ← SISTER	←			→	SISTER → SPOUSE
SPOUSE	←	CHILD	CHILD	→	SPOUSE
SPOUSE	←	DESCENDANT	DESCENDANT	→	SPOUSE

Settlements

20.26   A trustee of a settlement is connected with any individual who is a settlor in relation to that settlement, with any person who is connected with that settlor and with a body corporate which is deemed to be connected with that settlement. A body corporate is deemed to be connected with a settlement in any year of assessment if at any time in that year:

(*a*)   it is a close company (or only not a close company because it is not resident in the United Kingdom) and the participators then include the trustees of the settlement; or

(*b*)   it is controlled (within the meaning of *CTA 2010, s 1124* by a company falling within (a) above (*CAA 2001, s 575(3)*).

Partnerships

20.27 Except in relation to acquisitions or disposals of partnership assets pursuant to bona fide commercial arrangements, a person is connected with any person with whom he is in partnership, and with the spouse or civil partner or relative of any individual with whom he is in partnership (*CAA 2001, s575(4)*).

Companies

20.28 A company (including any body corporate or unincorporated association) is connected with another company:

(*a*) if the same person has control of both, or a person has control of one and persons connected with him, or he and persons connected with him, have control of the other; or

(*b*) if a group of two or more persons has control of each company, and the groups either consist of the same persons or could be regarded as consisting of the same persons by treating (in one or more cases) a member of either group as replaced by a person with whom he is connected (*CAA 2001, s 575(5)*).

20.29 A company is connected with another person if that person has control of it or if that person and persons connected with him together have control of it (*CAA 2001, s 575(6)*). In a winding-up, it is the liquidator rather than the shareholders who exercises control.

20.30 Any two or more persons acting together to secure or exercise control of a company are treated in relation to that company as connected with one another and with any person acting on the directions of any of them to secure or exercise control of the company (*s 575(7)*). 'Control' has the wide meaning given to it by *CTA 2010, s 450* (principally on the basis of voting rights taking into account the rights of associates). It is the circumstances *at the time of the sale* which are important. In most cases, a company pension fund will *not* be connected with the company itself.

CAPITAL ALLOWANCES BUYING: ANTI-AVOIDANCE

20.31 *FA 2010, Sch 4* inserted a new *Ch 16A* (*ss 212A to 212S*) into *Capital Allowances Act 2001*. These rules target perceived avoidance, where a company is sold (or its ownership otherwise changes) at a time when the tax written-down value of its plant and machinery exceeds the balance sheet value of that same plant and machinery. However, the legislation only targets specific instances where the main purpose, or one of the main purposes, of the change in ownership was the obtaining of a tax advantage. HMRC has confirmed that the legislation will not affect normal commercial arrangements.

20.32   Where the legislation has effect, the amount by which the tax written-down value of a pool exceeds the balance sheet value of the plant in that pool is transferred to a 'new pool', and future losses generated by allowances on that new pool may simply be carried forward against subsequent profits of the same trade, etc. They may not be surrendered by way of group relief, for example. Nor is it possible to transfer a trade (even a similar one) into the loss-making company in order to generate profits against which the 'new pool' allowances may be used.

20.33   HMRC interpretation of the legislation was provided in a Technical Note of 9 December 2009, entitled 'Capital allowance buying: anti-avoidance'.

Where the rules apply

20.34   *Section 212B* sets out the four criteria required for the restriction to apply, namely:

- a company carries on a trade;
- a 'qualifying change' (broadly, a change of ownership) affects the company;
- the company has a 'relevant excess of allowances'; and
- the qualifying change has an 'unallowable purpose'.

20.35   A 'qualifying change' is defined by *s 212C*. The basic position is where a company is acquired by another company (its 'principal company'). In effect the company will be part of a group after the change, whether or not it was a member of a group before the change is irrelevant.

20.36   The definition is extended to include (as well as an outright sale) situations where the company is owned by a consortium or by companies in partnership, and the ownership shares are altered.

20.37   Subsequent sections define relevant terms. Key among these is that a 'principal company' (and therefore the group, or so on, relationship) is defined in terms of 75% ownership (ie mirroring the group relief rules in *CTA 2010*).

Relevant excess of allowances

20.38   *Section 212J* defines a 'relevant excess of allowances' as the amount by which the relevant tax written-down value exceeds the balance sheet value (of the relevant plant).

20.39   One must exclude from the calculation any 'excluded plant and machinery', which is plant that is owned by the company but which is:

- let under a long funding lease (*CAA 2001, s 34A*); or

- hired out under an HP agreement (*CAA 2001, s 67*).

20.40   In each case, allowances would not be available to the lessor or hirer.

20.41   Relevant tax written-down value is defined as the total of any unrelieved expenditure in single asset pools, class pools or the main pool. Any expenditure which could have been added to a pool (but has not been) is deemed to have been added to the pool for the purpose of calculating relevant tax written-down value. It is not possible, therefore, to distort the calculation by failing to allocate expenditure to a pool (with the intention of so allocating it after the change in ownership).

Unallowable purpose

20.42   The rules apply only if the change in ownership, etc is effected for an 'unallowable purpose'. This section defines an unallowable purpose as being where the main purpose, or one of the main purposes, of the 'change arrangements' (transactions or other arrangements connected with the change) is to obtain a relevant tax advantage.

20.43   A relevant tax advantage is defined as becoming entitled to a reduction in profits (or increase in losses) for corporation tax purposes, in consequence of a claim for capital allowances on the plant and machinery relevant to the 'excess of allowances' calculation.

20.44   HMRC confirmed in the Technical Note that the rules will not be triggered simply by the existence of an 'excess of allowances' – the unallowable purpose test has to be in point. Helpful guidance was given in that Note regarding factors that HMRC will consider, including:

- the amount paid, compared to the balance sheet value;

- changes made prior to the change (eg attempts to isolate the 'excess of allowances' from other trading activities);

- whether the trade of the company sold is compatible with that of the acquirer (eg a financial institution acquiring a shipping company would attract attention); and

- the planned conduct of the business – whether the acquirer intends to run the acquired business in the long term.

20.45   HMRC confirmed that normal due diligence covering capital allowances does not imply that obtaining the capital allowances is a 'main purpose'.

Applying the rules in practice

20.46   The comparison of tax written-down value and balance sheet value must be done on a pool-by-pool basis, but the overall results may be netted off. For example, if one pool has excess capital allowances of £300,000 and another has an excess balance sheet value of £50,000, the net relevant excess of allowances is £250,000.

20.47   *Section 212P* sets out the mechanics for applying this new legislation.

20.48   Following the 'qualifying change', the unrelieved qualifying expenditure in each relevant pool is reduced by the amount of the excess of allowances relevant to that pool. The amount of that excess of allowances is transferred to a 'new pool' of the same type (ie singe asset, class or main pool). It will therefore be possible for an affected company to have two 'main pools'.

20.49   Allowances arising in the 'new pool' can be used only in calculating the profits of the existing trade – any trade transferred into the affected company will be regarded as a separate trade entirely. It should be noted that if the company merely expanded its trade, without acquiring an existing trade (previously carried on by another party), this rule would not seem to apply.

20.50   Any loss attributable to allowances in the 'new pool' cannot be surrendered by way of group relief, nor can it be offset against other profits of the relevant company, unless the activity generating those profits was carried on by the relevant company before the qualifying change.

Ships

20.51   These rules are extended to cover postponed allowances in respect of ships.

Later disposal

20.52   Where there is a later disposal of an asset owned at the time of the qualifying change, and affected by the calculation of the relevant excess of allowances, the disposal proceeds must be allocated between the 'relevant pool' (ie the old one) and the 'new pool' on a just and reasonable basis (*s 212R*).

ANTI-AVOIDANCE GENERALLY

20.53   Where *s 215* applies, no first-year allowances are available (*s 217*) and a purchaser's qualifying expenditure on plant is limited, generally, to the seller's disposal proceeds or the seller's original expenditure (see **20.8–20.10**).

20.54   *Finance Act 2012, Sch 9* replaced the existing *CAA 2001, s 215* with a new *s 215* more specifically defining avoidance, and introduced new *s 218ZA* stating how writing-down allowances may be restricted.

20.55   The 'sole or main benefit' test formerly set out in *s 215* was replaced by a new 'avoidance purpose' test that applies where the main, or one of the main, purposes of a party in entering into a transaction (or a scheme or arrangement of which the relevant transaction is part) is to enable any person to obtain a tax advantage (see **20.56**) that would not otherwise have been obtained. The tax advantage may arise to a party to the transaction or any other person.

20.56   A 'tax advantage' is defined in *s 577(4)*. The term includes allowances that are 'greater' or more favourable:

- because the amount of qualifying expenditure has been artificially increased;

- because the allowances have been a claimed at a rate that is too high; or

- because they have been claimed sooner than they should have been.

20.56A For transactions on or after 25 November 2015, *s 215* (see **20.55**) is amended so that the term 'avoidance purpose' includes not only the obtaining of a more favourable allowance, but also the avoidance of a liability for the whole or part of a balancing charge (see **12.46**) to which a person would otherwise be liable.

Furthermore, from the same date, where all or part of a receipt for the disposal of plant or machinery would be ignored in establishing the disposal value of that plant (and hence give rise to a tax advantage), the disposal value of the plant is adjusted in a just and reasonable manner to cancel out that advantage.

This is to nullify avoidance schemes which sought to reduce disposal values below the actual full value attributable to those assets, where the difference in value was being received, directly or indirectly, in such a way as to not form part of the disposal value for capital allowances purposes (*Finance (No 2) Act 2016 s 69*).

20.57 Where a transaction, scheme or arrangement has an avoidance purpose, then the buyer's (B's) allowances are restricted so as to cancel the tax advantage. To this end, the restriction may be:

- to reduce the rate at which B's allowances are calculated (if the tax advantage B would otherwise obtain is allowances at a rate that is too high);

- to reverse any timing advantage sought by B so that B is, in both cases, in the position that B would have been in without the tax advantage; or

- (in other situations) to restrict B's qualifying expenditure to an amount that has the effect of negating the tax advantage.

20.58 If appropriate, more than one restriction may be made to B's allowances.

20.59 If a transaction with an avoidance purpose is also a connected person (see **20.25** *et seq*) transaction or a sale and leaseback, the existing rules in *s 218* (see **20.8** *et seq*) or *s 228* (see **18.82**) must also be considered and the largest applicable restriction made.

Chapter 21

Claiming and disclaiming allowances

INTRODUCTION

21.1   Allowances are only given if claimed (*s 3(1)*). All of the most commonly claimed allowances must be claimed in a tax return.

21.2   In most circumstances, the taxpayer will wish to make the maximum claim for capital allowances. However, individual circumstances may mean that it is better to reduce the amount claimed (tantamount to wholly or partially disclaiming allowances) in any particular year, typically in order to make better use of other reliefs, or if the tax rate is expected to increase significantly (eg a sole trader moving to 40% or 45% marginal income tax). Allowances disclaimed are generally not lost forever; rather the benefit of them is deferred into subsequent years. Following the case of *Elliss v BP Tyne Tanker Co Ltd* (see **21.38**), it has been well established that the benefit of plant allowances may be deferred in this way.

21.3   However, it should be noted that the AIA (see **14.62** *et seq*) must be claimed in the year to which it relates. Any unused AIA may not be carried forward. One consequence of this is where qualifying expenditure is not identified in time to meet self-assessment deadlines for the filing of tax returns but is instead claimed in a subsequent year's return, no AIA is available, only writing-down allowances. Furthermore, land remediation relief (see **Chapter 24**) and research and development allowances (see **Chapter 19**) must be claimed in full in the year expenditure is incurred; otherwise the opportunity is lost.

21.4   Alongside the question of whether to claim, and how much, the taxpayer may also need to consider the further requirements and deadlines that potentially apply from April 2012, where fixtures are acquired second-hand (see **4.16** et seq).

TIME LIMITS FOR CLAIMS AND ENQUIRIES

Companies

21.5   Capital allowances must be claimed in the annual return of profits (*s 3*), for which the filing date is 12 months from the end of an accounting period (*FA 1998, Sch 18, para 14*).

21.6   However, the claimant then has a further 12 months to amend its claim (*FA 1998, Sch 18, para 82*) by amending its tax return (*FA 1998, Sch 18, para 81*) (CA, para 11140). The effect is therefore that a two-year time limit applies in most circumstances.

21.7   If a return is filed on time (ie on or before the due filing date), HMRC may challenge a claim within 12 months from the actual filing date (unless the company is a 'large company, in which case the claim may be challenged within 12 months from the due filing date). If a return is filed late, the time limit is extended to the 'quarter day' following the anniversary of the date the return was filed, ie the 31 January, 30 April, 31 July or 31 October that first occurs 12 months after the actual filing date. If a return is amended (see **21.5** *et seq*) the time limit is extended to the quarter day following the anniversary of the date the amendment was filed (*FA 1998, Sch 18, para 24*).

21.8   HMRC may amend a return to correct any obvious errors (eg arithmetical) within nine months of the day the return was filed, or if the correction is to an amended return, within nine months of the date that the amendment was filed (*FA 1998, Sch 18, para 16*). Also, where the return is subject to an enquiry and HMRC believes that the self-assessment is insufficient and there might otherwise be a loss of tax, it may amend the claim at any stage during the enquiry. Where this happens the company may appeal against the amendment within 30 days (*FA 1998, Sch 18, para 30*). Where HMRC amends a return, the company appeals against such an amendment, or where the return is subject to an enquiry by HMRC, the company may revise its capital allowances claim up to 30 days after notification of the amendment, determination of the appeal, or conclusion of the enquiry (*FA 1998, Sch 18, para 82*).

21.9   HMRC has additional powers to make a 'discovery assessment' where it has not been supplied with sufficient information (*FA 1998, ss 41–45*). For 'careless' actions the time limit is extended to six years from the end of the relevant accounting period (*FA 1998, s 46(2)*) or, in effect, 21 years if there has been negligence or fraud (*FA 1998, s 46(2A)*).

21.10   Some entries on tax returns depend on the valuation of an asset (eg, capital allowances apportionments). In such circumstances, the Court of

Appeal decided in *Veltema v Langham (Inspector of Taxes)* [2004] EWCA Civ 193 that stating the relevant figure on the return does *not* give HMRC the level of information that is necessary to prevent a later discovery assessment. This is because the court concluded that 'information made available' (as defined in statute) must make an Inspector aware of an actual insufficiency in the assessment for that information to be complete enough to prevent the making of a discovery assessment. Or put another way, HMRC must be clearly told that the taxpayer's self-assessment is insufficient (simply because a valuation has been used). Nevertheless, HMRC has provided guidance to give taxpayers some protection against discovery assessments. This guidance (SP1/06) states that:

> 'Most taxpayers who state that a valuation has been used, by whom it has been carried out, and that it was carried out by a named independent and suitably qualified valuer if that was the case, on the appropriate basis, will be able, for all practical purposes, to rely on protection from a later discovery assessment, provided those statements are true' (para 12).

21.11   Taxpayers are, therefore, recommended to make adequate disclosure of all relevant factors.

21.12   A revised claim may only be made by inclusion in an amended return of profits (*FA 1998, Sch 18, para 81*).

21.13   Prior to April 2010 a later claim could be made in some circumstances under the 'error or mistake' provisions. From April 2010, this system of relief was abolished and replaced with 'recovery of overpaid tax' provisions under which it is not possible to remedy capital allowances matters (see **21.23**).

Individuals

21.14   In income tax cases, capital allowances must be claimed in the income tax return (*s 3*) (CA, para 11120), for which the normal due filing date is 31 January next following the year of assessment (*TMA 1970, s 8*).

21.15   No income tax claim may be made more than four years after the 31 January next following the year of assessment to which it relates (*TMA 1970, s 43(1)*). However, this is a general long-stop date that is subject to other provisions, such as those for amending a return to claim capital allowances, which prescribe a shorter or longer date. Most capital allowances must be claimed in a tax return (*s 3(2)*). The only exceptions are allowances in respect of the special leasing of plant or machinery, and patent allowances in respect of non-trading expenditure.

21.16   With these rare exceptions, therefore, capital allowances claims must be made or amended at any time within the normal timeframe for amending an income tax return, which is 12 months after the 31 January following the year of assessment (*TMA 1970, s 9ZA*) (CA, para 11130). To illustrate, this means that a capital allowances claim for the tax year 2011/12 (ie 12-month period ended 5 April 2012) may be made or amended at any time up to 31 January 2014 because the normal tax return filing date of 31 January next following the year of assessment is 31 January 2013 and 12 months after that is 31 January 2014.

21.17   If a return is filed on time (ie on or before the due filing date), HMRC may challenge a claim within 12 months from the actual filing date. If a return is filed late, the time limit is extended to the quarter day (as defined) following the anniversary of the date that the return was actually filed, ie the 31 January, 30 April, 31 July or 31 October that first occurs 12 months after the actual filing date (*TMA 1970, s 9A*).

21.18   HMRC may also amend a return to correct any obvious errors (eg arithmetical) within nine months of the day the return was filed (*TMA 1970, s 9ZB*).

21.19   HMRC has additional powers to make a 'discovery assessment' where it has not been supplied with sufficient information (*TMA 1970, s 29*). For 'careless' actions the time limit is extended to six years from the end of the relevant year of assessment (*TMA 1970, s 36(1)*) or, in effect, 21 years if there has been negligence or fraud (*TMA 1970, s 36(1A)*).

21.20   Some entries on tax returns depend on the valuation of an asset (eg, capital allowances apportionments). In such circumstances, the Court of Appeal decided in *Veltema v Langham* (*Inspector of Taxes*) [2004] EWCA Civ 193 that stating the relevant figure on the return does *not* give HMRC the level of information that is necessary to prevent a later discovery assessment. This is because the court concluded that 'information made available' (as defined in statute) must make an Inspector aware of an actual insufficiency in the assessment for that information to be complete enough to prevent the making of a discovery assessment. Or put another way, HMRC must be clearly told that the taxpayer's self-assessment is insufficient (simply because a valuation has been used). Nevertheless, HMRC has provided guidance to give taxpayers some protection against discovery assessments. This (SP1/06) states that:

> 'Most taxpayers who state that a valuation has been used, by whom it has been carried out, and that it was carried out by a named independent and suitably qualified valuer if that was the case, on the appropriate basis, will be able, for all practical purposes, to rely on protection from a later discovery assessment, provided those statements are true' (para 12).

21.21   Taxpayers are, therefore, recommended to make adequate disclosure of all relevant factors.

21.22   Prior to April 2010, a later claim could be made in some circumstances under the 'error or mistake' provisions (see **21.16**). From April 2010, this system of relief was abolished.

Recovery of overpaid tax claims (previously error or mistake)

Claims made on or after 1 April 2010 – claims for recovery of overpaid tax

21.23   For claims made on or after 1 April 2010, the existing error or mistake rules are abolished and replaced by new 'recovery of overpaid tax' provisions (*FA 2009, s 100* and *Sch 52*). These rules expressly prevent taxpayers rectifying errors in returns that relate to capital allowances, ie where the tax paid or liable to be paid is excessive by reason of a mistake:

- in allocating expenditure to a capital allowances pool, or consisting of making or failing to make such an allocation; or

- bringing a disposal value into account, or consisting of making or failing to make such a value into account.

21.24   The change applies to income tax, capital gains tax and corporation tax.

21.25   It is understood that the legislation was drafted in this way because nothing in statute required a taxpayer who wanted to claim capital allowances to allocate the qualifying expenditure to a capital allowances pool in the period in which the expenditure was incurred. Therefore, flexibility already existed to allocate expenditure to the pool for a later period and it was considered that additional assistance via the recovery of overpaid tax rules was unnecessary. However, in respect of fixtures acquired second-hand from April 2012, additional requirements and deadlines were imposed (see **4.16** *et seq*) which, if not satisfied, mean that this flexibility is no longer available.

Claims before 1 April 2010 – error or mistake claims

21.26   Before 1 April 2010 where a taxpayer failed to claim capital allowances (or related reliefs, such as land remediation relief—see **24.1** *et seq*) within the normal statutory timeframe, it could be possible as a fall back to make a claim for 'error or mistake' relief. Error or mistake claims could cover factual mistakes, misunderstanding of the law, or errors of omission (eg neglecting to allocate expenditure to a capital allowances pool) or commission (eg computational or arithmetical errors).

21.27   The time limit for making an error or mistake claim was no later than six years after the end of the accounting period to which the return relates (corporation tax), or not later than five years after the 31 January next following the year of assessment to which the return relates (income tax) (*FA 1998, Sch 18, para 51* (corporation tax); *TMA 1970, s 33* (income tax)).

Example

A company acquired an office in its year ended 30 September 2004 but failed to claim any capital allowances. The company could claim error or mistake relief within six years after the end of the accounting period to which the return relates (ie by 30 September 2010). However, from 1 April 2010 the error or mistake provisions no longer exist, so any claim needed to have been made no later than 31 March 2010. After that date no claim for relief is possible for capital allowances related errors.

21.28   To claim error or mistake relief, there were several conditions to be satisfied, not least of which that errors of judgment were not protected, so where a deliberate choice was been made between two alternatives (such as claiming less than the full amount of capital allowances) there could be no error or mistake. Furthermore, no relief was available if:

- the return was made in accordance with the practice generally prevailing at that time, or

- in respect of a mistake in a claim or election which was included in the return.

21.29   For both income tax and corporation tax purposes, the relevant legislation sets out the circumstances in which error or mistake will apply, namely:

'If a person who has paid tax under an assessment (whether a self-assessment or otherwise) alleges that the assessment was excessive by reason of some error or mistake in a return, he may ... make a claim to the Board for relief.'

21.30   The legislation then goes on to state:

'No relief shall be given under this section in respect of ... an error or mistake in a claim which is included in the return'.

21.31   Note, the reference to *the* return, that is, the return previously referred to, which has given rise to the excessive assessment.

21.32   HMRC has sometimes sought to interpret this as meaning, in effect, 'a claim which is *required to be* included within *a* return'. That is not what the legislation says. The key issue is whether or not a claim was actually made within the actual return submitted.

21.33 In practice, therefore, error or mistake claims in respect of capital allowances claims were generally resisted by HMRC and only likely to be accepted by HMRC where a taxpayer had, unlike most other taxpayers of its class, failed to identify any expenditure that should have qualified for capital allowances (ie not allocating any expenditure to a capital allowances pool).

Example

Duncan acquired a nursing home in September 2003. The purchase contract included an allocation to fixtures of £10,000, on which Duncan claimed plant allowances. In 2009, Duncan had been advised that a just apportionment (see **4.12**) would have identified expenditure on plant of around £120,000. As more than two years had passed, he was out time for making an emended claim in the usual way, and instead sought to rely on the error or mistake provisions. Whilst some inspectors may accept the claim, others may consider that a valid claim had previously been made (on the £10,000 allocated by the contract), and that Duncan now simply wished to revise the amount claimed.

21.34 Where error or mistake relief was claimed in respect of missed capital allowances, Inspectors were instructed to invite taxpayers to give an undertaking that writing-down allowances and balancing charges due for future years should be computed as if the allowances subject to the error or mistake relief claim, had been claimed in the usual way. The relevant extract from HMRC's former guidance is set out below:

'IM3753a – Error or mistake relief: capital allowances

... If, however, a final and conclusive assessment is based on a return, even if the return shows no claim to capital allowances for that assessment, an error or mistake claim may be admitted provided that the remaining conditions of TMA70/S33 are satisfied and as regards machinery and plant both the terms of FA94/S118 are satisfied [ie notification within two years from the period end, which applied on or before 31 March 1998] the renewals basis has not been claimed or allowed for the period for which the error or mistake relief claim is made.

Where error or mistake relief is claimed by reference to capital allowances which have not otherwise been allowed, taxpayers should be invited to give an undertaking that any capital allowances and balancing charges due for future years should be computed as if the allowances in respect of which the error or mistake relief is claimed had been given in an assessment in the usual way.'

21.35   More recently, Revenue & Customs Brief 12/09 (March 2009) set out HMRC's view of error or mistake claims in the particular context of switching from IBAs to plant allowances, following the announced abolition of the former. It sets out, inter alia, the fact that where there is a choice of allowances, to choose one rather than another on the basis of information available at the time, is not an 'error or mistake'.

21.36   The Brief is set out in full below.

'RECLASSIFICATION OF CLAIMS TO CAPITAL ALLOWANCES

This Brief clarifies the HM Revenue & Customs (HMRC) view that once a business has exercised its choice to claim one type of capital allowance rather than another, that choice may not be revisited and effectively reversed in respect of expenditure incurred in a closed year, under the "error or mistake" provisions.

Introduction

Capital Allowances Act (CAA) 2001 expressly provides that if an allowance is made under one Part of the Act no further allowance may be made under another Part of the Act in respect of the same expenditure.

Following the Government's announcement at Budget 2007 that industrial and agricultural buildings allowances (IBAs & ABAs) would be gradually withdrawn, taxpayers have enquired about the possibility of submitting "error or mistake" claims in order to:

- substitute claims for plant and machinery capital allowances (PMAs) in respect of their expenditure on certain building fixtures;

- for part of their previous IBA or ABA claims on their expenditure on the building as a whole.

This Brief explains HMRC's view that it is not possible to use the "error or mistake" provisions in this way as:

- the error or mistake relief provisions specifically exclude relief for individuals and companies for a mistake in a claim made in a return;

- no relief is due for a mistake in a claim made in a partnership return where the partnership has failed to amend its capital allowances claim within the period allowed.

Background

Choice of allowances

It has always been the case that certain kinds of expenditure may qualify for capital allowances under more than one Part of CAA and that, in these circumstances, taxpayers may decide under which Part of the Act to claim. For example, expenditure on the fixtures incorporated in an industrial building may be included in a taxpayer's claim for IBAs on the building as a whole (under Part 3 of CAA), or the taxpayer may distinguish his expenditure on those fixtures that can qualify for PMAs (under Part 2) from his expenditure on the rest of the building in order to maximise his claim for PMAs.

No double allowances

However, in these cases where expenditure may qualify for allowances under more than one Part of CAA, the legislation makes it clear that double allowances, under different Parts of CAA in respect of the same expenditure, are expressly excluded (section 7 CAA).

A choice, once final, may not be changed

So, in these situations, the taxpayer has a choice about which allowance to claim. And, HMRC's official guidance makes it clear that: "Once a choice has been made to claim one type of allowance the taxpayer cannot change to another in later years." (See section CA31800 of the Capital Allowances Manual.)

Increased public interest since the withdrawal of IBAs & ABAs

However, since the announcement that IBAs and ABAs would be gradually withdrawn by 2011 (which was legislated in Finance Act 2008) there has been an increase of public interest in this area.

Some businesses have written to HMRC to say that, in the past, they had chosen to claim only IBAs (or ABAs, as the case might be) on their expenditure on qualifying buildings, simply for reasons of administrative convenience. In other words, they had been content to claim only IBAs (or ABAs) because those allowances would ultimately give relief on the whole expenditure incurred, albeit at a slower rate and over a longer period, to the extent that any part of that expenditure would also have qualified for PMAs. However, now that the "safety net" of IBAs (or ABAs) is to be withdrawn, they would like to revisit their earlier choices. They have asked HMRC whether they may do so using the "error or mistake" rules.

Error or mistake relief

The relevant "error or mistake" legislation is contained in section 33 and 33A of the Taxes Management Act, for income tax cases, and paragraph 51 of Schedule 18, Finance Act 1998, for Corporation Tax cases. In broad terms, these provisions allow persons who have grounds for believing that the tax they have paid is excessive because of some mistake made in a return to claim repayment of the amounts they have paid.

However, both section 33 TMA 1970 and paragraph 51 schedule 18 FA 1998 deny any relief in respect of an error or mistake in a claim which is included in a return. Claims by individuals and companies in respect of an IBA claim made in a return are therefore expressly excluded.

It is HMRC's view that relief is also not due where the claim was made in a partnership return for two reasons:

In such cases there has been no "error or mistake" where there has been a deliberate choice between permitted alternatives and, at the time that the choice was made, taking into account all the reasons for that choice, it did not clearly disadvantage the taxpayer. The outcome of any choice affecting later tax periods may be uncertain. A decision taken with that uncertainty is not mistaken if subsequent events show that the choice was not the most advantageous. It may be that in some cases where a partnership has claimed IBAs instead of PMAs in respect of some of its expenditure on building fixtures, the business would have obtained more relief had it chosen to maximise its claim to PMAs instead.

Clearly, there was no mistake within the meaning suggested by HMRC's guidance. That gives examples of mistakes which include computational errors, misunderstandings of the law or erroneous statements of fact (see the Self Assessment Claims Manual SACM) at 12015). The official guidance explains that:

"Where a deliberate choice has been made between two alternatives permitted by the Taxes Acts (such as claiming less that the full amount of capital allowances) there can be no error or mistake in the return.

The chosen alternative may not with hindsight prove to be to the best advantage of the taxpayer but it is not incorrect ..." (SACM 12045)

Also, the amount of relief must be reasonable or just having regard to all the relevant circumstances. HMRC considers that it would be neither just nor reasonable to allow partnerships to amend claims to capital allowances outside the period permitted by the Capital Allowances Act 2001 and beyond that available to other taxpayers.

Returns for open years

Finally, whilst it is HMRC's view that the "error or mistake" provisions do not permit a taxpayer to reverse a choice made for an earlier closed year, a taxpayer would nonetheless be able to amend a return in respect of qualifying expenditure incurred in a year for which the return was still open.'

21.37 HMRC has indicated that, where the tax return did not include an original capital allowances claim, an error or mistake claim can be settled within HMRC's 'collection and management' powers (*Commissioners for Revenue and Customs Act 2005, s 5*), as long as a figure is reached which is reasonable and just.

ALLOWANCES ARE NOT MANDATORY

21.38 In *Elliss v BP Tyne Tanker Co Ltd* (1986) 59 TC 474 (see **Appendix 4**), it was held that the company was not obliged to accept capital allowances. Thus, so long as the relevant allowance has not been included in a tax computation (such inclusion would constitute a formal claim), the allowance does not need to be formally disclaimed.

21.39 The legislation is now explicit that all types of allowances may be wholly or partly disclaimed. The relevant provisions are:

Section	*Allowance*
52(4)	Plant (FYAs)
56(5)	Plant (WDAs)
306(2)	Industrial buildings (initial allowances)
309(2)	Industrial buildings (WDAs)
372(3)	Agricultural buildings (WDAs)
441(3)	R&D allowances
458(4)	Know-how allowances
472(4)	Patent allowances.

CHOICE OF CLAIMS

21.40 If expenditure could qualify under two or more headings (eg as plant and as capital expenditure on R&D), double allowances are not possible, but the taxpayer may choose which type of allowances to claim. An exception is where expenditure is incurred on second-hand fixtures on or after 24 July 1996. In outline, such expenditure cannot qualify for allowances (as expenditure on plant) if the fixtures have previously been included in a claim for another type of allowance, for example IBAs or R&D allowances (*s 9*). This rule is disapplied, however, where a claim for IBAs or R&D allowances had previously been made and *s 186* or *187* (see **4.39**) operates to define the amount which a subsequent purchaser may include in a claim for allowances on plant (*s 9(2)*). Where expenditure on a fixture has once been included in a claim for plant allowances, it will henceforth (eg in the hands of a subsequent purchaser) only qualify for allowances as plant, and not under any other heading (*s 9(3)*).

21.41   Generally, no capital allowances are available in respect of expenditure for which a trading deduction is allowed (although see **7.37** *et seq*) (*s 4(2)*). This will apply, for example, to deductions under *CTA 2009*, *s 63* (for corporates) or *ITTOIA 2005*, *ss 60* and *61* (for non-corporates) in respect of short lease premia.

Disclaiming or not claiming allowances

21.42   At first sight, it may appear odd that a taxpayer should decline to take advantage of an allowance granted to him. However, the tax system operates in such a way that it can be advantageous either to disclaim allowances formally, or simply not to claim all that is due.

Avoiding a trading loss

21.43   It may be that capital allowances serve merely to create a trading loss which can only be carried forward to be set against future profits of the same trade. It can happen that losses remain unrelieved, whilst at the same time tax is payable on other sources of income.

Example

Snape Ltd had income and allowances as follows:

	Amount
	£
Year ended 31 March 2014	
Trading profits (before capital allowances)	150,000
Interest	200,000
Capital allowances	1,000,000
Year ended 31 March 2015	
Trading profits (before capital allowances)	750,000
Interest	200,000
Capital allowances	750,000

	Amount

If full allowances were claimed, the two years' tax computations would be as follows:

Year ended 31 March 2014	
Trading profits	150,000
Capital allowances	(1,000,000)
	(850,000)
Interest	200,000
Loss carried forward	(650,000)

Year ended 31 March 2015	
Trading profits	750,000
Capital allowances	(750,000)
	0
Interest	200,000
	200,000
Tax @ 20%	40,000
Loss carried forward*	(650,000)

*The loss carried forward may only be offset against trading profits and not against income generally (*CTA 2010, s 45(4)*). A current year loss may be set off against other income under *CTA 2010, s 37(3)* (see **22.35**).

If some of the 2014 allowances were disclaimed, the position could be as follows:

	Amount
Year ended 31 March 2014	£
Trading profits	150,000
Capital allowances	(350,000)
	(200,000)
Interest	200,000
Loss carried forward	0

	Amount
Year ended 31 March 2015	
Trading profits	750,000
Capital allowances (see note below)	(880,000)
	(130,000)
Interest	200,000
	70,000
Tax @ 20%	14,000

In this example, tax of £36,000 is saved.

Note

Capital allowances:

(a) as previously stated	750,000
(b) on increased expenditure b/fwd (£650,000 × 20%)	130,000
	880,000

21.44   There may be trading losses brought forward, which it is thought appropriate to utilise in the current year, rather than carry them forward. This could result from a variety of special circumstances.

Example

Clarke Ltd had the following income and allowances:

31 March	*Profit/loss Amount*	*CAs Amount*	*Net profit Amount*
	£	£	£
2010	400	400	–
2011	200	300	(100)
2012	200	200	–

At the end of March 2015, the shares in Clarke were sold to an unconnected person in circumstances such that any losses carried forward were likely to be lost, by operation of *CTA 2010, s 674*. Rather than waste losses of £100,000,

Clarke could disclaim allowances in 2015, so that the position in that year was as follows:

	Amount £	Amount £
Profits before CAs		200,000
CAs	200,000	
Less: disclaimed	(100,000)	
		(100,000)
Schedule D Case I		100,000
Losses b/fwd		(100,000)
		0

In this way, no losses will be wasted. In effect, the losses will have been converted into an increased general pool of expenditure to give increased capital allowances in the future. This might even increase the value of the company, and hence the amount the purchaser is willing to pay.

Generating or avoiding a balancing adjustment

21.45   On occasions, the taxpayer may know or believe that an asset is shortly to be sold, giving rise to a balancing allowance or charge. Disclaiming allowances will increase the tax written-down value of the asset carried forward and hence reduce a balancing charge (or increase a balancing allowance). A disclaimer is often worthwhile where a balancing charge would cause tax to be paid at a higher rate.

21.46   Balancing charges can arise in connection with plant and machinery, for example when dealing with short-life assets, or where disposal proceeds exceed the written-down value of the general pool. However, balancing charges have most commonly been an issue in connection with industrial buildings allowances. From 21 March 2007, the disposal of an industrial building no longer gave rise to a balancing event (ie a charge or allowance).

Impact of foreign taxes

21.47   Disclaiming allowances to increase profits may be advisable where some income has arisen abroad and has been charged to foreign tax. This foreign tax can normally be offset against UK tax, but where the foreign tax is greater, the excess is lost.

Example

Hughes Ltd, which is part of a large group, in the year ended 31 March 2015, has the following sources of income.

	Amount
	£
Trading profits	115,000
(before capital allowances)	
Less capital allowances	(100,000)
	15,000

Foreign tax of £8,000 has been paid on £40,000 of these profits. If no disclaimer of allowances is made, the position will be as follows:

	Amount
	£
Taxable profits	15,000
UK tax @ 20%	3,000
Less foreign tax	(3,000)
Tax payable	Nil

However the balance of the foreign tax (£5,000) is wasted. Hughes will effectively have paid tax on its total income at a rate of over 53%. If sufficient allowances were disclaimed, this could be avoided.

	Amount
	£
Profits	115,000
Capital allowances	(75,000)
Taxable profits	40,000
UK tax @ 20%	8,000
Less foreign tax	(8,000)
Tax payable	Nil

Tax suffered is still £8,000 but the value of the capital allowances pool (and hence tax saved in the following year) is greater.

Using group relief

21.48   A company in a group may be able to take advantage of group relief in one year but not in the next, and a disclaimer of allowances will ensure that the fullest advantage can be obtained.

Example

Moss Ltd and Boyd Ltd are in a 75% group until the end of the year ended 31 March 2014, when Boyd Ltd is sold. Relevant figures are as follows:

	2014 Amount £	2015 Amount £
Moss Ltd		
Profits	100,000	300,000
Capital allowances	(80,000)	(150,000)
	20,000	150,000
Tax payable (after group relief)	Nil	£30,000
Boyd Ltd		
Profits	20,000	
Capital allowances	(80,000)	
Available for group relief	60,000	

If Moss Ltd does not disclaim allowances, it will have 2014 profits of only £20,000. Potential group relief from Boyd Ltd of £40,000 will be lost. Tax payable in 2015 will be £30,000. Allowances could be disclaimed in 2014, however, to ensure the following position:

Moss Ltd	*Amount* £
2014	
Profit (before capital allowances)	100,000
Capital allowances	(40,000)
	60,000
Group relief	(60,000)
	Nil

Moss Ltd	*Amount*
	£
2015	
Profit (before capital allowances)	300,000
Capital allowances (note)	(158,000)
	142,000
Tax payable	£28,400
Note	
Capital allowances:	
As previously stated	150,000
Increase arising from disclaimer in previous year (£40,000 @ 20%)	8,000
	158,000

Tax of £1,600 has been saved in 2012 (ie a 5.3% reduction, with further allowances carried forward).

Making use of personal allowances

21.49   For an individual, it is possible that a full capital allowances claim may result in the wastage of personal allowances.

Example

In 2014/15, Wild was assessed on profits of £20,000 and had capital allowances available of £18,000. However the net profit of £2,000 was insufficient to make full use of his single person's allowance of £10,000. If capital allowances of £10,000 were disclaimed, this would be avoided, and higher capital allowances would be available in the following year.

Pension planning

21.50   An individual's personal pension plan contributions will qualify for tax relief only to the extent that they do not exceed that person's net relevant earnings. Disclaiming allowances can therefore be used to increase this figure, and hence increase the funding of the individual's pension.

Conclusion

21.51   Listed above are some of the most common instances of when it may be beneficial not to claim the maximum allowance due. However, there will be others, emanating from the taxpayer's individual circumstances, and the final claim should only be submitted after the taxpayer has considered whether the making of a capital allowances claim ties in with the overall minimisation of his tax liability.

Chapter 22

Interaction with other taxes

VAT

Introduction

22.1   The impact of VAT on capital allowances is often not fully considered by taxpayers or their advisers. Not only will the VAT amounts themselves be large (20% of the net asset cost) but there is also the risk of stringent penalties and interest should the rules be misapplied. Taxpayers who are unable to recover their input VAT fully should particularly take note of the impact of the capital goods scheme, where the capital allowances effect of adjustments is often overlooked.

General

22.2   Where input VAT has been reclaimed, it has not ultimately been borne by the taxpayer. It will not, therefore, attract tax relief, as a revenue deduction, or as expenditure qualifying for capital allowances. Consequently, no allowances will be due in respect of the VAT element of any purchase consideration in such circumstances. However, some taxpayers may not be registered for VAT (eg very small businesses, or landlords who have not 'opted to tax'), or may be making supplies which are exempt from VAT, and be unable to reclaim any input tax (eg the healthcare and financial industries). Where irrecoverable VAT has been charged on assets qualifying for capital allowances, that VAT will form part of the qualifying cost (CA, para 11530).

22.3   Where irrecoverable VAT is to be added to the cost of a new building, the taxpayer should ensure that any zero-rated elements of the construction have been identified. The zero-rating of certain constructions may extend to at least some of the fixtures installed by the builder.

22.4   Where a property is acquired second hand, and the qualifying expenditure on fixtures is based on an apportionment of the purchase price, that apportionment should take account of any irrecoverable VAT incurred by the vendor.

Partially exempt businesses

22.5 If the taxpayer is making a mixture of taxable and exempt supplies (ie a partially exempt business), the input VAT must be apportioned between taxable (ie recoverable) and exempt (non-recoverable) supplies. In fixing the appropriate proportion of the VAT on purchases which is not recoverable, and will therefore qualify for allowances, the deciding factor is not the nature of the goods, assets or services acquired, but rather the mix of the purchaser's sales or other outputs, and the use made of these goods, assets, etc. There are three possibilities:

(*a*)   Assets will be solely used in relation to the making of taxable supplies. The VAT on these assets should be recoverable in full, and will not, therefore, qualify for capital allowances.

(*b*)   Other assets will be used only for making exempt supplies. The VAT on these will not be recoverable, and will, therefore, be added to the net cost of the assets for capital allowance purposes.

(*c*)   Some assets will be of general or mixed use. The VAT on these will be recoverable in part, with the irrecoverable part qualifying for allowances.

22.6 For expenditure on certain assets, the recovery of input VAT by partially exempt businesses is subject to a set of rules known as the capital goods scheme.

Capital goods scheme

22.7 The capital goods scheme (CGS) was introduced from 1 April 1990. It is now set out in VAT Notice 706/2 (19 October 2011). An outline of CGS with an emphasis on its effect on capital allowances is given below, but VAT is a specialist area, and reference should be made to Bloomsbury Professional's *Core Tax Annual: VAT* by Andrew Needham or *VAT on Construction, Land and Property* by Martin Scammell.

22.8 The CGS initially related to two types of asset:

(*a*)   computers or items of computer equipment worth £50,000 or more; and

(*b*)   land and buildings worth £250,000 or more.

22.9 With effect from 1 January 2011 the CGS was extended to apply to capital expenditure on aircraft, ships, boats and other vessels with a VAT-exclusive value of £50,000 or more.

22.10 In the absence of the capital goods scheme, it would be possible for a partially exempt business to acquire such assets in a period when VAT recovery was abnormally high, for example, by using the assets only for producing taxable supplies in the first year, before resorting to more general use subsequently, once the VAT had been recovered. Consequently, in the case of items covered by the scheme, an adjustment is made to the recoverable portion of the VAT (and hence the amount qualifying for capital allowances) where the composition of a partially exempt business's use of the asset changes within a set period of time, this being five years for computers, and ten years for land and buildings. This may apply whether the change is an increase or a decrease in the taxable output as a percentage of the total. The amount qualifying for allowances may therefore, in the case of a building, increase or decrease up to ten years after the original expenditure was incurred.

Example

Manning Ltd purchased a computer for £100,000 plus VAT. The company makes a variety of supplies, 60% of which are taxable for VAT purposes. The total VAT charged on the computer was £100,000 × 20% = £20,000. Of this 60% will be recoverable. The balance will be added to the cost of the building for capital allowance purposes.

	£
Net cost	100,000
VAT (40% × £20,000)	8,000
	108,000
Writing-down allowance @ 20% =	£21,600

In the following year the mix of sales changes, such that the recoverable VAT fraction rises to 75%. An adjustment is made to the VAT recoverable on the computer as follows. Original VAT × change in recoverable proportion × 1/5. £20,000 × (75% – 60%) × 1/5 = £600. This amount will be repaid to Manning. The impact on capital allowances is as follows:

	£
Balance b/fwd (£108,000 – £21,600)	86,400
VAT rebate	(600)
	85,800
Writing-down allowance (£85,800 × 20%) =	£17,160

In year three, the mix of sales changes again, taxable supplies accounting for only 55% of the total. The VAT adjustment due under the capital goods scheme is as follows. £20,000 × (60% – 55%) × 1/5 = £200. Because the recoverable

VAT fraction has fallen below what it was on the purchase of the computer, this further amount will be payable by Manning. Capital allowances will be:

	£
Brought fwd (£85,800 – £17,160)	68,640
VAT liability	200
	68,840
Writing-down allowance (£68,840 × 20%) =	£13,768

These annual adjustments will continue for five years (unless, of course, the computer is sold before the end of that time).

The calculation is unaffected by changes to the rate of VAT itself.

Effective date of VAT rebate or additional liability

22.11   The general rule is that the date in question is the last day of the 'relevant VAT period of adjustment' (*s 548(1)*). These are those periods (normally one year) for which adjustments are made under the capital goods scheme, and the relevant one is the one in which a particular adjustment is made (*s 548(1)*). This date is the key one, therefore, for determining, inter alia, whether the event arises in the life of an enterprise zone, or whether the asset (if plant) has belonged to the claimant at the right time.

22.12   Because an additional liability or rebate will arise, in practice, some time after the event which triggered it and in a VAT interval not likely to coincide with a chargeable period, a number of practical difficulties have to be coped with. Consequently, a supplementary set of rules applies and applies for this purpose only.

22.13   An additional VAT liability or rebate is, for determining the chargeable period for capital allowances purposes, regarded as incurred or made at a time determined in accordance with the following paragraph. For all other purposes (eg determining the rate of allowance), the liability or rebate continues to be treated as incurred or made on the last day of the 'relevant VAT period' (see above). The chargeable period is derived from the following table (*s 549*):

Accrual of VAT liabilities and rebates

Circumstances	*Chargeable period*	*Time of accrual*
The liability or rebate is accounted for in a VAT return.	The chargeable period which includes the last day of the period to which the VAT return relates.	The last day of the period to which the VAT return relates.
The Commissioners of Customs and Excise assess the liability or rebate as due before a VAT return is made.	The chargeable period which includes the day on which the assessment is made.	The day on which the assessment is made.
The relevant activity is permanently discontinued before the liability or rebate is accounted for in a VAT return or assessed by the Commissioners.	The chargeable period in which the relevant activity is permanently discontinued.	The last day of the chargeable period in which the relevant activity is permanently discontinued.

22.14   In the Table:

(*a*)   'VAT return' means a return made to the Commissioners of Customs and Excise for the purposes of value added tax; and

(*b*)   'the relevant activity' means the trade or, in relation to Part 2, the qualifying activity to which the additional VAT liability or additional VAT rebate relates.

22.15   Where any allowance or charge is restricted under any capital allowance provision to a proportion only of the capital expenditure or to a proportion only of what an allowance or charge would otherwise have been, then the allowance or charge in respect of any additional VAT liability or rebate is similarly restricted (*s 550*). This will most commonly be seen in the context of non-trade use by individuals.

Example

Watts Bros makes up its accounts to 30 April each year. In January 2010, £70,000 was spent on a new computer and VAT was reclaimed in the quarter ended 31 March 2010. In the year to 31 December 2010, the taxable outputs of the business fell, and a further VAT liability of £3,000 became payable. This was accounted for in a return to HMRC for the quarter to September 2011. For the purpose of deciding in which year the £3,000 qualifies for allowances, it is necessary to look at when it was accounted for to HMRC, ie 30 September

2011. The amount will, therefore, first attract capital allowances in the year to 30 April 2012 (*s 549*). However, for other purposes, including determining what rate of allowance is available, the question is governed by *s 548*, so 31 December 2011 is the relevant date. Any additional VAT liability arising in respect of computer equipment will qualify for first-year allowance if the capital expenditure to which it relates also qualifies.

CAPITAL GAINS TAX

General

22.16　For most taxpayers faced with a large or unusual transaction, it is tempting to put different taxes (or different aspects of tax) into separate compartments, and deal with each in isolation. Consideration of CGT is necessary, however, in those instances where the capital allowances treatment and the capital gains treatment differ, or where one has an impact on the other. The term CGT is used throughout this section to denote both CGT proper, and also corporation tax on gains, which is the equivalent for companies.

22.17　An outline of the interaction between capital allowances and CGT is given below, but CGT is a specialist area, and reference should be made to Bloomsbury Professional's *Core Tax Annual: Capital Gains Tax* by Rebecca Cave and Iris Wünschmann-Lyall.

22.18　It is a common misconception that claiming allowances will reduce the CGT base cost, and hence increase any gain. That this is not the case is made clear by *TCGA 1992, s 41(1)*; HMRC Capital Gains Manual, hereafter CG, para 15401). Furthermore, the submission of a *s 198* joint election to agree the disposal value of plant and machinery fixtures (see **4.44** *et seq*) has no impact on the CGT computation (CA, para 26800). Where a capital loss arises, see **22.28**.

22.19　In most cases, the fact that expenditure qualifying for allowances can nonetheless form part of the CGT base cost will *not* result in double tax relief. This is because the disposal proceeds must be brought into the capital allowances pool, generally giving a reduction in allowances going forward, and in some cases a balancing charge. Therefore, although the capital gain is not increased, proceeds are taxed in another manner. However, this can be avoided where fixtures are concerned, and where an election under *s 198* is made for a low value (see **4.44**).

22.20　In some circumstances claiming land remediation relief can result in a CGT liability (see **24.35–24.36**).

Time of disposal

22.21   For capital allowance purposes, the time of disposal is the earlier of the date of completion and the date possession is given (*s 572* for most capital allowances; *s 451* for research and development allowances). However, for CGT purposes, disposal takes place at the time the contract is made (and not, if different, the time at which the asset is conveyed or transferred) (*TCGA 1992, s 28(1)*). If the contract is conditional (and in particular if it is conditional upon the exercise of an option), the time of disposal is the time the condition is satisfied (*TCGA 1992, s 28(2)*). The effect of these rules is that it is possible for the vendor of an asset to have a chargeable gain on that asset in one period and then a balancing charge in the next.

Example

Warren Ltd, which makes up accounts to 31 March each year, sold a building in such circumstances that gave rise to a balancing charge and a chargeable gain. Contracts were exchanged on 18 March 2010, and completion took place two weeks later. The chargeable gain will arise in the year ended 31 March 2010, and tax will be payable on 1 January 2011. However, the balancing charge (and the additional tax payable as a result) will not arise until one year later, as completion took place after an accounting year end.

Capital sums derived from assets

22.22   For CGT purposes, the realisation of a capital sum is in various circumstances deemed to be a disposal. This includes:

(*a*)   compensation for damage to assets, or for loss, destruction, dissipation or depreciation of assets;

(*b*)   insurance proceeds;

(*c*)   capital sums received for forfeiture or surrender of rights; and

(*d*)   capital sums received for the use or exploitation of assets (*TCGA 1992, s 22(1)*).

22.23   In such cases, the time of disposal for CGT purposes is the time at which the capital sum is received. Again, this could result in the CGT and capital allowances disposals being taken into account in different accounting periods, although in this case the capital allowances disposal would normally precede the chargeable gain.

Example

Stanley Ltd makes up accounts to 31 March each year. In March 2010, his premises burned down. Insurance proceeds were received six months later. The balancing adjustment for capital allowance purposes will be made in the year ended 31 March 2010. However, the chargeable gain will only arise in the following year upon receipt of the proceeds.

The amount of expenditure qualifying for relief

22.24   There is, of course, a fundamental difference between the time that tax relief is given for capital allowances purposes, and the time relief is given from CGT. Capital allowances are generally given over a period beginning with the acquisition of an asset; as far as CGT is concerned, relief is only given when the asset is disposed of, and various costs may be deducted from the proceeds.

22.25   The CGT cost may differ from the cost for capital allowances purposes. For example, it is unlikely that capital allowances would be available in respect of any right over an asset.

22.26   Alternatively, the cost of a second-hand industrial or agricultural building qualifying for capital allowances may have been limited to the original construction cost. This is not be the case for CGT. For CGT purposes, the deductible costs are:

(*a*)   the amount or value of the consideration given wholly and exclusively for the acquisition of the asset, or for the provision of the asset;

(*b*)   costs incidental to the acquisition of the asset such as fees, commission or remuneration paid for the professional services of any surveyor, valuer, auctioneer, accountant, agent or legal adviser, costs of transfer or conveyance (including stamp duty), and advertising costs;

(*c*)   the amount of any expenditure wholly and exclusively incurred on the asset for the purpose of enhancing its value;

(*d*)   expenditure incurred on establishing, preserving or defending title to, or a right over, the asset (*TCGA 1992, s 38*).

22.27   The capital allowances legislation contains no equivalent provisions to define incidental costs, but in practice those mentioned in (*b*) above will be allowed as part of the cost of an asset.

Restriction of capital losses by reference to capital allowances

22.28 The fact that expenditure has attracted capital allowances does not prohibit deduction of that expenditure in a capital gains computation. However, special rules apply where the result would be a capital loss (*TCGA 1992, s 41*). In the computation of a capital loss, there is excluded from the sums allowable as a deduction any expenditure to the extent that capital allowances have been made in respect of it (CG, para 15410). The allowances referred to comprise not only first-year or writing-down allowances, but also any balancing allowance or charge brought about as a result of the disposal itself (*TCGA 1992, s 41(6)*).

22.29 Where the asset involved is an item of plant which has been included in the pool of expenditure, a balancing adjustment will not generally arise. In such cases, allowances are deemed to have been given of an amount equal to the difference between the acquisition cost and the disposal proceeds. In most cases, this is tantamount to including a notional balancing allowance or charge.

Example

Andrew purchased a machine for use in his business in March 1982 at a cost of £30,000. Capital allowances were claimed and the machine was sold in May 2010 for £10,000. Due to the restriction of capital losses, as set out above, these transactions do not give rise (as would otherwise be the case) to an unindexed loss of £20,000. Instead, the result is as follows:

	£	£
Proceeds		10,000
Less: cost	30,000	
CAs	(20,000)	
		(10,000)
Unindexed 'loss'		0

For disposals prior to 30 November 1993, it was possible to create an indexed loss equal to the indexation allowance (*TCGA 1992, former s 53(1)(c)*). However, this has not been possible for disposals on or after 30 November 1993 (*TCGA 1992, ss 41 and 53(2A)*).

Under *TCGA 1992, s 41*, capital losses are restricted by any capital allowances given (see **22.28**). Where an asset is subject to a long funding lease (see **18.43**), no capital allowances will have been claimed by the lessor and relief for any fall in value will have been given in another form. Consequently, there is an alternative restriction equal to the fall in value of the asset during the term of any long funding leases (*s 41A*).

STAMP DUTY AND STAMP DUTY LAND TAX

General

22.30   An outline of the interaction between capital allowances and stamp duty land tax (SDLT) is given below, but SDLT is a specialist area, and reference should be made to Bloomsbury Professional's *Stamp Taxes* by Ken Wright. SDLT is a significant cost to purchasers of commercial property. Consequently, a large number of transactions have been structured to achieve SDLT savings. Often savings have been achieved only at the cost of losing or significantly reducing the capital allowances available. In many cases, the value of the allowances lost was greater than the SDLT savings made.

22.31   A common arrangement, for example, was for separate legal and beneficial interests to be created and sold to different entities within the purchasing group. In some cases, virtually the whole of the purchase price was allocated to the grant of a new lease, with the freehold (the qualifying interest for capital allowances purposes) being transferred for a merely nominal amount.

22.32   SDLT is a charge on transactions in land, including fixtures (see **11.17** *et seq*). However, it is not charged on chattels or goodwill, so another common technique for mitigating SDLT is to allocate part of the purchase price to these assets. In theory, this reduces the purchase price chargeable to SDLT and tax payable by the purchaser. Although, in practice, HMRC often accepts contract allocations of this kind it should be recognised that contract allocations are *not* always effective and do *not* provide the purchaser with the protection imagined. This is because just like capital allowances (see **4.12** *et seq*), the SDLT legislation requires a 'just and reasonable' apportionment (*FA 2003, Sch 4, para 4*). If a contract allocation is unreasonable, or makes a deduction for items that are not chattels (both of which are likely if arbitrary allocations are used) then HMRC may open an enquiry and revise the apportionment. In *Orsman v HMRC* [2012] UKFTT 277 (TC), the First-tier Tribunal reclassified purported chattels as fixtures, thereby causing the taxpayer to fall above a SDLT threshold.

22.33   It is not necessary for identical apportionments to be used for capital allowances and SDLT, because different types of apportionments are required. Capital allowances apportionments allocate the purchase price between expenditure that qualifies for capital allowances (which may be chattels or fixtures) and expenditure that does not; whereas SDLT apportionments allocate the purchase price between land (ie including fixtures) and non-land (ie chattels and goodwill).

22.34 It is advisable, before implementing *any* structure other than a straightforward purchase, to consider the impact on capital allowances. In particular, the purchaser should ensure that the qualifying interest is being acquired by the 'correct' purchaser, for the 'correct' price. *Section 562(2)* requires all property sold as a result of one bargain to be treated as sold together. Despite this, it is not always possible for capital allowances purposes to simply add together the various elements of consideration, and to ignore the involvement of different purchasers as if the structure did not exist.

LOSSES GENERATED BY CAPITAL ALLOWANCES

22.35 In most cases, capital allowances will be used to reduce current year profits, with tax payable on the reduced amount. Sometimes, however, capital allowances will create or augment a loss, in which case the loss is relievable as follows:

	Trading loss	*Loss from property business (to the extent it relates to capital allowances)*
Individual	Can set against general income, ie total income including employment income of current or *preceding* year (*ITA 2007, s 64*) and then against gains (*ITA 2007, ss 71*) of current or *preceding* year	Can set against general income, but not gains (*ITA 2007, s 120*) of current or *following* year
Company	Can set against total profits, ie all other income, including gains (*CTA 2009, s 2(2)*) of current or *preceding* year (*CTA 2010, s 37(3)*)	Can set against other income, including gains (*CTA 2009, s 2(2) and CTA 2010 s 62*) of current or *following* year

22.36 Losses may also be carried forward to relieve profits of the same trade (*ITA 2007, s 83* (individuals), *CTA 2010, s 45(4)* (companies)) or property business (*ITA 2007, s 118* (individuals), *CTA 2010, s 62* (companies)).

22.37 In the first four years of a trade (but not other types of businesses), an individual may carry back a loss against net income (but not gains) for up to three years (*ITA 2007, s 72*). This relief is restricted to cases where the trade is carried on on a commercial basis with a reasonable expectation of profit (*ITA 2007, s 74*). A terminal loss may be carried back for up to three years to offset profits of the same trade (*ITA 2007, s 89*).

Restrictions on trading losses

22.38 If the individual's involvement in a trade is a non-active one (ie less than ten hours per week), relief against other income under *s 64, 71* or *72* is restricted to £25,000 in any tax year (*ITA 2007, s 74A*).

22.39 Relief under *ITA 2007, s 64, 71* or *72* is not permitted where the loss arises directly or indirectly in consequence of, or otherwise in connection with, 'relevant tax avoidance arrangements', which are essentially arrangements aimed at obtaining relief under these sections (*ITA 2007, s 74ZA*).

Losses from furnished holiday lets

22.40 Since 6 April 2011, losses from a trade of letting furnished holiday accommodation (see **14.112**) may no longer be set against general income (*ITA 2007, ss 127* and *127ZA, FA 2011, Sch 14*). Such losses may only be carried forward (not back or sideways) against future profits from the same furnished holiday lettings business. UK-based furnished holiday lettings properties are treated as one business and European Economic Area (EEA) based properties are treated as an entirely separate business; losses on one cannot be set against the other.

Property losses in avoidance cases

22.41 From 24 March 2010, there are restrictions on the use of property losses to the extent they are attributable to the annual investment allowance (see **14.62** *et seq*), but only where anti-avoidance rules apply.

22.42 The restriction applies where:

- a person makes a loss in a UK property business or overseas property business;
- the loss has a capital allowances connection (defined by *ITA 2007, s 123(2)*); and
- the loss arises in consequence of, or in connection with, relevant tax avoidance arrangements (*s 127A(1)*).

22.43 *Interaction with other taxes*

22.43   If this section applies, no property loss may be relieved against general income to the extent that the loss is attributable to the annual investment allowance (assuming that the loss relates to the AIA before any other deductions or allowances) (*s 127A(2)*).

22.44   'Relevant tax avoidance arrangements' are those which have as their main purpose, or one of their main purposes, to make use of an annual investment allowance to reduce a tax liability by means of property loss relief against general income. Genuine commercial arrangements should not, therefore, be affected.

22.45   These rules apply for arrangements entered into on or after 24 March 2010, unless an unconditional obligation existed before that date.

Chapter 23

International matters

LOCATION OF ASSETS

General

23.1   Assets are often acquired for use abroad. This fact alone does not normally affect the calculation of capital allowances. A largely historical exception for leases finalised before 1 April 2006 is where plant is used for overseas leasing, where the rate of WDA is 10%, rather than the more usual 18%. However, plant allowances are only available for plant which is used for a trade or other qualifying activity (see **14.108**), etc taxable in the United Kingdom (*s 15(1)*) (see **14.111**). Furnished holiday letting properties potentially qualify for allowances provided they are situated in the European Economic Area (see **14.112**). Where overseas tax reliefs, rather than UK capital allowances, are relevant, see **23.25**.

23.2   Any local grant or subsidy has to be taken into account in just the same way as a grant or subsidy from a UK source (see **1.108** *et seq*). However, any equivalent of capital allowances computed for the purposes of foreign taxes does not affect the UK allowances.

23.3   Where UK assets are owned by an overseas person, allowances will still be due, provided of course, that person is taxable in the United Kingdom (*CTA 2009, s 5* for corporation tax, *ITTOIA 2005, s 269(1)* for income tax). In the case of real property, an overseas owner will generally have a UK tax presence. Non-resident investors in a UK property business will generally come within the non-resident landlords scheme (*SI 1995/2902*). Where relevant, capital allowances may be taken into account in determining the net rents on which any deduction of tax by an agent may be required.

Buildings and structures

23.4   Until April 2011, industrial buildings allowances were still available in respect of a building or structure outside the United Kingdom, so long as it was in use for purposes of a trade, the profits or gains of which were computed in accordance with the rules that apply in calculating trade profits for income tax or corporation tax purposes (*s 282*). HMRC's view is that this required those profits to be actually subject to UK tax (CA, para 32850). A company with an overseas trade or vocation chargeable or a person with an overseas trade, profession or vocation chargeable to income tax under *ITTOIA 2005, Pt 2* could still claim, however, because such profits are required to be computed in accordance with the rules of UK trades (*CTA 2009, s 5*) (for corporates) *or ITTOIA 2005, ss 7, 19* and *227* (for non-corporates)).

23.5   Industrial buildings allowances were abolished, following a gradual phasing-out, with effect from 1 April (corporation tax) and 6 April 2011 (income tax) – see **7.15** *et seq*.

ASSETS PURCHASED IN A FOREIGN CURRENCY

23.6   As a general rule, where the amount of expenditure is denominated in a foreign currency, the exchange rate to be used for conversion into sterling is the rate for the date on which the expenditure is treated as incurred for capital allowances purposes.

23.7   So far as the relevant expenditure is incurred under a hire-purchase contract, the rate to be used is therefore, with two exceptions, the rate in force when the asset is brought into use (CA, para 11750). The two exceptions are as follows:

(*a*)   Where the assets acquired are to be used for finance leasing (see **18.21** *et seq*), in which case the exchange rate to be used is that for the day on which each block of expenditure is actually incurred, regardless of the date the asset is brought into use.

(*b*)   Where expenditure is incurred prior to the commencement of a trade. Such expenditure is generally treated as incurred on the first day of trading (see **1.101**). For the purpose of conversion from a foreign currency, the rate to be used is that in force on the date the expenditure is actually incurred, and not that for the first day of trading (CA, para 11750).

IMMIGRATION OF TRADE

Machinery and plant

23.8   When an existing trade comes within the scope of UK taxation, for example, because the company carrying it on has become resident in the

UK, or begun to operate through a branch or agency, capital allowances are available in respect of machinery and plant subject to satisfaction of the normal conditions.

23.9   As regards assets already owned (and previously used abroad), the qualifying cost is deemed to be their market value on the date the trade comes within the scope of UK taxation. The authority for this practice is cited as *s 13*, which refers to plant or machinery being brought into use for the purposes of a qualifying activity. In the circumstances described the plant or machinery will have already been in such use (albeit outside the United Kingdom), however the occasion of a trade first coming within the charge to UK tax is deemed to be a commencement of that trade (*CTA 2009, s 41(2)*). Although *CTA 2009, s 41* only applies to companies, the same treatment is in practice applied to individuals and partnerships.

Industrial buildings and structures

23.10   WDAs will commence when liability to UK tax commences (or, if later, when the building or structure comes into use) and will cease at the end of the writing-down period (usually 25 years from the date of first use). It is not the case that the whole of the original cost may be written off over the period from immigration to the end of the 25 years. For example, if a trade using an industrial building first comes within the charge to UK taxation 15 years after the building's construction, it is *not* possible for the entire cost to be written off over the remaining ten years, as if the immigration of the trade were a balancing event. Though the legislation is unclear, HMRC would argue strongly that the original cost should be reduced to reflect notional allowances arising in the years before immigration to the United Kingdom, as is the case for UK-sited assets that are non-qualifying at the outset, before being brought into qualifying use.

Intangible fixed assets

23.11   Where a company becomes resident in the United Kingdom, any intangible fixed asset which it owns is treated as acquired for its accounting value at that time (*CTA 2009, s 863*).

EMIGRATION OF TRADE

Plant and machinery

23.12   When a company ceases to be within the charge to corporation tax in respect of a trade, that trade is deemed to have been discontinued

(*CTA 2009, s 41(2)*). *CAA 2001 s 61(2)*, *Table*, *items 6* and *7* then applies to require a disposal value to be brought into account (see **12.46** *et seq*). Although *CTA 2009, s 41(2)* deems there to have been only a discontinuance, whereas *s 61* requires there to have been a *permanent* discontinuance, no attempt to differentiate the two is made in practice.

23.13   There are no provisions similar to *CTA 2009, s 41(2)* applicable to persons subject to income, rather than corporation, tax. However, in most such cases there would be an actual discontinuance requiring a disposal value to be brought into account (see **12. 46** *et seq*).

Industrial buildings and structures

23.14   When a company ceases to be within the charge to corporation tax in respect of a trade, that trade is deemed to have been discontinued (*CTA 2009, s 41(2)*). Even prior to 21 March 2007 (when balancing events were generally abolished), such an event was not, however, an event giving rise to a balancing allowance or charge (see **12.9**). The WDAs will cease unless, for example, continued use of the building creates a UK tax liability by reason of there being a 'permanent establishment' in the United Kingdom.

23.15   Although *CTA 2009, s 41(2)* only applies to companies, the same treatment is, in practice, applied to individuals and partnerships.

Intangible fixed assets

23.16   Where a company ceases to be resident in the United Kingdom, any intangible which it owns is treated as realised for its market value at that time (*CTA 2009, s 863*).

Timing of disposals

23.17   Where a trade is leaving the United Kingdom, it may be that some of the assets used in that trade will not be transferred abroad, but will be sold or scrapped in the UK. If such disposal would give rise to a balancing allowance, the disposal should take place *before* emigration; if, on the other hand, a balancing charge would arise, the disposal should be deferred until *after* emigration. It should not be forgotten that if the trade carried on after emigration is substantially different from the previous UK trade, the UK trade will be regarded as having actually ceased, and not just deemed to have ceased.

TRANSFER OF A UK TRADE WITHIN THE EUROPEAN UNION

General

23.18   *EEC Mergers and Divisions Directive (90/434/EEC)* was brought in to ensure (inter alia) that no immediate capital allowance consequences arise on the transfer of a *business* within the EU. The resultant UK legislation (*s 561*) is, however, restricted to the transfer of *trades* (and not any of the other activities which qualify for plant allowances – see **14.108**). The legislation effectively, but not explicitly, ensures that transfers of trade between members of different member states are treated similarly for capital allowances purposes to a transfer between two UK companies under *CTA 2010, s 940*.

Conditions

23.19   *Section 561* applies when:

(*a*)   a qualifying company (A) resident in one EU member state transfers to another qualifying company (B) resident in another member state the whole or part of a trade carried on in the United Kingdom; and

(*b*)   *TCGA 1992, s 140A* applies, causing the transfer of the assets to be treated as made without gain or loss.

23.20   If company B is not resident in the United Kingdom immediately after the transfer it must be carrying on a trade (including whatever trade is transferred to it) in the United Kingdom through a permanent establishment (so that B is subject to UK taxation). A 'qualifying company' is a body incorporated under the law of a member state (*s 561(1)(c)*).

23.21   Relief under *s 140A* is conditional upon the transfer taking place on bona fide grounds and the avoidance of tax must not be the main or one of the main reasons for the transaction. It should be noted that the relief must be claimed jointly by both parties.

Effect

23.22   The application of *s 561* has a twofold effect:

(*a*)   The transfer does not give rise to either a balancing allowance or a balancing charge.

(*b*)   Company B takes over the capital allowances history of the assets so that when it disposes of the assets (other than in circumstances to which *s 561* also applies) there will be a balancing adjustment calculated on the basis that the assets had remained in one ownership spanning the date of the transfer (*s 561(2)*).

23.23 *Section 561A* (introduced by *F(No 2)A 2005, s 56*) ensures broadly the same effect where a SE (Société Européenne – European Company) is formed by a merger involving a UK company claiming capital allowances.

23.24 Where *s 561* applies the following provisions do not apply:

(i)   *s 266* (successions to trades: connected persons);

(ii)   *s 560* (insurance companies: transfers of business);

(iii)   *ss 567–570* (sales without change of control or between connected persons);

(iv)   *CTA 2010, s 628* (companies in liquidation).

OVERSEAS CAPITAL ALLOWANCES EQUIVALENTS

23.25 UK capital allowances are available only where the trade or qualifying activity is taxable in the United Kingdom. Where this is not the case, for example, because overseas assets are held in a foreign subsidiary, the prime concern will be to obtain tax relief in the local jurisdiction. Most countries do not recognise the term 'capital allowances' (Ireland and some commonwealth countries being exceptions). However, an equivalent deduction is usually available, generally in the form of tax depreciation.

23.26 It is useless to set out details of overseas tax depreciation systems, as legislation and practice is constantly changing in each jurisdiction, and action based on outdated information can be dangerous. Specialist professional advice should be sought. Although local tax specialists should be involved, most foreign countries do not have capital allowances specialists, and coordination by a UK-based specialist is likely to optimise the claim.

23.27 It should be helpful, however, to have a checklist of relevant issues. The following has proved useful in preparing claims under a number of European and other jurisdictions:

1   Entitlement   Is entitlement to depreciation based on economic (ie 'beneficial') or legal ownership?

Do different rules apply for fixtures and moveable plant?

Does tax depreciation 'belong to' the person bearing the wear and tear of the assets, even if he does not own them and has not incurred expenditure?

How are the terms 'moveable' and 'fixed' defined (by tax law, land law or commercial practice)?

Are fixtures automatically treated as part of the building, and depreciated over the same period?

Is depreciation permissible for leased property?

Is depreciation possible where a property as a whole is expected to increase in value?

What is the interaction with other taxes, eg VAT, stamp duty/transfer tax, capital gains tax or local taxes?

2	Basis	Does the depreciable cost include all costs of making an asset ready for use, including prime cost, transport, indirect 'on costs', commissioning, etc?

Can professional fees be depreciated?

Is it possible to depreciate taxes incurred on an acquisition (eg transfer tax/stamp duty)?

Can the whole cost be depreciated, or merely the net amount, after taking into account the estimated realisable value?

3	Timing	Does depreciation run from the time the asset is acquired, or when it is brought into use?

Where a project runs over a year-end, what is an acceptable basis for splitting the expenditure on a time basis?

Can estimated interim claims be submitted?

4	Calculation	In the year of acquisition, can a full year's depreciation be claimed?

If not, is expenditure apportioned on a time basis, or do other rules apply? (Eg some countries allow a full year's depreciation for expenditure in the first six months, but only half of the full year's depreciation for expenditure in the second half of the year.)

5	Method	Is depreciation calculated on a straight line or reducing balance basis, or on some other basis?

Does the taxpayer have a choice of depreciation method?

Can the method be changed during the asset's life?

Are second-hand assets subject to different rates?

6	Accounts	Is it necessary for depreciation to be reflected in the accounts, in order to qualify for tax relief?

437

Must the accounts and tax depreciation be identical?

(In some countries, less than the whole of the accounts depreciation may be claimed for tax purposes.)

If depreciation gives rise to a loss, can that be set against other income, carried back or forward, or surrendered to group companies?

What are the appropriate accounts categories?

How much detail must be filed or merely retained?

What are the filing deadlines?

Is there a requirement to make payments of tax 'on account' before the final accounts are filed?

Can rates of allowances be changed retrospectively?

What is the procedure and timescale for a claim to be 'agreed'?

Is there any procedure for obtaining an advance ruling on borderline issues?

7   Rates   Are permissible rates of depreciation set out by statute, or by commercial practice?

What are the permissible rates of depreciation?

Does depreciation of a building depend on the use to which it is put?

Is accelerated depreciation possible where an asset is used more than usual (eg where a factory operates in shifts, on a 24-hour basis)?

Many countries specify a range of depreciation rates for certain assets. How much discretion does the taxpayer have within that range?

Can depreciation be deferred if it is not needed, due to losses etc?

8   Incentives   Are incentives, such as increased or accelerated rates of depreciation, available for small businesses?

Is accelerated depreciation available for expenditure in prescribed geographical areas or development areas, or for certain types of businesses?

Are there incentives for energy-efficient or environmentally-friendly assets or expenditure?

9   Disposal   Is there a clawback of depreciation on disposal?

Can the clawback be 'rolled over' if replacement assets are acquired?

10   Planning   Opportunities for planning should be discussed with a local tax specialist. Various elections may be advisable.

11   Other   Local specialists should be asked for details of other 'quirks' peculiar to a particular jurisdiction.

Chapter 24

Contaminated land

INTRODUCTION

24.1   Tax relief at the rate of 150% is available for expenditure on cleaning up contaminated land and buildings ('land remediation relief'). Although this relief is not strictly a capital allowance, it is available equally on revenue and capital expenditure, and should not, therefore, be overlooked when acquiring land or constructing a building.

24.2   It is important to note that the expenditure must be incurred by a company, *not* by an individual or partnership (*CTA 2009, s 1143*). In appropriate circumstances, therefore, an individual who plans to buy and clean up contaminated land should consider routing the transactions through a company. Due to the different tax rates, this is only likely to be worthwhile where the expenditure would all be on capital account, such that the individual would himself qualify for no tax relief at all. If the individual is, say, a developer, such that the expenditure would attract a trading deduction, a 100% relief at the 40% rate of income tax will be better than a 150% relief at the small companies rate of corporation tax.

24.3   The relief is not available to individuals or partnerships. However, a company that is a member of a partnership can claim relief in respect of its share of the partnership's qualifying land remediation expenditure, provided it satisfies the relevant conditions (HMRC Corporate Intangibles Research & Development Manual, para 60015).

24.4   The legislation operates firstly by allowing capital expenditure to be treated as revenue expenditure, and secondly by granting a deduction equal to 150% of relevant revenue expenditure (including any capital expenditure treated as such under these provisions).

24.5   In Budget 2011, it was announced that the government intended to abolish land remediation relief after 2012, with the final date to be set after consultation. However, this proposal was subsequently dropped.

24.6   The relief is only available where the expenditure is incurred on or after 11 May 2001 (*CTA 2009, Sch 2, para 125*).

DEDUCTION FOR CAPITAL EXPENDITURE

24.7 Capital expenditure on land remediation may be deducted in computing the profits of a trade or UK property business, provided the taxpayer elects in writing for such treatment within two years of the end of the relevant accounting period. This will generally be the period in which the expenditure is incurred, unless the trade is yet to commence, in which case the expenditure is deemed to have been incurred on the first day of trading (*CTA 2009, s 1147*). The claimant company must acquire, or have acquired, a 'major interest' in land in the UK. This is the freehold, or a lease of at least seven years (or where an existing lease is assigned, at least seven years must remain) (*CTA 2009, ss 1147, 1178A*).

24.8 See pro forma election, **Appendix 5**.

QUALIFYING EXPENDITURE

24.9 Expenditure qualifies for the deduction if it relates to employee costs, direct materials, or sub-contractors' costs incurred on relevant land remediation undertaken by the company or on its behalf (*CTA 2009, s 1144*). In *Dean & Reddyhoff Ltd v HMRC Comrs* [2013] UKFTT 367 (TC), it was held that the correct approach in determining whether expenditure was incurred 'in relation to' land was to examine the individual works carried out and to determine whether those particular works met the qualifying conditions (rather than considering as a whole all of the works carried out as part of a wider project).

24.10 The relevant land must be *contaminated*, which means that, because of 'something' in, on or under the land, there is actual or potential 'relevant harm' being done. Relevant harm includes death or significant injury or damage to living organisms, water pollution, a significant adverse effect on the ecosystem, and structural or other significant damage to buildings or other property or interference that significantly compromises their use (*CTA 2009, s 1145*). From 1 April 2009, dealing with arsenic, arsenical compounds and radon also qualifies (*SI 2009/2037*).

24.11 Typical contaminants include hydrocarbons (eg oil, petrol, diesel, bitumen), asbestos, cyanide and chromium.

24.12 However, land cannot be contaminated because of the presence of living organisms or decaying matter deriving from them (*CTA 2009, s 1145(2)*), which means that, for example, the removal of burials or animal droppings does not qualify. An exception is remedying or mitigating the effects of Japanese Knotweed, even if it was not present at the time of acquisition (*SI 2009/2037*).

24.13 *Contaminated land*

The removal of hydrocarbons such as oil or petrol also qualifies because they are too remote from the original living organisms.

24.13 From 1 April 2009 the relief was extended to land in a derelict state (*CTA 2009, s 1146A*). It must have been derelict since the earlier of 1 April 1998 or when the site was acquired. Derelict land is not in productive use and cannot be put to such use without the removal of buildings or other structures, including post-tensioned concrete heavyweight construction, building foundations and machinery bases, reinforced concrete pilecaps and basements and certain below ground redundant services (*CTA 2009, s 1145A* and *SI 2009/2037*).

24.14 From 1 April 2009 it is necessary that the land must have been contaminated as a result of 'industrial activity', for example, construction, manufacturing, mining and quarrying, electricity, gas and water supplies, etc (*CTA 2009, s 1145(2)*). This does not mean that the site must have been in *use* for an industrial activity, as the contamination may be present as a result of industrial activity (eg the construction of a building), even if the land was used for other purpose (eg a retail park).

24.15 Qualifying land remediation has the purpose of preventing, minimising, remedying or mitigating the effects of any harm which contaminates the land, or of returning the land to its former state. Expenditure for this purpose will qualify for the deduction, along with any associated preparatory work, for example, in assessing whether land is contaminated (*CTA 2009, s 1146*). It should be noted that preparatory work of this nature only qualifies for the deduction where the land does, in fact, prove to be contaminated (*CTA 2009, s 1147(3)*). The relief is available for qualifying work on buildings, as well as land itself. Consequently, 150% tax relief may be claimed, for example, on the cost of removing asbestos. This is because although the land remediation legislation only explicitly uses the word 'land', the *Interpretation Act 1978, s 1(5)* states that in any Act, unless the contrary intention appears, words and expressions are to be construed in accordance with *Sch 1* to the *Interpretation Act 1978*, which defines 'land' as including 'buildings and other structures'.

EXCLUSIONS

24.16 The deduction is not available where:

- the land is contaminated due to anything done, or omitted to be done, by the company or a connected person, even if the contamination was normal industry practice, so was not considered to be contamination at the time (*CTA 2009, s 1150*). However, depending upon the facts, HMRC may relax this condition if the contaminant is Japanese Knotweed that has spread, but the company took appropriate specialist advice and acted as soon as practically possible;

- the expenditure has already attracted a tax deduction in a previous accounting period (*CTA 2009, s 1149(7)*);

- the expenditure would have been incurred irrespective of the contaminated land issue (*CTA 2009, ss 1144(3)* and *1147*);

- the expenditure is subsidised (*CTA 2009, s 1144(6)*);

- the land in question is a nuclear site (*CTA 2009, s 1145B*); or

- a capital allowance has been, or may be, made in respect of the expenditure (*CTA 2009, s 1147(8)*).

24.17   It is unclear what is intended by the final exclusion. HMRC's interpretation is that no expenditure on assets which might otherwise qualify for capital allowances (eg plant, or in connection with an industrial building or building qualifying for research and development allowances, etc) can qualify for the deduction.

24.18   However, this would seem to be a narrow interpretation that is unduly harsh on 'industrial' enterprises, if for example, stripping asbestos from an office is to qualify in year one for a 150% deduction, whereas the same work in a factory would qualify only at a maximum of 4% pa, and then only until the impending abolition of industrial business allowances (IBAs) (see **7.15** *et seq*). It is relatively easy to determine whether an allowance *has been* made, but more difficult to assess whether a capital allowance *may be* made. It could rightly be said that even a dwelling *may* attract a capital allowance at some future time if it were used instead for an industrial activity.

24.19   A more logical and pragmatic reading is that the exclusion is simply intended to prevent double-counting by denying land remediation relief where that expenditure has been allocated to a capital allowances pool (given that an allowance may not be made until qualifying expenditure has first been pooled – see **14.3**).

24.20   Capital allowances are of course given for capital expenditure, so if the land remediation expenditure is revenue in nature, the availability of capital allowances is not an issue. If the expenditure is capital, an election is required in order to claim land remediation relief (see **24.7**). The effect of this election is that the capital expenditure is treated as a deduction in computing profits. *Section 4(2)* precludes the claiming of capital allowances for any expenditure treated as a deduction in computing profits, so by definition, once the election has been made, no future capital allowance may be made.

24.21 It has been suggested that where property is acquired at a reduced price because of contamination, any later expenditure on land remediation has, in effect, been subsidised. In most cases, purchase documentation is unlikely to mention the contamination, and consequently this issue is likely to occur only rarely in practice. Indeed, such an argument would be contrary to the spirit of the relief – the government is keen to establish its 'green' credentials, and might therefore take a dim view of a HMRC argument that sought to deny relief in precisely the type of scenario envisaged by the relief.

EMPLOYEE COSTS

24.22 The costs which qualify for the deduction are all earnings consisting of money, certain expenses, pension contributions and secondary Class 1 National Insurance (*CTA 2009, s 1170*).

24.23 Where an employee spends only part of his time in dealing with land remediation, his remuneration, etc qualifies for the deduction in accordance with the following table:

Proportion of time spent dealing with land remediation	*Proportion of remuneration, etc qualifying for deduction*
20% or less	Nil
Between 20% and 80%	The appropriate proportion
80% or more	100%

24.24 The deduction for employee costs does not extend to administrative or secretarial functions (*CTA 2009, s 1171(6)*).

SUB-CONTRACTORS

24.25 Provided the company and the sub-contractor are not connected, the whole of the company's payment to the sub-contractor will qualify for the deduction (*CTA 2009, s 1176*).

24.26 If the company and the sub-contractor are connected, the whole of the company's payment to the sub-contractor will only qualify if (*CTA 2009, s 1175*):

● the sub-contractor has brought the payment into account in calculating his profits; and

- the whole of the expenditure incurred *by* the sub-contractor has been brought into account in computing profits, ie it is not capital in nature, is not subsidised, and has been incurred on materials or employee costs.

RELIEF AT 150%

24.27   Where a company has acquired land in the United Kingdom for the purposes of a trade or UK property business, and then incurs land remediation expenditure, it may make a claim to treat that expenditure as if it were 150% of the actual amount. This applies initially to revenue expenditure, but covers also capital expenditure allowed as a deduction by election under *CTA 2009, ss 1147– 1148 (CTA 2009, s 1149)*.

24.28   It should be noted that the legislation does *not* require the land to be owned by the company at the time the expenditure is incurred. If a company acquires land, then sells it on condition that it will clean it up, it does not matter that the clean-up expenditure is incurred after ownership has passed to the buyer.

24.29   A claim for this relief must be made in the relevant tax return, and can only be amended by amending the return (*FA 1998, Sch 18, para 83H*). The time limit is up to four years after the end of the accounting period for which the claim is made (*FA 1998, Sch 18, para 55*; CIRD, para 60060).

24.30   The detailed rules relating to claims, and penalties for fraudulent or negligent claims, are in *FA 1998, Sch 18, Pt 7*. One important factor is that the amount of the claim must be quantified at the time it is made.

LOSS RELIEF

24.31   If the land remediation relief (ie the 150% deduction) gives rise to a loss, the company may surrender the loss and instead claim a 'land remediation tax credit' equal to 16% of the loss (ie £240 for every £1,000 of expenditure). The company may claim for the tax credit to be repaid to it.

24.32   The loss for this purpose is reduced by any set-off (including group relief) in the current year, but no account is taken of losses brought forward or carried back (*CTA 2009, s 1153*). The effective value of the tax relief available from the loss may be higher though (eg 39% at the full corporate tax rate, or 30% at the small profits rate) and can be carried back, group relieved, or carried forward. So, unless cash flow is the priority, it may be better to wait and offset losses against taxable profits rather than surrendering them for cash.

24.33 A claim for land remediation tax credit must be made in the relevant tax return, and can only be amended by amending the return (*FA 1998, Sch 18, para 83H*). The time limit is up to two years after the end of the accounting period for which the claim is made (*FA 1998, Sch 18, para 83K*).

24.34 The detailed rules relating to land remediation tax credit claims, and penalties for fraudulent or negligent claims, are in *FA 1998, Sch 18, Pt 9B*. One important factor is that the amount of the claim must be quantified at the time it is made.

SALE OF REMEDIATED LAND

Expenditure on capital account

24.35 Where a land remediation tax credit is paid for capital expenditure, on disposal of the asset the tax credit will be partially clawed back or a tax liability may be suffered (depending upon the claimant company's tax rate, eg for every £100 of surrenderable loss, a company taxable at the full 26% rate may have received a £24 tax credit in a loss-making period, but suffer future corporation tax on the additional chargeable gain of £26 on disposal of the asset). This happens because although *TCGA 1992, s 38(1)* allows enhancement expenditure to be included in the capital gains base cost, the land remediation expenditure surrendered to HMRC must be excluded from the calculation in accordance with *TCGA 1992, s 39* (ie it is not an allowable deduction for capital gains purposes) (*CTA 2009, s 1157*; CIRD, para 60115).

24.36 Similarly, although this is not explicitly mentioned in the land remediation legislation, it appears that a land remediation deduction given in relation to capital expenditure will also effectively be partially clawed back on disposal. This is because, as mentioned above, *TCGA 1992, s 39* excludes any expenditure allowable as a deduction in computing the profits or losses of a trade. As land remediation relief for capital expenditure is given as a trading deduction (*CTA 2009, s 1147*) and there is no specific override provision to the contrary that puts land remediation outside the scope of *s 39*, then any land remediation claimed should be deducted from the capital gains base cost on disposal. However, this would only result in a partial claw-back, as 150% tax relief is given, but the expenditure incurred that must be deducted from the capital gains base cost is only two thirds of this amount. Furthermore, a timing benefit still arises from making the claim.

Expenditure on trading account

24.37   Where remediated land is sold as part of a trading activity, there is no provision to claw-back the additional 50% tax credit relating to land remediation relief.

ANTI-AVOIDANCE

24.38   No land remediation relief is given, to the extent that a transaction is carried out for a disqualifying purpose (*CTA 2009, s 1169*). This primarily catches transactions whose aim is to create an entitlement to land remediation relief where it would not otherwise exist, or to artificially inflate the amount of such a claim.

Chapter 25

Goodwill and other intangible fixed assets

INTRODUCTION

25.1   Prior to 1 April 2002, expenditure on most intangible fixed assets did not qualify for tax relief, other than in calculating a gain or loss on a subsequent sale. The only exceptions were computer software (see **15.73** *et seq*) patents and know-how (see **19.104** *et seq* and **19.119** *et seq*).

25.2   For *companies* chargeable to corporation tax, with effect from 1 April 2002 (*CTA 2009, s 889*), relief is given for expenditure on such assets (including goodwill) on the basis of amortisation shown in accounts, or (on election) at a fixed rate of 4% pa. This equally applies to patents and know-how, such that the 'old' capital allowances are not available for new expenditure incurred *by a company*. The allowances remain in place for individuals and others chargeable to income tax.

25.3   From December 2014, tax relief is no longer available where a company acquires goodwill or other intangible assets from related individuals and partnerships. This restriction applies to all direct transfers on or after 3 December 2014 unless made pursuant to an unconditional obligation entered into before that date. Where an accounting period commences before 3 December 2014, the accounting period is split so that this measure only applies to debits arising from the notional accounting period commencing on that date (*CTA 2009, s 849B–D*, inserted by *FA 2013, s 26*).

25.4   Certain assets are specifically excluded from these rules (see **25.20**).

25.5   *FA 2002, Sch 29* (now incorporated into *CTA 2009*) set out a complete system for dealing with both debits and credits relating to intangibles—this chapter concentrates primarily on the debits, to the extent that, like capital allowances, they aim to provide relief for capital expenditure.

25.6   It should be remembered, however, that the amortisation of intangibles is not a capital allowance as such, and consequently the general principles outlined in other chapters may not apply where intangible assets are concerned.

RELIEF FOR COMPANY EXPENDITURE ON INTANGIBLES

25.7   With effect from 1 April 2002, amortisation under *CTA 2009* is the only way that relief is given for capital expenditure by a company on intangibles. So far as patents and know-how are concerned, *CTA 2009* amortisation replaces the capital allowances previously available (*CTA 2009, s 711*). However, *CTA 2009* applies only to companies, consequently 'old style' allowances are still available to individuals, etc chargeable to income tax.

25.8   The amount relieved is:

- the amount of expenditure written off in the accounts on the acquisition of an intangible asset (*CTA 2009, s 728*);

- the amortisation shown in the accounts, pro-rated if the cost for tax purposes differs from the cost in the accounts (*CTA 2009, s 729*); or

- fixed rate amortisation (whether or not charged in the accounts), provided an election is made (*CTA 2009, s 730*) (see **25.11**).

25.9   The accounts must be drawn up in accordance with generally accepted accounting practice – if they are not, such amortisation will be permitted as would have been the case if generally accepted accounting practice had been applied (*CTA 2009, s 716*).

25.10   The taxpayer can elect to write down the cost of an intangible fixed asset at a fixed rate of 4% pa, whether or not the asset is written down for accounting purposes.

25.11   This election must be made within two years of the end of the accounting period in which the asset is acquired or created, and once made, is irrevocable (*CTA 2009, ss 730, 731*). See pro forma election, **Appendix 5**.

25.12   From December 2014, tax relief is no longer available where a company acquires goodwill or other intangible assets from related individuals and partnerships. This restriction applies to all direct transfers on or after 3 December 2014 unless made pursuant to an unconditional obligation entered into before that date. Where an accounting period commences before 3 December 2014, the accounting period is split so that this measure only applies to debits arising from the notional accounting period commencing on that date (*CTA 2009, s 849B–D*, inserted by *FA 2013, s 26*).

DEFINITION OF INTANGIBLE FIXED ASSET

25.13   An intangible asset is one which is regarded as such by generally accepted accounting practice, whether or not the asset is in fact capitalised in the accounts. It is a fixed asset if it is acquired or created for use on a continuing basis in the course of a company's activities (*CTA 2009, s 712*). An option to acquire such an asset is treated in the same way as the asset itself is, or would be, treated (*CTA 2009, s 713*).

25.14   The definition of an intangible asset specifically includes intellectual property, including:

- patents, trademarks, registered designs, copyright or design rights;

- foreign rights equivalent to the above;

- any other information or technique having industrial, commercial or other economic value; and

- a licence or other right relating to any of the above (*CTA 2009, s 712*).

Goodwill

25.15   The rules on intangibles also apply to goodwill, determined in accordance with generally accepted accounting practice (*CTA 2009, s 715*). In some businesses carried out from trade-related properties, such as pubs, hotels, nursing homes, petrol filling stations, restaurants and cinemas, it is common for the property to be sold along with the business that has been trading from the premises. In these circumstances, the sale price will reflect the combined value of the tangible assets, and goodwill will be relevant.

25.16   An HMRC Practice Note of 30 January 2009 confirms the HMRC view that, if a business operating from a trade-related property is sold as a going concern, the sale must include some element of goodwill. The total sale price will reflect the combined value of the tangible and other business assets (eg, contracts with customers, staff and suppliers, customer records, etc) and it is necessary to recognise the contribution that each asset makes to the combined whole. The value of goodwill (plus any other separately identifiable intangible assets) will usually be represented by the difference between the value of the business as a going concern and the value of the tangible assets (ie, the property, fixtures and chattels, etc).

25.17   This follows the decision in *Balloon Promotions Ltd v Wilson* [2006] SpC 524.

25.18 The question to be answered, according to HMRC published guidelines, is not whether goodwill exists but what is the value of that goodwill? That question has to be decided on the facts of each individual case. In some cases the value of the goodwill may be nominal but in some it may be substantial.

25.19 For capital allowances apportionment purposes it is normally appropriate to calculate the value of any goodwill first and deduct this from the total sale proceeds, and then carry out the apportionment of the residual value that relates to the tangible assets (ie, the property, fixtures and chattels, etc).

EXCLUDED ASSETS

25.20 A number of assets are excluded from the application of the *CTA 2009* rules in whole or in part (*CTA 2009, s 712(4)*). The excluded assets include (*ss 803–809*):

- rights over tangible assets;
- oil licences;
- financial assets;
- rights in companies, trusts, etc;
- assets held for non-commercial purposes;
- assets held for the life assurance business of an insurance company;
- assets held for the purposes of a mutual trade or business;
- films and sound recordings;
- computer software treated for accounting purposes as part of the cost of related hardware; and
- other computer software (on election).

Computer software

25.21 Computer software acquired with hardware, and accounted for as part of the cost of the hardware, will qualify as plant for capital allowances purposes, and is exempt from the *CTA 2009* rules (*CTA 2009, s 813*).

25.22 Other computer software qualifies for capital allowances under *s 71* (see **15.73**). However, from 1 April 2002, new expenditure on software will initially qualify for relief under *CTA 2009*, provided it is incurred by a company. If the company wishes to exempt such expenditure from *CTA 2009*, it must make an election within two years of the end of the accounting period in which the expenditure was incurred. Such an election is irrevocable (*CTA 2009, s 815*).

25.23 See pro forma election, **Appendix 5**.

25.24 For taxpayers other than companies, *CTA 2009* does not apply, and consequently, capital allowances are given without the need for an election.

25.25 Companies therefore can effectively choose between capital allowances under *CAA 2001, s 71* and amortisation under *CTA 2009*. Capital allowances will be more generous than fixed rate amortisation under *CTA 2009, s 730* (see **25.9**), but less generous than an immediate write-off under *CTA 2009, s 728* (see **25.8**) or a write-off over a period shorter than (approximately) ten to 15 years.

25.26 Where amortisation is charged in the accounts, the advisability of making an election will depend on the period over the accounting policy used, ie, the period over which the expenditure is written off. Ideally, the correct accounting policy should be determined first, without considering the choice of tax relief, then the advisability of making an election will be determined by a discounted cash-flow calculation.

QUALIFYING EXPENDITURE

25.27 Expenditure which qualifies for relief is:

- the cost of acquiring or creating an intangible asset;

- the cost of establishing, preserving or defending title to an intangible asset; and

- royalties in respect of the use of an asset.

25.28 Where expenditure is incurred only partly for the above purposes, the amount qualifying is to be determined by a just apportionment.

25.29 Where a qualifying intangible asset is acquired together with other assets, the amount qualifying shall be the value allocated by the company in accordance with generally accepted accounting practice. If there is no such allocation, the qualifying amount is determined by a just and reasonable apportionment (*CTA 2009, s 856*).

25.30 This is the case wherever assets are acquired as a result of a single bargain, even if there are, or purport to be, separate acquisitions or separate prices agreed between the parties.

REALISATION OF INTANGIBLE ASSETS

25.31   *CTA 2009* provides for debits or credits to be brought into account when an intangible asset is realised (*CTA 2009, s 733*). Realisation is defined as a reduction in the accounting value of an asset, including the asset ceasing to be recognised in the accounts. Assets without a balance sheet value are treated as if they did have a balance sheet value (*CTA 2009, s 734*).

25.32   A debit or credit (effectively a loss or gain) is brought into account, calculated as the difference between proceeds and net book value. If the asset is not shown in the balance sheet, the credit will be equal to the proceeds (*CTA 2009, ss 735–738*).

25.33   Where assets are sold together, the proceeds are to be allocated on the basis of a just and reasonable apportionment (*CTA 2009, s 856*).

25.34   Where proceeds are reinvested (within a period running from one year before the disposal to three years afterwards), the company may claim to reduce both the proceeds of the old asset and the cost of the new asset (*CTA 2009, s 758*).

25.35   See pro forma election, **Appendix 5**.

25.36   A claim for this relief must specify the old assets to which the claim relates, details of the new expenditure and the amount of the relief claimed (*CTA 2009, s 757*).

CONNECTED PERSONS, ETC

25.37   Where an intangible fixed asset is transferred between connected persons or related parties (see **20.25** *et seq*), the transfer will generally be treated as taking place at market value (*s 845*). However, there are a number of exceptions, where the transfer is treated as being tax-neutral. These include intra-group transfers (*CTA 2009, s 775*) and certain transfers of a business (*CTA 2009, s 818*).

EMIGRATION AND IMMIGRATION

25.38   Where a company ceases to be resident in the United Kingdom, any intangible which it owns shall be treated as realised for its market value at that time (*CTA 2009, s 859*).

25.39 Where a company becomes resident in the United Kingdom, any intangible which it owns shall be treated as acquired for its accounting value at that time (*CTA 2009, s 863*).

TAX AVOIDANCE

25.40 Arrangements aimed mainly at securing a debit (or avoiding a credit) are ignored for the purposes of the *CTA 2009* rules (*CTA 2009, s 864*).

25.41 From December 2014 tax relief is no longer available where a company acquires goodwill or other intangible assets from related individuals and partnerships. This restriction applies to all direct transfers on or after 3 December 2014 unless made pursuant to an unconditional obligation entered into before that date. Where an accounting period commences before 3 December 2014, the accounting period is split so that this measure only applies to debits arising from the notional accounting period commencing on that date (*CTA 2009, s 849B–D*, inserted by *FA 2013, s 26*).

Appendix 1

Rates of allowances

Various types of tax relief are available, depending on the type of expenditure incurred (ie whether capital or revenue) and the person incurring it (ie company or not). This appendix starts by listing the various reliefs available and presented in the order which the taxpayer should generally seek to claim the tax relief:

Type of relief	Qualifying expenditure	Available to	Type of expenditure	Tax relief available
Land remediation relief (see **Chapter 24**)	Cleaning up contaminated land and buildings	Companies only	Revenue and capital	Immediate 150% of expenditure incurred, or payable tax credit equal to 16% of loss
Revenue (see **1.9** *et seq*)	Repairs and maintenance	Companies and non-companies	Revenue	Up to immediate 100% of expenditure incurred
Annual investment allowance from April 2008 to April 2010 (see **14.62** *et seq*)	Capped £50,000 per annum of expenditure on plant or machinery (excluding cars)	Companies and non-companies	Capital	Immediate 100% of expenditure incurred
Annual investment allowance from April 2010 (see **14.62** *et seq*)	Capped £100,000 per annum of expenditure on plant or machinery (excluding cars)	Companies and non-companies	Capital	Immediate 100% of expenditure incurred
Annual investment allowance from April 2012 (see **14.62** *et seq*)	Capped £25,000 per annum of expenditure on plant or machinery (excluding cars)	Companies and non-companies	Capital	Immediate 100% of expenditure incurred

Annual investment allowance from January 2013 (see **14.62** *et seq*)	Capped £250,000 per annum of expenditure on plant or machinery (excluding cars)	Companies and non-companies	Capital	Immediate 100% of expenditure incurred
Annual investment allowance from April 2014 (see **14.62** *et seq*)	Capped £500,000 per annum of expenditure on plant or machinery (excluding cars)	Companies and non-companies	Capital	Immediate 100% of expenditure incurred
Annual investment allowance from January 2016 (see **14.62** *et seq*)	Capped £200,000 per annum of expenditure on plant or machinery (excluding cars)	Companies and non-companies	Capital	Immediate 100% of expenditure incurred
Enhanced capital allowance (see **14.31** *et seq*)	Energy-saving and environmentally beneficial (ie water conserving or quality improving) plant or machinery	Companies and non-companies	Capital	Immediate 100% of expenditure incurred, or payable tax credit equal to 19% of loss
Research and development allowance (see **Chapter 19**)	Equipment and buildings used for research and development	Companies and non-companies	Capital	Immediate 100% of expenditure incurred
Business premises renovation allowance (see **11.61** *et seq*)	Renovation of business premises	Companies and non-companies	Capital	Immediate 100% of expenditure incurred
Flat conversion allowance (see **6.24** *et seq*)	Conversion or renovation of flats (typically above shops)	Companies and non-companies	Capital	Immediate 100% of expenditure incurred
Enterprise zone allowance (see **Chapter 9**)	Commercial buildings in enterprise zones	Companies and non-companies	Capital	Immediate 100% of expenditure incurred
Short-life asset (see **14.179** *et seq*)	Plant and machinery with a short period of ownership	Companies and non-companies	Capital	Up to 100% of expenditure incurred

First-year allowance (see **14.14** *et seq*)	Plant and machinery owned by small or medium enterprises	Companies and non-companies	Capital	40% of expenditure incurred
Plant and machinery writing-down allowance before April 2012 (see **14.99** *et seq*)	Normal (main pool) plant and machinery	Companies and non-companies	Capital	20% per annum reducing balance
Plant and machinery writing-down allowance from April 2012 (see **14.99** *et seq*)	Normal (main pool) plant and machinery	Companies and non-companies	Capital	18% per annum reducing balance
Plant and machinery writing-down allowance before April 2012 (see **14.99** *et seq*)	Integral features plant and machinery and thermal insulation	Companies and non-companies	Capital	10% per annum reducing balance
Plant and machinery writing-down allowance from April 2012 (see **14.99** *et seq*)	Integral features plant and machinery and thermal insulation	Companies and non-companies	Capital	8% per annum reducing balance
Plant and machinery writing-down allowance before April 2012 (see **14.153** *et seq*)	Long-life asset plant and machinery (ie with an expected useful life of 25 years or more)	Companies and non-companies	Capital	10% per annum reducing balance
Plant and machinery writing-down allowance from April 2012 (see **14.153** *et seq*)	Long-life asset plant and machinery (ie with an expected useful life of 25 years or more)	Companies and non-companies	Capital	8% per annum reducing balance
Landlord's energy saving allowance (see **11.52** *et seq*)	Installation of energy-saving insulation to residential property	Companies and non-companies	Capital	Up to immediate maximum £1,500 per property

BUILDINGS

Initial allowances

	%
Buildings used for research and development (see **Chapter 19**)	100
Conversion of business premises into flats (see **6.24** *et seq*)	100
Business premises renovations (see **11.61** *et seq*)	100

Writing-down allowances

	%
Flat conversions (when initial allowance is disclaimed) (see **6.24** *et seq*)	25
Business premises renovations (when initial allowance is disclaimed) (see **11.61** *et seq*)	25

MACHINERY AND PLANT

The most common current allowances are shown in bold

First-year allowances (all enterprises)

	%
Expenditure incurred on or after 1 April 2001 on energy-saving plant or machinery	100
Expenditure incurred on or after 17 April 2002 on electric cars or cars with low CO_2 emissions, or on gas refuelling stations	100
Expenditure incurred between 1 April 2010 and 31 March 2018 (corporates) or 6 April 2010 and 5 April 2018 on zero emissions goods vehicles	100
Expenditure incurred on or after 17 April 2002 in a ring-fence trade	100
Expenditure incurred on or after 17 April 2002 in a ring-fence trade (long-life assets)	24
Expenditure incurred on or after 1 April 2003 on environmentally beneficial plant or machinery	100
First £50,000 (not necessarily earliest) pa of expenditure on plant or machinery, incurred in the two years beginning 1 April 2008 (corporation tax) or 6 April 2008 (income tax) ('annual investment allowance' – see **14.62**)	**100**

First £100,000 (not necessarily earliest) pa of expenditure on plant or **100**
machinery, incurred between 1 April 2008 (corporation tax) or 6 April
2008 (income tax) and 31 March 2012 (corporation tax) or 5 April 2012
(income tax) ('annual investment allowance' – see **14.62**)

First £250,000 (not necessarily earliest) pa of expenditure on plant **100**
or machinery, incurred between 1 January 2013 and 31 March
2014 (corporation tax) or 5 April 2014 (income tax) ('annual
investment allowance' – see 14.62)

First £500,000 (not necessarily earliest) pa of expenditure on plant **100**
or machinery, incurred between 1 April 2014 (corporation tax)
or 6 April 2014 (income tax) and 31 December 2015 (income tax)
('annual investment allowance' – see 14.62)

First £200,000 (not necessarily earliest) pa of expenditure on **100**
plant or machinery, incurred on or after 1 January 2016 ('annual
investment allowance' – see 14.62)

Final £1,000 in pool (so called 'small pools') **100**

Expenditure incurred on plant and machinery in designated assisted **100**
areas within enterprise zones (see **9.45** *et seq*)

Writing-down allowances (reducing balance basis)

	%
Long-life assets (before April 2008)	6
Long-life assets (from April 2008 to April 2012)	10
Long-life assets (from April 2012)	8
Plant used for overseas leasing (leases finalised prior to 1 April 2006)	10
Integral features (from April 2008 to April 2012)	10
Integral features (from April 2012)	8
Thermal insulation of existing buildings (from April 2008 to April 2012)	10
Thermal insulation of existing buildings (from April 2012)	8
Special rate solar panels (from April 2012)	8
Other (main pool) machinery and plant (before April 2008)	25
Other (main pool) machinery and plant (from April 2008 to April 2012)	20
Other machinery and plant (from April 2012)	18

(NB writing-down allowance on expensive cars restricted to £3,000 pa)

459

Land remediation

	%
Expenditure incurred by a company on or after 11 May 2001	150

Business Premises Renovation Allowance

	%
Expenditure incurred from 11 April 2007 to 10 April 2017 – see **11.61**	100

Landlord's Energy Saving Allowance

	%
Expenditure incurred by an individual from 6 April 2004 to 31 March 2015 (maximum £1,500 per dwelling-house) – see **11.52**	100
Expenditure incurred by a company from 8 July 2008 to (maximum £1,500 per dwelling-house) – see **11.52**	100

RESEARCH AND DEVELOPMENT

	%
Capital expenditure	100
Revenue expenditure incurred by a small or medium-sized enterprise between 1 April 2000 and 31 July 2008	150
Revenue expenditure incurred by a small or medium-sized enterprise between 1 August 2008 and 31 March 2011	175
Revenue expenditure incurred by a small or medium-sized enterprise between 1 April 2011 and 31 March 2012	200
Revenue expenditure incurred by a small or medium-sized enterprise between 1 April 2012 and 31 March 2015	225
Revenue expenditure incurred by a small or medium-sized enterprise from 1 April 2015	230
Revenue expenditure incurred by a large company between 1 April 2002 and 31 March 2008	125
Revenue expenditure incurred by a large company (or a small or medium-sized enterprise under the large company scheme rules) after 1 April 2008	130

Examples of machinery and plant

It is impossible to compile a comprehensive list of items qualifying for allowances as plant. This is because a claim is dependent upon many features, not least of which is the context in which the asset is used (see **Chapter 15**). At best, such a list can act as a catalyst in the compilation of an actual claim. The following items are listed for that purpose only. See also (as the context requires) **5.10** for offices and **6.14** for retail premises.

Those in italics are treated as integral features (see **14.5**) if the relevant expenditure was incurred on or after 1 April 2008 (corporation tax) or 6 April 2008 (income tax).

A

Advertising signs, billboards, and hoardings

Aerials

Agricultural drinking and feeding equipment

Air compressors and services

Air-conditioning including ducting and vents

Aquaria

Arc welding plant

Automatic exit doors and gates

B

Battery chargers

Beehives

Bicycle holders or racks

Blast furnaces

Blast tunnels

Blinds and curtains

Boilers

Bowser tanks

Brick elevators

Brick kilns

Bullet resistant screens

Burglar alarms

Bus bars

C

Cable TV provision and ducting

Cameras

Canteen fittings and equipment

Car park illumination and barrier equipment

Carpets and other loose floor coverings

Car wash apparatus, including housing

Cash dispensers (ATMs)

Catwalks

Ceilings – suspended, but only when performing a function, eg an integral part of a ventilation or air-conditioning system

Checkouts

Chilling equipment and insulation

Cleaning cradles (including tracks and anchorages)

Closed circuit television (CCTV) equipment

Compressed air systems

Computers and associated specialised flooring and ceilings

Communications equipment

Conduit for security alarm systems

Conveyor installations

Cooler rooms

Cold water systems for drinking and air-conditioning

Counters and fittings

Cranes, gantries and supports

Crush barriers for safety at sports grounds

D

Dark rooms (demountable)

Data installations

Derricks

Distribution systems

Document hoists and other hoists

Drainage (foul) – if trade-specific

Dry dock

Dry riser installation

Dumb waiters

Dust extraction equipment

Dynamos

E

Electric fences

Electric scoreboards

Electrically operated doors

Electrically operated roller shutters

Electrical substations and generators

Electrical wiring serving an accepted item of plant

Electrical systems

Emergency lighting

F

Fairground and similar amusements

Fans and heaters

Fascia lettering and signs

Fire alarms

Fire protection systems and sprinklers

Fire safety equipment to comply with the requirements of a fire authority

Fitted desks, writing tables and screens

Floodlighting

Floor covering (specialised)

Flooring (movable)

Flooring (raised, but only where incorporating special features necessary for trade)

Freezer rooms

Furnaces

G

Garden furniture (if trade-specific, at a public house, etc)

Gas installations

Generators

H

Hand dryers

Heating installations, fittings, pipes and radiators

Heating systems (post-April 2008)

Hoists

Hoses and hose reels

Hot water services and related plumbing

I

Incinerators

Intercom installations

Internal signs

K

Kitchen equipment

L

Laundry equipment and sluices

Lifts

Lifting and handling equipment

Light fittings and lamps (certain trades, eg hotels, for ambience)

Lighting

Lighting systems (post-April 2008)

Lightning protection systems

Loose floor coverings and doormats

Loose furniture

M

Mechanical gates

Mechanical vehicle barriers

Mezzanine storage platforms (movable)

Movable partitions (where commercial necessity)

Moving walkways

Murals (certain trades, eg hotels, for ambience)

O

Ornaments (certain trades, eg hotels, for ambience)

P

Passenger and goods lifts

Paging systems

Pictures (certain trades, eg hotels, for ambience)

Portable toilets

Power installations

Public address and piped music systems

R

Racking, cupboards and shelving (removable)

Radio and television receivers

Refrigeration installations and cold stores

S

Safety equipment and screens

Sanitary installations

Screens in a window display (movable)

Security screens

Silos

Smoke detectors and heat detectors

Soft furnishings

Software purchased at the same time as the hardware of a computer system

Solar panels

Solar shading (external)

Sound attenuation baffles

Spray and valeting booths

Sprinkler systems

Storage racks, etc

Strong rooms

Switchboards

Switch gear (electrical)

T

Tea and coffee dispensers, vending machines

Telecommunications equipment

Telephone booths and kiosks

Telex and fax systems

Thermal insulation of commercial buildings

Transformers (electrical)

Turnstiles

V

Vacuum cleaning installations

Ventilation equipment

Vents

Vibration control

Video equipment

W

WC partitions (if incidental)

Wash basins and associated plumbing

Waste disposal units

Water tower

Water treatment plant

Weigh bridge

Wet and dry risers

Winches

Window display lighting in shops

Window displays (movable)

Wiring and trunking to accepted items of plant

Works of art (at a museum, or hotel, etc)

Z

Zoo cages

Appendix 3

Location of enterprise zones

Old-style enterprise zone allowances (effectively a variety of industrial buildings allowances – IBAs) were withdrawn from 1 April 2011 (corporation tax) and 6 April 2011 (income tax). Previously, most capital expenditure (buildings as well as, by concession, fixed plant) qualified for 100% first-year allowances.

Although qualifying expenditure can, in some circumstances, be incurred up to ten years after expiry of the zone (subject to abolition in 2011), such instances will now be exceptional. The buyer of a second-hand property may find his claim for allowances on fixtures is restricted if enterprise zone allowances have previously been claimed (*s 186*). He should consider, therefore, whether this is likely to have been the case, and refer to the list of zones below.

In addition, it was announced in 2011 that new enterprise zones would be created – within those zones, there may be so-called 'designated assisted areas'. Expenditure on plant and machinery (but not other assets) used in those designated assisted areas will qualify for 100% first-year allowances.

The complete list of zones is as follows:

Former enterprise zones	*Expiry date*
Lower Swansea Valley (No 1)	10 June 1991
Corby	21 June 1991
Dudley	9 July 1991
Langthwaite Grange (Wakefield)	9 July 1991
Clydebank	2 August 1991
Salford Docks	11 August 1991
Trafford Park	11 August 1991
City of Glasgow	17 August 1991
Gateshead	24 August 1991
Newcastle	24 August 1991

Speke	24 August 1991
Belfast	20 October 1991
Hartlepool	22 October 1991
Isle of Dogs	25 April 1992
Delyn	20 July 1993
Wellingborough	25 July 1993
Rotherham	22 September 1993
Scunthorpe (Normanby Ridge and Queensway)	15 August 1993
Dale Lane and Kinsley (Wakefield)	22 September 1993
Workington (Allerdale)	3 October 1993
Invergordon	6 October 1993
North West Kent (Nos1–5)	30 October 1993
Middlesbrough (Britannia)	7 November 1993
North East Lancashire	6 December 1993
Tayside (Arbroath)	8 January 1994
Tayside (Dundee)	8 January 1994
Telford	12 January 1994
Glanford (Flixborough)	12 April 1994
Milford Haven Waterway (North Shore)	23 April 1994
Milford Haven Waterway (South Shore)	23 April 1994
Dudley (Round Oak)	2 October 1994
Lower Swansea Valley (No 2)	5 March 1995
North West Kent (Nos 6 and 7)	9 October 1996
Inverclyde	2 March 1999
Sunderland—Hylton and Southwick	26 March 2000
Sunderland—Castleford and Doxford Park	26 March 2000
Lanarkshire (Hamilton)	31 January 2003
Lanarkshire (Monkland)	31 January 2003
Lanarkshire (Motherwell)	31 January 2003
Dearne Valley (Nos 1–6)	2 November 2005
East Midlands (NE Derbyshire)	3 November 2005
East Midlands (Bassetlaw)	16 November 2005
East Midlands (Ashfield)	21 November 2005

East Durham (Nos 1–6)	29 November 2005
Tyneside Riverside (No 1)	19 February 2006
Tyneside Riverside (Nos 2–7)	26 August 2006
Tyneside Riverside (Nos 8–10)	21 October 2006

New (2011) designated assisted areas within enterprise zones

It has been announced that a number of new enterprise zones will offer enhanced capital allowances (100% allowances for investments in plant or machinery), or will include locations within designated assisted areas (European state aid rules stipulate that enhanced capital allowances within these areas cannot be offered alongside other forms of regional aid such as selective finance assistance, business rates discounts and so on. Enhanced capital allowances will therefore only be attractive for large, capital-intensive projects where the benefits from ECAs would outweigh other forms of available support) – see **Chapter 9**:

There are 44 enterprise zones across England, 15 in Scotland and 7 in Wales. Only a few of these offer enhanced capital allowances.

Useful further discussion is provided by House of Commons Library Briefing Paper 5942 by Matthew Ward (http://researchbriefings.files.parliament.uk/documents/SN05942/SN05942.pdf).

England:

http://enterprisezones.communities.gov.uk/enterprise-zone-finder.

Scotland:

www.scotland.gov.uk/Topics/Economy/EconomicStrategy/Enterprise-Areas/Incentives/Capital-Allowances.

Wales:

http://business.wales.gov.uk/enterprisezones.

Northern Ireland:

- University of Ulster, Coleraine campus. (In the 2016 Budget it was announced that the Northern Ireland Executive had set the boundaries for the zone and the first investors were expected on site later in 2016).

Appendix 4

Case summaries

Cases are listed in date order.

RE ADDIE & SONS (1875) 1 TC 1

Capital expenditure

The very first case in Volume One of Tax Cases was on the subject of relief (or the lack of it) for capital expenditure. The taxpayers carried on an iron and coal business, and owned a number of mineral fields. They claimed that there should be deducted from their profits for tax purposes amounts in respect of sinking pits and depreciation of buildings and machinery. These amounts were calculated on a percentage basis, not dissimilar to modern capital allowances. The Lord President observed: 'No sum shall be set against or deducted from ... profits or gains on account of any sum employed or intended to be employed as capital in a trade'. Almost identical provisions are now found in *CTA 2009 s 53* (corporation tax) and *ITTOIA 2005 s 33* (income tax). No allowance was therefore due, though of course this apparent injustice was to be remedied in subsequent years.

CALEDONIAN RAILWAY CO V BANKS (1880) 1 TC 487

Allowances/renewals basis

This early case does not sit easily alongside the complex modern system of capital allowances. The Customs and Inland Revenue Act 1878 introduced statutory allowances for wear and tear. The company claimed that it was entitled to such allowances in addition to a deduction for sums actually expended on repairs and renewals. It was held that this was not the case. Lord Gifford opined:

'... the Railway Company cannot get deduction for deterioration twice over—first by deducting the actual expenses of repair and renewal, and then by deducting an additional estimated sum for the same thing.'

However, although relief could not be given twice over, the taxpayer was entitled to choose by which method relief was obtained. The method must be consistently applied, ie it is not possible to claim 'capital allowances' in respect of some assets whilst dealing with others on a 'renewals basis'.

The importance of this case now is in its confirmation, unchallenged to this day, that the renewals basis remains a permissible alternative to formal capital allowances.

YARMOUTH V FRANCE (1887) 19 QBD 647

Plant

This case, though dealing with employer's liability, is renowned as being the source of the most commonly used definition of plant. It remains of great importance, and has been mentioned with approval in a number of higher court decisions, including *Wimpy* and *Scottish & Newcastle* (qv).

The asset in question was a horse. Lindley LJ stated:

'There is no definition of plant in the Act: but, in its ordinary sense, it includes whatever apparatus is used by a businessman for carrying on his business, not his stock-in-trade which he buys or makes for sale; but all goods and chattels, fixed or moveable, live or dead, which he keeps for permanent employment in his business.'

JOHN HALL JR & CO V RICKMAN [1906] 1 KB 311

Plant

The term 'plant' was held to encompass a hulk, which had formerly been a sailing ship, but which had been dismantled and had had its rudder removed and was now used as a floating warehouse for coal. This was not the main point considered by the court, and indeed was barely referred to at all. That the hulk qualified as plant cannot be said to be the outcome of protracted reasoning. The later case of *Benson v Yard Arm Club* is of greater import.

EARL OF DERBY V AYLMER (SURVEYOR OF TAXES) (1915) 6 TC 665

Plant

In this case the taxpayer claimed an annual allowance to represent the gradual diminution in value of two stallions used for breeding purposes. The relevant legislation at that time only envisaged allowances where the assets were subject to wear and tear. Rowlett J decided that the horses did not fall in value by reason of wear and tear, but merely by reason of the passing of time. He compared a horse to machinery which, if it were not used, would not diminish in value. The horses did not fall within the provisions of the legislation as it then stood and hence allowances were not granted. NB this case is often interpreted as showing that horses cannot be 'plant or machinery'.

This interpretation is wrong. Rowlatt J specifically declined to consider whether a horse could ever be plant or machinery. In practice, horses will normally be treated as plant where they perform some function in a business, for example, brewery dray horses, or even showjumpers used for advertising purposes. Capital allowances are not available for production animals dealt with under the herd basis set out in *CTA 2009 Chapter 8 of Part 3* or *ITTOIA 2005 Chapter 8 of Part 2 (s 38)*.

LAW SHIPPING CO LTD V IRC (1923) 12 TC 621

Capital/revenue – repairs

The taxpayer company purchased a second-hand ship at a time when the ship's periodical Lloyd's survey was overdue, but had been deferred pending completion of a voyage. Six months later the survey was carried out, and the company was obliged to spend a large sum on repairs. It was held that only part of the expenditure was properly chargeable to repairs, being in respect of repairs necessitated by the use of the ship since it was acquired by *Law Shipping*. The cost of repairs attributable to the period before *Law Shipping* acquired the ship was to be properly regarded as capital. The need for repairs would have been reflected in a lower purchase price upon acquisition. It is interesting, however, that if the ship had not changed hands, the repairs would have been allowable, even though they had been allowed to build up, and might represent more than one year's wear and tear. The Lord President (Clyde) said:

473

'Accumulated repairs are, in fact, nonetheless repairs necessary to earn profits, although they have been allowed to accumulate.'

The Revenue's published guidance (BIM paragraphs 35455 and 46906) is a reasonably accurate summary of the *Law Shipping* and *Odeon* principles, summarised in paragraph 46906:

- The fact that a taxpayer had repairs carried out just after they acquired the asset does not, of itself, mean that the cost of the repair is disallowable.

- The fact that the repairs were needed when the asset was acquired does not, of itself, mean that the cost of the repair is disallowable.

- The cost of the repair will be a capital expense if it is effectively part of the cost of acquiring the asset.

The Manual goes on to state that whether the cost of the repairs is part of the cost of the asset is a question of fact. It is important to establish the condition of the asset and how the price was arrived at.

Law Shipping is always linked with *Odeon Associated Theatres Ltd v Jones (Inspector of Taxes)* (1971) 48 TC 257(qv).

In that case, Buckley LJ in the Court of Appeal said of *Law Shipping*:

'The *Law Shipping* Co case is, in my view, more nearly analogous to the case of a trader who has bought a capital asset which at the date of acquisition was not in working order and has to put it into working order before being able to use it in his business.'

In practice, one may apply the following principles emerging from *Law Shipping* and *Odeon Associated Theatres*. Namely, that where the purchase price of an asset is reduced to reflect that asset's poor state of repair, and where repairs are necessary before that asset can be used for trading purposes, the cost of those repairs should be treated as capital. *However, where the state of repair is not reflected in the purchase price, and where the asset may be used in the trade without repair, the cost of any repairs should be charged against profits in accordance with normal commercial accountancy principles.*

Where a taxpayer chooses to carry out repairs immediately after acquisition, not because they are necessary, but because it makes commercial sense to do so (eg rather than spending a period of time building up trade, only for the premises to be closed for refurbishment a few months later), the costs should again be charged against profits, *provided of course that the acquisition price was not reduced to reflect the need for those repairs.*

DAPHNE V SHAW (INSPECTOR OF TAXES) (1926) 11 TC 256

Plant

The decision in this case was later overturned by *Munby v Furlong*, but remains of historical interest.

A solicitor incurred expenditure on his law library and claimed that this constituted expenditure on plant for capital allowances purposes. Daphne, who appeared for himself, referred to 'Coke upon Littleton', where there is reference to 'the utensils or instrument of [a] trade or profession, [such] as the axe of the carpenter, or the books of a scholar'. Sir Edward Coke (1552–1633) was a barrister, Chief Justice and some time Speaker of the House of Commons, remembered for his commentary on the Treatise on Tenures written by Sir Thomas Littleton in the sixteenth century. This must be one of the older authorities called upon in cases on the subject of capital allowances! The claim was rejected, with regret, by Rowlatt J and no appeal was made by the taxpayer. Rowlatt J attached great weight to the ordinary meaning of the word 'plant'. A flaw in this case was perhaps that no reference was made to *Yarmouth v France*. Although that case was heard in 1887 (39 years before *Daphne v Shaw*) it had related to the question of employer's liability and had never yet, in 1926, been referred to in a tax context.

The decision in *Daphne v Shaw* stood for some 50 years, until it was overturned by *Munby v Furlong* (qv) in 1977.

J LYONS & CO LTD V A-G [1944] 1 ALL ER 477

Plant

This case is often referred to, but is commonly misunderstood and is of little relevance post-*Wimpy*.

This case considered whether lamps and light fittings were 'land' under the *War Damage Act 1943*. That Act included within 'land' any plant and machinery as defined by rating legislation, so in effect the question was whether the lamps etc were 'plant'. Uthwatt J laid down the following principle:

'In the present case, the question at issue may, I think, be put thus: Are the lamps and fitments properly to be regarded as part of the *setting* in which the business is carried on, or as part of the *apparatus* used for carrying on the business? In this case the lamps and their fitments are owned by a caterer and used in premises exclusively devoted to catering purposes. But the presence of lamps in this building is not dictated by the nature of the particular trade these carried on, or by the fact that it is for trade purposes that the building is used. Lamps are required to enable the building to be used where natural light is insufficient. The actual lamps themselves, so far as the evidence goes, present no special feature either in construction, purpose or position and, being supplied with electricity from public suppliers, they form no part of an electric lighting plant in or to the hereditament.

In my opinion, these lamps are not, in these circumstances, properly described as "plant" but are part of the general setting in which the business is carried on. They would not, I think, in any catalogue of this trader's assets, fall under the heading "machinery and plant"...'

Ultimately, then, this case found that the lighting was neither plant nor premises, a decision which is largely irreconcilable with modern case law and practice.

ABBOTT (INSPECTOR OF TAXES) V ALBION GREYHOUNDS (SALFORD) LTD (1945) 26 TC 390

Plant

A company operating a greyhound track maintained a kennel of its own dogs for racing purposes. It claimed the dogs were trading stock, whilst the Revenue contended that the dogs were truly part of the fixed capital of the business. Wrottesley J mentioned in passing that the dogs were not plant or machinery. His comment, it appears, was not a particularly considered one, and capital allowances were not the subject of the case. The case is therefore of limited use as an authority on this subject.

IRC V LAMBHILL IRONWORKS LTD (1950) 31 TC 393

IBAs – definition of office

IBAs were claimed, and given, in respect of a drawing office. The drawing office in question occupied one floor of a two-storey building some 200 yards from the industrial buildings used for the purposes of a trade of structural steel engineering. The buildings were not physically connected. The people employed in the drawing office numbered between 20 and 35. Of these, two prepared drawings to be used for tenders sent to prospective customers; the remainder made drawings and lists necessary to the carrying out of orders received. The Lord President (Cooper) said '... the drawing office is ... to all outward semblance and in real substance an integral, and indeed a vital part of the industrial premises'. Further, the drawing office was not used for a purpose ancillary to the purposes of the general office—'a drawing office is no more an "office" within the meaning of the Act than a machine shop is a "shop"'. Lord Keith inferred that an office must be something which clearly has not got anything of an industrial character, or is not directly ancillary to the industrial operations conducted in the rest of the works.

DALE (INSPECTOR OF TAXES) V JOHNSON BROS (1951) 32 TC 487

IBAs – storage

Johnson Brothers acted as a selling agent for the products of various companies. Being required to have in stock certain quantities of each product, it constructed a warehouse for such purpose. Industrial buildings allowances were claimed under the equivalent of *s 274, Table A, item 3(c)*, ie 'the storage of goods or materials ... not yet delivered to any purchaser'. The claim was denied, and two important principles were laid down.

First, to qualify for IBAs, there must be a trade of storage—storage incidental to a wider trade was not sufficient: 'It will not do that the trade is storage plus something else or something else plus storage' stated Sheil J. Second, it was held that Johnson Brothers (by virtue of the transfer of title to it), even though it was a selling agent or intermediary, was nonetheless a purchaser within the meaning of the legislation.

IRC V GEORGE GUTHRIE & SON (1952) 33 TC 327

Expenditure incurred

The taxpayer made a payment to a motor dealer for a car to be used entirely for business purposes. However, he then discovered that the same car had already been sold to another person, and the car was subsequently delivered to that person. The motor dealer then went into liquidation and the taxpayer was unable to recover any of the money spent on the car which was never delivered. He claimed capital allowances in respect of this expenditure, whilst the Revenue argued that allowances were not due, as the 'provision' of the plant had never, in fact, taken place. The Lord President (Cooper) thought it significant that the effect of the legislation was:

'not that the benefits (ie the allowances) shall be claimable by the person who provides the prescribed improvement, but by the person who incurs capital expenditure on its provision'.

Allowances were rightly claimable, it being appropriate to look at the object of the expenditure, and not at the question of whether the intended object was actually realised.

KEMPSTER V MCKENZIE (INSPECTOR OF TAXES) (1952) 33 TC 193 AND CHAMBERS (GH) (NORTHIAM FARMS) LTD V WATMOUGH (INSPECTOR OF TAXES) (1956) 36 TC 711

Business/private use

These two cases are important in respect of what are now ss 205–207. Those sections operate to reduce the amount of any allowance in respect of assets which are used partly for the purposes of the trade and partly for other purposes. The allowances shall be reduced 'to such extent as may be just and reasonable having regard to all the relevant circumstances'.

These cases both dealt with cars used by farming businesses. In one case, allowances were not reduced to take account of the 'personal choice or preference' of the driver; in the other case they were, as the car (a Bentley) was far more expensive and luxurious than would have been necessary simply to meet the needs of the trade.

This issue has for many years been largely dealt with by the automatic restriction of allowances on cars costing more than £12,000. However, with effect from April 2009, that system has been replaced by one where allowances depend on emissions rather than cost. It remains to be seen whether this change will result in more claims being challenged on the basis of this case.

IRC V NATIONAL COAL BOARD (1957) 37 TC 264

IBAs – dwelling houses

The National Coal Board built a number of dwelling-houses for occupation by colliery workers, and claimed IBAs in accordance with the predecessor of *s 277(2), (3),* under which a dwelling-house is not excluded from being an industrial building by *s 277(1)* if it is:

'for occupation by … persons employed at, or in connection with the working of, a mine, oil well or other source of mineral deposits … if the building or structure is likely to have little or no value to the person carrying on the trade when the mine [etc] is no longer worked.'

It was held (in the House of Lords) that the houses did not qualify for IBAs. On the supposition that the mine closed (immediately) the houses did have an alternative use as general dwellings, and were therefore not 'of little or no value'.

The courts did not favour the National Coal Board's contention that it was necessary to look ahead to the date (2141) when the pit was likely to be exhausted, and quantify the value of the houses at that time. As Lord Radcliffe observed, by that time the houses would have ceased to exist.

The legislation is intended to compensate the taxpayer for the need to construct dwellings which have no value other than in connection with a trade; it is not intended to compensate for loss of value due to normal physical decay.

JACKSON (INSPECTOR OF TAXES) V LASKERS HOME FURNISHERS LTD [1957] 1 WLR 69

Capital/revenue – repairs

The company took a lease of premises which had been unoccupied for 18 years and were in a very bad state of repair and unfit for occupation. It agreed under the lease to reinstate the premises, including repairing the main roof and plaster, and installing electric lighting, heating and a new shop front. In return, the landlords agreed to substantial rent reductions (reducing what would otherwise have been a rent of £1,000 a year for 14 years to a peppercorn rent for the first year, £700 for the next six years and £1,000 a year thereafter).

The High Court held that in consideration of the rent reductions, the tenant did work which the landlord might otherwise have been required to do. This was work and expenditure of a capital nature that dealt with the accumulation of repairs and small alterations of the premises to suit the tenant's business.

HINTON (INSPECTOR OF TAXES) V MADEN AND IRELAND LTD (1959) 38 TC 391

Capital expenditure

Knives and lasts used by a shoe manufacturer, having an average life of three years, were held to be plant. The durability of the assets was sufficient to ensure that expenditure on them was capital in nature.

JARROLD (INSPECTOR OF TAXES) V JOHN GOOD & SONS LTD (1962) 40 TC 681

Plant

A company operating as a shipping agent and warehouse keeper, installed a quantity of movable partitions, which to all extents and purposes functioned as internal walls, albeit not load-bearing. The partitioning consisted of metal ribs into which insets of either hardboard sheeting, doors or windows were installed. It was then screwed to the floor and ceiling to form a room of any desired size. The taxpayer claimed these partitions were a commercial necessity (rather than commercial convenience) for the functioning of its trade, as departments could expand or contract, appear or disappear according to the volume of trade. At the planning stage, special instructions were given to the architects that the portion of the building to be devoted to offices was to be capable of the greatest degree of elasticity.

A key observation was made by Pennycuick J regarding the concept of setting:

'It appears to me that the setting in which a business is carried on, and the apparatus used for carrying on a business, are not always necessarily mutually exclusive.'

The partitions were not excluded from being plant merely by virtue of the fact that they might be 'setting', and on the facts of the case, allowances were deemed to be available. In practice, the partitions were moved only rarely or not at all, but the intention was held to be key.

Though not directly relevant to this case, another interesting comment was made by Ormerod LJ in the Court of Appeal: 'I am not satisfied that it is proper to say that the word "plant" in the Income Tax Acts must be construed as something capable of being the subject of wear and tear.'

BOURNE V AUTO SCHOOL OF MOTORING (NORWICH) LTD (1964) 42 TC 217

Cars – definition

The taxpayer made a claim for a now obsolescent investment allowance in respect of vehicles used in his trade as a driving instructor. The allowance was not generally available for motor cars, unless they were 'of a type not commonly used as private vehicles and not suitable to be so used' or alternatively were used 'wholly or mainly for hire to or for the carriage of members of the public in the ordinary course of a trade'.

Virtually identical wording is now contained in *s 81*, and so the case is still important in defining a motor car, for the purpose, for example, of deciding whether or not a vehicle should be included within the general plant and machinery pool.

It was held that a car fitted with dual controls was not of a type commonly used as a private vehicle and was unsuitable to be so used. Of wider import is the implication that one must look at the car in its current state, including any adaptations.

CYRIL LORD CARPETS LTD V SCHOFIELD
(1966) 42 TC 637

Grants

The taxpayer company traded as a textile and carpet manufacturer in Northern Ireland. In 1958–60, it incurred capital expenditure of £272,419, towards which it subsequently received government subsidies or grants of £84,555. The company claimed capital allowances in respect of the whole of its expenditure, ie ignoring the grants received, on the grounds that mere reimbursement by discretionary grant of expenditure already incurred did not mean that expenditure had been 'met directly or indirectly, by [a public body] etc', as provided for by the predecessor of *s 532*. The Court of Appeal held that the expenditure had in fact been 'met' by the grants. The word 'met' was held to be used with its everyday meaning.

KILMARNOCK EQUITABLE CO-OPERATIVE SOCIETY V
IRC (1966) 42 TC 675

IBAs – process – retail shop

The case dealt with whether the screening, sorting and packing of coal constituted a 'process' qualifying for IB As. In the building in question, coal was fed down a chute through a vibratory screen in order to remove dross. Thereafter, the coal was passed by conveyor belt to a weighing point, where it was packed into 28lb bags. It was held that this did constitute the subjection of goods or materials to a process, despite the fact that the coal itself did not change form.

It was also held that the process described above did not amount to use 'for a purpose ancillary to the purposes of a retail shop'. Customers did not resort to the coal depot to make purchases. Lord Guthrie described 'ancillary' as meaning 'subservient', and the purpose of the process outlined was 'a bigger and broader conception than the mere furtherance of the purposes of a retail shop'.

BOURNE (INSPECTOR OF TAXES) V NORWICH CREMATORIUM LTD (1967) 44 TC 164

IBAs – goods or materials

The taxpayer company claimed IBAs under a predecessor of *s 274, Table A, item 2*. The basis of the claim was that a crematorium was used for the destruction of human remains, ie the 'subjection of goods or materials to a process'. The claim was not allowed, neither the 'goods or materials' point nor the 'subject to a process' point being accepted by the courts. This case therefore limited the meaning of those phrases, but of perhaps greater import was the comment of Stamp J regarding the construction or interpretation of statute:

> 'English words derive colour from those which surround them. Sentences are not mere collections of words to be taken out of the sentence, defined separately ... and then put back into the sentence with the meaning which you have assigned to them as separate words so as to give the sentence or phrase a meaning which as a sentence or phrase it cannot bear without a distortion of the English language.'

MACSAGA INVESTMENT CO LTD V LUPTON (1967) 44 TC 659

Plant

Heating equipment, lifts, sprinklers, incinerators and fittings were held to be machinery or plant.

ROSE & CO (WALLPAPER & PAINTS) LTD V CAMPBELL (INSPECTOR OF TAXES) (1967) 44 TC 500

Capital expenditure – definition

The taxpayer company incurred expenditure on bound books of wallpaper designs used as a selling aid, and claimed these were plant for capital allowance purposes. This claim was turned down. Pennycuick J was of the clear opinion that the books, having a life expectancy of two years, did not represent capital expenditure. Following this, consideration of the 'plant' question was unnecessary.

SAXONE, LILLEY & SKINNER (HOLDINGS) LTD V IRC (1967) 44 TC 122

IBAs – storage

IBAs were claimed in respect of a central warehouse used for the storage of shoes by a number of group companies. Some of the goods stored had been manufactured by group companies and had not yet been delivered to any purchaser. Others had been purchased from third parties for resale. It was common ground that only the storage of the former would qualify for IBAs under the predecessor of *s 274, Table A, item 3(c)*. Shoes from both sources (ie manufactured and purchased) were stored together. It was not the case, for example, that shoes purchased from third parties were stored in particular, identifiable parts of the building. The Lord President (Clyde) said: 'a building may be an industrial building or structure if it is used for the purpose of a trade for storing qualified goods, even though it is in addition used for the purpose of a trade of storing unqualified goods as well ... There is nothing in the section about exclusive use ... Merely because it is also used for another purpose it does not cease to be used for the qualifying purpose.'

ABBOTT LABORATORIES LTD V CARMODY (1968) 44 TC 569

IBAs

This case concerned the question of whether industrial buildings allowances were available for expenditure on a building used for administration functions. The administration building was one of four buildings on a site, and although separate and complete in itself, was connected to another block 25 yards away by a covered passage. If, by virtue of the covered passage and connecting pipework, the administration building and the other building (which did qualify for IBAs) could be considered to be a single unit, allowances would be given on the whole cost, as expenditure on the non-qualifying part (the administration block) did not exceed 10% of the total.

The case reached the courts first in 1966, but was remitted to the Special Commissioners to decide whether or not the layout of buildings described above could be regarded as 'an industrial building or structure'. The Special

Commissioners decided that it could not. The administration block was not sufficiently physically integrated with the other structural units within the layout. The various units, including the administration block, were regarded as separate entities, though sharing the facilities provided by a common boiler-house and connected by made-up roads and pathways.

MCVEIGH (INSPECTOR OF TAXES) V ARTHUR SANDERSON & SONS LTD (1968) 45 TC 273

Plant

The taxpayer company incurred expenditure on wallpaper designs which it retained for a number of years. It was claimed that these constituted items of plant. The claim was rejected, but only because Cross J felt himself unable to overturn the decision of Rowlatt J in *Daphne v Shaw* (qv) which dealt with a law library. However, Cross J did express dissatisfaction with the earlier decision, but said that if any extension of the meaning of the word 'plant' beyond a purely physical object was to be made, it must be made by a higher court. Two decades later it was, in the case of *Munby v Furlong* (qv).

WOOD (T/A A WOOD & CO) V PROVAN (INSPECTOR OF TAXES) (1968) 44 TC 701

Plant – contract allocations

The taxpayer purchased machinery and plant along with other assets. In the purchase contract, a specific amount of consideration was stated to be in respect of the various items of plant. Subsequently the General Commissioners made a different apportionment of the consideration under the predecessor of *s 562*. The taxpayer then claimed that the transaction was one to which the precursor of *s 563* applied (see **4.12**), and that therefore it was not within the jurisdiction of the original Commissioners. It was held that:

(*a*) the Commissioners were entitled to make an apportionment, notwithstanding the fact that a separate price for the plant was shown on the purchase contract;

(*b*) *s 563* did not apply—although the apportionment was material to the tax liabilities of more than one person, one of the persons was not party to the original sale and purchase.

This case preceded the introduction of *s 198*, which provides for a joint (and binding) election fixing the amount allocated to fixtures (see **4.35**).

IRC V BARCLAY, CURLE & CO LTD (1969) 45 TC 221

Plant

The taxpayer company, which carried on a trade of shipbuilding and repairing on the River Clyde, constructed a dry dock. It claimed as plant not only the attendant machinery, but also the cost of excavation and concrete work. The House of Lords ruled (by a majority of three to two) that the whole qualified as plant. The Crown contended that the basin forming the dock should be regarded as the setting in which the trade was carried on. However, it was observed that a simple 'hole in the ground' would be of no use to the taxpayer in his trade.

Lord Reid noted two stages in the operations undertaken: 'Firstly, the ship must be isolated from the water and then the inspection and necessary repairs must be carried out.' The dry dock was perhaps merely the setting for the second stage, but the same could not be said with regard to the first stage, which was equally important. In this first stage, the dry dock did perform an essential function in the trade, leading Lord Reid to conclude: 'The whole dock is, I think, the means by which, or plant with which, the operation is performed.' The fact that the dock might also be a structure did not preclude it from being plant. Lord Reid again commented:

'I do not say that every structure which fulfils the function of plant must be regarded as plant, but I think that one would have to find some good reason for excluding such a structure. And I do not think that mere size is sufficient.'

Later legislation (now *ss 21–23*) limits the extent to which buildings or structures can be treated as plant (though existing case decisions are untouched).

WOODS V RM MALLEN (ENGINEERING) LTD (1969) 45 TC 619

IBAs – relevant interest

This case dealt with the question of the 'relevant interest' in an industrial building, and whether the relevant interests were transferred upon the creation of a lease. Mr Hodgkinson was the lessee of a plot of land, under a lease having a term of 99 years from 25 June 1950. He constructed an industrial building, his 'relevant interest', of course, being the 99-year lease. In 1962, Mr Hodgkinson granted a sub-lease in favour of Mallen (Engineering) Ltd, for a term of 99 years from 25 June 1950, less three days. Mallen claimed that it had acquired Hodgkinson's 'relevant interest' in the property, and was therefore entitled to industrial buildings allowances.

Plowman J looked at the respective interests of Hodgkinson and Mallen to determine whether they were, in fact, the same. He decided that they were not: one was for 99 years, whilst the other was for 99 years less three days. Although similar, they were not the same. The important point, twice quoted by Plowman J, was that contained in the predecessor of *s 288*: 'An interest shall not cease to be the relevant interest ... by reason of the creation of any lease or other interest to which that interest is subject.'

ICI AUSTRALIA AND NEW ZEALAND V TAXATION COMR (1970) 120 CLR 396

Plant

This Australian case was quoted with approval in *Cole Brothers* (qv). It dealt primarily with acoustic ceilings and electrical wiring. Special sound-absorbing ceiling tiles were added to an open-plan office. Kitto J noted the use of such tiles was standard practice in modern office buildings and that the tiles were therefore 'no more than part of the shelter' in which the taxpayer chose to carry on its activities. He continued:

'Every part of a building makes some contribution to the comfort and efficiency of those who work in it. To take it notionally to bits and describe as "plant" any bit that has a function which is useful in connection with the business carried on there seems to me indefensible.'

Regarding electric wiring, together with conduits, switchboards etc, Kitto J thought it formed no more than the reticulation system without which the building would be incomplete. Neither the ceilings nor the electrics were plant.

Note that with effect from April 2008, electrical systems are admitted as plant (integral features).

BRIDGE HOUSE (REIGATE HILL) LTD V HINDER (1971) 47 TC 182

Plant

The taxpayer company, which operated a hotel, contributed a capital sum towards the extension of a public sewer so that the sewer now served the hotel. Its claim for capital allowances was rejected on the grounds that these were itself merely a conduit for effluent, and not plant used in the treatment of that effluent. Lord Denning stated that sewage or drainage pipes were an essential ancillary to the building. Salmon LJ, though agreeing with Lord Denning, did not completely rule out the fact that sewers carrying trade effluent from a factory or a large hotel could be plant.

LUPTON V CADOGAN GARDENS DEVELOPMENTS LTD (1971) 47 TC 1

Plant

Various landlord's fixtures and services assets qualified as machinery or plant, including: air conditioning machinery and ducts, blinds, boiler house plant instruments, central heating pipes and radiators, a curtain rail with fittings, flagpoles, fire and sprinkler services, hanging rails, lifts, lighting, mirrors, partitions, sanitary ware (baths, lavatories and cisterns, washbasins, showers and fittings), ventilation machinery and ducts, and water heaters.

ODEON ASSOCIATED THEATRES LTD V JONES (INSPECTOR OF TAXES) (1971) 48 TC 257

Capital/revenue – repairs

The taxpayer's company's sole activity was the showing of films. After World War II, it incurred expenditure on the purchase and repair of cinemas. During and immediately after World War II, the building of theatres and cinemas was prohibited, as was any expenditure on repairs and maintenance, other than that which was essential. Two effects of this were:

(*a*) a company wishing to expand was forced to buy existing cinemas, rather than build new ones, and

(*b*) cinemas were invariably in a poor state of repair.

In contrast to the facts in the *Law Shipping* case (qv), the poor state of repair of cinemas acquired did not affect their purchase price nor did it render them useless for their intended purpose. Attendances at the cinemas would not be adversely affected as a result of the disrepair, because all cinemas were in the same state.

The Revenue, following the *Law Shipping* case, argued that the expenditure on repairs was properly regarded as capital, to the extent that it related to repairs which became necessary prior to the company's acquisition of the relevant cinemas. However, judgment was given in the taxpayer's favour.

See the summary of *Law Shipping Co Ltd v IRC* (1923) 12 TC 621 for the application in practice of the principles emerging from these two cases.

COOKE (INSPECTOR OF TAXES) V BEACH STATION CARAVANS LTD (1974) 49 TC 514

Plant

The taxpayer company, which owned and operated a caravan site, incurred expenditure on the construction of heated swimming pools. A claim for capital allowances was accepted in respect of the complex system of filtration, heating and recirculation. However the Inspector refused to accept that the cost of excavating and constructing the pools, together with the surrounding terraces, constituted expenditure on plant for capital allowances purposes. On appeal, Megarry J held that the whole expenditure did qualify as plant, basing his conclusion on three factors.

(i)   The pools could be considered as a unit, together with all the attendant apparatus for purifying and heating the water and so on.

(ii)   The pools had to be considered not on their own, but in relation to the business carried on. The function and purpose of the pools was to attract custom to the caravan site.

(iii)   The pools could not be regarded as merely passive, but instead performed an active function and were part of the means whereby the trade was carried on.

To conclude, Megarry J resorted to a 'relatively modern slang expression': 'The pools are not merely "where it's at", they are part of the apparatus used by the company for carrying on its business as caravan park operators.'

ST JOHN'S SCHOOL (MOUNTFORD & KNIBBS) V WARD (INSPECTOR OF TAXES) [1974] STC 69, 49 TC 524; AFFD [1975] STC 7N

Plant

The taxpayers operated a school from leased premises. They incurred expenditure on two prefabricated buildings; one a laboratory, the other a gymnasium. Both buildings had special features—the laboratory had fitted workbenches and sinks, while the gymnasium had a special floor, and walls and roof capable of supporting climbing equipment. The Commissioners held that neither building was an item of plant, and that (in the absence of supporting evidence) it was not possible to apportion the expenditure so as to determine that part incurred in connection with items of plant. Their decision was upheld by the courts. It was appropriate to look at the assets (ie the buildings) as whole entities, rather than on a piecemeal basis.

The result may have been different if there had been evidence to support an apportionment of the expenditure.

DIXON (INSPECTOR OF TAXES) V FITCH'S GARAGE LTD (1975) 50 TC 509

Plant

The taxpayer incurred expenditure on a canopy over its petrol pumps, and claimed capital allowances. It was contended that the canopy was plant, not in isolation, but because it formed part of an integral complex (the filling station), the whole of which was plant. Brightman J held that the canopy was not plant. Although sales had increased since construction of the canopy, petrol could nonetheless be supplied with a covering canopy. The comfort of customers was not a relevant consideration.

The correctness of this decision was doubted by Lord Hailsham LC in *Cole Bros Ltd v Philips* (qv) and by Lord Cameron in the *Scottish & Newcastle Breweries* case (qv). Furthermore, a garage canopy was held to be plant in the Irish case, *O'Culachain v McMullan Bros* (1991 – qv).

SCHOFIELD (INSPECTOR OF TAXES) V R & H HALL [1975] STC 353, 49 TC 538

Plant

Dockside silos were held to be plant. The primary purpose of the silos was not storage (grain was expected to be held there for only seven days) but was rather to hold the grain in a position from which it could be easily delivered into tankers. The silo housing was also considered part of the plant.

MUNBY V FURLONG (INSPECTOR OF TAXES) [1977] STC 232, 50 TC 491

Plant

A practising barrister incurred capital expenditure on his law library, and claimed that allowances were due because the library, or the books that made it up, constituted plant for this purpose. The claim was upheld, ultimately, by the Court of Appeal, reversing the decision in *Daphne v Shaw* (qv). A key argument was that, contrary to dicta in the earlier case, the meaning of 'plant' for tax purposes was something more than its everyday meaning, as the man in the street would have understood it. Lord Denning MR said that various sources showed quite conclusively that:

> 'in this taxing statute the courts do not apply the meaning to the word "plant" as the ordinary Englishman understands it. It has acquired by the course of decisions a special meaning in tax cases.'

Lord Denning used this 'special meaning' to include books within the definition of plant. The fact that the books were used intellectually, and not physically, was of no consequence. Sir John Pennycuick agreed with Lord Denning, and commented that *Yarmouth v France* had not been considered in the case of *Daphne v Shaw*.

BEN-ODECO LTD V POWLSON (INSPECTOR OF TAXES) (1978) 52 TC 459

Plant – definition of 'provision'

The taxpayer company acquired an oil drilling rig for use in its trade. Whilst the eligibility of direct expenditure on the rig itself for plant allowances was not doubted, the company had also capitalised the interest on borrowings taken out to finance the acquisition. The question put to the courts (ultimately to the House of Lords) was whether the interest could be regarded as expenditure incurred on the provision of machinery or plant, in accordance with the legislation, or whether it was in fact too remote to be so regarded. The courts took the latter view, ie that the incurring of the interest was too remote from the acquisition of the rig to be considered as part of the cost qualifying for allowances.

Lord Wilberforce put it that: 'The words "expenditure on the provision of" do not appear to me to be designed for this purpose. They focus attention on the plant and the expenditure on the plant – not limiting it necessarily to the bare purchase price, but including such items as transport and installation, in any event not extending to expenditure more remote in purpose ... the interest and commitment were expenditure on the provision of money to be used on the provision of plant, but not expenditure on the provision of plant.' Lord Russell conferred that: 'I do not seek to confine qualifying capital expenditure to the price paid to the supplier of the plant. I should have thought, for example, that if the cost of transport from the supplier to the place of user is directly borne by the taxpayer it would be expenditure on the provision of plant for the purposes of the taxpayer's trade. And there may well be other examples of expenditure, additional to the price paid to the supplier, which would qualify on similar grounds.'

BENSON (INSPECTOR OF TAXES) V YARD ARM CLUB LTD (1979) 53 TC 67

Plant

The taxpayer operated a floating restaurant on the Thames. It was claimed that the 'ship' constituted plant for capital allowance purposes. The case contained a significant review of decided cases in this area, with the emphasis on the question of whether the ship performed some 'function' in the trade, or whether it was merely the setting for a trade. Buckley LJ acknowledged that patrons came to the restaurant 'to get good food, somewhere different with views of the river etc and a shipboard feeling'. This did not mean, however, that the floating restaurant was plant, any more than a restaurant on land would be plant because its location offered attractive views. Templeman LJ agreed and referred to the restaurant atop the Post Office Tower:

'premises do not become plant merely because they float in the Thames or are suspended in the sky or are to be found on top of the Matterhorn. For the present purposes I can see no distinction between a restaurant in the Thames and a fish and chip shop in Bethnal Green. Premises only become plant if they perform the function of plant.'

Shaw LJ also in agreement, said: 'A characteristic of plant appears ... to be that it is an adjunct to the carrying on of a business and not the essential site or core of the business itself.'

BUCKINGHAM (INSPECTOR OF TAXES) V SECURITAS PROPERTIES LTD (1979) 53 TC 292

IBAs – process

The taxpayer was the lessor of a building used by Group 4 Total Security Ltd. Group 4 used the building for the storage of cash and making up wage packets, and it was claimed that this constituted 'the subjection of goods or materials to any process' within the meaning of what is now *s 274, Table A, item 2*. The claim was rejected, on the grounds that the notes and coins were not in this instance held as goods but as currency or 'valuable tokens'. Coins and notes could still be 'goods' in certain circumstances. For example, in the trade of a person printing bank notes.

CRUSABRIDGE INVESTMENTS LTD V CASINGS INTERNATIONAL LTD (1979) 54 TC 246

IBAs – process

Under the lease of a building the lessee covenanted to use it only as a warehouse within the meaning of Class X of the Town and Country Planning (Use Classes) Order 1972 and also within the meaning of 'industrial building or structure' as defined by the Capital Allowances Act. The lessee's business consisted for the greater part of purchasing used tyre casings, examining and grading them, and re-selling to remoulders. It also sold remoulds on a commission basis. The Revenue refused the lessor's claim for industrial buildings allowances, on the grounds that did not constitute a qualifying use, under the predecessor of *s 274*. The lessor therefore proceeded against the lessee for damages for breach of covenant.

It was held that the examination and grading of the casings did not amount to subjecting goods or materials to a process within the meaning of *s 274, Table A, item 2*. Finlay J distinguished the case from *Kilmarnock Equitable Co-operative Society v IRC* (qv). He did not believe that the examination and grading of tyres constituted a process: 'It is the very same tyre before the examination and after the examination. Nothing has happened to it that alters its nature or effects any kind of change in the tyre.'

However, the building did qualify as an industrial building by virtue of *s 274, Table A, item 3(b)*—the storage of goods or materials 'which are to be subjected, in the course of a trade, to a process' —in respect of the used casings and also by virtue of item 3(c) of that Act—the storage of goods or materials 'which, having been manufactured or produced or subjected, in the course of a trade, to a process, have not yet been delivered to any purchaser' —in respect of remoulds held for sale.

Finlay J held also that the person carrying on the process and the person effecting the storage need not be the same: 'In my view it matters not that the trade in which they are to be so subjected to a process is the trade of someone other than the company which is storing the casings with a view to that being eventually done.'

BROWN (INSPECTOR OF TAXES) V BURNLEY FOOTBALL & ATHLETIC CO LTD (1980) 53 TC 357

Plant – capital/revenue – repairs

The taxpayer company constructed a new stand, replacing one which had become unsafe. It claimed that the cost of this was properly chargeable to repairs. A second claim held that if the expenditure were not in respect of repairs, then the stand constituted an item of plant. Vinelott J quoted the words of Buckley LJ in *Lurcott v Wakeley and Wheeler* [1911] 1 KB 905:

'Repair is restoration by renewal or replacement of subsidiary parts of a whole. Renewal, as distinguished from repair, is reconstruction of the entirety, meaning by the entirety not the whole but substantially the whole subject-matter under discussion.'

In this case it was found that it was the stand, and not the football ground as a whole, that constituted the 'entirety'. Expenditure on the new stand was not, therefore, allowed as a repair.

On the second question of whether the stand was plant, it was held that it was not. Football matches took place and spectators came to watch within, rather than by means of, the stadium. The stand did not therefore function, either actively or passively in the trade.

The opposite conclusion was reached in an Irish case, *O'Grady v Roscommon Race Committee* (1992 – qv).

HAMPTON (INSPECTOR OF TAXES) V FORTES AUTOGRILL LTD [1980] STC 80, 53 TC 691

Plant

The operator of a number of restaurants installed, in public areas of those restaurants, false ceilings. The primary purpose of these ceilings was to act as cladding for pipes etc in the sense that the ceilings covered and connected the pipes. The Commissioners held that the ceilings were 'part and parcel' of the equipment which they supported and covered, and were therefore themselves 'plant'. This finding was overturned by the courts where Fox J laid emphasis on the 'function' test, and found no evidence that the ceilings performed any function in the trade. (NB suspended ceilings may qualify as plant under special circumstances, for example, where they form part of an air-conditioning or extraction system.)

Parts of the decision have been superseded by the *Scottish & Newcastle* decision (1982 – qv).

MASON V TYSON (INSPECTOR OF TAXES) [1980] STC 284, 53 TC 333

Definition – wholly and exclusively

Mr Mason, a chartered surveyor, furnished a flat above his office so that he could sleep there when he was required to work late. He claimed capital allowances on part of the amount expended. The court held, however, that no allowances were due, as the expenditure had not been incurred 'wholly and exclusively' for the purposes of the trade, as required (with slight amendment) by *s 11(4)*.

VIBROPLANT LTD V HOLLAND (INSPECTOR OF TAXES) (1981) 54 TC 658

IBAs – process – repair trade

The taxpayer company carried on a business of hiring out plant and machinery. It owned a number of depots used for storing the equipment between hirings and for cleaning, servicing and, if necessary, repairing the said equipment. It claimed industrial buildings allowances in respect of these depots, but without success. The claim was made under what is now *s 274, Table A, item 2* —the subjection of 'goods or materials to any process'. It was held in the first instance that premises used for servicing and repair were not a 'factory ... or similar premises', because, in essence, nothing was made or manufactured. Secondly, it was held that the repair and maintenance of items of plant according to their individual merits and requirements did not amount to a 'process'. Dillon J commented that, in his view, 'process' connotes a substantial measure of uniformity of treatment or a system of treatment.

IRC V SCOTTISH & NEWCASTLE BREWERIES LTD [1982] STC 296, 55 TC 252

Plant

The taxpayer company operated a chain of hotels and licensed premises, either purpose-built or purchased as a shell and fitted out to the company's specification. It was claimed that one element of the company's trade was the provision of a certain type of atmosphere, or ambience, conducive to attracting custom. This argument proved attractive to the courts, and consequently allowances were given in respect of items used to create this 'ambience', such as decor, murals and sculptures. In the Court of Session, Lord Cameron thought that the terms 'plant' and 'setting' could overlap, and also stated:

'... the question of what is properly to be regarded as "plant" can only be answered in the context of the particular industry concerned and, possibly, in light also of the particular circumstances of the individual taxpayer's own trade.'

Similar thoughts were expressed by Lord Wilberforce in the House of Lords: 'In the end each case must be resolved in my opinion by considering carefully the nature of the particular trade being carried on.'

For further comment, see *Wimpy* case (1989).

COLE BROS LTD V PHILLIPS (INSPECTOR OF TAXES) [1982] STC 307, 55 TC 188

Plant

John Lewis Properties Ltd incurred expenditure on an entire electrical system installed in a store at the Brent Cross shopping centre, leased to Cole Bros Ltd. It was accepted that certain items were plant (see **16.14**). These included:

- wiring to heaters, alarms, clocks, cash registers;

- telephone trunking;
- wiring to lifts and escalators;
- emergency lighting system;
- standby supply system.

Other items were disputed by the Revenue, being mainly lighting and wiring, some of it specially designed, and also transformers and switch gear.

The case eventually reached the House of Lords. It was held that the 'multiplicity of elements' in the installation and the differing purposes to which they were put precluded one from regarding the entire electrical installation as a single entity (that is, the entire electrical system was not a single item of plant). The claim therefore had to be approached on a piecemeal basis. The transformers and switch gear were held to be plant, other items were not, being a necessary part of the building or 'setting'. The judgment of Stephenson LJ in the Court of Appeal contains the well-known statement:

'The philosopher-statesman, Balfour, is reported to have said it was unnecessary to define a great power because, like an elephant, you recognised it when you met it. Unhappily, plant in taxing and other statutes is no elephant (though I suppose an elephant might be plant).'

In an unpublished decision of the Special Commissioners in 1992, another retailer's claim to treat an entire electrical system as plant was allowed, once it could be shown that certain conditions had been met. These conditions were that:

(*a*)   the electrical system is designed and built as a whole, it is a fully integrated system;

(*b*)   the electrical system is designed to meet the requirements of the trade, it is not a general purpose or standard system designed to meet the needs of a range of occupants;

(*c*)   the end user items of the installation function as apparatus in the trader's business;

(*d*)   the electrical installation is essential for the functioning of the business.

The principles of this case have been superseded by the integral features legislation (see **14.4**) with effect from April 2008.

LEEDS PERMANENT BUILDING SOCIETY V PROCTOR (INSPECTOR OF TAXES) (1982) 56 TC 293

Plant

A building society installed in its windows variously designed screens. This was part of an ongoing process of making the branches look more like retail shops, the aim being to attract the attention of customers or potential customers. The screens were demountable, but because they were designed to be of local interest, they were not often moved in practice. In addition to their advertising function, the screens served to provide privacy for customers inside the branch, and had a minor security function. It was held that the screens were plant, not setting. Goulding J stated:

'They were an adjunct to the carrying on of the business and not the essential site or core of the business itself [a phrase used in *Benson v Yard Arm Club* – qv]. They were not used as premises but were part of the means by which the relevant trade was carried out.'

O'CONAILL V WATERFORD GLASS LTD (1982) TL(I) 122

IBAs

This Irish case considered whether a computer building which served an industrial complex could by virtue of that fact itself be regarded as an industrial building. The taxpayer company carried on a trade consisting of the manufacture of crystal glass. On one site it occupied a number of buildings, the majority of which were used directly for the manufacturing process. One building, however, housed a computer, together with offices and showrooms. Ideally, the computer should have been located in the middle of the factory but could not be sited there owing to noise, dirt and vibration. The fact that it was housed in a separate building did not alter the fact that the computer's primary purpose was to assist in the manufacturing process. McWilliam J summed up that the computer building was 'a vital nerve centre for the whole industrial complex, and forms part of it'.

WHITE V HIGGINBOTTOM (1982) 57 TC 283

Definition – 'necessarily incurred'

A vicar purchased audio-visual equipment for use in church—there was no private use. He claimed capital allowances on the basis that the machines in question were necessarily provided for use in the performance of the duties of his office. This is now dealt with in *s 36(2)*. It was held that, although the machines were used wholly and exclusively for the office, they were not strictly necessary. Other vicars carried out their duties without the aid of such equipment, and its purchase was therefore a matter of personal choice. Allowances were not, therefore, given.

BOLTON (INSPECTOR OF TAXES) V INTERNATIONAL DRILLING CO LTD [1983] STC 70, 86 TC 449

Definition – 'qualifying expenditure'

The company (IDC) acquired a drilling barge in 1965, and entered into a contract with Amoco to drill for oil in the North Sea. At the same time, IDC granted Amoco an option to purchase the barge in 1969. In that year, the barge in question was the only one owned by IDC (another one was in construction) and so IDC, anxious to stay in business, paid Amoco some £500,000 for cancellation of the option. The two questions put to the courts were as follows:

(*a*) Did the £500,000 constitute expenditure on plant qualifying for allowances?

(*b*) Was the expenditure incurred in 1969 (therefore qualifying for an initial allowance)?

It was held that the answer to both questions was yes. IDC did already own the asset, but would have ceased to do so if the option cancellation payment had not been made. The payment was therefore made in connection with the provision (albeit the continued provision) of plant. Also, IDC continued to enjoy possession of the plant after 1969 in consequence of the expenditure, which therefore qualified for the initial allowance available in that year.

COPOL CLOTHING CO LTD V HINDMARCH (INSPECTOR OF TAXES) (1983) 57 TC 575

IBAs – storage

The taxpayer had for some years traded as a clothing wholesaler and distributor. About 90% of its purchases were imported. These goods were stored in a warehouse in Manchester. IBAs were claimed on the warehouse by virtue of what is now *s 274, Table A, item 3(d)*—'a trade consisting of storing goods or materials on their arrival in the United Kingdom from a place outside the United Kingdom'. Fox LJ agreed that 'on arrival' was not construed so narrowly that the allowance would only be given to buildings in the 'recognised dock area'. 'There may well be cases where a warehouse is situated some considerable distance from the coast but where it can conveniently serve a number of ports.' Fox LJ further concluded that the purpose of the allowance was to encourage the provision of storage for goods which have just arrived in the United Kingdom and before their onward transit. This was held not to apply to the Manchester warehouse, which simply provided the storage which any wholesaler might need for his goods. Consequently, the claim for IBAs was refused.

VAN ARKADIE (INSPECTOR OF TAXES) V STERLING COATED MATERIALS LTD [1983] STC 95, 56 TC 479

Expenditure – foreign currency

The taxpayer company (SCM) entered into an agreement to purchase plant from a Swiss company on deferred payment terms. The Swiss company, however, could not afford to fund construction of the plant, and so an arrangement was made with a Swiss bank. Under this arrangement, the bank paid the purchase price over to the Swiss supplier, and SCM was to repay the bank in instalments after installation of the plant. In effect, SCM was making payments as originally envisaged, albeit to the bank, rather than the supplier. Due to currency fluctuations, the price had effectively increased by the time payment was made, and SCM claimed allowances on this exchange loss. In contrast to the *Ben-Odeco* case (qv), it was held that this 'extra cost' did qualify for allowances. It was not in truth a 'loan', but was inextricably tied in with the purchase contract. However, it was also held that the extra amount was only incurred when repayment was made, and not on the date of the original contract.

O'SRIANIAN V LAKEVIEW LTD (1984) TL(I) 125

Plant

An Irish case considered whether a deep-pit poultry house was an item of plant. On the facts of the case, the claim for plant allowances succeeded. The entire design of the house was so made up as to create the most conducive and efficient environment in which hens would lay eggs, and without this design the hens would not lay so many eggs. A key feature pointed out by Murphy J was that the environment was designed for the benefit of the hens (and not the humans) and for the purpose of increasing egg production which was in fact the business carried on by the taxpayer.

Sections 21–23 restrict the extent to which buildings and structures may be treated as plant.

STOKES (INSPECTOR OF TAXES) V COSTAIN PROPERTY INVESTMENTS LTD (1984) 57 TC 688

Plant – fixtures

A company installed various items of plant (principally lifts and central heating) in two buildings. At the time this was done, the company was neither freeholder nor leaseholder of the building. However, upon completion of the works, it was to be entitled to the grant of a lease. Capital allowances were denied on the grounds that the plant in question did not 'belong' to the company, as required by what is now *s 11(4)(b)*. The word 'belong' must be given its ordinary meaning, and is not a term of art. In the High Court, Harmon J said it would not be true to say that he owned a Rolls Royce car if he were only renting it for the day, and the case here, though less extreme, was in essence the same: 'It seems to me plain and obvious as a matter of language that property of which the taxpayer has no right of disposition does not belong to him.' This view was supported by Fox LJ in the Court of Appeal, adding:

> 'Nor do I think it is an apt use of language to say that landlords' fixtures "belong" to the leaseholder. He cannot remove them from the building. He cannot dispose of them except as part of the hereditament and subject to the provision of the lease and for the term of the lease.'

However, Fox LJ thought the state of the law very unsatisfactory. The purpose of the statutory provisions was to encourage investment in machinery and plant, yet in this case no relief was given. The landlord could not claim allowances because he had not incurred any expenditure, and the (prospective) tenant could not because the plant did not belong to him. As a result of this unsatisfactory state of the law, 1985 saw the introduction of the provisions now contained with *CAA 2001, Chap 14* enabling the tenant to claim allowances.

ELLISS (INSPECTOR OF TAXES) V BP OIL NORTHERN REFINERY LTD; ELLISS V BP TYNE TANKER CO LTD (1986) 59 TC 474

Allowances not mandatory

These related cases dealt with the question of whether full capital allowances must be deducted for corporation tax purposes. The taxpayer companies were oil companies. Particular circumstances relating to oil companies at that time did not permit the carry-forward of losses. The companies contended that it was open to them not to claim part of the capital allowances to which they were entitled. The effect of this was to increase the tax written-down values of the assets carried forward, so that greater allowances were available in subsequent years when the companies were able to make use of them. The Revenue contended that in each accounting period the companies' profits should be reduced by the full amount of the allowances to which they were entitled. The effect of this would have been that allowances would have been wasted in earlier years (as taxable profits cannot be reduced below nil) and taxable profits would be increased in subsequent years. The companies' contention was accepted by the Special Commissioner, and upheld by the High Court and the Court of Appeal. Since the introduction of the modern capital allowances system to encourage post-war reconstruction the taxpayer could choose whether to take the allowances to which he was entitled. Walton J in the High Court applied the maxim that everyone is entitled to renounce any right intended for his benefit.

Section 3 now confirms that allowances will only be given if claimed. A taxpayer can choose not to claim.

GASPET LTD V ELLISS (INSPECTOR OF TAXES) [1987] STC 362, 60 TC 91

Research

This case dealt with the question of whether scientific research (now research and development) had been undertaken on behalf of the taxpayer (as required by *s 439*). It was held that in order to qualify there must be a link between the taxpayer and the research. Mere funding of the research was not sufficient.

PATRICK MONAHAN (DROGHEDA) LTD V O'CONNELL [1987] IR 661

IBAs

This Irish case considered whether bonded transit sheds used as a clearing house for goods unloaded from ships were industrial buildings in use for the purposes of a 'dock undertaking' (current English counterpart: *s 274, Table B, item 10*). It was held that they were. The storage of goods free of charge for short periods was not a separate trade but merely ancillary to the business of a dock undertaking.

THOMAS (INSPECTOR OF TAXES) V REYNOLDS & BROOMHEAD (1987) 59 TC 502

Plant

In this 'unfortunate little case', as Walton J called it, it was held that an inflatable tennis court cover was not plant. The taxpayers appeared in person, and supplied the court with certain facts which tended to show 'that the cover did have a function to play in the business of coaching … other than that of merely providing shelter from the weather'. However, these facts were not included in the case stated, and no judicial attention could therefore be paid to them. The decision was made with regret, and it is not inconceivable that subsequent similar claims have been resolved in the taxpayer's favour, without having reached the courts.

WIMPY INTERNATIONAL LTD V WARLAND (INSPECTOR OF TAXES); ASSOCIATED RESTAURANTS LTD V WARLAND (INSPECTOR OF TAXES) [1989] STC 273, 61 TC 51

Plant

Both taxpayers were members of the same group and operated restaurants under the names 'Wimpy' and 'Pizzaland'. Each refurbished their restaurants and claimed that various items should be treated as plant. The majority of the relevant items served, it was claimed, to attract custom and provide an atmosphere conducive to the enjoyment of meals. The claim in respect of most items was dismissed. Allowances were given in respect of special lighting (although normal in design) which served a business purpose, namely to 'create an atmosphere of brightness and efficiency, suitable to the service and consumption of fast food meals and attractive to potential customers looking in from outside'. Also allowed as plant was expenditure on carpets, cold water tanks and piping, fascia signs (in effect, advertising signs), built-in storage units and dispensers for food and drink, decorative wall panels/mirrors, electric wiring to plant, screens between tables, the rooftop brick housing for air cooling and extraction plant, and one very special suspended ceiling also designed for purposes of 'atmosphere by reducing the height of the ceiling and giving it visual interest'. The items not allowed as plant included:

(*a*) shop fronts;

(*b*) floor tiles and sheets (including ceramic, quarry and vinyl), and wall tiles;

(*c*)   some suspended ceilings;

(*d*)   mezzanine floor, raised floors, balustrading and stairs;

(*e*)   trapdoor and ladder;

(*f*)   decorative brickwork, plaster, artex, paint, varnish, and other wall finishes

(*g*)   fire doors and fireproofing of walls and other surfaces.

The main import of the Wimpy case has been the comments made by Hoffmann J regarding what has since become known as the 'premises test'. This is much misunderstood. Indeed, the published HMRC Capital Allowances Manual misrepresents Hoffmann J's comments in a number of ways, and it is worth setting out his statement in full:

'The question seems to me to be whether it would be more appropriate to describe the item as having become part of the premises than as having retained a separate identity. This is a question of fact and degree, to which some of the relevant considerations will be:

1.   whether the item appears visually to retain a separate identity,

2.   the degree of permanence with which it has been attached,

3.   the incompleteness of the structure without it, and

4.   the extent to which it was intended to be permanent or whether it was likely to be replaced within a relatively short period.

[Counsel for the company] submitted that if this was the proper test, those considerations constituted a series of separate hurdles which had to be overcome ... I do not agree.'

It is clear from this that Hoffmann J did not intend to set out four tests, all of which needed to be satisfied in order for an asset to be treated as plant (as has commonly been stated). Rather, his intention was to reaffirm the single test laid down by previous court decisions, namely 'whether it would be more appropriate to describe the item as having become part of the premises than as having retained a separate identity'. The four specific points mentioned are merely some of the considerations which may help to decide.

Regarding his second consideration, it is not the case that an asset will fail to qualify for wear and tear allowances because it is in some way 'attached', either to a building or to the land. *Yarmouth v France* refers to plant being 'goods and chattels, fixed or moveable' and no-one since has sought to suggest that plant cannot be fixed. Indeed, *Chapter 14* of the *Capital Allowances Act 2001* deals expressly with allowances on fixtures.

Equally, attachment to the land, rather than to a building or structure, does not preclude the claiming of plant allowances. Buckley LJ in *Benson v The Yard Arm Club* (Court of Appeal) observed that in determining whether an item was plant, 'it is no matter that it consists of some structure attached to the soil'.

Hoffmann J's fourth point is in essence concerned with the expected life of the assets claimed as plant. It has never been considered that an asset fails to be regarded as plant simply because it has a relatively lengthy period of use. Case law has always been clear on the point. *Yarmouth v France* spoke of plant including

'whatever apparatus is used by a businessman for carrying on his business ... which he keeps for permanent employment in his business.'

By way of illustration, the dock in *Barclay, Curle* was held to be plant despite that fact that it was agreed it might last for 80 to 100 years.

Hoffmann J expressly mentioned 'whether it (the alleged plant) was likely to be replaced within a relatively short period'. His intention was simply to suggest that a relatively short period of use would indicate that an asset has prima facie not become part of the premises; in the context of existing case law (referred to with approval by Hoffmann J), it cannot have been intended that assets not 'replaced within a relatively short period' were therefore premises. It is, of course, unclear what is meant by 'a relatively short period'. It must mean short by comparison with the life of the larger asset to which the plant is attached, in this case the land, which will endure infinitely longer than the structures.

The *Wimpy* case was subject to appeal, and consequently the comments of Hoffmann J were subject to review by a higher court.

The Court of Appeal unanimously endorsed the ratio of Hoffmann J, in particular his assertion that the key question was be whether it would be more appropriate to describe the item as having become part of the premises than as having retained a separate identity. Lord Justices Lloyd and Glidewell both acknowledged (as Hoffmann J had done) that the phrase 'something which becomes part of the premises' was borrowed from Lord Lowry in *Scottish & Newcastle*. Lloyd LJ observed (and in so doing affirmed the continuing applicability of *Yarmouth v France*):

'Of course, in one sense, everything on the premises, especially if it is fixed, may be said to form part of the premises. But obviously that is not what Lord Lowry had in mind. It would have been inconsistent with Lord Lindley's test in *Yarmouth v France* that plant includes all goods and chattels, fixed or movable.'

Glidewell LJ, after commenting that the decision in Scottish & Newcastle was binding on the Wimpy case, went on to say (our underlining):

'when Lord Lowry referred to "something which becomes part of the premises", he cannot have meant simply something which is affixed to the premises. He must have been expressing in other words the point made by Oliver LJ in *Cole Brothers v Phillips* about something which "performs simply and solely the function of housing the business".'

This echoes the comments of Brightman J in *Dixon v Fitch's Garage* [1975]:

'there is a clear thread running through the recent cases ... that a structure is not plant if its only purpose is to provide shelter and if it plays no part in what may be termed "the commercial process".'

To sum up, an asset only fails the premises test (ie it fails to qualify as plant) if its only function is to act as premises.

O'CULACHAIN V MCMULLAN BROS [1991] 1 IR 363

Plant

This Irish case dealt with the question of whether a petrol station canopy could be regarded as plant. Although similar in this respect to *Dixon v Fitch's Garage* (1975 – qv), the outcome was different. It was held that the canopy was plant by virtue of the fact that it fulfilled a function in the trade, namely:

'the provision of an attractive setting for the sale of ... products, the advertisement and promotion of those products, the creation of an overall impression of efficiency and financial solidarity in relation to the business of selling petrol and the attraction of customers to stop and purchase those products.'

It was appropriate to take a wider view of the trade carried on, rather than to look merely at whether the canopy assisted in the actual delivery of petrol.

CARR (INSPECTOR OF TAXES) V SAYER [1992] STC 396

Plant – IBAs

The taxpayers carried on the business of providing quarantine facilities for animals entering the United Kingdom. They incurred expenditure on the construction of kennels, both movable and permanent, and claimed that these kennels were plant, or industrial buildings. The General Commissioners held the movable kennels to be plant, and the Revenue did not appeal. The

High Court held that the permanent kennels were neither plant nor industrial buildings. As regards the former claim, Sir Donald Nicholls V-C observed:

'... buildings, which I have already noted would not normally be regarded as plant, do not cease to be buildings and become plant simply because they are purpose-built for a trading purpose.'

He also thought it was not possible to apportion the expenditure, so as to give tax relief for that part. The industrial buildings claim was based on what is now *s 274, Table A, item 3(d)*—ie 'a building or structure in use ... for the purposes of a trade which consists in the storage ... of goods or materials on their arrival by sea or air into any part of the United Kingdom'. The court held this did not apply. Sir Donald Nicholls decided that the taxpayers' service was provided to meet a need which existed, not as part of the ordinary process of physical transportation but because of statutory requirements. The claim for IBAs, like the claim for treatment as plant, was therefore dismissed.

ENSIGN TANKERS (LEASING) LTD V STOKES (INSPECTOR OF TAXES) [1992] STC 226

Qualifying expenditure

The taxpayer, which was not normally involved in film production, purchased into a tax scheme designed to take advantage of the availability of first-year allowances. Of total expenditure on the film (Escape to Victory) of $14 million, only $3.25 million was actually incurred by the taxpayer. The balance was lent to a production company on the understanding that it would be repaid out of the proceeds of the film, without recourse to partnership assets. The House of Lords held that an allowance was only due in respect of the $3.25 million, not on the whole $14 million. The fact that the taxpayer only engaged in the film trade for the fiscal purpose of obtaining a first-year allowance was of no import

HUNT (INSPECTOR OF TAXES) V HENRY QUICK LTD; KING (INSPECTOR OF TAXES) V BRIDISCO LTD [1992] STC 633

Plant

The facts in these two cases were practically identical and the appeals were heard together. Each taxpayer had erected a mezzanine platform in a warehouse in order to provide extra space for the storage of goods. These mezzanines comprised free-standing raised platforms on steel pillars with steel beams supporting wooden flooring. They were installed by a specialist firm, and it was admitted that it would have been difficult to buy an 'off the shelf' floor in the market place. The platform was bolted to the floor of the building only to ensure rigidity and safety, not for any reason of structural support. The company had applied for dispensation from building regulations, and in that application the platform was described as 'free-standing and not attached to the building in any way ... will be used exclusively for storage and no person will be resident on it'. The Commissioners had attached great weight to the lack of access by the public. On the grounds that the platforms were movable and temporary structures (they could be dismantled in three to four days if trading requirements changed) it was held that they did constitute plant for the purposes of capital allowances. However, lighting fixed to the underside of the platforms to illuminate the floor space below, did not so qualify, following dicta in *Wimpy International v Warland*, as the lighting was not specific to the trade.

O'GRADY V ROSCOMMON RACE COMMITTEE [1992] IR 425

Plant

This Irish case dealt with a new spectator stand at a racecourse. The facts were similar, therefore, to the English case *Brown v Burnley Football & Athletic Co Ltd* (1980 – qv). However the findings were different. It was held that expenditure on the new stand did constitute expenditure on plant. In contrast to the Burnley case, visitors to the racecourse did not sit in the stand throughout the entire event. Carroll J stated that:

'In my view the provision of an improved stand with accommodation which provides shelter from above and at the sides with new and improved viewing steps, must be considered as part of the means to get people to go to that racecourse for viewing horse races. It is very much akin to the swimming-pool provided by the caravan park owners [in *Cooke v Beach Stations Caravans* (qv)].'

GRAY (INSPECTOR OF TAXES) V SEYMOUR'S GARDEN CENTRE (HORTICULTURE) (A FIRM) [1995] STC 706

Plant

The taxpayers incurred expenditure on a 'planteria', effectively a greenhouse used for the nurturing and preserving of plants. Their claim that this constituted 'plant and machinery' for tax purposes was rejected by the Court of Appeal. Nourse LJ re-emphasised the importance of the 'premises test'. Note, however, that some greenhouses, notably those which are fully computer-controlled, have been accepted as plant by the Revenue. The Seymour's planteria did not even have integral heating, so the result should not deter other claimants.

MELLUISH (INSPECTOR OF TAXES) V BARCLAYS MERCANTILE INSURANCE FINANCE (NO 3) LTD [1995] STC 964

Plant – fixtures

The taxpayer company (BMI) and various associated companies leased items of equipment to local authorities. The court held that the equipment belonged to the lessors where they had the right to remove the equipment at the end of the lease term. Furthermore, it was held that the law of property prevailed to treat as fixtures certain items which the taxpayers had, by written agreement, sought to treat as chattels. The court's decision, however, that an election under what is now *s 177* could be made where the lessee was a non-taxpayer, so as to enable the lessor to claim allowances, was reversed (with effect from 23 July 1996) by subsequent amendment of *s 177(1)*. Also, the ownership requirement for plant was satisfied where the taxpayer was able to show it was in law or equity, the absolute owner of the equipment (that is, the beneficial owner) see **14.47**.

WEST SOMERSET RAILWAY PLC V CHIVERS (INSPECTOR OF TAXES) [1995] STC (SCD) 1

Entitlement to allowances

The onus of proving entitlement to allowances, and specifically that no person had previously been entitled to allowances, was held to fall on the claimant. This case is therefore often used by the HMRC to deny allowances where entitlement cannot be proved conclusively. However, the facts of this case were somewhat extreme, and it is not always appropriate to apply it in other circumstances. West Somerset Railway plc paid a capital sum to acquire a 99-year lease of a railway line and claimed plant and machinery allowances on the railway fixtures. However, the Special Commissioner held that the company failed to prove that no person had previously been entitled to claim capital allowances for the fixtures (whilst acknowledging that to do so would be an almost impossible task) and *on the balance of probabilities* it was likely that a prior freehold owner had become entitled to capital allowances. Therefore, no allowances were available to West Somerset Railway as the purchaser of the long lease. Where the *balance of probabilities* is that the claimant does have entitlement, allowances should be given.

BRADLEY (INSPECTOR OF TAXES) V LONDON ELECTRICITY PLC [1996] STC 1054

Plant

The taxpayer incurred expenditure on an electricity substation sited beneath Leicester Square, and claimed as plant not only the electrical equipment itself, but also the concrete housing. The latter claim was rejected on the grounds that the housing failed the premises test—other than housing the equipment, it performed no plant-like function. It was observed (at page 1079): 'The fact that the building in which a business is carried on is, by its construction, particularly well-suited to the business ... does not make it plant.' This echoes the conclusion in *Carr v Sayer* [1992] STC 396 (qv).

DECAUX (JC) (UK) LTD V FRANCIS [1996] STC (SCD) 281

Plant – fixtures

The taxpayer company carried on a trade of leasing automatic public conveniences (APCs) to local authorities. It also supplied bus shelters, etc which were not leased but which were provided on the understanding that Decaux could use them for advertising. The various items were securely fixed to the land and, in the case of the APCs, were connected to mains electricity and plumbing. Allowances were denied both under [*s 11*], because the assets, being fixed to the land, no longer belonged to Decaux, and under what is now [*s 176*], because Decaux did not have an interest in the land when it incurred the relevant expenditure. It was insufficient that the incurring of the expenditure brought into existence an interest in land. The right to enter in order to maintain the assets was in any case a mere contractual right which fell short of a 'licence to occupy land'. This case also considered the distinction between chattels and fixtures, and laid down principles subsequently enacted in *s 179*.

ENTERPRISE ZONE SYNDICATE V INSPECTOR OF TAXES [1996] STC (SCD) 336; BOSTOCK V TOTHAM (INSPECTOR OF TAXES) [1997] STC 764

IBAs – relevant interest and price paid

A building was bought by an enterprise zone syndicate, which was entitled to claim capital allowances on the 'net price paid' by it for the relevant interest, by making a 'just apportionment' excluding any expenditure on land.

The syndicate's apportionment compared the unit's floor area with other properties for which similar transactions had been undertaken and apportionments agreed with HMRC. Those previous agreements were calculated by deducting the original developer's cost to acquire the land from the actual purchase price paid to buy the finished building.

The Inspector rejected the syndicate's valuation on the grounds that it took no account of the statutory fiction that that there was a difference between the actual purchase price and the 'net price paid for the relevant interest'. Instead, the Inspector sought to use an alternative apportionment that borrowed the formula used to compute the gain on the part disposal of an asset. The excludable land value was calculated by dividing the value of the land by the same amount plus the market value of the building (ie its replacement cost).

It was held that the 'relevant interest' was a reference to the 'interest' relevant to the capital allowance (whether freehold or leasehold) and the 'net price paid' was the price paid for the building alone, excluding land, and so was distinct from the actual price paid. A just apportionment was required, which involved more than merely subtracting a land value from the price paid by the syndicate. In the absence of statutory guidance it was reasonable to borrow a 'not altogether inappropriate' formula from another statute.

Incidentally, the accepted total purchase price used for the apportionment included £17,575 of 'acquisition costs' which are understood to comprise stamp duty and legal and surveying fees.

BESTWAY (HOLDINGS) LTD V LUFF (INSPECTOR OF TAXES) [1998] STC 357

IBAs

The taxpayer operated wholesale cash-and-carry premises, and claimed industrial buildings allowances on the basis that part of its trade consisted of the storage of goods or materials, or alternatively that repackaging and labelling of products constituted 'the subjection of goods or material to a process'. The claim was rejected. It was held that in order to qualify for IBAs, storage had to be an end in itself—it was not sufficient that goods were stored for some other purpose, in this case sale to customers. Secondly, it was held that the repacking, labelling, etc did not constitute a 'process', but were 'mere preliminaries' to sale. Lightman J observed:

'... the activities in question were limited, mundane and of no substantial significance'.

Lightman J also observed that in order to qualify for IBAs by virtue of what is now *s 276* in respect of part of a trade, 'the activities in question must be a significant, separate and identifiable part of the trade'.

GIROBANK PLC V CLARKE (INSPECTOR OF TAXES) [1998] STC 182

IBAs – process – office

The bank claimed IBAs on a building in which information-bearing documents were subjected to a process consisting, inter alia, of sorting and batching the documents, and reading the information contained thereon. Some documents were then marked to indicate that they had been processed. The claim was rejected by the Court of Appeal on the grounds that the documents were not 'goods or materials'. The Court of Appeal, in contrast to the High Court, held that the term 'goods or materials' should be interpreted in the restricted sense of 'merchandise or wares' previously favoured in *Buckingham v Securitas Properties Ltd* (qv). The Court of Appeal said little about whether the activities constituted a process, but broadly supported Lindsay J in the High Court, who had found no authority for limiting the scope of the term 'any process' to indicate only those processes having an 'industrial character'. A qualifying process for IBA purposes certainly did not have to be a step in or towards the manufacture or sale of something.

The case also includes a useful debate on the meaning of the word 'office'. This was narrowly defined as 'the place where the central management emanates and where the manager and his staff do their work' (following a Canadian case, *Carter v Standard Ltd* (1915) 30 DLR 492).

SARSFIELD (INSPECTOR OF TAXES) V DIXONS GROUP PLC [1998] STC 938

IBAs – storage

One company within the Dixons Group used a warehouse for the purposes of a trade which consisted of receiving, storing and delivering goods purchased by Dixons for sale in its retail shops. Industrial buildings allowances were claimed, on the basis that the warehouse was in use for the purposes of a transport undertaking. This claim was rejected by the Court of Appeal on the grounds that any transport was merely ancillary to the purposes of a retail shop. It was stated in the High Court:

> 'A building is used for a purpose which is ancillary to the purposes of a retail shop if its user is confined to furthering the purposes of the retail shop, ie subservient and subordinate to retail selling.'

The transport undertaking was of a substantial size in terms of investment, number of employees and turnover, and made a taxable profit. However, the corporate relationship between the transport undertaking and its customers was a key consideration. The 'transport' company had no external customers, and the use of the warehouse was held to be 'subservient and subordinate and therefore ancillary to the purposes of the retail shops'.

ABC LTD V M (INSPECTOR OF TAXES) [2002] STC (SCD) 78

Entitlement – incurring expenditure

A taxpayer company entered into complex arrangements whereby a payment for plant and machinery was paid to the vendor, but was then (via a number of group companies) placed on deposit elsewhere within the purchaser's group.

Even though the individual taxpayer company was ignorant of the circular nature of the payment viewed from a group perspective, its claim for allowances was rejected on the basis that the transaction had no commercial reality, and that, in effect, no expenditure had been incurred on plant and machinery.

BARCLAYS MERCANTILE BUSINESS FINANCE LTD V MAWSON (INSPECTOR OF TAXES) [2002] EWHC 2466 (CH), [2003] STC 66, [2005] STC 1 (HL)

Plant – leasing

Sale and leaseback arrangements were unsuccessfully challenged by the Inland Revenue. In essence, it was held that a finance lessor may obtain allowances on plant, even though the availability of those allowances is a fundamental reason for the acquisition of the plant.

The Court of Appeal confirmed that provided the expenditure was incurred on the provision of machinery or plant wholly and exclusively for the purposes of the trade, it was irrelevant whether or not the trader's objective was or included the obtaining of capital allowances, and the Ramsay principle (ie that the scheme should be looked at as a whole to disregard any steps that have no business purpose, apart from avoiding tax) could not be applied. (*WT Ramsay Ltd v IRC; Eilbeck (Inspector of Taxes) v Rawling* [1981] STC 174.)

It was also irrelevant how the trader acquired the funds to incur the expenditure. Whilst the cost of finance will not itself qualify for allowances, the fact that finance has to be obtained by way of loan does not preclude allowances being claimed on the asset itself.

The House of Lords dismissed the Revenue's appeal.

TRANSCO PLC V DYALL (INSPECTOR OF TAXES) [2002] STC (SCD) 199

Capital/revenue – repairs – renewals

The taxpayer operated a gas distribution network, and claimed as a repair the cost of preventative maintenance. It had a policy of identifying pipes at risk, and inserting polyethylene (a thermoplastic material highly resistant to fracture and corrosion) into existing cast iron pipes as a matter of priority before failure actually occurred. The replacement was not of whole areas of pipes, but only of a 'mains unit' (the area which was between two joints in a cast iron pipe). In 2001 the Health and Safety Executive announced that Transco Plc would be required to replace all cast iron mains within 30m of property over a 30-year period. The introduction of the polyethylene did not enable the pipeline system to transport any different type of gas, nor did it alter the pressure at which gas could be transported in the system. Also, there was no increase in the longevity (or technical lifetime) of the system.

The Revenue considered that the expenditure was of a capital nature because it was incurred in connection with a long-term policy of renewal and improvement of the entire system. It was held, however, that the sections repaired were merely a part of the overall entirety, ie the network, and that there was no element of improvement. There was no significant prolongation of the network's useful life beyond that conferred by repair or maintenance: there was no increase in capacity; there was no substantial improvement in the quality of output or reduction in previously assessed operating costs; and there was no substantial increase in the open market value of the fixed asset.

SHOVE (INSPECTOR OF TAXES) V LINGFIELD PARK 1991 LTD [2004] STC 805

Plant

The taxpayer constructed an all-weather horse-racing surface and claimed it as plant. The High Court rejected the claim, on the grounds that the track functioned as part of the premises of the racecourse.

ANCHOR INTERNATIONAL LTD V IRC [2005] STC 411

Plant

The taxpayer successfully claimed plant allowances on artificial football pitches, which consisted of a 'carpet' of synthetic turf, on a specially prepared base. The carpet was held not to be a structure (inter alia, it was not fixed, and could be replaced without disturbing the base or foundation works). Furthermore, although the carpet could be regarded as the setting for the business, that did not prevent it from also being regarded as plant used in the trade.

It was also held that the relevant item for consideration was the carpet alone, rather than the whole asset consisting of carpet and base. As a result, the base for the carpet also qualified for plant allowances, as although it was a structure, it fell within the exemption of what is now *CAA 2001, s 23, item 22, List C* — 'the alteration of land for the purpose only of installing plant or machinery'.

REVENUE AND CUSTOMS COMMISSIONERS V MACO DOOR AND WINDOW HARDWARE (UK) LTD [2006] ALL ER (D) 267 (JUL); MACO DOOR AND WINDOW HARDWARE (UK) LIMITED V HER MAJESTY'S REVENUE AND CUSTOMS COMRS [2008] UKHL 54

IBAs – storage

The taxpayer imported into the UK door and window fittings manufactured by its Austrian parent company, which it stored and sold primarily to wholesalers. It built a warehouse and claimed industrial buildings allowances (IBAs) because the building was used for 'storage' [*s 274(1)(a), Table A, item 3*]. HMRC accepted that the building was used for the company's trade and that the hardware were goods or materials which were to be used in the manufacture of other materials. However, it disagreed that the building was in use for the purposes of a trade that consists in the storage of such goods. It argued that any storage was an inherent part of the company's wholesale activity and the decision in *Bestway (Holdings) Ltd* (qv) prevented wholesalers from claiming IBAs.

The High Court held that that although as a matter of ordinary language the goods were clearly 'stored', the expenditure did not qualify for IBAs, because to qualify any storage must itself be an activity in the nature of trade (ie a commercial trading activity carried out in its own right and directed toward making a profit) that is 'significant, separate and identifiable'. In this context physical separation was of no consequence; commercial separation was the key, and Maco's storage was simply carried out to support its wholesale trading operation and not as a trading activity in itself. The decision was reversed by the Court of Appeal who rejected the High Court's insistence on commercial separation. However, it was later upheld by the House of Lords who overturned the Court of Appeal's ruling.

This resulting narrow interpretation suggests that the provisions in *s 267* that extend IBAs to parts of a trade or undertaking are superfluous for taxpayers with 'composite' trades, undertaking various activities (some of which might qualify for IBAs), unless the potentially IBA qualifying activity is both significant, separate and identifiable and a commercial trading activity directed towards making a profit in its own right.

JD WETHERSPOON PLC V COMMISSIONERS FOR HM REVENUE AND CUSTOMS (2008) SPC 657; [2009] UKFTT 374 (TC); [2012] UKUT 42 (TCC)

Plant

The decision focused on sample pub fit-outs. JD Wetherspoon and the Revenue had failed to agree on whether more than 120 types of expenditure qualified for plant and machinery capital allowances. In determining the matter, the Commissioners/tribunal judges addressed three key issues:

(*a*)   whether assets were plant or machinery;

(*b*)   whether certain building alterations were incidental to the installation of plant or machinery (that is, qualifying under what is now *CAA 2001, s 25*);

(*c*)   to what extent, 'indirect' expenditure on contractor's preliminaries and consultants' professional fees could be allocated on to the builder's direct costs.

In addressing point (*a*), the Commissioners/First-tier Tribunal judges looked in detail at timber wall panelling as an example, in order to seek to establish general principles to be applied to other assets. They sought to apply the 'premises' tests put forward by Hoffmann J in *Wimpy*, but drew conclusions that appeared incompatible with the facts. They then appeared to add an additional test of their own devising (not put forward by either party), namely whether the panels were 'an unexceptional component which would not be an unusual feature of premises of [this] type'.

In other words, if it was not unusual to find a particular asset in a particular type of property, that asset must be part of the premises, and consequently not plant. On those grounds they rejected the taxpayer's claim for the timber panelling (despite all parties accepting that it was an embellishment to create ambience for Wetherspoon's trade) and other decorative assets, including cornices and architraves. This apparent test appeared to be inherently flawed; in practical terms, when applied to many common assets, the test gave results which were unequivocally wrong.

Wetherspoon appealed and contended that this represented a new wholly illegitimate legal test. However, the Upper Tribunal disagreed, concluding that the Commissioners were not seeking to lay down some principle of general application (ie a new test) but rather explaining their reasoning – which was that it was ordinary (so-called 'unexceptional') panelling which simply turned an un-panelled room into a panelled room. This decision is at odds with principles laid down by higher courts, which appear to have been overlooked by the tribunal. Lord Justice Oliver commented in the Court of Appeal in *Cole Bros* (subsequently endorsed by the House of Lords and referred to with approval by the House of Lords in *Scottish & Newcastle* and the Court of Appeal in *Wimpy*) that the 'premises' is something that 'simply and solely' houses the business. Therefore, given that the parties agreed the panelling created ambience, following binding precedent the tribunal should have had no option but to conclude that it was plant.

On point (*b*), the Upper Tribunal concluded that the purpose of *s 25* was that if plant is installed in an existing building it is possible that something will not fit, which will lead to alterations having to be made to the existing building. Therefore, *s 25* is intended to level the playing field between new and existing buildings by affording taxpayers relief for expenditure on existing buildings which would not be needed if the same plant was installed in new buildings or in the open air.

They considered a number of assets and held that the following qualified (some under general principles and some because they were incidental to the installation of plant):

- foul water drainage, including cold store drainage;

- strengthened upper floors to take the load of kitchen equipment;

- pattresses (that is, mountings) to support equipment;

- panelled toilet cubicles and back panelling to conceal cisterns and pipes (but the tribunal indicated that it would have found these ineligible if HMRC had appealed on that point);

- splashback wall tiling and plastering (ie small areas around sinks, lavatory basins or other equipment, but not apportioned amounts of fully tiled walls or floors);

- toilet and kitchen lighting; and

- PVC flooring in disabled WCs (having the 'special function' of assisting wheelchair traction).

Conversely, expenditure on the following was held not to qualify:

- brickwork and blockwork toilet cubicles (note that the tribunal indicated that it would have also have found panelled cubicles ineligible if HMRC had appealed on that point – given that HMRC and the taxpayer appeared to be in agreement, some commentators have taken this as indicative of the tribunal's limited understanding of the issues generally);

- wipe-clean wall-tiling in a kitchen, which the taxpayer argued was required due to hygiene requirements arising from the volume of grease-laden steam produced by cookers. This did not have a sufficient nexus with the installation of those cookers. A cooker could be used perfectly well (that is, 'serve its proper purpose', in the words of Lord Reid in *Barclay, Curle*) without the tiling. Consequently, expenditure on the tiling was not incidental to the installation of plant (ie the cookers);

- waterproof floor coatings and non-slip/wipe-clean floors (with the exception of PVC sheeting in disabled toilets);

- doors and frames relating to general areas of the toilets (not the toilet cubicles); and

- plastering and painting generally.

Turning to point (*c*), the Upper Tribunal rejected the Revenue's argument that preliminaries and professional fees qualified only if they were directly related to the acquisition and installation of assets that are plant, and '... to the extent that this sensible conclusion involved any issue of law at all' instead permitted claims based on a pro rata apportionment of the total preliminaries and fees incurred.

B&E SECURITY SYSTEMS LTD V COMMISSIONERS FOR HM REVENUE AND CUSTOMS [2010] UKFTT 146 (TC)

Plant – incidental expenditure

The taxpayer was a Northern Ireland-based company whose core business was the installation, maintenance and monitoring of domestic and commercial intruder alarm systems. However, it widened its activities to include sensitive surveillance work and won monitoring contracts for two undisclosed government agencies and a large town.

The pursuit of these contracts (particularly the first two) led directly to the construction of a specialised and specially constructed control room to house equipment from where the surveillance monitoring services could be carried out. The control room was formed by altering an existing room in a building already in occupation and use by the company. Its design and construction had to satisfy the requirements of the relevant British Standard Code of Practice and the finished facility was subject to regular inspections. Substantial alteration works were carried out over a six-month period including: strengthening walls, floors and ceilings; providing a raised access computer floor for extensive cabling; fire proof security doors and an interlock; providing independent amenities including washroom facilities and a kitchen; and independent power supplies including backup batteries and a generator in a newly constructed generator house. Computers, screens, monitoring devices and other equipment were then purchased and installed.

HMRC agreed that the security equipment qualified for plant and machinery allowances, but not the control room. The taxpayer argued that the control room itself qualified under the provisions of *s 25* because the expenditure was incurred on alterations to an existing building incidental to the installation of plant and machinery (ie the equipment).

The tribunal held that the control room expenditure was incidental to the equipment and so qualified for plant and machinery capital allowances. Following *Wetherspoon* the tribunal considered that there had to be a sufficient nexus between the installation of the security equipment and the construction of the walls, floors, ceilings etc. Firstly, the tribunal concluded that it was only because the company pursued and ultimately secured the two specialist security related contracts that any of the works needed to be carried out. Secondly, upon winning the contracts and needing to buy the equipment the control works became necessary and in practical terms inevitable. Thirdly, the company had little, if any, discretion as to the precise extent of the works required. Finally, the tribunal considered the issue of proportionality, because the word 'incidental' suggests something subordinate or secondary to the installation of the plant. They concluded that the total control room construction costs of £61,173 were not disproportionate to the total £78,658 spent on security equipment.

CHRISTOPHER WILLS V COMMISSIONERS FOR HM REVENUE AND CUSTOMS [2010] UKFTT 174 (TC)

Capital/revenue – repairs

The taxpayer spent about £100,000 renovating a listed-building outbuilding (attached to a residential rental property). The building was previously used as storage, a games room and additional living space and garage, but had become extremely run down and damp. Indeed, its state of disrepair was so dangerous it risked collapsing. Because the property was listed the only option was a "substantial repair scheme". The works brought the interior more up to date, including adding heating, electric power points and a water supply (but no basins, toilets, kitchen or anything that would allow the space to be anything more than additional living space ancillary to the main house). The taxpayer expensed about 40% of the cost as repairs and capitalised the remainder. The tribunal allowed the taxpayer's claim (that is, held the work was of "essential repair") and also allowed as repairs some further structural works not originally treated as such.

MOONLIGHT TEXTILES LTD V COMMISSIONERS FOR HM REVENUE AND CUSTOMS [2010] UKFTT 500 (TC)

Capital/revenue – repairs

The taxpayer manufactured and retailed curtains and accessories. It occupied a two-storey building with a showroom and warehouse on the ground floor, plus workshop, offices, boardroom and kitchen on the first floor. It spent about £70,000 renovating the property including completely replacing the roof, major alterations, redecoration and improvement of the kitchen, a reconfiguration of the stairs, removal of a wall, extension of the floor, installation of new steps, a false ceiling and disabled access. The alterations were designed to accommodate a shift in the business to providing a bespoke curtain/blind-making service along with their installation and resulted in a larger refurbished showroom and a reduced warehouse facility.

The taxpayer had expensed about 80% of the works as repairs and claimed a corresponding tax-deduction. It was accepted by both parties that the 'entirety' had not been replaced. HMRC agreed that the roof repairs and part of the kitchen alterations constituted repairs. But these comprised less than 15% of the expenditure. Otherwise, the tribunal held that the company had chosen to adapt the premises to its needs. This resulted in a significant improvement of the premises and changed the character of the building as a whole. Therefore, all of the broader expenditure was capital, some of which qualified for plant and machinery allowances.

MRS CA ANDREW V COMMISSIONERS FOR HM REVENUE AND CUSTOMS [2010] UKFTT 546 (TC)

Plant

A public house external timber 'gazebo' in use as a smoking shelter qualified as plant. The gazebo was freestanding, with a polygonal floor and roof, three foot high dado timber walls with latticework above (open to the elements), timber benching around the sides and no door. Because the gazebo was a relatively lightweight, moveable item it was held not to be a 'building' or 'fixed structure' (per *ss 21–22*). It was kept in the permanent employment of the business and was an embellishment of the garden that provided facilities for customers to sit and eat and drink. So in the context of the publican's business it satisfied the *Yarmouth v France* business apparatus test and it was more appropriate to regard it as plant, rather than premises (per *Wimpy International Ltd v Warland*).

MRS ME MCMILLIN V COMMISSIONERS FOR HM REVENUE AND CUSTOMS [2011] UKFTT 65 (TC)

Plant

A taxpayer unsuccessfully claimed plant allowances for entire holiday cottages, including specifically: stone floors, windows, painting and decorating, and an earth bund.

The taxpayer, who was a partner in a major accountancy firm and represented herself, carried out some building works on a house and built four stone cottages next door. The expenditure was incurred for holiday lettings purposes and the taxpayer described it as an 'eco holiday development' which was 'meant to demonstrate the benefits of green design, technology and living'. In the income tax return for 2006/07, plant and machinery allowances were claimed for various items and agreed with HMRC (eg, heating systems, including the screed laid above under floor heating). However, HMRC considered that about £55,000 of expenditure on the disputed items was not plant. The taxpayer contended that the whole site was plant, or alternatively each item must be.

The tribunal noted there were only rare cases (such as the *Barclay Curle* dry dock), where entire premises were themselves plant, and holiday cottages were not, in its view, one of them. Furthermore, the taxpayer contended that the cottages were analogous to caravans, which were excluded from the *s 21* definition of a 'building' by *s 23, List C, item 19*; the tribunal held that holiday cottages or 'eco holiday developments' could not be classed as caravans.

On the individual assets in contention:

- Stone floors – The taxpayer said that Brazilian slate floors had been laid as an integral part of the under floor heating in two of the properties. The tribunal found that the principal purpose was to provide an interior floor which was intended to remain permanently in place (in accordance with *s 23(4)*). Therefore, *s 21, List A, item 1* directed that the floor was an asset treated as 'building' that could not be plant;

- Windows – The taxpayer argued that the windows (which were argon filled and some faced south) were plant because, in addition to letting in light and keeping out draughts, they helped to control the level of heat in the buildings. Furthermore, solar shading was provided to some of the windows and if solar shading could be plant (*s 33A*) then so should the windows. The tribunal noted that most of the windows could be opened, which would defeat any insulation properties they had. It held that they were simply ordinary windows which part of the 'building' (*s 21, List A, item 1*);

- Painting and decorating – The taxpayer believed that the 'organic paint' applied to the cottage walls helped to 'clean the atmosphere'. She cited the Australian case of *Wanagratta Woolen Mills Ltd*, where dye house wall paint was held to be plant. The tribunal found that the claims made by the paint's manufacturer did not support the taxpayer's contention. The paint had no function beyond covering the walls and making them easier to clean. It had not retained a separate identity from the walls and, therefore, was part of the 'premises';

- Earth bund – This was made of spoil from works on the site. The taxpayer argued that the bund provided insulation to the north side of the cottages so was, in effect, part of the heating installation. Therefore, it constituted the alteration of land for the purpose only of installing plant or machinery (*s 23, List C, item 22*). The tribunal found that the bund's main purpose was to allow for the disposal of waste from the building works. Even if it had two purposes (also providing insulation) *s 23, List C, item 22* contained the word 'only'. The bund was excluded from plant allowances by virtue of being works involving the alteration of land (*s 22(1)(b)*).

Finally, the taxpayer bemoaned the perceived injustice of the legislation in force at the time allowing greater allowances to those who develop buildings in non-environmentally friendly ways. The tribunal, rather dryly, noted that it was not within its jurisdiction to amend the legislation and declined to comment on the fairness or otherwise of the law.

COMMISSIONERS FOR HM REVENUE AND CUSTOMS V TOWER MCASHBACK LLP 1 [2007] SPC 619; [2008] EWHC 2387 (CH); [2010] EWCA CIV 32; [2011] UKSC 19

Plant – first-year allowances

MCashback was a software development company that needed to raise money to develop its product, so entered into a complicated pre-ordained transaction devised by Tower Group, a financial services company. Four limited liability partnerships (LLPs) were established to purchase licences to use the software they intended to exploit. Individual investors into the LLPs funded one-quarter of their capital from their own resources and borrowed the other three-quarters on uncommercial terms via a series of circular transactions from MCashback using interest-free non-recourse loans put in place for tax purposes.

The tax efficiency for investors relied upon the LLPs qualifying for 100% first-year allowances available for expenditure by small enterprises on information and communications technology, so that an investment of £10,000 generated capital allowances of £40,000 and saved investors tax of £16,000 (at the 40% higher rate). Therefore, the economic reality was that the investors only risked the capital provided from their own resources, but if the scheme worked they could obtain tax relief on the gross amount contributed, which should be sufficient to recoup their initial investment and provide an adequate return, even if the software was not commercially successful.

First-year allowances were claimed in respect of the full amount of first-year qualifying expenditure but HMRC rejected this.

The Supreme Court overturned the findings of previous courts to hold that the composite transactions in the case did not, on a realistic appraisal of the facts, meet the statutory test which requires real expenditure for the real purpose of acquiring plant for use in a trade. Therefore, only the 25% provided by the investors had been incurred on the acquisition of the software (not the whole of the claimed expenditure) and only 25% of the claimed first-year allowances were available.

TAPSELL (MR & MRS) & LESTER (MR) (TRADING AS PARTNERSHIP 'THE GRANLEYS') V COMMISSIONERS FOR HM REVENUE AND CUSTOMS [2011] UKFTT 376 (TC)

Plant – apportionment

The taxpayers bought a second-hand care home in 2003 for £650,001. In the contract £40,000 was allocated to 'fixtures and fittings'. In the tax year ended April 2003, the buyers claimed capital allowances on plant and machinery expenditure of £146,014. This was based on a £106,014 apportionment of the purchase price for plant and machinery fixtures, plus the £40,000 contract allocation.

However, a couple of months later, the sellers also submitted a £68,811 capital allowances claim for the same tax year. No supporting details were provided. The sellers emigrated to the USA and could not be traced by the buyers. HMRC disallowed the buyers' capital allowances claim on the grounds that they had failed to show that the same expenditure on plant and machinery had not been claimed by the sellers.

The tribunal found against the buyers. It held that the burden of proof fell upon the buyers to prove that the sellers had not claimed on the same plant and machinery.

The fact that the sellers had claimed did not prevent the buyers from claiming. However, the buyers' claim had to be capped to the sellers' disposal value. The tribunal was not bound by the £40,000 contract allocation (*Fitton v Gilders & Heaton* (1955) 36 TC 233). However, despite the buyer having submitted an apportionment and the seller's claim also being known, the tribunal bizarrely '... could not find any just and reasonable basis upon which to make an apportionment'. Given the limited evidence and information about the sellers' capital allowances claim and disposal value, the tribunal found HMRC's approach was reasonable. The taxpayer's claim was limited to the £40,000 contract allocation. In essence, the purchaser suffered due to HMRC's failure to enquire into the seller's claim or to require the seller to account for an adequate disposal value.

BROCKHOUSE (MR PD, MRS J AND LD) V COMMISSIONERS FOR HM REVENUE AND CUSTOMS [2011] UKFTT 380 (TC)

Plant – personal security assets

The taxpayers' business sold fish, aquariums, ponds and associated products. Part of their site comprised a field with a storage lake. In their tax year ended April 2007, they spent about £81,000 on over 2,000 metres of galvanised palisade fencing around the field perimeter. The area was previously fenced by an insecure timber fence with barbed wire along the top that was already in disrepair when the land was bought in 1991.

The taxpayers claimed that the fence had been installed to meet a 'special threat' to Mr Brockhouse's personal physical security that had arisen because of the business and, therefore, was plant (see **15.90**). They said that Mr Brockhouse had felt threatened and vulnerable to attacks. There had been vandalism and poaching and he had had confrontations with poachers (that had resulted in him receiving a suspended prison sentence for carrying a loaded shotgun in public and assault). The stock lake was remotely located, which meant access was restricted and personal protection was offered to those tending the stocks. The taxpayers' home was also close by. They argued that although intruders were attracted by the valuable fish in the lake, the lake was netted, so theft was difficult, and the risk of property loss was low. Injury to Mr Brockhouse was said to be the main concern.

The taxpayers were represented by their accountant. However, unfortunately he had not been provided with all of the necessary factual detail about exactly what had happened and when (especially whether any incidents in the past had been targeted against the business or Mr Brockhouse personally).

The tribunal found against the taxpayers. It held that 'special' meant 'exceptional in quality or degree, unusual, out of the ordinary' (Shorter English Dictionary; *Lord Hanson v Mansworth* (2004) SpC 410). There was '… far too little evidence' to conclude that Mr Brockhouse faced a special threat to his personal security. Furthermore, what evidence there was led directly to the conclusion that the purpose of installing the fencing was to protect the land and stock, not solely to protect Mr Brockhouse's personal security.

G PRATT & SONS V COMMISSIONERS FOR HM REVENUE AND CUSTOMS [2011] UKFTT 380 (TC)

Capital/revenue – repairs

The taxpayers were a family partnership and ran a mainly dairy farm, which had been owned for many years. They repaired 239 metres of the farm drive that ran to the nearest public road. The drive was also used by suppliers delivering to the farm and on a daily basis by a 20,000 litre milk tanker collecting from the farm's dairy.

Amongst other costs, they spent £23,300 re-surfacing the drive with concrete. Originally the drive surface would have been stones laid on bare earth, but some time before had been covered by tarmac. The drive had last been surfaced about 30 years before and had deteriorated to the point that the local refuse collectors had refused to drive up it.

The repairs took four weeks. They comprised removing the top layer of tarmac until a stable sub-surface was reached, repairing the sub-surface potholes and creating a hard-core base over the original stone (using broken up pieces of the surface layers), and then re-surfacing with concrete. New kerbing was added to bring the drive up to modern standards. The drive was not widened and its load-bearing capacity was not increased.

The First-tier Tribunal found in favour of the taxpayers. It held that there was not a renewal of the entirety of the drive, but a repair to an existing asset. Before the work on the drive, the dairy sent 20,000 litre tankers for milk collections and that situation continued following its completion. Similar considerations applied to deliveries by suppliers to the farm. Albeit, the tribunal noted, that it might have taken a different view if the drive had been altered to accommodate larger milk tankers or supply lorries (which it had not). Therefore, the expenditure was tax-deductible revenue.

FARNELL ELECTRONIC COMPONENTS LTD V COMMISSIONERS FOR HM REVENUE AND CUSTOMS [2011] UKFTT 597 (TC)

IBAs – process

The company sought to claim IBAs on a distribution warehouse in which goods were purportedly subjected to a process consisting of storing, sorting, packaging and dispatch.

The company purchased products, mainly electrical components, in bulk quantities and handled them in the building in a sophisticated way that allowed it to sell products in very small quantities with a very short turnaround time.

The tribunal concluded that to determine what a trade consists of, it is necessary to consider the composite whole of the activities involved, rather than any one or more constituent activities, undertaken, however important or essential. The company's trade consisted in the purchase and sale of goods by way of distribution, not in the operations carried out at the building. Therefore, its trade did not consist in the subjection of goods to a process as required by *CAA 2001, s 274*. Furthermore, because each individual product was dealt with according to what it was, the products were not subjected to a sufficiently substantial measure of uniformity of treatment to cause the operations in the building to be a process in the relevant sense. So the operations carried out at the building were not the subjection of goods to any process.

HOARDWEEL FARM PARTNERSHIP V COMMISSIONERS FOR HM REVENUE AND CUSTOMS [2012] UKFTT 402 (TC)

AIA – mixed partnership

A farm operated in partnership by a husband and wife, and a connected company, was unsuccessful in claiming an annual investment allowance. The partnership was not a 'qualifying person' (that is, an individual, a partnership of which all the members are individuals, or a company) as required by *CAA 2001 s 38A*.

NEXT DISTRIBUTION LTD, NEXT GROUP PLC AND THE PAIGE GROUP LTD V COMMISSIONERS FOR HM REVENUE AND CUSTOMS [2014] UKUT 227 (TCC)

IBAs – process and storage

A business failed to claim IBAs on two enormous highly automated warehouses in which goods stored there were purportedly subjected to a process of 'stepping-down' a bulk delivery into smaller parcels, as well as the buildings being used to store goods on their arrival into the UK.

The tribunal held that the goods were the individual items and not the bulk. But the work done was essentially ancillary (ie unloading, checking, holding, labelling, transporting and dispatch). And overall nothing was physically done to most of the goods, which were simply unpacked, then selected by size, quantity and colour, and repacked into smaller retail quantities. Because the individual goods remained unchanged, they were not subjected to a process.

It was accepted that there was storage of goods in the buildings that was part of the company's trade, but it did not meet the IBA statutory requirement. First, because the goods were not subjected to a process, the trade did not consist in the storage of goods or materials which are to be subjected, in the course of a trade, to any process. Second, although the goods were in use for the purposes of a trade which consists in the storage of goods or materials, that trade did not consist in the storage on their arrival in the UK from a place outside the UK. This was because the goods arrived by ship and were transferred by road or rail, over distances of around 200 miles, to the buildings. Arrival connoted the act of instance of reaching a place. Therefore, they had arrived in the UK (at port) before being taken to the buildings, so there was no storage in the buildings on arrival in the UK from outside.

GRANT BOWMAN T/A THE JANITOR CLEANING COMPANY V COMMISSIONERS FOR HM REVENUE AND CUSTOMS [2012] UKFTT 607 (TC)

Capital expenditure – consultancy payments

The taxpayer was a litigant-in-person who failed to appear at the tribunal. He claimed that a 'consultancy payment' of £11,000 was tax-deductible. HMRC argued that it was capital. Mr Bowman contended that, if it was capital, it qualified for capital allowances.

The tribunal held that the payment had nothing to do with the day to day running of the business (The Janitor Cleaning Co) and was capital. £2,000 was to buy an identifiable asset (called Cleaner Times) and the other £9,000 was for assistance given in trying to win a long-term contract, which fell through. The evidence adduced by the taxpayer was 'threadbare' and he gave no rationale for his contention that any of the expenditure qualified for capital allowances. Predictably, the taxpayer's appeal failed.

MGF (TRENCH CONSTRUCTION SYSTEMS) LTD V COMMISSIONERS FOR HM REVENUE AND CUSTOMS [2012] UKFTT 739 (TC)

First-year allowances – leasing

A business successfully claimed first-year allowances (FYAs) for plant and machinery supplied without labour but with other services and benefits.

MGF supplied equipment to the construction industry to support temporary excavations (that is, earthworks shoring equipment). This included hydraulic struts, beams, piles and panels. Customers benefitted from a design service as well as the provision of equipment. The design was a very technical process specific to the individual excavation project, taking into account not only the type of shoring equipment to be provided, but also the excavation method and the process of installation.

HMRC contended that the equipment was used for leasing and, therefore, the company was not entitled to claim FYAs because of General Exclusion 6 set out in *CAA 2001 s 46*.

The tribunal noted that where leasing is provided together with something else the circumstances may be such that what is being provided can no longer be described simply as the leasing of plant. There could be circumstances where plant is supplied without labour, but with other services and benefits such that it could not be considered to be leasing. It held that what the company did could not fairly be described merely as the leasing of plant because it included a package of services. These comprised designing the solution and taking responsibility for the design, assembling plant before transportation to the construction site, providing plant for the contractor to implement the solution, and dealing with any issues during the construction project (eg, unforeseen ground obstructions or contractor errors).

CAIRNSMILL CARAVAN PARK V COMMISSIONERS FOR HM REVENUE AND CUSTOMS [2013] UKFTT 164 (TC)

Capital/revenue – repairs

A caravan park replaced a grassed area with hardcore and it was accepted that this was tax-deductible revenue expenditure for tax purposes.

Because the grass surface had deteriorated, Cairnsmill decided to restore the area of its caravan pitches that were used short-term by touring caravan customers. To allow the grass to become re-established would have required the area to be left largely vacant for about two holiday seasons. So instead, the business spent £89,201 on a hardcore foundation (made from the nearby former Leuchars air-base runway surface) with a top dressing of loose gravel.

It was held that the 'entirety' was the entire caravan park, and the area resurfaced was only a very small part of that entirety (three acres out of 51 acres). Therefore, the entirety was not replaced. Furthermore, there was no improvement. It was questionable whether the new surface was more durable, because the original grass surface had lasted about 50 years. Also, the new surface cost marginally more to maintain. The hardcore had less aesthetic appeal than grass, was not suitable as a recreation area for children, nor could the fixing pins be easily found to erect caravan awnings. This had generated customer complaints.

THE EXECUTORS OF LORD HOWARD OF HENDERSKELFE (DECEASED) V COMMISSIONERS FOR HM REVENUE AND CUSTOMS [2014] EWCA CIV 278

Plant – work of art

In this capital gains tax case, a work of art on display in a stately home was held to be plant.

The painting of Omai (a South Sea islander) was by Sir Joshua Reynolds. It was acquired by the fifth earl of Carlisle in 1776 and kept at Castle Howard in Yorkshire until its sale in 2001. The castle was owned by Castle Howard Estate Ltd since 1950. Its principal activity was land ownership, specifically opening the house and grounds and exhibiting its works of art to the public.

The question was whether the painting was a 'wasting asset' (meaning that no capital gains tax was due on its sale). The painting would be a wasting asset if it was plant or machinery. HMRC effectively accepted that the painting functioned as plant; its principal challenge was that it was used in the company's trade, whereas it was owned by Lord Howard's executors (who then disposed of the painting). That is, even though the company could say the painting was plant in its hands, the executors were unable to do so.

It was held that the trade was an unusual or specialised one and the painting was being used for the promotion of the trade and (until its sale) was kept for permanent employment in the company's business. Therefore, it was plant. For capital gains tax purposes an object can be plant even if it is used in the trade of a company controlled by the owner of the object, rather than used by the owner in his trade. This differs from the capital allowances legislation (*CAA 2001, s 11*) which expressly provides that the plant must belong to the person who incurs capital expenditure on the object for the purposes of his qualifying activity.

HOPEGAR PROPERTIES LTD V COMMISSIONERS FOR HM REVENUE AND CUSTOMS [2013] UKFTT 331 (TC)

Repairs

The taxpayer had a business of buying, developing, managing and letting land and buildings. An associated contracting firm spent 15 weeks carrying out works to the main entrance road of a 40-year-old industrial estate that it owned. This needed repair and widening because of an increase in traffic of heavier lorries, transporters and other vehicles which substantially exceeded the original weight expectations when the road was built. This caused a risk to underlaid fibre-optic cables. Footpaths were also breaking up.

HMRC accepted as repairs: diverting telephone and fibre-optic cables; and temporarily diverting the main carriageway and then re-laying and re-surfacing it. It disputed the remaining works: re-surfacing the car park and moving its entrance (for safety reasons, to avoid a steep entrance); and reinstating a footpath (new bollards and railings were installed for safety reasons, to protect pedestrians on the footpath and to prevent cars jumping the kerb and running down the steep incline of the road, and a new disabled ramp was built).

It was held that the disputed works were repairs (with the exception of the footpath bollards and railings, including painting, which were capital):

1. There was no 'scheme of alteration', and it would be incorrect to import an overall purpose of improving the site as the reason the work was undertaken. The itemised expenditure could be considered as individual pieces of work that were allowable as revenue deductions.

2.   The relevant 'entirety' was the road network, cable network and office (that is, car park and footpath works as 'appendages' to a property). There had not been a reconstruction, replacement or renewal of that asset or substantially the whole of that asset, and the character of the assets had not changed.

3.   Upholding modern standards of road repair, especially where required by law and the local authority, did not, of itself, make expenditure capital. Defective parts of the road were being repaired, as the re-laying and re-surfacing of the main carriageway was to provide, not a renewal of the entirety of the road network, but the repair of part of that network. The older material was dug up and replaced with a more modern equivalent which met current standards. It was a substantial repair, but not if one started with the entirety of 1,130 metres of road on the estate as a whole (only 120 metres were replaced). A cable network must be seen as a whole over the whole estate, and the part that was repaired and/ or replaced was of such a minimal amount that it could not be said that it created a new capital asset.

DEAN & REDDYHOFF LTD V COMMISSIONERS FOR HM REVENUE AND CUSTOMS [2013] UKFTT 367 (TC)

Land remediation relief

A company had the trade of constructing and operating marinas. Between 2007 and 2009, it spent about £8.8 million building a marina (including quayside buildings and facilities) at Portland, Dorset. The works were a system of sea defences comprising the construction of:

1.   an 875-metre dropped-stone sea wall on the seabed largely surrounding the marina. This acted as a breakwater to provide calmer water within the waterside part of the marina, and prevent wave, surge and flood damage to buildings, land, boats and other property;

2.   an additional sea wall on the foreshore (between mean low and high water). This was to protect dry reclaimed land from the erosive effects of the sea, wave damage and flooding;

3.   a 1.2-metre high plinth on dry land upon which buildings were constructed. This was built to prevent damage to the quayside buildings and property from wave, surge and flooding; and

4.   floodwater drainage systems, including storm drains and culverts draining onto the foreshore, to protect the quayside buildings and property flooding or storm surge damage.

The dropped-stone wall failed to qualify for land remediation relief because all the works were on the seabed or in the sea itself. This was not 'land' and therefore it could not be land in a contaminated state.

It was held that the foreshore was 'land' (despite it sometimes being covered with seawater). The additional sea wall was all built on land (partly on the foreshore and partly above mean high water). There was seawater on the foreshore and the possibility of harm being caused in terms of damage to property. Therefore, the land was in a contaminated state and land remediation relief was due.

The plinth and drainage systems were all built on dry land above the mean high water line. Despite there being the possibility of damage to property, this was not in a contaminated state because there was no seawater on it (the foreshore was contaminated by seawater, not the land beyond the mean high water line). So, these works did not qualify for land remediation relief.

Incidentally, the land remediation relief statute was changed in 2009 so that land could only be contaminated as a result of industrial activity (see **24.13**). The company would have been unable to claim if it had incurred its expenditure on or after 1 April 2009 (because its claim was based on natural seawater being the contaminant).

DAVID THOMSON V COMMISSIONERS FOR HM REVENUE AND CUSTOMS [2013] UKFTT 468 (TC)

IBAs – enterprise zone allowances

Lanarkshire Primary Care NHS Trust incurred expenditure building laundry facilities in an enterprise zone, which opened in November 2003. It entered into an arrangement to provide laundry services to two other Health Boards, as well as carrying out a relatively small amount of laundering for other customers.

It was conceded that a small part of the building was an office. This, therefore, qualified for 100% industrial allowances as a 'commercial building'.

Otherwise, despite being a NHS Trust, the defraying of overheads and other expenses approximated to a profit motive, and Lanarkshire had to view the enterprise as any entrepreneur would do. And the arrangements with the other Health Boards were at arm's length. Therefore, the laundry was a commercial building used for the purposes of a trade, and 100% industrial buildings allowances were available.

HMRC failed to persuade the Tribunal that, at first use, the building was not an industrial one (in this context, including a commercial building) on the grounds that it was for Lanarkshire alone and not the other Health Boards. The Tribunal found that it was only on the first day that the laundry processed Lanarkshire laundry alone. This was consistent with testing integral to the conduct of a trade with third parties. Lanarkshire had conducted that trade before moving to the new laundry, and its first use was a continuation of that trade. Also, the system operated was that laundered goods were not allocated to any one user but formed a shared supply.

ROGATE SERVICES LTD V COMMISSIONERS FOR HM REVENUE AND CUSTOMS [2014] UKFTT 312 (TC)

Plant – car valeting bay

A company was unsuccessful in claiming plant and machinery allowances for a car valeting bay.

The company was a dealer in new and second-hand Renault cars. Whilst valeting cars it had to apply, to Renault quality standards, a couple of glasscoat finishes. These waxing products had to be made at temperatures of between 16 and 21 degrees centigrade so they could be applied effectively. Hand buffing equipment was used.

The company built a double garage of standard concrete block construction, with a concrete floor raised a few centimetres above ground, and a flat roof set on wooden beams. The walls and door were insulated and the floor was raised to keep the internal temperature above the ambient temperature. It contained six electric wall-mounted heaters. There was nothing so unique about the building that it could only be used for the application of the glasscoat product (for example, it could have been used for storage).

The company argued that the garage was plant because it was a necessary part of the process which enabled glasscoat to be applied (ie it was a tool of the trade).

If the garage was a 'building' or 'structure' for the purposes of *CAA 2001, s 21* or *s 22* it could not be plant. The Tribunal found it was a building for the purposes of *CAA 2001, s 21*, and even if it was not a building for that purpose it was a structure for the purposes of *CAA 2001, s 22*. Furthermore, it found that the garage was not plant under general principles either because it did not perform a function like, for example, the dry dock in *Barclay Curle*. The building simply kept out the elements, and some dust and similar matters, and was like an office or workshop in the sense of being a place where people worked, rather than being apparatus.

DAVID ALEXANDER KEYL V COMMISSIONERS FOR HM REVENUE AND CUSTOMS [2014] UKFTT 493 (TC)

AIA – discontinuance of qualifying activity

A self-employed air conditioning engineer, Mr Keyl, bought a new van in July 2008 and claimed an annual investment allowance (AIA). At the beginning of that tax year he was a sole trader with an accounting year end of 31 March 2009, trading under the name "Changing Climates". On accountancy advice he incorporated a company called "Changing Climates Ltd" to take over his business, which started trading on 1 April 2009.

The Tribunal held that Mr Keyl transferred his business as a going concern to the company (retaining trade debtors and his continuing maintenance and warranty obligations to customers). That amounted to a permanent discontinuance of his trade in the chargeable period (in the scintilla of time before midnight on 31 March 2009 his trade ceased, and in the scintilla of time after midnight the new company commenced its trade). Therefore, an AIA was not available to him (*CAA 2001, s 38B, General Exclusion 1*).

DRILLING GLOBAL CONSULTANT LLP V COMMISSIONERS FOR HM REVENUE AND CUSTOMS [2014] UKFTT 888 (TC)

AIA – mixed partnership

A drilling engineering consultancy operated through a limited liability partnership (LLP) by a professional drilling engineer and connected company, was unsuccessful in claiming an annual investment allowance (AIA). Whilst for tax purposes an LLP is in general treated as a partnership (although under LLP law it is a body corporate), the LLP in question was not a 'qualifying person' (that is, an individual, a partnership of which all the members are individuals, or a company) as required by *CAA 2001, s 38A*.

COMMISSIONERS FOR HM REVENUE AND CUSTOMS V LLOYDS TSB EQUIPMENT LEASING (NO 1) LTD [2012] UK FTT 47 (TC); [2013] UKUT 0368 (TCC); [2014] EWCA CIV 1062; LLOYDS BANK LEASING (NO 1) LTD [2015] UKFTT 0401 (TC)

Plant – equipment leasing (ships) anti-avoidance

Under complicated arrangements, an equipment lessor spent in excess of £198 million on two seagoing vessels built to ship liquefied gas from Norway to Spain and the USA. After a tender process the mandate to own and operate the vessels was awarded to one of Japan's oldest shipping companies, Kawasi Kisen Kaisha Ltd ('K-Line'). This had a UK-incorporated and resident subsidiary company K-Line (Europe) Ltd ('K-Euro').

The equipment lessor claimed 25% plant and machinery writing-down allowances (WDAs), which was the usual rate of WDAs at the time. At the time, if plant was used by a person outside the scope of UK tax (overseas leasing) such allowances could be restricted either to 10% WDAs or no allowances at all (the latter applied in this case if 25% WDAs were not available). However, that restriction did not apply if the plant was used for a "qualifying purpose". The ships would be used for a qualifying purpose (regardless of the identity of their end users) if they were let on time charter terms by a person carrying on a trade of operating ships and that trade was within the charge to UK tax (*CAA 2001, s 123*).

There were four issues in dispute. If the equipment lessor was unsuccessful on issues 1, 2 or 4 then no WDAs would be available (issue 3 was an argument that issue 4 did not arise for consideration at all):

1   Whether K-Euro was responsible for defraying all, or substantially all, expenses in connection with the vessels under the time charter throughout the time charter period, within the meaning of *CAA 2001, s 123(1)*.

2   Whether K-Euro let the vessels on charter in the course of a trade which consisted of or included operating ships, within the meaning of *CAA 2001, s 123(1)*.

3   Whether *CAA 2001, s 123(4)* could apply in circumstances where *CAA 2001, s 110* was in point. Section 110 applies where there is overseas leasing but no qualifying purpose, but the taxpayer was entitled to no allowances rather than 10% WDAs. This was considered because *CAA 2001, s 123(4)* referred to the objective of obtaining WDAs determined without regard to *CAA 2001, s 109* (which denied 25% WDAs but instead allowed 10% WDAs where there was overseas leasing but no qualifying purpose).

4   Whether the main object, or one of the main objects, of any transaction or series of transactions which includes the letting of the vessels on charter was to obtain 25% WDAs (if issue 3 was determined so that in principle *CAA 2001, s 123(4)* applied).

The First-tier Tribunal ('FTT') decided issues 1,2 and 4 in favour of the equipment lessor (which was sufficient for it to succeed) and issue 3 against it. The Upper Tribunal upheld the FTT's decision.

The Court of Appeal dismissed the equipment lessor's appeal on issue 3. However, on issue 4 it concluded that whilst the FTT was entitled to find (as it did) that each transaction in the relevant series served a genuine commercial purpose, it did not follow that obtaining capital allowances was incapable of also being *a* main object of the transactions, even if it was not *the* main object of the transactions. In other words, a transaction could serve a genuine commercial purpose but still have a main object (or purpose) of obtaining capital allowances and, therefore, fall foul of relevant anti-avoidance legislation. The equipment lessor appealed back to the FTT to dispute that it was the main object or one of the main objects of any transaction or series of transactions which includes the letting of the vessels on charter to obtain writing-down allowances at 25%, and its appeal was dismissed.

BOWERSWOOD HOUSE RETIREMENT HOME LTD V COMMISSIONERS FOR HM REVENUE AND CUSTOMS [2015] UKFTT 0094 (TC)

Plant – conservatory over swimming pool

A company was unsuccessful in claiming plant and machinery allowances for a conservatory-type covering over a swimming pool.

The company bought a retirement home near Preston which had a swimming pool in its grounds. The swimming pool was enclosed on three sides and above by a conservatory. There was space to walk around the pool. The conservatory was built of a steel frame with uPVC glazed windows attached to low brick walls built on the three sides around the pool. One gable end was formed by an existing brick wall up to roof height. It had a low pitched roof of steel frame and polycarbonate sheeting panels. An old services room was incorporated within the indoor space which spanned the whole of the gable end. This included some pipework for the pool and seemed likely it was used as a changing area.

Surprisingly, the company did not rely on any evidence. But it submitted that the conservatory was plant because it was essential to the enjoyment of the pool (because the users would be septuagenarians or octogenarians). HMRC argued that it simply provided warmth and shelter which is one of the basic functions of a building.

If the conservatory was a 'building' or 'structure' for the purposes of *CAA 2001, s 21* or *s 22* it could not be plant. The tribunal found that the conservatory was plainly a building or fixed structure (indeed said it was difficult to describe it without using the word 'structure'). Those sections were not disapplied by *CAA 2001, s 23* because the conservatory did not fall within *CAA 2001, s 23(2)* (that is, adding thermal insulation against loss of heat to a building for the purposes of CAA 2001 s28) or s23 List C (expenditure unaffected by *ss 21* and *22*). Whilst the tribunal did not consider whether the conservatory may be plant under general principles, it pointed out there was extensive case law on the subject and to analyse how that applied to the present facts would be a "sterile exercise" (in other words, there was no prospect of success).

However, there was also a requirement to apportion part of the purchase price of the nursing home to plant, such as the swimming pool itself (which the parties agreed did qualify following *Cooke v Beach Station Caravans Ltd*).

Therefore, of probably greater interest and use to practitioners than whether the conservatory qualified (which was almost certainly doomed to fail) was that the tribunal endorsed the longstanding non-statutory formula approach to apportionments preferred by the Valuation Office Agency (VOA) (see **4.63**).

The taxpayer tried to argue that where the value of assets can be separately identified, an apportionment formula was not necessary. Instead it suggested all that was needed was to start with the £940,000 purchase price and subtract from this the agreed land value of £255,000, and a replacement (that is, rebuild) cost for the pool (with conservatory) of say, £216,000, and a replacement cost for other plant at the nursing home of say, £240,000. This would leave an amount for the non-qualifying building (that is, building/structure or 'premises') of £230,000. The tribunal concluded that this approach was flawed because it did not identify on the same basis the value of all assets purchased. It identified the value of assets qualifying for capital allowances on a new rebuild basis, but left all other assets to be valued by using a balancing figure of the total purchase price (ie market value of the freehold). Simply identifying the new replacement cost of assets qualifying for capital allowances was not the purpose of an apportionment.

The Tribunal accepted that the VOA's preferred apportionment formula had been used extensively over many years in the context. In the circumstances the tribunal was satisfied that it gave a just and reasonable result and the alternative proposed by the taxpayer did not.

Appendix 5

Pro forma elections

These pro forma elections are set out in the order in which they appear in the body of the book, and chapter and section numbers are given in each case. The following elections are included:

1.   fixtures: apportionment of consideration (*s 198*)

2.   sale of agricultural building (*s 381*)

3.   long lease of industrial building (*s 290*)

4.   fixtures: apportionment of consideration—leases (*s 199*)

5.   fixtures: grant of new lease (*s 183*)

6.   plant: succession to trade (*s 267*)

7.   assets other than plant—connected persons (*s 569*)

8.   group companies—pre-commencement integral features (*FA 2008, Sch 26, para 17*)

9.   short life assets (*s 83*)

10.   fixtures—equipment lessors (*s 177*)

11.   long funding leases—global election (*FA 2006, Sch 8, para 16*)

12.   energy services providers (*s 180A*)

13.   research & development—connected persons (*CTA 2009, s 1130*)

14.   acquisition of know-how with a trade (*CTA 2009, s 178(5)*)

15.   transfer of assets at tax written-down value (*s 569*)

16.   land remediation (*CTA 2009, s 1147*)

17.   intangibles—fixed-rate depreciation (*CTA 2009, s 730*)

18.   computer software (*CTA 2009, s 815*)

19.   intangibles—rollover relief (*CTA 2009, s 758*)

1   FIXTURES: APPORTIONMENT OF CONSIDERATION

Time limit: within two years of the completion date of the transaction (see 4.44)

HM Revenue and Customs

. . . .

. . . .

We hereby elect, in accordance with the provisions of *CAA 2001, s 198* that in connection with the sale and purchase of [*description of land, building etc*] on [*date*] for [*total consideration*], the amount regarded by both parties as the disposal value attributable to plant and machinery fixtures will be [£].

This represents expenditure in respect of the items shown on the attached schedule.

[*Property address*]

[*Interest acquired*]

[*Land Registry title number*]

[*Vendor's name*]

[*Vendor's Unique Tax Reference*] – or state if taxpayer does not have one

[*Date*]

[*Purchaser's name*]

[*Purchaser's Unique Tax Reference*] – or state if taxpayer does not have one

[*Date*]

2   SALE, DEMOLITION, DESTRUCTION OR CESSATION OF USE OF AGRICULTURAL BUILDING TO BE TREATED AS BALANCING EVENT

Time limit: within two years of the end of the accounting period in which the balancing event occurs (see 10.18)

Election must be completed by vendor and purchaser if building is sold/ acquired, but only by current owner if building is demolished, destroyed or ceases to be used.

HM Revenue and Customs

....

....

We hereby elect that the provisions of *CAA 2001, s 381* shall apply to the sale/demolition/destruction/cessation of use of the building [*address*] [*dated*].

For and on behalf of the vendor

Secretary

For and on behalf of the purchaser

Secretary

Dated

3   GRANT OF LONG LEASE OF INDUSTRIAL BUILDING TO BE TREATED AS SALE OF RELEVANT INTEREST BY LESSOR

Time limit: two years from date that lease takes effect (see 11.7)

HM Revenue and Customs

....

....

We hereby elect that the provisions of *CAA 2001, s 290* shall apply to the

grant [*dated*] of the long lease of the building [*address*] by [*the lessor*] to [*the lessee*]

For and on behalf of the lessor

Secretary

For and on behalf of the lessee

Secretary

Dated

4   FIXTURES: APPORTIONMENT OF CONSIDERATION (LEASES)

Time limit: within two years of the completion date of the transaction (see 11.35)

HM Revenue and Customs

…………

…………

We hereby elect, in accordance with the provisions of *CAA 2001, s 199* that in connection with the grant of a lease of [*description of land, building, etc*] on [*date*] for [*total consideration*], and pursuant to an election under *CAA 2001, s 183*, the amount regarded by both parties as the capital sum attributable to plant and machinery fixtures for the purposes of *s 183* will be [£].

[*Property address*]

[*Interest acquired*]

[*Land Registry title number*]

This represents expenditure in respect of the items shown on the attached schedule.

[*Lessor's name*]

[*Lessor's Unique Taxpayer Reference*] – where relevant

[*Date*]

[*Lessee's name*]

[*Lessee's Unique Taxpayer Reference*] – where relevant

[*Date*]

5   FIXTURES: GRANT OF NEW LEASE OR OTHER QUALIFYING INTEREST IN LAND

Time limit: within two years of the date on which the lease takes effect (see 11.35)

HM Revenue and Customs

…………

....

This is a claim under *CAA 2001, s 183* relating to fixtures at [*details of premises*]. On [*date of lease*], a lease of those premises for a period of [*x*] years was granted by [*the lessor*] to [*the lessee*] for consideration of [£].

We hereby elect, in accordance with *CAA 2001, s 183* for the assets specified below to be regarded as belonging to [*lessee*], and for the capital sum paid to be regarded as qualifying expenditure in respect of those assets.

[*Details of fixtures*]

[*Lessor*]

[*Date*]

[*Lessee*]

[*Date*]

6   TRANSFER OF PLANT ON SUCCESSION TO A TRADE

Time limit: within two years after the succession (see 13.10)

HM Revenue and Customs

....

....

[... Plc/Ltd (*the successor*)] succeeded to the trade of [... Plc/Ltd (*the predecessor*)] on [*date*]. We ... Plc/Ltd and ... Plc/Ltd who are connected persons for this purpose hereby elect under *CAA 2001, s 266* that the provisions of *CAA 2001, s 267* shall apply to the undernoted assets which were used for the purposes of the trade of ... Plc/Ltd prior to the succession and which were transferred to ... Plc/Ltd on the succession.

Description of the assets transferred

For and on behalf of the predecessor

Secretary

For and on behalf of the successor

Secretary

Dated

7   TRANSFER OF ASSETS OTHER THAN PLANT AT TAX WRITTEN-DOWN VALUE

Time limit: within two years of the disposal (see 13.22)

HM Revenue and Customs

. . . .

. . . .

We hereby elect that the provisions of *CAA 2001, s 569* shall apply to the transfer of the undernoted assets which took place in the accounting period ended [*date*].

Description of assets transferred at tax written-down value

For and on behalf of the transferor

Secretary

For and on behalf of the transferee company

Secretary

Dated

8   SALE BETWEEN GROUP COMPANIES OF A 'PRE-COMMENCEMENT INTEGRAL FEATURE'

Time limit: within two years of the date of sale (see 14.5, 13.14)

HM Revenue and Customs

. . . .

. . . .

We hereby elect that *FA 2008, Sch 26, para 17* shall apply to the sale and purchase of the assets shown on the attached list, being 'pre-commencement integral features', such that:

i.   the assets are treated as sold at a price which gives rise neither a balancing allowance nor a balancing charge; and

ii.   the purchaser's expenditure is treated as qualifying expenditure which is not special rate expenditure, and is to be allocated to the purchaser's general pool.

For and on behalf of the vendor

Secretary

For and on behalf of the purchaser

Secretary

Dated

9 ELECTION FOR PLANT TO BE TREATED AS SHORT-LIFE ASSET

Time limit: within two years of the end of the accounting period of expenditure (see 14.184)

HM Revenue and Customs

....

....

We [...] hereby elect to treat the following items of machinery or plant acquired in the accounting period ended [*date*] as short-life assets, in accordance with the provisions of *CAA 2001, s 83*.

Asset	*Date of expenditure*	*Expenditure description*
		£
		£

Secretary

Dated

10 FIXTURES: EXPENDITURE INCURRED BY EQUIPMENT LESSOR

Time limit: within two years of the end of the chargeable period in which the expenditure is incurred (by the lessor) (see 18.23)

HM Revenue and Customs

....

....

We hereby elect, in accordance with *CAA 2001, s 177* for the assets specified below to be regarded as belonging to [*equipment lessor*].

These assets are fixtures at [*details of premises*]. [*Details of fixtures*]. [*Date expenditure incurred*].

[*Lessor*]

[*Date*]

[*Lessee*]

[*Date*]

11   LONG-FUNDING LEASES: GLOBAL ELECTION

Time limit: within two years of the end of the accounting period to which the election relates (see 18.63)

HM Revenue and Customs

. . . .

. . . .

We hereby elect in accordance with *FA 2006, Sch 8, para 16* and Statutory Instrument 2007/304 for all eligible leases entered into by us to be treated as long-funding leases.

Secretary

Dated

12   ENERGY SERVICES PROVIDERS

Time limit: within two years of the end of the relevant chargeable period (see 18.71)

HM Revenue and Customs

. . . .

. . . .

The parties to this election, [*Client*] and [*Energy Services Provider*], have entered into an energy services agreement [*dated*] in respect of [*details of property*]. Under that agreement, [*Energy Services Provider*] has incurred capital expenditure on plant and machinery of [£]. We hereby jointly elect in accordance with *CAA 2001, s 180A* for [*Energy Services Provider*] to be regarded as the owner of the relevant plant and machinery.

Client

Secretary

Dated

Energy Services Provider

Secretary

Dated

13   REVENUE EXPENDITURE ON RESEARCH & DEVELOPMENT STAFF PROVIDERS: ELECTION FOR CONNECTED PERSON TREATMENT

Time limit: within two years of the end of the accounting period in which expenditure is incurred. (The accounting period referred to is that of the company paying for the research and development, not the staff provider) (see 19.44)

HM Revenue and Customs

…………

…………

[*The company*] has incurred expenditure of [£] on research and development, this being expenditure payable to [*staff provider*] for the provision of staff.

We hereby elect under *CTA 2009, s 1130* for that expenditure to be treated in accordance with *CTA 2009, s 1129*. Consequently, expenditure of [£] will qualify for relief under *CTA 2009, Pt 13*.

Company Secretary

Dated

Staff Provider

Dated

14 ACQUISITION OF KNOW-HOW WITH A TRADE

Time limit: within two years of the date of the transaction (see 19.126)

HM Revenue and Customs

…………

…………

On [*date*], the trade of [*description*] carried on by [*transferor*] was transferred to [*transferee*].

We hereby elect, in accordance with the provisions of *CTA 2009, s 178 (5)* for expenditure amounting to [£] arising on that transfer to be regarded as relating to the know-how described below.

[*Description of know-how*]

[*Transferor*]

[*Date*]

[*Transferee*]

[*Date*]

15 TRANSFER OF ASSETS AT TAX WRITTEN-DOWN VALUE

Time limit: within two years of the disposal (see 20.5)

HM Revenue and Customs

…………

…………

We hereby elect that the provisions of *CAA 2001, s 569* shall apply to the transfer of the undernoted assets which took place in the accounting period ended [*date*].

Description of assets transferred at tax written-down value

For and on behalf of the transferor

Secretary

For and on behalf of the transferee company

Secretary

Dated

16   CAPITAL EXPENDITURE ON LAND REMEDIATION

Time limit: within two years of the end of the accounting period in which expenditure is incurred (see 24.7)

HM Revenue and Customs

. . . .

. . . .

We hereby elect under *CTA 2009, s 1147* for capital expenditure incurred on land remediation to be deducted in computing the profits of the trade.

Details of the expenditure incurred, setting out the nature of the work undertaken and relevant dates are attached.

Secretary

Dated

17   INTANGIBLE FIXED ASSETS: ELECTION FOR FIXED RATE DEPRECIATION

Time limit: within two years of the end of the accounting period in which expenditure is incurred (see 25.11)

HM Revenue and Customs

. . . .

. . . .

We hereby elect under *CTA 2009, s 730* to write down the cost of certain intangible assets at a fixed rate of 4% per annum. The assets are/are not written down for accounting purposes.

Details of the assets acquired and the expenditure incurred are attached.

Secretary

Dated

18   COMPUTER SOFTWARE: EXEMPTION FROM CTA 2009, PART 8

Time limit: within two years of the end of the accounting period in which expenditure is incurred (see 25.22)

HM Revenue and Customs

....

....

The Company has incurred expenditure on computer software, as attached. We hereby elect under *CTA 2009, s 815* for that expenditure to be exempted from the provisions of *CTA 2009, Pt 8.*

Secretary

Dated

19   INTANGIBLE FIXED ASSETS: ELECTION FOR ROLL-OVER RELIEF

Time limit: within two years of the end of the accounting period in which expenditure is incurred (see 25.34)

HM Revenue and Customs

....

....

The company has realised intangible fixed assets and reinvested the proceeds in new intangible fixed assets. We hereby claim relief under *CTA 2009, s 758.*

Details of the assets realised and acquired are as follows:

Secretary

Dated

Appendix 6

Transaction checklists

The following checklists indicate *some* of the issues which should be considered for the more common transactions involving capital allowances. They are not exhaustive, and the taxpayer constructing a new building, for example, should read **Chapter 2** in its entirety. Depending on the precise facts of the transaction, this may then point to the relevance of, say, **Chapter 7** (industrial buildings), **Chapter 8** (hotels), **Chapter 9** (enterprise zones), **Chapters 14** to **16** (plant), and so on. General principles outlined in, inter alia, **Chapters 1** and **21** are also likely to be relevant.

With effect from April 2011, industrial buildings allowances, agricultural buildings allowances and enterprise zone allowances have been abolished. From that date, some of the considerations are no longer relevant, and are shown in italics below.

This highlights the interaction of the different types of allowances, and the benefit of an approach to capital allowances issues which is driven, not by the allowances themselves, but by the nature of the transaction.

CONSTRUCTION OF NEW BUILDING

Is it an industrial building?	*7.47 et seq*
Will it be used for research and development?	19.5 *et seq*
Is it in an enterprise zone?	*9.8 et seq,* *App 3*
Is there a system to identify and record relevant facts and decisions?	1.62 *et seq*
Has the date been established when the expenditure is incurred?	1.77 *et seq*
Are any contributions or subsidies due?	1.108 *et seq*
Has integral plant been identified?	Chs 15 and 16, App 2

Does any of the plant qualify for first year allowances, being energy efficient or environmentally beneficial?	14.14 *et seq*
Will any of the plant be a long-life asset?	14.153 *et seq*
Have preliminaries, fees and other similar costs been identified?	2.17 *et seq*
Has the tax impact of planning agreements, etc been assessed?	2.51 *et seq*
Is any of the expenditure in respect of 'integral features'?	14.5
Is there any expenditure on 'land remediation'?	Ch 24
Is a documentation manual being compiled?	2.55
If industrial, will part of the building be non-qualifying?	7.96 *et seq*, 7.114 *et seq*
Is there a single building, or more than one?	7.116 *et seq*
When is the building first used?	7.50

PURCHASE OF NEW BUILDING

Is it an industrial building?	7.47 *et seq*
Is it in an enterprise zone?	9.8 *et seq*, App 3
Will it be used for research and development?	19.5 *et seq*
Has integral plant been identified?	Chs 15 and 16
Is any of the plant a long-life asset?	14.153 *et seq*
Is any of the plant an 'integral feature'?	14.5
If the building is industrial, what part is non-qualifying?	7.96 *et seq*, 7.114 *et seq*
Has the date been established when the expenditure is incurred?	1.77 *et seq*
Are any contributions or subsidies due?	1.108 *et seq*
Have preliminaries, fees and other similar costs been identified?	2.17 *et seq*
When is the building first used?	7.50

PURCHASE OF SECOND-HAND BUILDING

Have IBAs or research and development allowances previously been claimed?	*4.39*
Has the vendor provided an IBAs history?	
What was the original cost?	
When was it constructed?	
If relevant, do tenants' trades qualify for IBAs?	*7.48 et seq*
Has plant within the building been identified?	Chs 15 and 16, App 2
Is any of the plant a long-life asset?	*14.153 et seq*
Is any of the plant an 'integral feature'?	*14.5*
Has a joint election been made regarding the value of fixtures?	*4.44 et seq*
Is the cost of fixtures restricted by claims made by the seller or a previous owner?	*4.35 et seq,* 11.51
Is the transaction subject to the provisions of *s187A*, requiring mandatory pooling by the seller (that is, where the seller was entitled to claim capital allowances but did not do so), or a formal fixed value statement (that is, where the seller has claimed and it is necessary for the buyer to formally establish a value for qualifying expenditure incurred) or both?	*4.16 et seq*
Has the land value been identified?	*2.7 et seq,* 15.108 *et seq*
Have relevant warranties been sought from the vendor?	*4.86 et seq,* 9.44
Have preliminaries, fees and other similar costs been identified?	*2.17 et seq*
Is just part of the building being used for non-qualifying purposes?	*7.96 et seq, 7.114 et seq*
When is/was the building first used?	*7.50*

RENTING PREMISES (LANDLORD)

Will the lessee's trade qualify for IBAs?	*7.48 et seq*
Can commencement of the lease be accelerated to fall within the current accounting period?	*11.6*
If industrial, is the building actually in use at the year end?	*7.50 et seq*
Has a *s 290* election been made?	*11.7 et seq*
Have fixtures been identified?	11.15 *et seq*, Ch 16, App 2
On a sale, does *s 325* limit a balancing allowance?	*12.24 et seq*
Has a capital value been realised?	*12.34 et seq*

RENTING PREMISES (TENANT)

Has a *s 290* election been made?	*11.7 et seq*
Is any sum payable in respect of fixtures?	11.15 *et seq*
Are you required to install your own fixtures?	11.26 *et seq*
What will happen to such fixtures at the end of the lease?	11.46

ACQUIRING PLANT

Were building alterations required?	14.119 *et seq*
Were there any installation costs?	2.38
Do any specific needs of the business influence the choice of plant?	15.14 *et seq*, 15.67 *et seq*
What is the expected useful economic life of the plant (>25 years)?	14.153 *et seq*
Has a short life asset election been considered?	14.179
Have the relevant costs (eg transport) been identified?	14.114 *et seq*
Is there irrecoverable VAT?	22.2 *et seq*
Are there any contributions or subsidies towards wear and tear?	1.108 *et seq*
Is the expenditure specifically allowed by statute?	15.67
Is any of the plant an 'integral feature'?	14.5

Is the 'plant' a motor car or another type of vehicle?   17.1 *et seq*

Is the plant being acquired on HP?   18.1

Is the plant to be leased out?   18.15 *et seq*

Are the allowances needed—should they be disclaimed or 'sold'?   18.77 *et seq*, 21.38

Typical amounts of allowances

PURCHASED PROPERTY

These indicative estimates of the capital allowances that may be available when second-hand property is purchased *depend on individual circumstances* and are influenced by a range of factors including, for example, the type of property, its tax history, its design and specification and its geographic location.

However, the following expenditure qualifying for tax relief would typically be expected (as a percentage of the purchase price). These indicative estimates are provided for guidance only and are *not* intended to be used for, nor are suitable for, filing tax returns, for which an appropriately qualified professional should be appointed to prepare a capital allowances analysis.

Property type	*Plant & machinery allowances*
Offices:	
Low to medium rise, not air conditioned	15%–30%
Air conditioned	25%–35%
Prestige air conditioned	30%–45%
Retail:	
Retail units, landlord's shell	1%–5%
Shopping centres, enclosed	10%–30%
Distribution warehouses	5%–10%
Hotels:	
Provincial	25%–40%
Luxury city centre	35%–50%
Industrial:	
Industrial units, landlord's shell	10%–15%
Office/industrial units (planning class B1)	15%–30%

Property type	Plant & machinery allowances
Healthcare:	
Hospitals	35%–45%
Nursing homes	30%–40%
Health centres/surgeries	30%–40%
Leisure:	
Bars, pubs and restaurants	20%–45%
Leisure centres and gyms	15%–30%

CONSTRUCTION PROJECTS

These indicative estimates of the capital allowances that may be available when carrying out construction works (ie new build, extension or conversion/ refurbishment projects) *depend on individual circumstances* and are influenced by a range of factors including, for example, the type of property and its design and specification.

However, the following expenditure qualifying for tax relief would typically be expected (as a percentage of the construction cost). These indicative estimates are provided for guidance only and are *not* intended to be used for, nor are suitable for, filing tax returns, for which an appropriately qualified professional should be appointed to prepare a capital allowances analysis.

Property type	Plant & machinery allowances
Offices:	
Low to medium rise, not air conditioned	25%–35%
Air conditioned	30%–40%
Prestige air conditioned	35%–45%
Fitting out landlord's shell	60%–90%
Retail:	
Fitting out retail units, landlord's shell	60%–90%
Shopping centres, enclosed	15%–30%
Distribution warehouses	5%–15%
Hotels:	
Provincial	35%–50%

Property type	Plant & machinery allowances
Luxury city centre	40%–55%
Industrial:	
Industrial units, landlord's shell	1%–5%
Shell office/industrial units (planning class B1)	10%–20%
Healthcare:	
Hospitals	35%–50%
Nursing homes	30%–40%
Health centres/surgeries	30%–40%
Leisure:	
Bars, pubs and restaurants	20%–50%
Fitting out landlord's shell bar/restaurant	55%–45%
Leisure centres and gyms	20%–45%
Fitting out landlord's shell gym	55%–85%

Pre-contract enquiries and warranties

PRE-CONTRACT ENQUIRIES

On any property acquisition, one would expect the purchaser, through his solicitor, to ask a number of standard questions of the vendor, some of which will relate to capital allowances. These questions need to be answered by the vendor to the purchaser's satisfaction—they are important and can have a significant impact on the purchaser's claim for allowances. Answers such as 'not applicable', 'don't know' or 'ask accountant' are unacceptable! The vendor should be pressed to explain *why* it thinks such an answer is appropriate. Readers' attention is drawn to *Clarke v Iliffes Booth Bennett (a firm)* [2004] EWHC 1731 (Ch), [2004] All ER (D) 369 (Jul), where it was held that a solicitor has a duty to understand a contract (for example, tax matters) to the extent necessary to give proper advice to the client (see **4.7**).

The most widely used version of these questions is form Commercial Property Standard Enquiries 1 (CPSE.1), 'General pre-contract enquiries for all commercial property transactions', prepared by members of the London Property Support Lawyers Group and endorsed by the British Property Federation (since 28 February 2014, capital allowances being dealt with in enquiry 32). The latest version (3.4 at the time of writing) is available online (http://uk.practicallaw.com/3-579-3225) and is free to use, subject to certain conditions.

Commentary on the individual CPSE questions is included in **Appendix 9**.

CONTRACT CLAUSES AND WARRANTIES

It is impractical to compile a definitive list of contract clauses and warranties because what is appropriate depends upon many factors, not least the circumstances of the particular transaction.

At best, illustrative clauses and warranties can act as a catalyst in the agreement of contract terms. The following are listed for that purpose only—it is essential that specific professional advice should be obtained.

Illustrative warranties

For transactions completing after March 2014 in particular, the required clauses and warranties will depend to a great extent on the history of the property and the proposed division of capital allowances between seller and purchaser.

Where the seller has claimed allowances and the parties will enter into a s 198/s 199 election on completion

On completion, the seller and the buyer shall make an election in respect of the fixtures under *CAA 2001, s 198.*

Both the buyer and the seller shall:

- provide all necessary information to each other and take all reasonable steps required to make the election,
- submit a copy of the election to HMRC with their tax return for the first period affected by the election,
- take all reasonable steps to ensure that the amounts fixed by the election are accepted by HMRC, and
- reflect the amounts fixed by the election in their respective tax computations and returns.

The seller warrants that no person has a 'prior right' as defined by *CAA 2001, s 181* in relation to any of the fixtures.

Where the seller has claimed allowances and the parties will apply to the Tax Chamber of the First-tier Tribunal for a just and reasonable allocation of allowances

The seller and the buyer agree that within [*six months*] of completion the [*seller/buyer*] shall make an application to the Tribunal for a just and reasonable apportionment of the purchase price to the fixtures.

Both the buyer and the seller shall reflect the amounts fixed by the Tribunal in their respective tax computations and returns.

The seller shall:

- use its best endeavours to supply such documents and information relating to the capital allowances history of the fixtures (including information relating to the entitlement of previous owners to capital allowances) as the buyer may request, and

- take such action as is reasonably necessary to assist the buyer in making the Application and any claim it may make for capital allowances.

The seller warrants that no person has a 'prior right' as defined by *CAA 2001, s 181* in relation to any of the fixtures.

Where the seller was entitled to claim allowances, but has not done so

The seller will provide all such information and assistance as is necessary for the buyer to claim capital allowances on any fixtures in respect of which the seller was entitled to claim capital allowances, but has not done so.

For all such fixtures, the seller will, in its tax return for the period in which completion takes place, allocate its expenditure on those fixtures to a pool in accordance with *CAA 2001, ss 53* and *54*.

The seller agrees to submit all returns and take all reasonable steps to ensure acceptance by HMRC of the pooling of expenditure.

The seller warrants that no person has a 'prior right' as defined by *CAA 2001, s 181* in relation to any of the fixtures.

The seller agrees that it will enter into an election under *CAA 2001, s 198* for an amount equal to the seller's qualifying expenditure on those fixtures.

Where the seller has not claimed allowances, and was not entitled to do so

The seller warrants that:

- it has not claimed, and has at no time been entitled to claim, allowances for capital expenditure on the provision of the fixtures,

- no person who is treated as having owned the fixtures during a period ending on or after [1/6] April 2014 has claimed, or was entitled to claim, allowances for capital expenditure on the provision of the fixtures, and

- no person has a 'prior right' as defined by *CAA 2001, s 181* in respect of any of the fixtures.

The seller acknowledges that after completion the buyer may seek to agree a just and reasonable apportionment of the purchase price to fixtures with HMRC. The seller shall:

- use its best endeavours to supply such documents and information relating to the capital allowances history of the fixtures (including information relating to the entitlement of previous owners to capital allowances) as the buyer may request, and

- take such action as is reasonably necessary to assist the buyer in any claim it may make for capital allowances in respect of the fixtures.

Comments on pre-contract enquiries

In most cases where a property is being sold or otherwise transferred, the purchaser's solicitor will make a number of standard enquiries covering a range of topics, including capital allowances. For anyone acquiring a property, proper completion of the pre-contract enquiries is essential, as they give the purchaser valuable information affecting any claim he may wish to make, albeit in a low-key manner. All too often, however, the capital allowances enquiries are answered incompletely, and are not pursued by purchasers' solicitors, in the belief that any capital allowances issues can be sorted out later by his accountant. Thus, important information is lost, and in many cases the scope to make a claim may be severely restricted, leading to an actual tax cost to the purchaser.

There is no 'official' version of the pre-contract enquiries, and solicitors are free to use their own version. However, the most commonly used is form Commercial Property Standard Enquiries 1 (CPSE.1), prepared by members of the London Property Support Lawyers Group and endorsed by the British Property Federation. The latest version is available online (http://property. practicallaw.com) and is free to use, subject to certain conditions.

A short-form version called CPSE.7 is also available for low value transactions, but is no practical use for capital allowances and should be avoided for that purpose.

The following notes (which adopt the numbering of CPSE.1) are intended to assist solicitors in understanding replies and knowing when to insist on further information. It should be noted that CPSE.1 is regularly updated, and advisers should always ensure that they use the current version from http://property. practicallaw.com.

The authors have become aware of an increasing number of cases where solicitors have been sued by clients for failing to deal appropriately with capital allowances. In many cases, inadequate understanding of income or corporation tax and the capital allowances pre-contract enquiries has been at the core of the problem. *Finance Act 2012* introduced additional conditions that the purchaser of a property must satisfy before they can claim capital allowances on fixtures.

These are the 'fixed value requirement' and the 'pooling requirement' (see **4.16–4.34**). With these new conditions, it is more essential than ever for conveyancing solicitors to be aware of, and deal with, capital allowances issues at the time of the property transaction. A new version of CPSE.1 was issued in February 2014 to take account of these changes.

ENQUIRY 32.1

Do you hold the Property on capital account as an investor/ owner-occupier, or on revenue account as a developer/ property trader as part of your trading stock? Please specify which.

This is the most fundamental tax question, relevant in all circumstances. It seeks to establish whether the Seller intended to retain the property (for own occupation or to generate rental income), or sell it with a view to making a profit. In other words, whether the Seller's expenditure on the property was 'capital' or 'revenue' for tax purposes. These are mutually exclusive – the answer must therefore be *either* capital *or* revenue; it cannot be both, and it cannot be neither.

This question is now more explicitly stated than in previous versions of CPSE.1, where sellers often responded that they were 'traders', meaning that they carried on a trade generally (rather than one of construction or property dealing).

In cases of doubt, the Seller's accountant should be able to confirm which treatment applies.

If the Seller's expenditure is capital, the Seller potentially *could* have claimed capital allowances (irrespective of whether the property is held as an investment or for own occupation).

If the Seller's expenditure is revenue, the Seller *could not* have claimed capital allowances (because capital allowances are given for capital expenditure). This also means that the Seller *cannot* enter into an election under *Capital Allowances Act 2001 (CAA 2001), s 198* or *199* to fix the disposal value of plant and machinery fixtures (see **4.44** *et seq*). Furthermore, if the Seller's expenditure is revenue, the transaction will not (subject to prior history) be subject to the 'fixed value requirement' and the 'pooling requirement' (see **4.16–4.34**).

Unacceptable answers to this question include 'not applicable', 'don't know', 'yes', 'no', 'accountant to advise', 'buyer should make their own enquiries', and so on.

ENQUIRY 32.2

Have you claimed capital allowances on plant or machinery fixtures or allocated any expenditure on such fixtures to a capital allowances pool? If so, please answer the supplementary questions in enquiry 32.9 in respect of that expenditure.

Enquiry 32.1 establishes whether the Seller *could* have claimed capital allowances. Enquiry 32.2 looks to establish whether the Seller actually *did* claim any capital allowances on fixtures.

Claiming capital allowances is, in effect, a two-stage process. The first step is that the expenditure is 'pooled'. This effectively means telling HM Revenue & Customs that the business has spent money on those qualifying items by reflecting that qualifying expenditure in a tax return (see **14.3**). The second step is that the business actually claims the tax relief on that qualifying expenditure in a tax return, for example by claiming a 'writing-down allowance' (see **14.99** *et seq*) or 'annual investment allowance' (see **14.62** et seq). It is not obligatory to go through with the second step and actually claim the tax relief (see **21.38** *et seq*).

If the Seller *has* pooled any expenditure on fixtures:

- the Buyer's qualifying expenditure on those fixtures will be limited by *CAA 2001, s 185* to the Seller's disposal value for those items (limited to the Seller's original expenditure) (see **4.35** *et seq*); and

- the 'fixed value requirement' introduced by *Finance Act 2012* will apply (see **4.24**).

An acceptable answer to this enquiry is 'yes' or 'no'. If the answer is 'yes', supplementary enquiry 32.9 should also be completed (see below).

Unacceptable answers include 'not applicable', 'don't know', 'accountant to advise', 'buyer should make their own enquiries', and so on.

ENQUIRY 32.3

If you have not pooled any expenditure on plant or machinery fixtures:

(a) will you do so if the Buyer asks you to?

(b) if so, by when?

(c) if not, why not?

This question deals with the pooling requirement introduced by *Finance Act 2012* (see **4.27** *et seq*), which applies to property sales and purchases from 1 April 2014 (corporation tax) or 6 April 2014 (income tax), where the Seller (or an earlier owner since April 2014) *could* have pooled qualifying expenditure on plant and machinery fixtures (irrespective of whether it actually *did*). Broadly, that means circumstances where the Seller (or earlier owner since April 2014) is a business subject to tax. It does *not* apply where that owner:

- was not within the charge to tax (for example, a charity, pension fund or local authority);

- was only able to claim capital allowances because it had contributed towards another person's expenditure (for example, a landlord paying some or all of the cost of a tenant's plant); or

- would not have been entitled to claim because the fixture (or fixtures) in question would not have been treated as plant in its hands.

If there are any fixtures upon which the Seller was not entitled to pool qualifying expenditure (as above), the Buyer's claim is calculated by means of a 'just and reasonable apportionment' – under *CAA 2001, s 562* – of the total purchase price to buy the whole property. The Buyer may simply pool the expenditure in its tax return. It is not possible to agree a *CAA 2001, s 198* election.

Where it applies, the pooling requirement dictates that, before the Buyer is able to claim plant and machinery allowances for fixtures, the Seller must first pool the qualifying expenditure in its own tax return (based on its original expenditure). Once the expenditure has been pooled by the Seller, the fixed value requirement applies. If the pooling requirement applies but the Seller does not pool the expenditure, the Buyer's qualifying expenditure is deemed to be nil. Thereafter, the fixture, or fixtures, in question permanently have a value of nil for capital allowances, even if they change hands again in future.

It is therefore critical to establish whether the pooling requirement applies and, if so, that it is met.

Pooling does not have to be before the completion date of the transaction, although it may be prudent for a Buyer to insist upon this if there is any risk that the Seller might fail to comply. In practice, the Seller's expenditure may be pooled up to two or three years after the completion date of the transaction (depending on transaction and year-end dates).

If the Seller has already pooled the expenditure (as indicated by an affirmative answer to enquiry 32.2), an acceptable response is 'not applicable'.

Otherwise, an acceptable answer to enquiry 32.3(*a*) is 'yes' or 'no'. Enquiry 32.3(*b*) requires a timescale, such as a specific date or a number of days, weeks or months. Where relevant, enquiry 32.3(*c*) requires a brief explanation of why the Seller cannot, or will not, pool its qualifying expenditure.

Unacceptable answers include 'don't know', 'accountant to advise', 'buyer should make their own enquiries', 'not necessary' (where the Seller was entitled to claim), and the like.

ENQUIRY 32.4

If you bought the Property and cannot pool any expenditure on plant and machinery fixtures:

(a) please provide the name and contact details of everyone who has owned the Property since April 2014;

(b) please provide evidence that the most recent previous owner who was entitled to claim allowances pooled any expenditure on plant and machinery fixtures? Please answer the supplementary questions in enquiry 32.9 in respect of that previous owner's expenditure.

This enquiry focuses on instances where the Seller is not entitled to pool any expenditure on plant and machinery fixtures (for example, because its expenditure was revenue or because it is outside the charge to tax). In such cases, it looks through the Seller to consider the capital allowances treatment of the fixtures by previous owners of the property (for example, the predecessor in title that sold the property to the current Seller).

The pooling requirement only applies to transactions from April 2014. So, this enquiry just seeks the name and contact details of anyone who has owned the property since then.

If the Seller *was* entitled to pool expenditure (that is, broadly, where it is an owner-occupier or investor within the charge to tax), an acceptable answer is 'not applicable'.

Otherwise, if the Seller *was not* entitled to pool expenditure, an acceptable answer to enquiry 32.4(*a*) is the name and contact details of anyone known to have owned the property since April 2014. In many cases, the Seller ought to be able to provide relevant information in respect of its immediate predecessor in title. An acceptable answer to enquiry 32.4(*b*) is to provide evidence that the most recent owner who was entitled to pool expenditure on plant and machinery did so. In many cases, this should be possible because CPSE.1 has, for a number of years, requested details of the predecessor in title's capital allowances treatment.

ENQUIRY 32.5

Please provide details of any plant and machinery fixtures which were paid for by a tenant, including any contributions made by you towards their cost.

Where an asset has been installed and paid for by a tenant, *s 176* normally deems the fixture to belong to the tenant for capital allowances purposes (see **11.26**). This means that the tenant is entitled to claim capital allowances, and *not* the landlord. Where the landlord's interest changes hands, the entitlement to capital allowances on such tenant's fixtures remains with the tenant, and does not pass to the Buyer.

If the Seller has contributed towards a tenant's plant or machinery (both chattels and fixtures), the Seller may have been able to claim capital allowances under the 'contributions' rules set out in *CAA 2001, ss 537* and *538* (see **1.119** *et seq*). If that is the case, entitlement to claim allowances on that plant and machinery will pass to the Buyer under the transaction.

Where the property has not been let out, the appropriate answer will be 'not applicable'. Otherwise, where known, details of any such tenant's assets or contributions made should be provided.

ENQUIRY 32.6

Please provide details of any plant and machinery fixtures which are leased to you by an equipment lessor.

Sometimes, plant and machinery is leased under an equipment lease, rather than belonging outright to the property owner. This means that it is the equipment lessor who is entitled to claim capital allowances, rather than the property owner (see **Chapter 18**).

Where a property changes hands, and some of the plant and machinery is leased like this, ownership for capital allowances purposes of those assets will *not* pass under the transaction. Entitlement to allowances will remain with the equipment lessor, and the Buyer will therefore need to exclude any such assets from its capital allowances claim.

Where no assets are leased under an equipment lease, the appropriate answer will be 'not applicable'. Otherwise, details of any such leased assets should be provided.

ENQUIRY 32.7

If the transaction is the grant of a new lease at a premium, and you are entitled to do so and the buyer asks you to, will you enter into a *Capital Allowances Act 2001 section 183* election for the buyer to be treated as the owner of the plant and machinery fixtures for capital allowances purposes?

This question is only relevant if the transaction is the grant of a new lease for a premium (that is, a capital sum).

If the Grantor was entitled to claim capital allowances, or would have been if it had been subject to tax, then ownership for capital allowances purposes is automatically treated as being retained by the Grantor after the grant of the lease. However, as long as the Grantor and Grantee are not connected for tax purposes, they may enter into an election under *CAA 2001, s 183* to treat the Grantee as the owner of those plant and machinery fixtures for capital allowances purposes (see **11.35**). This means that the Grantee will be able to claim capital allowances for its capital expenditure.

If the question is not relevant (because the transaction is not the grant of a lease for a premium), an acceptable answer is 'not applicable'. If the question is relevant, an acceptable answer is 'yes' or 'no'. Unacceptable answers include 'don't know', 'accountant to advise', 'buyer should make their own enquiries', and the like.

ENQUIRY 32.8

Please provide details of any expenditure on plant and machinery that you have treated as long-life assets, or any expenditure upon which you have claimed another type of capital allowances (for example, industrial buildings allowances, research and development allowances, business premises renovation allowances and so on).

This is really two questions in one. Most of the questions in enquiry 32 focus on capital allowances for plant and machinery. However, alternative types of allowances are available which may affect the Buyer's capital allowances claim if they have been claimed by someone else previously. Where a property has previously been subject to a claim for a different type of allowances to plant and machinery allowances (such as the above), this can affect the Buyer's claim and restrictions may apply.

Long-life assets are plant and machinery which can reasonably be expected to have a useful economic life, when new, of at least 25 years (in all owners' hands). If a previous owner has treated any plant or machinery as a long-life asset in its tax return, the Buyer is obliged to follow this treatment (see **14.153** *et seq*).

Enquiry answers

If the question is not relevant (because the property has not previously been subject to another type of allowance), an acceptable answer is 'not applicable'.

If the question is relevant, an acceptable answer is to provide details of that previous claim (for example, the type of capital allowance claimed, the amount of qualifying expenditure, when this was incurred and so on).

Similarly, if any assets have been treated as 'long-life assets', full details are required.

ENQUIRY 32.9

For each plant and machinery fixture for which a claim has been made or expenditure has been pooled, please:

(a) provide a description of that fixture;

(b) state when that fixture was acquired;

(c) state whether that fixture was installed by you, or already installed by a previous owner (please specify which);

(d) state the amount of expenditure pooled in respect of that fixture; and

(e) (where enquiry 32.2 applies) confirm that you will enter into a *Capital Allowances Act 2001 section 198* election in that amount (or other appropriate amount, to be agreed) if asked to do so by the Buyer.

OR

(f) (where enquiry 32.4 applies) confirm whether the most recent previous owner who was entitled to claim allowances entered into a *Capital Allowances Act 2001 section 198* election and, if so, in what amount.

This enquiry is supplementary to enquiries 32.2 and 32.4(*b*). Where expenditure on plant and machinery has been pooled previously, this question requests full details of that claim; or, where the most recent previous owner who was entitled to claim plant and machinery allowances entered previously into a *CAA 2001, s 198* election, it requests confirmation that this was the case and the amount of that election.

Capital allowances for plant and machinery must be formally claimed in a tax return, and a taxpayer is obliged to retain appropriate records in support of that claim. Therefore, where enquiry 32.2 is relevant, in most cases the Seller or the Seller's tax accountant should be able to provide some details of capital allowances claims made. However, 'perfect' information is unlikely – particularly if the property has been owned for many years or the Seller has changed accountants during its period of ownership.

Enquiry 32.9(*a*) requests a *meaningful description* of each fixture upon which capital allowances qualifying expenditure has been pooled by the Seller. In practice, it would be burdensome to list each individual fixture separately, so in appropriate circumstances HM Revenue & Customs (HMRC) will normally accept a degree of amalgamation where this does not distort the tax computation. Therefore, the use of sensible elemental descriptions such as 'hot water system', 'sanitary ware' and the like will usually suffice.

Enquiry 32.9(*b*) requests details of the date or chargeable period in which the Seller incurred expenditure on the fixtures described in answer to 32.9(*a*). Different fixtures may well have different dates of acquisition. Therefore, a date or period is required against each elemental description set out in response to enquiry 32.9(*a*).

Enquiry 32.9(*c*) asks whether the fixture was already in the property when the Seller bought the property second-hand, or whether it was installed by the Seller (for example, during refurbishment works). Therefore, for each elemental description set out in response to enquiry 32.9(*a*), it should be made clear whether that fixture already existed when the property was bought, or was added to the property by the Seller.

Enquiry 32.9(*d*) asks how much capital expenditure the Seller incurred, and pooled, for each fixture. Therefore, for each elemental description set out in response to enquiry 32.9(*a*), the expenditure originally incurred and pooled by the Seller should be provided.

Enquiry 32.9(*e*) refers back to enquiry 32.2, which only applies where the Seller has pooled qualifying expenditure on a plant or machinery fixture, and therefore the 'fixed value requirement' applies. Where this is relevant, the Seller and Buyer have the option of jointly entering into a *CAA 2001, s 198* (or *s 199*) election to establish a value for those fixtures. Alternatively, they can use an apportionment (restricted as appropriate) and either party must send this to the Tax Chamber of the First-tier Tribunal for ratification.

This question simply seeks to establish whether the Seller will enter into an election if the Buyer asks it to do so. Therefore, a simple 'yes' or 'no' answer will suffice. This enquiry proposes that the election amount will be the qualifying expenditure originally incurred and pooled by the Seller. However, the parties have the flexibility to agree an alternative appropriate amount. Where that is relevant, the enquiry response should say so and state the alternative amount proposed.

The Buyer should consider carefully whether it is in its interests to enter into a *s 198* election and, if so, at what figure, because there are serious consequences if the wrong choice is made. In practice, *s 198* elections are rarely to a Buyer's advantage. There are several problems with elections.

In most practical circumstances, *s 198* elections favour Sellers. This is because, without an election, a Seller's capital allowances claimed will generally be clawed back and transfer to the Buyer by default. An election agreed at a low amount (such as £1, £2 or tax written-down value) gives a Seller the opportunity to keep some or all of the tax relief, despite selling the qualifying assets at a profit. Furthermore, the Buyer may still need to carry out an apportionment to any assets which cannot be included in an election, such as chattels or fixtures on which the Seller claimed no allowances.

ENQUIRY 32.10

Please provide the name and contact details of your capital allowances adviser. Please confirm that we may make contact with him/her in order to obtain information about the matters dealt with in this enquiry 32.

Whilst many accountants have a basic understanding of capital allowances for fixtures, few will have the expert knowledge required to identify all potential issues. Specialist capital allowances advisers and valuers do exist (such as the authors of this book!), and advisers may wish to recommend at the outset that the Buyer of a property should consider consulting a suitably qualified and experienced specialist capital allowances adviser.

This enquiry simply asks for the name and contact details of the person giving capital allowances advice to the Seller (if they have anyone).

Index

[all references are to paragraph number]

573